Preface

The contribution of foreign direct investment to development is now widely recognized. There is a perception, however, that this contribution may be affected by the way investment enters a country. It may come in the form of a new enterprise or the expansion of an existing enterprise; it may also come through a merger or an acquisition. Acquisitions, in particular, arouse concerns, especially over employment, ownership and market structure. And the concerns become urgent when the host economy is a developing one.

Given the recent explosion in cross-border mergers and acquisitions, UNCTAD's 10th *World Investment Report* is a highly timely and important document. This phenomenon calls for just the sort of careful and dispassionate analysis that has become the hallmark of the WIRs.

Cross-border mergers and acquisitions are a part of economic life in a liberalizing and globalizing world. But accepting a more open market in the interests of growth and development does not mean relaxing the requirements of public vigilance. On the contrary, a freer market — and particularly the emerging global market for enterprises — calls for greater vigilance as well as stronger and better governance. To this end, *World Investment Report 2000* provides us with a valuable resource.

Kofi A. Annan
Secretary-General of the United Nations

New York, July 2000

Acknowledgements

The *World Investment Report 2000* was prepared by a team led by Karl P. Sauvant and coordinated by Anne Miroux. Its member included Victoria Aranda, Persephone Economou, Wilfried Engelke, Torbjörn Fredriksson, Masataka Fujita, Kálmán Kalotay, Mark Knell, Gabriele Köhler, Padma Mallampally, Ludger Odenthal, Marko Stanovic, James Xiaoning Zhan and Zbigniew Zimny. Specific inputs were received from Kumi Endo, Boubacar Hassane, Abraham Negash and Katja Weigl.

Principal research assistance was provided by Mohamed Chiraz Baly, Lizanne Martinez and Bradley Boicourt. Research assistance was also provided by Tadelle Taye and Alke Gijrath. Three interns assisted with the *WIR2000* at various stages: Raluca Maxim, Ghitu I. Mundunge and Ronald Wormgoor. The production of the *WIR2000* was carried out by Jenifer Tacardon-Mercado, Maria Lourdes Pasinos, Mary McGee, Zenaida Lugon and Atsedeweyn Abate. Graphics were done by Diego Oyarzun-Reyes. *The WIR2000* was copy-edited by Betty Hamnett and desktop-published by Teresita Sabico.

Sanjaya Lall was the principal consultant and adviser to Part Two of *WIR2000*. Experts from both within and outside the United Nations provided inputs. Major inputs were received from Daniel Chudnovsky, Jaime Crispi, Andrés López and Bernard Yeung. Inputs were also received from Douglas van der Berghe, Peter Brimble, Teresa Chudy, Joel Davidow, Christian Dery, David M. Eisenberg, Celso Garrido, David Hall, Mongi Hamdi, Gabriela Llobet, Emanuele Lobina, Chris McIntyre, Stilpon Nestor, Terutomo Ozawa, Carlos Romero, Jörg Simon, Rob van Tulder, Carlos Vidotto and Ted Zahavich.

A number of experts were consulted on various chapters. Evidence on the special topic of Part Two was gathered at regional seminars, for which Katalin Antalóczy, JD Soediono Basuki, Sonia Ferencikova, David Floyd, David Hendrix, Gábor Hunya, Martin Jarolim, Nagesh Kumar, Peter Mihályi, Raghav Naraslay, Shoko Negishi, Matija Rojec, Valdas Samonis, Magdolna Sass, Miklós Szanyi, Stanislaw Uminski, Kittipong Urapeepatanapong, Tony Wesolowsky, Mikyung Yun and Alena Zemplínerová prepared papers. Comments were also received during various stages of preparation from Christian J. Bellak, Magnus Bild, George Bittlingmayer, Richard Bolwijn, Philippe Brusick, Alfred Chandler, John Cuddy, Jarko Fidrmuc, Chris Freeman, Massimiliano Gangi, Vishwas Govitrikar, H. Peter Gray, Anthony Hill, Wee Kee Hwee, Azizul Islam, Anna Joubin-Bret, Ku-Hyun Jung, Nam-Hoon Kang, John Kelly, Gudrun Kochendoerfer-Lucius, Ari Kokko, Hans-Peter Lankes, Ignacio de Leon, Maura Liberatori, Robert E. Lipsey, Pradeep Mehta, Ricardo Monge, Michael Mortimore, Rajneesh Narula, Gesner Oliveira, Maria Pigato, Stephen Pursey, Hassan Qaqaya, Eric D. Ramstetter, Pedro Roffe, Tagi Sagafi-nejad, Eric Sahlin, Hans Schenk, Joseph Smolik, Marjan Svetlicic, Anh-Nga Tran-Nguyen, Obie Whichard, Mira Wilkins and Xia Youfu.

Numerous officials of national central banks, statistical offices, investment promotion agencies and other government offices, officials of international organizations and non-governmental organizations, and the executives of a number of companies, also contributed to *WIR2000*, especially through the provision of data and other information. Data on cross-border M&As were provided by Eileen Ciesla and Carrie Smith in Thomson Financial Securities Data Company.

The regional seminars discussing the special topic of Part Two were hosted by the Austrian National Bank in Vienna, Austria, and by the Chulalongkorn University in Bangkok, Thailand. The global seminar was co-sponsored by the Germany Policy Forum (DSE).

The *WIR2000* benefited generally from the advice of John H. Dunning, Senior Economic Advisor.

The financial support of the Governments of Germany, Netherlands, Norway and Sweden is gratefully acknowledged.

Table of contents

Page

PART TWO
CROSS-BORDER MERGERS AND ACQUISITIONS
AND DEVELOPMENT

Page

Page

Annexes

PART ONE

Boxes

Page

Figures

Page

Tables

Page

List of box figures

PART TWO

Boxes

Page

Figures

Tables

Page

List of box tables

Overview

Transnational corporations, the firms driving international production,...

International production by transnational corporations (TNCs), now numbering some 63,000 parent firms with around 690,000 foreign affiliates and a plethora of inter-firm arrangements, spans virtually all countries and economic activities, rendering it a formidable force in today's world economy. The world's top 100 (non-financial) TNCs (with General Electric in first place), based almost exclusively in developed countries, are the principal drivers of international production. The $2 trillion in assets of their foreign affiliates accounted for about one-eighth of the total assets of all foreign affiliates worldwide in 1998. The foreign affiliates of the top 100 TNCs employ over 6 million persons, and their foreign sales are of the order of $2 trillion. They are concentrated mainly in electronics and electrical equipment, automobiles, petroleum, chemicals and pharmaceuticals.

Despite the prominence of the top 100, the universe of TNCs is quite diverse, and includes a growing number of small and medium-sized enterprises, TNCs from countries in Central and Eastern Europe that have only recently begun to engage in international production, and large TNCs based in the developing world. Although less transnational overall than the world's top 100

TNCs, some of the developing-country TNCs are quite sizeable — witness, for example, the size of the foreign assets ($8 billion) of Petroleos de Venezuela, the largest TNC from the developing world and the only developing-country firm to appear in the top 100 list.

The expansion of international production has been facilitated by virtually all countries through changes in their regulatory environments. Over the period 1991-1999, 94 per cent of the 1,035 changes worldwide in the laws governing foreign direct investment (FDI) created a more favourable framework for FDI. Complementing the more welcoming national FDI regimes, the number of bilateral investment treaties — concluded increasingly also between developing countries — has risen from 181 at the end of 1980 to 1,856 at the end of 1999. Double taxation treaties have also increased, from 719 in 1980 to 1,982 at the end of 1999. At the regional and interregional levels, an increasing number of agreements (most recently between the European Community and Mexico) are helping to create an investment environment more conducive to international investment flows.

Evidence on the expansion of international production over the past two decades abounds. Gross product associated with international production and foreign affiliate sales worldwide, two measures of international production, increased faster than global GDP and global exports, respectively. Sales of foreign affiliates worldwide ($14 trillion in 1999, $3 trillion in 1980) are now nearly twice as high as global exports, and the gross product associated with international production is about one-tenth of global GDP, compared with one-twentieth in 1982. The ratio of world FDI inflows, which stood at $865 billion in 1999, to global gross domestic capital formation is now 14 per cent, compared with 2 per cent twenty years ago. Similarly, the ratio of world FDI stock to world GDP increased from 5 per cent to 16 per cent during the same period. And the number of transnational parent firms in 15 developed home countries increased from some 7,000 at the end of the 1960s to some 40,000 at the end of the 1990s.

The ascendance and deepening of international production have given rise to new policy challenges. The distribution of international production, and of the corresponding benefits associated with it, is one of the most important of these. While the size of international production has risen significantly over the past few decades, not all countries have participated in it to the same extent. FDI, albeit an imperfect measure of international production, is concentrated in a handful of countries — ten countries received 74 per cent of global FDI flows in 1999. Just ten developing countries received 80 per cent of total FDI flows to the developing world. The trans-nationalization index, a more complex measure of the extent of a country's involvement in international production, shows a similar picture. More importantly, there are no signs that the concentration of international production across countries has been declining over time. However, in many least developed countries that have received only small amounts of FDI, such investment is important vis-à-vis the size of domestic investment. What remains a challenge for these countries is the ability to attract not only more, but also higher-quality FDI — broadly defined as investment with strong links to the domestic economy, export orientation, advanced technology and skill or spillover effects.

Another challenge is posed by issues arising from the ability of TNCs to internalize cross-border transactions and bypass national controls and scrutiny. For example, TNCs can use transfer pricing on intra-firm trade to minimize their tax exposure, depriving host or home countries of tax revenues. Furthermore, cross-holdings, share listings in several stock exchanges, the location of headquarters in countries other than the

country of origin, and sourcing of inputs from facilities in multiple countries are all examples of how the ownership and nationality of TNCs have become less clear-cut. Finally, given that the micro-economic interests of TNCs and the development objectives of host countries do not necessarily coincide, governments need to ensure that policies are in place to ensure that they maximize the benefits gained from FDI. This means creating dynamic locational advantages so as to attract especially higher-quality FDI. It also means creating an integrated and coherent framework of policies conducive to development, implementing it properly and establishing a framework for property rights and dispute settlement. However, it requires effective bargaining capabilities in host countries.

...invested record amounts abroad in 1999, but mostly in the developed world.

Driven by the recent wave of cross-border mergers and acquisitions (M&As), global FDI outflows reached $800 billion in 1999, an increase of 16 per cent over the previous year. Indications are that FDI flows in 2000 may well surpass the one-trillion-dollar mark. (Beyond that year, predictions are difficult to make.) After stagnating in 1998, FDI flows to developing countries have resumed their earlier growth trend. In 1999, developing countries received $208 billion in FDI, an increase of 16 per cent over 1998 and an all-time high. The share of developing countries in global FDI inflows has, however, fallen, going from 38 per cent in 1997 to 24 per cent in 1999.

Developed countries attracted $636 billion in FDI flows in 1999, nearly three quarters of the world's total. The *United States* and the United Kingdom were the leaders as both investors and recipients. With $199 billion, the United Kingdom became the largest outward investor in 1999, forging ahead of the United States. Large M&As in the United States, driven partly by the continuing strength of its economy, rendered it the largest recipient of FDI with $276 billion, nearly one-third of the world total.

TNCs based in the *European Union* (EU) invested $510 billion abroad in 1999, or nearly two-thirds of global outflows. Within the EU, the United Kingdom, France and Germany were the largest outward investors, while the United Kingdom and Sweden were the largest recipients — in the case of the latter, owing to one single large acquisition. In the case of outflows, extra-EU FDI has been more important than intra-EU investment since 1997, owing to a few large M&A deals, but intra-EU FDI remained significant as TNCs were still adjusting their investment plans to the various EU directives deregulating and opening up new industries. The EU's single currency, the euro, has stabilized exchange rates, contributing in this manner to a reduction of transaction costs for investors in the region; but it has also increased competition, which has exerted more pressure on firms to restructure and consolidate their operations.

FDI flows to *Japan* quadrupled, reaching a record $13 billion in 1999, the largest annual inflow to date. Dispelling the image of Japan as a country where M&As are either unwelcome or difficult to undertake, most of these inflows arrived through cross-border M&A deals. As for Japanese FDI outflows, they declined in 1999 by 6 per cent, to $23 billion, although Japanese TNCs, among the most affected by the Asian financial crisis, are beginning once again to increase production in Asia.

FDI rebounded in East and South-East Asia, and gained momentum in Latin America and the Caribbean,...

Contrary to general expectations, FDI flows to *East and South-East Asia* increased by 11 per cent, to reach $93 billion in 1999. The increase was mainly in newly industrializing economies (Hong Kong, China; Republic of Korea; Singapore; and Taiwan Province of China), whose inflows increased by almost 70 per cent. In the Republic of Korea, FDI inflows reached an unprecedented $10 billion. Inflows to Singapore and Taiwan Province of China experienced a significant recovery after a sharp decline in 1998. FDI in Hong Kong (China), now the second largest recipient in the region, increased significantly — by more than 50 per cent — to reach $23 billion in 1999. This increase was largely due to the 1998 wave of "re-domiciling" funds owned by Hong Kong investors and foreign investors based in Hong Kong (China) and also to a large amount of reinvested earnings as a result of the distinct turnaround in local economic activity in 1999.

Nevertheless, FDI flows declined in three of the five countries most affected by the recent financial crisis (Indonesia, Thailand and the Philippines). Flows to China, which had been well above $40 billion for four consecutive years, dropped by nearly 8 per cent, to just over $40 billion in 1999. South-East Asian low income countries which are dependent on other countries in the region for FDI continued to be adversely affected by the negative impact of the crisis on Asian outward investment.

Behind the recovery of FDI in the region lies intensified efforts to attract FDI, including greater liberalization at the sectoral level and increased openness to cross-border M&As. Cross-border M&As in the five countries (Indonesia, Malaysia, the Philippines, Republic of Korea and Thailand) most affected by the recent crisis reached a record level of $15 billion in 1999. Indeed, M&As have become an important mode of entry for TNCs investing in the region, averaging $20 billion during the period 1997-1999, compared with an average of $7 billion during the period 1994-1996.

FDI in *South Asia* declined in 1999 by 13 per cent, to $3.2 billion. Inflows to India, the single largest recipient in the sub-region, were $2.2 billion (a 17 per cent decrease). FDI flows to *Central Asia* declined slightly in 1999 to $2.8 billion, losing the momentum exhibited during the initial phases of liberalization and regulatory reform. The *Pacific Island* economies saw an improvement in their inflows in 1999, which rose to $250 million. FDI flows to *West Asia* increased to $6.7 billion, with Saudi Arabia receiving most of the new investment.

Outward FDI from developing Asia recovered from its recession during the financial crisis (increasing by 64 per cent in 1999 to an estimated $37 billion), still lower than the pre-crisis level. Hong Kong (China) remained the major outward investor, accounting for over half of the total outflows from the region. Divestment by Asian TNCs continued in 1999. In some cases, Asian TNCs sold their existing overseas businesses; in others, they were themselves acquired by foreign TNCs. Many Asian TNCs have been unable to take advantage of the cheap assets available due to the crisis; exceptions were those based in Hong Kong (China), Singapore and Taiwan Province of China, which managed to maintain their financial strength to engage in M&As, mostly in neighbouring countries.

FDI flows to *Latin America and the Caribbean* continued to increase in 1999, reaching a new record level of $90 billion, a 23 per cent increase over 1998. For the fourth consecutive year, Brazil was the largest recipient in the region, with $31 billion in investment inflows, mostly in non-tradable services and domestic-market-oriented manufacturing. Argentina's inflows more than tripled, reaching $23 billion in 1999; it overtook Mexico as the region's second largest recipient. Mexico received $11 billion in 1999, mainly in export-oriented manufacturing. A significant part of FDI flows to Latin America has entered through M&A deals, which reached a value of $37 billion in 1999. Some $16 billion of it involved the acquisition of local private companies by foreign-based TNCs. Privatization, however, remained important in Argentina, Brazil and to a lesser extent Chile, with a significant participation by TNCs based in Europe. For the Andean Community countries, FDI through privatization remained low.

...but flows to Central and Eastern Europe rose only modestly, while Africa continued to receive no more than a marginal share of FDI inflows.

In 1999, FDI flows into *Central and Eastern Europe* increased for the third consecutive year, reaching $23 billion in 1999. Still, the region accounted for less than 3 per cent of global FDI flows. As in 1998, Poland, the Czech Republic and the Russian Federation continued to be the top recipients of FDI flows. In the case of the last, FDI flows have rebounded, but they are still half the level of their 1997 figure of $6 billion. In relation to the size of their economies, Estonia, Hungary and the Czech Republic are the region's leaders. TNCs based in the European Union are the principal investors in Central and Eastern Europe, and services are gaining in importance over manufacturing. The size of the domestic market in the case of large recipients, such as Poland, or privatization programmes allowing the participation of foreign investors, as in the case of the Czech Republic, are the principal determinants of FDI in the region. Central and Eastern European countries are not significant outward investors, registering less than $3 billion of outflows in 1999.

Despite a modest rise in FDI flows to *Africa* — from $8 billion in 1998 to $10 billion in 1999 — the region's performance remains lackluster. On a more positive note, though, FDI flows to Africa have stabilized at much higher levels than those registered in the early 1990s, in response to the sustained efforts of many countries to create more business-friendly environments. Some countries, such as Angola, Egypt, Morocco, Nigeria, South Africa and Tunisia, have attracted sizeable amounts of FDI in recent years. Angola and Egypt, in particular, have been especially successful, overtaking Nigeria to become the largest FDI recipients in the region in 1999. Although the absolute levels of FDI were small for most countries, they were nevertheless often significant in relation to the size of their domestic economies, as measured by both GDP and gross domestic capital formation. Finally, there is more diversification in terms of both source countries — with the United States being the most important one, followed by European countries — and in terms of sectors — with manufacturing and services gaining in importance over natural resources. On the negative side, FDI in Africa continues to be highly concentrated in five countries (whose composition, however, has changed over the years), with the bulk of African countries receiving meager amounts and the continent's share of world FDI inflows languishing at 1.2 per cent.

The responses to a survey of 296 of the world's largest TNCs carried out jointly by UNCTAD and the International Chamber of Commerce at the beginning of 2000 indicate that the modest increase in the level of FDI flows into Africa observed in recent years may well be sustained in the future. One-third of the 65 respondents intend to increase investment in Africa in the next three to five years, and more than half expect their investment to remain stable. More than 43 per cent of the respondents expect that Africa's overall prospects for attracting FDI will improve in the next three-to-five years, but another 46 per cent expect no change. South Africa and Egypt are viewed as the most attractive African locations. In general, the more developed countries in the region ranked higher than those at the bottom of the ladder, but a few least developed countries, notably Mozambique, Uganda, the United Republic of Tanzania and Ethiopia, were also viewed as attractive FDI destinations. Tourism, natural resource industries, or industries for which the domestic market is important — such as telecommunications — were viewed as the most promising in their potential to attract FDI. Textiles and clothing industries for which the international market is important ranked low. The survey findings also pointed out that the negative image of Africa persists and acts as a disincentive for foreign investors. But they also underline the need to differentiate among the countries of the continent.

The findings of the survey are broadly in line with those of an earlier survey of African investment promotion agencies conducted in 1999. There are, however, some interesting differences as regards the determinants of FDI decisions. TNCs ranked the size of domestic markets high and access to international markets low, while it was the belief of African investment promotion agencies that TNCs placed more emphasis on access to global markets, regulatory frameworks and incentives. Both TNCs and investment promotion agencies, however, recognized that corruption, the high costs of doing business, the poor state of the physical infrastructure and difficulties in accessing capital will be obstacles to attracting FDI in the foreseeable future.

Cross-border M&As, transacted in an emerging global market for firms, are the main force behind the latest rise of FDI,...

Over the past decade, most of the growth in international production has been via cross-border M&As (including the acquisitions by foreign investors of privatized state-owned enterprises) rather than greenfield investment: the value of completed cross-border M&As rose from less than $100 billion in 1987 to $720 billion in 1999. It should be cautioned, however, that data on the value of cross-border M&As and FDI flows are not truly comparable, for a variety of reasons that relate to how M&As are financed and to the balance-of-payments methodology used in calculating FDI flows, which is not applicable to M&As. Still, regardless of whether investments take place through greenfield establishments or M&As, they add to the size of international production.

Less than 3 per cent of the total number of cross-border M&As are officially classified

as mergers (although many of them are so only in name) — the rest are acquisitions. Full acquisitions account for two thirds of the total number of cross-border acquisitions. Minority acquisitions (10-49 per cent) account for about one-third of cross-border acquisitions in developing countries, compared with less than one-fifth in developed countries. Cross-border M&As can be classified functionally as horizontal (between firms in the same industry), vertical (client-supplier or buyer-seller M&As), or conglomerate (between companies in unrelated industries). In terms of value, about 70 per cent of cross-border M&As are horizontal. In terms of number, that share is 50 per cent. Vertical M&As have been increasing in numbers in recent years. While many of the cross-border M&As in the late 1980s were driven by the quest for short-term financial gains, most M&As today appear to have strategic and economic rather than immediate financial motives. Also, most of the recent cross-border M&As are not hostile: hostile M&As accounted for less than 5 per cent of the total value and less than 0.2 per cent of the total number of M&As in 1999.

The total *number* of all M&As worldwide (cross-border and domestic) has grown at 42 per cent annually between 1980 and 1999. The *value* of all M&As (cross-border and domestic) as a share of world GDP has risen from 0.3 per cent in 1980 to 8 per cent in 1999. Two big M&A waves can be distinguished during this period: one in 1988-1990 and another from 1995 onwards. The recent wave has taken place alongside a boom in domestic M&As. Consequently, during the 1990s, the share of cross-border M&As in all M&A deals has not changed: it averaged about 25 per cent in terms of both value and number of completed transactions. (In 1999, however, that share in terms of value was nearly 31 per cent.) Apart from traditional bank loans, the recent M&A boom has been facilitated by the increased use of such financing mechanisms as the issuance of common stocks, the exchange of stocks and corporate debt. In addition to the traditional bank loans, venture capital funds have also been significant as a source of finance, enabling many new firms or small and medium-sized enterprises to engage in M&A activity.

Following earlier trends, cross-border M&As increased by 35 per cent in 1999, reaching — according to UNCTAD estimates

— $720 billion in over 6,000 deals. About one-sixth of these M&A transactions (in terms of number) involved foreign affiliates already present in host countries. Cross-border M&As are expected to increase further in 2000, with several mega deals already announced or completed (e.g. Vodafone AirTouch-Mannesmann). The year 2000 may well see a total value of cross-border M&As above $1 trillion.

The ratio of the value of cross-border M&As to world FDI flows reached over 80 per cent in 1999. M&As are particularly significant as a mode of entry for FDI in developed countries. In the developing world, greenfield FDI is still dominant. FDI flows to developing countries associated with M&As have been on the rise, however, their value increased roughly from one-tenth of the value of total FDI inflows at the end of the 1980s to one-third at the end of the 1990s. In Central and Eastern Europe, due to fluctuations in cross-border acquisitions associated with privatizations, the share of M&As in total FDI inflows has varied widely from year to year.

Some interesting parallels can be drawn between the current M&A boom and the one that occurred in the United States at the turn of the nineteenth century, reaching its climax between 1898 and 1902. Both M&A waves have been affected by major technological developments, new means of financing M&As and regulatory changes. But while the recent wave is an international one, the older one was confined to the United States. And just as the earlier boom in the United States contributed to the emergence of a national market for goods and services and a national production system, complemented by a national market for firms, so is the current international boom reinforcing the emergence of a global market for goods and services and the emergence of an international production system, complemented by an increasingly global market for firms.

...driven by strategic corporate objectives ...

The current spate of cross-border M&As is occurring despite the fact that many M&As have not delivered the anticipated positive results to the acquiring firms in terms of both share prices and "real" economic effects such as profits and productivity. Although the impact on the target firms often appears to be more favourable, the growth of cross-border M&As as a mode of expansion may still be regarded as somewhat paradoxical. In order to understand the phenomenon more fully, both basic motivations for M&As and changes in the economic environment — and their interaction — need to be taken into account.

In general, from a foreign investor's perspective, cross-border M&As offer two main advantages compared with greenfield investment as a mode of FDI entry: speed and access to proprietary assets. The crucial role of speed in today's business life is illustrated by such quotes from top executives as: "In the new economy in which we live, a year has 50 days" or "Speed is our friend — time is our enemy". Cross-border M&As often represent the fastest means of building up a strong position in a new market, gaining market power — and indeed market dominance — increasing the size of the firm or spreading risks. At the same time, financial opportunities may be exploited and personal gains be reaped by top management. Moreover, cross-border M&As may allow firms to realize synergies by pooling the proprietary resources and capabilities of the firms involved, with potential static and dynamic efficiency gains. The relatively poor financial performance record of M&As suggests, however, that there may be other reasons to consider.

They have to do with advances in technology, liberalization and changes in capital markets. The rapid pace of technical change has intensified competitive pressures on the world's technological leaders, which are often TNCs. By merging with other TNCs with complementary capabilities, firms can share the costs of innovation, access new technological assets and enhance their competitiveness. The spreading and deepening of the international production system through cross-border M&As has furthermore been facilitated by the ongoing removal or relaxation of restrictions on FDI (including restrictions on cross-border M&As) in many countries. Trade liberalization and regional integration efforts have added an impetus to cross-border M&As by setting the scene for more intense competition and by prompting regional corporate restructuring and consolidation. Capital market liberalization, in turn, and the proliferation of new methods of financing M&As, have made cross-border M&As easier.

Finally, the idea that there is an increasingly global market for firms, in which firms are bought and sold, has become more widely accepted.

The current wave of unprecedented global and regional restructuring through cross-border M&As reflects a dynamic interaction between the various basic factors motivating firms to undertake M&As and changes in the global economic environment, in the pursuit of strategic corporate objectives. For many firms, the quest to survive and prosper in the emerging global market for firms becomes the key strategic issue and, hence, drives the M&A trend. In the market for firms, sanctions can await those that fail to deliver growth and profits. One such sanction is to be taken over. All the basic motivations for firms to undertake cross-border M&As then combine to become key elements in the overarching strategic goal to defend and develop competitive market positions. Cross-border M&As are growing so rapidly in importance precisely because they provide firms with the fastest way of acquiring tangible and intangible assets in different countries, and because they allow firms to restructure existing operations nationally or globally to exploit synergies and obtain strategic advantages. In brief, cross-border M&As allow firms rapidly to acquire a portfolio of locational assets which has become a key source of competitive strength in a globalizing economy. In oligopolistic industries, furthermore, deals may be undertaken in response to the moves or anticipated moves of competitors. Even firms that would not want to jump on the bandwagon may feel that they have to, for fear of becoming targets themselves.

...and concentrated mainly in a handful of developed countries and industries.

Some 90 per cent of all cross-border M&As (by value in 1999), including most of the 109 mega deals with transaction values of more than $1 billion, were carried out in developed countries. These countries have had the highest share of M&As in their GDPs and have witnessed a parallel increase in FDI flows.

Western European firms engaged actively in cross-border M&As in 1999, with a total of $354 billion in sales and $519 billion in purchases. Intra-European-Union M&A activity accounts for a significant share of these transactions, driven by the introduction of the single currency and measures promoting greater regional integration. Most of the purchases outside the region involve United Kingdom firms acquiring United States firms. The United Kingdom, Sweden, Germany and the Netherlands were the largest target countries, while Germany and France were the largest acquirers after the United Kingdom.

The United States continued to be the single largest target country with M&A sales of $233 billion to foreign investors in 1999. More than a quarter of all M&A deals in the United States in 1999 were concluded by foreign acquirers in 1999, compared with 7 per cent in 1997. Cross-border M&As are today the dominant mode by which FDI enters the United States market. M&A-associated investment in foreign affiliates in the United States accounted for 90 per cent in terms of value and 62 per cent in terms of the number of projects of all FDI in 1998. On the outward side, United States firms acquired foreign firms valued at $112 billion in 1999, $25 billion less than in 1998. The decline reflects a lower number of mega deals.

The value of Japanese M&A purchases overseas increased significantly in 1999, primarily due to a single transaction. In general, Japanese TNCs still prefer greenfield investments to M&As, especially when investing in developing countries. Cross-border M&A sales in Japan have risen rapidly in recent years, and were larger than purchases during the period 1997-1999. This is due to changes in the regulatory framework for M&As, corporate strategies favouring M&As pursued by foreign-based TNCs, and the changing attitudes of Japanese firms towards M&As.

Automobiles, pharmaceuticals and chemicals, and food, beverages and tobacco were the leading industries in the manufacturing sector in terms of worldwide cross-border M&A activity in 1999. Most M&As in those industries were horizontal, aiming at economies of scale, technological synergies, increasing market power, eliminating excess capacity, or consolidating and streamlining innovation strategies and R&D budgets. In most of the industries in which horizontal M&A activity is strong, concentration ratios have intensified. In automobiles, M&A activity between car makers and suppliers has also led to greater vertical consolidation.

Telecommunications, energy and financial services were the leading industries in M&A activity in the services sector, largely as a result of recent deregulation and liberalization in these industries. In financial services, competitive pressures and mounting information technology costs have given an added impetus to M&As.

It was not until the late 1990s that developing countries emerged as important locations for incoming cross-border M&As in terms of value. While their share in world cross-border M&As remained constant at less than 10 per cent in terms of value almost every year until the mid-1990s, in terms of the number of deals, it increased from 5 per cent in 1987 to 19 per cent in the late 1990s. The value of cross-border M&As undertaken by firms *from* developing countries rose from $3 billion in 1987 to $41 billion in 1999.

Among the developing regions, Latin America and the Caribbean dominate cross-border M&A sales, with Brazil and Argentina as the main sellers. Privatization has been the main vehicle for M&As in both countries. In Asia, cross-border M&A sales gathered pace in 1999. In the Republic of Korea, acquisitions by foreign firms exceeded $9 billion in 1999, making it the largest recipient of M&A-associated FDI in developing Asia. In Africa, Egypt, Morocco and South Africa have been the targets of most foreign acquisitions. In the other African countries, M&A activity has been slow, due partly to the slow pace of privatization and partly for broader reasons related to the investment climate and limited availability of attractive firms for purchase in the private sector.

The principal acquirers of firms based in developing countries have traditionally been TNCs based in developed countries. European Union firms became the largest acquirers during 1998-1999, replacing United States firms and accounting for more than two-fifths of all cross-border M&As in developing countries. Cross-border M&A purchases by firms based in developing countries nearly doubled in 1999 after dipping in 1998 in response to the Asian financial crisis. Asian firms in fact became the principal targets of these purchases in 1999, with Singapore the leading buyer. Cross-border M&A purchases by firms from the five Asian countries most affected by the financial crisis also increased, reflecting improvements in their liquidity position. The same trend can be observed in Latin America and the Caribbean, with significant increases in purchases by firms from this region in recent years.

In Central and Eastern Europe, M&A activity has fluctuated widely, doubling in 1999 to $10 billion. Poland, the Czech Republic and Hungary have been the major target countries owing to their large privatization programmes. European Union firms are the principal acquirers in this region.

Among developed countries, the sectoral patterns of cross-border M&A activity differ significantly between the European Union and the United States. In the former, chemicals, food, beverages and tobacco are the most targeted industries for M&As by foreign firms. In the latter, electrical and electronic equipment and chemicals are the preferred target industries. In the European Union and the United States, financial firms are the most aggressive acquirers. In Latin America and the Caribbean, M&A activity is concentrated in public utilities, finance, petroleum products, transport, storage and communications. In the five countries most affected by the Asian financial crisis, finance is the dominant industry in foreign acquisitions. Finance, but also food, beverages and tobacco, are the principal target industries in Central and Eastern Europe.

The special features of cross-border M&As raise concerns about the balance of benefits for host countries...

Cross-border M&As, particularly those involving large firms, vast sums of money and major restructurings of the activities of firms, are among the most visible faces of globalization. And, as with globalization generally, the impact of M&As on development can be double-edged and uneven. Indeed, perhaps to a greater extent than many other aspects of globalization, cross-border M&As — and the expanding global market for firm ownership and control in which these transactions take place — raise questions about the balance of their benefits and costs for host countries (box). These concerns are further accentuated in the prevailing context of globalization and the rapid changes associated with it. TNCs are seen to benefit disproportionately from globalization, while local SMEs in host developing countries are affected adversely. M&As, and in particular their cross-border variety, appear to be little more than a vehicle for the expansion of big business.

Concerns related to cross-border M&As are not confined to developing countries. They are also expressed in many developed countries, often more vehemently. When Japanese investors acquired the Rockefeller Center in New York and film studios in Hollywood, the press reacted with indignation. When Vodafone AirTouch (United Kingdom) recently sought to acquire Mannesmann (Germany), the reaction was similar in some quarters. While nationalistic reactions to foreign takeovers are diminishing in force, they can be strong enough to lead host governments to intervene, particularly if takeovers are hostile.

All these concerns need to be considered carefully. They are examined in *WIR2000* by focussing on the impact of cross-border M&As in key areas of economic development, and whether it differs from that of greenfield FDI. A good part of the discussion in this volume is conceptual, and more empirical work is needed to understand the matter fully.

The starting point of the examination is the impacts of FDI in general on different key areas of development, as identified in UNCTAD's *WIR99*. The *Report* then compares the impact of FDI through M&As with that of FDI through greenfield ventures. Comparing cross-border M&As with greenfield FDI often means considering counterfactuals — what might have happened if cross-border M&As had not taken place. Such counterfactuals need to take account of not just the industry and host-country context, but also of the broader setting of trade, technology and competition.

Not all cross-border M&As are FDI. Some are portfolio investments (acquisitions of less than 10 per cent equity, for measurement

---

What concerns do cross-border M&As raise for host countries?

In a number of host countries, concern is expressed in political discussions and the media that FDI entry through the takeover of domestic firms is less beneficial, if not positively harmful, for economic development than entry by setting up new facilities. At the heart of these concerns is that foreign acquisitions do not add to productive capacity but simply transfer ownership and control from domestic to foreign hands. This transfer is often accompanied by layoffs of employees or the closing of some production or functional activities (e.g. R&D capacities). It also entails servicing the new owner in foreign exchange.

If the acquirers are global oligopolists, they may well come to dominate the local market. Cross-border M&As can, moreover, be used deliberately to reduce competition in domestic markets. They can lead to strategic firms or even entire industries (including key ones like banking) falling under foreign control, threatening local entrepreneurial and technological capacity-building.

Concerns over the impact of cross-border M&As on host-country development arise even when M&As go well from a corporate viewpoint. But there can also be additional concerns related to the possibility that M&As may not, in fact, go well. Half of all M&As do not live up to the performance expectations of parent firms, typically when measured in terms of shareholder value. Moreover, even in M&As that do go well, efficient implementation from an investor's point of view does not necessarily mean a favourable impact on host-country development. This applies to FDI through M&As as well as to greenfield FDI. The main reason is that the commercial objectives of TNCs and the development objectives of host economies do not necessarily coincide.

The areas of concern transcend the economic and reach into the social, political and cultural realms. In industries like media and entertainment, for example, M&As may seem to threaten national culture or identity. More broadly, the transfer of ownership of important enterprises from domestic to foreign hands may be seen as eroding national sovereignty and amounting to recolonization. When the acquisitions involve "fire sales" — sales of companies in distress, often at low prices considered abnormally low — such concerns are intensified.

Source: UNCTAD.

purposes). Yet others are akin to portfolio investments, being solely or primarily motivated by financial considerations, regardless of the equity share involved. Portfolio or near-portfolio M&As are not considered here, since the focus is on M&As as a mode of *FDI* entry, not on cross-border M&As *per se*. In any event, the share of portfolio or near-portfolio M&As in the total value of cross-border M&As is small.

For some direct investors there is a genuine choice between entering a host country through greenfield FDI and entering it through M&As. However, the two modes of entry are not always realistic alternatives for either TNCs or host countries, as for example when a telecommunication network is privatized or a large ailing firm needs to be rescued and no domestic buyers can be found. Hence *WIR2000* also considers situations in which cross-border M&As are the only realistic way for a country to deal with a given situation, focusing on how M&As affect the performance of the acquired enterprise and the host economy.

...especially at the time of entry and shortly thereafter,...

The essential difference between cross-border M&As and greenfield FDI is that the former involve, by definition, a change of assets from domestic to foreign hands and, at least initially, do not add to the productive capacity of host countries. The discussion in *WIR2000* suggests that, especially *at the time of entry and in the short term*, M&As (as compared to greenfield investment) may involve, in some respects, smaller benefits or larger negative impacts from the perspective of host-country development. To summarize:

- Although FDI through both M&As and greenfield investment brings foreign financial resources to a host country, the financial resources provided through M&As do not always go into additions to the capital stock for production, while in the case of greenfield FDI they do. Hence a given amount of FDI through M&As may correspond to a smaller productive investment than the same amount of greenfield FDI, or to none at all. However, when the only realistic alternative for a local firm is closure, cross-border merger or acquisition can serve as "life preserver".

- FDI through M&As is less likely to transfer new or better technologies or skills than greenfield FDI, at least at the time of entry. Moreover, it may lead directly to the downgrading or closure of local production or functional activities (e.g. R&D), or to their relocation in line with the acquirer's corporate strategy. Greenfield FDI does not *directly* reduce the technological assets and capabilities in a host economy.

- FDI through M&As does not generate employment when it enters a country, for the obvious reason that no new production capacity is created in a merger or an acquisition. Furthermore, it may lead to lay-offs, although it can conserve employment if the acquired firm would have otherwise gone bankrupt. Greenfield FDI necessarily creates new employment at entry.

- FDI through M&As can increase concentration in host countries and lead to anti-competitive results; in fact, M&As can be used deliberately to reduce or eliminate competition. It can, however, prevent concentration from increasing when takeovers help preserve local firms that might otherwise have gone under. Greenfield FDI, by definition, may increase the number of firms in existence and cannot directly increase market concentration upon entry.

...but these fade in the longer term, when both direct and indirect effects of M&As come into play,...

Most of the shortcomings of FDI through M&As in comparison with greenfield FDI relate to effects at entry or soon after entry. *Over the longer term*, when direct as well as indirect effects are taken into account, many differences between the impacts of the two modes diminish or disappear. To summarize:

- Cross-border M&As are often followed by sequential investments by the foreign acquirers — sometimes large, especially in special circumstances such as privatizations. Thus, over the longer term, FDI through M&As can lead to enhanced investment in production just as greenfield FDI does. The two modes are also likely to have similar effects regarding the crowding in and crowding out of domestic enterprises.

- Cross-border M&As can be followed by transfers of new or better technology (including organizational and managerial practices), especially when acquired firms are restructured to increase the efficiency of their operations. To the extent that TNCs invest in building local skills and technological capabilities, they do so regardless of how those affiliates were established.

- Cross-border M&As can generate employment over time, if sequential investments take place and if the linkages of acquired firms are retained or strengthened. Thus, in the longer run, differences between the two modes as regards employment generation tend to diminish and depend more on the motivation for entry than on the mode of entry. If employment reductions occur due to restructuring for greater efficiency, the consequences may be less disruptive than when greenfield FDI eliminates uncompetitive firms.

- The effects on market structure, whether negative or positive, can persist after entry. The capacity to engage in anticompetitive practices is greater with M&As that increase concentration, especially when they occur in weakly regulated oligopolistic industries.

In sum, host-country impacts of FDI are difficult to distinguish by mode of entry once the initial period has passed — with the possible exception on market structure and competition.

In addition to the principal effects on the important *individual* aspects of economic development summarized above, the overall impact of cross-border M&As as against greenfield investment also needs to be considered, taking into account the specific economic context and the development priorities of individual host countries. Particularly important here is the impact on economic restructuring. The restructuring of industries and activities is necessary for growth and development, especially under conditions of rapid technological change and increasing global competition. It can also be important

under exceptional circumstances, such as financial crises or transitions to market-based economic systems. Cross-border M&As may have a role to play here since they provide a package of assets that can be used for various types of restructuring and, furthermore, have the attributes of speed and the immediate involvement of local (acquired) firms; they can thus usefully supplement domestic resources and efforts. Greenfield investment, of course, can also help economic restructuring; but it has no role to play in conserving domestic enterprises and may, indeed, hasten the demise of weaker domestic firms if and when it out-competes them.

...although concerns regarding foreign control and ownership generally may linger.

Finally, there are the broader apprehensions regarding a weakening of the national enterprise sector and a loss of control over the direction of national economic development and the pursuit of national social, cultural and political goals. These issues acquire urgency when cross-border M&As result in industries thought to be strategic coming under the control of foreign TNCs. They may acquire a yet further edge in developing countries since these countries are predominantly host rather than home countries for FDI in general and cross-border M&As in particular.

The basic question here is what role foreign firms should play in an economy, regardless of whether they enter through greenfield investment or cross-border M&As. It has to do with the extent of foreign ownership that a country can accept comfortably, and the economic, social, cultural and political consequences of such ownership. Many governments, local enterprises and civil-society groups feel that certain activities (e.g. the media) should be exclusively or primarily in local hands.

There are no *a priori* solutions to these concerns. Each country needs to make its own judgement in the light of its conditions and needs and in the framework of its broader development objectives. It also needs to be aware of — and to assess — the trade-offs involved, whether related to efficiency, output growth, the distribution of income, access to markets or various non-economic objectives.

And it needs to note as well that some of these concerns are raised by *all* FDI, although the specific nature of M&As may exacerbate them. Trade-offs between economic objectives and broader, non-economic ones, in particular, require value judgements that only countries alone can make.

The circumstances of host countries are particularly important for determining impact.

Apart from consideration related to the time at entry versus the longer run, circumstances in which host countries find themselves deserve underlining when it comes to the assessment of the costs and benefits of cross-border M&As:

• Under *normal circumstances* (i.e. in the absence of crises or systemic changes), and especially when cross-border M&As and greenfield investments are *real* alternatives, greenfield FDI is more useful to developing countries than cross-border M&As. Other things (motivations, capabilities) being equal, greenfield investment not only brings a package of resources and assets *but* simultaneously creates additional productive capacity and employment; cross-border M&As may bring the same package but do not create immediate additional capacity. Furthermore, certain types of cross-border M&As involve a number of risks at the time of entry, from reduced employment through asset stripping to the slower upgrading of domestic technological capacity. And when M&As involve competing firms, there are, of course, the possible negative impacts on market concentration and competition, which can persist beyond the entry phase.

• Under *exceptional circumstances*, cross-border M&As can play a useful role, a role that greenfield FDI may not be able to play, at least within the desired time-frame. Particularly relevant here is a situation of crisis in which firms in a country experience several severe difficulties or face the risk of bankruptcy and no alternative to FDI (including public funding) to M&As by foreign investors is available to help them. Large capital-intensive privatizations (or a large number

of privatizations within the framework of a comprehensive privatization programme) may also fall in this category, because domestic firms may not be able to raise the required funds (including in international financial markets) or have other assets (such as modern managerial practices or technology) that are needed to make the privatized firms competitive. The need for rapid restructuring under conditions of intense competitive pressures or overcapacity in global markets may also make host countries find the option of FDI through cross-border acquisitions of some of their firms useful. The advantage of M&As in such conditions is that they restructure existing capacities. In some of these circumstances, host countries have thus found it useful to relax cross-border M&A restrictions, extend incentives previously reserved for greenfield investment to FDI through M&As, and even make active efforts to attract suitable cross-border M&A partners.

Although there are countries in which exceptional circumstances may be overriding for some time (for example, for economies in transition implementing massive privatization programmes or countries experiencing financial crises), most countries face a mixture of normal and exceptional circumstances. Thus, even countries in sound economic condition might have a number of enterprises (or even entire industries) that are uncompetitive and require restructuring. And, of course, competitive enterprises can also be targets of cross-border M&As. The factors that influence the impact of cross-border M&As on development — regardless of circumstances — were summarized in June 2000 in the "Outcome" of an intergovernmental Expert Meeting on Mergers and Acquisitions as follows (UNCTAD, 2000e, para. 7):

"The economic policy framework and the country's level of development are key. Other factors affecting the impact are: whether a short or long-term perspective is taken to evaluate effects; the normal or exceptional circumstances (such as privatization programmes or financial crises) in which cross-border M&As take place; motivation of the investor (e.g. market seeking vs. efficiency seeking); the situation of the acquired enterprise; and the availability of alternatives as regards modes of entry of investment."

Regardless of circumstances, policy matters — and competition policy takes pride of place among policies addressing cross-border M&A concerns.

Many of these factors — and the specific consequences of cross-border M&As — can be influenced by policy measures. This underlines the central message of the *World Investment Report 1999,* which dealt with FDI and development generally, namely that policy matters. Policy matters especially when it comes to the risks and negative effects associated with cross-border M&As. This is not to minimize the importance of various alternatives to cross-border M&As. For example, while cross-border M&As are an alternative to greenfield FDI, the viability of other options such as strategic alliances or public intervention must also be considered carefully. There may even be a role for international assistance, especially for firms in distress because of developments over which they have no influence.

Policy also matters (as in the case of domestic M&As) in that sectoral policies need to address a number of potential negative effects, e.g. as regards employment and resource utilization. In addition, FDI policies in general can be used to maximize the benefits and minimize the costs of cross-border M&As, through sectoral reservations, ownership regulations, size criteria, screening and incentives. Specific cross-border M&A policies can also be used for some of the same purposes, e.g. the screening of cross-border M&As to ensure that they meet certain criteria.

The most important policy instrument, however, is competition policy. The principal reason is that M&As can pose threats to competition, both at the time of entry and subsequently. The search for increased market shares and indeed market domination is one of the characteristics of business behaviour. In the new knowledge-based economy, the search for market power — or even monopoly — is accentuated by the nature of the costs of knowledge-based production. As was recently observed: "the constant pursuit of that monopoly power becomes the central driving thrust of the new economy" (Summers, 2000, p. 2). Indeed, the threat of monopoly, or tight oligopoly, is potentially the single most important negative effect of cross-border M&As and therefore poses the single most important policy challenge. The challenge, more precisely, is to ensure that policies are in place to deal with those M&As that raise competitive concerns, and that they are implemented effectively.

Indeed, as FDI restrictions are liberalized worldwide, it becomes all the more important that regulatory barriers to FDI are not replaced by anticompetitive practices of firms. This means that, as observed in *WIR97,* "the reduction of barriers to FDI and the establishment of positive standards of treatment for TNCs need to go hand in hand with the adoption of measures aimed at ensuring the proper functioning of markets, including, in particular, measures to control anticompetitive practices by firms" (UNCTAD, 1997a, p. XXXI). This puts the spotlight squarely on coordinated competition policy as a means to assess and address the impact of cross-border M&As on host-country economies, although policies aimed at maintaining a well-defined contestability of markets also have a role to play. It also suggests that the culture of FDI liberalization that has become pervasive, combined with the growing importance of cross-border M&As as a mode of entry, has to be complemented by an equally pervasive culture recognizing the need to prevent anticompetitive practices of firms. In the context of cross-border M&As, this requires the adoption of competition laws and their effective implementation, paying full attention not only to domestic, but also to cross-border M&As, both at the entry stage and subsequently. M&A reviews are indeed the principal interface between FDI and competition policy. Thus, there is a direct, necessary and enlarging relationship between liberalization of FDI entry through M&As on the one hand and the importance of competition policy on the other.

Increasingly, however, competition policy can no longer be pursued effectively through national action alone. The very nature of cross-border M&As — indeed the emergence of a global market for firms — puts the phenomenon into the international sphere. This means that competition authorities need to have in place, and to strengthen, cooperation mechanisms among themselves at the bilateral, regional and multilateral levels, in order to respond effectively to M&As and anti-competitive practices of firms that affect their countries. International action is particularly important when dealing with cross-border M&As with global dimensions, especially for smaller countries that lack the resources to mount and enforce such policies on their own.

A postcript

WIR2000 draws an intriguing parallel between the emergence of a *national* market and production system in the United States during the last decade of the nineteenth century, in the wake of a massive domestic M&A wave, and the emergence at the present time of a *global* market for firms, as a complement of the evolving global market for products and services and the development of an international production system. The United States wave, and the quest for increased market power that was part and parcel of it, caused the courts of that country to interpret the Sherman Antitrust Act to cover M&As and, eventually, Congress to adopt the Clayton Act, which prohibited M&As likely to lessen competition, and the Federal Trade Commission Act, which created the Federal Trade Commission to police violations of the Act. This marked the beginning of M&A control in the United States and of a process which has, over the nearly 100 years since then, led to a further strengthening of that country's competition control system. The Sherman Act also was the antecedent of similar legislation in other countries. Today, some 90 countries have adopted antitrust laws, most of which were introduced in the 1990s.

The world economy today may well be seeing the beginning of a similar challenge in terms of global market structure and competition. If the parallel with the United States experience is indicative, this could mean that what is already happening may be only the beginning of a massive consolidation process at the regional and global levels. If so, it is all the more important to put in place the necessary policy instruments to deal with this process. Among these policy instruments, competition policy has pride of place. In the end, a global market for firms may need a global approach to competition policy, an approach that takes the interests and conditions of developing countries fully into account.

Geneva, July 2000

Rubens Ricupero
Secretary-General of UNCTAD

PART ONE

TRENDS

Global Trends:
The Expanding International Production System

Foreign direct investment (FDI) flows continue to set new records. In 1999, global inflows reached $865 billion, an increase of 27 per cent over the previous year. FDI flows to developing countries, after stagnating in 1998, seemed set to resume their earlier growth trend. Their value reached $208 billion, an increase of 16 per cent over 1998. The driving force behind the 1999 increase in FDI continued to be cross-border mergers and acquisitions (M&As), accounting for a substantial share of total flows — a higher share in developed and a lower share in developing countries.

This is the short-term picture. The long-term picture is that FDI is playing a larger and more important role in the world economy. International production — production under the common governance of transnational corporations (TNCs) — is growing faster than other economic aggregates. The nature of international production is changing, responding to rapid technological change, intensified competition and economic liberalization. Falling transportation and communications costs are allowing TNCs to integrate production and other corporate functions across countries in historically unprecedented ways. Previous *World Investment Reports (WIRs)* have termed this process "deep integration", which is giving rise to a *cohesive global production system*, with specialized activities located by TNCs in different countries linked by tight, long-lasting bonds. The system is unevenly spread across industries, countries and TNCs, but it is growing rapidly to span many of the most dynamic activities in the world. If it represents "best practice" in international economic activity — and this may be so, given the strong economic rationale behind its growth — then all countries have to come to grips with its dimensions and implications.

A. The growth of international production remains unabated

International production now spans — in different degrees — virtually all countries, sectors, industries and economic activities. While it is difficult to quantify its magnitude because of its many facets, broad indicators show its spread. At the end of 1999, the stock of FDI, a broad measure of the capital component of international production, stood at $5 trillion (table I.1). Sales by foreign affiliates, a broad measure of the revenues generated by international production, reached an estimated $14 trillion in 1999, while their gross product (value added) stood at an estimated $3 trillion. The gross product of all TNC systems together — that is, including parent firms — was an estimated $8 trillion in 1997, comprising roughly a quarter of the world's gross domestic product (GDP).[1]

International production is thus of considerable importance to the world economy. Global sales of foreign affiliates alone were about twice as high as global exports in 1999,

Table I.1. Selected indicators of FDI and international production, 1982-1999

(Billions of dollars and percentage)

Item	Value at current prices (Billion dollars)			Annual growth rate (Per cent)				
	1982	1990	1999	1986-1990	1991-1995	1996-1999	1998	1999
FDI inflows	58	209	865	24.0	20.0	31.9	43.8	27.3
FDI outflows	37	245	800	27.6	15.7	27.0	45.6	16.4
FDI inward stock	594	1 761	4 772	18.2	9.4	16.2	20.1	18.8
FDI outward stock	567	1 716	4 759	20.5	10.7	14.5	17.6	17.1
Cross-border M&As[a]	..	151	720	26.4[b]	23.3	46.9	74.4	35.4
Sales of foreign affiliates	2 462	5 503	13 564 [c]	15.8	10.4	11.5	21.6[c]	17.8[c]
Gross product of foreign affiliates	565	1 419	3 045 [d]	16.4	7.1	15.3	25.4[d]	17.1[d]
Total assets of foreign affiliates	1 886	5 706	17 680 [e]	18.0	13.7	16.5	21.2[e]	19.8[e]
Exports of foreign affiliates	637	1 165	3 167 [f]	13.2	13.9	12.7	13.8[f]	17.9[f]
Employment of foreign affiliates (thousands)	17 433	23 605	40 536 [g]	5.6	5.0	8.3	11.4[g]	11.9[g]
Memorandum:								
GDP at factor cost	10 611	21 473	30 061 [h]	11.7	6.3	0.6	-0.9	3.0[h]
Gross fixed capital formation	2 231	4 686	6 058 [h]	13.5	5.9	-1.4	-2.1	-0.3[h]
Royalties and fees receipts	9	27	65 [h]	22.0	14.2	3.9	6.3	0.5[h]
Exports of goods and non-factor services	2 041	4 173	6 892 [h]	15.0	9.5	1.5	-1.8	3.0[h]

Source: UNCTAD, based on FDI/TNC database and UNCTAD estimates.

[a]   Data are only available from 1987 onwards.
[b]   1987-1990 only.
[c]   Based on the following regression result of sales against FDI inward stock for the period 1982-1997:
    Sales = 636 + 2.71 * FDI inward stock.
[d]   Based on the following regression result of gross product against FDI inward stock for the period 1982-1997:
    Gross product = 239 + 0.59 * FDI inward stock.
[e]   Based on the following regression result of assets against FDI inward stock for the period 1982-1997:
    Assets = -714 + 3.86 * FDI inward stock.
[f]   Based on the following regression result of exports against FDI inward stock for the period 1982-1997:
    Exports = 129 + 0.64 * FDI inward stock.
[g]   Based on the following regression result of employment against FDI inward stock for the period 1982-1997:
    Employment = 13 287 + 5.71 * FDI inward stock.
[h]   Estimates.

Note: Not included in this table are the value of worldwide sales by foreign affiliates associated with their parent firms through non-equity relationships and the sales of the parent firms themselves. Worldwide sales, gross product, total assets, exports and employment of foreign affiliates are estimated by extrapolating the worldwide data of foreign affiliates of TNCs from France, Germany, Italy, Japan and the United States (for sales and employment) and those from Japan and the United States (for exports), those from the United States (for gross product), and those from Germany and the United States (for assets) on the basis of the shares of those countries in the worldwide outward FDI stock.

compared to almost parity about two decades ago. Global gross product attributed to foreign affiliates is about one tenth of global GDP, compared to 5 per cent in 1982. The ratio of the stock of FDI to global GDP has risen from 6 per cent to 16 per cent over this period. The ratio of FDI flows to world gross domestic capital formation was 14 per cent in 1999; this ratio is significantly higher for manufacturing (22 per cent in 1998) (table

I.2). [2] In relation to private capital formation, the share varies (for the countries for which data are available) from 0.4 per cent in Japan to 98 per cent in Djibouti.[3] This share is typically higher in developing countries.[4] Global sales and gross product associated with international production have increased faster than global exports and GDP — by 3.2 percentage points and 4.1 percentage points, respectively, during the period 1982-1999 (figure I.1).

Table I.2. The importance of FDI flows in capital formation, by region and sector, 1980, 1990 and 1998

Region/economy	FDI inflows as a percentage of gross domestic capital formation: all industries	FDI inflows as a percentage of gross domestic capital formation: manufacturing	FDI inflows as a percentage of private capital formation: all industries
World			
1980	2.3	9.0[a]	3.4[d]
1990	4.7	14.0[b]	5.4[e]
1998	11.1	21.6[c]	13.9[f]
Developed countries			
1980	2.7	8.5	3.4
1990	4.9	11.9	5.2
1998	10.9	16.6	12.9
Developing countries			
1980	1.2	11.7	3.6
1990	4.0	22.3	6.7
1998	11.5	36.7	17.7
Central and Eastern Europe			
1980	0.1	..	..
1990	1.5	..	0.7[g]
1998	12.9	..	16.2

Source: UNCTAD, based on information from the World Bank, 1999 and 2000b; International Finance Corporation, Economics Department Database, (taken from their web site http://www.ifc.org/economics/data/dataset.htm); OECD, various issues and IMF, 1999.

[a] Based on data for the following economies: Bangladesh (1981), Bolivia (1981), Canada (1984), Chile, Colombia, Costa Rica, Ecuador (1986), France (1987), Germany (1987), Hong Kong (China) (1986), India, Italy (1989), Malaysia (1985), Mexico (1984), Nepal (1987), the Netherlands (1988), Pakistan (1986), Peru (1982), the Philippines, the Republic of Korea, Singapore (1981), Sri Lanka, Sweden (1987), Thailand (1989), Trinidad and Tobago (1981), the United Kingdom (1987), the United States, and Venezuela (1981).

[b] Based on data for the following economies: Australia, Bangladesh, Bolivia, Canada, Chile, Colombia, Denmark, Ecuador, Ethiopia (1992), Finland (1992), France, Germany, Hong Kong (China), India (1991), Indonesia, Italy, Malaysia, Mexico, Mongolia (1991), Morocco (1992), Nepal, the Netherlands, Norway (1994), Pakistan (1988), Peru, the Philippines, the Republic of Korea, Singapore, Spain (1992), Sri Lanka, Sweden (1987), Thailand, Trinidad and Tobago, Tunisia, the United Kingdom, the United States, Venezuela and Zimbabwe (1993).

[c] Based on data available for the most recent year in the economies as follows : 1987 for Sweden; 1991 for Denmark, Mexico and Pakistan; 1992 for Bangladesh; 1993 for Argentina, Germany, the Netherlands and Sri Lanka; 1994 for Bolivia, India, Italy, Mongolia, Norway, Peru, the Republlic of Korea, Thailand and Tunisia; 1995 for Australia, Chile, Colombia, Ethiopia, Finland, Hong Kong (China), Indonesia, Malaysia, the Philippines, Spain, Trinidad and Tobago, the United Kingdom, the United States and Zimbabwe; 1996 for Belgium, Ecuador, France, Morocco, Nepal, Singapore and Venezuela.

[d] Includes only 71 countries (14 developed and 57 developing) for which data are available for 1980.

[e] Includes only 100 countries (14 developed, 84 developing and 2 in Central and Eastern Europe), for which data are available for 1990.

[f] Includes only 113 countries (13 developed, 93 developing and 7 in Central and Eastern Europe), for which data are available for 1998 or the most recent year.

[g] Based on data for Bulgaria and Poland.

While there are several reasons behind the expansion and deepening of international production,[5] the ongoing liberalization of FDI (and related) regimes and the recognition that FDI can contribute to firm competitiveness stand out as the principal pull and push factors. They exercised their influence in 1999 in the context of a relatively healthy world economy, including the recovery in Asia.

FIGURE I.1
The growth of sales and gross product associated with international production, GDP and exports, 1982-1999
(Index, 1982=100)

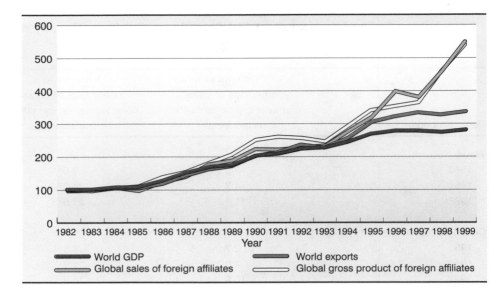

Source: UNCTAD, FDI/TNC database.

B. Countries continue to liberalize FDI regimes

Given the economic importance of FDI, it is not surprising that all countries today seek to attract it and to make their policies more favourable to investors. Of the 140 changes in FDI laws in 1999, 131 liberalized conditions for foreign investors (table I.3) (box I.1); over the period 1991-1999, 94 per cent of the 1,035 policy changes favoured investors.

These changes in national FDI laws were complemented by the conclusion of new bilateral investment treaties (BITs), an increasing number between developing countries. The total number of BITs rose from 1,726 at the end of 1998 to 1,856 at the end of 1999 (figure I.2 and box I.2). These treaties were often accompanied by double taxation treaties

(DTTs), which rose in number to 1,982 at the end of 1999, compared to 1,873 at the end of 1998 (see figure I.2 and box I.3).[6] BITs and DTTs together were concluded at a rate of one every two working days during 1999 — an impressive rate of treaty-making. At the regional level, an increasing number of agreements are creating more favourable FDI regimes as well (UNCTAD, 1996b). Thus, during the second half of 1998 and 1999, free trade and investment agreements between Chile and Mexico, and between the members of the European Community and Mexico, expanded and deepened the existing network of agreements (UNCTAD, 2000a). More broadly, investment issues increasingly permeate international economic agreements. For example, many of the free trade, association, partnership and cooperation agreements signed by the European Community with third countries also contain FDI provisions (box I.4).

Table I.3. **National regulatory changes, 1991-1999**

Item	1991	1992	1993	1994	1995	1996	1997	1998	1999
Number of countries that introduced changes in their investment regimes	35	43	57	49	64	65	76	60	63
Number of regulatory changes	82	79	102	110	112	114	151	145	140
of which:									
More favourable to FDI [a]	80	79	101	108	106	98	135	136	131
Less favourable to FDI [b]	2	-	1	2	6	16	16	9	9

Source: UNCTAD, based on national sources.

[a]   Including liberalizing changes or changes aimed at strengthening market functioning, as well as increased incentives.
[b]   Including changes aimed at increasing control as well as reducing incentives.

Box I.1. Developments in national FDI frameworks during 1999

Changes in government policies on FDI during 1999 confirm and strengthen the trend towards the liberalization, protection and promotion of FDI. Most new measures by developing and transition economies reduced sectoral restrictions to foreign entry, or liberalized operations in industries earlier closed or restricted to FDI (box figure I.1.1). Notable among them are petroleum, mining, energy, airports, telecommunications, tourism, film making, banking and insurance, retail trading and pharmaceuticals. Other restrictions, such as on the ownership of land

Box figure I.1.1. Types of changes in FDI laws and regulations, 1999

(Percentage)

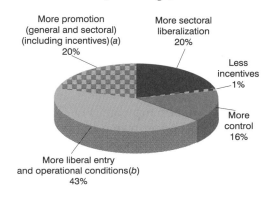

Source: UNCTAD, based on national sources.

a   Includes free-zone regulations.
b   Operational conditions include performance requirements as well as other operational measures.

and real estate, employment of foreigners and foreign exchange controls, were also reduced or removed. In some countries, legal guarantees on the protection of intellectual property rights and against expropriation and unfavourable changes in legislation, were strengthened. Some incentive regimes were revised and rationalized while additional incentives — mainly tax incentives — were offered to promote investment in priority industries and activities. In most cases, these measures were an extension of changes undertaken in previous years.

A number of countries, however, also substantially revised their FDI regimes to make them more attractive, e.g. Cambodia, India, the Russian Federation, Slovenia, the Sudan and Thailand. There was some opening up in the Islamic Republic of Iran after years of restriction. At the same time, there was a noticeable trend in developing and transition economies towards greater consumer and environmental protection and disclosure of financial information.

In developed countries, where FDI regimes are largely open, there was further deregulation of activities where foreign entry had been limited (e.g. electricity, gas and banking). The emphasis of regulatory changes, however, was on strengthening competition laws, corporate governance, consumer and environmental protection. A few countries introduced new incentives targeting, in particular, R&D and investment in underdeveloped regions. Most new fiscal measures, however, were related to the general tax regime.

Source: UNCTAD.

FIGURE I.2
Cumulative number of DTTs and BITs, 1980-1999

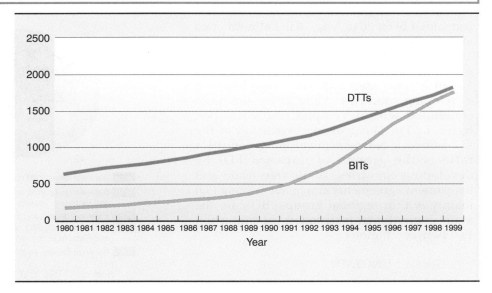

Source: UNCTAD, BITs and DTTs databases.

C. Enterprises seek to become more international

The quest of countries to attract more FDI is matched by the desire of companies to enhance competitiveness by spreading activities over different locations — to acquire a good portfolio of "locational assets". Capturing new markets is one important motivation, allowing firms to serve customers better by setting up local facilities. (In many services, where supply necessarily requires a local presence, this becomes the major driver of foreign investment.) Another is the search for new sources of knowledge and skills ("created assets") abroad.

Firms venturing abroad seek to match their competitive strengths ("ownership advantages") with the resources and capabilities in other countries ("locational advantages"). In many cases, where selling firm-specific advantages at arm's length is costly, cumbersome or simply unfeasible, firms expand by internalizing facilities in affiliates they control. Then FDI becomes the preferred way for firms to remain competitive in the new global environment. It is not, however, the only way. Where arm's length arrangements with overseas firms are a cheaper and more efficient way of exploiting ownership advantages, firms also undertake externalized transactions (such as licensing) with firms in other countries. Typically TNCs engage in the whole range of internal and external transactions

internationally: the decision on the type of transaction depends on the nature of a firm's advantages, the capabilities of the overseas firm and conditions in the foreign location. Over time, however, as FDI policies have been liberalized, innovation costs have risen and international transaction costs fallen, internalized transactions by TNCs have grown in significance.

As a result, the number of firms that have become transnational has risen exponentially over the past three decades. In the case of 15 developed countries, that number increased from some 7,000 at the end of the 1960s to some 40,000 in the second half of the 1990s (figure I.3). The number of parent firms worldwide is now in the range of 60,000 (table I.4). These parent firms form a diverse universe that spans all countries and industries, and include a large and growing number of small and medium-sized enterprises. More and more TNCs hail from countries that have only recently begun to undertake international production - witness the growth of TNCs from some developing countries and economies in transition (table I.4 and chapter III).

The ownership of FDI, however, remains highly concentrated in both host and home countries. The concentration ratio increased even further in recent years in FDI inflows (UNCTAD, 1999a). A mere one hundred (non-financial) parent firms, based mainly in developed countries, account for roughly one-eighth of the total assets of all

---

Box I.2. BITs in 1999

During 1999, the number of BITs increased substantially. A total of 96 countries concluded BITs: 30 in Asia, 20 in Latin America and the Caribbean, 13 in Africa, 11 in Central and Eastern Europe, 4 in developing Europe and 18 developed countries. Nearly half the 130 BITs concluded that year were between developing countries, while 43 treaties were concluded with developed countries (box figure I.2.1). The growing expansion of the BIT network between developing countries reflects the growth of outward FDI by developing countries. While free trade and investment agreements aim at liberalizing FDI mainly within regional groups, BITs are the main international instrument for protecting FDI between regions.

Source: UNCTAD.

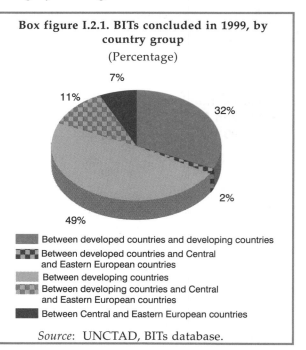

Box figure I.2.1. BITs concluded in 1999, by country group

(Percentage)

- Between developed countries and developing countries
- Between developed countries and Central and Eastern European countries
- Between developing countries
- Between developing countries and Central and Eastern European countries
- Between Central and Eastern European countries

Source: UNCTAD, BITs database.

foreign affiliates (chapter III). This means that the locational decisions of these few companies can have important repercussions for international production in the world economy, as well as in individual host (and, for that matter, home) countries. The extent of concentration by destination is also high as far as the absolute value of FDI inflows is concerned.[7] It is even higher for participation by host countries in integrated global production systems.

The 63,000 parent firms have an estimated 690,000 affiliates (defined in terms of a minimum of equity ownership by parent firms) (table I.4). In addition to these affiliates, TNCs have, as noted, a variety of non-equity arrangements with other firms, such as franchising, licensing, subcontracting and management contracts.[8] Inter-firm agreements like strategic alliances and partnerships also play a growing role, mostly with other large firms with strong ownership advantages. With

---

Box I.3. DTTs in 1999

In 1999, 88 countries signed a total of 109 DTTs (box figure I.3.1); 25 developed countries, 28 Asian developing countries, 12 Central and Eastern European countries, 11 countries from Africa, six from Latin America and the Caribbean and 4 from developing Europe.

Box figure I.3.1. DTTs concluded in 1999, by country group

(Percentage)

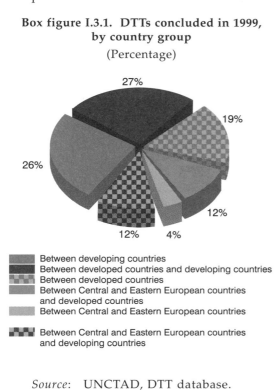

- Between developing countries
- Between developed countries and developing countries
- Between developed countries
- Between Central and Eastern European countries and developed countries
- Between Central and Eastern European countries
- Between Central and Eastern European countries and developing countries

Source: UNCTAD, DTT database.

---

the rise of the internet, new types of cooperation, such as internet-based procurement systems, are developing, even among fierce competitors. The on-line exchange planned by General Motors, Ford and Daimler Chrysler is an example. To the extent that TNCs can exercise control through non-equity arrangements — at least for the duration of the arrangement — local producers also fall under their common governance, creating interlocking relationships that expand the size and scope of international production.

Transnational corporations adopt a variety of strategies in undertaking international production. These strategies have changed over time. Independent "satellite" production facilities abroad by firms pursuing "stand alone" strategies are being increasingly replaced by integrated production structures by firms pursuing "deep integration" strategies (UNCTAD, 1993a, 1999a). Deep integration can take several forms. It may mean the location abroad of corporate functions like R&D, marketing or accounting. It may mean an integrated production system in which different steps of a production process are undertaken in different countries according to their relative cost and logistic advantages. It may also mean that service functions are broken up into different segments and are located inter-nationally to minimize cost or increase flexibility.

The progress of deep integration is uneven by activity, firm and location. Some activities lend themselves more readily to the division of specialized processes across countries than do others; for example, engineering industries with many discrete processes can be divided more efficiently than heavy process industries. Some TNCs are more likely to locate important functions overseas than are others. Those that do relocate transfer some tasks more than others; for instance, the relocation of top management and R&D activities has proceeded far more slowly than that of other functions. Similarly, some host countries can be integrated into global systems more easily than others, depending on their locational advantages, FDI and other policies, infrastructure, risk and so on. Thus, the overall structure of international production remains fairly hybrid, with deep integration strategies being pursued alongside traditional shallow integration strategies (involving merely the integration of markets). However, with barriers to investment, trade and information falling, it makes economic sense - indeed, there is increased competitive pressure to do so — for TNCs to place any activity (or segment of an activity) wherever it is most economically performed — as long as efficiency, control and responsiveness remain the same. Growing competition and increasing familiarity with different locations should therefore lead inexorably to more deep integration.

Box I.4. FDI provisions in association, partnership, free trade and cooperation agreements of the European Community, March 2000

The European Community and its member States have concluded, since 1966, a number of association, partnership, free trade and cooperation agreements with non-member States. From the start, many of these instruments included provisions dealing with FDI. Thus, for example, article 74 of the 1995 Association Agreement with the Republic of Latvia provides as follows:

"Investment promotion and protection

1.   Cooperation shall aim at maintaining and, if necessary, improving a legal framework and a favourable climate for private investment and its protection, both domestic and foreign, which is essential to economic and industrial reconstruction and development in Latvia. The cooperation shall also aim to encourage and promote foreign investment and privatization in Latvia.

2.   The particular aims of cooperation shall be:

- for Latvia to establish a legal framework which favours and protects investment;

- the conclusion, where appropriate, with Member States of bilateral agreements for the promotion and protection of investment;

- to proceed with deregulation and to improve economic infrastructure;

- to exchange information on investment opportunities in the context of trade fairs, exhibitions, trade weeks and other events.

Assistance from the Community could be granted in the initial stage to agencies which promote inward investment.

3.   Latvia shall honour the rules on Trade-Related Aspects of Investment Measures (TRIMs)."

Source: UNCTAD, 2000a, vol. V.

D. M&As take the lead

Over the past decade, most of the growth in international production has been via cross-border M&As rather than greenfield investment (chapter IV). The value of completed cross-border M&As (defined as the acquisition of more than 10 per cent equity share) rose from less than $100 billion in 1987, to $720 billion in 1999 (figure I.4).[9] As a percentage of GDP, the increase was from a negligible proportion in 1987 to 2.4 per cent in 1999. Individual M&A deals can be quite substantial. Take the biggest cross-border deal until early 2000 - the takeover of Mannesmann (Germany) by Vodafone AirTouch (United Kingdom): this nearly $200 billion deal came to 6 per cent of the combined GDPs of the two countries in 1999.

It is not possible to determine precisely the share of cross-border M&As in FDI inflows. M&As can be financed locally or directly from international capital markets; neither is included in FDI data. FDI data are reported on a net basis, M&A data are not. Moreover,

FIGURE I.3
Number of parent TNCs in 15 developed home countries,[a] 1968/1969 and second half of the 1990s[b]

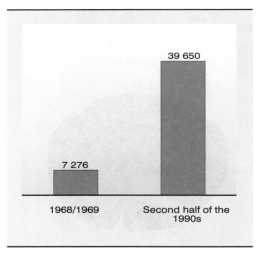

Source: UNCTAD, based on United Nations, 1973 and table I.4.

[a]   Austria, Belgium, Denmark, France, Germany, Italy, Luxembourg, the Netherlands, Norway, Portugal, Spain, Sweden, Switzerland, the United Kingdom and the United States.
[b]   1993 for the Netherlands, 1995 for Switzerland, 1997 for Austria, Belgium, Italy, the United States and Norway, 1998 for Denmark, France, Germany, Spain and the United Kingdom, 1999 for Portugal and Sweden. Luxembourg is not included.

Table I.4. **Number of parent corporations and foreign affiliates,**
by area and economy, latest available year
(Number)

Area/economy	Year	Parent corporations based in economy[a]	Foreign affiliates located in economy[a]
Developed economies		**48 791** [b]	**94 269** [b]
Western Europe		**37 580** [b]	**61 594** [b]
European Union		**32 096** [b]	**52 673** [b]
Austria	1997	896	2 464
Belgium/Luxembourg	1997	988 [c]	1 504 [c]
Denmark	1998	9 356	2 305 [d]
Finland	1998	1 200	1 491 [d]
France	1998	1 695	9 494
Germany	1998	8 492	12 042 [e]
Greece	1991	..	798
Ireland	1998	39 [f]	1 140 [g]
Italy	1997	806 [h]	1 769 [h]
Netherlands	1993	1 608 [i]	2 259 [i]
Portugal	1999	1 100 [j]	3 500 [j]
Spain	1998	857 [k]	7 465
Sweden[l]	1999	3 965	3 759
United Kingdom [m]	1998	1 094	2 683
Other Western Europe		**5 484** [b]	**8 921** [b]
Iceland	1999	78	47
Norway	1998	900 [n]	3 100 [n]
Switzerland	1995	4 506	5 774
North America		**5 109** [b]	**23 665** [b]
Canada	1997	1 722	4 562
United States	1997	3 387 [o]	19 103 [p]
Other developed countries		**6 102** [b]	**9 010** [b]
Australia	1999	610	2 539
Japan	1998	4 334	3 321 [q]
New Zealand	1998	217	1 106
South Africa	1998	941	2 044
Developing economies		**12 518** [b]	**355 324** [b]
Africa		**167** [b]	**3 669** [b]
Ethiopia	1998	..	21 [r]
Lesotho	1999	..	411
Mali [s]	1999	3	33
Seychelles	1998	-	30
Swaziland	1999	12	53
Tunisia	1999	142	1 906
Zambia	1999	2 [t]	1 179
Zimbabwe	1998	8	36
Latin America and the Caribbean		**2 019** [b]	**24 345** [b]
Bolivia	1996	..	257
Brazil	1998	1 225	8 050
Chile	1998	478 [u]	3 173 [v]
Colombia	1995	302	2 220
El Salvador	1990	..	225

Table I.4. (continued)

Area/economy	Year	Parent corporations based in economy[a]	Foreign affiliates located in economy[a]
Guatemala	1985	..	287
Guyana	1998	4	56
Jamaica	1998	..	177
Mexico	1993	..	8 420
Paraguay	1995	..	109
Peru	1997	10 [w]	1 183 [x]
Trinidad & Tobago	1999	..	65 [y]
Uruguay	1997	..	123
Asia		**10 332** [b]	**327 310** [b]
South, East and South-East Asia		**9 883** [b]	**317 147** [b]
Bangladesh	1999	..	161 [z]
Bhutan	1997	..	2
Cambodia	1997	..	598 [aa]
China	1997	379 [ab]	235 681 [ac]
Hong Kong, China	1998	819 [ad]	6 247 [ae]
India	1995	187 [af]	1 416
Indonesia	1995	313	2 241 [ae]
Lao People's Democratic Republic	1997	..	669 [ag]
Malaysia	1999	..	15 567 [ah]
Mongolia	1998	..	1 400
Myanmar	1998	..	299 [ai]
Nepal	1999	..	224 [aj]
Pakistan	1998	59	644
Philippines	1995	..	14 802 [ak]
Republic of Korea	1999	7 460	6 486
Singapore	1997	..	24 114
Sri Lanka	1998	..	305 [al]
Taiwan Province of China	1994	666 [am]	2 026
Thailand	1998	..	2 721 [an]
Viet Nam	1996	..	1 544
West Asia		**449** [b]	**1 948** [b]
Oman	1995	92 [ao]	351 [ao]
Saudi Arabia	1989	..	1 461
Turkey	1995	357	136
Central Asia		**-**	**7 663**
Armenia	1999	..	1 604 [ap]
Georgia	1998	..	190 [aq]
Kazakhstan	1999	..	1 865 [ar]
Kyrgyzstan	1998	..	4 004 [as]
The Paciifc		**-**	**552** [b]
Fiji	1997	..	151
Papua New Guinea	1998	..	345 [at]
Solomon Islands	1996	..	56 [au]
Central and Eastern Europe		**2 150** [b]	**239 927** [b]
Albania	1995	..	2 422 [av]
Armenia	1999	..	1 657 [aw]
Belarus	1994	..	393
Bulgaria	1994	26	918
Croatia	1997	70	353
Czech Republic	1999	660 [t]	71 385 [ax]

Table I.4. (continued)

Area/economy	Year	Parent corporations based in economy[a]	Foreign affiliates located in economy[a]
Estonia	1999	..	3 066 [ay]
Hungary	1998	..	28 772 [az]
Lithuania	1999	16 [ab]	1 893
Poland	1998	58 [ba]	35 840 [bb]
Romania	1998	20 [ba]	71 318 [bc]
Russian Federation	1994	..	7 793
Slovakia	1997	..	5 560 [bd]
Slovenia	1997	1 300 [ae]	1 195 [az]
Ukraine	1999	..	7 362
World		**63 459**	**689 520**

Source: UNCTAD, based on national sources.

a   Represents the number of parent companies/foreign affiliates in the economy shown, as defined by that economy. Deviations from the definition adopted in the *World Investment Report* (see section on definitions and sources in the annex B) are noted below.

b   Includes data for only the countries shown below.

c   Provisional figures by Banque Nationale de Belgique.

d   Directly and indirectly owned foreign affiliates.

e   Does not include the number of foreign-owned holding companies in Germany which, in turn, hold participating interests in Germany (indirect foreign participating interests).

f   As of 1994.

g   Refers to the number of foreign-owned affiliates in Ireland which receive assistance from the Industrial Development Agency (IDA).

h   Relates to parent companies and foreign affiliates in agriculture and industrial activities (*source*: REPRINT database, Polytechnics University of Milano/CNEL).

i   As of October 1993.

j   Preliminary estimate. The number of foreign affiliates in Portugal as of 1998.

k   Includes those Spanish parent enterprises which, at the same time, are controlled by a direct investor.

l   Data provided by Sveriges Riksbank. Includes those Swedish parent companies which, at the same time, are controlled by a direct investor. The number of foreign affiliates relates only to majority-owned firms.

m   Data on the number of parent companies based in the United Kingdom, and the number of foreign affiliates in the United Kingdom are based on the register of companies held for inquiries on the United Kingdom FDI abroad, and FDI into the United Kingdom conducted by the Central Statistical Office. On that basis, the numbers are probably understated because of the lags in identifying investment in greenfield sites and because some companies with small presence in the United Kingdom and abroad have not yet been identified.

n   Approximation by Norges Bank. The number of parent companies as of 1997.

o   Represents a total of 2,618 non-bank parent companies in 1996 and 60 bank parent companies in 1994 with at least one foreign affiliate whose assets, sales or net income exceeded $3 million, and 709 non-bank and bank parent companies in 1994 whose affiliate(s) had assets, sales and net income under $3 million. Each parent company represents a fully consolidated United States business enterprise, which may consist of a number of individual companies.

p   Data for 1996. Represents a total of 13,108 bank and non-bank affiliates in 1996 whose assets, sales or net income exceeded $1 million, and 5,551 bank and non-bank affiliates in 1992 with assets, sales and net income under $1 million, and 534 United States affiliates that are depository institutions. Each affiliate represents a fully consolidated United States business entreprise, which may consist of a number of individual companies.

q   Only foreign affiliates that have over 20 per cent stake in their affiliates located in Japan, plus the number of foreign affiliates, insurance and real estate industries in November 1995 (284).

r   Represents the number of foreign affiliates that received permission to invest during 1992-May 1998.

s   As of April 1999

t   As of 1997.

u   Estimated by Comite de Inversiones Extranjeras.

v   Number of foreign companies registred under DL600.

w   Less than 10.

x   Out of this number, 811 are majority-owned foreign affiliates, while 159 affiliates have less than 10 per cent equity share.

y   An equity stake of 25 per cent or more of the ordinary shares or voting power.

z   Number of investment projects registered with the Board of Investment.

aa   Number of projects approved, both domestic and foreign, since August 1994.

ab   As of 1989.

ac   Number of registered industrial enterprises with foreign capital.

ad   Number of regional headquarters as at 1 June 1998.

ae   As of 1996.

af   As of 1991.

ag   Number of projects licensed since 1988 up to end 1997.

payments for M&As (including those involving privatizations) can be phased over several years (UNCTAD, 1999a, p. 8). It is therefore possible for the ratio of the value of cross-border M&As to total FDI flows — for the world as a whole or for individual countries — to be higher than 1.[10] Taking the extreme case in which all cross-border M&As are financed by FDI (certainly incorrect for developed countries, but less so for developing countries), the share of total cross-border M&As in world FDI flows has increased from 52 per cent in 1987 to 83 per cent in 1999 (figure I.5). This figure varies considerably between developed and developing countries. For the former, the ratio is higher, having risen from 62 per cent in 1987 to more than 100 per cent in 1999.[11] For developing countries, the ratio is lower, but is also rising (figure I.5), with considerable variation among developing regions and countries (figure I.6). While these ratios do not show the exact share of FDI flows accounted for by M&As in any given year, they do suggest that M&As contribute an increasing share of FDI flows to all groups of countries.

This makes it imperative for developing host countries to understand the forces driving M&As and the impact they have on development. Only then will they be able to formulate appropriate policies. The latest M&A wave — especially where it has taken the form of hostile acquisitions or "fire sales" — has heightened concerns on the part of host governments. As the Prime Minister of Malaysia phrased it in his address to UNCTAD X in February 2000:

"...mergers and acquisitions .. are making big corporations even bigger. Now many of these corporations are financially more powerful than medium sized countries. While we welcome their collaboration with our local companies, we fear that if they are allowed into our countries unconditionally they may swallow up all our businesses" (Mahathir, 2000, p. 6).

The basis of concern is that M&As represent a change of ownership from domestic to foreign hands, while greenfield FDI represents an addition to the capital stock. This leads to such worries as the extent to which M&As (when compared to greenfield FDI) bring resources to host countries that are needed for development; the denationalization of domestic firms; employment reduction; loss of technological assets; crowding out of domestic firms and increased market concentration and its implication for competition.

Table I.4. **(concluded)**

ah May 1999. Refers to companies with foreign equity stakes of 51 per cent and above. Of this, 3,787 are fully owned foreign affiliates.
ai Number of permitted foreign enterprises up to end-February 1998.
aj June 1999.
ak This figure refers to directly and indirectly owned foreign affiliates.
al Number of projects approved under section 17 of the BOI law which provides for incentives.
am Number of approved new investment projects abroad in 1998.
an Data refer to the number of BOI-promoted companies which have been issued promotion certificates during the period 1960-1998, having at least 10 per cent of foreign equity participation.
ao As of May 1995.
ap Accumulated number of joint ventures and foreign enterprises registered as of 1 November 1999.
aq Number of cases of approved investments of more than 100,000 dollars registered during the period of January 1996 up to March 1998.
ar Joint ventures and foreign firms operating in the country.
as Joint venture companies established in the economy.
at Number of applications received since 1993.
au Number of foreign investment projects approved in 1996.
av 1,532 joint ventures and 890 wholly-owned foreign affiliates.
aw The number refers to the registered firms.
ax Out of this number 53,775 are fully-owned foreign affiliates. Includes joint ventures.
ay As of 15 March 1999. Only registered affiliates with the Estonian Commercial Register.
az Data are for the number of investment projects.
ba As of 1994.
bb Number of firms with foreign capital.
bc The number of affiliates established during December 1990-December 1999.
bd Includes joint ventures with local firms.

Note: The data can vary significantly from preceding years, as data become available for countries that had not been covered before, as definitions change, or as older data are updated.

Indeed, perhaps the most common concern about cross-border M&As — in distinction to greenfield FDI — is their impact on domestic competition. The sheer size of many of the firms involved, and their large share of global markets, raise fears about growing international oligopolies and market power. Governments therefore increasingly realize that effective competition policy is vital, and a large number of countries have adopted (or are in the process of preparing) competition laws. If anything, this policy instrument will become more important as a global market for firms is emerging, leading to the consolidation of industries on a global scale.

The mode of entry of foreign investors raises therefore important policy issues. What is driving cross-border M&As? How do they perform? Does it matter for developing countries and economies in transition whether FDI comes in the form of M&As or greenfield ventures? What policies help to minimize the negative impacts of cross-border M&As? What policies help to maximize the positive impacts? These and related issues are examined in some detail in the present report.

E. International production expands in scope and depth

Regardless of whether the mode of entry into a foreign market is M&As or greenfield FDI, the outcome is still an increase in the extent of international production under the common governance of TNCs. International production involves a gamut of cross-border flows by TNCs. The principal ones are finance, trade and flows of know-how, personnel and technology. The usual way to measure these flows is by its financial element — the value of FDI flows. This is an incomplete measure of the spread of international production; in fact, it does not even measure correctly the value of all investments undertaken abroad by TNCs (because some of them can be financed from local or international capital markets). However, FDI is the only aspect of international production on which comparable data are available at the country level, and this section focuses thereon.

Global FDI flows, as noted earlier, have continued to rise steadily. Inflows of FDI reached $865 billion worldwide[12] in 1999, a new record (figure I.7). The current FDI boom is now in its seventh year (since 1993). It is expected to continue into the year 2000.

Equity capital accounted for 72 per cent of global FDI inflows and reinvested earnings for 8 per cent in 1998 (figure I.8). This distribution has changed little over the past five years. Continuing last year's trend, FDI inflows to developed countries in 1999 rose faster than to other countries and set a new record of $636 billion. Most of this increase reflected cross-border M&As between firms based within the developed world. Flows of FDI, both inward and outward, for the European Union and the United States were at record levels in 1999. For Japan, inward flows quadrupled to reach also a record high, but outflows declined slightly.

FIGURE I.4
Value of cross-border M&As and its share in GDP, 1987-1999

Source: UNCTAD, FDI/TNC database and cross-border M&A database (based on data provided by Thomson Financial Securities Data Company).

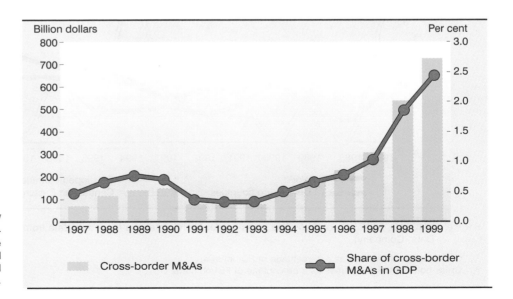

In contrast to 1998, FDI flows to developing countries increased as well — by 16 per cent, to a total of $208 billion in 1999. Africa (including South Africa) continued to attract small amounts of FDI flows, accounting only for 5 per cent of the developing country total (including South Africa). FDI increased however in 1999, with Angola, Egypt, Nigeria and South Africa being major recipients in that year. FDI inflows to Latin America and the Caribbean (where privatization is still a major magnet) increased by 23 per cent, to reach $90 billion. This increase meant that Latin America and the Caribbean had almost reached the amounts that developing Asia (including West Asia and Central Asia) had received that year,

$106 billion, out of which $40 billion went to China alone; cross-border M&As influenced significantly the level of FDI flows in this region, in particular in the Republic of Korea.

Over the past two decades, firms from developing countries have also increasingly invested abroad — $66 billion in 1999, compared to $1.7 billion in 1980. As a result, their share in global FDI flows has risen from 3 per cent to 8 per cent during that period (figure I.9). Outflows of FDI from developing countries are dominated by firms from Asia, although firms from Latin America are increasingly venturing abroad as well.

FIGURE I.5

Value of cross-border M&As in relation to the value of FDI flows, world and by group of economies, 1987-1999

(Percentage)

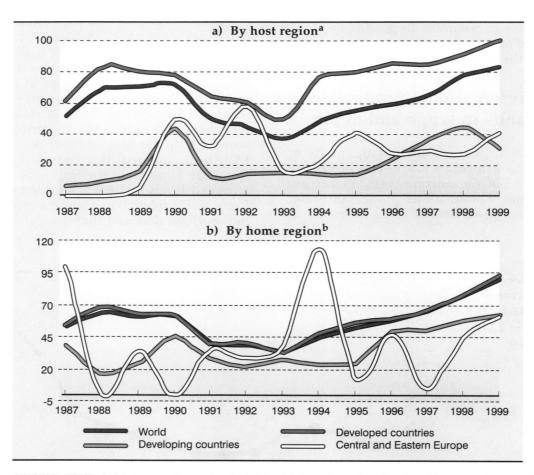

Source: UNCTAD, FDI/TNC database and cross-border M&As database (based on data from Thomson Financial Securities Data Company).

a   Cross-border M&A sales as a percentage of FDI inflows.
b   Cross-border M&A purchases as a percentage of FDI outflows.

Flows to the economies in transition of Central and Eastern Europe[13] also reached a record level of $23 billion in 1999, with 70 per cent going to Central Europe. Furthermore, those flows concentrated on a limited number of countries in this sub-region (the Czech Republic, Hungary and Poland). Flows to the Russian Federation have not yet recovered fully to the previous levels.

By sector, services have for some years been the largest recipient of FDI (figure I.10), accounting for an estimated 53 per cent of global FDI outflows of 23 important outward investors in 1998. As services become more tradable, FDI is no longer the only means of reaching customers in different countries; hence one might expect a decline in FDI services. On the other hand, as services become more tradable — and here the internet plays an important role — firms can split the production process of services and, as in the case of manufacturing, locate parts of it abroad, increasing FDI in services (Sauvant, 1990). In addition, there are many services where proximity to the customer is still vital. Moreover, the ongoing deregulation and privatization of infrastructure continues to spur the growth of FDI in services. As a result, several infrastructure providers from developed and more advanced developing countries — many themselves newly privatized — have emerged as major TNCs in this industry, which is traditionally reserved for local firms.

An important feature of international production is the overwhelming importance of TNCs in trade and innovative activities. FDI and international trade are more and more determined simultaneously by TNCs as part of their decision of where they access resources and locate production, distribution or other activities (UNCTAD, 1996a). The location decisions of TNCs increasingly involve international trade as they rationalize and distribute facilities across national borders to maximize economies of scale, scope and location. TNCs are responsible for an estimated two-thirds of world trade (UNCTAD, 1996a). About half of TNC trade takes place between parent firms and their affiliates abroad, or among affiliates (UNCTAD, 1999a). TNCs also account for a large proportion of global R&D, perhaps as much as 75-80 per cent (UNCTAD, 1995a). Judging from German, Japanese and United States data — between two-thirds and nine-tenths of inter-country technology flows (approximated by royalties and fees) are also intra-firm, that is, within TNC systems (annex table A.I.1).

In addition, FDI is also the largest source of external finance for developing countries (box I.5). Moreover, in recent years, and especially during financial crises, developing countries have found FDI to be more stable than portfolio investment and bank lending. In fact, FDI inflows remained almost unchanged during the crisis in the five most seriously affected Asian countries, when other private inflows fell dramatically (figure I.11). The principal reason is that FDI is less directly influenced by factors that place countries under financial duress: the main requirement for receiving FDI is a match between the markets and productive factors that TNCs want and those that countries offer. Unlike other forms of private capital, access to which is influenced

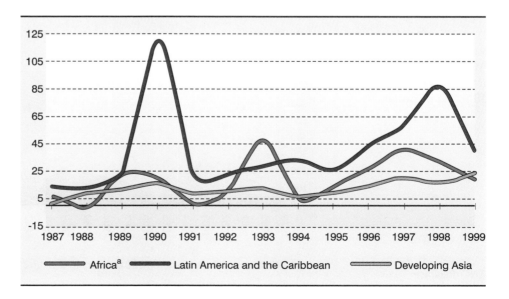

FIGURE I.6

Value of cross-border M&As in relation to the value of FDI inflows in developing countries, by region, 1987-1999
(Percentage)

Source: UNCTAD, FDI/TNC database and cross-border M&A database (based on data from Thomson Financial Securities Data Company).

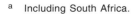

a Including South Africa.

by investment ratings and short-term financial considerations, FDI therefore responds more to underlying economic fundamentals.

This feature of FDI is important for countries at the bottom of the development ladder that do not have access to other investible resources. At the same time, there are common influences on FDI and other private capital flows, such as growth performance and prospects or macro-economic and political stability. In normal times, therefore, there is likely to be a high correlation between all forms of private financial flows: countries that receive more of one also tend to receive more of the other (table I.5). However, the correlation is not perfect. Some countries may get much more of one flow than of another, and FDI is more likely to go to low income countries than portfolio flows or commercial loans (Hausmann and Fernandez-Arias, 2000; Dunning and Dilyard, 1999).

In sum, a significant portion of cross-border transactions in the world economy is internalized within international production systems under the common governance of TNCs. The absolute and relative importance of international production raises a number of policy challenges.

F. Challenges

International production is a growing and powerful force in today's global economy. Liberalization and new technologies increasingly allow TNCs to locate their production and other functions wherever it is most efficient and strategically appropriate for them. To benefit from the emerging system of international production, countries seek to attract FDI and pursue policies that allow them to benefit from it (UNCTAD, 1999a). This gives rise to three major challenges for policy.

The distribution challenge. The faster growth of international as compared to domestic production in the world means that economies too have become more transnational. The sum of world inward and outward FDI stocks, calculated as a percentage of world GDP, has risen from 10 per cent in 1980 to 31 per cent in 1999 (figure I.12). A more complex measure, the transnationalization index (imperfect as it may be) yields a similar picture:[14] for 23 developed and 30 developing host economies, the index rose by 0.8 percentage points for the former and 0.5 percentage points for the latter between 1996 and 1997 (figure I.13).

Despite those increases, however, the degree of transnationalization is not converging across individual countries or groups of countries. The FDI inward stock/GDP ratio is higher for developing than for developed countries (figure I.12), perhaps showing differences in the strength of local enterprises in the latter. The difference is growing over time. The ratio in 1999 was 1.7 times higher for developing than developed host countries, compared to 1.1 times twenty years ago (1980). Of course, there are significant variations among regions and countries. Similarly, the transnationalization index for host countries was 14.2 per cent in 1997 for developing countries, compared to 12.8 per cent for developed countries. Again, there were large

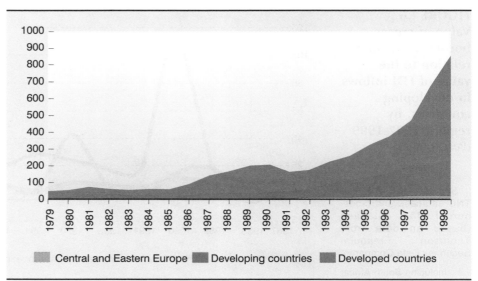

FIGURE I.7
**World FDI inflows,
1979-1999**
(Billions of dollars)

Source: UNCTAD, FDI/
TNC database.

FIGURE I.8
Components of FDI inflows, 1990-1998

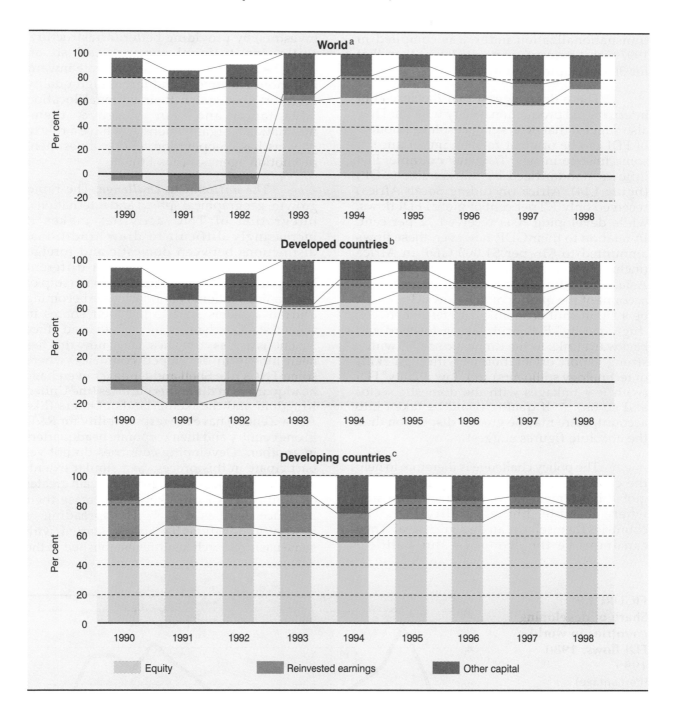

Source: UNCTAD, based on IMF, June 2000 International Financial Statistics CD-ROM.

a   Including two economies in Central and Eastern Europe: Estonia, for which data start in 1992, and Poland.
b   Including: Australia, Finland, Germany, Iceland, Israel, the Netherlands, Portugal, Switzerland, the United Kingdom and the United States.
c   Including: Antigua and Barbuda, Argentina, Barbados, Benin, Botswana, Brazil, Costa Rica, Dominica, Fiji, Grenada, Guatemala, Guinea, Honduras, Jamaica, Kazakhstan, Malta, Mexico, Morocco, Namibia, Panama, Paraguay, Saint Lucia, Saint Vincent and the Grenadines, Senegal, Swaziland, and Trinidad and Tobago. 1996 data are not available for the Netherlands Antilles and Trinidad and Tobago. Data from 1997 are not available for Antigua and Barbuda, Grenada, Saint Lucia and Saint Vincent and the Grenadines. 1998 data are not available for Benin and Senegal. Data for Kazakhstan are not available prior to 1995.

Note: Figures are based on 39 countries for which the data on each component of FDI inflows are available throughout the period.

variations within each group, with the developed country group showing a smaller variance. The standard deviation for the 23 developed countries for which the transnationalization index was compiled in 1997 was 4 percentage points lower than that for 30 developing countries.

These data suggest that the spread of international production is very uneven. They also suggest that even small absolute amounts of FDI can be of great relative importance to some host countries. Take, for example, FDI inflows standardized by market size (GDP) (figure I.14). Africa (including South Africa) received only 1.2 per cent of global FDI flows, while developing Asia received 12 per cent. In relation to their GDP, however, these flows amounted to $16 per $1,000 GDP in Africa (including South Africa) and $26 in developing Asia. These figures do not, of course, take account of the quality of FDI flows. There can be a significant economic difference between "high quality" FDI (with strong forward and backward links to the domestic sector, with a strong export orientation or with high skills or technology spillovers) and "low quality" FDI (with few linkages with the domestic sector and so on).[15] If quality could be taken into account, there may be greater dispersion than the absolute figures suggest.

The policy challenge is therefore to help the countries that are relatively marginal to global investment flows to attract more and, where feasible, higher quality FDI. The countries themselves can do a great deal. They can improve the economic and political environment for private sector activity in general, which would also be conducive for foreign investors. They can improve their economic attractiveness to international investors, by providing better infrastructure, skills, institutional support and so on (UNCTAD, 1999a). They can promote inward FDI more effectively, and target high quality investors that match their national location advantages and can improve them. International organizations also have a role to play, as has co-operation among investment promotion agencies (box I.6).

The nationality challenge. The rapid growth, geographical spread and international integration of TNC activities makes it increasingly difficult to draw traditional distinctions between domestic and foreign firms or between production in different locations. Take, for instance, the ownership of companies. National boundaries are becoming blurred as firms start to list their shares in several stock exchanges and spread head office functions across countries. Until now this has been mostly in developed countries, where some TNCs like Shell and Unilever even have headquarters in different countries (the United Kingdom and the Netherlands). Others (like Astra-Zeneca) have the responsibility for R&D in one country and their corporate headquarters in another. Developing countries do not yet participate in this process to a similar extent, but as their stock markets grow and gain greater credibility, TNCs are likely to increase their presence there as well.[16] The spreading of head-office functions has already started, with some basic research facilities established in the

FIGURE I.9
Share of developing countries in world FDI flows, 1980-1999
(Percentage)

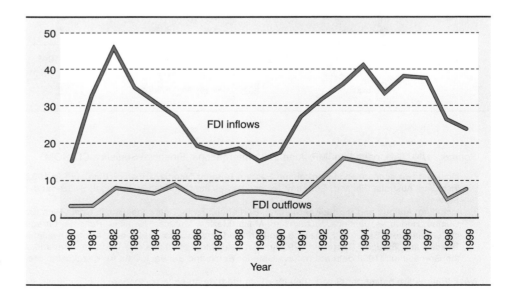

Source: UNCTAD, FDI/ TNC database.

more advanced developing countries (for examples see UNCTAD, 1999a, pp. 213-214).

Over time, some companies may disperse ownership so widely that their "nationality" becomes very difficult to define. The spread of cross-border M&As, with extensive share swaps, and the rise of conglomerate cross-holding of shares make this even more complex. Thus, while firms become larger and more visible, where they are headquartered becomes less important — a very different scenario from the traditional transnational corporation with clear national origins, loyalties and culture. TNCs have not become stateless, but their spread and interests place them increasingly above individual national interests. This raises difficult challenges for national policies, which are not necessarily geared to transnational issues. The policy focus of national Governments will have

to change, as it becomes more important to provide competitive conditions for businesses in general in the country rather than only for the country's firms in particular.

Similarly, the growth of integrated production systems means that it is difficult to define where a "product" actually comes from. Is a Ford made in the United Kingdom, when inputs come from all over Europe or further afield, design is done jointly in the United States and Europe, and stages of processing are spread over many locations, British, American or European? In some instances, as with television sets or videos, the whole product may have been manufactured by an independent local company, say, in the Republic of Korea, and sold under the brand of a Japanese TNC as part of an original equipment or contract manufacturing arrangement. Moreover, the sourcing of

FIGURE I.10
Flows and stocks of FDI, by sector, 1988 and 1998
(Percentage)

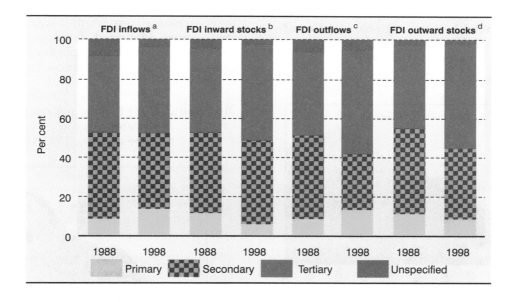

Source: UNCTAD, FDI/TNC database.

Notes: In order to represent as many countries as possible for each period, whenever data for the given years were not available, those for the latest year available close to 1988 and 1998, respectively, were chosen. Furthermore, in the absence of actual data, approval data were used in some countries.

[a] Data cover 40 countries in 1988 and 61 countries in 1998, accounting, respectively, for 73 and 91 per cent of world inward flows. Totals in 1988 do not include the countries in Central and Eastern Europe.

[b] Totals are based on data for 41 countries in 1988 and 60 countries in 1998. They account, respectively, for 71 and 81 per cent of world inward stocks.

[c] Flows in 1988 cover 15 countries with a 66 per cent share in world outward flows. In 1998, the total, composed of 23 countries, had an 89 per cent share in world outward flows.

[d] Data for 25 countries make up the total for outward stocks in 1988, and their share in world outward stocks is 77 per cent. The total in 1998 is based on data for 25 countries, which accounted for 80 per cent of world outward stocks.

products and components may shift rapidly over time, as cost and demand conditions change. Again, traditional policies — e.g. rules of origin — based on a clear demarcation of national origin can become redundant, inefficient or distorting.

As a result of their international spread, TNCs are more insulated from national conditions and policies than national firms. They are more flexible in placing productive resources or functions in different countries, and are thus able to respond more quickly to

---

Box I.5. Financial flows to developing countries

The trend of rising private capital flows and declining official flows to developing countries was interrupted in 1998. In 1999, private external financing continued to decrease, following the disruption created by the outbreak of the Russian crisis in August 1998 (box figure I.5.1). Official flows to developing countries have grown since 1997 as a result of large-scale financial assistance packages organized for the various countries at the centre of the Asian, Russian and the later Brazilian crises. Grants (including technical cooperation grants) — part of official development assistance (mostly to the least developed countries) — nevertheless continued their now well established trend decline.

Box figure I.5.1. Total net resource flows[a] to all developing countries,[b] by type, 1990-1999

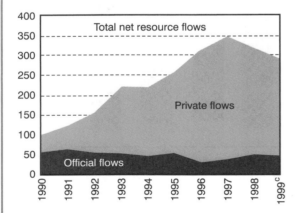

Source: UNCTAD, based on World Bank, 2000a.

While total private flows experienced a decline in both 1998 and 1999 (box figure I.5.2), there were marked differences in the pattern of net flows as regards the major categories of direct investment, portfolio investment and commercial bank financing. Inflows of FDI remained remarkably resilient, registering a

Source: UNCTAD.

marginal increase in 1998 and a rebound in 1999. Most of the decline in private external financing reflected a reduction in portfolio investment flows (including equity and bonds) in 1998 and commercial bank lending in 1999. The debt part of portfolio investment has continued to decline since 1997, while portfolio equity investment increased in 1999 after a decline during that period 1997-1998. The differentiated trends among these categories in the past few years reflects in particular the sensitivity of portfolio investment in debt securities and commercial bank lending with regard to default risk perceptions, which were dramatically revised in light of the Russian debt default of August 1998 and the Brazilian crisis in February 1999. Net financing by commercial banks remained especially unstable for some large, more advanced developing countries embroiled in financial crisis since 1998, which caused large negative balances on commercial bank loans in 1999.

Box figure I.5.2. Private net resource flows[a] to developing countries,[b] by type of flow, 1990-1999

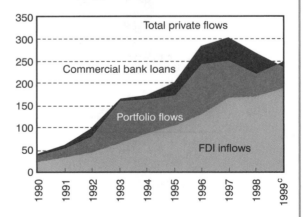

Source: UNCTAD, based on World Bank, 2000a.

a   Defined as net liability transactions or original maturity of greater than one year.
b   The World Bank's classification on developing countries is different from that of UNCTAD. Central and Eastern Europe is included in the former classification.
c   Preliminary.

differences in economic conditions and policies. They can source inputs, information and personnel more readily across the world. They can thus bring international market forces to bear on national economies more quickly than other firms (and so exercise discipline on local markets and policy makers); at the same time, they are becoming less subject to national policies. Their large internalized markets mean that a large part of their international transactions can bypass national controls and scrutiny. For example, TNCs can use transfer pricing on intra-firm trade to minimize their tax exposure, so depriving host or home countries of tax revenue. The tax authorities of the United States, home to many of the largest TNCs, made income adjustments of $1.5 billion for 156 United States-controlled TNCs and $2 billion for 236 non-United States controlled TNCs in 1994 (UNCTAD, 1999b, p. 31). Perhaps this is not unrelated to the fact that 61 per cent of United States controlled TNCs and 67 per cent of non-United States

controlled TNCs paid no income taxes in 1995 (United States, General Accounting Office, 1999, p. 5).

The development challenge. Governments of both home and host countries of TNCs have to develop responses to the challenges raised by the rapid growth of international production. Some are mentioned above, but there are several others, relating, for instance, to technology transfer,

FIGURE I.11
Private financial flows to the five Asian countries most seriously affected by the financial crisis,[a] 1995-1999
(Billions of dollars)

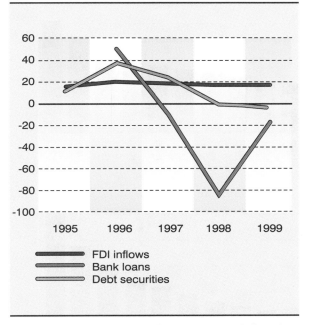

- FDI inflows
- Bank loans
- Debt securities

Source: UNCTAD, FDI/TNC database and BIS, various issues.

Note: Data for bank loans are available in the BIS statistics only from 1996 and up to September 1999. Debt securities include international money market instruments, bonds and notes.

[a] Indonesia, Malaysia, the Philippines, the Republic of Korea and Thailand.

Table I.5. **Pattern of private financial flows in developing and transition economies[a], 1993-1998**
(Percentage of total[b])

Rank	Economy	FDI inflows	Portfolio equity	Bonds	Bank and trade-related lending
1	China	25.7	10.8	4.4	1.3
2	Brazil	7.6	9.6	5.9	39.3
3	Mexico	6.5	10.9	10.8	13.0
4	Argentina	3.8	3.9	18.5	6.4
5	Malaysia	3.7	5.3	1.6	6.6
6	Poland	2.6	2.9	1.9	1.4
7	Chile	2.4	1.0	1.7	7.4
8	Indonesia	2.2	5.9	2.2	-3.7
9	Thailand	2.1	6.6	2.5	1.3
10	Russian Federation	1.8	3.0	15.2	6.8
11	Colombia	1.7	0.4	3.4	0.8
12	Hungary	1.6	1.9	2.1	2.1
13	Venezuela	1.6	1.1	1.8	1.5
14	Republic of Korea	1.6	14.1	12.1	-3.1
15	Peru	1.4	3.0	-0.2	1.2
16	Viet Nam	1.4	0.3	0.0	-0.3
17	India	1.4	6.1	5.6	-0.2
18	Czech Republic	1.1	0.4	1.2	1.8
19	Philippines	1.0	3.2	2.1	0.3
20	Nigeria	1.0	0.0	0.0	-0.5
21	Kazakhstan	0.7	0.0	0.3	1.3
22	Egypt	0.6	2.1	0.0	-0.7
23	Turkey	0.5	3.0	1.4	4.9
24	Romania	0.5	0.1	0.4	0.2
25	Panama	0.4	0.1	0.4	0.0
26	Pakistan	0.4	1.2	0.2	1.0
27	Ecuador	0.4	0.0	-0.0	-0.1
28	Trinidad and Tobago	0.4	0.0	0.0	-0.1
29	Morocco	0.4	0.6	0.1	0.6
30	Azerbaijan	0.4	0.0	0.0	0.1
	Total above	77.0	97.5	95.6	90.6
	Top 10	58.5	59.9	64.8	79.9
	Top 20	72.3	90.5	93.0	83.4

Source: UNCTAD, FDI/TNC database and World Bank, 2000a.

[a] 30 economies chosen and ranked on the basis of the magnitude of FDI inflows.
[b] Cumulative total of developing economies and countries in Central and Eastern Europe during 1993-1998. Excluding Bermuda, Cayman Islands, Hong Kong (China), Saudi Arabia, Singapore and Taiwan Province of China.

FIGURE I.12
Inward plus outward FDI stock as a percentage of GDP, 1980-1999
(Percentage)

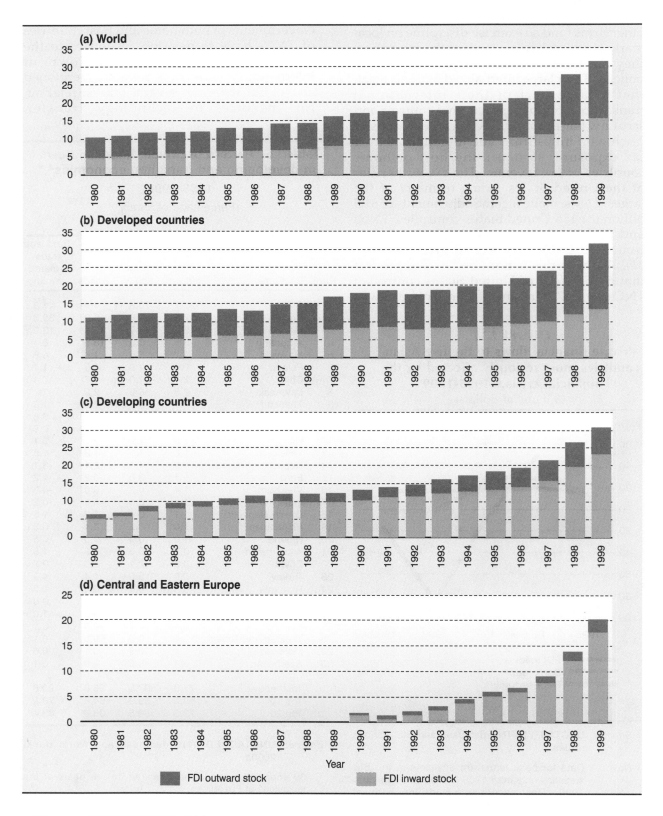

Source: UNCTAD, FDI/TNC database.

FIGURE I.13
Transnationality index[a] of host economies,[b] 1997
(Percentage)

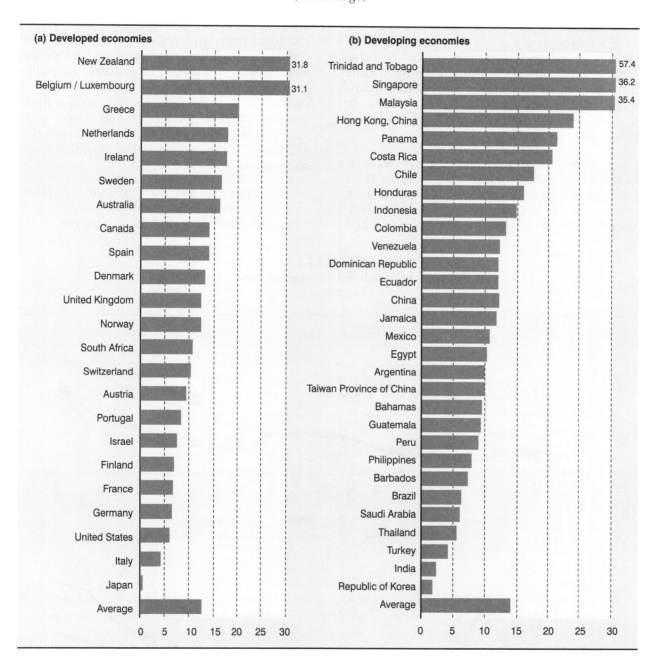

Source: UNCTAD estimates.

[a]   Average of the four shares : FDI inflows as a percentage of gross fixed capital formation for the past three years (1995-1997); FDI inward stocks as a percentage of GDP in 1997; value added of foreign affiliates as a percentage of GDP in 1997; and employment of foreign affiliates as a percentage of total employment in 1997.

[b]   Only the economies for which data for all of these four shares are available were selected. Data on value added are available only for Finland (1996), France (1996), Italy, Japan, Norway, Portugal (1996), Sweden (1996), the United States, China, India (1995), Malaysia (1995), Mexico (1993), Singapore and Taiwan Province of China (1994). For other economies, data were estimated by applying the ratio of value added of United States affiliates to United States outward FDI stock to total inward FDI stock of the country. Data on employment are available only for Austria, Denmark (1996), Finland, France (1996), Germany, Ireland, Italy, Japan, Portugal (1996), Sweden (1998), the United States, Brazil (1995), China, Hong Kong (China), Indonesia (1996), Mexico (1993) and Taiwan Province of China (1995). For other economies, data were estimated by applying the ratio of employment of German and United States affiliates to German and United States outward FDI stock to total inward FDI stock of the economy.

employment, skills, local linkages and the like (UNCTAD, 1999a). A number of policies used traditionally to deal with TNCs are less used today, for instance offering protected markets or subsidies, engaging in extensive bargaining or discriminating against TNCs in favour of domestic enterprises. Not only do new international rules of trade and investment limit the freedom of national governments, many governments feel that their main function is to provide an efficient setting for market-based enterprises to operate.

Markets and supporting institutions, however, do not work perfectly — far from it. Moreover, the interests of TNCs and host countries do not always coincide. Policy therefore matters. Governments have to make

sure that they create conditions in which their economies gain the maximum benefits from FDI and suffer a minimum of losses. The issue of cross-border M&As is very relevant here (see chapter VI below). So is the issue of increasing the local roots and spillovers of TNCs, with corresponding benefits for the development of domestic enterprise. In general, the policy challenge with respect to FDI is twofold: to create the locational assets that would build genuine competitiveness and so attract more and better quality FDI; and to make sure that FDI benefits host country development as much as possible.

Because markets are not perfect, moreover, it is important for countries to preserve a "policy space" for themselves in the

FIGURE I.14
FDI inflows standardized by market size,[a] 1979-1998
(Dollars)

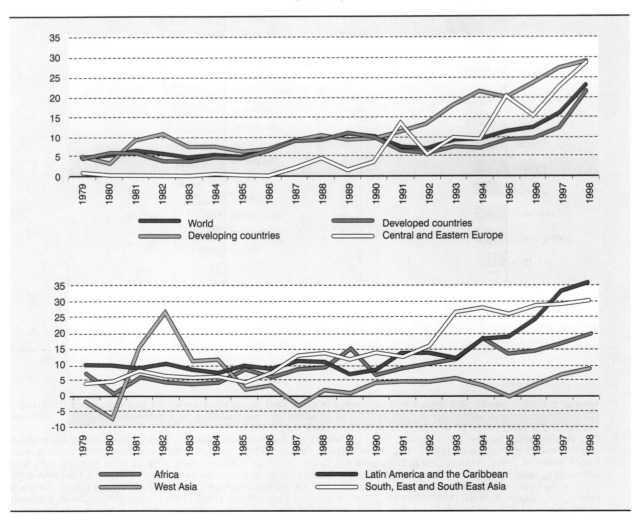

Source: UNCTAD, FDI/TNC database.

[a]   FDI inflows per $1,000 GDP.

new international environment. They should, for instance, keep room for manoeuvre when negotiating international investment agreements in order to ensure that they are able to further national economic interests.[17] They should use the grace period provided in various WTO agreements to ensure that they are able to participate more effectively in international production, rather than withdraw from it. As was suggested in *WIR99*, however, simply participating in international production in a static way is not the way to develop: sustained growth requires that the base of domestic capabilities be dynamic. This calls for a number

of policies which, while not directly related to FDI, are critical to benefiting from it.[18]

Finally, the spread of international production also raises complex and challenging broader policy management issues. There is no ideal or universal policy towards FDI, and each country has to mount its own to suit its needs and capabilities. This calls for considerable skill, information and flexibility on the part of national governments. Bargaining with TNCs remains vital in a number of areas, such as large resource extraction projects, infrastructure projects or large privatizations.

Box I.6. World Association of Investment Promotion Agencies

After its establishment in 1995, the World Association of Investment Promotion Agencies (WAIPA), headquartered in Geneva, Switzerland, has grown to a membership of 110 investment promotion agencies (IPAs) from 105 countries. Although IPAs compete worldwide for investment capital, they have many concerns in common, and there is considerable need for enhanced cooperation among them. Therefore, participating agencies in WAIPA have agreed to promote and develop understanding and cooperation amongst them; strengthen information gathering systems and information exchange; share country and regional experiences in attracting investment; assist each other to gain access to technical assistance and training through referrals to relevant agencies; facilitate access to funding and other assistance, through referrals to relevant bilateral and multilateral agencies, for the development and implementation of investment promotion programmes; and assist IPAs in advising their respective governments in the formulation of appropriate investment promotion policies and strategies. To this end, seminars, training courses and workshops, as well as conferences, are organized by WAIPA in cooperation with UNCTAD and other international organizations, and reports on specific investment promotion issues published.

The new work programme of WAIPA, defined at its Fifth Annual Conference in Bangkok, Thailand, in February 2000, reflects the challenges with which IPAs will be faced during the next decade, as well as issues related to investors' perception regarding the role of

IPAs, regional strategies for investment promotion, and assistance that can be provided by international organizations.

While in most countries new policies and instruments for effective investment promotion have been put in place, not all countries have been equally able to benefit from these changes. For IPAs to meet the challenges of the future will require continuous evaluation and improvement in their operational structures as well as quick adaptation of investment related policies and strategies. In addition, regional cooperation in investment promotion will assume a more important role. Many IPAs already take advantage of the opportunities offered by increased regional economic integration and harmonization of policies, and several country groupings are promoted as single investment locations. Indeed, for many IPAs a regional strategy can assist to overcome such location disadvantages as small market size, accessibility problems or supply capacity limitations.

Financial support to the implementation of WAIPA activities is provided by the Governments of Ireland and the Netherlands. Furthermore, the following five international agencies established a Consultative Committee to support WAIPA activities and advise on its work programme: Foreign Investment Advisory Services (FIAS) of the World Bank, Multilateral Investment Guarantee Agency (MIGA), Organisation of Economic Co-operation and Development (OECD), United Nations Conference on Trade and Development (UNCTAD), and United Nations Industrial Development Organization (UNIDO).

Source: UNCTAD.

So does regulating TNCs in natural monopolies and providing a modern legal framework for property rights or dispute resolution. Effective competition policy is one of the most important tools in handling the spread of TNCs, particularly through cross-border M&As (see

chapters IV-VI). Moreover, it is no longer sufficient to have a patchwork of good policies - they have to be integrated across traditional ministerial and departmental lines to achieve the coherence needed to raise competition and promote national development.

NOTES

1   The value added of all TNC systems in the world is estimated by extrapolating the data of foreign affiliates and parent firms of United States TNCs.

2   Calculated on the basis of 39 countries for which data for both manufacturing FDI and gross domestic capital formation are available.

3   Figures showing high shares (even exceeding 100 per cent in the case of Malawi) may result from the fact that the reported data on capital formation do not necessarily reflect accurately the actual value of capital formation and that FDI flows do not necessarily translate into capital formation.

4   Calculated on the basis of 113 countries for which data on private capital formation are available for 1998.

5   See UNCTAD, 1999a for a more thorough discussion.

6   The total number of DTTs, 1982 include the following types of DTTs: Income and Capital, 1754; Income, 4; Individuals/Legal Entities, 3; Air and Sea Transport, 97; Air Transport, 9; Air Services, 1; Transport, 2; Cooperation and Exchange of Information, 15; Inheritance and Gift, Specific, 56; Inheritance, 1; Technical/Administrative/ Arbitration, 12; Tax Implementation Agreement, 1; Taxation of Frontier Workers Agreement, 1; and Protocols, 26.

7   The ten largest host countries, for example, accounted for 75 per cent of world FDI inflows in 1999, compared with 61 per cent in 1997 and 71 per cent in 1998.

8   Some of these are especially important in service industries, e.g. management contracts in the hotel industry.

9   The value of all cross-border M&As on an announcement basis was $1.1 trillion in 1999. It should be noted that the value and number of cross-border M&As differ, depending on whether they are given on an announcement or completion basis, or whether they cover all deals (i.e. including those of less than 10 per cent) or not. Data prior to 1987 are not systematically collected. For details see chapter IV.

10   For a more detailed discussion, see chapter IV.

11   It is a typical case that one dollar of cross-border M&As does not correspond to one dollar of FDI.

12   In current prices. In constant 1995 world import prices, this would have been higher.

13   Includes countries that are classified under developing Europe (i.e. countries of the former Yugoslavia), according to the United Nations classification.

14   Measured as the average of FDI inflows as a percentage of gross fixed capital formation over the past three years; FDI inward stock as a percentage of GDP over the latest available year; value added of foreign affiliates as a percentage of GDP over the latest available year; and employment by foreign affiliates as a percentage of total employment over the latest available year. The index is calculated for 53 countries for which data are available.

15   In practice it is very difficult to distinguish "high" from "low" quality FDI. Other conditions remaining equal, FDI projects with a high technology content or strong export-orientation are considered by most developing countries to be of higher "quality" than projects with low technology contents and no exports. Many countries would consider FDI with strong linkages to domestic enterprises that help upgrade or build up local capabilities as being of higher quality than that with weak linkages and little technological upgrading. However, priorities can vary by specific circumstances. Countries with high unemployment rates, for instance, may regard employment-creating FDI as high quality. Countries with large unexploited natural resources may regard extractive FDI as high quality. Those with weak skills and ample cheap labour may regard skill- and technology-intensive FDI as low quality, and so on. The generalization about quality being associated with linkages, skills, technology and export promotion does nevertheless apply to most developing countries with established industrial bases.

16   The reverse is certainly happening. A number of start-up companies from developing countries like India now have their initial public offerings in the United States.

17   For the discussion of the issue of flexibility in international investment agreements, see UNCTAD, 2000b.

18   See UNCTAD, 1999a, for a discussion of such policies.

II | Regional Trends

Developed countries attracted $636 billion in FDI inflows in 1999, $156 billion more than in 1998, accounting for nearly three-quarters of the world's total. The United States and the United Kingdom continued to lead in both inward and outward FDI. The United Kingdom became the largest outward investor in 1999, replacing the United States for the first time since 1988. These two countries also were the principal host countries. Total flows between the European Union (EU) and the United States increased significantly in 1999, after doubling in 1998. Inflows of FDI to the EU as a region were an estimated $305 billion, a 23 per cent increase over the previous year. Inflows of FDI to Japan quadrupled: from $3 billion in 1998 to $13 billion in 1999. Japanese outflows showed a slight decline, from $24 to an estimated $23 billion. The countries of *Central and Eastern Europe*, still in transition to a market economy, managed to retain a stable inflow of about $23 billion in 1999.[1]

Flows of FDI to *developing countries* increased by 16 per cent in 1999 after stagnating in 1998. However, given the rise in flows to developed countries in 1999, their share in world FDI inflows continued to decline, falling in 1999 to 24 per cent from 38 per cent in 1997. Total flows to developing countries amounted to $208 billion, some $106 billion went to developing Asia (including Central Asia and West Asia), $40 billion of it to China alone. Latin America and the Caribbean pulled in 23 per cent more than in 1998; of the region's estimated total flows of $90 billion, some $31 billion went to Brazil, which was the regional leader for the fourth consecutive year. In Africa, large increases in FDI were recorded in Morocco and South Africa; the continent (including South Africa) is estimated to have attracted $10 billion in inward investment.

Flows of FDI to the 48 least developed countries (LDCs) increased slightly from $3.7 billion in 1998 to $4.5 billion in 1999. Despite this positive development, the LDCs as a group remain marginalized as they account for only 0.5 per cent of global FDI inflows and 2.2 per cent of FDI inflows to developing countries. Angola, Mozambique, the Sudan and Myanmar were the most important recipients, with FDI inflows of $1.8 billion, $0.4 billion, $0.4 billion and $0.3 billion respectively. Within the LDC group the 33 African LDCs accounted for a share of 84 per cent in the total flows to LDCs in 1999, representing no change to the previous year.

A. Developed countries

1. United States

For the third consecutive year, FDI *outflows* from the United States continued to increase, reaching a record $151 billion in 1999, though the pace of growth slowed down compared with the two previous years (a 3 per cent increase). With this performance, the United States fell to second place behind the United Kingdom (figure II.1). The stock of

FIGURE II.1
Developed countries: FDI *outflows*, 1998 and 1999ª
(Billions of dollars)

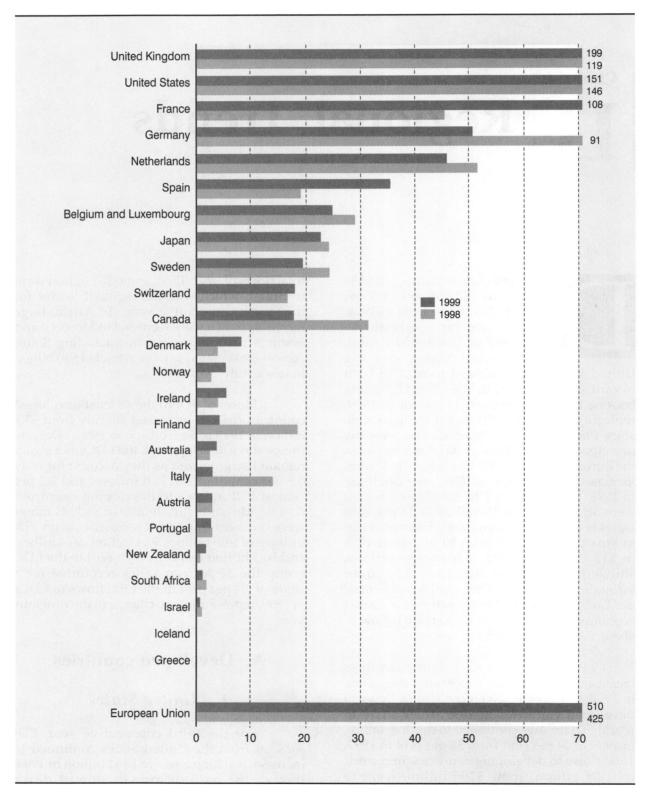

Source: UNCTAD, FDI/TNC database and annex table B.2.

ª   Ranked on the basis of the magnitude of 1999 FDI outflows.

United States FDI abroad (at historical cost) as of 1999 stood at $1.1 trillion. During that year, the United Kingdom was the largest beneficiary of FDI outflows from the United States, receiving one-fifth of the total. Japan, where United States TNCs had registered net outflows (i.e. divestments) in both 1996 and 1997, received about $4 billion in FDI in both 1998 and 1999. Latin America and the Caribbean continues to be the biggest developing recipient region of United States FDI flows ($23 billion in 1999[2]). As in previous years, finance, insurance and real estate were the most important industries for outward investment, and accounted for almost one-third of total United States outflows. Altogether, the service sector accounted for 59 per cent of total outflows from the United States, against 31 per cent for the manufacturing sector.

Since 1996, FDI *inflows* into the United States have exceeded outflows. In 1999, they again registered a substantial increase of 48 per cent (which is, however, less than the 1998 increase of 77 per cent). With a record $276 billion, the United States was the largest host country in the world in 1999 (figure II.2), accounting by itself for one-third of global FDI inflows. The United Kingdom was the largest investor in the United States, accounting for 39 per cent of the total, followed by the Netherlands with 14 per cent.

After a decline in 1997 and 1998, Japanese FDI flows into the United States rose to $13 billion in 1999, a level comparable to that of 1996. In 1999, the services sector replaced the manufacturing sector (which was by far the largest recipient sector in 1998, accounting for about two-thirds of all inflows), primarily because of the acquisition of AirTouch Communications by the Vodafone Group (United Kingdom) with a transaction value of $60 billion, the largest completed cross-border M&A deal in 1999 (annex table A.IV.4).

These large FDI inflows into, and outflows from, the United States, unperturbed by the financial crisis, have placed that country at the centre of the current FDI boom. Cross-border M&As, especially between companies based in the European Union and the United States, lie in the heart of recent United States FDI in both directions (table II.1). But both the number and the value of cross-border M&A transactions by United States TNCs exceeding one billion dollars fell in 1999: from 26 to 21

in terms of number and from $74 billion to $55 billion in terms of value.[3] On the inward side, about 90 per cent of investment outlays by foreign investors in United States businesses in recent years were attributed to the acquisition of United States companies by foreign-based TNCs (annex table A.IV.8). Some of these inflows reflected capital contributions to existing affiliates in the United States, which were in turn used to acquire local companies. This raises the question of whether recent levels of FDI flows for 1999 can be sustained in the future. They may be sustained in the short-term if the present M&A boom persists with similar large M&A transactions: indeed, even if the pace of M&A activity subsides, a few large transactions can still lead to very high values of FDI activity, as in 1999.

There are, however, signs that both sales and purchases of cross-border M&A activity are slowing down, reflecting the lower number of large-scale transactions that characterized the United States cross-border M&As until 1998. This could suggest that a decline in United States FDI flows, both inward and outward, could take place in the next 1 or 2 years. For example, while outflows dropped to $35 billion in the first quarter of 2000 compared with $38 billion of the quarterly average of 1999, the corresponding figures for inflows were $42 and $69 billion, respectively.

From a longer-term perspective, however, United States FDI outflows are likely to remain robust, as the country's TNCs continue to seek to improve their competitiveness by accessing new markets and resources and to generate strong ownership advantages at home. Given the size of its domestic economy, the United States still lags behind other developed countries with a long history of outward investment. The ratio of outward FDI flows to gross domestic fixed capital formation for the United States during the period 1996-1998, at 8 per cent, was considerably below that of Sweden and the Netherlands for instance, or even the United Kingdom; on the inward side, the picture is similar (figure II.3). As regards inward investment, with the value of the United States dollar virtually unchanged in 1999 (it appreciated by a mere 1 per cent on a trade-weighted basis against a group of seven major countries),[4] it is unlikely that the burst of FDI flows was dictated by low asset prices. The rates of return earned by non-financial foreign

FIGURE II.2
Developed countries: FDI *inflows*, 1998 and 1999ᵃ
(Billions of dollars)

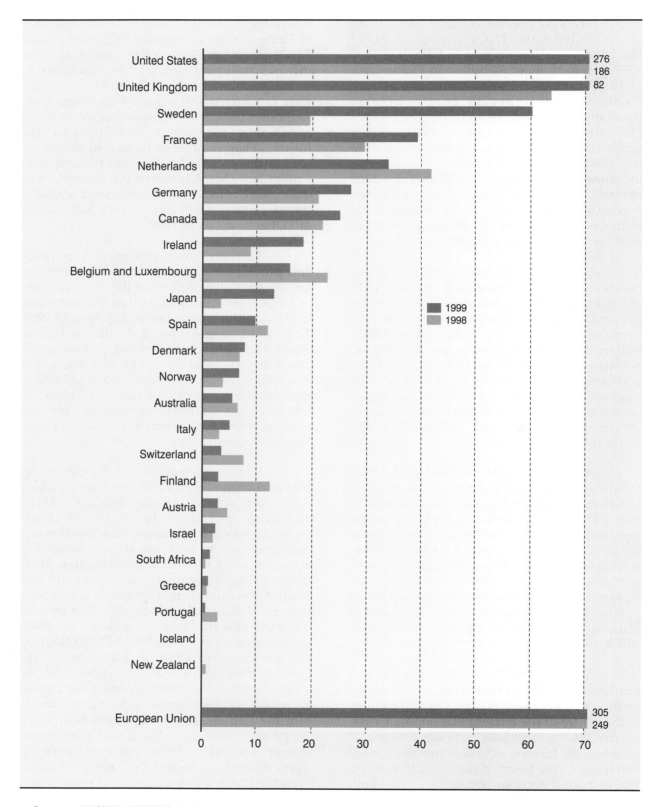

Source: UNCTAD, FDI/TNC database and annex table B.1.

ᵃ   Ranked on the basis of the magnitude of 1999 FDI inflows.

affiliates in the United States were also consistently lower than for non-financial local companies, although the gap appeared to be narrowing (Mataloni, 2000). The main motives

for high FDI inflows were clearly access to the huge and rapidly growing market and the pull of dynamic technological activity there. These attractions are likely to persist in the future.

Table II.1. Sales and purchases of cross-border M&As in the United States, by home region/country, 1987-1999

(Billions of dollars)

(a) Sales

| Year | World | Developed countries | | | | Developing countries | | | | Central and Eastern Europe[b] |
		Total	EU	Japan	United States[a]	Total	Africa	Latin America and the Caribbean	South, East and South-East Asia	
1987	51.8	50.5	23.0	3.2	21.8	1.3	0.1	-	1.0	-
1988	63.9	63.1	19.0	10.8	17.7	0.7	-	-	0.7	-
1989	68.8	66.6	35.9	5.7	19.3	2.2	-	0.9	1.3	-
1990	54.7	50.9	26.8	7.7	10.8	3.8	-	0.4	1.8	-
1991	28.2	27.7	12.7	10.5	3.6	0.5	-	0.1	0.3	-
1992	15.8	14.6	6.7	3.4	3.5	1.2	-	1.0	0.1	-
1993	20.0	18.5	9.2	0.8	6.4	1.5	-	0.7	0.4	-
1994	44.7	42.6	19.0	0.4	9.2	2.1	-	1.0	0.8	-
1995	53.2	49.3	19.3	2.1	13.4	3.9	-	2.0	1.6	-
1996	68.1	66.0	42.1	4.4	8.8	2.0	-	1.0	1.1	-
1997	81.7	78.7	39.2	1.6	16.8	3.0	-	0.4	2.0	-
1998	209.5	206.1	148.4	0.7	22.7	3.4	-	2.5	0.7	-
1999	233.0	215.1	184.3	0.4	10.9	17.9	0.4	16.8	0.6	-

(b) Purchases

| Year | World | Developed countries | | | | Developing countries | | | | Central and Eastern Europe[b] |
		Total	EU	Japan	United States[c]	Total	Africa	Latin America and the Caribbean	South, East and South-East Asia	
1987	28.4	27.3	2.1	-	21.8	1.2	-	1.1	0.1	-
1988	24.2	23.9	4.4	-	17.7	0.3	-	0.1	0.2	-
1989	38.9	38.3	12.4	1.6	19.3	0.6	-	0.1	0.5	-
1990	27.6	24.5	6.5	-	10.8	2.9	0.4	2.2	0.3	0.2
1991	16.6	14.5	7.9	0.1	3.6	2.0	-	2.0	-	0.1
1992	15.0	12.5	5.9	0.1	3.5	2.1	-	1.3	0.8	0.4
1993	21.4	17.9	9.5	0.1	6.4	3.2	-	2.7	0.5	0.3
1994	28.5	25.6	12.3	0.3	9.2	2.6	-	2.3	0.3	0.2
1995	57.3	52.4	26.3	0.4	13.4	4.6	-	3.8	0.7	0.3
1996	60.7	50.3	28.2	0.3	8.8	8.9	0.2	7.1	0.4	1.5
1997	80.9	60.0	24.9	0.3	16.8	20.4	0.1	16.3	3.9	0.5
1998	137.4	115.6	62.8	4.0	22.7	20.8	-	15.6	5.2	0.3
1999	112.4	98.0	51.5	8.7	10.9	13.7	-	7.9	5.8	0.7

Source: UNCTAD, cross-border M&A database, based on data from Thomson Financial Securities Data Company.

[a] Sold by foreign affiliates operating in the United States to United States firms and/or sold by United States firms to foreign affiliates operating in the United States.

[b] Includes the countries of the former Yugoslavia.

[c] Acquisition of United States firms by foreign affiliates operating in the United States and/or acquisition of foreign affiliates operating in the United States by United States firms.

FIGURE II.3

Developed countries: FDI flows as percentage of gross fixed capital formation,1996 and 1998[a]

(Percentage)

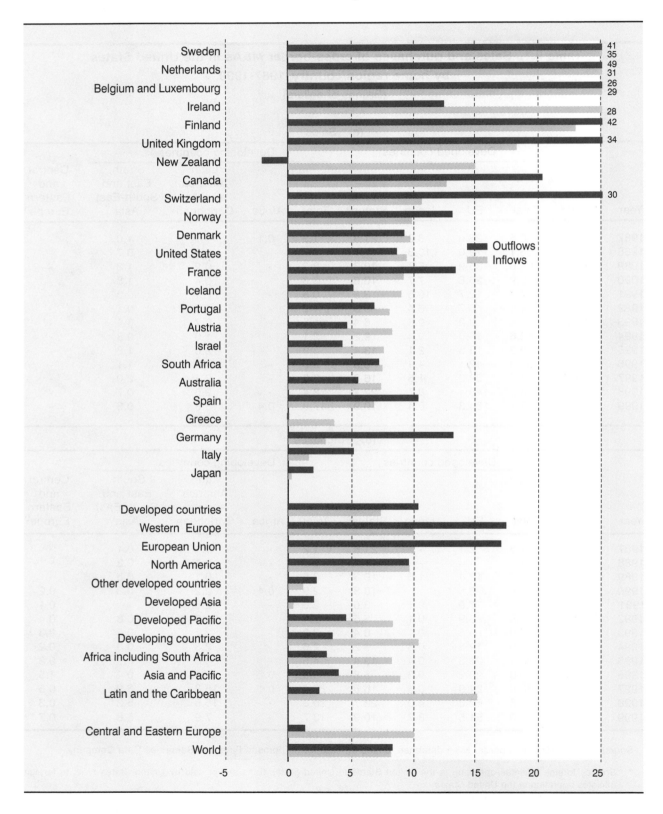

Source: UNCTAD, FDI/TNC database and annex table B.5.

[a]   Ranked on the basis of the magnitude of 1996-1998 FDI inflows as a pecentage of gross fixed capital formation.

2. *European Union*

The position of the EU as the world's most important source of FDI was reconfirmed in 1999 as *outflows* of FDI rose for the sixth year in a row. Firms of the EU accounted for outward flows of $510 billion, an increase of 20 per cent over 1998. The United Kingdom maintained its status as the largest investor this year not only in Europe, but globally. The United Kingdom, which alone accounted for 39 per cent of total EU outflows, was followed by two other large economies, France and Germany, and by the Netherlands (figure II.1 and annex table B.2). In terms of growth, Denmark, France and Spain reported the largest increases, while FDI from Finland, Italy and Germany fell significantly in 1999. As in earlier years, FDI outflows from EU countries greatly surpassed the level of EU inflows. The discrepancy continued to expand from $95 billion in 1997 and $177 billion in 1998 to reach $205 billion in 1999.

Inflows of FDI to the EU countries increased by 23 per cent to a total of $305 billion, higher than inflows into the United States (annex table B.1). The United Kingdom remained the largest recipient in the EU, with the small economy of Sweden as the runner-up with a growth rate of more than 200 per cent compared with 1998. France and the Netherlands were in third and fourth places, respectively (figure II.2). The remarkable increase in inward investment to Sweden was mainly the result of the merger between the two pharmaceutical companies Astra (Sweden) and Zeneca (United Kingdom). Inflows to

Ireland more than doubled, in which M&As (e.g. the acquisition of Telecom Eireann by Iranian investors with an acquisition value of $4.4 billion) played an important role. On the other hand, inflows to Portugal, Finland, Austria, Belgium and Spain declined markedly compared with the year before.

Distinguishing between intra-EU and extra-EU flows, it appears that FDI between the EU and other parts of the world is gaining in importance. In the case of both outward and inward flows, the intra-EU share of total FDI was at its lowest level in 1998 since 1992 (figure II.4). In 1998, extra-EU FDI was dominated by the United States, which accounted for 59 per cent of total outflows and 69 per cent of total inflows. About one-quarter of flows in both directions was related to Central and South America and the EFTA countries, while the share of the rest of the world was only some 10 per cent (Eurostat, 2000).

European FDI developments in 1999 were more than ever driven by M&As. The value of cross-border M&A sales and purchases within Europe increased by 83 per cent and 75 per cent, reaching $345 and $498 billion respectively.[5] The EU accounted for almost half of all global cross-border sales of M&As and as much as 70 per cent of global purchases (table IV.3). Companies of the EU were involved in all but one of the ten largest cross-border M&As in 1999 (table IV.4), with Vodafone's takeover of AirTouch Communications and the merger between Astra and Zeneca topping the list.

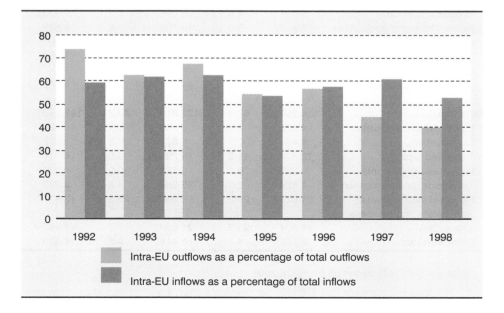

FIGURE II.4
Intra-EU FDI flows, 1992-1998
(Percentage of total EU FDI)

Intra-EU outflows as a percentage of total outflows

Intra-EU inflows as a percentage of total inflows

Source: Eurostat, 2000.

These cross-border FDI flows in Europe are partly a response to the ongoing integration and liberalization affecting much of European industry. The implementation of the various single market directives and subsequent deregulation efforts at both national and EU levels have made national borders increasingly obsolete. The industries that have been the most affected during the late 1990s are in the service sector, including financial intermediation, telecommunications, electricity, media and transportation. The sectoral breakdown of FDI flows reveals the growing importance of these industries in European FDI (table II.2). During the period 1997-1998, services accounted for more than 70 per cent of both intra- and extra-EU FDI inflows, with financial intermediation, real estate and other business activities the main recipient industries. In terms of outward FDI, there was a marked difference between intra-EU and extra-EU flows. While services accounted for 67 per cent of total intra-EU outflows, the share in total extra-EU outflows was only about 44 per cent. Financial intermediation was the primary

generator of service-related FDI, accounting for 62 per cent of the EU outflow of all FDI in services in 1998. Throughout the 1990s, services have accounted for a greater proportion of inflows to the EU compared with EU firms' FDI outside of the Union. This discrepancy has widened in recent years (figure II.5).

Due to the merger between BP (United Kingdom) and Amoco (United States) in the petroleum business, primary industries grew in importance in extra-EU outflows of FDI in 1998. Within manufacturing, the share of the motor vehicles industry in extra-EU outflows rose considerably. The 1998 merger between Daimler (Germany) and Chrysler (United States) played an important role, making motor vehicles by far the most important industry in German FDI outflows that year. For the first time, motor vehicles also became the largest manufacturing sector in EU outflows, taking the lead from the chemical industry (Eurostat, 2000). The consolidation of the automotive industry continued at a high pace in 1999 and 2000, examples of which are the following:

Table II.2. Sectoral distribution of intra-EU and extra-EU flows, 1997-1998

	Outflows				Inflows			
	Intra-EU		Extra-EU[a]		Intra-EU		Extra-EU[a]	
Sector/industry	ECU million	Per cent	ECU million	Per cent	ECU million	Per cent	ECU million	Per cent
All industries[b]	**199 323**	**100.0**	**281 190**	**100.0**	**163 963**	**100.0**	**131 432**	**100.0**
Primary	**-2 919**	**-1.5**	**70 861**	**25.2**	**548**	**0.3**	**-594**	**-0.5**
Manufacturing	**65 545**	**32.9**	**87 186**	**31.0**	**38 450**	**23.5**	**38 498**	**29.3**
Food products	1 015	0.5	4 228	1.5	5 545	3.4	1 532	1.2
Textiles and wood	9 567	4.8	6 098	2.2	6 633	4.0	3 051	2.3
Petrol, chemicals and rubber	17 922	9.0	13 702	4.9	10 625	6.5	9 535	7.3
Metal and mechanical	12 635	6.3	6 902	2.5	5 504	3.4	4 111	3.1
Office machinery and radio	6 286	3.2	3 950	1.4	1 854	1.1	14 280	10.9
Motor vehicles, other transport equipment	3 091	1.6	44 344	15.8	4 567	2.8	2 878	2.2
Services	**134 259**	**67.4**	**122 819**	**43.7**	**121 730**	**74.2**	**93 148**	**70.9**
Electricty, gas and water	4 622	2.3	5 203	1.9	34	-	12 460	9.5
Construction	1 431	0.7	871	0.3	952	0.6	884	0.7
Trade and repairs	22 824	11.5	16 897	6.0	14 111	8.6	6 829	5.2
Hotels and restaurants	277	0.1	-2 651	-0.9	596	0.4	2 499	1.9
Transports, communication	4 124	2.1	13 385	4.8	8 363	5.1	9 051	6.9
Financial intermediation	51 012	25.6	66 068	23.5	43 811	26.7	29 988	22.8
Real estate and business activities	41 204	20.7	21 630	7.7	49 493	30.2	27 682	21.1
Other services	8 765	4.4	1 416	0.5	4 370	2.7	3 755	2.9

Source: UNCTAD, based on Eurostat, 2000.

a   FDI flows which are not intra-EU, thus including flows which are not classified as either intra- or extra-EU.
b   Includes FDI flows which are not allocated according to industry.

Ford's acquisitions of Volvo Cars and Land Rover (the latter from BMW); Volkswagen's acquisition of Scania, the Swedish heavy truck-maker; Renault's takeover of Samsung Motor Inc. (Republic of Korea); the acquisition of a 33 per cent stake of Mitsubishi Motors by DaimlerChrysler; Renault's 37 per cent equity acquisition of Nissan; and Volvo's acquisition of Renault's truck division (chapter IV).

Although it is difficult to assess the full impact of the Euro on FDI, the current reshaping of European industry is likely to be affected by the single currency. It has created a liquid market in European corporate bonds, which companies are increasingly using to refinance bank debt and to raise money for M&A activity.[6] The single currency will also contribute to greater price transparency and increased competition in Europe, putting more pressure on firms to restructure and consolidate their operations.

Contrary to expectations, however, it does not appear that the launch of the Euro has had a major negative impact on the inflow of FDI to EU members that have not participated in the European Monetary Union (EMU). Inward FDI to the EMU countries decreased somewhat (-2 per cent) between 1998 and 1999, though the level of flows remained high (figure II.6). On the other hand, FDI inflows to the non-EMU members increased by 66 per cent. Inflows to the United Kingdom, Sweden and Denmark have increased every year since 1996 (figure II.6). However, this does not mean that the Euro will not affect FDI flows in the longer term. First, as the dominance of M&As in FDI makes the data

highly sensitive to individual business transactions, FDI statistics should be interpreted with caution. Second, it is still too soon to assess the longer-term impact of the single currency on FDI (UNCTAD, 1999a). There are several studies suggesting that the non-EMU countries may suffer from staying outside. For example, in a survey of leading British economists, two-thirds of 164 respondents stated that joining the European single currency would be beneficial for the economy of the United Kingdom.[7] The major advantage provided by the Euro, they said, would be a more stable exchange rate. This, in turn, would enable United Kingdom companies, whose major source of revenue are exports to other EMU countries, to reduce risk and related foreign exchange transaction costs. TNCs whose United Kingdom affiliates export to other EMU countries would probably be in favour of the United Kingdom joining the EMU. The same message was given by foreign affiliates in Sweden. Whereas none expected a Swedish membership in the EMU to lead to a reduction of FDI into Sweden, more than one quarter of foreign affiliates stated that joining the EMU membership would result in more investment into Sweden (Invest in Sweden Agency, 2000).

To conclude, FDI is a central element in the current European restructuring process. Cross-border M&As play an important role as a way for firms to respond to deregulation and increased competition. Major M&A transactions announced or completed in the beginning of 2000 (e.g. Vodafone AirTouch-Mannesmann) suggest that FDI flows will remain at historically high levels. Nevertheless,

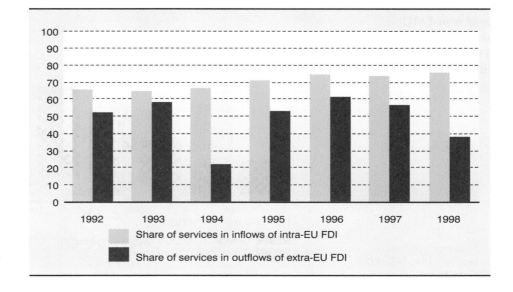

FIGURE II.5
Share of services in intra-EU and extra-EU FDI flows, 1992-1998
(Percentage)

Share of services in inflows of intra-EU FDI

Share of services in outflows of extra-EU FDI

Source: UNCTAD, based on Eurostat, 2000.

the EU continues to attract considerably less FDI than what it undertakes abroad, with the United States receiving most of the outward FDI of the EU.

3. Japan

Cross-border M&As dominated Japanese FDI inflows and outflows in 1999. Outflows of FDI from Japan declined by 6 per cent, to $23 billion in 1999, while inflows quadrupled, to reach a record level of $13 billion. The imbalance between inflows and outflows fell to the lowest level since Japanese authorities started to collect FDI statistics (figure II.7) comparable to other major developed countries (e.g. France, Germany, and the United Kingdom). This is a remarkable and sudden shift: only a few years ago, foreign investors regarded Japan as extremely difficult to enter. More surprisingly, in spite of the traditional Japanese view that M&As are not suited to the country's business culture, most of the new FDI inflows came through a spate of large M&As. For example, the purchase of Japan Leasing Corporation by General Electric Capital, with a transaction value of $6.6 billion, was alone equivalent to about twice the value of the inflows registered in 1998. The purchase of a 37 per cent stake of Nissan by Renault was valued at $5.4 billion. Cable and Wireless invested $700 million in IDC.

Both the number and the value of inward FDI projects increased significantly in 1999. This mirrors strategic changes in Japanese companies, which are increasingly viewing M&As as a means to revitalize and restructure their companies. This stance is encouraged by a series of recent incentives and deregulation measures related to M&A FDI (box IV.7).

Inflows of FDI in the financial industry grew dramatically beginning in 1997, when Japan started to liberalize financial services. Inflows of FDI were relatively small in manufacturing as compared to services, but inflows into specific manufacturing industries, e.g. automobiles, have been rising lately. These have been mainly on account of some large-scale M&As – Ford-Mazda in 1998, Renault-Nissan in 1999 and DaimlerChrysler-Mitsubishi Motors in 2000. As a result, the shares of financial industries and transport equipment in FDI inflows increased from 4 per cent in 1996 to 21 per cent in 1999 in the former, and from 20 per cent in 1996 to 36 per cent in 1999 in the latter.[8]

With regard to FDI *outflows*, two features should be noted. On the one hand, FDI outflows were seriously affected by restructuring in the financial services industry.[9] On the other hand, the relative importance of M&As as a mode of entry by Japanese TNCs declined over the past few years. Since the late 1980s, Japanese companies have increasingly used M&As as a mode of entry into developed countries, notably the United States. However, the number of foreign affiliates established through M&As as a share of total new Japanese foreign affiliates declined from 17 per cent in 1983 to 12 per cent in 1995

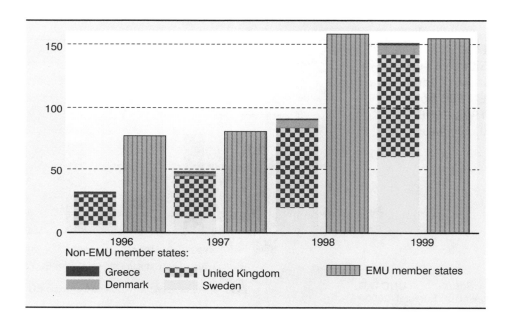

FIGURE II.6
FDI inflows to EMU and non-EMU member states, 1996-1999
(Billions of dollars)

Source: UNCTAD, FDI/ TNC database.

(UNCTAD, 1999a, p. 99). The decline was the result of the increasing number of greenfield affiliates in developing countries. The number of affiliates created through M&A as a share of the number of new Japanese affiliates in developing countries was halved from 17 per cent in 1983 to 8 per cent in 1995. Even though M&As by Japanese TNCs increased in Asia after the financial crisis (as noted elsewhere — UNCTAD, 1999a), this was mainly in the form of additional equity or intra-company loans to existing affiliates affected by the crisis. Few new affiliates were established through M&As in 1998 and 1999.[10]

It should be noted, however, that on a value basis outward FDI through M&As increased in importance recently, mainly due to a few large deals. For example, the value of the ($7.8 billion) purchase of the international tobacco business of RJR Nabisco by Japan Tobacco — the largest cross-border M&A involving a Japanese firm — alone was equivalent to about a third of Japanese outward FDI in 1999.[11]

Some broader implications of these changes are worth noting. An indication of the possible decline of Japanese international competitiveness is its serious slippage in the rankings of the International Institute for Management Development's *World Competitiveness Yearbook*: from number 1 in 1989-1993 to 16 in 1999 (IMD, 1999). This reflects weaknesses in the performance of the domestic economy, especially in financial and corporate management. With declining (new) domestic capital expenditures since 1997, what Japanese industry seems to need to regain global competitiveness is not new investment as much as management know-how and practices in a globalizing world. Cross-border M&As may assist this process.

In 1999, Japanese TNCs started to increase production and hire or rehire employees in the Asian countries most seriously affected by the financial crisis.[12] The slow-down of the domestic economy and the rise of the yen have encouraged them to further expand and deepen their international

FIGURE II.7
Japanese FDI flows and ratio of FDI inflows to FDI outflows, 1980-1999

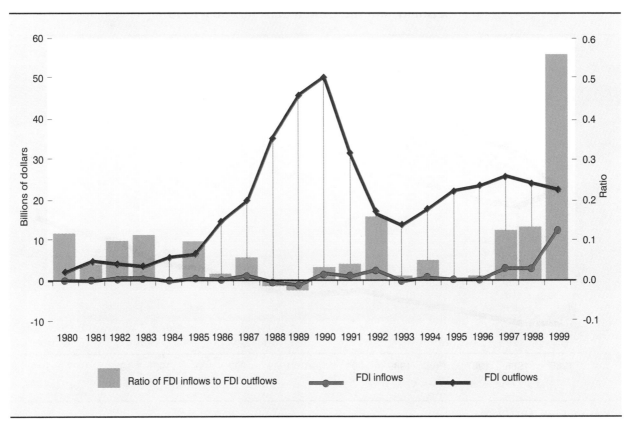

Source: UNCTAD, FDI/TNC database.

production networks. The allocation of specific
functions to foreign affiliates has accelerated.
The number of foreign affiliates designated as
regional headquarters doubled in 1995 and rose
by 59 per cent in 1996. This number was stable
in 1997. As a result, one quarter of all Japanese
foreign affiliates functioned as regional
headquarters in 1997 (Japan, MITI, 2000).

While international production by
Japanese TNCs is continuing to grow, its share
in total production still lags behind other major
home countries such as Germany or the United
States (figure II.8). Prospects for further
increases in international production in the near
future are limited. Only about one-fifth of
Japanese TNCs surveyed in 1999 plan to
increase their investments in the next three
years, compared to 38 per cent in 1998.[13] For
inward FDI, about one-third of foreign affiliates
operating in Japan planned to expand their
business (JETRO, 2000); this compares to two-
fifths of those surveyed in the previous year.[14]
For the moment, foreign firms in Japan are
trying simply to maintain their operations.

B. Developing countries

1. Africa

Inflows of FDI into Africa (including
South Africa)[15] rose by 28 per cent, from $8
billion in 1998 to $10 billion in 1999 (figure II.9).
This growth rate is higher than that of other
developing countries. However, this was not
enough for Africa to increase its share in global
FDI inflows. It remained at the low level of
1.2 per cent in 1999, compared to 2.3 per cent
in 1997 and 1.2 per cent in 1998. This
performance should, however, be seen against
the backdrop of dramatic increases in FDI
inflows to developed countries in 1998-1999.

Recent FDI inflows to Africa have been
growing faster than at the beginning of the
1990s, a result, among other things, of the efforts
of many African Governments to create a more
business-friendly environment after the
turbulent 1970s and 1980s. But the real
challenge for the continent lies ahead:
integration into the global economy, including

FIGURE II.8
**International production as a percentage of total production in Japan,
Germany and the United States^a, 1985-1998**

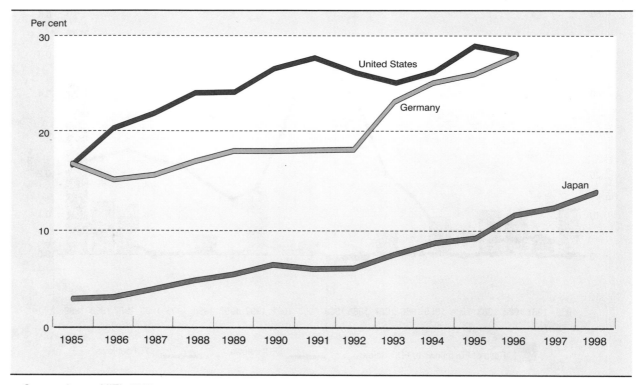

Source: Japan, MITI, 2000.

a   The share of sales by affiliates abroad in total sales of the country.

integration into the regional or global production networks of TNCs. Only then will the continent become a more prominent player in the world market and benefit more from FDI.

Given the limited amounts of FDI flows in absolute terms it is not surprising that most African countries receive small FDI flows. However, Angola, Egypt, Morocco, Nigeria, South Africa and Tunisia have attracted sizeable amounts of FDI in recent years (figure II.10). In 1999 the amounts received by Angola and Egypt were particularly impressive: for the former because of investment in petroleum, and for the latter, mainly on account of deregulation and privatization. As a result, these two countries became the largest recipients of FDI flows in 1999 in Africa, overtaking Nigeria, which had been traditionally the largest. Increases in FDI flows to Ghana and South Africa are also noteworthy.

The *distribution* of FDI inflows between the different regions in Africa has changed somewhat. North Africa (led by Egypt) attracted a slightly higher share of FDI flows during 1997-1998 than in the previous years. In 1999, this share rose to 29 per cent. The oscillations in recent FDI inflows into Morocco reflect its privatization programme, with large projects determining their lumpiness. The Libyan Arab Jamahiriya has matched the lifting of the external embargoes with a liberalization of internal policies, permitting FDI in some industries. If this continues, it might have rising FDI inflows in the future.

Sub-Saharan Africa (including South Africa) had its share in total FDI inflows to Africa slightly reduced from 72 per cent in 1998 to 71 per cent in 1999. However, the development in the sub-region was not uniform; some countries managed to attract rapidly increasing FDI inflows in recent years. Angola and Mozambique have been particularly successful (annex table B.1).

Measured against other indicators, such as GDP or gross domestic capital formation, FDI in a number of small African countries appears much more sizeable than figures for absolute inflows might suggest. Angola, Equatorial Guinea, Lesotho and Zambia rank high if FDI inflows are related to gross domestic capital formation (figure II.11). A similar ranking emerges when FDI inflows are measured against GDP. The two rankings give different pictures of locational attractiveness, although neither has changed much in the past few years.

There is evidence of diversification in *sources* of FDI to Africa. In 1998, the United States maintained its position as the most important investor; it had lost this position to the United Kingdom and to France for a number of years up to 1995: in the period 1994-1998, its FDI outflows to Africa totalled $7.6 billion (figure II.12). France and the United Kingdom ranked second and third, with outflows to Africa of $2.5 billion each. However, the combined share of France, the United Kingdom and the United States decreased from 77 per cent of total FDI flows from OECD countries to Africa in 1984-1988 to 71 per cent in 1989-1993 and 65 per cent in 1994-1998. Other countries, notably such as Germany and the Netherlands, gained in importance. Thus, at least as far as Europe is concerned, the basis for FDI flows to Africa is widening over time, with an increasing number of countries becoming important sources for FDI into Africa.

Evidence on the *sectoral* distribution of FDI outflows to African countries remains patchy. United States FDI is mainly in natural resources, led by petroleum (UNCTAD, 1999b). French FDI also shows an increased share for natural resource extraction. On the other

FIGURE II.9
FDI inflows to Africa, 1990-1999
(Billions of dollars)

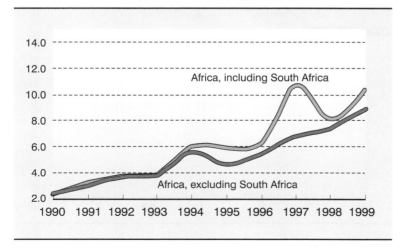

Source: UNCTAD, FDI/TNC database.

hand, FDI from Germany, the Netherlands and Switzerland has gone mainly into manufacturing, while outflows from the United Kingdom have gone mainly into service industries.

In addition, there is evidence that ongoing privatization programmes have triggered an increasing number of FDI projects. Approximately 14 per cent of FDI flows going into Africa during 1990-1998 have been linked to privatization (Pigato and Liberatori, 2000, p. 1). In 1998 alone, foreign investment through privatization triggered a total of $694 million in foreign exchange reserves in sub-Saharan Africa.[16] This figure was only exceeded in 1997, an exceptional year marked by large privatization projects in South Africa. In sub-Saharan Africa, South Africa ($1.4 billion), Ghana ($769 million), Nigeria ($500 million), Zambia ($420 million) and Côte d'Ivoire ($373 million) were the most important recipients of privatization-related FDI during the period 1990-1998. In terms of industries, the bulk of privatization (including projects with domestic as well as with foreign participation) took place in telecommunications (with a total volume of $2.5 billion during the period 1990-1998) and mining ($1.4 billion) (Pigato and Liberatori, 2000).

Although there has been a slowdown in privatization-related FDI in 1999 as compared to the mid-1990s mainly due to fewer privatization projects being offered, this trend is likely to be reversed in the near future. Some countries in sub-Saharan Africa, such as Kenya, Nigeria, Lesotho and South Africa, are preparing for major privatizations in the next few years, offering opportunities for FDI in the power, telecommunications and transport industries.

As to FDI *outflows* from Africa, they stood at $2 billion in 1999, $0.3 billion lower than in 1998 (annex table B.2). Major home countries for FDI outflows from Africa are – as in previous years – South Africa, the Libyan Arab Jamahiriya and Nigeria (figure II.13). In 1999, Uganda was also among the top countries in terms of FDI outflows, partly reflecting a large acquisition in the United States in 1999 (acquisition of Vistana by Starlight Communications with a transaction value of $406 million).

A joint survey by UNCTAD and the International Chamber of Commerce (ICC) of 296 of the world's largest TNCs at the beginning of 2000 provides insights into the prospects for

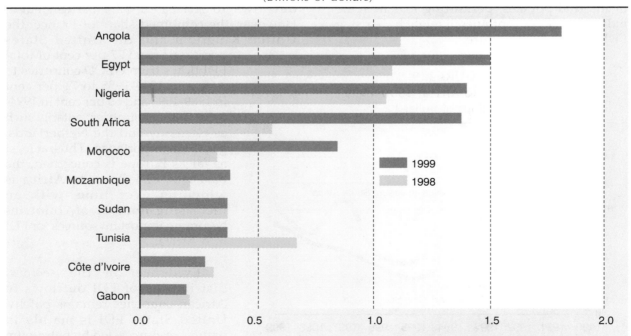

FIGURE II.10
Africa: FDI inflows, top 10 countries, 1998 and 1999[a]
(Billions of dollars)

Source: UNCTAD, FDI/TNC database and annex table B.1.

[a]   Ranked on the basis of the magnitude of 1999 FDI inflows.

FIGURE II.11
Africa: FDI flows as percentage of gross fixed capital formation, top 20 countries, 1996-1998ᵃ
(Percentage)

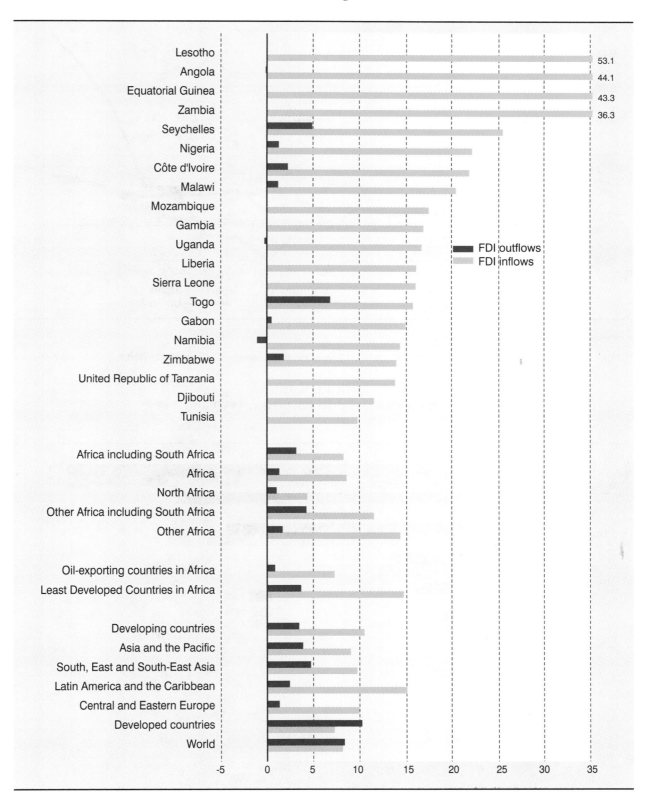

Source: UNCTAD, FDI/TNC database and annex table B.5.

ᵃ   Ranked on the basis of the magnitude of 1996-1998 FDI inflows as a percentage of gross fixed capital formation.

FIGURE II.12
The most important countries for FDI outflows to Africa, 1981-1998
(Millions of dollars)

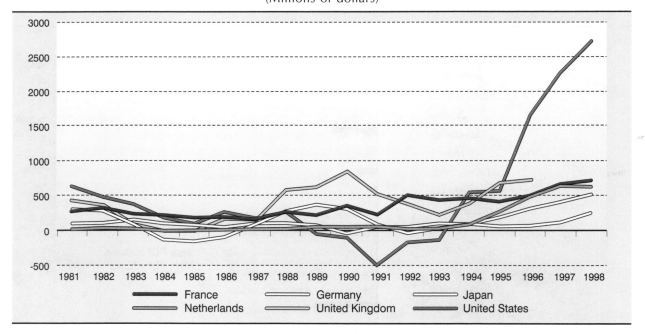

Source: OECD, unpublished data.

Note: FDI flows figures 1981-1997 are calculated as 3-year moving average. Data for the United Kingdom are not available for 1998

FIGURE II.13
Africa: FDI *outflows*, top 10 countries, 1998 and 1999[a]
(Billions of dollars)

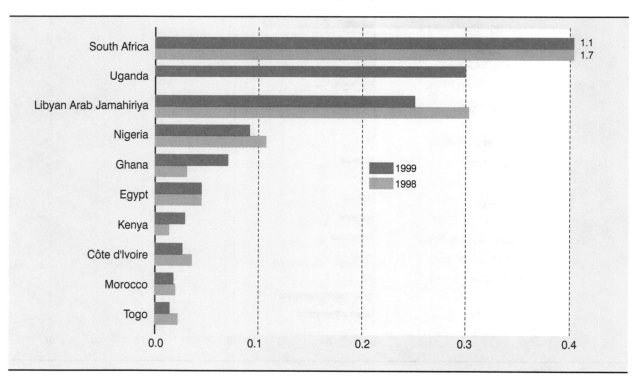

Source: UNCTAD, FDI/TNC database and annex table B.2.

a   Ranked on the basis of the magnitude of 1999 FDI outflows.

FDI in the continent (box II.1). Overall, the assessment of the TNCs that responded to the survey suggests that the increase in FDI inflows into Africa in recent years might be sustained in the future. One-third of the TNCs that responded said that they intended to increase investment in the next three to five years (figure II.14), while more than half expect their investments to remain stable.

Box II.1. Who was surveyed?

All in all, a total of 296 companies were contacted between November 1999 and January 2000. The sample included 196 companies from the database of the top 100 TNCs of UNCTAD and the 50 largest TNCs from developing countries. The top 100 and top 50 databases do not include companies from the financial industry (including banks and insurance companies) for statistical reasons, but this industry accounts for a significant share in worldwide FDI flows – 50 financial companies were also included in the survey.

All in all, 63 useful responses were received, representing a 21 per cent response rate. The responding firms had a total of $658 billion in foreign assets in 1997, which corresponded to 5 per cent of total foreign assets worldwide that year. These companies had 1.6 million employees abroad (or 5 per cent of total foreign employment by all TNCs) and foreign affiliate sales of $625 billion (7 per cent of total foreign sales by the foreign affiliates of all TNCs). About 59 per cent of the companies that responded are based in Europe, 14 per cent in North America, 11 per cent in Japan and 13 per cent in developing countries. Some 3 per cent of the responding companies are headquartered in Africa. Compared to the overall sample, the share of European companies in the group of companies that responded was higher, while that of North American and Japanese firms was considerably lower. In terms of industrial sectors, 6 per cent of the industries included in the survey were companies from the primary sector, 56 per cent were manufacturing companies, and 37 per cent service companies.

Some 81 per cent of the responding TNCs produce mainly for the local market, while 24 per cent produce mainly for export to countries outside Africa.

Source: UNCTAD.

Though a number of companies did not respond to the survey, which should caution against undue generalization, it is encouraging that only 6 per cent of the responding companies were considering reducing their investment from current levels or pulling out completely. More than 43 per cent of the respondents expected that Africa's overall prospects for attracting FDI would improve in the next three to five years, compared with the past three years. Slightly more (46 per cent) did not expect prospects to change. A majority of the companies (73 per cent) assessed the overall potential for FDI in Africa as "limited" and only 12 per cent found it to be "very large" or "large", implying that there is potential in Africa, but that it is not obvious.

South Africa topped the list of the most attractive countries for FDI in Africa (figure II.15a), followed by Egypt and — at some distance — by Morocco and Nigeria. In general, countries with a relatively high level of development or relatively large domestic markets dominate the list of the most attractive countries. This preference is also reflected in

FIGURE II.14
Investment plans for Africa in 2000-2003
(Share in overall responses[a])

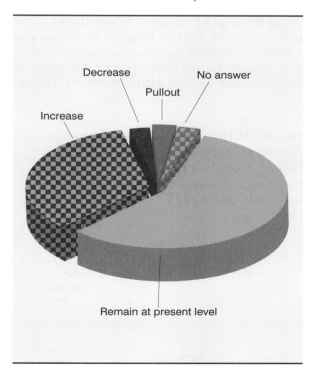

Source: UNCTAD/ICC survey conducted in November 1999-January 2000.

[a]   Responding TNCs only.

the rating of countries expected to make the most progress in creating a business-friendly environment in the next three to four years. South Africa was the most frequently cited (figure II.15b), followed by Morocco and Egypt. Next on the list are Tunisia, Côte d'Ivoire and Ghana, in that order. However, Mozambique and the United Republic of Tanzania, two of the least developed countries, are also ranked relatively high. This might be an indication that some TNCs are beginning to take a differentiated view of the 53 countries that make up the African continent. Overall, the ranking is in line with the list of the main recipients of FDI in Africa, since South Africa and Nigeria, together with the two North African countries of Egypt and Morocco, account for most inflows into Africa (figure II.10 and annex table B.1). The survey suggests that this order will not change dramatically in the near future.

The growth and size of local markets and access to regional markets rank next to the profitability of FDI as the most enticing factors and were mentioned most frequently as influencing corporate investment decisions in a positive way (figure II.16a).

On the negative side, the incidence of extortion and bribery and the difficulty of access to global markets were the most discouraging factors cited (figure II.16b). This was followed by the overall political and economic outlook — poor access to capital, high administrative costs of doing business and deficiencies in the state of the physical

infrastructure. Most of the responding TNCs were already located in Africa and most of them in countries with attractive markets, which might explain the fact that factors related to the characteristics of the market rank relatively low in their list of negative determinants, while other factors, such as access to global markets, access to capital and skilled labour, cost of doing business, and the state of the physical infrastructure ranked prominently.

The findings on the industries where TNCs see the greatest potential for FDI in 2000-2003 support this result (figure II.17). The most frequently mentioned industries for Africa are either natural-resource-seeking or market-seeking, with the exception of tourism, which is difficult to classify according to the motives of FDI decisions. Industries such as textiles and clothing, where FDI is efficiency-seeking, are low on this list. The results confirm that Africa's investment opportunities are perceived to be broader than those suggested by the traditional image of the continent as a mere provider of natural resources.

The assessment of investment potential by industry varied according to region. The poll gave the following regional profiles:[17]

•   North Africa: petroleum, gas and related products, telecommunications and tourism were the most frequently mentioned industries with investment potential, followed by agriculture and motor vehicles;

FIGURE II.15a

African countries ranked according to their attractiveness for FDI in 2000-2003
(Percentage of replies[a])

Source: UNCTAD/ICC survey conducted in November 1999-January 2000.

a   Replies as a percentage of responding TNCs.

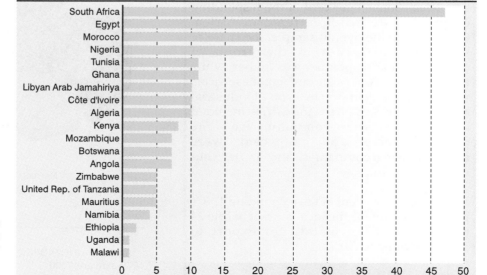

- West Africa: petroleum, gas and related products, as well as mining, quarrying, agriculture, forestry and telecommunications;
- East Africa: tourism, followed at a considerable distance by telecommunications;
- Central Africa: a few opportunities in mining and quarrying, and forestry;
- Southern Africa: tourism and transport and storage, followed by telecommunications, mining and quarrying, metals and metal products, motor vehicles, food and beverages, pharmaceutical and chemical products and agriculture.

The results of the survey also point to a severe "image" problem for Africa. More than half of the respondents (56 per cent) stated that the actual business environment is better than the continent's image would suggest, in at least some African countries, while a quarter made the same observation about "many" African countries. Only a small minority (6 per cent) thought that in *no* African country is the actual business climate better than the external image. These results call for more efforts on the part of the international community to change the image of Africa and to provide investors with a more differentiated picture of the continent.

When comparing the results of the TNC survey with those of the survey UNCTAD carried out in 1999 among African investment promotion agencies (IPAs), some interesting differences, as well as similarities, come to the fore:

- With respect to the most promising industries, the top ten industries named by TNCs are similar to those named by IPAs. While both mentioned a wide range of industries, TNCs give a little more weight to industries from natural-resource-based industries, such as petroleum and metal, as well as metal manufacturing industries;

- As for the most attractive countries for FDI, the bias towards North African countries and large as well as more developed countries in sub-Saharan Africa is accentuated on the TNC list, while the IPA list also features a number of smaller countries, such as Botswana, Namibia and Mauritius — as well as a least developed country, Mozambique;

- As regards the *positive* determinants influencing investment decisions, while TNCs ranked markets high and efficiency-seeking low, IPAs rated access to global markets, along with the regulatory framework and incentives, much higher;

- The findings concerning the factors that are expected to have a *negative* impact on FDI during the period 2000-2003, largely overlap and coincide: both TNCs and IPAs mention extortion and bribery most frequently as having a negative impact on

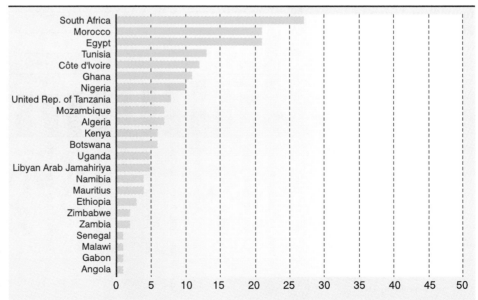

FIGURE II.15b
African countries ranked according to their progress in improving the business environment in 2000-2003
(Percentage of replies[a])

Source: UNCTAD/ICC survey conducted in November 1999-January 2000.

[a] Replies as a percentage of responding TNCs.

FIGURE II.16a
Positive determinants for FDI in Africa in 2000-2003
(Percentage of replies[a])

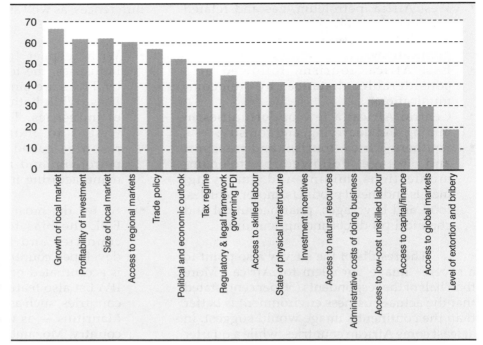

Source: UNCTAD/ICC survey conducted in November 1999-January 2000.

[a] Replies as a percentage of responding TNCs.

FDI in the coming years, and also agree that high costs of doing business, deficiencies in access to capital, and the relatively poor state of the physical infrastructure represent major obstacles.

While there is considerable overlap between the views of TNCs and IPAs, the different perceptions as to the most attractive countries and industries may hint at a certain degree of wishful thinking on the part of the IPAs. TNCs are less inclined to invest in smaller

African countries and in globally integrated industries, such as textiles or mechanical and electric equipment, than most IPAs assume.

As for the policy conclusions to be drawn from the survey, many African countries that seek to attract FDI need to continue to improve investment conditions, in particular for efficiency-seeking investment. This includes (apart from general efforts to increase economic and political stability) the reduction of red tape and serious efforts to fight

FIGURE II.16b
Negative determinants for FDI in Africa in 2000-2003
(Percentage of replies[a])

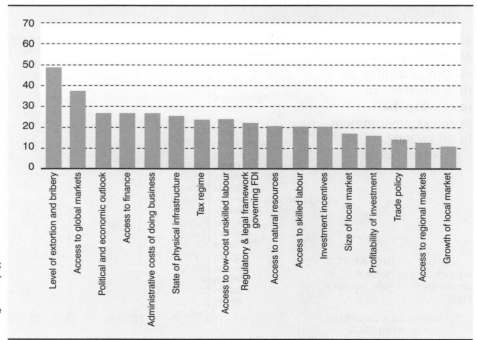

Source: UNCTAD/ICC survey conducted in November 1999-January 2000.

[a] Replies as a percentage of responding TNCs.

corruption, improvement of physical infrastructure and a better-trained workforce. In addition, smaller African countries and LDCs need to accelerate regional integration to create sizeable and attractive markets. At the same time, given the fact that the majority of TNCs think Africa has an image problem, African countries have to make efforts, individually and jointly, to change their image and to persuade investors to differentiate among them. Assistance in projecting a better and more differentiated image of Africa is needed.

Recently UNCTAD has undertaken several initiatives to this effect. Together with the ICC, the Multilateral Investment Guarantee Agency (MIGA) of the World Bank and the United Nations Development Programme (UNDP), it has produced a fact sheet on FDI in Africa, based on the UNCTAD publication *FDI in Africa: Performance and Potential* (UNCTAD, 1999b). Also, jointly with the ICC, UNCTAD is working on a project on investment guides and capacity-building for LDCs, in which guides to Ethiopia and Mali have already been produced and others are to follow. These

efforts need to be complemented by efforts on the part of developed countries to liberalize access to their markets for African products. The "African Growth and Opportunity Act", which would *inter alia* guarantee African textile exporters better access to the United States market, is a case in point.[18]

2. *Asia and the Pacific*

Inflows of FDI to developing Asia (South, East and South-East Asia, Central Asia and West Asia) increased by 9 per cent in 1999, to reach a record level, of $106 billion. This was contrary to the decline that was widely anticipated in the wake of the 1997-1998 financial crisis (figure II.18). This regional increase, however, masks considerable variations in flows to individual countries. China saw a drop of nearly 8 per cent in 1999. Compensating for this were the FDI boom in the Republic of Korea and the recovery of flows into Singapore and Taiwan Province of China (figure II.19). Among the five countries most affected by the crisis, flows declined in the Philippines and Thailand, while increasing

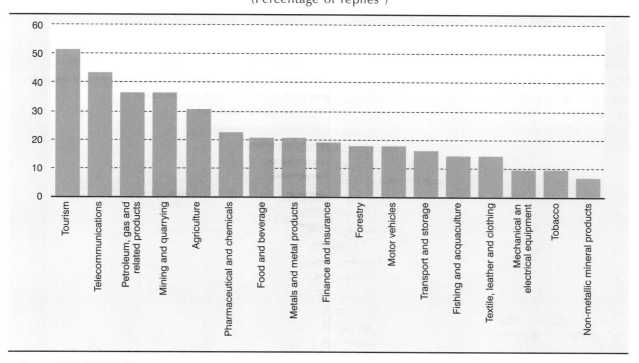

FIGURE II.17
**Industries offering the best opportunities
for FDI in Africaᵃ in 2000-2003**
(Percentage of repliesᵃ)

Source: UNCTAD/ICC survey conducted in November 1999-January 2000.

ᵃ   This category is a cumulative expression of the data obtained from the responses of TNCs to the category 'Africa as a whole' and/or to one or more of the following sub-regions: North, Central, East, West and Southern Africa.

FIGURE II.18
**FDI inflows to
developing Asia,
1991-1999**
(Billions of dollars)

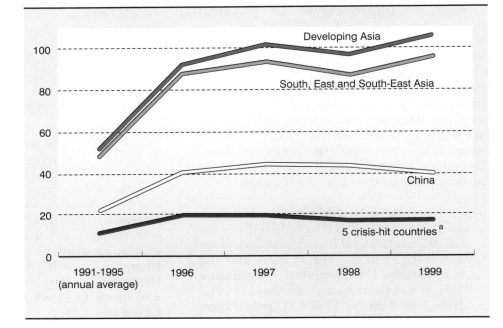

Source: UNCTAD, FDI/
TNC database and annex
table B.1.

a   Indonesia, Malaysia,
the   Philippines,
Republic of Korea and
Thailand.

significantly in Malaysia and skyrocketing in
the Republic of Korea. Indonesia registered a
further decrease of FDI flows — negative flows
in two consecutive years (annex table B.1). On
balance, all five together gained 4 per cent, to
reach $17 billion.

Efforts to attract FDI intensified further
in   most   Asian   economies.   Sectoral
liberalization was reinforced by more flexible
modes of entry such as cross-border M&As.

A number of countries also strengthened their
competition policies and authorities with a
view towards maximizing the benefits of
liberalization. FDI retained its crucial role as
a source of development finance for the region,
dominating the composition of net private
capital flows with over 80 per cent share in
the total (World Bank, 2000a). The share of
FDI in host countries' gross fixed capital
formation continued to increase, particularly
in crisis-hit countries (figure II.20).

FIGURE II.19
**Asia and the Pacific:
FDI *inflows*, top 20
economies, 1998
and 1999[a]**
(Billions of dollars)

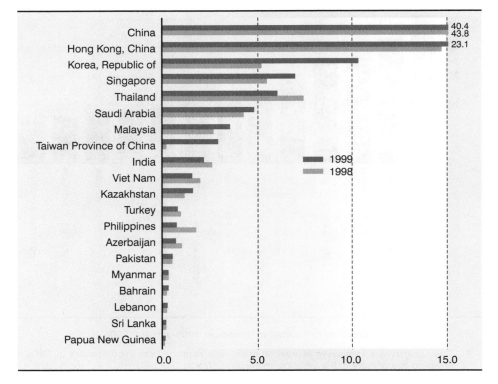

Source: UNCTAD, FDI/
TNC database and annex
table B.1.

a   Ranked on the basis
of the magnitude of
1999 FDI inflows.

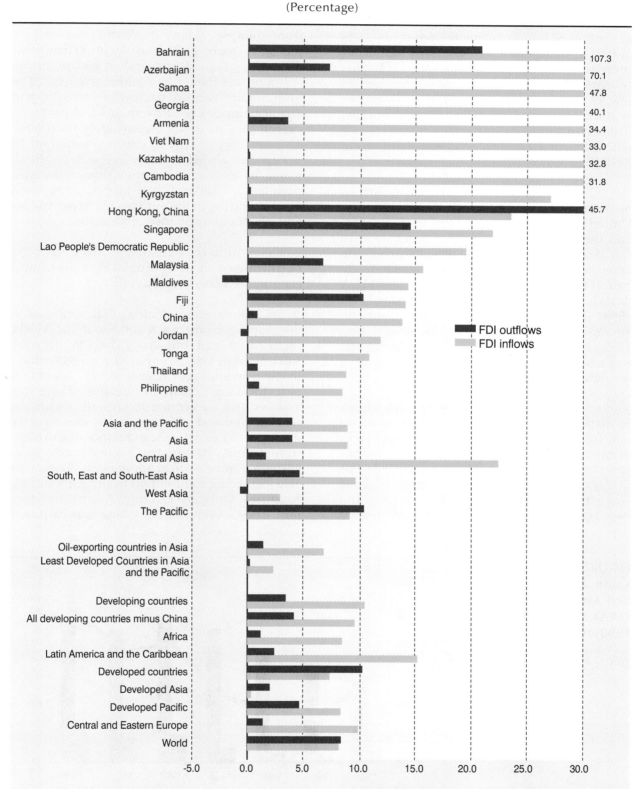

FIGURE II.20
**Asia and the Pacific: FDI flows as a percentage of gross capital formation,
top 20 economies, 1996-1998ª**
(Percentage)

Source: UNCTAD, FDI/TNC database and annex table B.5.

ª   Ranked on the basis of the magnitude of 1999 FDI inflows as a percentage of gross fixed capital formation.

Cross-border M&As became an important mode of entry in developing Asia. Cross-border M&As in South, East and South-East Asia reached an annual average of $20 billion during 1997-1999, compared to an average of $7 billion during the pre-crisis years of 1994-1996 (figure II.21). The most significant increases occurred in the five crisis-hit countries. Their share of total cross-border M&As in developing Asia jumped to 68 per cent in 1998 compared to 19 per cent in 1996. Cross-border M&As in the five countries as a whole reached a record level of $15 billion in 1999 (figure II.22).

The distribution of cross-border M&As by country of origin saw a significant shift. The United States, the United Kingdom, Singapore and the Netherlands — in that order — were the largest purchaser countries during the financial crisis, and together accounted for nearly half of the total value of all cross-border M&A deals in the five crisis-hit countries during 1998-1999. They overtook Malaysia and Germany among the front-runners before the crisis during 1995-1996 (figure II.23). TNCs from France, the Republic of Korea and Switzerland also accelerated their pace of acquisition.

Two types of cross-border M&As can be distinguished: acquisitions of local firms by new foreign investors and acquisitions of shares in existing joint ventures by the foreign joint-venture partners (Zhan and Ozawa, 2000). The first was encouraged by the low prices of firms when translated into foreign currencies, the new openness to M&As and the favourable

long-term prospects of the crisis-affected countries. The second took place either through acquiring more equity from a domestic partner or through buying new issues, motivated by changes in the law or to prevent a joint venture from collapse. Many domestic joint-venture partners were either in serious financial difficulties or had undertaken restructuring, spinning off their non-core businesses. The foreign joint-venture partners were willing to acquire equities held by their local partners, even if they were not immediately profitable. This category of acquisitions accounted for 39 per cent of all M&A deals in the Republic of Korea in 1998. Such acquisitions were also popular in Thailand, typically in component manufacturing in the automobile or electronic-and-electrical-appliances industries.

Within the overall regional trends, the performance of individual sub-regions and economies varied considerably.

China, the principal FDI recipient in developing countries throughout the 1990s, retained its lead, but saw a drop to just over $40 billion in 1999, compared with $44 billion in the previous year (figure II.19). A number of factors help explain this decline. There was a slowdown of economic growth leading to weaker demand. There was excess capacity in certain manufacturing industries due to over-investment during the past decade (e.g. garments and electrical appliances). There was also increasing competition from neighbouring countries. Outward FDI from Asian economies fell. The Government of China was cautious

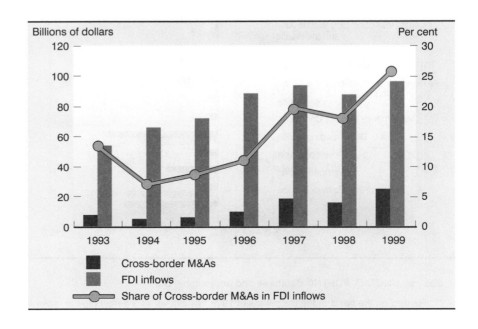

FIGURE II.21
South, East and South-East Asia: cross-border M&As and FDI inflows, 1993-1999
(Billions of dollars and per cent)

Source: UNCTAD, FDI/TNC database and cross-border M&A database, based on data provided by Thomson Financial Securities Data Company.

FIGURE II.22

Cross-border M&As in the five crisis-hit countries[a] and developing Asia, 1993-1999

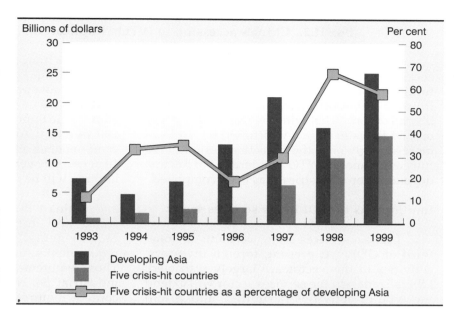

Source: UNCTAD, cross-border M&A database, based on data provided by Thomson Financial Securities Data Company.

[a] Indonesia, the Philippines, Malaysia, Republic of Korea and Thailand.

FIGURE II.23

Cross-border M&A sales in the five crisis-hit countries[a] by selected home economy, 1995-1996 and 1998-1999[b]

(Millions of dollars)

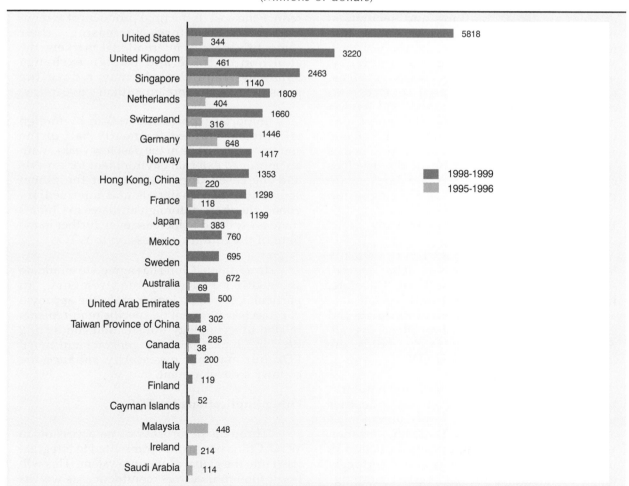

Source: UNCTAD, cross-border M&A database, based on data provided by Thomson Financial Securities Data Company.

[a]   Indonesia, the Philippines, Malaysia, Republic of Korea and Thailand.
[b]   Ranked on the basis of the magnitude of sales in 1998-1999.

Box II.2. China's accession to WTO: implications for inward FDI

The negotiation process for China's accession to WTO is in its final phase. The fulfilment of the WTO obligations by China will involve substantial trade and investment liberalization. This will have several impacts on FDI flows to China, which will be felt even more strongly once the transition period to the full compliance of WTO standards (2 to 5 years, depending on industries) has been completed.

Implications for FDI in the services sector

China's services sector accounts for one-third of GDP. At present, foreign investors' activities in this sector are largely restricted. Liberalization in the services sector will extend the type of activities permitted, and it will eliminate or reduce geographic and ownership restrictions. Liberalization will gradually allow foreign investors to operate in such service industries as distribution (wholesaling and retailing) and related services (e.g. warehousing, packaging, advertising, and express services); banking and securities; insurance (both life and non-life); information technology services and telecommunications; professional services (e.g. accountancy, management consultancy, legal services, engineering, business related services and computer maintenance); tourism; and motion pictures and audio-visual distribution. China will also participate in the WTO Basic Telecommunications and Financial Services Agreements. Liberalization in the services sector will set the stage for a large-scale participation of FDI in this fast growing sector.

Implications for FDI in manufacturing

China's manufacturing sector is already largely open to foreign investors. It has, indeed, attracted a significant amount of FDI. Therefore, liberalization in the aftermath of China's accession to WTO may not have immediate and substantial investment-creation effects overall. Some changes, however, might reduce the incentive for market-oriented FDI.

Over the past decades, tariff and non-tariff barriers have protected certain key industries in China, such as petrochemicals, automobiles and consumer electronics. Trade liberalization — and particularly a significant reduction in import licensing and quotas could seriously erode the incentive for the "barrier-jumping" type of FDI, as the principal motivation for such

FDI comes from a desire to gain access to trade-protected markets by producing within the tariff or quota protected area. The automotive industry is a case in point: tariffs for automobile imports will be phased down from 100 per cent to 25 per cent, and for auto components from an average of 24 per cent to 10 per cent by year 2006. Quotas on automobile imports will be phased out by 2005.

China will also have to bring to an end trade and foreign exchange balancing requirements, as well as local content requirements (under the TRIMs Agreement). Those requirements are part of China's existing industrial policies. The elimination of local content requirements will, on the one hand, facilitate the import of foreign inputs, thereby reducing the incentive for some foreign investors to develop linkages with domestic subcontractors or for foreign suppliers of intermediary inputs to invest in China. On the other hand, it could help insure the quality and reduce the cost of the final products of foreign affiliates, therefore increasing their competitiveness in international markets, the abolition of trade and foreign exchange balancing requirements may reduce the pressure on some foreign affiliates to exports.

Imports/exports undertaken by foreign affiliates accounted for nearly half of the country's total trade in the past few years. With an improved external environment for exports and increased opportunities for the global sourcing of raw materials and intermediary goods, the share of foreign affiliates in China's trade is expected to increase even further in the light of the country's accession to WTO.

In addition, China has agreed to eliminate some other FDI entry requirements. In particular, it will no longer make the approval of projects contingent on specific requirements related to technology transfer and conducting R&D in China. This may generate additional FDI, but may not necessarily enhance the country's development.

Other implications for FDI

Through the process of its accession to WTO, China has further committed to integrate itself into the global economic system. This will boost foreign investors' confidence, as well as improve the overall investment environment.

/...

in opening service industries to FDI.[19] Most of these are short-term factors. In the longer run, China can be expected to remain an attractive location for FDI, particularly in the light of its expected accession to the WTO (box II.2) and a further liberalization of its services sector.

In *East Asia* (Hong Kong (China), the Republic of Korea; and Taiwan Province of China), FDI flows increased by nearly 80 per cent in 1999. In the Republic of Korea FDI reached another record level (it nearly doubled), over $10 billion, four times its pre-crisis level (1996). The recent liberalization of FDI policies led to higher M&A-driven FDI growth. The Government's public-sector reforms and its urgent need to supply financing at the time of the crisis led to large-scale

privatization — another important attraction for foreign investors. The Republic of Korea is now being integrated more tightly into the regional and global production networks of TNCs. Inflows to Taiwan Province of China recovered to $2.9 billion from their exceptionally low level of $222 million in 1998. In Hong Kong (China), the second largest recipient in the region, FDI increased significantly over the period of 1998-1999. Its inflows reached a record level of $15 billion in 1998 and $23 billion in 1999.[20] In 1998, large inflows came from overseas tax-haven economies; some of the increase might be attributable to returning investment by foreign and Hong Kong domestic investors, which flew out before the return of Hong Kong to mainland China. As investors' confidence in Hong Kong's future gradually recovered, they

---

(Box II.2, concluded)

In turn it encourages longer-term investment commitments by foreign investors in the Chinese market. For instance, the relaxation of restrictions on foreign participation in terms of equity share in a number of industries (e.g. automobile, distribution, construction, hotel) will not only attract new investors, but also enable foreign joint venture partners to increase their equity shares in existing affiliates.

China will probably phase out preferential tax policies, following its accession to the WTO – in an effort towards levelling the playing field for foreign and local companies alike. Although this may not affect those foreign affiliates already operating in China, newcomers would be entitled to fewer fiscal incentives.[a] Foreign investors will be faced with fiercer competition in the Chinese market, as the market becomes more contestable due to the dramatic liberalization in investment and trade. Furthermore, the rise of domestic firms increases competitive pressures on foreign affiliates. This has been a widespread phenomenon in a number of manufacturing industries, such as garments, toys, travel goods and electronic and electrical appliances in recent years, where, following the "lost decade" between the mid-1980s and mid-1990s,

domestic producers are gradually regaining market shares. In the services sector, Chinese firms have long-established business networks and infrastructure. As cross-border M&As are not yet encouraged in China, partnerships with domestic players would be the best way for a quick start-up and immediate access to the existing domestic business networks.

In conclusion, China's accession to WTO will make China more attractive for FDI. The services sector may well replace the manufacturing sector as the engine of FDI growth; within the manufacturing sector, foreign affiliates in China will most likely undergo a process of consolidation in response to the development of a more competitive landscape in the country. As foreign investors may adopt a wait-and-see approach until the new reforms are in place and liberalization is fully implemented, in the short-term, however, FDI may remain at a level close to the one achieved in recent years. In the medium-term, however, another FDI boom may well be forthcoming, with FDI flows perhaps reaching an annual level of over $60 billion. If cross-border M&As should be permitted, annual inflows could even reach $100 billion.

Source: Based on Zhan, forthcoming.

[a]   Under the current law, all corporations in China are taxed at the flat rate of 33 per cent; but, after various deductions, most foreign affiliates pay only around 15 per cent. In special economic zones, foreign affiliates have been enjoying an even lower rate.

responded to the need for capital injections in the light of the financial crisis. In 1999, however, investments were mainly in the form of reinvested earnings, which accounted for over half of the total FDI.[21] This was mainly due to the distinct turnaround in local economic activity, with investment earnings of foreign affiliates doubling that year.

In *South-East Asia (ASEAN 10)*, FDI decreased by 17 per cent in 1999. Flows of FDI to Thailand dropped 18 per cent, to $6.1 billion, due in part to the flattening of the wave of massive recapitalizations in the banking industry, which had reached exceptionally high levels in 1998. Manufacturing continued to attract considerable FDI to Thailand. Singapore was again the largest FDI recipient in this sub-region; inflows into the country increased by 27 per cent, to $7 billion. Flows to Malaysia ($3.5 billion) increased by 31 per cent in 1999. The Philippines experienced a decline and its overall level of inflows is still relatively low compared with some other economies in the region. Divestment continued in Indonesia, about $3 billion in 1999. Countries whose primary sources of FDI have been other countries in the region continued to suffer from the negative effects of the crisis – e.g. Viet Nam and Myanmar. Growth of inflows to Asian LDCs as a whole remained sluggish in 1999.

In *South Asia*, FDI in 1999 declined by 13 per cent to $3.2 billion, and $1.7 billion lower than the peak level of 1997 ($4.9 billion). Inflows to India, the single largest recipient in the sub-region, were $2.2 billion. The ongoing liberalization of FDI policies is expected to raise inflows in the years to come. FDI to Bangladesh declined after increases in the previous two years. Inflows to Pakistan and Sri Lanka remained at a very low level. In the longer term, the sub-region has considerable potential. Its realization will depend very much on the pace of liberalization and economic reform, as well as on domestic and regional stability.

Inflows of FDI to *West Asia* continued their upward trend in 1999, following their recovery in 1997 and 1998. Inflows to the sub-region reached $6.7 billion, an 8 per cent increase over 1998. The large increases in FDI since 1997 have gone mainly to Saudi Arabia, by far the single largest recipient in that region. Tourism, electrical and electronic plants, and various high-technology industries were particularly attractive. Recent improvements in the macroeconomic and political environment in the region, combined with the opening up of the oil industry to foreign investors, particularly in Kuwait and in Saudi Arabia (box II.3), are likely to mean larger flows to the region. Similarly, Kuwait is seeking to attract international oil companies to invest up to $7 billion to develop oil fields close to the border with Iraq. A large number of international oil companies have already expressed their strong interest to invest in the upstream part of the oil industry in both Kuwait and Saudi Arabia. Saudi Arabia has also been attracting foreign investors to invest in its rapidly growing power industry under build-operate-own and build-operate-transfer schemes. The Government of the Islamic Republic of Iran decided to allow foreign oil and gas companies to develop its natural resources for the first time since 1979. The development of further phases of South Pars valued at $1.5 billion is on the way with foreign companies.[22]

Central Asia lost the FDI momentum it had enjoyed at its initial stage of liberalization and reforms. Inflows to the sub-region in 1999 were slightly lower than in 1998 ($2.8 billion). The share of the two leading recipient countries (Kazakhstan and Azerbaijan) increased further, from about 70 per cent in 1998 to over 80 per cent in 1999. The share of oil and gas in FDI inflows in both Kazakhstan and Azerbaijan rose to 80 per cent. Other industries in these countries, and the other (non-oil) economies of the region, fared much worse, due to problems of transition (in Uzbekistan and Turkmenistan) and to bleak economic prospects.

After two to three years of subdued FDI flows to the *Pacific Island* economies, partly due to spillover effects of the financial crisis, a turn-around in business sentiment seemed to have emerged in 1999. Inflows are estimated at $248 million, a $17 million increase over the 1998 level. Papua New Guinea accounts for the bulk of FDI inflows to the sub-region (more than two-thirds in 1999), owing to its large-scale development in mining and petroleum. The opening of a stock exchange in April 1999 for the trading of large companies may attract some foreign investors.[23]

Looking ahead, the investment prospects for developing Asia remain bright, given the quality of the underlying economic determinants of FDI, the rapid recovery of the

Box II.3. A new FDI law in Saudi Arabia

In recent years, a fundamental change of attitude towards the role of the private sector has emerged in a number of oil-exporting countries in the Middle East, including as regards the role of FDI in development. The countries of the Middle East are, however, at different stages of integrating FDI into their development, particularly when it comes to the petroleum industry. The Islamic Republic of Iran and Kuwait have either already signed contracts with foreign oil companies or are contemplating moves to allow foreign participation in this industry. Saudi Arabia, the world's biggest oil producer and exporter, has established a General Investment Authority and introduced in April 2000 a new foreign investment law aimed at improving the investment climate and attracting FDI. The newly created Authority is expected to establish a one-stop-shop for foreign investors to speed up the process of approving investment projects. The new law provides incentives to court long-term investment, including by reducing the top rate of corporate profits tax on foreign companies from 45 per cent to 30 per cent (the same as for national companies).

International oil companies have already been invited to submit proposals for investment in the Kingdom following negotiations with 12 of them. As a result, project proposals containing investments worth more than $100 billion over a period of 20 years have been received.[a] These projects are expected to be reviewed and finalized before the end of the year. Although details are not known, the main focus is on natural gas development, processing and distribution and other associated projects involving the use of gas as a feedstock for petrochemical plants and as a fuel for power generation and water desalination plants. Notwithstanding these reforms, the Government has made it clear that the upstream part of the oil industry, i.e. exploration and production, would remain off limits to foreign investment.

Source: UNCTAD.

[a] Middle East Economic Digest, 19 May 2000, p.19.

region from the financial crisis, and the ongoing liberalization and restructuring efforts that are now widespread in the region.

Outward FDI from developing Asia and the Pacific recovered from its recession since the onset of the financial crisis, but is still lower than the pre-crisis level. Outflows increased by nearly two-thirds in 1999, to an estimated $ 37 billion (annex table B.2). Hong Kong (China) remained the major outward investor, accounting for over half of the total outflows from the region. Nevertheless, its outflows to China, where it is still the largest investor, have been declining over the past few years (figure II.24). Divestment by Asian TNCs, particularly in the United States and Europe, also increased in 1999.[24] Two types of such divestment could be observed. One is that Asian TNCs sold their existing overseas businesses; the other is that parent firms were acquired by a foreign TNC and, subsequently, the overseas affiliates of the acquired firm were taken over by the acquirer. Such divestment does not necessarily imply that foreign affiliates are in an unhealthy state; they may be more a function of corporate restructuring and financial difficulties. Even within the region most Asian TNCs have been unable to take advantage of the cheap assets available. The exceptions are TNCs based in Hong Kong (China), Singapore and Taiwan Province of China, which managed to maintain their financing strength to engage in such activities, mostly in neighbouring countries.

As noted in *WIR99* (UNCTAD, 1999a), Asian TNCs are likely to continue their inward focus on restructuring and spinning off non-core activities. The revitalization of their outward investment may take some time.

3. *Latin America and the Caribbean*

Aggregate FDI *inflows* to Latin America and the Caribbean continued to expand in 1999 to reach a new record of $90 billion, nearly a quarter higher than in 1998. A significant part of FDI flows came through M&As. As in preceding years, FDI had an important stabilizing effect on the region's balance of payments, more than offsetting the $56 billion current account deficit posted in 1999.[25]

Changes in the distribution of FDI within the region point to an apparent paradox: inflows into the relatively stagnant South American sub-region increased by 40 per cent, while inflows into the faster-growing Mexican and Caribbean Basin economies declined somewhat. As a result, the share of South American countries in the region's FDI inflows increased from 70 per cent in 1998 to 80 per cent in 1999. This above-average growth in FDI inflows to South America in 1999 does not necessarily reflect a permanent change in the composition of inflows to the region. It can be explained by a few very large acquisitions in the southern cone by Spanish TNCs (box II.4). If these operations are excluded, FDI flows into South America would have been about the same as in 1998, consistent with overall regional trends.

The MERCOSUR countries (Argentina, Brazil, Paraguay and Uruguay, with Bolivia and Chile as associates) increased their weight in total Latin American FDI inflows in 1999. Among them, despite economic stagnation and the instability surrounding the flotation of its currency in January 1999, Brazil continued for the fourth year to be the regional leader with

around $31 billion of inflows in 1999 (figure II.25). This was close to the level registered in 1998 and equivalent to more than one-third of the regional total. In terms of FDI inflows as a percentage of gross fixed capital formation, however, Brazil is not ranked among the top 20 countries (figure II.26).

Most new inflows continued to go into non-tradable service and manufacturing industries producing mostly for domestic markets. As regards modes of investment, in contrast to 1998, a relatively low proportion of inflows went into the acquisition of state enterprises. Total privatization operations involving foreign M&As decreased from over $29 billion in 1998 to $21 billion in 1999 (annex table A.IV.22). Large amounts of new resources went instead into the restructuring of previously acquired service companies, mostly in telecommunications. The acquisition of private companies through M&As also gathered pace.

FIGURE II.24
Asia and the Pacific: FDI outfows, top 10 economies, 1998 and 1999[a]
(Billions of dollars)

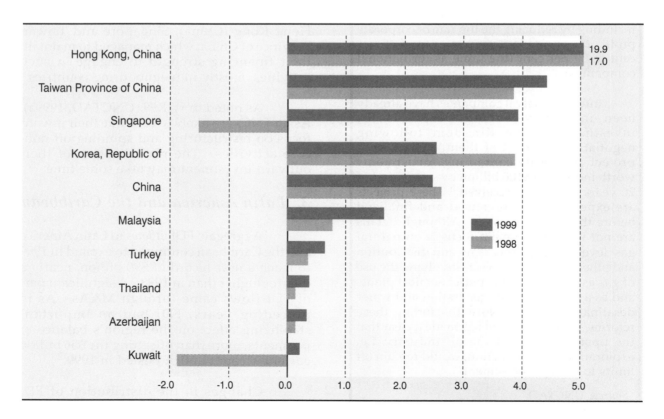

Source: UNCTAD, FDI/TNC database and annex table B.2.

[a] Ranked on the basis of the magnitude of 1999 FDI outflows.

Box II.4. Consolidation strategies of Spanish firms

One of the most important developments in Latin America in the late 1990s has been the strong surge in the acquisitions of private companies by Spanish TNCs in the services sector, reflecting an effort by these companies to consolidate their competitive position in the region. Large Spanish companies clearly favoured Latin America for their international expansion throughout the 1990s, with a significant impact on the region's capital stock. Seven large Spanish companies — *Telefónica* (telecommunications), *Endesa España* (electricity), *Repsol* (oil and natural gas), *Iberdrola* (electricity), *Banco Bilbao Vizcaya Argentaria* and *Banco Santander Central Hispano* (banking) and *Iberia* (air transport) — accounted for over $50 billion of investment in Latin America between 1991 and 1999. As a result, investment in Latin America in 1999 accounted for around 40 per cent of *Endesa España's* total assets, and over 30 per cent of the assets of *Telefónica* and *Banco Bilbao Vizcaya Argentaria* and *Banco Santander Central Hispano*.

The largest M&A operation by a Spanish company in Latin America in 1999 was the acquisition by *Repsol* (Spain's largest company) of Argentina's oil giant *Yacimientos Petrolíferos Fiscales* (YPF). This operation started in January 1999 when *Repsol* acquired from the Government a 15 per cent share in YPF for $2 billion, followed in April 1999 by the purchase of the remaining 85 per cent of YPF for almost $13.2 billion (annex table A.IV.4). With this acquisition, *Repsol* became the largest operator in Argentina's oil industry and prepared itself for further expansion into the rest of the region. Soon after this, the company announced plans for an aggressive expansion into the oil industries of Brazil, Chile and Mexico, with investment plans of $7 billion before 2002.

The second largest operation by a Spanish TNC in the region during 1999 was the acquisition by *Endesa España* of majority control in the Chilean electricity holding *Enersis* for a total amount of about $3.5 billion. *Endesa España's* involvement in the region started in Argentina in 1992 and extended over the decade to Brazil, Colombia, Chile, the Dominican Republic, Peru and Venezuela (largely through its participation in privatization operations). In 1997 it entered into a strategic alliance with *Enersis* (which has a strong presence in the region), by buying a 29 per cent stake in it. Differences between the management of the two companies led *Endesa España* to obtain majority control in

1999. *Endesa España*, now the largest regional operator in the electricity industry with investments of over $8 billion and over 25 million customers, plans to restructure and consolidate its regional holdings under the umbrella of *Enersis* so as to improve its overall regional competitiveness.

Telefónica's strategy in the region is similar. It first became involved in the region in 1990 in Argentina and Chile, and continued its expansion through participation in privatization programmes in Brazil, El Salvador, Guatemala, Peru, Puerto Rico and Venezuela. By 1999, it had accumulated investments in the region of over $10 billion and a customer base of 49 million. In 1998, *Telefónica* had the largest consolidated sales of TNCs in Latin America. The company's strategy today is to consolidate operations and use its extensive regional base for expansion into new businesses. The simultaneous launch of its internet operation *Terra Networks* in most countries of the region in 1999 demonstrates the competitive edge it has obtained from its combined regional operations. *Terra Networks* is rapidly becoming a leading internet provider in Latin America, and the price of its stocks tripled during their first trading day on the Madrid and New York exchanges in November 1999. Plans for further expansion over the next two years include substantial investments in fixed and mobile telephones, as well as in cable television and the internet.

Spanish banks have also penetrated financial industry markets in Latin America. *Banco Bilbao Vizcaya Argentaria* and *Banco Santander Central Hispano* are the most aggressive banking acquirers. The strategy of Spanish banks is to deepen their core activity — commercial banking as well as investment banking and pension fund management — rather than to provide financial services for non-financial firms to expand their internationalization. Examples include the acquisitions of *Banco Excel Economico* (Brazil) and *Banco Santa Cruz* (Bolivia) with values of $0.9 billion and $0.2 billion, respectively, in 1998.

These examples point to some important common features. Large Spanish companies mostly started and expanded in the region through participation in privatization programmes. They are now also acquiring private companies and expanding into new areas. The strategy is marked by a regional rather than a national perspective.

Source: UNCTAD, based on ECLAC, 2000 and UNCTAD, cross-border M&A database.

Argentina more than tripled its 1998 level of FDI inflows, to reach $23 billion. The country replaced Mexico as the second largest regional recipient in the region. Though precise figures for the share of privatization-related FDI in total FDI are difficult to calculate (see chapter IV), it is clear that privatization contributed significantly to the increase of FDI inflows into Argentina: in 1999, the Spanish TNC Repsol acquired the oil company Yacimientos Petrolíferos Fiscales (YPF) for over $13 billion (box II.4). The case of Chile is similar. That country increased its relative importance as a host country significantly, almost doubling its total receipts to more than $9 billion in 1999.

This was largely the result of the acquisition of the Chilean electricity generator and distributor Enersis-Endesa Chile by the Spanish TNC Endesa España for $3.5 billion (ECLAC, 2000).[26] As in recent years, most FDI in both countries was concentrated in services (including energy) and natural-resource-intensive activities. Among the smaller countries in the southern cone, Uruguay, which has promoted itself as a regional headquarters location for MERCOSUR, received levels of FDI higher than those of 1998, while inflows into Paraguay, which suffered from political and financial instability, fell by more than a quarter from 1998.

FIGURE II.25

Latin America and the Caribbean: FDI *inflows*, top 20 economies, 1998 and 1999[a]

(Billions of dollars)

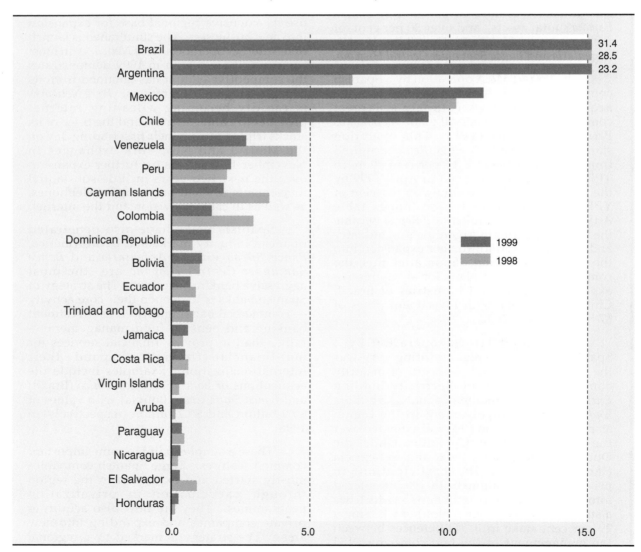

Source: UNCTAD, FDI/TNC database and annex table B.1.

a   Ranked on the basis of the magnitude of 1999 FDI inflows.

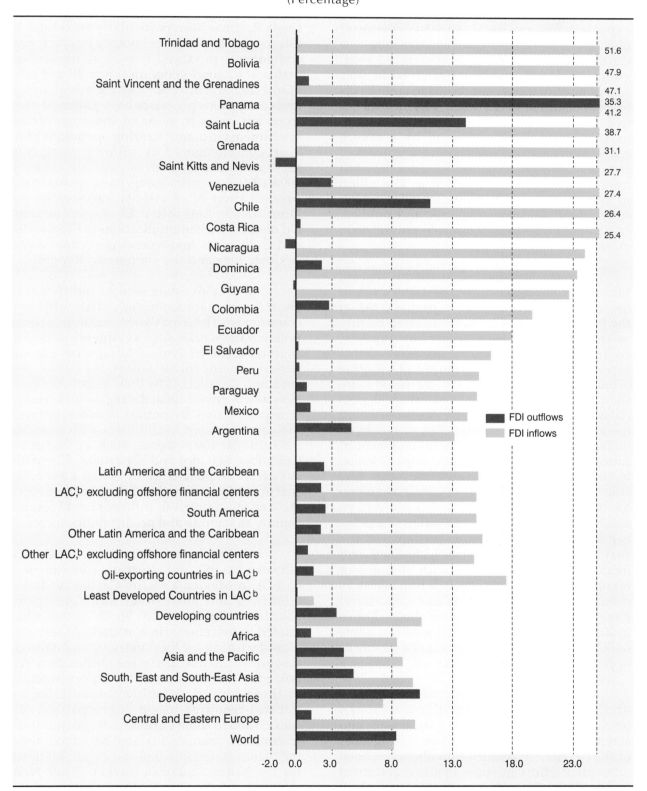

FIGURE II.26
Latin America and the Caribbean: FDI flows as percentage of gross fixed capital formation, top 20 countries, 1996-1998[a]
(Percentage)

Source: UNCTAD, FDI/TNC database and annex table B.5.

[a]   Ranked on the basis of the magnitude of 1996-1998 FDI inflows as a percentage of gross fixed capital formation.
[b]   Latin America and the Caribbean.

Within the Andean Community (Bolivia, Colombia, Ecuador, Peru and Venezuela), Bolivia and Peru maintained relatively stable levels of FDI inflows of $1.0 billion and $2.1 billion, respectively. The other three countries, experiencing political and institutional instability, suffered a sharp contraction. In Colombia, the insecurity associated with guerrilla activity, high levels of crime and economic difficulties contributed to large levels of disinvestment. As a result, FDI inflows fell from $2.9 billion in 1998 to around $1.4 billion in 1999. Venezuela, affected by a severe economic crisis and undergoing a process of radical institutional change, experienced a fall from more than $4 billion in 1998 to $2.6 billion in 1999. Inflows of FDI into Ecuador, which suffered from a deep economic and political crisis in 1999, fell by a quarter to around $636 million.

In the Northern end of the region, Mexico received $11 billion in 1999, close to the average of the 1995-1998 period. As in the past, FDI continued to be directed mainly to the manufacturing sector for exports, contributing to the rapid expansion of this sector: Mexico's exports to the NAFTA market (Canada and the United States) increased more than five-fold during the period 1990-1998 (UNCTAD, 2000c). This process, initially led by TNCs from the United States, has been increasingly sustained by the involvement of European and Asian TNCs investing in Mexico to comply with NAFTA rules of origin. The free trade agreement concluded between Mexico and the European Union could have similar effects in terms of FDI inflows. Under-capitalization and under-provision in some service industries (including energy and infrastructure), combined with changes in regulatory frameworks are attracting investors in banking, commerce, telecommunications and energy among other industries. These industries still receive relatively small amounts of FDI, but may provide significant investment opportunities in coming years.

Flows of FDI into the smaller economies of Central America and the Caribbean (excluding offshore financial centres) went into assembly operations for re-export during most of the decade. In recent years, there has been an explicit effort in some of these countries (particularly Costa Rica and the Dominican Republic) to upgrade their manufacturing and export base by attracting investment in high-technology industries. These involve higher levels of domestic value added, particularly in human capital, and can generate large positive externalities in the domestic economy. Costa Rica has been particularly successful in this respect, and high-technology products and components produced largely by the United States TNC Intel generated over 40 per cent of total exports in 1999.[27] As the privatization and concessions processes have gathered pace in recent years in some of these countries, investments in manufacturing operations have been complemented by inflows going into services (including infrastructure). During 1998-1999, foreign investors participated in the privatization of electricity services in the Dominican Republic, El Salvador and Guatemala, telecommunications in El Salvador and Guatemala, and won airport concessions in Costa Rica and the Dominican Republic.

Direct investors seemed indifferent to short-term macroeconomic difficulties in countries with relatively stable institutional and policy frameworks, such as Argentina, Brazil, Bolivia, Chile or Peru. Long-term growth prospects in these countries were not substantially affected by their recent economic slowdown. Investors in the region took a long-term perspective. In contrast, investors reduced their involvement in countries with unstable institutional frameworks, such as Paraguay, Colombia, Ecuador and Venezuela. Given the investment potential of these countries (particularly in the oil industry in the case of the Andean countries), inflows should resume rapidly as stability and predictability increase.

There is an interesting difference between the role and structural consequences of FDI in Mexico and the Caribbean Basin countries and most other Latin American countries. Recent FDI in South America has tended to concentrate in non-tradable services, manufacturing for local markets and natural-resource-intensive activities. It has thus not helped much to transform the export structure of these countries, highly concentrated on natural-resource-based commodities. In Mexico and in some Caribbean Basin countries, in contrast, manufacturing TNCs have used the region as a production and export platform for the North American market. They have transformed the competitive position of the host economies and are shifting their production and trade structures towards exports in dynamic automobile, electronics and textile industries.

As regards the modes of entry in Latin America and the Caribbean, cross-border M&A sales reached $37 billion in 1999 (annex table A.IV.6), a $27 billion decline from the previous year due to the slowdown of privatization in much of the region in 1999.

The southern cone countries were the most advanced in privatization in the region. In value terms, privatization in 1998-1999 was concentrated in Argentina and Brazil (annex table A.IV.21): these two countries accounted for more than four-fifths of all privatization operations involving foreign firms during this period in the region. In 1999, the most important operation in Argentina was the sale of a residual of public participation in the ownership of YPF (box II.4) to Repsol. Argentina had three privatization deals involving foreign TNCs in that year. In Brazil, following the large sale of Telebras in 1998, the largest privatization deal was the sale of a gas distribution company in São Paulo (Cia de Gas do Estado de São Paulo) for almost $1 billion to United Kingdom investors in 1999. There were sales of some regional electricity generators to United States and European companies. Chile sold two large sanitary and water companies (Empresa Metropolitana de Obras Sanitarias and Empresa de Servicios Sanitarios) to Spanish firms in 1999.

Partially reflecting economic and political difficulties, privatization in the Andean group was very low in 1999. Only Peru, Ecuador and Venezuela had privatization operations involving $100 million or more. The Government of Peru sold concessions for the development of electricity-generating capacity to a Brazilian and a Swedish company; Venezuela sold the concession for some oil fields to the Chinese National Petroleum Corporation; and Ecuador sold a concession for electricity-generation to a Finnish corporation. In Mexico, the only operations of more than $100 million in 1999 involved the concession of airport services to TNCs from Denmark, France and Spain. Central American countries started relatively late with their privatization processes, and the total amount of FDI raised through privatization reached

only about $2 billion in 1999 — a level very similar to that registered in 1998 (ECLAC, 2000).

The interest shown by extraregional TNCs in the acquisition of leading Latin American private companies in recent years has also had consequences on the internationalization of the region's companies, partially reversing the process of intraregional investment observed earlier in the decade. The cases of YPF and Enersis illustrate this trend (box II.4). With its acquisition of YPF in 1999, *Repsol* was not only aiming at the market of Argentina but, through the holdings of YPF in other South American countries, positioned itself to penetrate in the region at large. The operation thus may have truncated an incipient process of internationalization of the company in Argentinean hands. The case of *Enersis* in Chile is even more striking. The Chilean holding company had developed through the 1990s one of the most successful processes of intraregional expansion by a Latin American company, acquiring important interests in the electricity industries of Argentina, Brazil, Colombia and Peru. The acquisition of a controlling stake in the company by *Endesa España* will serve to consolidate this process of regional expansion, but not as part of intraregional investment. More generally, Latin American companies — which expanded through the region in the 1990s and fostered the process of intraregional investment — seem to be facing increasing difficulties to compete with leading extraregional TNCs, which have found in the acquisition of these Latin American firms a platform for their own regional expansion.

TNCs based in Latin America have engaged in *outward* investment. Bermuda was the largest home country in 1999, followed by Chile, Virgin Islands, Brazil and Argentina (figure II.27). Much of outward FDI originating in this region is intraregional. For example, more than 70 per cent of outward FDI stock from Colombia is concentrated in the region. Traditional investors such as those based in Brazil and Mexico, however, do invest in countries other than those in the region: in 1999, three-quarters of M&A deals made by Brazilian TNCs took place outside the region, while the largest four cross-border M&As from Mexico were concluded either in the United States or the Philippines.

C. Central and Eastern Europe

In 1999, FDI flows into Central and Eastern Europe[28] increased for the third consecutive year. For the second time since the transition to the market economy started, annual inflows exceeded $20 billion (annex table B.1). The Czech Republic, Hungary, Poland and the Russian Federation continued to be leading recipients of FDI inflows (figure II.28).

By the end of 1999, the inward FDI stock of Central and Eastern Europe reached $110 billion. This stock was mainly concentrated in four countries: Poland ($30 billion), Hungary ($19 billion), the Russian Federation ($17 billion) and the Czech Republic ($16 billion), together accounting for almost three-fourths of total inward FDI stock in Central and Eastern Europe (annex table B.3). The FDI stock in Central and Eastern Europe continued to be dominated by EU investors, whose share accounted for 60 per cent of the total (figure II.29). The United States accounted for 16 per cent of the region's total (figure II.29) and was

in the leading position only in Croatia, Ukraine and the Russian Federation (annex table A.II.1).

In the sectoral breakdown of inward FDI stocks, the share of services increased at the expense of manufacturing to about 56 per cent (figure II.30 and annex table A.II.2) compared to less than 50 per cent in 1998. This may have a positive impact on the economic transition as efficiency gains in manufacturing are now being complemented by efficiency gains in services, improving the performance of the host economies more generally.

In Poland, by far the leading recipient ($7.5 billion) for a second consecutive year (figure II.28), FDI inflows have increased in every year since 1990. Foreign investors were obviously attracted by the large domestic market (the second after the Russian Federation in terms of GDP and the third largest after the Russian Federation and Ukraine in terms of population). Inflows of FDI into the Czech Republic in 1999 ($5.1 billion) exceeded the previous record of 1998, owing largely to a recent turnaround in privatization policies

FIGURE II.27

Latin America and the Caribbean: FDI outflows, top 10 economies, 1998 and 1999[a]

(Billions of dollars)

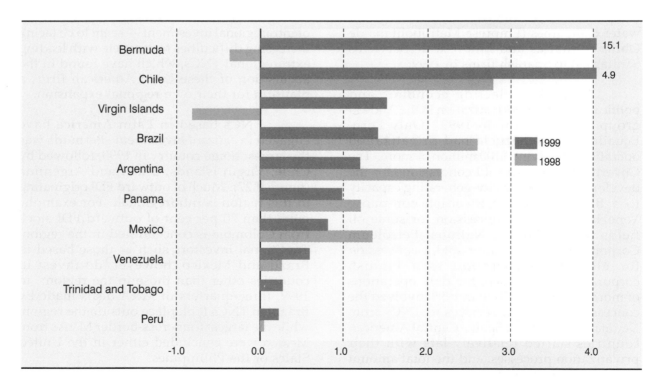

Source: UNCTAD, FDI/TNC database and annex table B.2.

[a]   Ranked on the basis of the magnitude of 1999 FDI outflows.

(figure II.28). While privatization policies during the first half of the 1990s excluded foreign participation in the Czech Republic, the second round of privatization followed the example of other countries such as Hungary, which had successfully involved foreign firms.

In the Russian Federation, after the dramatic drop in 1998 (from $6.6 billion to $2.8 billion), FDI inflows rose again in 1999 (to $2.9 billion), but were still far from the previous record and low relative to the size of that economy. "Round-tripping" was still prevalent, as suggested by the continued high share of inflows from Cyprus (8 per cent in the first half of 1999, compared to 23 per cent in inward FDI stock) (annex table A.II.1). Nonetheless,

1999 saw the second highest level of inflows into the Russian Federation since economic transition began. At the same time, portfolio and other investment inflows continued to decline and turned negative in 1999. FDI regained its dominant position among capital inflows.

In the light of a series of crises (Asia, Russian Federation, Kosovo) that shook confidence in emerging markets generally, the resilience and continued increase of Central and Eastern European FDI inflows is quite remarkable. In 1998, the Russian crisis did not keep the rest of the region from setting a new record. And in 1999, even in the most affected South-Eastern European countries such as

FIGURE II.28
Central and Eastern Europe: FDI *inflows*, 1998 and 1999[a]
(Billions of dollars)

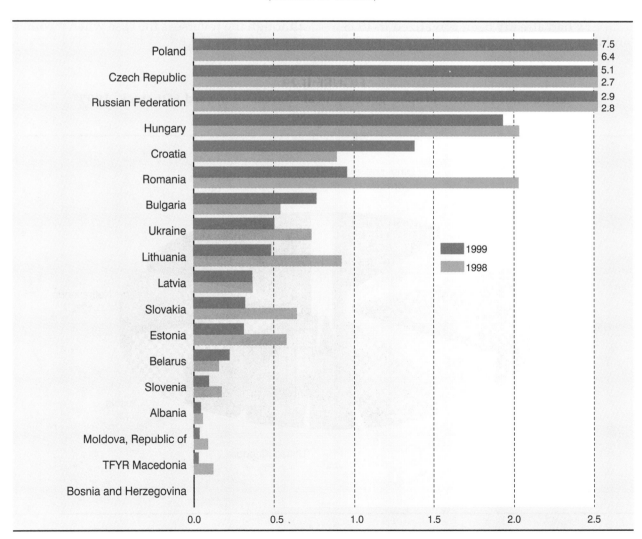

Source: UNCTAD, FDI/TNC database and annex table B.1.

[a]   Ranked on the basis of the magnitude of 1999 FDI inflows.

Bulgaria and Croatia, FDI inflows were resilient (annex table B.1).

In South-Eastern Europe, the experience varied country-by-country. In Bulgaria and Croatia, inflows increased significantly. In other countries there was a decline of varying degrees. This was only partly due to the Kosovo conflict, which prompted some investors to put projects on hold. Some countries reacted to the crisis with an increased openness to FDI, an increased focus on privatization and an increased readiness to implement major privatization projects involving foreign investors. In many countries major privatization deals were accelerated (e.g. Bulgarian and Croatian telecommunications companies, a Macedonian oil refinery, a Romanian car producer), although some of these deals did not materialize in actual FDI inflows before the beginning of 2000. And in Romania, where the telecommunication company had already been privatized in 1998 (and that transaction alone had accounted for

almost half of the cash equity FDI inflows in that year), total inflows decreased significantly in 1999. In Albania and Bosnia and Herzegovina, FDI inflows remained very low.

A disaggregation by type (equity in cash, equity in kind, reinvested earnings and intra-company loans) of reported FDI inflows shows two types of situations (annex table A.II.3): in the Czech Republic and Hungary, where some of the components are not reported (intra-company loans in the Czech Republic, reinvested earnings in Hungary), equity flows account for at least 90 per cent of registered inflows; in Poland, the Russian Federation and Romania, where all types of flows are reported, they account for only around 60 per cent. Consequently, judged solely by equity inflows, the lead of Poland over the Czech Republic is much smaller than its lead in all inflows. In the same vein, Hungary's equity cash inflows are higher than those of the Russian Federation, although the reverse is the case when it comes to total inflows.

FIGURE II.29

Central and Eastern Europe: geographical sources of inward FDI stock, 1999[a]

(Percentage)

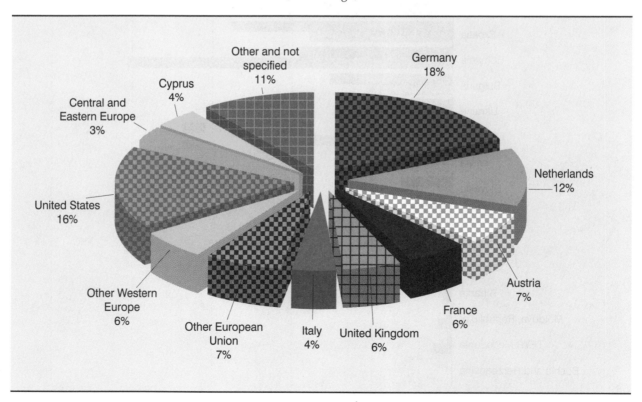

Source: UNCTAD, FDI/TNC database.

[a] Estimates.

In relative terms — FDI inflows as a percentage of gross fixed capital formation and FDI stocks compared with the size of GDP — smaller countries continue to be more internationalized by way of FDI than bigger ones. In terms of FDI inflows as a percentage of gross fixed capital formation (figure II.31), Bulgaria, Estonia and Latvia are the region's leaders, while the Russian Federation and Ukraine are among the region's laggards. (They are the two biggest economies of the region in terms of population.) In terms of FDI stocks as a percentage of GDP in 1999, the small countries (Hungary: 40 per cent; and Czech Republic: 31 per cent) and very small countries (Latvia: 31 per cent; and Estonia: 42 per cent) again show higher ratios than bigger countries (Poland: 18 per cent; Russian Federation: 9 per cent; and Ukraine: 11 per cent).

In 1999, FDI *outflows* from Central and Eastern Europe recovered somewhat from the decline of 1998. But the current level ($2.6 billion) is still lower than that of 1997 ($3.6 billion). In the Russian Federation, FDI outflows started to recover in 1999. In the Czech Republic too, they increased. But in Hungary and Poland, they temporarily decreased (figure II.32). Not all countries report on the destination of FDI outflows. Data indicate that the share of Central and Eastern Europe in outward FDI varies from country to country: it accounts for an overwhelming majority of outflows and outward stocks in Croatia, Estonia and Slovenia, is also dominant in Slovakia and the Czech Republic, and is sizeable (though only in second position) in the case of Hungary and the Russian Federation (annex table A.II.4). On the other hand, the share of Central and Eastern Europe was minimal in Latvia's outward FDI stock in 1999. In most cases, intraregional FDI takes place between countries that are each other's neighbours (annex table A.II.4). The rest of outward FDI is typically directed to Western Europe.

FIGURE II.30

Central and Eastern Europe: industry composition of inward FDI stock, 1999[a]
(Percentage)

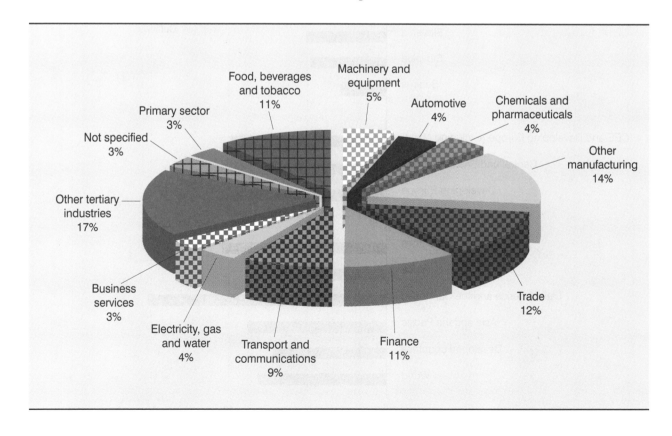

Source: UNCTAD, FDI/TNC database.

[a]   Estimates.

FIGURE II.31
Central and Eastern Europe: FDI flows as percentage of gross fixed capital formation, 1996-1998ᵃ
(Percentage)

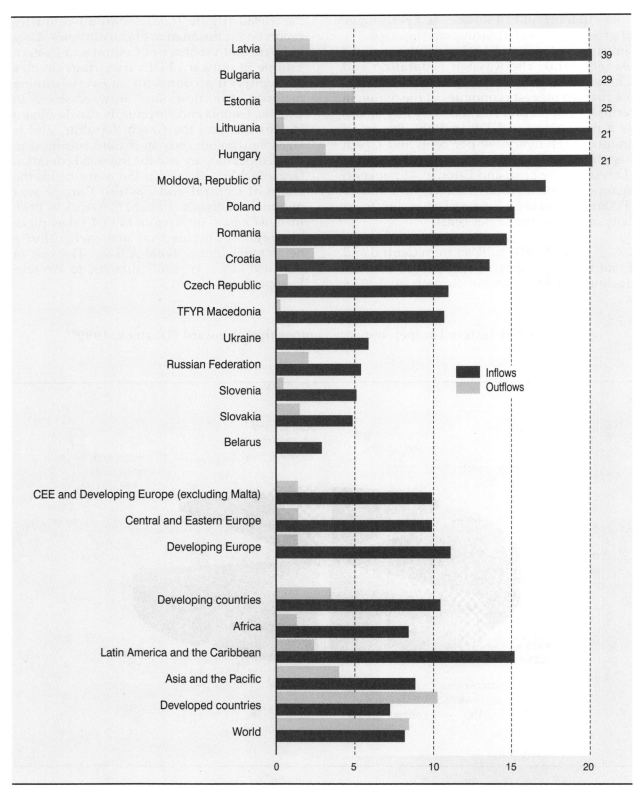

Source: UNCTAD, FDI/TNC database and annex table B.5.

ᵃ   Ranked on the basis of the magnitude of 1996-1998 FDI inflows as a percentage of gross fixed capital formation.

FIGURE II.32
Central and Eastern Europe: FDI outflows, top 10 countries, 1998 and 1999[a]
(Billions of dollars)

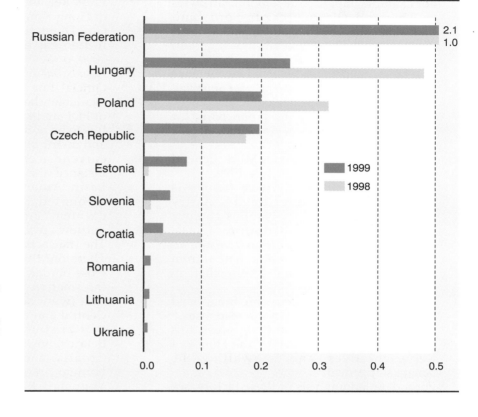

Source: UNCTAD, FDI/TNC database and annex table B.2.

[a]   Ranked on the basis of the magnitude of 1999 FDI outflows.

Notes

1   Including the countries of the former Yugoslavia.

2   Excluding tax heavens, this region received $12 billion in 1999.

3   UNCTAD, cross-border M&A database, based on data from Thomson Financial Securities Data Company.

4   Data from *Survey of Current Business*, March 2000.

5   Data on cross-border M&As can not be directly compared with FDI figures. For a discussion on the comparability of the two sources of statistics, see box IV.3.

6   "Europe's new capitalism", *The Economist*, 12 February 2000.

7   "Economists for EMU", *The Economist*, 17 April 1999. In addition, a recent survey of 15 important inward investors in the United Kingdom indicated that all but one were in favour of the United Kingdom joining the Euro. A number of them expressed warnings about the impact of currency fluctuations on future investment in the United Kingdom. The survey included companies such as Robert Bosch, Caterpillar, Siemens, SCA, Toyota, Samsung and Sony. (Kevin Brown and Peter Marsh, "Top executives warn on euro", *Financial Times*, 27 June 2000).

8   The data are on a notification basis and for the fiscal year. Transport equipment here includes general and electric machinery as well.

9   All of the 17 city (major) banks recorded income deficits in the fiscal year 1998 (end-March 1999). The mergers among these banks is an example of restructuring in this industry: examples include the mergers of Dai-Ichi Kangyo Bank, Fuji Bank and the Bank of Japan planned in 2001; Sanwa Bank, Tokai Bank and Asahi Bank planned in 2002; and Sumitomo Bank and Sakura Bank planned in 2002.

10 For example, the number of foreign affiliates newly established by Japanese companies in fiscal year 1999 was only 1,713, compared to 2,489 in fiscal year 1997 (1,597 in fiscal year 1998). A significant decline was recorded in FDI by SMEs; they established only 47 new affiliates in 1998 and 80 in 1999, compared to 476 in 1997 (Japan, Small and Medium-sized Enterprise Agency, 1999 and 2000).

11 It is to be noted that it is not possible to calculate precisely what percentage of FDI flows are accounted for by cross-border M&As. For details, see box IV.4.

[12]   For example, Japanese automobile affiliates in Thailand (Isuzu, Mazda-Ford) and Malaysia (Mitsubishi Motors), and various other manufacturing affiliates (e.g. an affiliate of Toshiba in Thailand) which were affected by the crisis, started to increase employment in 1999 (*Nihon Keizai Shimbun*, 29 September 1999, p. 1).

[13]   Survey conducted by the Japan Bank for International Cooperation, 2000, of 472 Japanese manufacturing TNCs.

[14]   Survey conducted by Japan's MITI. Quoted in *Nihon Keizai Shimbun*, 7 July 1999.

[15]   In this section, South Africa (which is categorized as a developed country according to the United Nations country classification) is included in Africa.

[16]   These figures include portfolio investment. Therefore, they are different in nature from the data on privatization used elsewhere in WIR00.

[17]   All of the industries cited were mentioned in more than 10 per cent of the responses.

[18]   After two years of legislative process, this bill was adopted recently by the House of Representatives, and is awaiting the Senate's approval.

[19]   For a detailed analysis of these factors, see UNCTAD, 1998a, pp. 202-204.

[20]   Hong Kong (China) reported FDI data (both flows and stocks) for the first time in 2000 for the data for 1998 and 1999. For details, see definitions and sources in annex B.

[21]   Press Release issued by the administration of Hong Kong (China), 19 June 2000.

[22]   Guy Dinmore, "Total and Gazprom tipped in Iran gas deal", *Financial Times*, 9 May 2000, p. 8.

[23]   *Islands Business*, June 1999, p. 25.

[24]   Official data on overseas divestment are not available; therefore, the net outward flows of FDI are likely to be over-estimated.

[25]   It is to be noted that payments of dividends and distributed branch profits contribute to current account deficits. In 1998, for instance, the current account deficit of the Latin America and Caribbean region amounted to about $89 billion, while dividend and distributed branch profit outflows reached about $13 billion.

[26]   The transaction was not completed in 1999. Therefore this deal is not included in the cross-border M&A database of UNCTAD.

[27]   Information from Banco Central de Costa Rica (www.bccr.fi.cr).

[28]   Central and Eastern Europe includes (both in statistics and in analysis) Albania, Belarus, Bosnia and Herzegovina, Bulgaria, Croatia, the Czech Republic, Estonia, Hungary, Latvia, Lithuania, the Former Yugoslav Republic of Macedonia, the Republic of Moldova, Poland, Romania, the Russian Federation, Slovakia, Slovenia, Ukraine and the Federal Republic of Yugoslavia (Serbia including Kosovo and Montenegro). No FDI data are available for the Federal Republic of Yugoslavia.

Chapter III The Largest Transnational Corporations

DI and corporate size are closely related. Large companies dominate both outflows and inflows of direct investment. For instance, the 50 largest TNCs from the major home countries account for over half of their FDI outflows — indeed, for some countries, the share exceeds 90 per cent (UNCTAD, 1997a, p. 34). In the past 14 years, cross-border M&As, dominated by large companies in value terms, and FDI have grown in parallel (chapter IV). In 1998-1999, for instance, mega-deals (i.e. deals of more than $1 billion) accounted for more than 60 per cent of the total value of cross-border M&As.

It is therefore of some interest to analyse the assets, sales and employment of the world's largest TNCs, as illustrated by the list of the 100 largest non-financial TNCs[1] published annually by UNCTAD since 1990. The list ranks non-financial TNCs by foreign assets (table III.1). The role of these firms in international production is illustrated by the fact that the foreign assets, sales and employment of the top 100 account for roughly 13, 19 and 18 per cent of foreign assets, sales and employment of the whole TNC universe, which contains an estimated 60,000 companies.[2]

In addition to the 100 largest TNCs in the world, the present chapter also examines the 50 largest TNCs from developing economies and the 25 largest TNCs from Central Europe. The former group has gained in significance during the past decade as the share of the developing economies in outward FDI has risen from some 3 per cent at the beginning of the 1980s to some 9 per cent in 1999. The latter group shows some interesting developments in what used to be centrally planned economies, with some members of the group beginning to make inroads into international production.

A. The 100 largest TNCs worldwide

1. Highlights

In 1998, General Electric again held the top position among the world's 100 largest non-financial TNCs (table III.1) ranked by foreign assets. General Motors moved to the second position from the fourth, with Royal Dutch Shell remaining in the third. Overall, the ranking remained fairly stable. Only a few changes have occurred among the top 10 TNCs: BP Amoco (rank 8) has replaced Volkswagen Group (now rank 11) and Nestlé (10) changed places with DaimlerChrysler (9).

Foreign assets. Growth in the total amount of foreign assets held by the 100 largest TNCs resumed in 1998. They increased by seven per cent compared to 1997, to $1.9 trillion (table III.2). There were noticeable variations, however, among regions and companies. TNCs from the European Union

Table III.1. The world's 100 largest TNCs, ranked by foreign assets, 1998

(Billions of dollars and number of employees)

Ranking 1998 by: Foreign assets	Ranking 1998 by: TNI[a]	Ranked in 1997 by: Foreign assets	Ranked in 1997 by: TNI[a]	Corporation	Country	Industry[b]	Assets Foreign	Assets Total	Sales Foreign	Sales Total	Employment Foreign	Employment Total	TNI[a] (Per cent)
1	75	1	84	General Electric	United States	Electronics	128.6	355.9	28.7	100.5	130 000	293 000	36.3
2	85	4	91	General Motors	United States	Motor vehicles	73.1	246.7	49.9	155.5	...	396 000	30.9
3	45	3	44	Royal Dutch/Shell Group[c]	Netherlands/United Kingdom	Petroleum expl./ref./distr.	67.0	110.0	50.0	94.0	61 000	102 000	58.0
4	76	2	80	Ford Motor Company	United States	Motor vehicles	...	237.5	43.8	144.4	171 276	345 175	35.4
5	19	5	29	Exxon Corporation[d]	United States	Petroleum expl./ref./distr.	50.1	70.0	92.7	115.4	...	79 000	75.9
6	60	6	75	Toyota	Japan	Motor vehicles	44.9	131.5	55.2	101.0	113 216	183 879	50.1
7	54	7	54	IBM	United States	Computers	43.6	86.1	46.4	81.7	149 934	291 067	53.0
8	21	30	42	BP AMOCO	United Kingdom	Petroleum expl./ref./distr.	40.5	54.9	48.6	68.3	78 950	98 900	74.9
9	59	10	71	DaimlerChrysler	Germany	Motor vehicles	36.7	159.7	125.4	154.6	208 502	441 502	50.4
10	3	9	4	Nestlé SA	Switzerland	Food/beverages	35.6	41.1	51.2	52.0	225 665	231 881	94.2
11	51	8	50	Volkswagen Group	Germany	Motor vehicles	...	70.1	52.3	80.2	142 481	297 916	53.8
12	7	18	5	Unilever	Netherlands/United Kingdom	Food/beverages	32.9	35.8	39.4	44.9	240 845	265 103	90.1
13	63	-	-	Suez Lyonnaise Des Eaux	France	Diversified/utility	...	84.6	12.9	34.8	126 500	201 000	45.6
14	73	-	-	Wal-Mart Stores	United States	Retailing	30.2	50.0	19.4	137.6	...	910 000	37.2
15	8	14	2	ABB	Switzerland	Electrical equipment	...	32.9	23.1	27.7	154 263	162 793	89.1
16	43	11	39	Mobil Corporation[d]	United States	Petroleum expl./ref./distr.	...	42.8	29.7	53.5	22 100	41 500	58.6
17	17	42	25	Diageo Plc	United Kingdom	Beverages	27.9	46.3	10.5	12.4	65 393	77 029	76.7
18	38	24	32	Honda Motor Co Ltd	Japan	Motor vehicles	26.3	41.8	29.7	51.7	...	112 200	60.2
19	52	19	56	Siemens AG	Germany	Electronics	...	66.8	45.7	66.0	222 000	416 000	53.6
20	41	21	34	Sony Corporation	Japan	Electronics	...	52.5	40.7	56.6	102 468	173 000	59.3
21	34	33	68	Renault SA	France	Motor vehicles	23.6	43.2	25.4	39.8	92 854	138 321	61.8
22	12	28	21	News Corporation[e]	Australia	Media/publishing	22.9	33.6	10.5	11.7	...	50 000	78.7
23	40	25	38	BMW AG	Germany	Motor vehicles	22.9	35.7	26.8	37.7	53 107	119 913	59.9
24	81	22	78	Mitsubishi Corporation	Japan	Diversified	21.7	74.9	43.5	116.1	3 668	11 650	32.7
25	67	17	60	Nissan Motor Co Ltd	Japan	Motor vehicles	21.6	57.2	25.8	54.4	...	131 260	42.6
26	33	15	9	Bayer AG	Germany	Pharmaceuticals/chemicals	21.4	34.3	21.9	31.1	80 900	145 100	62.8
27	13	20	10	Roche Holding AG[d]	Switzerland	Pharmaceuticals	21.2	40.6	16.7	17.0	57 142	66 707	78.7
28	23	13	16	Hoechst AG[d]	Germany	Pharmaceuticals/chemicals	21.2	33.5	21.0	26.2	...	96 967	71.6
29	56	16	48	Elf Aquitaine SA	France	Petroleum expl./ref./distr.	20.7	43.2	21.8	37.9	42 000	85 000	51.6
30	50	37	55	Viag AG	Germany	Diversified	...	34.8	16.3	27.9	41 990	85 694	55.3
31	26	36	30	Rhone-Poulenc SA[d]	France	Pharmaceuticals/Chemicals	...	28.4	12.0	14.7	36 421	65 180	69.1
32	27	32	20	Total Fina SA	France	Petroleum expl./ref./distr.	...	27.0	20.8	28.6	35 100	57 166	69.0
33	14	27	8	Philips Electronics	Netherlands	Electronics	19.0	32.8	32.1	33.9	189 210	233 686	77.8
34	1	23	1	Seagram Company	Canada	Beverages/media	18.8	22.2	9.1	8.7	...	24 200	94.8
35	28	34	18	Cable And Wireless Plc	United Kingdom	Telecommunications	17.7	28.5	8.8	13.2	37 426	50 671	67.5
36	53	31	57	Hewlett-Packard	United States	Electronics/Computers	17.6	33.7	25.2	46.5	...	124 600	53.2
37	78	35	79	Mitsui & Co Ltd.	Japan	Diversified	17.3	56.5	46.5	118.5	...	7 288	34.9
38	80	45	88	ENI Group	Italy	Petroleum expl./ref./distr.	...	48.4	12.0	33.2	24 602	78 906	34.1
39	91	46	86	Chevron Corporation	United States	Petroleum expl./ref./distr.	16.9	36.5	2.0	29.9	8 956	39 191	25.3
40	46	38	41	BASF AG	Germany	Chemicals	...	30.4	24.2	32.4	46 730	105 945	57.9

/....

Table III.1. The world's 100 largest TNCs, ranked by foreign assets, 1998 (continued)
(Billions of dollars and number of employees)

Ranking 1998 by: Foreign assets	Ranking 1998 by: TNI[a]	Ranked in 1997 by: Foreign assets	Ranked in 1997 by: TNI[a]	Corporation	Country	Industry[b]	Assets Foreign	Assets Total	Sales Foreign	Sales Total	Employment Foreign	Employment Total	TNI[a] (Per cent)
41	69	41	72	Du Pont (E.I.) de Nemours	United States	Chemicals	16.7	38.5	11.7	24.8	35 000	101 000	41.7
42	42	26	31	Alcatel	France	Electronics	16.7	34.6	14.5	23.6	80 005	118 272	59.1
43	65	53	77	Peugeot SA	France	Motor vehicles	15.9	39.8	24.4	37.5	43 300	156 500	44.2
44	77	-	-	Texas Utilities Company	United States	Utility	15.8	39.5	4.0	14.7	8 300	22 055	35.0
45	96	39	82	Itochu Corporation	Japan	Trading	15.1	55.9	18.4	115.3	...	5 775	21.5
46	89	44	94	Sumitomo Corporation	Japan	Trading/machinery	15.0	45.0	17.6	95.0	...	5 591	26.3
47	25	-	-	Coca-Cola Company	United States	Beverages	14.9	19.2	11.9	18.8	...	29 000	70.6
48	24	-	-	Nortel Networks[f]	Canada	Telecommunications	14.3	19.7	12.2	17.6	...	75 052	70.8
49	92	40	76	Nissho Iwai	Japan	Trading	14.2	38.5	9.1	71.6	...	4 041	24.9
50	82	12	74	Fiat Spa[c]	Italy	Motor vehicles	14.2	76.1	19.4	51.0	87 861	220 549	32.1
51	62	57	63	Motorola Inc	United States	Electronics	14.0	31.0	14.0	31.3	66 800	141 000	45.8
52	86	-	-	Telefonica SA	Spain	Telecommunications	13.8	42.3	6.1	20.5	27 802	101 809	29.9
53	83	80	95	Vivendi SA	France	Diversified/utility	...	57.1	11.5	35.3	94 310	235 610	31.5
54	11	63	46	Rio Tinto Plc[g]	United Kingdom/Australia	Mining	12.4	16.1	7.1	7.1	22 478	34 809	80.4
55	72	55	83	Matsushita Electric	Japan	Electronics	12.2	66.2	32.4	63.7	133 629	282 153	38.9
56	79	59	85	Fujitsu Ltd	Japan	Electronics	12.2	42.3	15.9	43.3	74 000	188 000	34.9
57	2	52	3	Thomson Corporation	Canada	Media/Publishing	12.1	12.5	5.8	6.2	36 000	39 000	94.6
58	97	56	99	Hitachi Ltd	Japan	Electrical equipment/Electronics	12.0	76.6	19.8	63.8	58 000	331 494	21.4
59	36	66	49	McDonald's Corporation	United States	Eating places	12.0	19.8	7.5	12.4	...	284 000	60.7
60	48	72	53	Robert Bosch GmbH	Germany	Motor vehicle parts	...	21.9	19.6	30.2	94 180	189 537	56.3
61	74	-	-	RJR Nabisco Holdings	United States	Food/tobacco	...	28.9	5.6	17.0	...	74 000	36.9
62	6	89	11	Holderbank Financière Glarus	Switzerland	Construction materials	11.6	12.8	7.0	8.0	37 779	40 520	90.5
63	22	-	-	Stora Enso Oys	Finland	Paper	11.5	18.0	10.8	11.7	25 189	40 987	72.8
64	18	76	43	Michelin	France	Rubber/tires	...	15.0	12.3	14.6	87 160	127 241	76.0
65	88	61	92	VEBA Group	Germany	Diversified	...	52.2	14.7	49.0	39 220	116 774	28.2
66	95	-	-	RWE Group	Germany	Utility	10.8	57.2	8.2	41.2	42 681	155 576	22.1
67	20	71	14	Glaxo Wellcome Plc	United Kingdom	Pharmaceuticals	10.8	15.5	10.9	13.3	42 562	56 934	75.5
68	90	58	90	Marubeni Corporation	Japan	Trading	10.6	53.8	31.4	98.8	...	8 618	25.8
69	5	77	37	British American Tobacco Plc[h]	United Kingdom	Food/tobacco	10.5	12.4	13.8	15.3	99 204	101 081	91.0
70	57	47	52	Dow Chemical	United States	Chemicals	10.4	23.8	11.0	18.4	19 125	39 029	50.8
71	9	94	24	SmithKline Beecham Plc	United Kingdom	Pharmaceuticals	10.4	15.0	12.4	13.4	50 900	59 500	82.3
72	29	88	47	Danone Groupe SA	France	Food/beverages	10.3	17.6	8.8	14.4	58 602	78 945	64.6
73	49	-	-	Carrefour SA	France	Retailing	10.3	20.3	17.2	30.4	86 846	144 142	55.9
74	66	69	64	Johnson & Johnson	United States	Pharmaceuticals	...	26.2	11.1	23.7	...	93 100	43.0
75	30	-	-	Compart Spa	Italy	Food	10.2	21.6	10.5	15.0	24 097	33 076	63.4
76	100	-	-	SBC Communications	United States	Telecommunications	...	75.0	...	46.2	...	200 380	13.5
77	16	87	12	Akzo Nobel NV	Netherlands	Chemicals	10.1	14.0	11.6	14.6	67 800	85 900	76.8

/....

Table III.1. The world's 100 largest TNCs, ranked by foreign assets, 1998 (concluded)

(Billions of dollars and number of employees)

Ranking 1998 by: Foreign assets	Ranking 1998 by: TNI[a]	Ranked in 1997 by: Foreign assets	Ranked in 1997 by: TNI[a]	Corporation	Country	Industry[b]	Assets Foreign	Assets Total	Sales Foreign	Sales Total	Employment Foreign	Employment Total	TNI[a] (Per cent)
78	71	65	66	Procter & Gamble[i]	United States	Chemicals/cosmetics	10.0	31.0	17.9	37.2	...	110 000	40.3
79	31	54	26	Montedison Spa	Italy	Chemicals/agriindustry	...	19.4	9.9	14.3	20 050	28 672	63.1
80	37	67	36	Ericsson LM	Sweden	Electronics/telecommunications	9.6	20.7	17.8	22.8	58 688	103 667	60.4
81	98	-	-	Southern Company	United States	Utility	9.6	36.2	1.8	11.4	...	31 848	21.0
82	4	74	7	Electrolux AB	Sweden	Electrical equipment/electronics	...	10.3	13.8	14.5	89 573	99 322	92.7
83	47	62	40	Volvo AB	Sweden	Motor vehicles	...	25.2	23.8	26.3	35 313	79 820	57.4
84	32	91	22	Royal Ahold NV	Netherlands	Retailing	9.3	13.3	20.9	29.4	133 716	279 255	62.9
85	84	79	87	Merck & Co	United States	Pharmaceuticals	...	31.9	6.6	26.9	22 800	57 300	31.1
86	15	83	15	L'Air Liquide Groupe	France	Chemicals	...	10.6	5.1	6.8	20 306	28 600	77.0
87	64	86	67	Mannesmann AG	Germany	Telecommunications/engineering	...	20.3	10.8	21.2	43 821	116 247	44.4
88	58	70	81	Mitsubishi Motors	Japan	Motor vehicles	8.4	25.4	16.8	29.1	18 251	29 945	50.6
89	61	-	-	Broken Hill Proprietary	Australia	Steel manufacturing	8.0	20.6	8.7	12.6	20 000	50 000	49.3
90	35	78	33	Crown Cork & Seal	United States	Packaging	8.0	12.5	5.0	8.3	...	38 459	61.8
91	87	73	70	Petroleos de Venezuela SA	Venezuela	Petroleum expl./ref./distr.	7.9	48.8	11.0	25.7	6 026	50 821	23.7
92	55	96	59	Canon Electronics	Japan	Electronics/office equipment	7.4	23.4	17.8	24.4	41 834	79 799	52.3
93	44	93	51	Bridgestone	Japan	Rubber/tires	7.4	14.7	11.3	17.1	...	97 767	58.2
94	99	84	100	GTE Corporation	United States	Telecommunications	7.3	43.6	3.3	25.7	22 000	120 000	16.0
95	94	92	97	Atlantic Richfield	United States	Petroleum expl./ref./distr.	...	25.2	1.6	10.3	4 300	18 400	22.5
96	39	60	17	Imperial Chemical Industries	United Kingdom	Chemicals	7.2	14.9	10.9	15.1	...	59 100	60.2
97	68	-	-	Compaq Computer Corp.	United States	Computers	7.0	21.7	16.4	31.2	...	71 000	42.6
98	10	-	-	SCA	Sweden	Paper	7.0	9.7	7.0	7.7	25 346	32 211	80.8
99	70	-	-	ALCOA	United States	Aluminium manufacturing	...	17.0	6.6	15.3	...	103 500	41.7
100	93	98	96	Toshiba Corporation	Japan	Electronics	6.8	48.8	14.5	44.6	...	198 000	23.3

Source: UNCTAD/Erasmus University database.

a   TNI is the abbreviation for "transnationality index", which is calculated as the average of three ratios: foreign assets to total assets, foreign sales to total sales and foreign employment to total employment.

b   Industry classification for companies follows the United States Standard Industrial Classification as used by the United States Securities and Exchange Commission (SEC).

c   Foreign assets, sales and employment are outside Europe.

d   Mergers between Exxon and Mobil into ExxonMobil, and Hoechst AG and Rhone-Poulenc SA into Aventis are not documented yet as they took place in 1999.

e   Foreign assets, sales and employment are outside Australia and Asia.

f   Nortel Networks replaces BCE due to internal restructuring and reduction of BCE's ownership in Nortel Networks.

g   Foreign employment is outside Europe, Australia and New Zealand.

h   British American Tobacco demerged a large part of their services business, which explains decrease of total assets.

i   Foreign assets, sales and employment are outside North-America.

...   Data on foreign assets, foreign sales and foreign employment were not made available for the purpose of this study. In case of non-availability, they are estimated using secondary sources of information or on the basis of the ratios of foreign to total assets, foreign to total sales and foreign to total employment.

Note: The list includes non-financial TNCs only. In some companies, foreign investors may hold a minority share of more than 10 per cent.

slightly increased their share in the total foreign assets of the top 100 TNCs, by 2.3 percentage points (table III.3), whereas North American and Japanese TNCs retained their relative positions. Nine out of the top ten increases in foreign assets originated in European companies (e.g. BP Amoco, Diageo and Vivendi). The only non-European company among the top 10 increases in foreign assets is General Electric (United States). However, with the exception of Dow Chemical and Nissan Motor, the largest decreases were also displayed by European TNCs, with declines of up to 33 per cent (Imperical Chemical). The European record is certainly a result of the massive recent M&A wave in the major markets. The current relative weakness of the Japanese economy and the constraints it has placed on Japanese TNCs might explain their stagnation compared with the other TNCs from the Triad.

Foreign sales. The total foreign sales of the largest TNCs amounted to $ 2.1 trillion (table III.2). Compared with the slight decline of 0.7 per cent in 1997, the decline of foreign sales in 1998 was even more pronounced (3.2 per cent). As with foreign assets, however, individual company experiences varied widely. Seven out of the ten largest increases in foreign sales were among TNCs from the European Union — Peugeot, Renault, BP Amoco, Roche, Vivendi, Rio Tinto and Volkswagen — which registered increases in foreign sales of between 23 and 54 per

cent. The largest decreases in foreign sales offer a mixed picture: TNCs experiencing them come from a variety of countries and a variety of industries, so that no clear pattern can be discerned.

Foreign employment. Total foreign employment by the largest TNCs increased by almost 10 per cent, as did their total employment (table III.2), reversing for the first time in three years the previously observed trend of declining overall employment with rising foreign employment (figure III.1). Michelin, BP AMOCO and Renault more than doubled their foreign employment. Six out of ten companies with the largest increase in foreign employment originate in the European Union. Four Japanese companies (Itochu Corp., Nishho Iwai, Mitsui and Sumitomo Corp.) are among the top 10 companies showing a decline in foreign employment of up to 50 per cent. For these companies in particular, the decline in foreign employment was in line with a decline in foreign assets.

For the list as a whole, 17 new entries and exits were registered (tables III.4 and III.5), of which 10 were caused by mergers or acquisitions (Suez Lyonnaise des Eaux, Wal-Mart Stores, Texas Utility, Nortel, Telefonica, Stora Enso, RWE, Carrefour, Southern Company and Compaq Computer). In 1998, only one firm among the top 100 TNCs, Petróleos de Venezuela (PDVSA), was headquartered in a developing country. PDVSA descended 18 rungs to end up 91st in the top 100 list. Daewoo left the top 100 listing, although it remains in its proximity. This company, which has encountered serious difficulties in the wake of the Asian financial crisis, is currently undergoing comprehensive restructuring.

The most striking feature of this group of companies, however, is its relative stability in terms of geographic origin and membership since 1990, the first reporting year:

- The national origins of the group were fairly stable, with almost 90 of the top 100 being headquartered in the Triad of the European Union, Japan and the United States (table III.3). Triad countries — not surprisingly given the connection between corporate size and FDI volume — accounted for 85 per cent of total FDI outflows in 1999. The share of the

Table III.2. Snapshot of the world's 100 largest TNCs, 1998

(Billions of dollars, number of employees and percentage)

Variable	1998	1997	Change 1998 vs. 1997 (Percentage)
Assets			
Foreign	1 922	1 793	7.2
Total	4 610	4 212	9.4
Sales			
Foreign	2 063	2 133	-3.3
Total	4 099	3 984	2.9
Employment			
Foreign	6 547 719	5 980 740	9.5
Total	12 741 173	11 621 032	9.6
Average index of transnationality	53.9	55.4	-1.5 [a]

Source: UNCTAD/Erasmus University database.

[a] The change between 1997 and 1998 is expressed in percentage points.

Table III.3.   **Country composition of the world's 100 largest TNCs by transnationality index, foreign assets and number of entries, 1990, 1997 and 1998**

(Percentage)

Country	Average TNI [a]			Share in total of foreign foreign assets of top 100			Number of entries		
	1990	1997	1998	1990	1997	1998	1990	1997	1998
European Union	**56.7**	**62.5**	**61.5**	**45.5**	**40.9**	**43.2**	**48**	**45**	**47**
France	50.9	58.4	58.8	10.4	9.8	10.5	14	13	12
Germany	44.4	55.7	51.4	8.9	12.7	12.6	9	11	12
United Kingdom [b]	68.5	70.8	75.7	16.8	11.2	12.3	12	11	10
Netherlands [b]	68.5	77.7	73.1	8.9	7.3	7.2	4	5	5
Italy	38.7	47.0	48.2	3.5	3.2	2.7	4	3	4
Sweden	71.7	70.1	72.8	2.7	1.6	1.9	5	3	4
Finland	-	-	72.8	-	-	0.6	-	0	1
Spain	-	-	29.9	-	-	0.7	-	0	1
Belgium	60.4	92.3	-	1	0.4	-	1	1	0
North America	**41.2**	**47.9**	**46.2**	**32.5**	**35.1**	**35.3**	**30**	**30**	**29**
United States	38.5	44.2	41.6	31.5	32.4	32.9	28	27	26
Canada	79.2	81.2	86.7	1	2.7	2.4	2	3	3
Japan	**35.5**	**39.5**	**38.7**	**12**	**15.7**	**14.5**	**12**	**17**	**17**
Remaining countries	**73.0**	**74.8**	**73.8**	**10**	**8.3**	**7.7**	**10**	**8**	**8**
Switzerland	84.3	85.3	88.1	7.5	6.1	5.1	6	5	4
Australia [a]	51.8	72.8	69.5	1.6	1.1	2.3	2	1	3
Venezuela	-	44.5	29.7	-	0.5	0.4	-	1	1
New Zealand	62.2	-	-	0.5	-	-	1	-	-
Republic of Korea	-	54.5	-	-	0.6	-	-	1	-
Norway	58.1	-	-	0.4	-	-	1	-	-
Total [c] of all 100 listed TNCs	**51.1**	**55.4**	**54.0**	**100**	**100**	**100**	**100**	**100**	**100**

Source: UNCTAD, 1993a and Erasmus University database.

[a]   TNI is the abbreviation for "transnationality index", which is calculated as the average of three ratios: foreign assets to total assets, foreign sales to total sales and foreign employment to total employment.
[b]   Due to dual nationality, Royal Dutch Shell and Unilever are counted as an entry for both the United Kingdom and The Netherlands. In the aggregate for the European Union and the total of all listed TNCs they are counted once. Rio Tinto Plc is counted as an entry for both the United Kingdom and Australia.   In the aggregate for the total of all 100 listed TNCs it is counted once.
[c]   Numbers may not add up exactly due to rounding.

FIGURE III.1
Snapshot of the world's 100 largest TNCs, 1990-1998

Source: UNCTAD/Erasmus University database.

Note: The ratios represent the averages of the individual ratios of foreign assets/total assets, foreign sales/total sales, foreign employment/ total employment of the top 100 expressed in percentages. The average transnationality index (TNI) of the top 100 TNCs is the average of the 100 individual company transnationality indices.

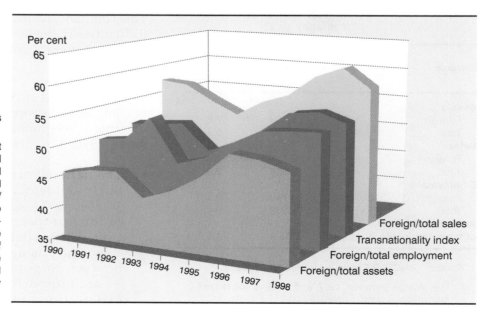

Table III.4. Newcomers to the world's 100 largest TNCs, ranked by foreign assets, 1998

Ranked by Foreign assets	Ranked by TNI [a]	Corporation	Country	Industry	TNI [a] (Percentage)
13	63	Suez Lyonnaise des Eaux	France	Diversified	45.6
14	75	Wal-Mart Stores	United States	Retailing	37.2
47	77	Texas Utilities Company	United States	Utility	35.0
48	25	Coca-Cola Company	United States	Beverages	70.6
47	24	Nortel Networks	Canada	Telecommunications	70.8
52	86	Telefónica SA	Spain	Telecommunications	29.9
61	74	RJR Nabisco Holdings	United States	Food/tobacco	36.9
63	22	Stora Enso Oys	Finland	Paper	72.8
66	95	RWE Group	Germany	Utility	22.1
73	49	Carrefour SA	France	Retailing	55.9
75	30	Compart Spa	Italy	Food	63.4
76	100	SBC Communications	United States	Telecommunications	13.5
81	98	Southern Company	United States	Utility	21.0
89	61	Broken Hill Proprietary	Australia	Steel manufacturing	49.3
97	68	Compaq Computer Corporation	United States	Computers	42.6
98	10	SCA	Sweden	Paper	80.8
99	70	ALCOA	United States	Aluminium manufacturing	41.7

Source: UNCTAD/Erasmus University database.

[a] TNI is the abbreviation for "transnationality index", which is calculated as the average of three ratios: foreign assets to total assets, foreign sales to total sales and foreign employment to total employment.

Table III.5. Departures from the world's 100 largest TNCs, ranked by foreign assets, 1998[a]

Ranked in 1997 by Foreign assets	Ranked in 1997 by TNI [b]	Corporation	Country	Industry	TNI [b] (Percentage)
29	58	Philip Morris	United States	Food/tobacco	51.1
43	19	Novartis	Switzerland	Pharmaceuticals/chemicals	74.4
48	69	Texaco Incorporated	United States	Petroleum expl./ref./distr.	45.3
49	61	BCE Inc	Canada	Telecommunications/electronics	50.9
50	65	Xerox Corporation	United States	Photo equipment	48.7
51	45	Saint-Gobain SA	France	Industrial material	58.7
64	23	Lafarge SA	France	Construction	71.3
68	93	AMOCO Corporation [c]	United States	Petroleum expl./ref./distr.	25.9
75	62	Daewoo Corporation	Republic of Korea	Diversified	50.8
81	98	AT&T Corp	United States	Telecommunications/electronics	21.9
82	6	Solvay SA	Belgium	Chemicals/pharmaceuticals	92.3
85	89	International Paper	United States	Paper	30.7
90	13	BTR Plc [d]	United Kingdom	Plastics and foam	78.2
95	35	LVMH SA	France	Diversified	62.1
97	73	American Home Products	United States	Pharmaceuticals	41.3
99	28	Gillette Company	United States	Drugs, cosmetics & health	65.9
100	27	Pharmacia & Upjohn Inc.	United States	Pharmaceuticals	66.6

Source: UNCTAD/Erasmus University database.

[a] This also includes companies that could not be considered in 1998 because of the late arrival of the response to the UNCTAD questionnaire and for which estimates could not be derived.

[b] TNI is the abbreviation for "transnationality index", which is calculated as the average of three ratios: foreign assets to total assets, foreign sales to total sales and foreign employment to total employment.

[c] AMOCO merged with BP into BP AMOCO.

[d] BTR merged with Siebe into Invensys.

Triad in total FDI outflows decreased from 87 per cent in 1990 to 75 per cent in 1996 to rebound in 1999. The most recent rise is mainly due to the current cross-border M&A wave, in which the top 100 have a considerable role.

- During the past nine years, 57 of the top 100 TNCs have continued to feature in the list. Ten TNCs that were in the first list did not appear in the 1998 list because of M&As. The successor companies (e.g. DaimlerChrysler, BP Amoco and Diageo) replaced them.

The list was dominated in 1998 by the same three industries as in previous years: electronics/electrical equipment, motor vehicles and petroleum exploration and distribution (table III.6). In 1998, 57 of the top 100 TNCs were in one of these four industries, with 31 in the first two. The emergence of large transnational utility and telecommunication companies in the list, resulting from the increasing liberalization of their markets, as well as a worldwide consolidation in the pharmaceuticals, reduced the number of pharmaceutical firms in the list from 13 to 8 entries in 1998.

2. Transnationality

The TNC "transnationality index" is the average of three ratios: foreign assets/total assets, foreign sales/total sales and foreign employment/total employment. It is intended to capture the foreign dimension of assets, sales and employment in a firm's overall activities. Between 1990 and 1998, the average transnationality index of the world's top 100 TNCs[3] rose from 51 per cent in 1990 to 55 per cent in 1997 and declined to 54 per cent in 1998 (figure III.2). The slight decline is mainly due to the emergence of large transnational utility and telecommunication companies, whose average transnationality index in 1998 was 37 percentage points as compared to 54 percentage points for the top 100 in total. The small decrease in total foreign sales in 1998, accompanied by a marginal increase in domestic sales, also helps account for the decline in the overall transnationality index.

In 1998, as in earlier years, the index is led by firms from countries with small domestic markets: of the top 10 TNCs in

Table III.6. Industry composition of the top 100 TNCs, 1990, 1997 and 1998

Industry	Number of entries			Average TNI [a] per industry (Percentage)		
	1990	1997	1998	1990	1997	1998
Electronics/electrical equipment/computers	14	18	17	47.4	55.0	52.6
Motor vehicle and parts	13	14	14	35.8	46.7	49.0
Petroleum exploration/refining/distribution and mining	13	13	11	47.3	48.9	52.7
Food/beverages/tobacco	9	8	10	59.0	72.7	74.3
Chemicals	12	8	8	60.1	63.3	58.5
Pharmaceuticals	6	13	8	66.1	67.5	64.3
Diversified	2	7	6	29.7	42.3	38.0
Telecommunications	2	4	6	46.2	40.7	40.4
Trading	7	3	4	32.4	34.0	24.6
Retailing	-	1	3	-	71.5	52.0
Utilities	-	-	3	-	-	26.0
Metals	6	-	2	55.1	-	45.5
Media	2	1	2	82.6	72.8	86.7
Construction	4	3	1	58.8	70.3	90.5
Machinery/engineering	3	2	-	54.5	35.8	-
Other	7	5	5	57.6	60.8	69.9
Total/average	100	100	100	51.1	55.4	53.9

Source: UNCTAD, 1993a and Erasmus University database.

a   TNI is the abbreviation for "transnationality index", which is calculated as the average of three ratios: foreign assets to total assets, foreign sales to total sales and foreign employment to total employment.

terms of transnationality (table III.7), only one was headquartered in a single, relatively large, economy (United Kingdom). This is not surprising, as TNCs from smaller home countries tend to go abroad to overcome the constraints of their home markets and to make full use of their ownership advantages. The top 10 rises and declines in the transnationality index mostly feature TNCs from smaller home countries (figures III.3 and III.4).

Looking at transnationality by industry, one finds great variations (table III.6). Food and beverages topped the list with 74 per cent, while trading was at the bottom with 25 per cent. The degree of transnationality of the top five firms in all industries that have at least five entries in the lists of both 1990 and 1998 increased substantially over the period 1990-1998 (table III.8). Food and beverages firms exhibited the largest gains (25 percentage points), while petroleum firms the smallest (6 percentage points). The top five motor vehicle companies remained among the least transnationalized, whereas the top five food and beverages firms, closely followed by pharmaceutical and electronic firms, had gained substantially over the period. The different allocation and use of capital in the various industries could explain this

FIGURE III.2
**Average transnationality
index of the world's
100 largest TNCs,
1990-1998**

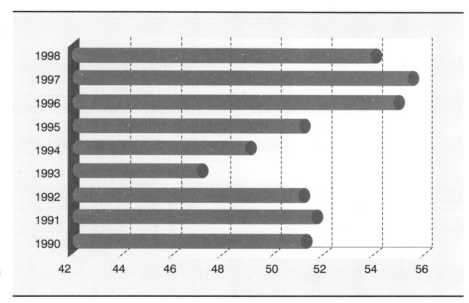

Source: UNCTAD/Erasmus University database.

Table III.7. **The world's top 10 TNCs in terms of transnationality, 1998**

Ranking 1998 by		Ranking 1997 by					
Foreign assets	TNI [a]	Foreign assets	TNI [a]	Corporation	Country	Industry	TNI [a]
34	1	23	1	Seagram Company	Canada	Beverages/media	94.8
57	2	52	3	Thomson Corporation	Canada	Media/publishing	94.6
10	3	9	4	Nestlé SA	Switzerland	Food/beverages	94.2
82	4	74	7	Electrolux AB	Sweden	Electrical equipment/electronics	92.7
69	5	77	37	British American Tobacco Plc	United Kingdom	Food/tobacco	91.0
62	6	89	11	Holderbank Financière Glarus	Switzerland	Construction materials	90.5
12	7	18	5	Unilever	Netherlands/ United Kingdom	Food/beverages	90.1
15	8	14	2	ABB	Switzerland	Electrical equipment	89.1
71	9	94	24	SmithKline Beecham Plc	United Kingdom	Pharmaceuticals	82.3
98	10	New	New	SCA	Sweden	Paper	80.8

Source: UNCTAD/Erasmus University database.

a   TNI is the abbreviation for "transnationality index", which is calculated as the average of
    three ratios: foreign assets to total assets, foreign sales to total sales and foreign employment to total employment.

FIGURE III.3
The top 10 increases in transnationality among the world's 100 largest TNCs, 1997-1998
(Percentages)

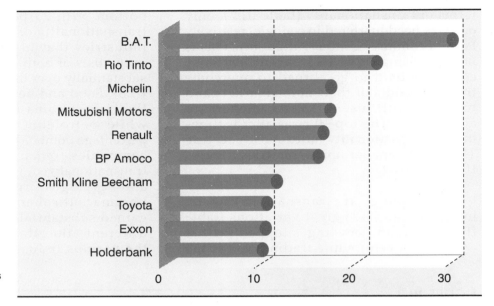

Source: UNCTAD/Erasmus University database.

Table III. 8.   **Averages in transnationality index, assets, sales and employment of the top 5 TNCs in each industry, [a] 1990, 1997 and 1998**

(Percentage points, and per cent of top 100 total)

Industry	Year	Transnationality index	Assets Foreign	Assets Total	Sales Foreign	Sales Total	Employment Foreign	Employment Total
Petroleum	1990	57.7	15.1	10.6	15.8	11.9	5.5	4.2
	1997	60.2	11.2	7.8	12.8	10.7	3.5	3.2
	1998	63.8	10.8	7.0	11.8	9.0	4.0	3.2
Motor vehicles	1990	34.7	11.9	15.3	10.4	11.8	9.7	14.2
	1997	41.1	13.1	17.6	11.2	13.9	10.5	14.7
	1998	44.1	13.1	18.4	15.8	15.5	11.6	13.1
Electronics/ electrical equipment	1990	36.1	6.4	7.4	4.7	6.3	6.5	9.6
	1997	59.5	12.1	12.6	8.6	7.8	12.5	11.3
	1998	58.3	13.1	12.9	8.9	8.1	11.6	10.5
Pharmaceuticals	1990	47.1	1.5	1.3	1.6	1.4	2.4	2.3
	1997	63.8	4.4	3.6	3.5	2.7	4.5	3.5
	1998	71.5	4.9	3.3	4.0	2.5	4.4	3.4
Chemicals	1990	51.6	5.3	4.2	5.9	4.5	4.8	5.4
	1997	63.4	5.8	3.7	5.1	3.9	4.8	4.5
	1998	53.5	3.3	3.0	3.7	3.1	3.2	3.5
Food/beverages	1990	60.8	7.2	5.6	5.8	5.0	11.7	7.6
	1997	81.1	6.4	4.2	7.1	4.6	11.2	6.5
	1998	85.3	6.8	3.6	5.9	3.3	8.8	4.9

Source: UNCTAD, 1993a and Erasmus University database.

[a]   Only industries that have at least five entries in the lists of the top 100 TNCs of 1990, 1997 and 1998.

structural phenomenon. Actually, only the motor vehicle companies still maintain a transnationality index below 50 per cent at the end of the 1990s whereas all the other five manufacturing industries moved their industry-specific transnationality indices substantially above 50 per cent. The motor vehicle industry will certainly catch up within the next five years, given the trend towards global consolidation in that industry.

B.   The largest 50 TNCs from developing economies

The 1998 list of the top 50 non-financial TNCs from developing economies, ranked by foreign assets, naturally features some of the best-known enterprises from Asia, Latin America and Africa (table III.9). As in 1997, Petróleos de Venezuela (Venezuela) tops the list, followed by Daewoo Corporation (Republic of Korea). Although these two corporations have also figured among the world's largest 100 TNCs since 1995, this year, Daewoo missed the $6.8 billion mark, which was the threshold for entry into the top 100.

The next four largest developing-economy TNCs have foreign assets ranging from $4.6 to $6.0 billion, a level that is not too far from the lowest-ranked TNCs in the top 100. In general, however, the biggest TNCs from developing economies are relatively small, judged by foreign assets. Their median foreign-asset holdings are

around 1.5 billion — far below the median foreign-asset level of the top 100, which was around 14 billion in 1998. Table III.10 illustrates some changes in the main variables of the top 50 TNCs group over 1997 — 1998.

The performance of the group as a whole changed somewhat in 1998. In 1998, movements in the main variables were mixed with the ratio of foreign-assets-to-total assets increasing significantly, while the ratio of foreign-sales-to-total-sales and foreign-employment-to-total-employment experienced another decline (figure III.5). In addition, foreign employment and especially foreign sales declined significantly. These movements seem to be linked to the financial crises in the major home countries of the top 50 TNCs. Nevertheless, the trend towards increasing transnationalization resumed in 1998, as indicated by the 2.4 per cent increase over 1997 in the average index of transnationality of the top 50 TNCs from developing countries (table III.10 and figure III.5). This result reflects the increase in the top 50 stock of foreign assets, from $103 to $109 billion in 1998, as compared to total assets which declined by 1 percentage point.

In terms of the degree of transnationality, the top five companies in the list of the largest TNCs from developing countries were from Asia (table III.11). As in the case of the world's 100 largest TNCs, those of the top 50 list headquartered in the smaller developing countries were among the most transnationalized in their group.

FIGURE III.4
The top 10 decreases in transnationality among the world's 100 largest TNCs, 1997-1998
(Percentages)

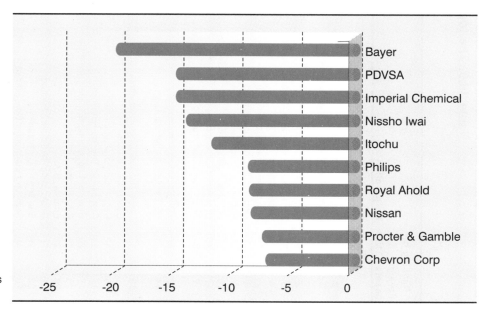

Source: UNCTAD/Erasmus University database.

/...

Table III.9. The top 50 TNCs from developing economies, ranked by foreign assets, 1998

(Millions of dollars, number of employees)

Ranking by Foreign assets	Ranking by TNI [a]	Corporation	Economy	Industry [b]	Assets Foreign	Assets Total	Sales Foreign	Sales Total	Employment Foreign	Employment Total	TNI [a] (Per cent)
1	34	Petróleos de Venezuela S.A.	Venezuela	Petroleum expl./ref./distr.	7 926	48 816	11 003	25 659	6 026	50 821	23.7
2	14	Daewoo Corporation	Republic of Korea	Trade	..	22 135	..	30 547	..	15 000	49.4
3	6	Jardine Matheson Holdings, Limited [d]	Hong Kong (China)/Bermuda	Diversified	5 954	9 565	7 921	11 230	..	160 000	67.6
4	12	Cemex, S.A.	Mexico	Construction	5 639	10 460	2 334	4 315	9 745	19 761	52.4
5	35	PETRONAS - Petroliam Nasional Berhad	Malaysia	Petroleum expl./ref./distr.	5 564	26 184	3 757	11 133	2 700	18 578	23.2
6	8	Sappi Limited	South Africa [c]	Pulp and Paper	4 574	6 475	3 246	4 308	10 725	23 640	63.8
7	19	Hutchison Whampoa, Limited	Hong Kong (China)	Diversified	..	13 389	2 191	6 639	20 845	39 860	39.4
8	9	First Pacific Company Limited	Hong Kong (China)	Other	4 086	7 646	2 527	2 894	15 063	30 673	63.3
9	39	Sunkyong Group	Republic of Korea	Diversified	3 851	36 944	12 029	38 274	2 400	29 000	16.7
10	49	Petroleo Brasileiro S.A. - Petrobras	Brazil	Petroleum expl./ref./distr.	3 700	33 180	1 300	15 520	417	42 137	6.8
11	45	New World Development Co., Limited	Hong Kong (China)	Construction	3 414	13 465	376	2 628	30	16 512	13.3
12	31	China State Construction Engineering Corporation	China	Construction	3 290	7 300	1 950	5 890	5 535	239 102	26.8
13	36	YPF Sociedad Anonima	Argentina	Petroleum expl./ref./distr.	3 278	13 146	880	5 500	1 754	9 486	19.8
14	21	LG Electronics, Incorporated	Republic of Korea	Electronics and electrical equipment	3 127	12 824	4 841	12 213	27 819	60 753	36.6
15	17	China National Chemicals Import & Export Corporation	China	Trade	3 000	4 950	7 920	13 800	510	8 415	41.4
16	43	Keppel Corporation Limited	Singapore	Diversified	2 598	17 321	376	2 127	1 700	11 900	15.7
17	24	Companhia Vale do Rio Doce	Brazil	Transportation	1 947	13 539	3 025	4 321	7 076	40 334	34.0
18	20	Hyundai Engineering & Construction Co.	Republic of Korea	Construction	1 842	7 094	..	3 815	7 639	22 787	37.6
19	15	Citic Pacific, Limited	Hong Kong (China)	Diversified	1 697	8 771	908	1 755	9 342	11 871	45.7
20	28	Enersis, S.A.	Chile	Electric utilities or services	1 695	16 117	306	3 406	16 015	14 336	28.2
21	3	Guangdong Investment Limited	Hong Kong (China)	Diversified	1 676	2 577	614	812	4 338	17 330	77.9
22	26	San Miguel Corporation	Philippines	Food and beverages	..	3 552	287	1 811	..	15 923	30.1
23	40	Samsung Electronics Co., Limited	Republic of Korea	Electronics and electrical equip.	1 610	17 213	..	16 640	..	42 154	16.3
24	44	Shougang Group	China	Steel and iron	1 574	6 990	830	4 270	1 548	212 027	14.4
25	16	Barlow Limited	South Africa [c]	Diversified	1 517	2 624	1 734	3 769	..	27 804	43.9
26	25	Singapore Airlines Limited	Singapore	Transportation	1 473	9 944	3 284	4 508	3 115	27 386	33.2
27	7	Fraser & Neave Limited	Singapore	Food and beverages	1 449	3 993	1 069	1 507	13 037	15 082	64.8
28	10	Acer Incorporated	Taiwan Province of China	Diversified	1 270	3 304	4 192	5 267	9 373	16 326	60.3
29	18	Sime Darby Berhad	Malaysia	Diversified	1 247	3 198	1 959	3 178	..	32 490	41.3
30	2	Orient Overseas (International) Limited	Hong Kong (China)	Transportation	1 145	1 801	1 820	1 833	3 314	3 935	84.3
31	37	Perez Companc, S.A.	Argentina	Petroleum expl./ref./distr.	1 139	4 822	219	1 309	836	4 450	19.8
32	27	Gener, S.A.	Chile	Electric utilities or services	..	3 477	185	599	217	910	29.1
33	29	Tatung, Co.	Taiwan Province of China	Electronics and electrical equipment	..	4 483	..	2 921	..	19 719	28.1

Table III.9. The top 50 TNCs from developing economies, ranked by foreign assets, 1998 (concluded)

(Millions of dollars, number of employees)

Ranking by Foreign assets	TNI [a]	Corporation	Economy	Industry [b]	Assets Foreign	Assets Total	Sales Foreign	Sales Total	Employment Foreign	Employment Total	TNI [a] (Per cent)
34	46	Companhia Cervejaria Brahma	Brazil	Food and beverages	..	3 862	..	2 639	..	10 708	12.5
35	23	Dong-Ah Construction Ind. Co., Limited	Republic of Korea	Construction	..	5 435	..	2 147	..	4 291	34.8
36	42	China Harbor Engineering Company	China	Construction	860	2 420	150	1 540	1 963	62 652	16.1
37	32	China National Metals and Minerals Imp and Exp Corp.	China	Trade	850	2 260	880	3 180	142	1 409	25.1
38	48	Reliance Industries Limited	India	Chemicals and pharmaceuticals	..	5 741	..	3 160	..	15 985	7.7
39	47	Compania de Petroleos de Chile (COPEC)	Chile	Diversified	842	6 459	142	2 896	485	7 841	8.0
40	11	Gruma, S.A. de C.V.	Mexico	Food and beverages	731	1 738	833	1 394	7 736	13 652	52.8
41	30	South African Breweries plc.	South Africa [c]	Food and beverages	..	3 812	2 423	5 877	11 222	49 431	27.3
42	13	NatSteel Group	Singapore	Steel and iron	685	1 296	208	885	8 598	11 695	50.0
43	22	Hong Kong and Shanghai Hotels, Limited	Hong Kong (China)	Tourism and hotel	642	2 346	58	274	3 606	6 249	35.4
44	50	CLP Holdings Limited	Hong Kong (China)	Electric utilities or services	630	7 115	180	3 101	..	4 420	4.9
45	33	Souza Cruz, S.A.	Brazil	Diversified	..	2 154	689	1 535	..	7 200	24.6
46	4	WBL Corporation Limited	Singapore	Electronics and electrical equip.	545	752	264	407	9 021	9 875	76.2
47	5	Asia Pacific Breweries Limited	Singapore	Food and beverages	544	857	618	839	3 449	3 955	74.8
48	38	Metalurgica Gerdau, S.A.	Brazil	Steel and iron	520	2 849	357	1 802	1 335	9 974	17.1
49	41	Sadia S.A. Industria e Comercio	Brazil	Food and beverages	..	1 738	..	2 204	..	22 331	16.2
50	1	Want Want Holdings, Limited	Singapore	Food and beverages	452	465	262	271	4 708	4 713	97.9

Source: UNCTAD, FDI/TNC database.

a   TNI is the abbreviation for "transnationality index", which is calculated as the average of three ratios: foreign assets to total assets, foreign sales to total sales and foreign employment to total employment.

b   Industry classification for companies follows the United States Standard Industrial Classification which is used by the United States Securities and Exchange Commission (SEC).

c   Within the context of this list, South Africa is treated as a developing country.

d   The company is incorporated in Bermuda and the group is managed from Hong Kong (China).

.. Data on foreign assets, foreign sales or foreign employment were not made available for the purpose of this study. In case of non availability, they are estimated using secondary sources of information or on the basis of the ratios of foreign to total assets, foreign to total sales and foreign to total employment.

Typically, companies enter or leave the list either because the level of their foreign assets changes relative to other companies on the list, or because they merge, or otherwise leave the marketplace. Mobility among the top 50 used to be considerable during the first years of the list (1993 to 1996). Since then it has stabilized. In 1998, five new entries and corresponding exits (tables III.12 and III.13) were registered, compared to seven in 1997 and twelve in 1996.

The most strongly represented industries (in terms of numbers) in the top 50 group in 1998 were : construction, food and beverages, diversified, and petroleum exploration, refining and distribution. These industry groups together accounted for about 60 per cent of the foreign assets, foreign sales and foreign employment of the top 50 group as a whole in 1998 (figure III.6). This has been a significant increase compared

Table III.10. Snapshot of the top 50 TNCs from developing economies, 1998

(Billions of dollars, percentage and number of employees)

Variable	1998	1997	Change [a] 1998 vs. 1997 (Percentage)
Assets			
Foreign	109	103	5.8
Total	449	453	-1.0
Sales			
Foreign	109	136	-19.7
Total	289	306	-5.7
Employment			
Foreign	400 475	483 129	-17.1
Total	1 546 883	1 737 756	-11.0
Average index of transnationality	36.6	34.2	2.4 [a]

Source: UNCTAD, FDI/TNC database.

[a]   Change is measured in percentage points.

FIGURE III.5
Snapshot of the top 50 TNCs from developing economies, 1993-1998

Source: UNCTAD, FDI/TNC database.

Note: The average transnationality index (TNI) of the top 50 TNCs is the average of the 50 individual company transnationality indices.

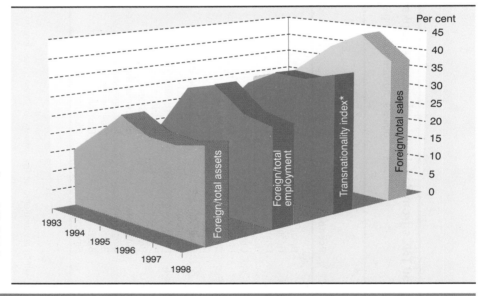

Table III.11. The top five TNCs from developing economies in terms of transnationality, 1998

Ranking by TNI [a]	Foreign assets	Corporation	Economy	Industry	TNI [a] (Per cent)
1	50	Want Want Holdings, Limited	Singapore	Food and beverages	97.9
2	30	Orient Overseas (International) Limited	Hong Kong (China)	Transportation	84.3
3	21	Guangdong Investment Limited	Hong Kong (China)	Diversified	77.9
4	46	WBL Corporation Limited	Singapore	Electronics and electrical equipment	76.2
5	47	Asia Pacific Breweries Limited	Singapore	Food and beverages	74.8

Source: UNCTAD, FDI/TNC database.

[a]   TNI is the abbreviation for "transnationality index", which is calculated as the average of three ratios: foreign assets to total assets, foreign sales to total sales and foreign employment to total employment.

Table III.12.   **Newcomers to the top 50 TNCs from developing economies, 1998**

Number	Ranked by Foreign assets	TNI[a]	Corporation	Economy	Industry	TNI[a] (Per cent)
1	47	5	Asia Pacific Breweries Limited	Singapore	Food and beverages	74.8
2	44	50	CLP Holdings Limited	Hong Kong (China)	Electric utilities or services	4.9
3	48	38	Metalurgica Gerdau, S.A.	Brazil	Steel and iron	17.1
4	42	13	NatSteel Group	Singapore	Steel and iron	50.0
5	46	4	WBL Corporation Limited	Singapore	Electronics and electrical equipment	76.2

Source: UNCTAD, FDI/TNC database.

[a] TNI is the abbreviation for "transnationality index", which is calculated as the average of three ratios: foreign assets to total assets, foreign sales to total sales and foreign employment to total employment.

to just five years earlier, when the same industry groups accounted for only about 40 per cent of the foreign assets, foreign sales and foreign employment of the top 50 TNCs (figure III.6).

This increase of 50 per cent in these industries' combined share in the top 50's foreign assets, foreign sales and foreign employment in a span of only five years suggests that they are at the forefront of the transnationalization process. Indeed, if one looks at the average transnationality index of these four industry groups (figure III.7), this impression is confirmed. The transnationality index increased for all four over the five-year period 1993-1998 and very substantially so for two of the four: for food and beverages, it nearly tripled, going from 16 to 47 per cent, while for the petroleum group, it jumped by a multiple of six, from 3 to 19 per cent (table III.14).

In 1998, the most transnationalized industries among the top 50 TNCs were transport, pulp and paper, diversified, and food and beverages, with transnationality indices ranging from 40 to almost 64 per cent (table III.14). These results contrast with the findings for the top 100 (table III.6), where food and beverage as well as chemicals and pharmaceuticals had significantly higher transnationality indices than they did for the top 50 group. The difference between the top 50 and the top 100 in their transnationality indices for the petroleum exploration, refining and distribution group is also remarkable: 19 in the former as against more than 50 in the latter.

The top 50 are in general much less transnationalized than the top 100, reflecting the fact that firms from developing economies began investing abroad much later than their developed-country counterparts. Their

Table III.13.   **Departures from the top 50 TNCs from developing economies, 1998**

Number	Ranked in 1997 by Foreign assets	TNI[a]	Corporation	Economy	Industry	TNI[a] in 1997 (Per cent)
1	40	22	China National Foreign Trade Transportation Corp.	China	Transportation	31
2	35	36	Empresas CMPC, S.A.	Chile	Pulp and paper	18
3	47	47	SABIC - Saudi Basic Industries Corp.	Saudi Arabia	Chemicals and pharmaceuticals	12
4	49	44	Vitro S.A. de C.V.	Mexico	Other	15
5	50	27	Wing On International Holdings Limited	Hong Kong (China)	Diversified	28

Source: UNCTAD, FDI/TNC database.

[a] TNI is the abbreviation for "transnationality index", which is calculated as the average of three ratios: foreign assets to total assets, foreign sales to total sales and foreign employment to total employment.   ·

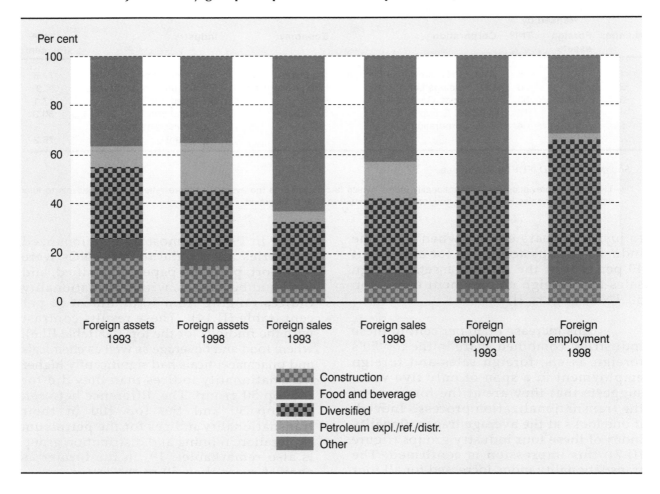

FIGURE III.6
Major industry groups as per cent of the top 50 totals, 1993 and 1998

Source: UNCTAD, FDI/TNC database.

FIGURE III.7

Major industry groups of the top 50 TNCs and their average transnationality index, 1993-1998

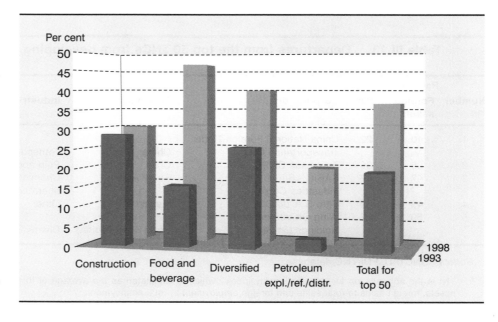

Source: UNCTAD, FDI/TNC database.

Table III.14. **Industry composition of the top 50 TNCs from developing economies, 1993, 1997 and 1998**

Industry	Number of entries			Average TNI [a] per industry (Percentage)		
	1993	1997	1998	1993	1997	1998
Diversified	12	16	11	25.6	35.8	40.1
Food and beverages	7	7	8	15.6	40.8	47.0
Construction	4	6	6	28.8	31.5	30.2
Petroleum expl./ref./distr.	3	5	5	3.1	21.8	18.6
Electronics and electrical equipment	7	4	4	28.1	37.2	39.3
Electric Utilities or Services	1	2	3	2.0	32.2	20.8
Steel and iron	5	..	3	11.6	..	27.2
Trade	..	..	3	..	..	38.6
Transportation	1	4	3	23.2	46.6	50.5
Chemicals and pharmaceuticals	1	2	1	17.0	9.9	7.7
Other	4	1	1	23.6	15.3	63.3
Pulp and paper	2	2	1	26.0	39.8	63.8
Tourism and hotel	3	1	1	33.1	32.7	35.4
Average/total [b]	50	50	50	19.8	34.2	36.6

Source: UNCTAD, FDI/TNC database.

Note: This list does not include countries from Central and Eastern Europe.

[a]   TNI is the abbreviation for "transnationality index", which is calculated as the average of three ratios:foreign assets to total assets, foreign sales to total sales and foreign employment to total employment.
[b]   Numbers may not add up exactly due to rounding.

Table III.15. **Country composition of the top 50 TNCs from developing economies, by transnationality index and foreign assets, 1993, 1997 and 1998**

Economy	Average TNI [a] per country (Percentage)			Share in total foreign assets of the top 50 (Percentage)		
	1993	1997	1998	1993	1997	1998
South, East and South-East Asia	**21.8**	**42.5**	**35.8**	**70.6**	**66.1**	**65.7**
China	..	36.5	24.8	..	10.8	8.8
Hong Kong (China)	36.5	61.4	56.6	22.0	24.9	22.0
India	6.4	17.1	7.7	0.4	0.9	0.8
Korea, Republic of	20.2	41.0	31.9	24.8	19.6	16.7
Malaysia	20.0	34.0	32.3	4.7	2.3	6.3
Philippines	6.9	33.8	30.1	1.4	1.0	1.5
Singapore	43.0	63.2	58.9	5.3	4.5	7.2
Taiwan Province of China	19.6	53.1	44.2	12.3	2.2	2.4
Latin America	**14.0**	**28.3**	**27.3**	**29.9**	**28.5**	**28.2**
Argentina	..	17.2	19.8	..	3.7	4.1
Brazil	17.4	17.5	18.5	12.0	6.0	7.6
Chile	12.1	22.5	21.8	1.0	3.9	3.4
Mexico	12.5	39.7	52.6	16.9	6.3	5.9
Venezuela	..	44.5	23.7	..	8.6	7.3
Africa	**..**	**31.8**	**45.0**	**..**	**5.4**	**6.3**
Average/total [b]	19.8	34.2	36.6	100.0	100.0	100.0

Source: UNCTAD, FDI/TNC database.

Note: This list does not include countries from Central and Eastern Europe.

[a]   TNI is the abbreviation for "transnationality index", which is calculated as the average of three ratios:foreign assets to total assets, foreign sales to total sales and foreign employment to total employment.
[b]   Numbers may not add up exactly due to rounding.

average index value stood at 37 per cent in 1998 as against 54 per cent for the top 100. The smaller economies, Singapore and Hong Kong (China) (table III.15), exhibit the greatest transnationality, as might be expected given the size of their domestic markets.

With respect to national origins, the list continues to be dominated by TNCs from South, East and South-East Asia, accounting for 66 per cent of the top 50 total foreign assets (table III.15), with Hong Kong (China), the Republic of Korea, China and Singapore, in that order, being the most

important home countries (figure III.8). They were followed by firms from Latin America. Africa's share in the foreign assets of the top 50 TNCs remains very low.

C. The largest 25 TNCs from Central Europe

The list presented in this report (table III.16) is a revision of the largest Central European TNCs list included in *WIR99*. It is based on 1998 data, confirming, and in some cases revising, the data provided last year by the firms responding to the UNCTAD survey of the largest TNCs in Central Europe.[4]

FIGURE III.8

Foreign assets of the biggest investors from developing economies, 1997, 1998

(a) Asia

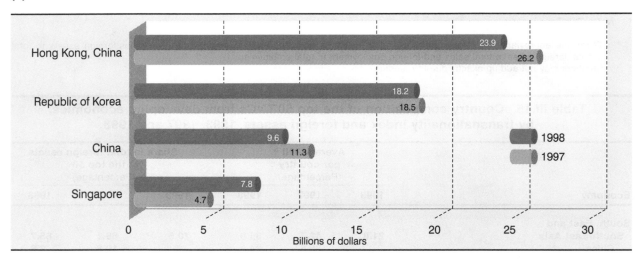

(b) Latin America

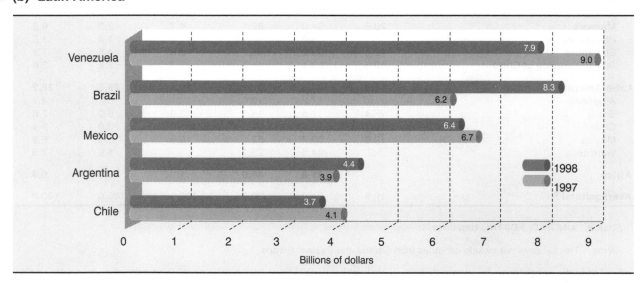

Source: UNCTAD, FDI/TNC database.

Table III.16. The top 25 non-financial TNCs based in Central Europe,[a] ranked by foreign assets, 1998

(Millions of dollars and number of employees)

Ranking by Foreign assets	Ranking by TNI [b]	Corporation	Country	Industry [c]	Assets Foreign	Assets Total	Sales Foreign	Sales Total	Employment Foreign	Employment Total	TNI [b] (Per cent)
1	3	Latvian Shipping Co.	Latvia	Transportation	493.0	504.0	214.0	214.0	1 631.0	2 275.0	89.8
2	23	Hrvatska Elektroprivreda d.d.	Croatia	Utilities	363.0	2 924.0	0.2	898.0	..	15 728.0	4.1
3	11	Podravka Group	Croatia	Food & beverages/ pharmaceuticals	285.9	477.1	119.4	390.2	501.0	6 898.0	32.6
4	8	Gorenje Group	Slovenia	Domestic appliances	256.4	645.9	642.2	1 143.3	607.0	6 717.0	35.0
5	5	Motokov a.s.	Czech Republic	Trade	163.6	262.5	260.2	349.1	576.0	1 000.0	64.8
6	1	Atlantska Plovidba d.d.	Croatia	Transportation	152.0	167.0	47.0[d]	47.0	...	528.0	95.5
7	6	Pliva Group	Croatia	Pharmaceuticals	142.1	855.1	334.3	463.0	1 616.0	6 680.0	37.7
8	19	Skoda Group Plzen	Czech Republic	Diversified	139.1	973.4	150.7	1 244.5	1 073.0	19 830.0	10.6
9	2	Adria Airways d.d.	Slovenia	Transportation	129.4	143.7	97.7	97.7	0.0	585.0	95.0
10	24	MOL Hungarian Oil & Gas Plc	Hungary	Petroleum & natural gas	128.3	2 881.6	203.4	2 958.1	628.0	20 140.0	5.1
11	7	Krka d.d.	Slovenia	Pharmaceuticals	118.4	490.4	226.9	300.3	375.0	3 253.0	37.1
12	13	VSZ a.s. Kosice	Slovakia	Iron & steel	110.0	1 445.0	815.0[d]	1 528.9	58.0	26 191.0	20.4
13	20	Petrol d.d.	Slovenia	Petroleum & natural gas	70.6	584.2	112.4[d]	706.0	10.0	3 349.0	9.4
14	14	Slovnaft a.s.	Slovakia	Petroleum & natural gas	65.5	1 496.0	518.6	984.5	124.0	5 734.0	19.7
15	18	Matador j.s.c.	Slovakia	Rubber & plastics	51.9	304.9	34.0	203.4	5.0	3 878.0	11.3
16	15	Zalakerámia Rt.	Hungary	Clay product & refractory	35.0	125.0	9.0	35.0	...	4 500.0	17.9
17	17	KGHM Polska Miedz S.A.	Poland	Mining & quarrying	34.0	1 536.0	401.0	1 236.0	25.0	33 000.0	11.6
18	9	Malev Hungarian Airlines Ltd.	Hungary	Transportation	32.9	149.1	238.0	316.9	49.0	3 215.0	32.9
19	16	TVK Ltd.	Hungary	Chemicals	31.6	542.9	122.6	401.3	181.0	6 099.0	13.1
20	4	Graphisoft	Hungary	Software consultancy	28.0	50.0	25.0	25.0	188.0	188.0	85.3
21	10	Croatia Airlines d.d.	Croatia	Transportation	27.6	211.4	97.4[d]	121.2	188.0	846.0	32.7
22	25	Elektrim S.A.	Poland	Trade and diversified	21.0	1 228.0	42.0	874.0	40.0	26 475.0	2.2
23	21	Pilsner Urquell a.s.	Czech Republic	Food & beverages	20.0	251.0	16.0	253.0	62.0	2 918.0	8.8
24	22	Moldova Steel Works	Republic of Moldova	Iron & steel	19.9	335.9	1.0	15.6	356.0	4 562.0	4.2
25	12	Budimex Capital Group	Poland	Construction	17.8	153.9	55.8[d]	316.4	644.0	1 095.0	29.3

Source: UNCTAD survey of top TNCs in Central Europe.

a   Based on survey responses.
b   TNI is the abbreviation for "transnationality index", which is calculated as the average of three ratios: foreign assets to total assets, foreign sales to total sales and foreign employment to total employment.
c   Industry classification for companies follows the United States Standard Industrial Classification as used by the United States Securities and Exchange Commission (SEC).
d   Including export sales by parent firm.
...   Data on foreign assets, foreign sales and foreign employment were not made available for the purpose of this study. In case of non-availability, they are estimated using secondary sources of information or on the basis of the ratios of foreign to total assets, foreign to total sales and foreign to total employment.

While reflecting some improvement in reporting in various Central European countries, the list confirms the findings of last year's report as regards the basic characteristics of the largest TNCs from Central Europe. Latvian Shipping Company (transport) continues to be the biggest TNC in terms of foreign assets. The second place is now held by a newly reporting company, Hrvatska Elektroprivreda (Croatia; utilities), while previously second Podravka (Croatia; food and beverages and pharmaceuticals) appears third on the list. In terms of degree of transnationality, Atlantska Plovidba (Croatia) and Adria Airways (Slovenia) are the leaders, as indicated last year, while revised data put Latvian Shipping in third place. It is to be noted that all these firms are in the transport industry.

The diversity of country composition is also confirmed (table III.17). Nine countries were represented in the 1997 list and eight in the 1998 list. Firms from Estonia, Lithuania, TFYR Macedonia, Romania and Ukraine were too small to qualify for the top 25 list. Their largest TNCs are shown separately in table III.18.

As was the case last year, the number of Russian firms participating in the survey is not representative enough to include firms from the Russian Federation. Data on the Russian firms that did report are presented separately (table III.18). Had they been included, two of them (Lukoil Co. and Primorsk Shipping) would have appeared as the largest and fifth largest TNCs of the region. The degree of transnationality of Lukoil is below the average transnationality index of the top 25 Central European TNCs, while that of Primorsk Shipping, a transport firm, is high.

The data in this year's survey confirm most of the trends highlighted last year: the fast growth in foreign assets, and negative growth in total assets, total sales, and both foreign and total employment. The revised data also show a slight decline in foreign sales, as compared to an increase reported last year. This change is due to the fact that newly reporting firms typically had decreasing foreign sales and other companies revised their 1998 figures downwards. The large decline in total employment is due to the fact that, in 1998, the Romanian oil

firm, Petrom S.A., with a total employment of 90,000, departed from the list. There is in fact a great diversity among firms from the region in employment, with the number of employees ranging from 188 (Graphisoft) to 33,000 (KGMM Polska Miedz). The data confirm, as noted last year, that foreign employment is the weak point of Central European TNCs. All firms, except Latvian Shipping Co. and Budimex Capital Group in the list, have a ratio of foreign to total employment of less than 0.24 which is clearly below the average ratio of 0.35 of the top 50 TNCs from developing countries.

Revised data also confirm the relatively low value of the average transnationality index, 32 per cent (table III.19), and of its median, 20 per cent, which suggests that the transnationalization of these firms is still fairly limited.

As regards industry composition, transport is the most strongly represented industry, followed by mining including petroleum and gas, and chemicals and pharmaceuticals (table III.20).

Preliminary data for 1999 are available on 13 of the top 25 TNCs on the 1998 list. They seem to confirm the trends of the previous years. The foreign assets of these firms continued to increase in 1999, and their total and foreign sales have also increased, reversing previous trends.

Table III.17. **Country composition of the top 25 TNCs based in Central Europe, 1997 and 1998**
(Number of entries)

Country	1997	1998
Croatia	5	5
Hungary	5	5
Slovenia	4	4
Poland	3	3
Slovakia	3	3
Czech Republic	2	3
Latvia	1	1
Republic of Moldova	1	1
Romania	1	-
Total	25	25

Source: UNCTAD survey of top 25 TNCs in Central Europe.

Table III.18. The top non-financial TNCs of the Russian Federation, Estonia, Lithuania, Macedonia (TFYR), Romania and the Ukraine, ranked by foreign assets, 1998

(Millions of dollars and number of employees)

Year	Potential ranking by foreign assets	Corporation	Country	Industry [b]	Assets		Sales		Employment		TNI [a]
					Foreign	Total	Foreign	Total	Foreign	Total	(Per cent)
1998	1 [c]	Lukoil Oil Co.	Russian Federation	Petroleum & natural gas	2 266.0	6 609.0	2 590.0	8 393.0	5 000	102 000	23.3
1998	5 [c]	Primorsk Shipping Co.	Russian Federation	Transportation	267.1	454.3	69.9	103.7	1 247	2 807	56.9
1998	35 [c]	Alrosa Co. Ltd.	Russian Federation	Diamond mining & processing	9.7	1 501.2	83.1	1 731.0	177	36 400	2.0
1998	28 [c]	Petrom SA National Oil Co.	Romania	Petroleum & natural gas	17.0	3 790.0	128.0	2 700.0	140	88 350	1.8
1998	29 [c]	Lifosa AB	Lithuania	Chemicals	13.2	55.2	93.1	100.0	0	1 339	58.5
1998	34 [c]	Norma AS	Estonia	Automotive	10.0	34.0	1.0	36.0	21	1 368	11.2
1998	43 [c]	Alkaloid AD	The Former Yugoslav Republic of Macedonia	Pharmaceuticals	1.0	78.3	24.7	64.7	58	1 720	14.3
1998	45 [c]	Azovstal Iron & Steel Works	Ukraine	Iron & steel	0.6	839.1	..	775.4	..	24 850	..

Source: UNCTAD survey of top TNCs in Central and Eastern Europe.

[a] TNI is the abbreviation for "transnationality index", which is calculated as the average of three ratios: foreign assets to total assets, foreign sales to total sales and foreign employment to total employment.

[b] Industry classification for companies follows the United States Standard Industrial Classification as used by the United States Securities and Exchange Commission (SEC).

[c] Including Russian firms.

... Data on foreign sales and foreign employment were not made available for the purpose of this study. In case of non-availability, they are estimated using secondary sources of information or on the basis of the ratios of foreign to total assets, foreign to total sales and foreign to total employment.

The top 25 firms are actively pursuing both greenfield investments and foreign acquisitions as a mode of international expansion, as illustrated by the fast increase in their foreign assets. Between 1 January 1997 and 30 June 2000, 7 of the top 25 firms undertook foreign acquisitions. The average size of these deals is still fairly small. Until June 2000, the acquisition by MOL Hungarian Oil & Gas Plc. of Slovnaft, a company from Slovakia, for $262 million was the biggest publicly announced deal (box III.1).

Table III.19. Snapshot of the top 25 TNCs based in Central Europe, 1997 and 1998

(Millions of dollars, number of employees, percentage)

Variable	1997	1998	Change of 1998 versus 1997
Assets			
Foreign	2 669	2 937	10.0
Total	21 054	18 738	-11.0
Sales			
Foreign	4 907	4 784	-2.5
Total	18 041	15 122	-16.2
Employment			
Foreign	9 814	8 754	-10.8
Total	302 157	205 684	-31.9
Average transnationality index	32.3	32.3	-0.1

Source: UNCTAD survey of top 25 TNCs in Central Europe.

Table III.20. Industry composition of the top 25 TNCs based in Central Europe, 1997 and 1998

(Number of entries)

Industry	1997	1998
Transportation	5	5
Mining and petroleum	5	4
Chemicals and pharmaceuticals [a]	4	4
Other or diversified manufacturing [a]	4	4
Metallurgy (iron and steel)	2	2
Trade [a]	2	2
Food and beverages [a]	1	2
Business services	1	1
Construction	1	1
Machinery and equipment	1	1
Utility	1	1
Total [b]	25	25

Source: UNCTAD survey of top 25 TNCs in Central Europe.

[a]   Firms can be listed under more than one industry.
[b]   The total does not add up to 25 because of some limited double listing.

Box III.1. The acquisition of Slovnaft by MOL Hungarian Oil & Gas Plc.

On 31 March 2000, MOL Hungarian Oil & Gas Plc. acquired a 36 per cent stake in Slovnaft, a Slovakian oil company, for $262 million (MOL, 2000a). This intra-regional deal illustrates the fact that, after a decade of transition, some advanced Central European firms have developed sufficient managerial skills and financial strength to carry out major cross-border acquisitions. Prior to the Slovnaft acquisition, MOL had changed both its management style and its strategic directions. It decided to stop high-cost exploration, and concentrate on refining and marketing (MOL, 1999). In 1999, MOL was in merger talks with the Croatian oil firm INA. But that deal did not materialize (*The Economist*, 2000).

The two companies together are expected to consolidate their market lead in Hungary (with an estimated 36 per cent retail market share in oil products) and Slovakia (38 per cent), and strengthen their position in Romania and the Czech Republic. In qualitative terms, MOL and Slovnaft together would control some of the most complex and modern refining assets in the region (MOL, 2000b). They would also match the size of major competitors (box table).

The MOL-Slovnaft deal may also signal a change in national attitudes towards the downstream oil industry, which had been seen as too sensitive to qualify for foreign strategic investments (*The Economist*, 2000). Still, the MOL deal is not yet a majority acquisition. Two years after the initial acquisition, however, MOL would have the option to buy a majority stake in Slovnaft.

It seems that, in the longer term, MOL intends to pursue a strategy of consolidation in the downstream oil industry of Central

/...

Box III.1. The acquisition of Slovnaft by MOL Hungarian Oil & Gas Plc. (concluded)

Europe (*The Economist*, 2000). At the press conference on the Slovnaft deal, this acquisition was presented as *"the first in a series* *of initiatives that position MOL as a driving force in the future regional consolidation"* (Central Europe Online, 2000).

Box table III.1. Financial performance of selected oil companies, 1999-2000

(Millions of dollars)

Company	Country	Market capitalization 24 April 2000	Sales 1999	Pre-tax profit 1999	Price/earnings ratio
Lukoil[a]	Russian Federation	9 920	10 452	260	38.2
PKN[b]	Poland	2 154	3 579	235	9.2
ÖMV[b]	Austria	2 077[c]	5 515	206	10.1
MOL[b]	Hungary	1 849	2 973	325	5.7
Unipetrol[b]	Czech Republic	303[c]	1 564	68	4.5
Slovnaft[b]	Slovakia	277[c]	1 031	32[d]	8.7

Source: *Financial Times* 500, May 2000.

[a]   Exploration and extraction company.
[b]   Refining and marketing (downstream company).
[c]   3 April 2000.
[d]   Without foreign-exchange losses of $ 65 million.

Sources: UNCTAD based on Central Europe Online (2000); "Oil in Eastern Europe: MOL's milestone", *The Economist,* 8 April 2000; Expert (2000); MOL (1999); MOL (2000a); MOL (2000b).

Notes

[1]   Financial firms are excluded because of the different economic functions of assets of financial and non-financial firms and the unavailability of relevant data for the former.

[2]   These estimates are based on the estimates of the 1998 sales, assets and employment of foreign affiliates of TNCs, as given in table I.2 of *WIR 99*. These ratios, especially those relating to sales and assets, should be treated with caution, as the data on the foreign assets and sales of the top 100 TNCs, mostly obtained through a questionnaire filled out by firms, may not necessarily correspond exactly to the definition of foreign assets and sales used in table I.2 of *WIR 99*.

[3]   The average transnationality index of the world's top 100 TNCs is the average of the 100 individual transnationality indices.

[4]   These data were collected through a questionnaire survey organized by UNCTAD that took place in February-May 2000 and covered over 100 firms from 15 Central European countries.

PART TWO

CROSS-BORDER M&As AND DEVELOPMENT

Cross-border M&As are playing an increasingly important role in the growth of international production. Not only do they dominate FDI flows in developed countries, they have also begun to take hold as a mode of entry into developing countries and economies in transition. The reasons for, and the full extent of, the world-wide growth of cross-border M&As have not yet been fully explored, nor have the implications of this shift in the preference of TNCs regarding the choice of entry mode for expanding internationally been considered in a systematic fashion.

Against this background, Part Two of *WIR2000* is devoted to an examination of the trends, determinants and performance of cross-border M&As. It then proceeds to examine, most importantly, the impact of FDI through cross-border M&As on development, more specifically as compared with greenfield investment as a mode of entry. In turn, it addresses the question of how to formulate policies in order to maximize the positive effects and minimize the possible negative effects of cross-border M&As.

The concept of cross-border M&As underlying the discussion is introduced in chapter IV by relating the phenomenon to data on FDI and explaining the various ways of classifying M&As. While FDI flows and cross-border M&As have followed parallel paths in the past decade, a straightforward comparison between the two sets of data is almost impossible to make. Factors influencing the link between cross-border M&As and FDI statistics include the method of financing and the timing of a transaction. Chapter IV describes trends in the volume, direction and characteristics of cross-border M&As worldwide, with particular focus on differences between regions, sectors and types of M&As. Whereas cross-border M&As are still primarily concentrated in developed countries, a steady increase of such deals in other regions can also be observed. In some developing countries and many economies in transition, this increase is closely related to the privatization of state-owned enterprises.

The dramatic growth of cross-border M&As raises an obvious set of questions. How do they affect the performance of firms? What drives them? And what can one expect in the future? The initial section of chapter V focuses on a controversial area: how M&As affect corporate performance. It is widely held that most deals produce relatively poor results. How is success measured? Are there differences between the performance of acquiring and acquired firms and between domestic and cross-border M&As? The chapter then asks why firms engage in cross-border M&As. While M&As can be undertaken for many different reasons, the role of speed and the quest for strategic assets are pointed out as being especially important. To explain fully why M&As have become more common as a means by which firms expand their activities internationally, both economic and non-economic reasons need to be considered. These general motivations behind M&As constitute a useful complement to the received FDI literature when analysing cross-border M&As, and "mega mergers" in particular. The current expansion of cross-border M&As, which is seen as part of an upward trend, deserves special attention. It reflects the interaction between the basic driving forces that motivate firms to engage in cross-border M&As and the important changes that have taken place in the economic environment in which firms operate (especially the liberalization of trade, finance and investment, regional integration, deregulation and privatization), technological change and increased global competitive pressure. The concluding section of chapter V explores an intriguing historical parallel between the M&A wave at the end of the nineteenth century in the United States and what one observes on a global scale now.

As cross-border M&As are becoming more common as a mode of entry for TNCs in developing countries, questions arise as to the role of M&As, as opposed to greenfield FDI, in economic development. Indeed, cross-border M&As, particularly those involving large TNCs from developed countries and major reorganizations of economic activities, figure among the most striking features of the globalization process. As with globalization in general, the impact on economic development of M&As differs among countries and industries, and raises concerns. There is a commonly held perception that FDI entry through greenfield investment is beneficial for host economies, while FDI entry through M&As is not. The current M&A wave – especially where it has sometimes taken the form of hostile acquisitions or "fire sales" – has heightened concerns on the part of host governments. Worries include issues such as the denationalization of domestic firms, downsizing of acquired enterprises, employment reduction, loss of technological assets, crowding out of domestic firms and increased market concentration. Chapter VI examines the impact of FDI through M&As on the economic development of host countries as compared with that of greenfield FDI. The effects are analyzed in terms of the impacts on key areas related to development (UNCTAD, 1999a) – external financial resources and investment, technology, employment and skills, export competitiveness and trade, and market structure and competition – as well as broader impacts, including those on economic restructuring, national economic sovereignty and social, political and cultural aspects of development. The main policy implications that can be drawn on the basis of the analysis are considered, and policy options for countries are outlined. As the empirical evidence on the linkages between cross-border M&As and development, and how they may differ compared with other modes of FDI entry, is still very limited, the analysis is largely conceptual and should be seen as a first attempt at assessing the role of cross-border M&As in development.

Finally, the discussion in Part Two is subject to certain limitations. First, unless otherwise stated, throughout the text cross-border M&As refer only to FDI through M&As. Thus, portfolio investment, defined for measurement purposes as an acquisition of less than 10 per cent of the voting shares of an enterprise, is not dealt with in the discussion, although the distinction between portfolio investment and FDI is not always obvious. Second, when examining the impact of cross-border M&As, greenfield FDI is the main alternative with which a comparison is made. Non-internalized modes of international production, such as strategic alliances and various non-equity arrangements, as well as trade and purely domestic alternatives, are not considered explicitly. In practice, the latter are all obviously alternatives, to varying extents, to FDI through cross-border M&As, as well as greenfield FDI, but the control situation examined here is the narrow one of whether the mode of entry makes a difference. It is important to emphasize, however, that, where the greenfield option is lacking, the impact of cross-border M&As (including, especially, privatization to foreign firms) must be evaluated in the light of the non-FDI options open to potential host countries. In any event, it needs to be recalled (UNCTAD, 1999a) that FDI itself, whatever its mode of entry, serves to supplement and complement domestic resources and efforts, which are key for the development process.

Chapter IV | Trends in Cross-border M&As

A. Definitions and classifications

A firm can undertake FDI in a host country in either of two ways: greenfield investment in a new facility, or acquiring or merging with an existing local firm.[1] The local firm may be privately or state owned: privatizations involving foreign investors count as cross-border M&As, which entail a change in the control of the merged or acquired firm. In a cross-border merger, the assets and operations of two firms belonging to two different countries are combined to establish a new legal entity. In a cross-border acquisition, the control of assets and operations is transferred from a local to a foreign company, the former becoming an affiliate of the latter. (For a schematic representation of different types of cross-border M&As, see figure IV.1.)

To the extent that both greenfield investment and cross-border M&As place host country assets under the governance of TNCs — and, hence, contribute to the growth of an international production system — there is no reason to distinguish between them. Both involve management control of a resident entity in one country by an enterprise resident in another. To the extent, however, that the assets placed under TNC control are newly created in the case of greenfield FDI, and existing assets are transferred from one owner to another in the case of cross-border M&As, then there is reason to consider them separately. This is the subject of chapter VI.

The normal definitions of FDI apply to entry through M&As as well. The country of the acquirer or purchaser is the "home country" and the country of the target or acquired firm is the "host country". In mergers, the headquarters of the new firm can be in both countries (e.g. the Netherlands and the United Kingdom, in the case of Royal Dutch/Shell) or in one (e.g. the United Kingdom, in the case of BP-Amoco; Germany, in the case of Daimler-Chrysler).[2] Acquisitions can be minority (foreign interest of 10 to 49 per cent of a firm's voting shares), majority (foreign interest of 50-99 per cent), or full or outright acquisitions (foreign interest of 100 per cent).[3] Acquisitions involving less than 10 per cent constitute portfolio investment and, therefore, are not considered in the present analysis (box IV.1). Consequently, unless otherwise specified, cross-border M&As in Part Two of *WIR2000* refer to FDI through M&As only.

The data on M&As show that acquisitions dominate the scene. Less than 3 per cent of cross-border M&As by number are mergers (table IV.1). In reality, even when mergers are supposedly between relatively equal partners, most are in fact acquisitions with one company controlling the other. The number of "real" mergers is so low that, for practical purposes, "M&As" basically mean "acquisitions". Full or outright (100 per cent) acquisitions accounted for more than half of all cross-border M&As in 1999. In developing countries, about one-third of acquisitions by foreign firms were minority (10-49 per cent) acquisitions, compared to less than one-fifth

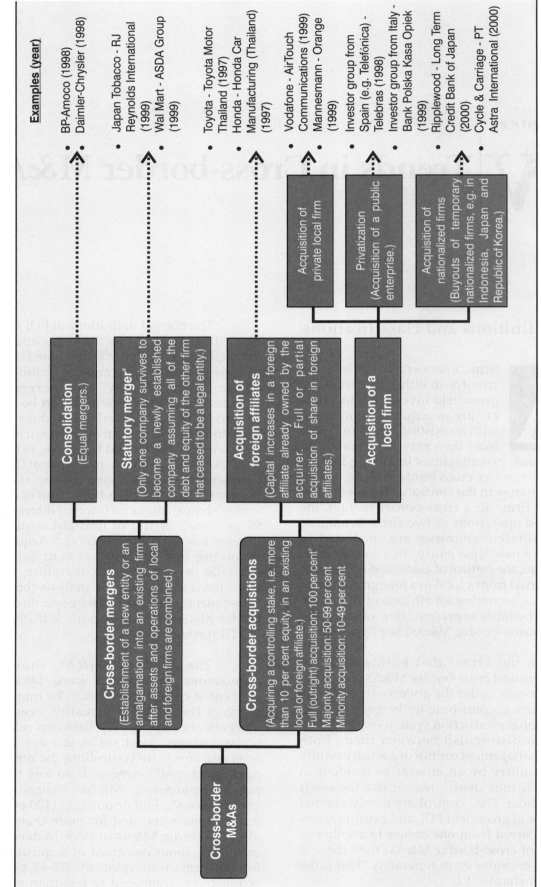

FIGURE IV.1
The structure of cross-border M&As

Examples (year)

- BP-Amoco (1998)
- Daimler-Chrysler (1998)

- Japan Tobacco - RJ Reynolds International (1999)
- Wal Mart - ASDA Group (1999)

- Toyota - Toyota Motor Thailand (1997)
- Honda - Honda Car Manufacturing (Thailand) (1997)

- Vodafone - AirTouch Communications (1999)
- Mannesmann - Orange (1999)

- Investor group from Spain (e.g. Telefónica) - Telebras (1998)
- Investor group from Italy - Bank Polska Kasa Opiek (1999)
- Ripplewood - Long Term Credit Bank of Japan (2000)
- Cycle & Carriage - PT Astra International (2000)

Consolidation (Equal mergers.)

Statutory merger[a] (Only one company survives to become a newly established company assuming all of the debt and equity of the other firm that ceased to be a legal entity.)

Acquisition of foreign affiliates (Capital increases in a foreign affiliate already owned by the acquirer. Full or partial acquisition of share in foreign affiliates.)

Acquisition of a local firm

Acquisition of private local firm

Privatization (Acquisition of a public enterprise.)

Acquisition of nationalized firms (Buyouts of temporary nationalized firms, e.g. in Indonesia, Japan and Republic of Korea.)

Cross-border mergers (Establishment of a new entity or an amalgamation into an existing firm after assets and operations of local and foreign firms are combined.)

Cross-border acquisitions (Acquiring a controlling stake, i.e. more than 10 per cent equity, in an existing local or foreign affiliate. Full (outright) acquisition: 100 per cent[a] Majority acquisition: 50-99 per cent Minority acquisition: 10-49 per cent)

Cross-border M&As

Source: UNCTAD.

a   The key difference between statutory mergers and full acquisitions lies in the fact that a new legal entity is established in the former case, but not in the latter. These two forms, however, may otherwise be treated as identical.

in developed countries. Differences in the equity share of foreign firms largely reflect the nature of government regulations as well as corporate strategies.

Cross-border M&As can be functionally classified as:

- *Horizontal* M&As (between competing firms in the same industry). They have grown rapidly recently because of the global restructuring of many industries in response to technological change and liberalization (see chapter V). By consolidating their resources, the merging firms aim to achieve synergies (the value of their combined assets exceeds the sum of their assets taken separately) and often greater market power. Typical industries in which such M&As occur are pharmaceuticals, automobiles, petroleum and, increasingly, several services industries.

- *Vertical* M&As (between firms in client-supplier or buyer-seller relationships). Typically they seek to reduce uncertainty and transaction costs as regards forward and backward linkages in the production chain, and to benefit from economies of scope. M&As between parts and components makers and their clients (such as final electronics or automobile manufacturers) are good examples.

- *Conglomerate* M&As (between companies

Table IV.1. **Cross-border M&As, by percentage ownership, 1987-1999**

(Percentage of the total number of deals)

Year	Total M&As[a]	Cross-border mergers	Cross-border acquisitions			
			Total	Full (100%)	More than 50%	10-49%
1987	100	4.2	94.1	70.1	8.7	15.3
1988	100	2.9	95.6	72.4	9.7	13.6
1989	100	3.2	95.6	69.1	10.9	15.6
1990	100	2.1	96.5	67.4	11.8	17.3
1991	100	0.8	98.6	64.1	14.5	19.9
1992	100	0.6	98.6	62.5	16.9	19.1
1993	100	0.5	99.1	61.2	17.2	20.6
1994	100	0.5	98.6	60.4	16.7	21.5
1995	100	1.2	98.0	59.6	17.9	20.5
1996	100	1.1	98.4	61.2	17.2	20.1
1997	100	1.7	97.5	64.8	16.3	16.3
1998	100	1.8	97.5	68.3	14.7	14.5
1999	100	2.3	96.9	65.3	15.4	16.2

Source: UNCTAD, cross-border M&A database, based on data from Thomson Financial Securities Data Company.

a Includes the deals in which acquirers acquire the whole remaining interest of their foreign affiliates.

in unrelated activities). They seek to diversify risk and deepen economies of scope.

The balance between these types of M&As has been changing over time. The importance of horizontal M&As has risen somewhat over the years (figure IV.2 and annex table A.IV.I): in 1999, 70 per cent of the value of cross-border M&As were horizontal compared to 59 per cent ten years ago. Vertical M&As have been on the rise since the mid-1990s, but staying well below 10 per cent. In the late-1980s M&A boom, conglomerate M&As were very popular, but they have diminished in importance as firms have tended increasingly to focus on their core business to cope with intensifying international competition. They declined from a high of 42 per cent in 1991 to 27 per cent in 1999 (figure IV.2).

The distinction among these three categories, however, is not always clear-cut. [4] Recent developments related to the Internet may make it even more difficult, and could significantly affect formal corporate links (box IV.2).

Box IV.1. **Portfolio investment**

Portfolio investment is usually associated with purely financial investment. Such investment flows are not dealt with in *WIR2000*. However, the distinction between portfolio and direct investments is not always obvious. While FDI involves a long-term relationship reflecting an investor's lasting interest in a foreign company, portfolio acquisitions can also involve management control, e.g. if there are accompanying non-equity arrangements, especially where non-institutional investors are involved. Cross-border portfolio acquisitions (i.e. deals that result in an acquisition of less than 10 per cent of a firm's voting shares) were $105 billion, accounting for about 13 per cent of the total cross-border M&As in 1999.

Source: UNCTAD.

Cross-border M&As may also be classified differently:

- M&As can be driven primarily by short-term financial gains, rather than strategic or economic motivations such as the search for efficiency. Typical examples include deals where buyout firms and venture capital companies acquire other firms. It is not possible to determine what percentage of M&As consists of transactions driven primarily by the quest

for short-term financial gains, as available data do not usually allow a determination of motives. If all transactions by finance companies (including commercial banks) involving target firms whose main activity is in non-financial industries are regarded as investment aiming at short-term financial gains, then available data suggest that deals motivated by the quest for such gains are losing in importance in cross-border M&As (figure IV.3 and annex table A.IV.2). [5]

FIGURE IV.2

World cross-border M&As, by type (horizontal, vertical, conglomerate),[a] 1987-1999

(Percentage of the total value)

Source: UNCTAD, cross-border M&A database (based on data from Thomson Financial Securities Data Company).

[a] For the definition of each type of M&As, see annex table A.IV.1.

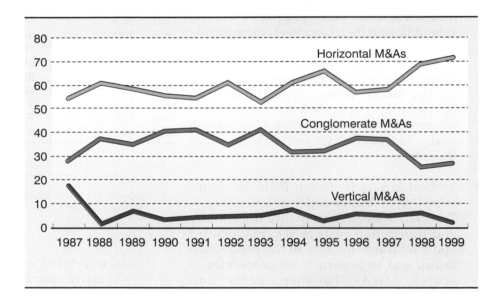

Box IV. 2. The impact of the Internet on formal corporate links

In the past year, a number of deals have been concluded between companies, often competing in the same industry, to create internet-based business-to-business exchanges. In such arrangements, companies come together on a functional basis to build internet-based market places without having to establish formal corporate links. Such exchanges enable companies to achieve various objectives, beginning with cost savings, without having those activities housed in the same corporate shell. This applies particularly to internet-based procurement systems, through which, by streamlining the procurement process, companies aim at reducing procurement expenditures.

Examples of internet business-to-business exchanges include the tie-up between Hitachi, IBM, LG Electronics, Matsushita

Electronics, Nortel Networks, Seagate Technology Selection and Toshiba, known as e2open.com, and the tie-up still under discussion between DaimlerChrysler, Ford and General Motors, known as Covisint. Covisint, for instance, would offer to its members a comprehensive online market place for the procurement of automotive parts and supplies and other services (e.g. catalogue purchasing and Internet bid events). The respective purchasing departments of the member firms would remain separate, using the exchange as a tool to conduct their independent procurement.

The development of such exchanges raises a number of questions, especially as regards their impact on competition. The combined purchasing power of their members also can significantly affect the bargaining position of suppliers.

Source: UNCTAD, based on "The urge to merge takes on a different form", *Financial Times*, 30 June 2000; "Purchasing: technical hits stalls "Big Three" trading site", *Financial Times*, 14 June 2000 and, Covisint webpage, www.covisint.com.

• Friendly M&As can be distinguished from those that are hostile. In friendly M&As, the board of a target firm agrees to the transaction. (This does not exclude the possibility that, initially, the management of the target firm was against the transaction.) Hostile M&As are undertaken against the wishes of the target firms, i.e. the boards of the latter reject takeover/merger offers. Regardless of whether hostile M&As involve bidding by several prospective acquirers, the price premium tends to be higher than in friendly transactions.[6] The overwhelming number of M&As, both domestic and international, are friendly. In 1999, according to data from Thomson Financial Securities Data Company, there were only 30 hostile takeovers out of 17,000 M&As between domestic firms. Hostile cross-border M&As that were completed accounted for less than 5 per cent of the total value and less than 0.2 per cent of the total number of M&As during the 1990s (figure IV.4 and annex table A.IV.3). In fact, according to the same source, 1999 saw only 10 hostile cross-border cases out of a total of some 6,200, all in developed countries (annex table A.IV.3).[7] But some, such as the takeover of Mannesmann by Vodafone AirTouch that succeeded in 2000, involve high-profile battles. Over the period 1987-1999, out of the 104 hostile cross-border M&As, 100 targeted developed country firms, four targeted developing country firms,[8] while none targeted firms in Central and Eastern Europe. The number of hostile acquisitions in the late 1980s was somewhat higher, despite the significantly smaller numbers of M&As, than in the late 1990s. Target companies have developed various

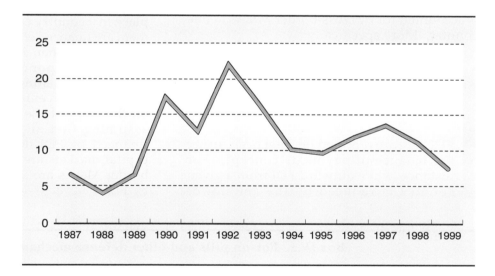

FIGURE IV.3

Share of M&As motivated by short-term financial gains[a] **in cross-border M&As, 1987-1999**

(Percentage of the total value)

Source: UNCTAD, cross-border M&A database (based on data from Thomson Financial Securities Data Company).

[a]   For the definition of financial motivated cross-border M&As, see annex table A.IV.2.

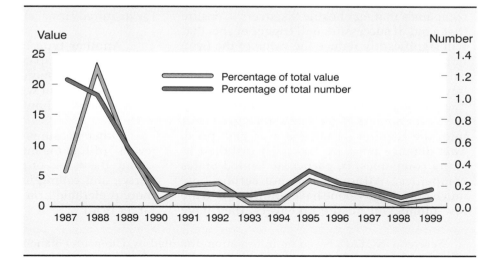

FIGURE IV.4

Share of hostile take-overs in cross-border M&As, 1987-1999

(Percentage of total)

Source: UNCTAD, cross-border M&A database (based on data from Thomson Financial Securities Data Company); and annex table A.IV.3.

defence mechanisms, including "poison pills", selling off "crown jewels" and calling in "white knights" to avoid becoming a target (box IV.3).

It is difficult to estimate precisely what share of FDI flows is accounted for by cross-border M&As because one cannot compare directly the values of cross-border M&As with FDI flows registered in the balance of payment (box IV.4). If data on the sources of financing of cross-border M&As were separately available, it would be possible to distinguish them from greenfield FDI flows. But they are not. There are also several problems in comparing cross-border M&A data reported by various sources. Similarly, only a few countries provide data on FDI that distinguish greenfield investments from M&As. As a result, it is not possible to get a straightforward and accurate comparison between data series on cross-border M&As and FDI flows and to assess precisely what share of FDI flows in one year is accounted for by cross-border M&As in one country. More specifically:

• The value of cross-border M&As includes funds raised in local and international financial markets; by definition, FDI data do not;

• FDI data are reported on a net basis, using the balance-of-payments concept. For instance, while outward FDI from a given country is reduced by the amount of

disinvestment undertaken by firms from that country abroad, data on cross-border M&A purchases report only the total value of purchases abroad (i.e. they do not subtract the amounts received from the sales of foreign affiliates);

• Payments for cross-border M&As are not necessarily made in a single year, but can be phased over several years.

As a result, calculating the value of cross-border M&As as a percentage of FDI inflows in a given year may be quite misleading. Take an extreme case. Foreign M&As in a given country can amount to $10 billion, while FDI inflows are zero; this can happen if the M&As were financed locally — including an existing foreign affiliate using funds other than reinvested earnings — or from international capital markets. The other extreme case, which may well happen, is when the only direct investment activities that take place in a country comprises M&As *and* all of them are financed entirely and during the same year by FDI; then $10 billion in cross-border M&As corresponds to $10 billion of FDI inflows. Calculating the value of cross-border M&As as a percentage of FDI flows proceeds on the basis of the second extreme case, i.e. assuming that all cross-border M&As are financed by FDI flows. In countries where capital markets are poorly developed, cross-border M&As are more likely to be financed by FDI.

Box IV.3. Poison pills and other defense mechanisms

Companies adopt various measures to avoid takeovers. Poison pills are used by companies that fear hostile takeovers to ensure that a bid, if successful, will trigger events that will significantly reduce the value of the firm. For instance, *flip-in* poison pills allow all existing holders of target company shares to buy additional shares at a bargain price. *Flip-over* poison pills allow holders of common stock to buy (or holders of preferred stock to convert into) the acquirer's shares at a bargain price. This defence measure has been installed in many companies, in particular United States companies. Although it is not certain how much poison pills alone have contributed to the low number of hostile takeovers, they have

forced raiders to negotiate with the board of target firms to agree to a fair market price for the acquired firms' shares.

Another type of defense mechanism is when a target company warns an acquirer that, in the event of a successful takeover, the entire management team will resign at once, leaving the company without experienced leadership.

Other measures include selling off "crown jewels" (dilute the intention of the acquirer by selling the assets of the target firm to a third party); and calling in "white knights" (find a more preferable firm and ask it to acquire the target firm).

Source: UNCTAD, based on information provided by Thomson Financial Securities Data Company.

Box IV.4. Cross-border M&A data: how to make sense of them

It is conceptually easy to distinguish cross-border M&As from greenfield FDI. However, this distinction is nearly impossible to apply to available statistics. Although M&A data are compiled and reported by a number of providers (including investment banks and consulting firms), there is no common definition of M&As, and the nature and the type of data collected are different. For instance, M&A statistics are compiled either on an announcement basis (recorded when the deals are announced) or a completion basis (recorded when the deals are completed or the definite agreement between the parties of a deal is reached). Different forms of M&As may be included by some sources and not others (e.g. management buyouts, acquisition of properties, and acquisition of convertible stocks that do not have voting control). The treatment of additional acquisitions (further increases in stock holdings by firms that already own more than 50 per cent or increases in stakes in joint ventures in which one party owns a certain share) may differ. Despite all these differences, however, the various sources show rather similar trends.

The available data on cross-border M&As include portfolio investments. It is therefore necessary to extract transactions that correspond to the FDI definition (10 per cent or more foreign control) from the reported M&A data. The data on cross-border M&As used in *WIR2000* are from the UNCTAD database on cross-border M&As, compiled from information provided by Thomson Financial Securities Data Company. These data conform to the FDI definition as far as the equity share is concerned. However, they do include purchases financed via both domestic and international capital markets. Although it is possible to distinguish types of financing (syndicated loans, corporate bonds, venture capital etc.) for M&As, it is not possible to trace the origin or country sources of the funds used. Therefore, the data here almost certainly include funds not categorized as FDI.

FDI is a balance-of-payments concept, i.e. FDI flows are recorded on a net basis (capital account credits less debits between direct investors and foreign affiliates) in a particular year. On the other hand, M&A data are expressed as the total transaction amounts of

particular deals, not as differences between gross acquisitions and divestment abroad by firms from a particular country. Transaction amounts recorded in M&A statistics are for the time of the announcement or closure of the deals, and the values are not necessarily for a single year.

The United States provides data on M&As approximating the FDI definition. The data from the United States Department of Commerce are for investment outlays by foreign direct investors to acquire or establish new United States businesses regardless of whether the invested funds are raised in the United States or abroad. (The data cover United States business enterprises that have total assets of over $1 million or that own at least 200 acres of United States land.) A United States enterprise is categorized as "acquired" if a foreign parent firm or its United States affiliate obtains a voting equity interest in an existing business enterprise, or purchases a business segment or an operating unit of an existing United States enterprise that it organizes as a new separate legal entity or merges into the affiliate's own operations. (The data do not include a foreign parent firm's acquisition of additional equity in its United States affiliates or its acquisition of an existing United States affiliate from another foreign investor. They do not include expansions of existing United States affiliates. Sell-offs or other disinvestment are not netted against the new investment. Reinvested earnings are not included.) A United States enterprise is categorized as "established" (in this context "greenfield") if a foreign parent firm or its existing United States affiliate creates a new legal entity that is organized and begins operating as a new United States business enterprise. There are no similar data reported by the United States Department of Commerce for United States outward investments established through M&As or greenfield investments.

A few other countries provide some information on cross-border M&As. For instance, Japan's Ministry of International Trade and Industry compiles statistics on the establishment form of Japanese affiliates abroad. However, the reported data are only for the number of affiliates creating a new legal entity, and there is no further information

/...

B. Trends and characteristics

1. Global trends

M&As completed worldwide, between domestic firms or between domestic and foreign firms, have grown over the past two decades (1980-1999) at an average annual rate of 42 per cent, to reach $2.3 trillion in 1999. [9] More than 24,000 such deals took place. There have been two M&A waves in this period: during the late 1980s (1988-1990) and since 1995 (figure I.4). Both periods experienced relatively high economic growth and widespread industrial restructuring.

Although a number of "mega deals" (M&As worth $1 billion or more) have taken place in the latter half of the 1990s, recent M&As are not exceptionally large by historical standards. For example, the creation of US Steel at the beginning of the twentieth century would be worth around $600 billion at today's prices (Smith and Sylla, 1993); this compares to some $200 billion paid by Vodafone AirTouch for the

acquisition of Mannesmann in 2000. Overall, the ratio of M&As relative to the country's GDP was some 10 per cent in the United States at the beginning of the twentieth century. [10] By comparison, the value of all M&As (domestic and cross-border) in the world in relation to world GDP in the past two decades rose from 0.3 per cent (1980) to 2 per cent (1990) and to 8 per cent (1999) (figure IV.5). Increases have been particularly dramatic in the last few years.

Within this total, the share of cross-border M&As has remained almost constant, at about one-quarter in terms of both the value and number of deals throughout the 1990s, although the years 1990 and 1999 saw peaks of above 30 per cent (figure IV.6). [11] In value terms, cross-border M&As rose from $75 billion in 1987 to $720 billion in 1999. [12] This period covers the two booms (during the latter half of the 1980s and in the years since the mid-1990s) and an interim period of FDI recession. The two waves were marked by a large number of mega deals. These accounted for about 1.5 per cent of the number of cross-border M&As in both periods, but for 40 per cent of their

---

Box IV.4 (concluded)

available on such affiliates (Japan, MITI, 1999 and its earlier issues).

The above-mentioned statistical problems make the direct comparison of the magnitude of cross-border M&As with FDI very difficult. To illustrate, if data for

privatizations only are taken, FDI inflows to finance privatization-linked acquisitions in Brazil, for instance, amounted to $6 and $8.8 billion in 1998 and 1999, while the total value of privatization involving foreign TNCs amounted to, respectively, $20 and $3 billion in those years (box table IV.4.1).

Box table IV.4.1. Comparison of privatization-related FDI flows and privatization-related cross-border acquisitions in Brazil, 1996-1999

(Billions of dollars)

Year	Privatization-related FDI inflows [a]	Privatization-related cross-border acquisitions
1996	2.6	2.9
1997	5.2	6.0
1998	6.1	19.9
1999	8.8	2.8

Source: UNCTAD, FDI/TNC database and cross-border M&A database.

[a] On a balance-of-payments basis.

Source: UNCTAD.

value in the former and 60 per cent in the latter (table IV.2). In 1999, the value of cross-border M&As increased again by 35 per cent (table IV.3); the number of deals exceeded 6,000. Nearly one-fifth of these cross-border M&As involved acquiring and target companies located in the same country, but with different ultimate parent countries. This reflects the fact that foreign affiliates also engage themselves in M&As, largely to purchase other domestic firms (box IV.5). The value of cross-border M&As in 2000 is expected to grow even faster, as several large deals have been announced or completed (e.g. the Vodafone AirTouch acquisition of Mannesmann for some $200 billion; the France Telecom acquisition of Orange for $46 billion) in the first half of that year. Their completed value between January and mid-June 2000 ($508 billion) was more than

80 per cent higher than that during the corresponding period in the previous year. [13] Some 90 per cent of cross-border M&As (by value of sales and purchases) were in developed countries. There were 109 mega deals in 1999 (table IV.2; annex table A.IV.4).[14] Most were among firms from developed countries (table IV.4).

As with FDI flows, outward M&As for developed countries are larger than inward M&As, while the opposite is true for the developing countries and those of Central and Eastern Europe. However, the imbalance between purchases (outflows) and sales (inflows) is smaller for cross-border M&As than for total FDI for both developed and developing countries. This is because the bulk of cross-border M&As takes place among developed

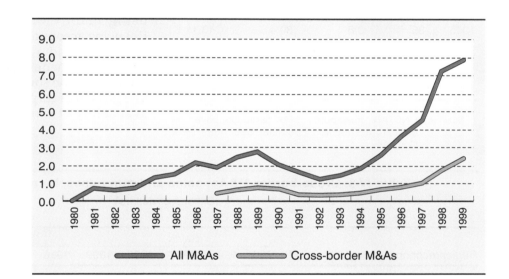

FIGURE IV.5
Value of world M&As as a percentage of GDP, 1980-1999

Source: UNCTAD, cross-border M&A database (based on data from Thomson Financial Securities Data Company).

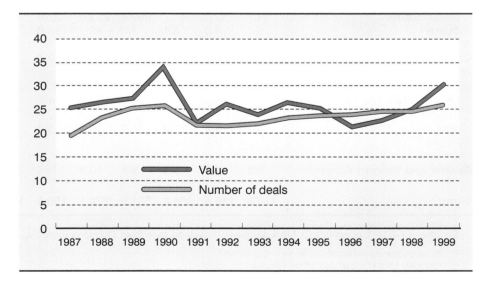

FIGURE IV.6
Cross-border M&As as a percentage of all M&As in the world, 1987-1999

Source: UNCTAD, cross-border M&A database (based on data from Thomson Financial Securities Data Company).

countries. In developing countries, most purchases are intra-regional.

If the value of cross-border M&As is put in relation to world GDP, the ratio quadrupled from 0.5 per cent in 1987 to over

Table IV.2. Cross-border M&As with values of over $1 billion, 1987-1999

Year	Number of deals	Percentage of total	Value (billion dollars)	Percentage of total
1987	14	1.6	30.0	40.3
1988	22	1.5	49.6	42.9
1989	26	1.2	59.5	42.4
1990	33	1.3	60.9	40.4
1991	7	0.2	20.4	25.2
1992	10	0.4	21.3	26.8
1993	14	0.5	23.5	28.3
1994	24	0.7	50.9	40.1
1995	36	0.8	80.4	43.1
1996	43	0.9	94.0	41.4
1997	64	1.3	129.2	42.4
1998	86	1.5	329.7	62.0
1999	109	1.7	500.8	69.6

Source: UNCTAD, cross-border M&A database, based on data from Thomson Financial Securities Data Company.

2 per cent in 1999 (figure IV.7). Not surprisingly, developed countries have been consistently above this world average as both host and home regions. Developing countries reached the world average in 1993 and 1997 as host region, while, as home region, they gradually increased their ratio until 1997; in both cases, the financial crisis explains this performance. Central and Eastern Europe experienced peaks as a host region in 1995 fairly soon after the region's transition to a market economy began, as well as in 1997-1998; in both cases, privatizations played the key role.

M&A activity has been facilitated by new ways of raising capital. While bank loans are still the most important source for finance for M&As, direct financing by issuing common stocks and corporate debt have gained in importance because of the improved environment for corporate fund-raising. Deals using mainly one of these two types of financing accounted for about one-third of the total value and a half of the total number of the cross-border M&A deals for which information on sources of funds is available.[15] The growth of corporate funds and the broader availability of venture capital have paved the

Table IV.3. Cross-border M&As: sales and purchases, by region, 1990-1999

(Billions of dollars)

Region/economy	Sales					Purchases				
	1990	1995	1997	1998	1999	1990	1995	1997	1998	1999
Developed countries	**134.2**	**164.6**	**234.7**	**445.1**	**644.6**	**143.2**	**173.7**	**272.0**	**511.4**	**677.3**
of which :										
European Union	62.1	75.1	114.6	187.9	344.5	86.5	81.4	142.1	284.4	497.7
United States	54.7	53.2	81.7	209.5	233.0	27.6	57.3	80.9	137.4	112.4
Japan	0.1	0.5	3.1	4.0	15.9	14.0	3.9	2.7	1.3	9.8
Developing countries	**16.1**	**15.9**	**64.3**	**80.7**	**63.4**	**7.0**	**12.8**	**32.4**	**19.2**	**41.2**
of which :										
Africa	0.5	0.2	1.7	0.7	0.6	-	0.1	-	0.2	0.4
Latin America and the Caribbean	11.5	8.6	41.1	63.9	37.2	1.6	4.0	10.7	12.6	24.9
Europe	-	-	-	-	0.3	-	-	-	-	-
Asia	4.1	6.9	21.3	16.1	25.3	5.4	8.8	21.7	6.4	15.9
Pacific	-	0.1	0.3	-	0.1	-	-	-	-	-
Central and Eastern Europe[a]	**0.3**	**6.0**	**5.8**	**5.1**	**10.3**	**-**	**0.1**	**0.3**	**1.0**	**1.6**
World[b]	**150.6**	**186.6**	**304.8**	**531.6**	**720.1**	**150.6**	**186.6**	**304.8**	**531.6**	**720.1**

Source: UNCTAD, cross-border M&A database, based on data from Thomson Financial Securities Data Company.

a   Includes the countries of the former Yugoslavia.
b   Includes amounts that cannot be allocated by region.

way for new firms and established small and medium-sized enterprises (SMEs) to engage in M&As. The number of small-scale cross-border M&As with a transaction value less than $100 million has steadily increased, accounting for one-third of the total number of deals in 1999. The share of the number of deals with $1 million or less rose from 1.5 per cent in 1990 to about 3 per cent in 1999.

Growth of cross-border M&As has been further facilitated by the availability of the exchange-of-stock options, which has become a popular method of financing M&A deals, particularly big ones (box IV.6). Deals consisting of stock swaps (and no cash) have increased over the years (annex table A.IV.5); 26 of the 109 mega deals in 1999 used this option.

2. Regional trends

As discussed in section A of this chapter, although it is not possible to assess precisely the share of FDI flows that are accounted for by cross-border M&As, it is interesting to compare the trends of these two flows over

---

Box IV.5. Domestic or cross-border M&As?

As the transnationalization of firms gathers pace, the form and type of FDI have become more complex. In the case of cross-border M&As, nationality is a complex issue. The ultimate parent firm or the ultimate host country may be different from the immediate parent firm or the immediate host country. In FDI statistics, data are usually compiled on the basis of the immediate host and immediate home countries involved. The data on cross-border M&As that the *WIR00* uses include the following combinations of immediate and ultimate countries:

1.   A domestic firm in country X acquires (or merges with) a domestic firm in country Y.
2.   A domestic firm in country X acquires (or merges with) a foreign affiliate in country X.
3.   A domestic firm in country X acquires (or merges with) a foreign firm in country Y.
4.   A foreign affiliate in country X acquires (or merges with) a domestic firm in country Y.
5.   A foreign affiliate in country X acquires (or merges with) another foreign affiliate in country X.
6.   A foreign affiliate in country X acquires (or merges with) a domestic firm in country X.
7.   A foreign affiliate in country X acquires (or merges with) a foreign affiliate in country Y.

The M&As that fall under the deal categories 2, 5 and 6 above show the same nationality for immediate home and immediate host countries. The growth of such deals is particularly noteworthy in Latin America and the Caribbean (box table IV.5.1), implying that foreign affiliates established in that region are actively involved in M&As in the region as acquirers and target firms. These deals look like domestic M&As, but in reality the ultimate beneficiaries of such deals are from different countries. The impacts of these seemingly domestic M&As go beyond the country in which the firms involved operate.

Box table IV.5.1. Number of cross-border M&As whose immediate host and immediate home countries are the same

Year	World	Developed countries			Developing countries			Central and Eastern Europe
		Total	European Union	United States	Total	Latin America and the Caribbean	South, East and South-East Asia	
1987	187	178	43	108	9	2	6	-
1990	497	473	178	222	24	7	16	-
1995	817	723	352	227	83	30	50	11
1999	1044	852	430	262	147	82	58	45
Memorandum: (value in $billion)								
1990	20.7	20.1	6.2	10.8	0.7	0.4	0.3	-
1999	64.9	57.2	37.4	10.9	6.8	2.6	4.2	0.9

Source: UNCTAD, cross-border M&A database, based on data from Thomson Financial Securities Data Company.

Source: UNCTAD.

Table IV.4. The top 50 cross-border M&A deals completed during 1987-1999

	Year	Value ($bill.)	Acquiring company	Home economy	Industry of the acquiring company	Acquired company	Host economy	Industry of the acquired company
1	1999	60.3	Vodafone Group PLC	United Kingdom	Telecommunications	AirTouch Communications	United States	Telecommunications
2	1998	48.2	British Petroleum Co PLC(BP}	United Kingdom	Oil and Gas; Petroleum Refining	Amoco Corp	United States	Oil and Gas; Petroleum Refining
3	1998	40.5	Daimler-Benz AG	Germany	Transportation Equipment	Chrysler Corp	United States	Transportation Equipment
4	1999	34.6	Zeneca Group PLC	United Kingdom	Drugs	Astra AB	Sweden	Drugs
5	1999	32.6	Mannesmann AG	Germany	Metal and Metal Products	Orange PLC	United Kingdom	Telecommunications
6	1999	21.9	Rhone-Poulenc SA	France	Chemicals and Allied Products	Hoechst AG	Germany	Chemicals and Allied Products
7	1998	18.4	Zurich Versicherungs GmbH	Switzerland	Insurance	BAT Industries PLC-Financial	United Kingdom	Insurance
8	1999	13.6	Deutsche Telekom AG	Germany	Telecommunications	One 2 One	United Kingdom	Telecommunications
9	1999	13.2	Repsol SA	Spain	Oil and Gas; Petroleum Refining	YPF SA	Argentina	Oil and Gas; Petroleum Refining
10	1999	12.6	Scottish Power PLC	United Kingdom	Electric, Gas, and Water Distribution	PacifiCorp	United States	Electric, Gas, and Water Distribution
11	1998	10.9	Texas Utilities Co	United States	Electric, Gas, and Water Distribution	Energy Group PLC	United Kingdom	Electric, Gas, and Water Distribution
12	1999	10.8	Wal-Mart Stores (UK) Ltd	United Kingdom	Investment & Commodity Firms,Dealers,Exchanges	ASDA Group PLC	United Kingdom	Retail Trade-Food Stores
13	1999	10.8	Aegon NV	Netherlands	Insurance	TransAmerica Corp	United States	Insurance
14	1998	10.2	Universal Studios Inc	United States	Motion Picture Production and Distribution	PolyGram NV(Philips Electrn)	Netherlands	Electronic and Electrical Equipment
15	1998	10.2	Roche Holding AG	Switzerland	Drugs	Corange Ltd	Bermuda	Drugs
16	1999	10.1	Global Crossing Ltd	Bermuda	Telecommunications	Frontier Corp	United States	Telecommunications
17	1999	9.8	ABB AG	Switzerland	Electronic and Electrical Equipment	ABB AB	Sweden	Electronic and Electrical Equipment
18	1998	9.3	Nortel Networks Corp	Canada	Communications Equipment	Bay Networks Inc	United States	Computer and Office Equipment
19	1999	9.1	Deutsche Bank AG	Germany	Commercial Banks, Bank Holding Companies	Bankers Trust New York Corp	United States	Commercial Banks, Bank Holding Companies
20	1999	8.4	Mannesmann AG	Germany	Metal and Metal Products	Ing C Olivetti-Telecom Int	Italy	Telecommunications
21	1999	8.2	Suez Lyonnaise des Eaux SA	France	Electric, Gas, and Water Distribution	Tractebel SA	Belgium	Electric, Gas, and Water Distribution
22	1997	8.0	ICI PLC	United Kingdom	Chemicals and Allied Products	Quest International,3 Others	Netherlands	Chemicals and Allied Products
23	1989	7.9	Beecham Group PLC	United Kingdom	Drugs	SmithKline Beecham Corp	United States	Drugs
24	1987	7.9	BP America(British Petroleum)	United States	Oil and Gas; Petroleum Refining	Standard Oil Co(British Petro)	United States	Mining
25	1999	7.8	Japan Tobacco Inc	Japan	Tobacco Products	RJ Reynolds International	Netherlands	Tobacco Products

/...

Table IV.4. (concluded)

	Year	Value ($bill.)	Acquiring company	Home economy	Industry of the acquiring company	Acquired company	Host economy	Industry of the acquired company
26	1999	7.7	HSBC Holdings PLC	United Kingdom	Commercial Banks, Bank Holding Companies	Republic New York Corp,NY	United States	Commercial Banks, Bank Holding Companies
27	1999	7.5	British American Tobacco PLC	United Kingdom	Tobacco Products	Rothmans Intl BV(Richemont)	Netherlands	Tobacco Products
28	1991	7.4	Matsushita Electric Industrial	Japan	Electronic and Electrical Equipment	MCA Inc	United States	Motion Picture Production and Distribution
29	1995	7.3	Hoechst AG	Germany	Chemicals and Allied Products	Marion Merrell Dow Inc	United States	Drugs
30	1995	7.0	Upjohn Co	United States	Drugs	Pharmacia AB	Sweden	Drugs
31	1999	6.8	TRW Inc	United States	Transportation Equipment	LucasVarity PLC	United Kingdom	Business Services
32	1999	6.6	General Electric Capital Corp	United States	Credit Institutions	Japan Leasing Corp	Japan	Credit Institutions
33	1988	6.5	Campeau Corp	Canada	Real Estate; Mortgage Bankers and Brokers	Federated Department Stores	United States	Retail Trade-General Merchandise and Apparel
34	1999	6.5	Ford Motor Co	United States	Transportation Equipment	Volvo Passenger Cars	Sweden	Transportation Equipment
35	1998	6.4	Teleglobe Inc	Canada	Telecommunications	Excel Communications Inc	United States	Telecommunications
36	1996	6.3	Metro Vermoegensverwaltung	Malaysia	Construction Firms	ASKO Deutsche Kaufhaus, Deutsch	Germany	Retail Trade-General Merchandise and Apparel
37	1999	6.3	Vivendi SA	France	Electric, Gas, and Water Distribution	United States Filter Corp	United States	Machinery
38	1999	6.2	New Holland(New Holland Hldg)	Netherlands	Machinery	Case Corp	United States	Machinery
39	1999	6.1	Dexia Belgium	Belgium	Investment & Commodity Firms,Dealers,Exchanges	Dexia France	France	Investment & Commodity Firms,Dealers,Exchanges
40	1998	6.1	Astra AB	Sweden	Drugs	Astra Merck Inc(Merck & Co)	United States	Wholesale Trade-Nondurable Goods
41	1989	5.8	Grand Metropolitan PLC	United Kingdom	Food and Kindred Products	Pillsbury Co	United States	Retail Trade-Eating and Drinking Places
42	1995	5.7	Seagram Co Ltd	Canada	Food and Kindred Products	MCA Inc(Matsushita Electric)	United States	Motion Picture Production and Distribution
43	1999	5.7	Sun Life and Provincial	United Kingdom	Insurance	Guardian Royal Exchange PLC	United Kingdom	Insurance
44	1999	5.4	Renault SA	France	Transportation Equipment	Nissan Motor Co	Japan	Transportation Equipment
45	1994	5.3	Roche Holding AG	Switzerland	Drugs	Syntex Corp	United States	Drugs
46	1999	5.3	Total SA	France	Oil and Gas; Petroleum Refining	Petrofina SA	Belgium	Oil and Gas; Petroleum Refining
47	1997	5.3	Tyco International Ltd	United States	Miscellaneous Manufacturing	ADT Ltd	Bermuda	Business Services
48	1988	5.2	BATUS Inc(BAT Industries PLC)	United States	Tobacco Products	Farmers Group Inc	United States	Insurance
49	1998	5.1	Aeropuertos Argentina 2000	United States	Investment & Commodity Firms,Dealers,Exchanges	Argentina-Airports(33)	Argentina	Air Transportation and Shipping
50	1998	5.1	Allianz AG	Germany	Insurance	AGF	France	Business Services

Source: UNCTAD, cross-border M&A database, based on data from Thomson Financial Securities Data Company.

FIGURE IV.7
Cross-border M&As as a percentage of GDP, by group of economies, 1987-1999
(Percentage)

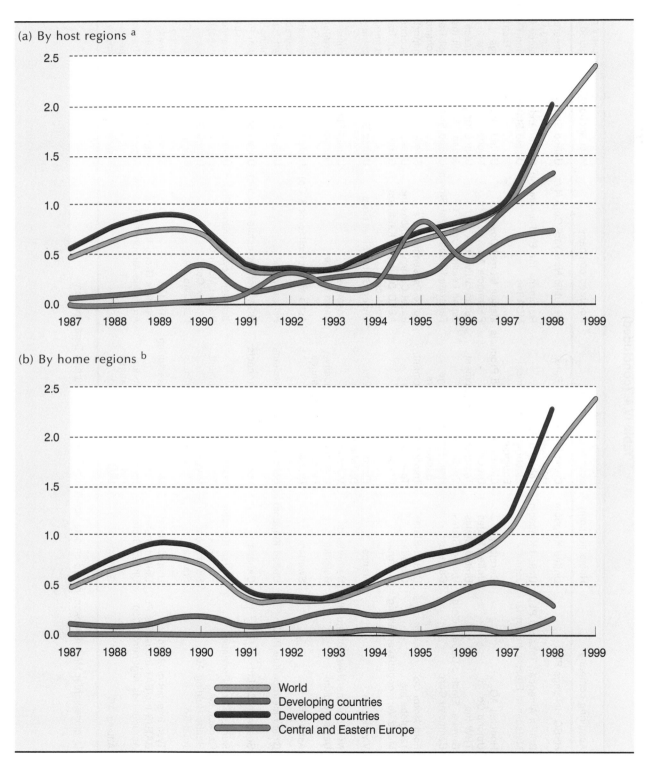

(a) By host regions [a]

(b) By home regions [b]

Legend: World; Developing countries; Developed countries; Central and Eastern Europe

Source: UNCTAD, cross-border M&A database (based on data from Thomson Financial Securities Data Company).

[a] Cross-border M&A sales as a percentage of GDP.
[b] Cross-border M&A purchases as a percentage of GDP.

time, as well as differences across regions. Worldwide FDI flows and cross-border M&As have followed a similar path since the mid-1980s (figure IV.8a). In 1999 the value of world cross-border M&As in relation to that of world FDI flows yielded a ratio of over four-fifths. If all M&As were financed by FDI, this would mean that four-fifths of world FDI flows took the form of M&As. This picture is largely influenced by the performance of the developed countries where the relationship between FDI inflows and cross-border M&As is closer (figure IV.8b). (In the case of the developed countries, it is also quite reasonable to say that the bulk

---

Box IV.6. Cross-border M&As through the exchange of stocks

Paying for M&As through an exchange of stocks has become increasingly popular in recent years. This option is frequently used to finance large M&A deals in which their sheer size makes cash payment virtually impossible.[a] Most of these deals took place either in 1998 or 1999 (box table IV.6.1). For example, in the case of the Daimler-Chrysler deal with a transaction value of $40 billion in 1998 common shareholders of Chrysler Corp received 0.62 new ordinary shares of Daimler-Chrysler (DC) and shareholders of Daimler-Benz AG received a new ordinary share of DC per share held. Upon completion, shareholders of Daimler-Benz owned 57 per cent of the new company.

Cross-border M&As financed in this manner result in large, but almost entirely offsetting, capital flows in the balance of payments of the two countries involved: the inflow of capital that results from a foreign direct investor's acquisition of stock in an acquired firm is offset by the outflow of capital recorded in the portfolio investment account that results from the distribution to the shareholders in the acquired company of the stock in the newly established foreign company (UNCTAD, 1999a). Thus, there is no direct impact on the balance of payments of the countries involved. This option is used also by firms based in developing countries. For example, in 1999, Corcemar (Argentina) bought Interactive ConEd.com (United States) and Excel Machine Tools (Singapore) purchased GarAgent Garazsipari Keresked (Hungary) using this option.

As actually no funds flow between the countries involved, cross-border M&A deals using the stock-swap option can be distinguished from other deals involving flows of funds in terms of their financial impact on host economies.

Box table IV.6.1. The top 20 stock-swap cross-border M&A deals completed during 1987-1999

Rank	Year	Value in billion dollars	Acquiring company	Home country	Acquired company	Host country
1	1999	60.3	Vodafone Group PLC	United Kingdom	AirTouch Communications	United States
2	1998	48.2	British Petroleum Co PLC{BP}	United Kingdom	Amoco Corp	United States
3	1998	40.5	Daimler-Benz AG	Germany	Chrysler Corp	United States
4	1999	34.6	ZENECA Group PLC	United Kingdom	Astra AB	Sweden
5	1999	32.6	Mannesmann AG	Germany	Orange PLC	United Kingdom
6	1999	21.9	Rhone-Poulenc SA	France	Hoechst AG	Germany
7	1999	12.6	Scottish Power PLC	United Kingdom	PacifiCorp	United States
8	1999	10.8	Aegon NV	Netherlands	TransAmerica Corp	United States
9	1999	10.1	Global Crossing Ltd	Bermuda	Frontier Corp	United States
10	1999	9.8	ABB AG	Switzerland	ABB AB	Sweden
11	1998	9.3	Nortel Networks Corp	Canada	Bay Networks Inc	United States
12	1999	8.2	Suez Lyonnaise des Eaux SA	France	TRACTEBEL SA	Belgium
13	1989	7.9	Beecham Group PLC	United Kingdom	SmithKline Beecham Corp	United States
14	1999	7.5	British American Tobacco PLC	United Kingdom	Rothmans Intl BV(Richemont)	Netherlands
15	1995	7.0	Upjohn Co	United States	Pharmacia AB	Sweden
16	1998	6.4	Teleglobe Inc	Canada	Excel Communications Inc	United States
17	1996	6.3	Metro Vermoegensverwaltung	Malaysia	ASKO Deutsche Kaufhaus	Germany
18	1999	6.1	Dexia Belgium	Belgium	Dexia France	France
19	1997	5.3	Tyco International Ltd	United States	ADT Ltd	Bermuda
20	1998	4.9	Enso Oy	Finland	Stora Kopparbergs Bergslags AB	Sweden

Source: UNCTAD, cross-border M&A database, based on data from Thomson Financial Securities Data Company.

Source: UNCTAD.

[a]   Obviously if companies have lots of cash and a low debt/equity ratio, they may not use this option. The Unilever-Bestfoods deal is a good example of this.

of FDI inflows enter through M&As.) In developing countries, the value of cross-border M&As has also been growing rapidly since the mid-1990s, but is still below that of greenfield FDI; in this group of countries, at least two-thirds of FDI inflows finance greenfield projects (figure IV.8c). Overall, the ratio of the value of cross-border M&As to FDI inflows in developing countries has risen from one-tenth in 1987-1989 to more than one-third in 1997-1999. Among developing regions this ratio is the highest in Latin America and the Caribbean: it increased from 18 per cent to 61 per cent between these two periods, while in developing Asia it increased from 8 per cent to 21 per cent between the same periods. In the case of Central and Eastern Europe, however, the overall trend indicates that greenfield FDI is becoming increasingly more important than M&As (figure IV.8d).

These data suggest (within the framework of the qualifications made in section A) that, indeed, cross-border M&As account for a very important part of FDI inflows to developed countries and are also becoming more important for developing countries. They also suggest that, in general the more developed a host region (and the more active privatization activity), the higher the share of M&As in FDI inflows (figure IV.9).

The text below elaborates this picture further for each major region.

a. Developed countries

Between 1987 and 1999, the value of cross-border M&As in developed countries (sales and purchases) grew at an annual rate of 20 per cent. During that period, their share in world cross-border M&As was never below 77 per cent (nearly 87 per cent in the case of purchases), peaking at 98 per cent in the late 1980s. Within this group, the share of the European Union in cross-border M&A sales in developed countries increased markedly — from less than 20 per cent in 1987 to about 65 per cent in 1992, the year of the formation of the single market — and has remained around 50 per cent since then (figure IV.10). A similar trend can be observed as regards the share of the EU in the cross-border M&A purchases of developed country firms. Reflecting large-scale M&A purchases by EU firms during 1998-1999, the EU share increased considerably, to become higher than that at the peak years before the formation of the single market (figure IV.10).

In 1999, *Western European* firms were particularly active, with a total of $354 billion of sales and $519 billion of purchases. Intra-European Union deals accounted for a significant share (figure IV.11). The notable imbalance at times between sales and purchases of cross-border M&As in Western Europe is largely explained by the fact that United Kingdom firms often targeted United States firms. Excluding M&A deals involving United

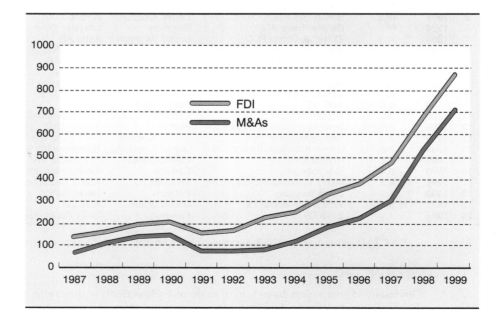

FIGURE IV.8a
World: FDI inflows and cross-border M&As^a, 1987-1999
(Billions of dollars)

Source: UNCTAD, cross-border M&A database and FDI/TNC database.

Note: As there is no unique relationship between FDI and cross-border M&As, a direct comparison is not possible.

^a Cross-border M&As that result in acquiring more than 10 per cent equity share.

FIGURE IV.8b

Developed countries : FDI inflows and cross-border M&As,[a] 1987-1999
(Billions of dollars)

Source: UNCTAD, cross-border M&A database and FDI/TNC database.

Note: As there is no unique relationship between FDI and cross-border M&As, a direct comparison is not possible.
a   Cross-border M&As that result in acquiring more than 10 per cent equity share.

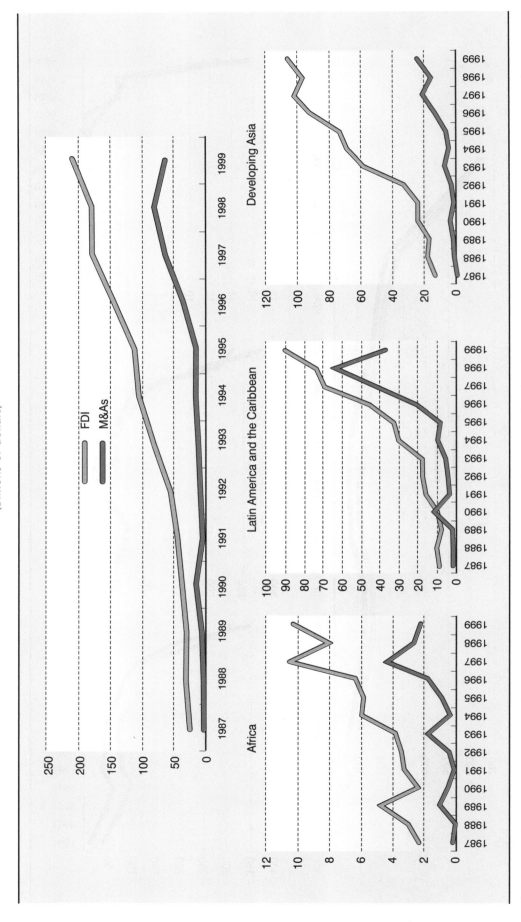

FIGURE IV.8c

Developing countries : FDI inflows and cross-border M&As,ᵃ 1987-1999

(Billions of dollars)

Source: UNCTAD, cross-border M&A database and FDI/TNC database.

Note: As there is no unique relationship between FDI and cross-border M&As, a direct comparison is not possible.
ᵃ   Cross-border M&As that result in acquiring more than 10 per cent equity share.

FIGURE IV.8d

Central and Eastern Europe[a]: FDI inflows and cross-border M&As[b], 1987-1999
(Billions of dollars)

Source: U N C T A D ,
cross-border M&A database
and FDI/TNC database.

Note: As there is no
unique relationship between
FDI and cross-border M&As,
a direct comparison is not
possible.

[a] Includes the countries of
    the former Yugoslavia.
[b] Cross-border M&As that
    result in acquiring more
    than 10 per cent equity
    share.

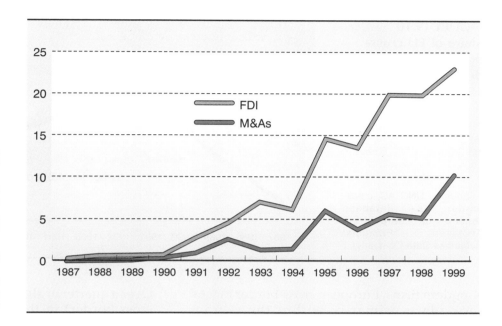

FIGURE IV.9
Cross-border M&As as a percentage of FDI inflows, 1997-1999
(Percentage)

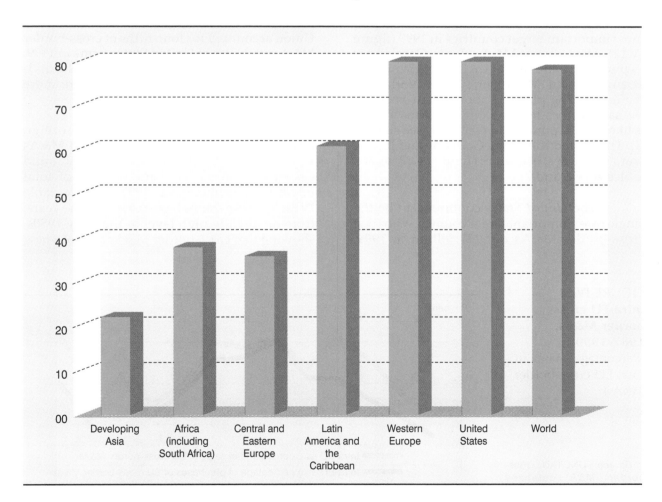

Source: UNCTAD, cross-border M&A database (based on data from Thomson Financial Securities Data Company).

FIGURE IV.10

Share of EU cross-border M&As in developed countries, 1987-1999

(Percentage)

Source: UNCTAD, cross-border M&A database (based on data from Thomson Financial Securities Data Company).

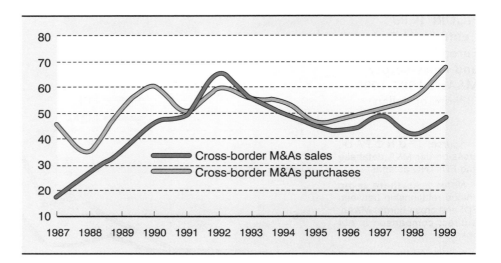

Kingdom firms, European cross-border M&As took place primarily within the region. Consolidation among continental European firms was partly a natural response to deregulation, regional integration and the introduction of the single currency.

The United Kingdom, Sweden, Germany and the Netherlands were Europe's most important target countries in 1999 (figure IV.12). The value of M&A sales in Germany is expected to be high in 2000, given the acquisition of Mannesmann by Vodafone AirTouch. The planned abolition of taxes on the sale of cross-holdings among firms in 2001 is likely to encourage M&A further (see chapter II). The United Kingdom, Germany and France were the largest acquirers (figure IV.13; annex tables A.IV.6 and 7).

The *United States* continued to be the single most important target country, with total cross-border M&As of $233 billion in 1999.

Over a quarter of all M&As (both domestic and cross-border) in the United States were by foreign acquirers, compared with 7 per cent in 1997 and 14 per cent in 1998. [16] European firms in particular have become more active in taking over or merging with United States enterprises, driven by the globalization of their industries and attracted by the rapid growth of the United States market. The European Union accounted for four-fifths of cross-border M&A purchases of United States firms in 1999, compared with less than a half before the mid-1990s, when Japanese companies were more active.

Investment expenditures in foreign affiliates in the United States through M&As accounted for 90 per cent in terms of value and 62 per cent in terms of the number of total inward investments in 1998 (annex table IV.8). [17] These shares have risen over the years, from an already high level in the early 1980s, showing that cross-border M&As are not a new

FIGURE IV.11

Intra-EU cross-border M&As, 1987-1999

(Percentage shares in total EU cross-border M&As)

Source: UNCTAD, cross-border M&A database (based on data from Thomson Financial Securities Data Company).

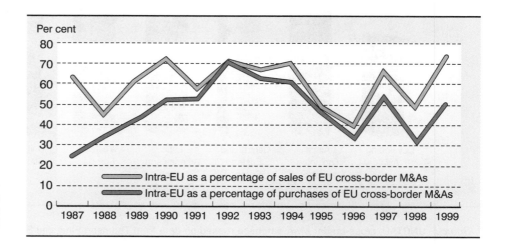

phenomenon in the United States. The picture for outward United States FDI is similar. The share of affiliates established abroad through M&As has fluctuated over time, but it was already high during the period 1951-1975, ranging from 30 per cent to more than a half (table IV.5).

In 1999, United States firms spent $112 billion on acquiring foreign firms, about $100 billion less than United Kingdom firms, and $25 billion less than in 1998. In 1999, four out of the 15 largest cross-border deals were undertaken by United Kingdom firms, while no United States firms entered that list (compared to three in 1998) (annex table A.IV.4). The decline in the value of outward M&As by United States firms reflects the lower involvement of United States companies as acquirers in mega-deals during that year. About 12 per cent of United States cross-border M&A purchases involved developing country firms in 1999.

Japanese overseas M&A purchases increased significantly in 1999, but largely because of the acquisition of the international tobacco business of RJ Reynolds for $7.8 billion,

FIGURE IV.12
Developed countries: cross-border M&A *sales*, top 10 countries, 1998 and 1999[a]
(Billions of dollars)

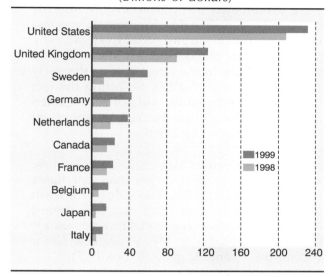

Source: UNCTAD, cross-border M&A database (based on data from Thomson Financial Securities Data Company).

a   Ranked on the basis of the magnitude of sales in 1999.

the fifteenth largest cross-border M&A in the world that year (annex table A.IV.4). Although this signals a shift from the traditional Japanese preference for greenfield investment (see chapter II), the latter remains the preferred mode of FDI entry (UNCTAD, 1999a). Japanese

FIGURE IV.13
Developed countries: cross-border M&A *purchases*, top 10 countries, 1998 and 1999[a]
(Billions of dollars)

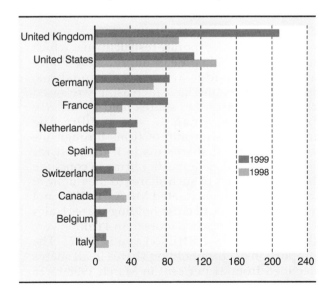

Source: UNCTAD, cross-border M&A database (based on data from Thomson Financial Securities Data Company).

a   Ranked on the basis of the magnitude of sales in 1999.

Table IV.5. Type of United States foreign affiliates established through M&As and greenfield investment, 1951-1975
(Number)

Year	Total	M&As	Greenfield	Share of M&As
1951-55	989	301	507	30.4
1956-60	1 957	645	1 009	33.0
1961-65	3 225	1 314	1 430	40.7
1966	669	309	288	46.2
1967	912	457	366	50.1
1968	1 006	534	423	53.1
1969	945	452	437	47.8
1970	853	403	402	47.2
1971	905	479	388	52.9
1972	646	319	282	49.4
1973	693	354	307	51.1
1974	619	212	365	34.2
1975	376	135	234	35.9

Source: Curhan, Davidson and Suri, 1977.

TNCs tend to use the M&A option more in developed than in developing countries. As of March 1996, about a quarter of Japanese manufacturing affiliates in developed countries were established through M&As, while the comparable figure in developing Asia was less than one-tenth (Japan, MITI, 1998). The purchase value of cross-border M&As in 1999 was lower than in the late 1980s or the early 1990s (annex table A.IV.7), reflecting the fact that Japanese companies had not yet regained the growth dynamism (backed by abundant liquidity) of the early 1990s.

Cross-border M&A sales in Japan rose much faster and were larger than purchases in each year since 1997. The value of inward M&As is now higher than that of outward M&As, which is not true of FDI flows overall.[18] Changing attitudes to M&As are one factor behind this dramatic growth (box IV.7).

b. *Developing countries*

Developing country firms are still not large players in terms of *acquiring* firms abroad, although they can be important in a regional context, especially in Asia and Latin America. Their share of the value of global M&A purchases reached just over 10 per cent during 1996-1997, but dropped to less than 5 per cent in the period 1998-1999. In contrast to FDI outflows, of which developing countries account for some one-tenth of the world total, firms based in developing countries prefer greenfield FDI to M&As when investing abroad. Nevertheless, in absolute values, cross-border M&A purchases by firms from developing countries nearly doubled in 1999 to record levels, at $41 billion, after dipping in 1998 in response to the Asian financial crisis (table IV.3). This compares to $7 billion in 1990. The ratio of cross-border M&As to FDI outflows

---

Box IV.7. The cross-border M&A market in Japan

Three principal factors explain the recent growth of cross-border M&As in Japan: changes in business culture, changes in the regulatory framework for M&As and corporate factors. These changes have significantly facilitated M&As in Japan, contributing to make Japan the ninth largest M&A target country in the world in 1999.

Changes in business culture:

Japan's business culture used to be resistant to M&As, mainly for the following reasons: i) a business was considered to be a collection of human resources and not of funds. Human beings cannot be bought nor sold; and ii) a business used to be considered as a family, where workers were loyal to management in return for life-time employment. This business culture has been gradually changing, however, thereby facilitating M&As.

Changes in the regulatory framework:

With changes in the Commercial Law in 1999, a target company can become a wholly owned subsidiary, foreign or domestic, of the acquiring company through exchange of shares. It was previously virtually impossible to purchase all shares of the acquired firms as there were always some shareholders unwilling to sell their shares. With the introduction of the exchange of shares introduced by this law, all

shares of the target firm have to be exchanged with the shares of the acquirer. As a result, foreign firms can now establish wholly owned foreign affiliates through M&As. Holders of new shares acquired through an exchange of shares from the acquirer are also allowed to defer tax payments on capital gains until they sell those shares. This tax deferral attracts M&As via exchanges of stocks, which have already become a popular option in other major countries.

Changes in corporate structure:

Pushed by corporate restructuring, which has led firms to dispose of unprofitable shares and to reconsider *keiretsu* relationships, Japanese companies have increasingly released cross-held shares, i.e. shares held by *keiretsu* firms in each other, to the public. The interlocking relationship of firms through the cross holding of shares made it difficult for foreign (as well as domestic) firms to conclude M&As. The sales of such shares to the public at large has greatly facilitated M&As. In 1999, net sales to the public of cross-holding shares (sales less purchases) reached more than 4 trillion yen; this compares to 1.5 trillion yen in 1997. The proportion of cross-holding shares in all shares declined from 21 per cent in March 1998 to 16 per cent in March 1999 for firms listed on the stock exchange.[a] This trend continues.

Source: UNCTAD.

[a] *Nihon Keizai Shimbun*, 28 December 1999, p. 1.

from developing countries also increased from 45 per cent in 1990 to 63 per cent in 1999.

Asian firms are important acquirers in developing countries; Singapore was the main base for acquiring firms, and the targets were primarily firms in developing countries in the Asian region. Firms from the five Asian countries most affected by the financial crisis also increased their cross-border M&A purchases, reflecting improvements in their liquidity situation. Latin America saw significant increases in cross-border purchases of M&A activity; Bermuda was the largest base for acquiring firms in the region, indeed in the developing world as a whole (figure IV.14). [19] Through cross-border M&As, some firms from developing countries have become world leaders in their industries (box IV.8).

On the inward side, it was not until the late 1990s that developing countries emerged as important recipients of FDI in the form of cross-border M&As. Their share in the value of world cross-border M&As was less than 10 per cent almost every year until the mid-1990s. In terms of the number of cross-border M&A

FIGURE IV.14

Developing countries: cross-border M&A *purchases*, **top 10 countries, 1998 and 1999**[a]
(Billions of dollars)

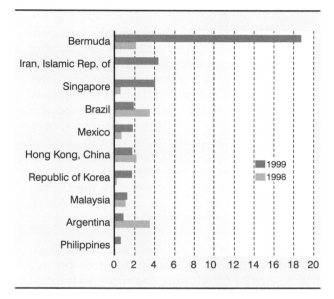

Source: UNCTAD, cross-border M&A database (based on data from Thomson Financial Securities Data Company).

[a]   Ranked on the basis of the magnitude of sales in 1999.

Box IV.8. Cemex: reaching the world's top level through M&As

Cemex S.A. de C.V. is not only Mexico's largest cement giant, but also the world's third-largest cement company, operating 56 cement plants in 30 countries in 2000. Founded in 1906, Cemex went through several domestic M&As until it gained the number one position in Mexico in the late 1980s. In the 1990s, the company repeatedly used cross-border acquisitions to expand its overseas operations.

In less than a decade, Cemex acquired all or part of three entities in developed countries and ten in developing countries outside Mexico. Through these acquisitions, its production capacity more than doubled and its net sales almost tripled. While the company controls about a 60 per cent share of the Mexican market, the domestic sales now account for less than half of the company's total revenues.

As a strategy to strengthen its capital structure, Cemex aims at making effective use of its presence in Spain, whose operation was established through its first cross-border acquisition deal in 1992. Indeed, when

comparing its financial results with competitors, Cemex's leverage is comparable to or lower than its European rivals. Nevertheless, the perception of international investors is affected by the fact that Cemex's operations are heavily concentrated in emerging markets. Unlike Mexico, however, Spain has better investment ratings and lower interest rates. Cemex can borrow at much lower interest through its Spanish affiliate than through its Mexican operation.

Over the last few years, Cemex has gradually shifted ownership control of its non-Mexican affiliates (i.e. Cemex USA, Panama's Bayano, the Philippines' Rizal, Venezuela's Vencemos, which consolidates Dominican Republic's Cementos Nacionales, Colombia's Diamante, which consolidates Samper's operations, and Indonesia's Semen Gresik) to its Spanish affiliate, Valenciana. This corporate structure allows Cemex to benefit from lower-interest rates, to improve capital structure and to make a better matching in debt obligations and operating cash flows.

Source: UNCTAD based on information available from Cemex (www.cemex.com).

deals, the developing countries' share increased over the 1990s from 5 per cent in 1987 to almost 20 per cent in the late 1990s (annex table A.IV.2). In terms of value, their share was 2 per cent in 1987 and 9 per cent in 1999.

These relative shares mask, however, that cross-border M&A *sales* in developing countries have grown significantly since 1996. In 1999 there was a 21 per cent decline after three years of rapid growth (table IV.3), mainly caused by the lower volume of cross-border M&A purchases by United States firms. European Union enterprises were the largest acquirers during 1998-1999, accounting for more than two-fifths of cross-border M&As in developing countries, followed by the United States (table IV.6). Japanese M&As in developing countries were marginal.

The Latin American and Caribbean region continued to dominate cross-border M&A sales by developing countries. In the past two years, Argentina and Brazil were the largest sellers (figure IV.15). Privatization was the main vehicle in both countries (discussed below), exemplified by the privatization of Telebras in Brazil (1998) and YPF in Argentina (1999). In Argentina, one of the few countries for which information on the breakdown of FDI by mode of entry is available, the share of cross-border M&As financed by FDI in total FDI inflows (on an approval basis) rose from

one-fifth during 1990-1996 to nearly one half during 1997-1999 (Argentina, CEP, 2000).

In Asia a rapid rise in cross-border M&A sales took place in recent years, partly as a result of the financial crisis (chapter II). Acquisitions by foreign firms in the Republic of Korea exceeded $9 billion in 1999, making it the largest recipient of M&A-based FDI in developing Asia. By contrast, M&As played a relatively small role in FDI inflows into China – only at most $2 billion out of total FDI of $40 billion in 1999. In Indonesia, the Republic of Korea and Thailand, foreign acquisitions of some firms temporarily nationalized during the financial crisis took place. For example, 40 per cent of the equity of PT Astra International, the largest car producer in Indonesia, owned by the Indonesian Bank Restructuring Agency since the financial crisis, was sold in 2000 to Cycle & Carriage Ltd. of Singapore for $506 million. In the transition economies of Central Asia, cross-border M&A sales were largely influenced by large privatization deals. Significant M&A sales in Kazakhstan during 1996-1997 are explained by the acquisition of Kaztelekom by Daewoo Corp (with a transaction value of $1.4 billion) (annex table A.IV.6). [20]

In West Asia there have been steady (but small) M&A sales in Turkey since the late 1980s. In other countries in the region, there is

---

Table IV.6. **Cross-border M&As in developing countries, by home region/country, 1987-1999**

(Billions of dollars)

| Year | World | Developed countries | | | | Developed countries | | | | |
		Total	EU	Japan	United States	Total	Africa	Latin America and the Caribbean	South, East and South-Asia	Central and Easterm Europe[a]
1987	1.7	1.5	0.4	-	1.2	0.2	-	-	0.2	-
1988	2.9	2.7	1.1	0.2	0.3	0.2	-	0.1	0.1	-
1989	5.1	3.9	2.5	0.2	0.6	1.1	-	-	1.1	-
1990	16.1	14.5	9.7	1.6	2.9	1.5	-	0.7	0.8	-
1991	5.8	4.9	1.7	0.2	2.0	0.9	-	0.2	0.7	-
1992	8.0	5.5	1.6	0.6	2.1	2.5	-	0.9	1.6	-
1993	12.8	6.2	1.8	0.2	3.2	6.6	-	1.5	4.9	-
1994	14.8	9.5	3.6	0.3	2.6	5.3	-	1.8	3.0	-
1995	15.9	10.3	4.1	0.5	4.6	5.5	-	1.6	3.4	-
1996	34.6	21.3	9.2	0.8	8.9	13.2	0.1	6.5	6.4	-
1997	64.3	42.4	15.8	0.8	20.4	21.9	-	8.6	13.1	-
1998	80.7	67.6	31.9	0.2	20.8	13.1	-	9.0	4.0	-
1999	63.4	49.5	32.0	0.7	13.7	13.8	-	4.3	8.9	0.1

Source: UNCTAD, cross-border M&A database, based on data from Thomson Financial Securities Data Company.

[a]   Includes the countries of the former Yugoslavia.

FIGURE IV.15
Developing countries: cross-border M&A *sales*, top 10 countries, 1998 and 1999[a]
(Billions of dollars)

Source: UNCTAD, cross-border M&A database (based on data from Thomson Financial Securities Data Company).

[a] Ranked on the basis of the magnitude of sales in 1999.

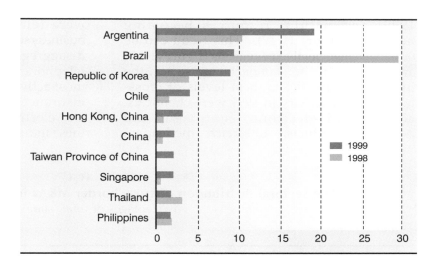

generally very little M&A activity, with occasional one-off cases.

In Africa, Egypt, Morocco and South Africa attracted most foreign acquisitions. None of the other African countries attracted more than $1 billion of M&As, though Zambia and Ghana have had some M&A-based inflows since the mid-1990s. The low level of M&A activity is partly explained by the slow pace of privatization programmes.

c. Central and Eastern Europe[21]

While greenfield FDI is increasingly important in Central and Eastern Europe, cross-border M&A sales also rose in 1999 (table IV.3), doubling from $5 billion to $10 billion.[22] As earlier, most were privatization and infrastructure related. Because of the lumpy nature of these sales, cross-border M&As (as well as FDI inflows) into the region have fluctuated widely over the years (figure IV.8d). Poland, the Czech Republic and Croatia were the major target countries in 1999 (figure IV.16), reflecting relatively large privatization programmes.

M&As by Western European firms led the field. United States firms gradually got involved through M&As, but the size of their purchases remained small (less than $1 billion). As some countries (e.g. Hungary) have nearly completed their privatization programmes mostly in the manufacturing sector, TNCs are increasingly buying local privately-owned businesses; these deals are generally small compared with those involved in privatization. However, in this region, privatization in the services sector has not yet been completed. For example, the restructuring and rationalization

of the banking industry in the Czech Republic and Poland continue to attract cross-border M&As. Cross-border M&As in the Baltic States, in particular in Lithuania, are noteworthy (annex table A.IV.6).

3. Sector and industry trends

The sectoral distribution of cross-border M&As mirrors the development of the pattern of FDI flows in general: there has been a trend towards more services (accounting for 60 per cent in 1999) on a sales basis, with the share of manufacturing declining (to 38 per cent in

FIGURE IV.16
Central and Eastern Europe:[a] cross-border M&A *sales*, top 10 countries, 1998 and 1999[b]
(Billions of dollars)

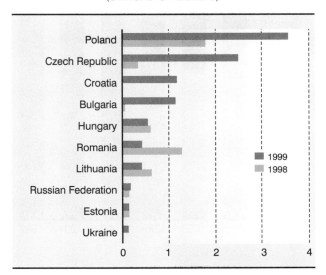

Source: UNCTAD, cross-border M&A database (based on data from Thomson Financial Securities Data Company).

[a] Includes the countries of the former Yugoslavia.
[b] Ranked on the basis of the magnitude of sales in 1999.

1999) and natural resources becoming negligible (figure IV.17). This trend can be observed irrespective of regions (figures IV.18 and IV.19). In the *manufacturing* sector, the industries with the highest levels of cross-border M&A activity in 1999 were chemicals, electric and electronic equipment and petroleum products. In *services*, the leaders

were telecommunications, financial and business services (annex table A.IV.9). At a more disaggregated level, radiotelephone (mobile telephones) communications were by far the most active, followed by pharmaceuticals, life insurance, other telephone communications and electrical power (figure IV.20). Some of these industries have long attracted large-scale

FIGURE IV.17

The sectoral distribution of cross-border M&As in the world, 1987-1999

(Percentages of total value)

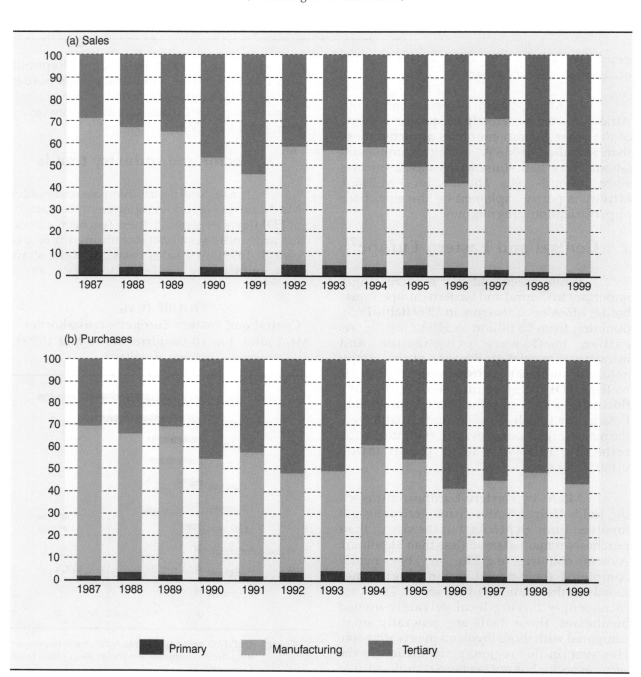

Source: UNCTAD, cross-border M&A database and annex tables A.IV.9 and A.IV.10.

cross-border M&As, partly because of the corporate strategies pursued by main players and partly because of liberalization and deregulation.

The sectoral breakdown of cross-border M&A purchases tends to mirror that of sales, but there are some notable differences at the industry level. In services, for instance, the financial services industry accounted for the highest expenditures in cross-border M&A purchases in 1999 (annex table A.IV.10), while transport, storage and communications were the largest sellers (annex table A.IV.9). Indeed, as this example shows, cross-border M&A deals also take place between different industries. Wholesale and retail trade, as well as business services, sold twice as much as they purchased,

FIGURE IV.18
The sectoral distribution of cross-border M&As in developed countries, 1987-1999
(Percentages of total value)

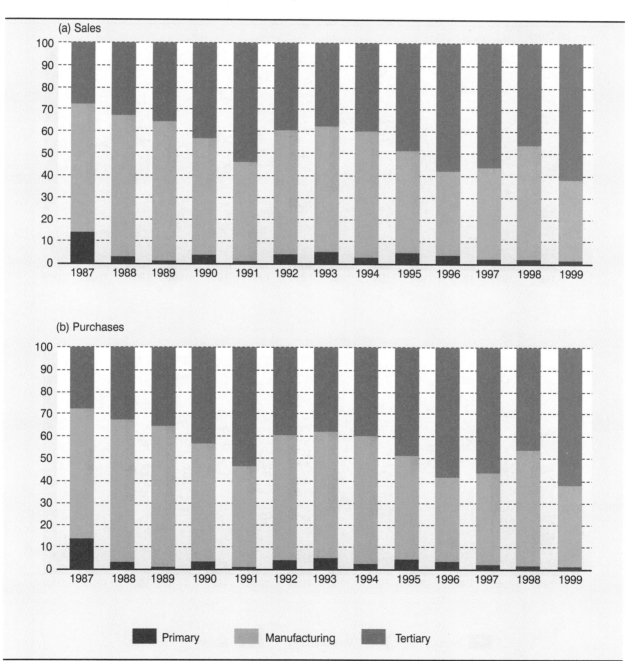

Source: UNCTAD, cross-border M&A database (based on data from Thomson Financial Securities Data Company).

reflecting the fact that the parties involved in cross-border M&As were not from the same industry. In manufacturing, the chemical industry was the largest purchaser, as well as the largest seller.

Horizontal M&As are prevalent in activities like automobiles, defence, pharmaceuticals, telecommunications and banking. In capital and technology-intensive activities, firms may undertake M&As to remain competitive by eliminating excess capacity (e.g. automobiles or defence) and to spread huge investments in information technology and/or R&D (pharmaceuticals, telecommunications and banking). Horizontal M&As also take place in less technology-intensive industries like food, beverages and tobacco, textile and clothing. Economic motivations here seem to be to increase market

FIGURE IV.19

The sectoral distribution of cross-border M&As in developing countries, 1987-1999
(Percentages of total value)

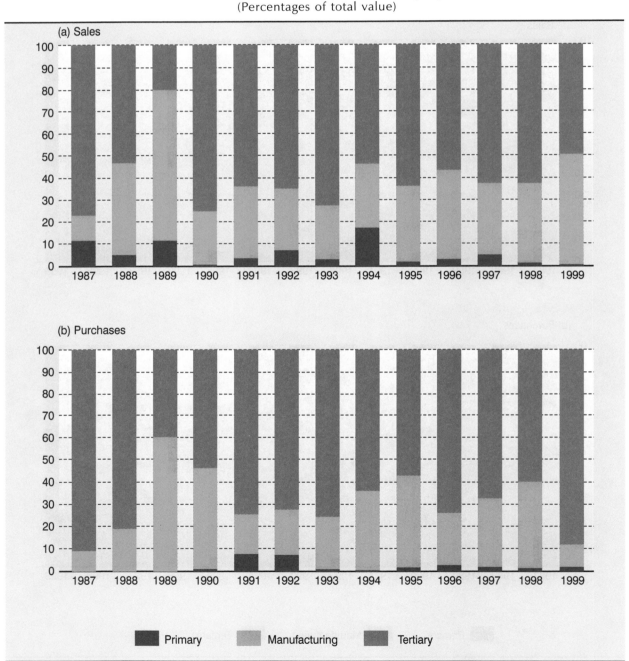

Source: UNCTAD, cross-border M&A database (based on data from Thomson Financial Securities Data Company).

FIGURE IV.20
Cross-border M&A sales, top 10 industries, 1998 and 1999[a]
(Billions of dollars)

Source: U N C T A D , cross-border M&A database (based on data from Thomson Financial Securities Data Company).

[a] Ranked on the basis of the magnitude of sales in 1999.

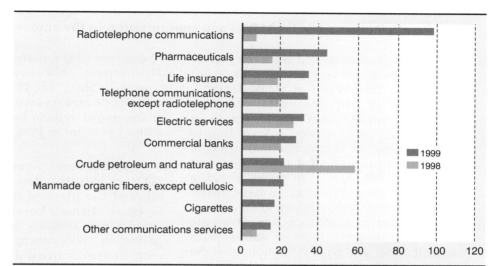

power by reducing competition, realize scale economies in marketing, distribution and procurement or increase negotiating power vis-à-vis buyer and suppliers as well as financial institutions.

In industries characterizing intense horizontal M&A activity, market concentration is rising. Much of this is driven by the large number of M&As concluded by a few major

TNCs. During 1987-1999, the top 10 TNCs concluding the largest cross-border M&A deals accounted for 13 per cent of the total value of deals (table IV.7). Because of mega deals in recent years, this share increased from 15 per cent during 1996-1997 to 31 per cent during 1998-1999. The companies involved in such deals change each year, reflecting the industries that underwent consolidation in a given year. Thus, in 1999, three out of the top 10 TNCs

Table IV.7. **The 20 largest TNCs with cross-border M&A activity[a], 1987-1999**

Rank	Name	Home	Industry	Value in billion dollars[b]	Number of deals
1	BP Amoco PLC	United Kingdom	Petroleum	65.0	76
2	Vodafone Group PLC	United Kingdom	Telecommunications	60.3	9
3	Mannesmann AG	Germany	Metal and metal products	44.7	44
4	Daimler-Benz/DaimlerChrysler AG	Germany	Transportation equipment	42.9	67
5	ZENECA Group PLC	United Kingdom	Chemicals	35.8	12
6	Aventis SA	France	Chemicals	26.8	13
7	Roche Holding AG	Switzerland	Chemicals	24.7	20
8	Zurich Versicherungs GmbH	Switzerland	Insurance	21.9	36
9	General Electric Co	United States	Electronic and electrical equipment	21.6	183
10	Seagram Co Ltd	Canada	Food and kindred products	20.2	23
11	AXA/AXA-UAP	France	Insurance	19.1	44
12	Suez Lyonnaise des Eaux SA	France	Electric, gas and water distribution	17.8	77
13	News Corp Ltd	Australia	Printing, publishing and allied services	17.4	64
14	Koninklijke	Netherlands	Diversified	17.5	301
15	Aegon NV	Netherlands	Insurance	17.1	22
16	Allianz AG/Allianz AG Holding	Germany	Insurance	16.9	72
17	Repsol SA	Spain	Oil and gas	16.4	24
18	Deutsche Bank AG	Germany	Commercial banks	16.3	57
19	Hoechst AG	Germany	Chemicals	15.9	117
20	Texas Utilities Co	United States	Electric, gas and water distribution	15.7	18
Top 10				363.9	483
Top 20				533.8	1 279
Total				2 821.5	44 583

Source: UNCTAD, cross-border M&A database, based on data from Thomson Financial Securities Data Company.

[a] Includes cross-border M&As concluded by their affiliates.
[b] Includes only the deals for which information on transaction values is available.

Box IV.9. Cross-border M&As and concentration in the automotive industry

The automotive industry has gone through substantial restructuring in recent years, partly as a result of weak demand, overcapacity and environmental pressures (e.g. production of "clean cars"). This is an industry where size matters. According to some estimates, an automobile maker has to produce a minimum of 4 million cars to survive (JETRO, 2000). In recent years, a number of automobile makers have either merged, or entered into strategic alliances. For example, General Motors has strategic alliances (with acquisition of shares) with Vauxhall, Opel and Saab Automobile — the latter two now being 100 per cent subsidiaries. Ford Motor Company has acquired Jaguar and Volvo Cars and has a strategic alliance with Mazda.[a] This trend continued in 2000 with the acquisition of a 20 per cent equity of Fiat by General Motors; the acquisition of a 33 per cent equity of Mitsubishi Motors by DaimlerChrysler; and Renault's acquisition of

70 per cent of the shares in Samsung Motor. The impact on concentration has been considerable. In 1999, the 10 largest automobile makers accounted for 80 per cent of the world vehicle production, compared with 69 per cent in 1996 (box table IV.9.1).

Similar developments have characterised the truck industry. After the EU Commission blocked the planned merger between two Swedish firms, Volvo and Scania, for competition reasons, Scania found a new partner in Volkswagen, and Volvo joined up with Renault's truck division, creating the world's second largest truck maker after DaimlerChrysler. There are also numerous strategic alliances involving a small share of equity involvement in the automobile industry. In addition, consolidation, competition and outsourcing in this industry have triggered the restructuring in its supplier industries through M&As.

Source: UNCTAD.

　[a]　See also UNCTAD, 1999a, chapter II.C.1.

Box table IV.9.1. Automobiles:[a] degree of concentration of the 10 largest TNCs, 1996 and 1999
(1,000 vehicle production units)

TNCs	1996	TNCs	1999
General Motors	8 400	General Motors	8 336
Ford Motor	6 750	Ford Motor	7 220
Toyota Motor	4 756	Toyota Motor	5 401
Volkswagen	3 977	Volkswagen	4 853
Chrysler	2 861	DaimlerChrysler	4 827
Nissan	2 742	Renault[b]	4 720
Fiat	2 586	Fiat[c]	2 596
Honda Motor	2 084	PSA	2 496
Mitsubishi Motor[d]	1 943	Honda Motor	2 423
Renault	1 804	Hyundai Motor	2 081
Total 5 largest	26 744	Total 5 largest	30 637
Share in the world total	49	Share in the world total	54
Total 10 largest	37 903	Total 10 largest	44 955
Share in the world total	69	Share in the world total	80
World total	55 036	World total	56 286

Source:　UNCTAD, based on *Automotive News*,1997, 2000.

　[a]　Includes cars and trucks.
　[b]　Includes Nissan. Renault purchased a 37 per cent equity share in 1999.
　[c]　General Motors purchased a 20 per cent equity share in 2000.
　[d]　DaimlerChrysler purchased a 33 per cent equity share in 2000.

(Vodafone Group, Mannesmann and Deutsche Telekom) were in the telecommunications industry; none of these ranked among the top 10 in the previous years. On the other hand, firms in chemicals and pharmaceuticals appeared almost every year among the top 10 TNCs during 1987-1999, suggesting a prolonged restructuring in this industry.

Concentration has increased in various industries such as automobiles (box IV.9), banking (box IV.10) and pharmaceuticals (box IV.11) because of M&As. Telecommunications, insurance and energy (including petroleum) are other major industries in which concentration has increased with mega cross-border M&A deals contributing significantly (annex table A.IV.4). Liberalization and deregulation have also driven M&As in the services sector (figures IV.17 - IV.19).

There are interesting differences by region and country groups. In developed countries, finance, transport, storage and communications, and chemicals were the largest recipient industries during 1997-1999 (figure IV.21). However, patterns of cross-border M&A sales in the European Union differ from those in the United States even when the values are almost the same (annex tables A.IV.11 and 12). In the European Union, firms in chemicals, and food, beverages and tobacco were the most targeted for M&As by foreign firms. In the United States, the preferred targets were electrical and electronic equipment and chemicals. As acquirers, financial firms were the most aggressive in both the European Union and the United States, accounting for a quarter of total purchases of cross-border M&As (annex table A.IV.13 and 14).

Box IV.10. Cross-border M&As and concentration in the banking industry

M&As, both domestic and cross-border, are changing the structure of the banking industry. Deregulation and liberalization, as well as competitive pressures to cope with mounting information technology costs, have spurred M&A activity. Although the largest banks are still created through domestic M&As, a number of large banks were born through cross-border M&As. Thus, in 1999, Deutsche Bank – Bankers Trust New York, HSBC – Republic New York, HSBC – Safra Republic, and three other cases were all mega deals with a transaction value of more than $1 billion each (annex table A.IV.4). The result is increased concentration among the top banks. For example, the largest 25 banks measured by assets accounted for 33 per cent of the assets of the 1,000 largest banks in 1999, compared with 28 per cent in 1996.[a] The factors driving M&As in the banking industry differ between regions. The abolition of the Glass-Stegall Act in the United States in 1999 dismantled the wall between banking and securities. Deregulation and the introduction of the single currency in the European Union, financial liberalization in Japan (the Japanese "big bang"), and the restructuring of banking in countries affected by the financial crisis all contributed to large-scale M&As.

Source: UNCTAD.

[a] Data from "Top 1000", *The Banker*, July 2000.

Box IV.11. Cross-border M&As and concentration in the pharmaceutical industry

The need to share the costs for expensive R&D and to derive synergies is driving the spate of cross-border M&A activity in this industry. All the largest pharmaceutical companies have grown through M&As rather than organic growth. Most recently two giants, AstraZeneca and Aventis (Hoechst and Rhône Poulenc), were established through cross-border mergers. Those and other consolidations have led to a further concentration of the industry. In 1999, the top five and ten largest TNCs accounted for 28 and 46 per cent of the world sales of pharmaceutical products, respectively, compared to 19 and 33 per cent respectively, in 1995.[a] The ageing population in developed countries, growing demand for pharmaceutical products in developing countries and advances in biology (genomics) have led pharmaceutical firms to reconsider their corporate strategies. As the United States accounts for 40 per cent of global sales and has in many therapeutic areas the leading R&D clusters, it is attracting foreign firms to invest in the country.

Source: UNCTAD.

[a] "Life sciences & pharmaceuticals", *The Financial Times*, 6 April 2000; and "Pharmaceuticals", *The Financial Times*, 24 April 1997. Pharmaceuticals was a $350 billion industry in world sales in 1999 ($218 billion in 1995).

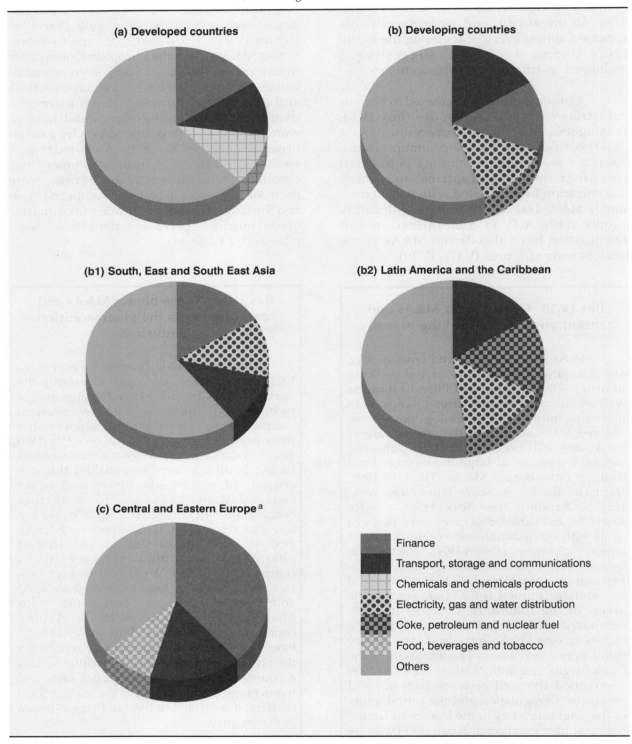

FIGURE IV.21

Three largest recipient industries in cross-border M&A sales, by region, 1997-1999
(Percentages of total value)

Source: UNCTAD, cross-border M&A database and annex tables A.IV.9 and A.IV.10.

a   Includes the countries of the former Yugoslavia.

Japan is in a different situation altogether. Although M&As are growing, the values of cross-border sales and purchases remain relatively small. Because of this, a few large M&As strongly affected the industry distribution in individual years. In 1999, the finance industry dominated on the sales side (annex table A.IV.15), while the food, beverages and tobacco industries were predominant on the purchase side (annex table A.IV.16). In previous years, the pattern was quite different.

It is difficult to identify any clear trends in developing countries. In developing Asia the ranking of recipient industries has changed each year (annex table A.IV.17). During 1997-1999, finance, electricity, gas and water distribution and transport, storage and communications, were the largest targeted industries (figure IV.21). In Latin America and the Caribbean, transport, storage and communication, coke and petroleum products, and utilities (electric, gas and water) received sizeable cross-border M&As (figure IV.21 and annex table A.IV.19). The differences between the regions are partly explained by differences in liberalization and deregulation, privatization and investor attitudes.

After the Asian financial crisis, cross-border M&As in the five main crisis-hit countries, accounting for more than 60 per cent of the Asian total in 1998-1999, influenced the level and distribution of M&As by industry in developing Asia. For example, finance became the largest industry for foreign acquisitions after the crisis (annex table A.IV.18). In Central and Eastern Europe, finance was also strongly targeted (figure IV.21). Partly due to large capital requirements, petroleum products and motor vehicles attracted large cross-border M&A deals (annex table A.IV.20). The relatively large volume of cross-border M&As in food, beverages and the tobacco industries is also noteworthy in Central and Eastern Europe.

4. Privatization and cross-border M&As

Privatization is a special form of acquisitions, involving domestic and/or foreign firms taking over a part or the whole of the equity of state-owned firms. Sales to foreign firms constitute cross-border M&As. In Latin America and Central and Eastern

Europe, privatization has been an important means of attracting FDI and it is growing in developing Asia.

The amounts involved over the years in privatization programmes in developed countries have been larger than those in developing countries. In 1998, for example, only $28.5 billion out of $114.5 billion privatization sales (total, not just cross-border) in the world were in non-OECD countries (OECD, 1999),[23] of which the bulk ($25.5 billion) was in Brazil. In 1998 privatization in developing Asia fell, but remained robust in Latin America, while a sharp decline in Latin America in 1999 led to declining privatization revenues in the developing world as a whole. The increase in sales in the developed world continued. While the value of cross-border M&As through privatization has continued to increase in recent years, the number of deals reached a plateau by the early 1990s (figure IV.22).

Foreign acquisitions of privatized firms as a percentage of the total value of cross-border M&As in the world reached about one-tenth in the mid-1990s, but fell to 6 per cent in 1999. In developed countries, the bulk of privatization is to domestic buyers, while in developing countries foreign participation has been higher than domestic participation.[24] Of the world's 50 largest privatizations involving foreign buyers during 1987-1999, less than half (23) were in developed countries. As a result, the amount raised through privatization to foreign buyers by developing countries sometimes exceeds those achieved by developed countries by a factor of two during 1997-1998 (annex table IV.22). In Central and Eastern Europe, privatization has been an integral part of the transition to a market economy, accounting for a substantial share of cross-border M&As (figure IV.23). Nevertheless the majority of privatized assets has been acquired by or distributed to domestic stakeholders, depending on the methods used when privatizing. Although a number of countries sold state enterprises to foreign firms, foreign acquisitions of state-owned enterprises, on a value basis, were concentrated in a handful of countries: 11 countries sold more than $5 billion each worth of privatized firms during 1987-1999 (annex table A.IV.21). Brazil, Argentina and Australia were the largest sellers, receiving $32 billion, $26 billion and $24 billion, respectively, during that period (annex table A.IV.21).

Privatizations of capital-intensive infrastructure activities such as telecommunications and utilities, and those related to the restructuring of industries such as automobiles and petroleum, have attracted substantial amounts of capital to some countries. In fact, most of the cross-border mega deals in developing countries are privatization-related (see annex table A.IV.4 for 1999). The two largest cross-border acquisitions of privatized firms made in the past were in Latin America: Brazil and Argentina (table IV.8). In

Brazil, for instance, in the case of the privatization of the telecommunications company Telebras, more than half of the privatization revenues (about $11 billion) were raised through cross-border acquisitions. The participation of foreign firms in the Brazilian privatization programme continued strongly in 1999, attracting acquisitions of $2.8 billion, just behind Argentina, Germany and Australia (annex table A.IV.21). The removal of restrictions on foreign ownership, as well as the start of a new phase in privatizations in

FIGURE IV.22
Transaction values and the number of cross-border M&As of privatized firms in the world and by region, 1987-1999

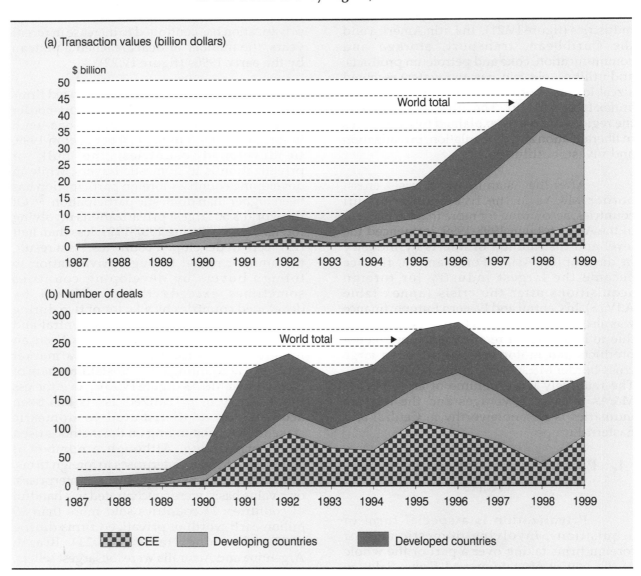

Source: UNCTAD, cross-border M&A database (based on data from Thomson Financial Securities Data Company).

Note: CEE includes the countries of the former Yugoslavia.

1995, account for this performance in Brazil. In the case of Argentina the privatization of YPF was a prominent case in 1999.

Examples of other countries with large-scale privatizations of telecommunications through cross-border M&As were Austria, Belgium, the Czech Republic, Mexico, Peru, South Africa and Venezuela. Energy-related and mining (including petroleum) activities also attracted large cross-border M&As for privatization in developed and developing countries (table IV.8).

* * * *

To conclude, cross-border M&As have risen significantly in importance. Given the number, value and spread of the transactions involved, one can now speak of a market for firms, a market that is increasingly global in nature and in which firms are bought and sold, as they merge, acquire or divest. To be sure, most of this market is in and among developed countries and even there not all countries are equally involved. It is also uneven in terms of industries, reflecting differences in economic structure, corporate governance and corporate strategies. But more and more countries, including developing countries and countries in Central Europe, are drawn into it, as are more and more industries and firms, large or small.

Since cross-border M&As have become an important element in the expansion of the international production system, there is a need for a better understanding of what factors drive these transactions and what distinctive impacts they have on host country development. The following chapters address these issues.

FIGURE IV.23
Total FDI and cross-border M&As in Central and Eastern Europe,[a] 1990-1999
(Billions of dollars)

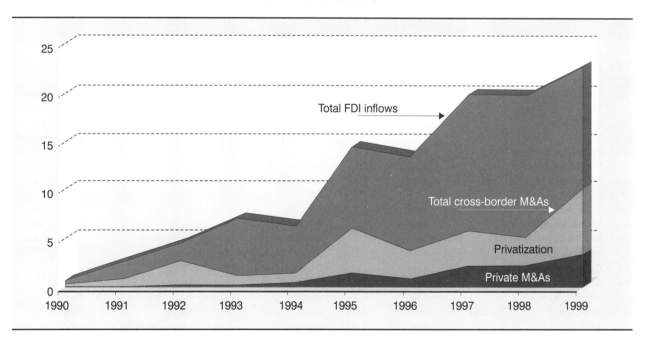

Source: UNCTAD, FDI/TNC database and cross-border M&A database

[a] Includes the countries of the former Yugoslavia.

Table IV.8. The world's 50 largest privatization deals involving foreign firms, 1987-1999

Rank	Privatized firm	Year	Value of acquisition (billion dollars)	Country	Acquiring foreign firm	Acquiring country[a]
1	YPF SA	1999	13.2	Argentina	Repsol SA	Spain
2	Argentina-Airports(33)	1998	5.1	Argentina	Aeropuertos Argentina 2000	United States
3	TELESP(Telebras)	1998	5.0	Brazil	Investor Group	Spain
4	Victoria-Loy Yang A Power	1997	3.8	Australia	Investor Group	United States
5	Energie Baden-Wuerttemberg AG	1999	3.4	Germany	Investor Group	France
6	Telesp Celular Participacoes	1998	3.1	Brazil	Investor Group	Portugal
7	Credit Communal de Belgique SA	1996	3.1	Belgium	Credit Local de France SA	France
8	Nobel Industrier Sweden AB	1994	3.0	Sweden	Akzo NV	Netherlands
9	Coca-Cola Bottlers Philippines	1997	2.7	Philippines	Coca-Cola Amatil Ltd	Australia
10	Belgacom	1996	2.5	Belgium	ADSB Telecommunications BV	United States
11	Telekom Austria	1998	2.4	Austria	Telecom Italia SpA	Italy
12	Embratel(Telebras)	1998	2.3	Brazil	MCI Communications Corp	United States
13	YPF SA	1999	2.0	Argentina	Repsol SA	Spain
14	PowerNet Victoria(GPU Inc)	1997	2.0	Australia	GPU Inc	United States
15	Entel Peru SA,Cia Peruana	1994	2.0	Peru	Investor Group	Spain
16	Stockholm Energi AB	1998	2.0	Sweden	Gullspangs Kraft(Imatran Voim)	Sweden
17	CA Nacional Telefonos de VE	1991	1.9	Venezuela	VenWorld Telecom CA	United States
18	Svyazinvest	1997	1.9	Russian Federation	Mustcom Ltd	Cyprus
19	Yallourn Energy	1996	1.8	Australia	Investor Group	United Kingdom
20	Hazelwood Power Station	1996	1.8	Australia	Hazelwood Power Partnership	United Kingdom
21	Sidor	1998	1.8	Venezuela	Consorico Siderurgia Amazonia	Argentina
22	Telecentro Sul (Telebras)	1998	1.8	Brazil	Investor Group	Italy
23	Light SE	1996	1.7	Brazil	Investor Group	United States
24	Telmex	1990	1.7	Mexico	Investor Group	United States
25	Australia-Dampier to Bunbury	1998	1.6	Australia	Epic Energy Inc	Canada
26	Eastern Energy Ltd	1995	1.6	Australia	Texas Utilities Co	United States
27	Cia de Electricidade do Estado	1997	1.6	Brazil	Investor Group	Spain
28	Powercor Australia	1995	1.6	Australia	Investor Group	United States
29	Elsag Bailey Process	1999	1.5	Netherlands	ABB Transportation	Netherlands
30	SPT Telecom	1995	1.5	Czech Republic	Telsource consortium	Netherlands and Switzerland
31	Ferrocarril del Noreste	1997	1.4	Mexico	Transportacion Ferroviaria	Mexico
32	Cie Centro Oeste	1997	1.4	Brazil	AES Corp	United States
33	Kaztelekom	1997	1.4	Kazakhstan	Daewoo Corp	Republic of Korea
34	Citipower Ltd(Entergy Corp)	1996	1.3	Australia	Entergy Corp	United States
35	Telkom South Africa	1997	1.3	South Africa	Investor Group	United States
36	Ikon Energy/Multinet Gas	1999	1.3	Australia	Energy Partnership	United States
37	Santa Fe Exploration	1996	1.2	United Kingdom	Saga Petroleum AS	Norway
38	Codensa	1997	1.2	Colombia	Investor Group	Spain
39	Retevision	1997	1.2	Spain	Investor Group	Italy
40	OK Petroleum AB	1994	1.2	Sweden	Corral Petroleum Holdings AB	Sweden
41	Telesudeste Celular(Telebras)	1998	1.2	Brazil	Investor Group	Spain
42	FSM	1992	1.1	Poland	Fiat Auto SpA(Fiat SpA)	Italy
43	Ceskoslovenska Obchodni Banka	1999	1.1	Czech Republic	KBC Bancassurance Holding NV	Belgium
44	Tengizchevroil	1996	1.1	Kazakhstan	Mobil Corp	United States
45	Bank Polska Kasa Opieki SA	1999	1.1	Poland	Investor Group	Italy
46	ASLK-CGER Insurance,ASLK-CGER	1993	1.1	Belgium	Fortis International NV	Netherlands
47	Cemig(Minas Gerais)	1997	1.1	Brazil	Southern Electric Brazil	United States
48	Cellulose du Pin-Paper & Pkg	1994	1.0	France	Jefferson Smurfit Group PLC	Ireland
49	Cia Riograndense de Telecomun	1998	1.0	Brazil	Investor Group	Spain
50	Kinetik Energy/Westar	1999	1.0	Australia	Texas Utilities Australia Pty	Australia

Source: UNCTAD, cross-border M&A database, based on data from Thomson Financial Securities Data Company.

a   For deals whose host and acquiring countries are the same, the ultimate parent country is different. For details, see box IV.4.

Notes

1   In addition to these two modes of entry, the concept of "brownfield investment" can also be found in the literature. It denotes a hybrid situation, between greenfield and acquisition, where investments that are formally an acquisition resemble greenfield projects. In such "brownfield projects", the foreign investor acquires a firm, but almost completely replaces plant and equipment, labour and product line (Meyer and Estrin, 1998). This concept has been applied in particular in cases of acquisitions in transition economies.

2   There are also some cases in which the headquarters are placed in a third country (e.g. the United Kingdom in the case of Pharmacia (Sweden) and Upjohn (United States).

3   In the case of full (100 per cent) acquisitions, deals may also be referred to as (statutory) mergers, though there is a distinction between these two forms (figure IV.1).

4   In addition, the classification of M&As into horizontal, vertical and conglomerate types may lose some of its relevance as a new type of M&A seems to be emerging. Internet companies, or internet holding companies, are investing in a large number of other internet companies, taking usually minority shares. For example, Softbank of Japan has invested in more than 100 internet firms, both at home and abroad, taking less than 30 per cent shares of the companies. Since these internet firms are engaged in many different segments of the internet industry, they are not vertical investments. They could be related with each other in business, making them difficult to be classified as "conglomerate". They can be horizontal, but not exactly in the same line of business. What some of these internet holding companies are trying to do with a series of minority acquisitions is to create an "econet" or economic network, in which various firms linked through minority equity holdings formulate a loose network of affiliated firms and have influence (in such activities as setting standards) in shaping the future of the industry. This would be a new concept of business in the sense that the firms involved are not interested in "control" *per se*, i.e. in formulating a hierarchical organization, but organizing a horizontal network of like-minded companies (Jung, 2000).

5   It should be stressed that the data in figure IV.3 and annex table A.IV.2 are just indicative of the trend. The share of financially motivated deals may well be underestimated as short-term financial

gains can be important motives also in the case of cross-border M&As by non-financial firms.

6   This, in turn, can have implications for how M&As are implemented, not only because the target firms may be less prepared to proceed, but also because the acquirers may have to recoup some of the premiums paid by selling some assets.

7   On a completion basis the value of hostile cross-border takeovers accounted for 1 per cent in 1999 for all cross-border M&As (figure IV.4), compared with 3 per cent for domestic hostile takeovers. In that year, however, a number of high-profile hostile M&As were *announced*, including Vodafone AirTouch's bid for Mannesmann (which succeeded in 2000). Therefore, in terms of announced value, hostile M&As accounted for 14 per cent of *all* M&As (cross-border and domestic) in 1999. "The world is not enough … to merge", press release by Thomson Financial Securities Data Company, 5 January 2000.

8   One case in Chile (Banco Santiago) in 1995 by a Spanish bank (Banco Central Hispanoamericano), two cases in Cayman Islands (GT Chile Growth Fund) by a firm based in the United Kingdom (Regent Kingpin) in 1995 and 1996, and one case in Papua New Guinea (Highlands Gold Ltd.) by a Canadian firm (Placer Dome) in 1997.

9   Unless otherwise noted, *WIR2000* uses data on a completion basis. In addition, transaction values are used in *WIR2000*. They do not, therefore, take into account the value of any liabilities of target firms.

10   "20th century: survey", *The Economist*, 11 September 1999, p. 39.

11   Data for cross-border M&As are systematically collected only from 1987 onwards.

12   KPMG reports $787 billion in cross-border M&As for 1999 (including portfolio M&As), of which $659 billion were majority-owned M&As. Data provided by KPMG Corporate Finance in the Netherlands. The differences between the data reported by KPMG and the data used in the present report essentially lie in the different treatment of cross-border M&A data. While the former do not include increases in stakes in joint ventures in which the target firm remains as a joint venture, the latter do.

13   The data are provided by Thomson Financial Securities Data Company. The period is between 1 January and 13 June. They refer to all cross-border M&As (including portfolio cross-border M&As).

14   Since 1998, 16 deals have had a value of

more than $10 billion: six in 1998 and ten in 1999. There were no such deals before (table IV.4).

[15]   Based on about 200 deals for which information on sources of funds is available (UNCTAD, cross-border M&A database).

[16]   Reported by J.P. Morgan, quoted in "International mergers and acquisitions", *Financial Times*, 22 September 1999.

[17]   In this calculation of investment expenditures, invested funds include those raised in the United States and abroad. For details, see box IV.3.

[18]   This reflects the fact that greenfield FDI is still dominant in outward FDI even though M&As have been rising.

[19]   There is also one large acquisition from the Islamic Republic of Iran – a 50 per cent acquisition of Telecom Eireann (Ireland) for $4.4 billion.

[20]   However, this investment proved to be short-term. In 1998, Daewoo sold its shares to portfolio investors and back to the Government.

[21]   Includes the countries of the former Yugoslavia.

[22]   The figures for Central and Eastern European cross-border M&A sales may significantly underestimate the real volume of such sales because a number of deals, especially at the local level, go unreported.

[23]   Data for the Czech Republic, Hungary, Republic of Korea, Mexico, Poland and Turkey are included in the OECD total as they are OECD member States. The World Bank reports $49.3 billion in privatization revenues in 1998 for developing countries (including Central and Eastern Europe) (World Bank, 2000a).

[24]   For example, during the period 1990-1998 in Brazil, three-quarters of privatizations involved foreign buyers, while in Poland nearly 80 per cent of privatization sales involved foreign firms. The data on privatization revenues are from World Bank, 2000.

Chapter V | Performance, Motivations and Outlook

A. Corporate performance of M&As

The increase in cross-border M&As documented in the preceding chapter is taking place against a widespread perception that most M&As fail to deliver the expected gains set out at the time deals are announced.[1] For example, several management surveys of predominantly cross-border M&As in the mid-1990s concluded that the value of shares held by owners declined in more than half of the cases examined, while increases in the value of shares followed only a small proportion of all M&As (AT Kearney, 1999; KPMG, 1999). There is much controversy surrounding the question of post-M&A performance, however. This section looks at the evidence in the literature to shed light on how *corporate* performance is affected by M&As.

There are several ways of measuring performance. It is therefore important to keep a few points in mind. First, most studies in this area focus on *domestic* M&As and are based on data from the United States and the United Kingdom, where M&As have been prevalent since the beginning of the past century. There is only scant evidence from developing countries and economies in transition. Second, except for a few recent surveys, the experience in the 1990s has not yet been fully explored in the literature. Third, it is impossible to factor in what would have happened to a firm had a merger or acquisition not taken place. Fourth,

it is important to distinguish the impact on firms from the impact on host and home economies. M&As that produce poor results from a strictly financial point of view may still exert a positive impact on an acquired firm and, under certain conditions, the host country. This section deals with the impact on corporations; broader economic impacts will be discussed in the next chapter.

The bulk of the empirical studies of the impact of M&As on corporate performance can broadly be classified into two categories. The first group can be found in the finance literature, and comprises what are called "event studies", which use changes in share prices to gauge changes in firm value. The second group belongs to the industrial organization literature and consists of studies that measure corporate performance mainly by comparing various measures of profitability before and after transactions. The rates of success or failure are typically assessed by comparing the performance with a relevant control group of companies.

The "event studies" generally assume that stock markets are efficient, meaning that changes in the share prices of the firms involved, after controlling for market movements in general and systematic risk, represent the value of the event. Corporate performance is measured by comparing the share prices from before and after M&As relative to a relevant control group. Evidence from a large number of articles analyzing short-term stock reactions to merger announcements indicates that a target firm's shareholders benefit, and a bidding firm's shareholders generally lose or break even. [2] Only about one-third of published shareholder value studies were able to find positive effects for the bidding firm (Schenk, 2000). [3] Other studies have noted that the rates of return earned on common stock tend to deteriorate when the period after the merger is extended to one year or more (Jensen and Ruback, 1983; Magenheim and Mueller, 1988). Moreover, a survey of studies covering different time periods suggested that returns going to the acquirer deteriorated in the 1980s, as compared with the preceding decades (Sirower, 1997).

The results from various event studies are inconclusive with regard to the factors influencing the outcome of M&As. Some researchers have noted that the chances of a positive impact on performance increases if the firms involved are in related industries,[4] while others have reached the opposite conclusion.[5] Moreover, some studies indicate that returns to the acquiring company develop more favourably in cross-border M&As than in domestic ones,[6] whereas others do not support that finding.[7]

The industrial organization literature offers an alternative assessment of performance by using accounting data to measure, e.g. profitability or market shares a few years before and after M&As.[8] Empirical evidence here is also rather sobering. Although industrial organization studies normally consider longer time horizons than those in the financial literature, most of them do not show significant improvement in long-term profitability after acquisition (Scherer, 1988). For example, a study of United Kingdom firms over a 10 to 18 year period indicated little improvement in profitability relative to the period before acquisition and a decline in profitability relative to firms relying on internal growth (Dickerson et al., 1997).[9] Similarly, a survey of 22 accounting data studies from nine countries showed that the average acquiring firm does not earn a significantly higher return than the industry average (Bild, 1998). The most exhaustive study of post-merger performance, covering almost 6,000 M&As by 471 corporations in the United States and 900 divestitures, again found poor financial results from M&As (Ravenscraft and Scherer, 1987).[10]

The industrial organization literature does not provide any clear evidence in regard to how the relatedness of activities of the bidder and target firms affect M&A performance (Bild, 1998). In fact, some studies have concluded that conglomerate M&As provide more favourable results than horizontal or vertical M&As (e.g. Reid, 1968; Mueller, 1980b). Moreover, in the case of cross-border M&As, large cultural differences between bidder and target companies have been found to be positively related to acquisition performance in terms of sales growth (Morosini et al., 1998).

In addition to the above mentioned studies, which mainly focus on the performance of a firm as a whole following a merger or an acquisition, there is some evidence on how the target companies, or even target plants, are affected by takeovers. Although various studies have produced mixed results, ownership changes have been noted to exert positive impacts on the productivity of the acquired units.[11] For example, Canadian plants that were taken over in the 1970s achieved higher productivity increases than those that did not experience a change in ownership (Baldwin, 1995). United States data from the 1960s to the early 1980s indicate that productivity performance may be related to the size of the target (Caves, 1998). It appears that acquisitions can either lift the performance of an unproductive large unit or supply resources needed to leverage the strength of a highly productive small one (Caves, 1998, p. 1962). These conclusions are partly supported by a Swedish study of ownership changes undertaken during 1980-1994 and which, interestingly, distinguished between cross-border and domestic M&As (Modén, 1998). The study found that, prior to a takeover, average labour productivity of the target firms of both domestic and foreign acquirers was lagging behind the industry average. After an acquisition, however, firms taken over by foreign investors showed a substantial increase in labour productivity relative to the industry average, while productivity in domestically acquired firms stayed about the same, or declined somewhat. In addition, compared with both the industry average and with the acquired firms in domestic takeovers, foreign acquisitions developed more favourably in terms of total factor productivity, employment and market shares.

Similar observations have also been made in Argentina. Compared with companies that were not taken over, acquired companies experienced stronger growth rates of sales, productivity, employment and exports (box

VI.14). Moreover, acquired firms reported greater organizational and technological improvements. These results apply to both domestic and cross-border M&As vis-à-vis non-acquired companies. However, sales, employment and exports developed more favourably in the case of foreign takeovers, while the technological and organizational improvements were particularly noteworthy following domestic M&As.

Based on the above discussion, a few important points can be made:

• Studies in the finance and industrial organization literature lend support to the common perception that a large number of M&As "fail" in the sense that firms engaging in M&As do not produce better results, in terms of share prices and profitability, than those that do not enter into M&As. The picture is more positive, however, with regard to the performance of the target companies specifically. This suggests that improved performance at the level of the acquiree, if any, is often compensated by negative effects of the merger at the level of the newly formed firm as a whole. Moreover, some evidence indicates that cross-border M&As may outperform domestic ones, although

several recent management surveys have found a high "failure" rate also among cross-border deals.

• The extent of "failure" crucially depends on the success criteria. As one study (Hopkins, 1999, p. 220) recently concluded:

> "There seems to be clear evidence that mergers and acquisitions often fail. But this depends on how one defines failure. If failure is used in an extreme sense, such as the sale or liquidation of the business, then the rate of failure is relatively low. If failure is the lack of attainment of management's financial objectives, then the rate of failure is high."

• It is difficult to say to what extent the observed rates of "failure" are abnormal in any sense. As all investments have an element of risk associated with them, it is to be expected that a certain proportion of M&As will not live up to the expectations of those who have undertaken them, just as many new ventures, product development projects and greenfield investments do (box V.1). Whether the observed ratios of success are high or low given the associated risk is impossible to

---

**Box V.1. The "failure" of a greenfield FDI: the closure of Siemens'
computer chip plant in Tyneside, United Kingdom**

In May 1997, Siemens AG (Germany) opened a new computer chip plant in Tyneside, near Newcastle in the United Kingdom. The new project was to create 1,100 jobs at the factory, at a cost of about $1.9 billion once completed.[a] The investment was welcomed by the local community, which had suffered economically from the steady decline in the region's traditional industries of coal, steel and shipbuilding. Hopes, however, were dampened soon, as the world price of the type of semiconductors to be produced in this plant declined from around $60 in 1995, when the plant construction was first announced, to $1.50 in 1998.[b] In early July 1998, Siemens' chief executive warned that the group's semiconductor business worldwide stood to lose around DM 1 billion, unless ways could

be found to cut excess capacity. Then, later that month, the head of Siemens' semiconductor business announced that the Tyneside plant — the construction of which had started less than fifteen months ago and which had been tested — would not be opened for volume production.

This is an example of a decision to make a greenfield investment which, subsequently, is overtaken by industry developments. In this case, it was the slump of prices combined with rapidly changing technology which required new production facilities. In the semiconductor industry, a new generation of chips is put in production roughly every three years; a production facility that is not fully operational two years into a new generation is often too expensive to be reconfigured.

Source: UNCTAD.

[a] Matthew Rose, "For a short time, U.K. town's motto was 'Fish into chips': promise of a Siemens plant revived North Tyneside but then cost it dearly", *Wall Street Journal*, 20 October 1998.
[b] Mark Milner and Peter Hetherington, "Jobs blow to high-tech hopes: 1,100 to go as factory closure rocks recovery plans in North-east", *The Guardian*, 1 August 1998.

determine. To merge two separate companies, with different cultures and that previously may have been fierce rivals, into one single business entity is indeed a difficult task. Any merger or acquisition is a complex procedure from pre-deal planning to post-deal integration. The challenge is to create additional value through the transaction, a value that exceeds the premium paid plus the costs for making the deal work. The result depends to a great extent on the successful integration of the two work forces; taking over a major firm is like hiring a large number of new employees at once. This aspect is particularly important for acquisitions in which the skills and capabilities of the target firms are the main source of anticipated gains.

• Other criteria have to be taken into account to assess the extent to which M&As can be regarded as having succeeded or not. In that respect, the right counterfactuals must be considered. What would have happened if a firm had not undertaken a particular merger or acquisition? Even if a merger or an acquisition fails to deliver the expected financial returns in the short-term, the deal may still be motivated by specific strategic reasons, e.g. if the act prevents a competitor from securing a critical asset.

In view of the above, an examination of the broad set of motivating factors is required to explain what appears to be a paradox, i.e. the growth of M&As in spite of their performance results in terms of share prices and profitability. To explore this issue further, the following sections look more closely at the motivations underlying M&As.

B. Why do firms engage in cross-border M&As?

Why are firms increasingly engaging in cross-border M&As when undertaking FDI? Although cross-border M&As represent one mode of FDI entry into foreign locations, the received literature on international production can only partly explain this phenomenon. Indeed, the "OLI paradigm" — the most prominent explanation of FDI — does not distinguish between different modes of entry

and was formulated primarily in reference to greenfield FDI (box V.2). Thus, it is useful to consider first the basic reasons for M&As in general, and for cross-border M&As in particular. As the acquisition behaviour of firms is closely affected by shifts in the business environment, the second part of this section addresses some of the major changes that have taken place in recent years with important implications for the cross-border M&A activity.

1. Motivations for conducting M&As

To explain why firms may prefer to grow via M&As rather than through organic growth, two factors stand out as being particularly important: speed and access to proprietary assets.[12]

Speed is crucial. M&As often represent the fastest means of reaching the desired goals when expanding domestically or inter-nationally. For example, when time to market is vital, the takeover of an existing firm in a new market with an established distribution system is far more preferable to developing a new local distribution and marketing organization. For a latecomer to a market or a new field of technology, M&As can provide a way to catch up rapidly. Enhanced competition and shorter product life cycles accentuate the necessity for firms to respond quickly to opportunities in the economic environment, preferably before competitors move. The pressure of time and the feeling of urgency are highlighted in the observations often made in the information technology (IT) industry today that, in the new economy in which we live, a year has only 50 days, or in the business slogan that "Speed is our friend — time is our enemy". While erstwhile planning may have taken place in five-year intervals, the watchword today is "plaction" — plan and act at once.

The second main motivation for firms to merge with or acquire an existing company, rather than to grow organically, is the *quest for strategic assets,* such as R&D or technical know-how, patents, brand names, the possession of local permits and licences, and supplier or distribution networks. Ready made access to proprietary assets can be important because, by definition, they are not available elsewhere in the market and they take time to develop.[13]

Box V.2. The OLI paradigm and cross-border M&As

The OLI paradigm (Dunning, 1993) addresses three questions related to FDI:

Which firms undertake FDI? Firms investing abroad must possess specific proprietary or ownership ("O") advantages to overcome the extra costs of operating in a different, less familiar environment. These advantages are generally costly to create, but can be transferred to new locations at relatively low cost. The analysis of "O" advantages draws on industrial organization, resource based, evolutionary and management theories, with advantages residing mainly in firm-specific technology, brand names, privileged access to factor or product markets or superior technological or management skills. Initial "O" advantages allow firms to grow and invest abroad, but size and international spread can, in turn, feed back and provide new advantages (accessing capital markets and information, spreading risks and so on). In some cases, firms may go overseas to supplement or enhance their existing "O" assets ("asset-seeking" FDI) seeking synergies between their own strengths and those of foreign firms or institutions.

Where do firms choose to exploit their advantages, in the home country (by exports) or abroad, and in which foreign locations? They select sites with location ("L") advantages that best match the deployment of their "O" assets. The analysis of "L" advantages draws on trade and location theory, the main factors determining comparative costs being factor and transport costs, market size and characteristics, and government policies (e.g. stability, predictability, tariffs, taxes and FDI regulations). Asset-seeking FDI is drawn to locations with strong technological, educational or information creation activities.

Why do firms choose to internalize their advantages by direct investment in preference to selling them to other firms? The analysis of internalization ("I") draws on transaction-cost theories of the firm, and centres on the feasibility of and returns to contracting the sale of intangible advantages to other firms. The most valuable and new advantages tend to be internalized, since these are the most difficult to price and contract over time. The more mature ones are easier to price, less subject to uncertainty and less valuable to the owner: these are licensed more readily. Internalization can also explain vertical FDI, where a particular

process or function is located abroad by TNCs to serve its production system (rather than subcontracted to independent suppliers). Transaction-cost analysis can also help explain why it is difficult or costly to contract independent firms for such arrangements, particularly in technology-intensive or strategic activities.

While the paradigm does not explicitly distinguish between different modes of FDI entry, the origins of the paradigm were more in greenfield investments than M&As. On the "ownership" side, the original thesis on which it draws explained the growth of United States companies in terms of an industrial organization analysis of barriers to entry in setting up new facilities (Hymer, 1960). The extension made to multi-plant operations again was conceived in terms of firms setting up new plants (Caves, 1971). The "internalization" analysis was based upon work explaining how firm boundaries were drawn in terms of the costs of hierarchical control (internalization) versus market control (externalization) of their assets (Coase, 1937; Williamson, 1971). The implicit setting was the expansion of firms by the building of new facilities rather than the joint internalization of assets by different firms involved in M&As. With regard to international investment in developing host countries, the analysis was entirely conducted in terms of greenfield FDI. Until recently, cross-border M&As in these countries were rare.

It is therefore useful to consider OLI factors specifically for M&As, and to distinguish mergers from acquisitions (box table V.2.1). Mergers are taken to involve firms of roughly similar size and capacity that jointly internalize their "ownership" advantages to gain economies of synergy, size and scope. Acquisitions are taken to involve larger, more powerful or better capitalized firms taking over smaller or weaker ones, and using this to gain speedy access to the latter's "ownership" and "locational" assets. The OLI factors can be considered separately for the three main types of M&As (horizontal, vertical and conglomerate), bearing in mind that horizontal transactions account for nearly two-thirds of cross-border M&A activity (figure IV.2).

Cross-border M&As and their characteristics call for an adaptation of the conventional analysis. The fact that M&As

/...

Box V.2. The OLI paradigm and cross-border M&As (concluded)

allow investors much faster access to, or offer new, ownership advantages accounts partly for their growing use in the current international competitive environment. The internalization factors are also different in that there is *joint* internalization, particularly in M&As between similar firms. In addition, the traditional OLI paradigm does not take into account non-economic explanations, such as personal motivations of managers or corporate responses under strategic interdependence.[a]

The traditional OLI analysis of locational factors is thus not particularly relevant in explaining mega mergers between TNCs, pooling not only their ownership-specific advantages, but also the global locational advantages of their worldwide production networks. The framework can still be applied to acquisitions by more advanced firms of less advanced ones — and so to FDI flows from developed to developing countries or economies in transition.

Box table V.2.1. The OLI paradigm and cross-border M&As

Type	Horizontal	Vertical	Conglomerate
Mergers	O: Both firms have O advantages complementing each other in scale, synergy, finance or market power. L: Standard location factors are not relevant where two TNCs merge their global production systems. I: Both firms seek to gain economies of scale by internalizing joint advantages. Joint internalization differs from "internalization" in usual OLI terms, but determinants (transaction costs in some sense) are similar. Mergers provide a much faster way of exploiting each other's advantages.	O: Both firms have O advantages that complement each other in different processes of the production chain. L: As with greenfield FDI, but also see horizontal mergers. I: Merging firms both seek to gain security, information, finance or market power, and to reduce transaction costs.	O: Both firms have O advantages in unrelated activities that may have economies of scope, but not technological complementarity. A merger is thus not based on O advantages in the usual sense; it may just involve access to finance. L: Mainly market size/ growth or prospects of capital appreciation, not location advantages in the OLI sense. I: Merging firms seek a larger capital base or economies of scope, but are not internalizing their O assets to save on transaction costs.
Acquisitions	O: Acquiring firms tend to have greater O advantages than acquired firms, or seek specific new O advantages (technology, contacts, etc.). L: As with greenfield FDI, except that many L advantages are "embodied" in the acquired firm. I: As with greenfield FDI, acquiring firms strengthen their competitive positions by internalization.	O: Acquiring firms have a stronger financial or managerial base that allows them to acquire vertically linked firms abroad. L: As with horizontal acquisitions. I: As with greenfield FDI, acquiring firms strengthen their competitive positions by internalization.	O: Acquiring firms have greater financial and/or managerial resources, but no O advantages in the usual sense. L: Mainly market size and growth and prospects of capital appreciation, not location advantages. I: Acquiring firms seek diversification or economies of scope, but are not internalizing in an OLI sense.

Source: UNCTAD.

Source: UNCTAD.

[a]   In recent work, the need for adapting the OLI framework to meet new situations has been acknowledged; see Dunning (1998 and 2000).

Such assets may be crucial to advance a firm's *static* advantages, i.e. its income-generating resources and capabilities at a given moment in time, or to strengthen its *dynamic* advantages, i.e. its ability to sustain and increase the income-generating assets over time (Dunning, 2000). To take just one example of where the need for speed — the alternative between "build" or "buy" — and the search for proprietary assets came together: the main reason for the Indian company Tata Tea to acquire Tetley Ltd. in the United Kingdom was to obtain access to a global brand name and a global distribution network; reaching the same objective through organic growth would have been more or less impossible. To quote Tata Tea's Vice-Chairman who engineered the acquisition:

"For us to develop a global market in the time frame we had in mind, the acquisition of Tetley, with its brand name and distribution system, was the only option."[14]

These two main advantages of M&As interact with a number of other driving forces, which play out differently in different industries and markets, and which often simultaneously affect the decision to undertake M&As. Many of the driving forces listed below can also motivate FDI in general, but, when speed enters the picture, they tend to favour M&As, as the objectives sought for can be realized more quickly:

- The search for new markets, increased market power and market dominance;
- Efficiency gains through synergies;
- Greater size;
- Diversification (spreading of risks);
- Financial motivations; and
- Personal (behavioural) motivations.

The *search for new markets and market power* is a constant concern for firms. Where domestic markets are saturated, in particular, foreign ones beckon. High transaction costs associated with arm's-length transactions involving intangible assets may explain why firms possessing ownership specific capabilities often prefer to exert direct control (instead of exporting or licensing) when exploiting them in new geographical locations or industry segments. Through M&As, firms can quickly access new market opportunities and develop critical mass without adding additional capacity to an industry. By taking over an existing company, immediate access to a local network of suppliers, clients and skills can be obtained. This motivation is of particular importance for cross-border M&As as the need for knowledge about local conditions increases when leaving the home market. Beyond this, and especially in markets characterized by oligopoly, M&As can also be motivated by the pursuit for market power and *market dominance*. Especially in the case of horizontal M&As, the motivation can well be the search for oligopolistic positions; in addition, consolidated market control may provide opportunities for anti-competitive practices and increased barriers to entry.

Anticipated *efficiency gains through synergies* are probably the most cited justification for M&As. Synergies can be static (cost reduction or revenue enhancement at a given point in time) or dynamic (e.g. innovation-enhancing) in character. Examples of the former kind of synergies include the pooling of management resources (one head office instead of two), revenue enhancement by using each others' marketing and distribution networks, purchasing synergies (greater bargaining power), economies of scale in production leading to cost reductions, and the avoidance of duplication of production, R&D or other activities. Dynamic synergies may involve the matching of complementary resources and skills to enhance a firm's innovatory capabilities with long-term positive effects on sales, market shares and profits. The search for static synergies may be particularly important in industries characterized by increased competitive pressure, falling prices and excess capacity, such as in the automotive and defence industries. Meanwhile, dynamic synergies may be crucial in industries experiencing fast technological change and that are innovation-driven, such as in information technology and pharmaceuticals. The efficiency-through-synergy motive is present for both domestic and cross-border M&As. However, the scope for rationalization and improving company performance by achieving an international specialization of the value chain can be particularly high in the case of cross-border investments that allow firms to locate different activities in places with appropriate mixes of locational advantages.

In a globalizing economy, *greater size* can be a crucial parameter, particularly in operations requiring economies of scale, large expenditures for R&D and the expansion of distribution networks for example.[15] Size in itself can also make it more difficult to be taken over and, therefore, can have a protective function. Large size can furthermore create financial, managerial and operational synergies that reduce the operational vulnerability of firms. Sheer size normally means lower-cost access to investible funds as there are economies of scale in capital raising.[16] Information asymmetries between corporate insiders and investors can make internal financing more favourable.[17] A company can use its internal capital market by letting cash rich divisions with few profitable projects finance capital expenditures in cash poor divisions with better growth opportunities. Another advantage of size is that larger firms with multiple operations across geographical locations and segments can have an advantage in the collection and adoption of new information and innovation. The size motive can apply to both domestic and cross-border M&As.[18]

A fourth driver behind M&As is the desire for risk reduction (operational risks, foreign exchange risks, etc.) through product or geographical market *diversification*. Firms may make cross-border M&As on the basis that industry returns across countries may be less correlated than within an economy (Vasconcellos and Kish, 1998). By acquiring foreign companies, a firm may be able to circumvent tariff and non-tariff barriers and thereby lower the level of uncertainty. As intensified global competition and rapid technology development have led firms to focus on their core activities, however, the product diversification motive has become less important (Morck and Yeung, 1999), although geographical diversification plays a role.

There can be important *financial motives* behind M&As. Stock prices do not always reflect the true value of a firm. A potential acquirer can, for example, value a company's anticipated earnings stream higher than current shareholders do. Bad management of a firm, imperfections in the capital market and major exchange rate realignments may provide short-term capital gains to be made by acquiring an undervalued firm, or affect the timing of planned M&As. Such motivations are particularly important in the case of portfolio-type M&As and in economies with poorly developed capital markets or in financial crisis. In addition, some M&As are undertaken partly for tax considerations, e.g. to exploit unused tax shields.

The *personal gains (or behavioural)* explanation argues that corporate managers pursue their own self-interest, especially where corporate governance is weak (a manifestation of what economists have denoted the "principal-agent problem").[19] They may seek expansion or "empire building" to enhance executives' power, prestige, job-security or remuneration, even when this is not technically efficient or in the interest of shareholders (Baumol, 1967). They can also be under the pressure of financial markets — especially where double-digit growth rates are considered the norm — to show high growth and profit rates; M&As can provide the easiest route in this respect, compared to organic greenfield investment growth. Individual managers may also overestimate their ability to manage acquisitions and think that they are especially well equipped to make a merger-deal work.

The factors discussed so far basically apply to both domestic and cross-border M&As. In the case of the latter, a number of empirical studies have specifically analyzed the determinants of the choice between takeover M&As and greenfield investments as a mode of entry into foreign locations. In addition to the basic motivations identified above, many of these studies have also taken firm-specific, host country-specific as well as industry-specific aspects into account (box V.3).

While all factors mentioned here are important to consider when explaining why firms undertake cross-border M&As, it is seldom only one factor that is decisive. In fact, in a cross-national comparison testing several of the motives for M&As discussed above, no hypothesis examined received consistent confirmation, suggesting that there are multiple reasons simultaneously at work (Mueller, 1980a). To put it differently (Scherer and Ross, 1990, p. 159):

"Mergers occur for a myriad of reasons, and in any given case, several different motives may simultaneously influence the merging parties' behavior".

2. Changes in the economic environment

So far the principal basic motivations for undertaking cross-border M&As have been examined. But the acquisition behaviour of firms is also greatly affected by changes in the economic and regulatory environment and, when it comes to cross-border M&As, by the international economic and regulatory environment. This section considers some of the major changes — as regards technology, the regulatory framework and capital markets — that have taken place in the past decade and that have facilitated cross-border M&As and, indeed, encouraged firms to pursue them.

a. Technology

The rapid pace of technological change has intensified competitive pressures on the world's technology leaders. Consequently, the costs and risks of innovation have risen in most industries, as has the need to incorporate continuously new technologies and manage-

ment practices. Firms thus need more efforts to maintain innovative leads, to find new areas of technological leadership, and to keep up with new knowledge and shorter product-life cycles. In an environment characterized by rapid technological change and rising expenditures for risky R&D projects, many firms feel compelled to enter into cross-border M&As as a way of sharing the costs of innovation and accessing new technological assets to enhance their innovatory capabilities. M&As allow firms to do this quickly. Such asset-seeking FDI by TNCs from developed (and increasingly from developing) countries is a rising form of FDI. It is likely to become more common as intangible, knowledge-based assets and access to a pool of skilled people and work teams become more important in the world economy.[20]

Box V.3. Determinants of the mode of FDI entry

The literature (see e.g. Harzing, 1999) has identified a number of firm-specific, host-country-specific and industry-specific-factors that affect the mode of entry of firms into foreign markets:

- Firms with lower R&D intensity are more likely to buy technological capabilities abroad by acquisition, while those with strong technological advantages tend to prefer greenfield ventures to a greater extent.
- More diversified investing firms are likely to enter new markets through acquisitions.
- Larger TNCs are traditionally more prone to acquire than smaller ones, although the latter have shown an increased tendency to acquire in recent years.
- There is weak support that high advertising intensity leads to more acquisitions. This propensity is strengthened where local firms can provide access to distribution systems and extensive knowledge of the local market.
- The greater the cultural and economic distance between home and host countries, the lower the probability of an acquisition. Most M&As concentrate in developed home and host countries with similar cultural and business practices.
- Acquisitions are encouraged by imperfections of capital markets that lead to the undervaluation of company assets (Gonzalez et al., 1998). By similar reasoning, they are also encouraged by economic crises that lead to sharp falls in asset prices generally.

- TNCs that already have an affiliate in a host country are more likely to prefer takeovers as a way of expansion in the same country, to avoid adding local production capacity and competition. This finding helps to explain why the continuous increase in transnational activity would lead to a stronger preference for M&As (Andersson and Svensson, 1994).
- In developing countries, the advantage of M&As is rarely access to proprietary technology or skills (with the exception of some newly industrializing economies). The advantage lies more in rapid market entry, local market knowledge, established distribution systems and contacts with the government, suppliers or customers.
- For firms to choose M&As instead of entry through greenfield investment, there has to be a supply of suitable target companies to acquire. This may not always be the case, most notably in a number of developing countries.
- Slow growth in an industry favours M&As. A number of the cross-border deals in the late 1990s have been undertaken in industries characterized by over-capacity, falling prices and slow growth. Under such conditions, firms may be reluctant to add new capacity as that could further deteriorate the situation. This applies, e.g. to raw material-based industries, such as paper and pulp, steel, metal mining, petroleum as well as to military equipment and the automotive industries (Kang and Johansson, 2000; UNCTAD, 1999a).

Source: UNCTAD.

But technological developments also have other implications. Some of the most important changes relate to the new information and communication technologies. They enable a better management of operations distributed worldwide, and provide new ways of organizing contacts within and between firms as well as with consumers. The use of electronic commerce, for example, makes it possible to restructure the supply chain and reduces the costs of reaching large consumer markets. By lowering transport, information-access and communication costs, technical progress has dramatically shrunk economic space. One result is more intense competition, as foreign competitors may be able to deliver goods and services more cheaply, technologies are diffused more rapidly and information is more broadly available. Another, however, is that TNCs can compete more effectively. They can communicate better across their international production systems, transfer goods and personnel across borders more cheaply and break up production and management processes to locate sub-processes in different countries to minimize cost. Even between different headquarters operations — finance, strategy, R&D, design, marketing — locational links are being loosened, as some TNCs place some of these operations in dispersed sites.[21]

Technological change thus has an impact on the size of firms, reduces costs and facilitates better management of far-flung transnational operations. It allows new management systems to be applied more effectively across the globe, and makes globally integrated production systems more feasible and cost-effective. Cross-border M&As play a critical role in allowing TNCs to set up and expand these systems to develop a portfolio of locational assets. As a result, too, TNCs gain more experience in "digesting" acquired enterprises into existing corporate systems which, in turn, makes the M&A route more enticing than before.

b. Changes in the policy and regulatory environment

If the crucial role of technology makes asset-seeking FDI more important and technological changes have facilitated the operation of international production systems, changes in the policy and regulatory environment during the past decade have provided more space for these systems to expand, including through M&As. Key here are the liberalization of FDI and trade regimes, regional economic integration, privatization and the deregulation of various industries.

(i) Policies on FDI and cross-border M&As

The liberalization of FDI regimes has continued apace, typically on a unilateral basis. Most countries are now trying to attract direct investment, not just by removing restrictions, but also through active promotion and by providing high standards of treatment, legal protection and guarantees. Of the 1,035 FDI regulatory changes between 1991 and 1999 in over 100 countries in all regions, 974 went in the direction of facilitating FDI inflows (chapter I). Examples of such changes relevant to M&As include the removal of compulsory joint venture requirements, restrictions on majority ownership and authorization requirements. The international regulatory framework has also been strengthened, especially through the conclusion of bilateral investment protection and double taxation treaties (chapter I). Multilateral agreements support these trends. For instance, WTO agreements limit the use of certain investment-related measures that affect trade, like local content requirements on TNCs, and certain types of export requirements. World Bank and IMF programmes encourage countries to adopt more open, transparent and welcoming regimes towards foreign investors.

As FDI regimes typically apply to both greenfield investment and cross-border M&As, the latter have also been facilitated by FDI policy liberalization in developed and developing countries. A survey of the literature dealing with more than 100 national FDI regulatory frameworks reveals that most laws dealing with FDI do not explicitly make a distinction between greenfield investment and M&As.[22] Thus, when industries are removed from closed lists, both forms of FDI are typically permitted; and when restrictions on foreign ownership are removed, majority acquisitions of domestic firms are also allowed. Within this overall trend, however, a number of host countries have various policy instruments to deal with cross-border M&As, including special authorization requirements for cross-border M&As under their FDI laws, as e.g. in Malaysia (box V.4), Canada (box V.5) and, until recently, New Zealand and Sweden. Some countries also have instruments to screen cross-border M&As for particular purposes, e.g. national security considerations (box V.6). Moreover, governments may reserve the right to approve some proposed investment projects and reject or modify others to preserve important public interests. Furthermore, when governments screen FDI projects, it may well be that more greenfield proposals have been approved than M&As; but as the relevant bodies do not normally publish their results and reasoning, no precise conclusions are possible. Finally, governments have sometimes kept "golden shares" in privatized companies in order to be able to preserve essential strategic interests; golden shares have been used to veto undesirable further changes in ownership and control of the privatized company.

Box V.4. Malaysia's guidelines for the regulation of acquisition of assets, mergers and takeovers

The Foreign Investment Committee (FIC) Guidelines of 1974 were formulated to establish a set of rules regarding the acquisition of assets or any interest, mergers or takeovers of companies and businesses. Through these Guidelines, the Government endeavours to reduce the imbalances in the distribution of the corporate wealth and to encourage those forms of private investment that would contribute to the development of the country in consonance with its economic objectives. The Guidelines provide that the proposed acquisition of assets or any interest, mergers or takeovers:

(a) Should result directly or indirectly in a more balanced Malaysian participation in ownership and control;

(b) Should lead directly or indirectly to net economic benefits in relation to such matters as the extent of Malaysian participation, particularly Bumiputera participation, ownership and management, income distribution, growth, employment, exports, quality, range of products and services, economic diversification, processing and upgrading of local raw material, training, efficiency, and research and development; and

(c) Should not have adverse consequences in terms of national policies in such matters as defence, environmental protection or regional development.

They also provide that the onus of proving that the proposed acquisition of assets or any interest, mergers or takeovers of companies and businesses is not against the objectives of the New Economic Policy is on the acquiring parties concerned.

The Guidelines apply to the following:

(a) Any proposed acquisition by foreign interests of any substantial fixed assets in Malaysia;

(b) Any proposed acquisition of assets or any interest, mergers and takeovers of companies and businesses in Malaysia by any means, which will result in ownership or control passing to foreign interest;

(c) Any proposed acquisition of 15 per cent or more of the voting power by any one foreign interest or associated group or by foreign interests in the aggregate of 30 per cent or more of the voting power of a Malaysian company or business;

(d) Control of Malaysian companies or businesses through any form of joint-venture agreement, management agreement and technical assistance agreement or other agreement;

(e) Any merger and takeover of any company or business in Malaysia whether by Malaysians or foreign interests; and

(f) Any other proposed acquisition of assets or interests exceeding in value of RM5 million whether by Malaysians or foreign interests.

The Guidelines, however, do not apply to specific projects approved by the Government comprising the following:

(a) Acquisition by Ministries and Government Departments;

(b) Acquisition by Minister of Finance Incorporated, Menteri Besar Incorporated and State Secretary Incorporated; and

(c) Privatization projects approved by the Federal or State Government.

Source: Malaysia, Ministry of Finance, 2000.

But the practice of countries in this respect has also changed over time. An example is the Republic of Korea which, until 1998, did not experience foreign purchases of majority interests in local firms, but which, in the face of the Asian financial crisis, opened all industries to M&As, except for a few sensitive ones (box V.7). Thailand represents another country that, in response to the financial crisis, liberalized its regulatory environment for cross-border M&As and even promoted them.[23] The ASEAN Investment Area, also in response to the financial crisis, extended in December 1998, and for a specified period of time, various incentives to cross-border M&As (ASEAN, 1998).

While FDI policies are being liberalized, cross-border M&As are increasingly reviewed as part of competition policy. By June 2000,

some 90 countries have adopted competition laws or were in the process of doing so (table V.1). Merger review systems have been widely used for this purpose in a number of developed countries for many years (UNCTAD, 1997a). During the past fifteen years or so, such systems have also been adopted or strengthened in developing countries and economies in transition.[24] Thus, rather than the blanket restrictions on foreign takeovers imposed in past years under FDI laws, M&A reviews under competition laws proceed on a case-by-case basis, with competition concerns constituting the key benchmark. By and large, competition-based M&A reviews do not tend to discriminate between cross-border and domestic M&As. Thus, a switch from investment to competition control virtually always represents a step towards liberalization.

Box V. 5. Canada's regulatory regime on cross-border M&As

Canada has traditionally relied heavily on FDI to further its economic development. In the 1950s, it began to measure the level of foreign control in certain industries and to analyze the costs and benefits of foreign investment, primarily foreign takeovers. As a result, Canada introduced certain laws and policies to regulate foreign investment. During the 1980s, however, most of these regulations were removed except for a few, including the 1986 *Investment Canada Act*.

Under the *Investment Canada Act*, all foreign takeovers of Canadian companies are subject to notification to the Government; however, only significant ones are formally reviewed. Foreign takeover proposals are assessed on the basis of their "net benefit" to Canada. The factors of net benefit on which the assessment is based include:

(a) The effect of the investment on the level and nature of economic activity in Canada, including the effect on employment, on resource processing, on the utilization of parts, components and services produced in Canada and on exports from Canada;

(b) The degree and significance of participation in the Canadian business or new Canadian business and in any industry or industries in Canada of which the Canadian business or new Canadian business forms or would form a part;

(c) The effect of the investment on productivity, industrial efficiency, technological development, product innovation and product variety in Canada;

(d) The effect of the investment on competition within an industry or industries in Canada;

(e) The compatibility of the investment with national industrial, economic and cultural policies, taking into consideration industrial, economic and cultural policy objectives enunciated by the Government or legislature of any province likely to be significantly affected by the investment; and

(f) The contribution of the investment to Canada's ability to compete in world markets.

Most proposals for foreign takeovers of Canadian firms are reviewed and approved quickly (i.e. within 45 days), although large and complex ones sometimes need longer time for review. In 1999, there were 700 foreign takeovers of Canadian businesses, and between 5 and 10 per cent were reviewed. As a rule, reviewability is based on the asset value of the Canadian business to be acquired, which was 184 million Canadian dollars in 1999 and has been set at 192 million Canadian dollars for 2000. Canada's laws on foreign takeovers are applicable to investors from all countries.

Source: UNCTAD based on Chudy, *et al*, 2000.

(ii) Other changes in the regulatory environment

Trade liberalization gathered pace in the 1990s with the conclusion of the Uruguay Round. The cumulative effect has been a radical change in the signals and competitive setting for international investors. Firms now face more intense competition at home as well as abroad.

The formation of regional free trade areas has facilitated both greenfield investment and cross-border M&As in several ways. Regional trade agreements enlarge the size of the immediately accessible market for firms, and

---

Box V. 6. Control of cross-border M&As in the United States: the Exon-Florio provision

Section 5021 of the United States Omnibus Trade and Competitiveness Act of 1988 amended Section 721 of the Defense Production Act of 1950 and provides authority to the President of the United States to suspend or prohibit any foreign acquisition, merger or takeover of a United States corporation that is determined to threaten the national security of the United States. The Government can exercise this authority under section 721, also known as the "Exon-Florio provision", to block a foreign acquisition of a United States corporation only if the President finds that:

- There is credible evidence that the foreign entity exercising control might take action that threatens national security; *and*

- The provisions of law, other than the International Emergency Economic Powers Act, do not provide adequate and appropriate authority to protect national security.

The Exon-Florio provision is implemented by the Committee on Foreign Investment in the United States (CFIUS), an inter-agency committee chaired by the Secretary of the Treasury. To assist in making a determination, the Exon-Florio provision provides for written notice of an acquisition, merger or takeover of a United States corporation by a foreign entity. After reviewing the notified transaction, in some cases it may be necessary to undertake an investigation. This must begin no later than 30 days after notification. Any investigation is required to end within 45 days. Information provided by companies is held confidential and cannot be made public except in the case of an administrative or judicial action.

The Exon-Florio provision lists the following factors that the President or a designee may consider in determining the effects of a foreign acquisition on national security:

- The domestic production needed for projected national defense requirements;

- The capability and capacity of domestic industries to meet national defense requirements, including the availability of human resources, products, technology, materials, and other supplies and services;

- The control of domestic industries and commercial activity by foreign citizens as it affects the capability and capacity of the United States to meet the requirements of national security;

- The potential effects of the transaction on the sales of military goods, equipment or technology to a country that supports terrorism or proliferates missile technology or chemical and biological weapons; and

- The potential effects of the transaction on United States technological leadership in areas affecting United States national security.

The Exon-Florio provision was amended by Section 873(a) of the National Defense Authorisation Act for 1993 which requires an investigation in cases in which:

- The acquirer is controlled by, or acting on behalf of, a foreign government; and

- The acquisition "could result in control of a person engaged in interstate commerce in the U.S. that could affect the national security of the U.S.."

According to the latest statistics published by the General Accounting Office of the United States (box table V.6.), 1,258 notifications of foreign M&As were made to the CFIUS under the Exon-Florio provision between 1988 and 1999. Of these, 17 were investigated, seven were withdrawn before the final determination was made and the President blocked one.

/...

so attract foreign investors to serve them by setting up new facilities. They can enhance market transparency and, if they link national currencies, lower the costs of cross-border transactions. If they incorporate investment agreements, they make M&As more feasible. From a TNC perspective, the need to establish

a local presence is particularly strong if an integrating area sets up high common external tariffs; but even low external barriers to trade can be a powerful magnet in rich or expansive regional markets. The formation of the European Community, for instance, provided a major stimulus to inward FDI and promoted

---

Box V. 6. Control of cross-border M&As in the United States: the Exon-Florio provision (concluded)

Box table V.6.1. Disposition of CFIUS notifications, October 1988 - December 1999

Year	CFIUS notifications	Notifications investigated	Notifications withdrawn	President blocked
1988	14	1	-	-
1989	200	5	2	1[a]
1990	295	6	2	-
1991	152	1	-	-
1992	106	2	1[b]	-
1993	82	-	-	-
1994	69	-	-	-
1995	81	-	-	-
1996	55	-	-	-
1997	62	-	-	-
1998	63	2	2	-
1999	79	-	-	-
Total	1 258	17	7	1

Source: United States, General Accounting Office, 1995, p. 4, based on CFIUS data as of January 1995, and United States , CFIUS data up to December 1999.

[a] In this case, the President ordered the China National Aero-Technology Import and Export Corporation, an aerospace company of China, to divest from MAMCO, which involved a United States aircraft parts manufacturer.

[b] The investors withdrew their offer on the last day of the investigation of this case, which involved the acquisition of LTV Missiles Division by Thomson-CSF.

Source: United States, Department of the Treasury, Office of International Investment, 2000

Box V.7. The Republic of Korea's shift in policy on cross-border M&As

In the wake of the 1997 financial crisis, the country's policy towards FDI through M&As changed as the Government sought to overcome the crisis by increasing foreign exchange liquidity. By May 1998, the restrictions on the foreign acquisition of domestic shares in the stock market, and restrictions on M&As and land acquisition by foreigners, had been abolished. Controls remain only in a few industries sensitive to national security, public health and environment protection. Restrictions on foreign equity ownership were abandoned in most industries, and even hostile takeovers by foreign investors have become possible.

The new investment policy, however, still slightly favours greenfield over M&A investment. For example, most of the newly introduced measures (other than the abolitions in share acquisitions), such as the creation of a foreign investment zone and tax incentives, basically imply investments in greenfield form. Thus, the tax regime favours greenfield FDI rather than M&As by allowing reductions of taxes on corporate income, acquisitions, registration, property and land under various laws. This benefits acquisition of assets, which are considered to be greenfield investment (as opposed to acquisition of shares, which are not) under the laws of the Republic of Korea.

Source: UNCTAD, based on Yun, 2000; and information provided by the Republic of Korea, Ministry of Commerce, Industry and Energy.

Table V.1. Countries that have adopted competition laws, as of June 2000

Africa	Asia and the Pacific	Central and Eastern Europe	Developed countries	Latin America and the Caribbean
Algeria (1995)	Azerbaijan [b]	Albania (1995	Australia (1974)	Argentina (1923, 1980, 1999)
Benin [a]	Bahrein [b]	Belarus (1992)	Austria (1988, 1993, 1999)	Barbados [a]
Botswana [a]	China (1993)	Bosnia and Herzegovina [a]	Belgium (1991, 1999)	Bolivia [a]
Cameroon [b]	Cyprus (1990, 1999)	Bulgaria (1991, 1998)	Canada (1986, 1999)	Brazil (1962, 1990, 1994, 1998)
Central African Republic (1994)	Fiji (1993)	Croatia (1995)	Denmark (1997)	Chile (1959, 1973, 1980)
Chad [a]	Georgia (1996)	Czech Republic (1991, 1992, 1993)	Finland (1992, 1998)	Colombia (1959, 1992,1996, 1998)
Côte d'Ivoire (1978, 1991)	India (1969)	Estonia (1993, 1998)	France (1986, 1995)	Costa Rica (1994)
Gabon (1989)	Indonesia (1999)	Hungary (1984, 1990, 1996)	Germany (1957, 1998)	Cuba [a]
Ghana [a]	Iran, Islamic Republic of [a]	Latvia (1991, 1993, 1998)	Greece (1977, 1995)	Dominican Republic [a]
Egypt [a]	Jordan [a]	Lithuania (1992, 1999)	Iceland (1993)	Ecuador [a]
Ethiopia [a]	Kazakhstan (1999)	Poland (1990)	Ireland (1978, 1991, 1996)	El Salvador [a]
Kenya (1988)	Kyrgyzstan (1994)	Republic of Moldova (1992)	Israel (1959, 1988,1989)	Guatemala [a]
Lesotho [a]	Lebanon (1967)	Romania (1991, 1996)	Italy (1990)	Honduras [a]
Malawi (1998)	Malaysia [a]	Russian Federation (1991, 1992, 1995, 1998, 2000)	Japan (1947, 1998)	Jamaica (1993)
Mali (1997)	Malta (1994)	Slovakia (1991, 1994, 1998)	Liechtenstein (1992, 1995)	Mexico (1992, 1998)
Mauritania (1991, 1999)	Mongolia [b]	Slovenia (1993, 1998)	Luxembourg (1970, 1981)	Nicaragua [a]
Mauritius (1980, 1999)	Pakistan (1970)	The Former Yugoslav Republic of Macedonia [b]	Netherlands (1997)	Panama (1996, 1999)
Morocco (1999)	Philippines (1992)	Ukraine (1992, 1996, 1998)	New Zealand (1986)	Paraguay (1997)
Namibia [a]	Republic of Korea (1980)	Yugoslavia (1996)	Norway (1993)	Peru (1991)
Niger (1992)	Saudi Arabia [a]		Portugal (1993)	Trinidad and Tobago [a]
Rwanda [a]	Sri Lanka (1987)		Spain (1989, 1996, 1999)	Uruguay [a]
Senegal (1994)	Taiwan Province of China (1992, 1999)		Sweden (1993)	Venezuela (1973, 1992, 1996)
Sudan [a]	Tajikistan (1993)		Switzerland (1962, 1985, 1995, 2000)	
South Africa (1955, 1998, 1999)	Thailand (1979, 1999)		United Kingdom (1973, 1994, 1998)	
Tunisia (1991)	Turkey (1994, 1998)		United States (1890, 1976)	
United Republic of Tanzania (1994)	Turkmenistan (1993)			
Zambia (1994, 1998)	Uzbekistan (1992, 1996)			
Zimbabwe (1996, 1999)	Viet Nam [a]			
	Yemen [a]			

Source: UNCTAD, based on information provided by Governments; White & Case, 2000; United States, International Competition Policy Advisory Committee, 2000; and UNCTAD sources.

[a] Competition law is under preparation.
[b] Date of adoption of law not available.

restructuring by national, regional (intra-EU) and cross-border (non-EU) M&As (UNCTC, 1993). The initial impetus was greatly strengthened by the creation of a single market and, more recently, the launch of the Euro, which adds to competitive pressures and to the restructuring of previously segmented markets. Increased competition underlines the role of rapid responses by companies, thus favouring cross-border M&As in particular. Regional trade agreements in the developing world, like ASEAN in South-East Asia and MERCOSUR in Latin America, are stimulating similar restructuring, even if the markets involved are not as large and the integration processes less intense.

In parallel with trade liberalization and regional integration processes, there has been widespread *privatization* and *deregulation* of activities, most notably in such service industries as telecommunications, transportation, power generation and financial services. These changes have provided another stimulus to M&As in general and cross-border ones in particular. Privatization programmes in many developing countries and economies in transition have increased the availability of domestic companies for sale. In fact, the combination of privatization and deregulation has created a number of new TNCs. Previously state-owned utility companies, for example, facing new competitive pressures at home, have responded by becoming dynamic international investors. In Europe, activities that have long been strongly homebound, like water supply, power generation, rail transports, telecommunications, and airport construction, are now populated by transnational operators. The

first wave of expansion (with foreign participation in privatization) is being followed by further consolidation and restructuring, with M&As again set to play a vital role.

c. Changes in capital markets

Cross-border M&As have been facilitated by changes in world capital markets. The liberalization of capital movements, new information technology providing instant information across the globe, more active market intermediaries, and new financial instruments have had a profound impact on M&A activity worldwide. Whereas the liberalization of capital markets since the mid-1980s had already greatly facilitated the growth of cross-border M&As, most developed countries now have completely liberalized their capital accounts, with virtually unrestricted facilities for cross-border loans and credits, foreign currency deposits and portfolio investment. More recently, financial transactions have also been substantially liberalized in many developing countries.

In addition, the increased use of cross-border M&As mirrors changes in the market for corporate ownership. The number of available targets, both among publicly listed and non-listed firms, is rising. Financial advisors have been expanding their operations and are more widely presenting potential "deal opportunities" to prospective clients. The bulk of the major cross-border deals are handled by a small number of large deal makers, most of which are based in the United States (table V.2). The growing demand for acquisition targets is adding to a sense of urgency.

Table V.2. Worldwide M&A advisor rankings (deals completed, January-June 2000)

Rank	Advisor	Nationality	Value of deals (Billion dollars)	Number of deals
1	Goldman Sachs	United States	901	168
2	Morgan Stanley Dean Witter	United States	808	195
3	Merrill Lynch	United States	757	124
4	Credit Suisse First Boston	Switzerland	386	173
5	JP Morgan	United States	359	107
6	UBS Warburg	Switzerland	345	105
7	Rothschild	Luxembourg	255	73
8	Deustche Bank	Germany	240	97
9	Salomon Smith Barney	United States	227	156
10	Lazard	United States	214	77
11	Chase Manhattan	United States	208	82
12	Bear Stearns	United States	206	37
13	Lehman Brothers	United States	184	97
14	Donaldson, Lufkin & Jenrette	United States	118	157
15	RBC Dominion Securities	Canada	77	12

Source: UNCTAD based on *Financial Times*, 5 July 2000, p. 15.

Meanwhile, corporate executives are also under increased pressure from the stock market to participate actively in the global restructuring process to seize potential opportunities. This combines with new ways of financing major transactions. The liberalization of foreign equity ownership has facilitated M&As based on stock swaps rather than cash deals. (As noted in chapter IV, a number of mega deals have been financed in this way; see box IV.6.) Major M&As have also been facilitated by the rise of stock markets and ample liquidity in capital markets, which has allowed firms to raise large amounts of money through banks and bond issues. This was accentuated by the introduction of the single European currency, which has created a liquid market in European corporate bonds. Companies are increasingly issuing Euro-denominated bonds to refinance debt and to raise money for takeovers. For example, the rise of the Euro-denominated corporate bond market and the underlying Euro-syndicated loan market greatly facilitated Olivetti's acquisition of Telecom Italia (Ciucci, 1999).

It appears also that the increasing globalization of capital markets is contributing to a certain convergence of different systems of corporate governance and financing patterns (Maher and Andersson, 1999). One indication of this is the increased acceptance of M&As around the world. As noted earlier (chapter IV.B), the United States and the United Kingdom remain the most active countries with regard to M&As, but the incidence of takeovers (domestic as well as cross-border) has also increased in both continental Europe and Japan. The frequency of M&As also raises questions related to corporate governance, including as regards the protection of minority shareholders and the role of other stakeholders.[25]

C. A secular trend

The forces underlying the dramatic growth of cross-border M&As are complex and vary by industry and country. In essence, they reflect a *dynamic interaction* between changes in the global environment observed in the preceding section – new technologies, policy liberalization, deregulation and privatization, and changes in the capital market – and the multitude of basic factors motivating firms to undertake cross-border M&As (figure V.1). M&As are part of a process of regional and global restructuring, in which actions by national and international policy-makers trigger responses by firms and vice versa.

While this process is far from complete and its incidence is highly uneven, its direction is quite clear. The major changes that have simultaneously taken place in the international business environment have profoundly affected the setting in which firms are operating and have provided new and expanded business opportunities, as well as risks.

The advent of the internet has added to this as it stimulates M&A activity between "old economy" and "new economy" firms in search of opportunities and as it may lead firms to try to find new solutions to some of the problems to which M&As have traditionally represented the solution. An example is the business-to-business exchanges, which may be akin to functional mergers.

In this new and continuously evolving environment, the key strategic issue for firms becomes how to survive and prosper, knowing that there is a market for firms and that sanctions await them if they fail to deliver growth and profits. One such sanction is to be taken over. All the basic motivations for firms to undertake cross-border M&As then combine to become key elements in the overarching strategic goal to defend and develop competitive positions. Cross-border M&As are growing so rapidly in importance precisely because they provide firms with the fastest way of acquiring tangible and intangible assets in different countries, and because they allow firms to restructure existing operations nationally or globally to exploit synergies and obtain strategic advantages. In brief, cross-border M&As allow firms rapidly to acquire a portfolio of locational assets, which has become a key source of competitive strength in a globalizing economy (UNCTAD, 1995a).

The fact that a considerable part of the current expansion of M&A activity consists of major deals in industries in which a limited number of companies dominate the market, leading to a consolidation at the regional or global level, suggests that strategic interactions among the leading firms also play an important role. Indeed, under conditions of strategic interdependence and uncertainty, once the established equilibrium is disturbed by the move of a major player (say, to acquire a foreign company) it can be expected to have a strong impact on key competitors and to trigger a chain reaction of countermoves at both

FIGURE V.1
The driving forces of cross-border M&As

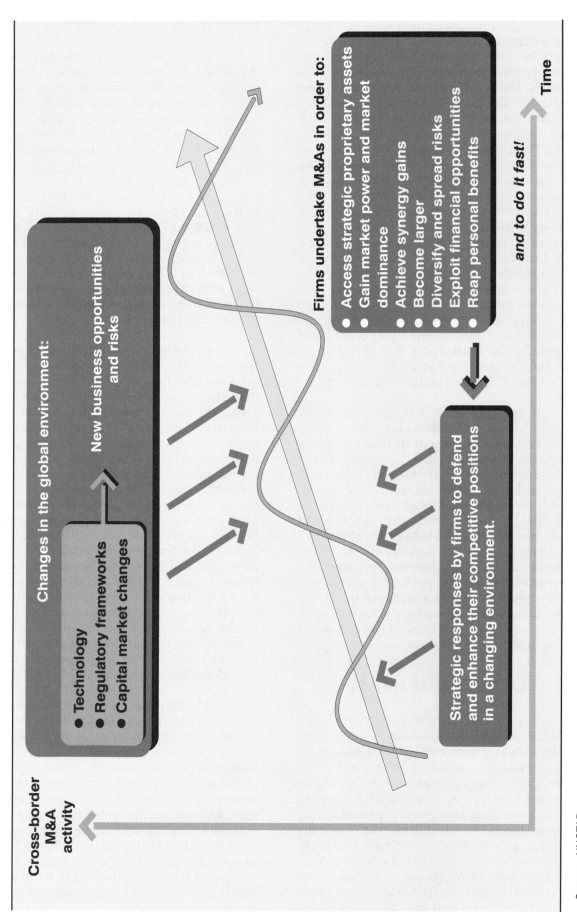

Source: UNCTAD.

domestic and international levels by rivals anxious to protect their positions (Schenk, 1996).[26] By pursuing a merger or acquisition, management minimizes the largest possible regret, which occurs when *ex post* successful moves by other players have not been imitated, or when they themselves become a target for a takeover. Thus, even firms reluctant to pursue this course may be forced into it for fear of becoming an acquisition target themselves. Such pre-emptive actions can be intended to create "strategic comfort" rather than shareholder value or economic wealth (Schenk, 1999). Moreover, if they do not move quickly enough, there may be fewer desirable partners left. By moving, however, they will help amplify a merger wave that has just started.

Like most previous major M&A waves, the current M&A boom has coincided with strong economic growth and buoyant stock prices. This suggests that the present level of M&A activity is likely to be affected by changes in the business cycle, by stock market corrections and by possible interventions by antitrust authorities.[27] However, as long as changes in the business environment continue to facilitate cross-border M&As – indeed, compel firms to pursue them – the volume of cross-border M&As may well oscillate over time, but it can be expected to do so on an upward trend.

D. An intriguing historical parallel

Major changes in the ownership structure of firms by means of M&As are not a new phenomenon. In fact, one of the largest and most significant waves of M&As in history took place in the United States around the end of the nineteenth century, reaching its climax between 1898 and 1902 (Chandler, 1990). During these five years, firms accounting for perhaps as much as one-half of the United States manufacturing capacity were involved in M&As (Bittlingmayer, 1985). That wave radically changed the industrial structure of the United States, setting the stage for the role of "big business" in United States industry in the twentieth century. National Biscuit, US Steel and International Harvester were among the many firms born out of the M&As that took place during this boom.

What were the main factors behind the wave of the end of the nineteenth and early twentieth century in the United States? Is it possible to draw parallels between it and the current worldwide increase in cross-border M&A activity? The two waves do seem to have much in common.

1. Factors behind the United States wave at the turn of the past century

There have been many attempts to explain this United States merger wave, and several major driving forces have been identified.[28] The main factors are related to important changes in the business environment that set off a series of corporate responses. These changes fall into three categories: technology, financial markets and regulatory factors.

- **Technology.** The United States M&A boom coincided with the overlap of two "long waves" of technological development. The last quarter of the nineteenth century marked the end of one long wave, which included the development of steam power, the railway and the telegraph, and the beginning of the next: the rise of electrical and heavy engineering (Freeman and Perez, 1988). The growth of the railroad and telegraph network significantly reduced information and transportation costs and brought firms from various regional markets together in direct competition in a single national market, increasing the incentives for firms to enhance their market power (Bain, 1944). The electrical and heavy engineering industries opened the way for the development of a variety of new products, as well as significant innovations in the production process, with unparalleled cost advantages through economies of scale and scope in production and distribution as a result. These innovations led to the creation of new industries and the transformation of many old ones. Thus, technology affected acquisitions in two ways. First, lower costs of transporting goods and people and of communicating over long distances made it possible for firms to compete in a larger national market, and to seek the benefits from economies of scale and grasp first-mover advantages in building a national production system. Second, new industries were born out of technological progress and firms in traditional industries were forced to respond to new production and market opportunities, often through consolidation.

- **Financial markets.** The second factor relates to changes in capital markets and the way investment was financed. Prior to the M&A wave, most new enterprises relied on local businesses and venture capitalists for the initial capital, and on local banks for working capital. At the end of the nineteenth century, new ways of financing were introduced as investment bankers, especially those experienced in railroad finance, became increasingly more involved in instigating and financing industrial M&As.[29] At the same time, the organized securities exchanges emerged as important institutions in the financial market. During the M&A wave, which was then characterized by a buoyant stock market, large-scale consolidations were greatly facilitated by the exchange of shares, which became the predominant mode of financing major M&As.

- **Regulatory factors.** This third category of explanatory factors concerns changes in the legislative environment concerning, in particular, competition and incorporation laws. The most important was the passage of the Sherman Antitrust Act in 1890 and a number of subsequent court rulings. The Sherman Antitrust Act was passed in response to widespread anti-competitive collusion between manufacturers in many industries in the last quarter of the nineteenth century, first through informal agreements on price and output and then formalized in trade-association cartels.[30] While a series of Supreme Court rulings between 1895 and 1899 established that close inter-firm cooperation through trade associations was anti-competitive and actionable under the Act, M&As remained unchallenged by the courts until 1903.[31] This window of opportunity, together with increasing difficulties in enforcing contractual agreements by trade associations, made M&As the main means of achieving greater market control, and hastened the transformation of trade associations into merged corporations (Chandler, 1990).[32]

The consolidation process was further facilitated by changes in the general incorporation laws, which permitted the formation of holding companies that might operate on a national scale. In this way it became possible to centralize the administration of constituent companies and concentrate production in a small number of large plants (Chandler, 1990). Such changes were first enacted in the state of New Jersey, which, as a result, accounted for almost 80 per cent of all consolidation

capitalizations between 1895 and 1904 (Nelson, 1959).

2. Parallels with the current wave

The three factors that explain a good part of the M&A wave in the United States at the end of the nineteenth century also seem to be at work today:

- **Technology.** As at the end of the nineteenth century, recent decades have been characterized by major technological change. In particular, the 1980s and 1990s witnessed the blossoming – and convergence – of information and communication technologies. Falling costs of transportation and communication, with improved telecommunications and the internet, again led to an expansion of the markets in which firms act, this time involving many national markets, and allowing them to manage worldwide production systems. The new information technologies are prompting firms to merge in order to find new solutions in areas such as electronic business, the development of new products and services and the integration of different lines of business. At the same time, firms in traditional industries characterized by excess capacity, slow growth and greater domestic and international competition, are consolidating in order to attain a stronger global market position and to exploit economies of scale in various activities.

- **Financial markets**. Both waves were facilitated by developments in financial markets. In the current wave, the sweeping liberalization of capital movements has been crucial. In both cases, changes in the ways M&As were financed played an important role. For instance, while the evolution of the securities market opened the possibility of financing M&As through an exchange of shares in the United States wave, the liberalization of foreign ownership of shares has facilitated the financing of international M&As through stock swaps.

- **Regulatory factors.** Undoubtedly, like the end of the previous century, the end of the twentieth century also witnessed significant adjustments in the regulatory environment facilitating M&As, albeit of a different character. Whereas in 1898-1902, it was the interpretation of the 1890 Sherman Antitrust Act that barred cartel agreements, but did not bar M&As that had encouraged consolidation, the recent wave of M&As has been made possible by the worldwide liberalization of FDI and trade regimes, deregulation and privatization (described earlier in this chapter), which create more space for undertaking M&As and allow the organization of international production systems. At the same time, international production is more protected and facilitated through bilateral, regional (including in particular the formation of the EU single market) and multilateral agreements.

***

To conclude, there are indeed interesting parallels between the two merger waves. Common denominators are increased competition and major changes in the economic and government-business environment facing firms that have triggered corporate responses on a large scale. First, both waves were enabled by a combination of a significant lowering of technical barriers to wider geographic investment and trade, and technological change permitting reductions in the costs of transportation and communication and more

integrated management of dispersed production facilities. In both periods, such circumstances led to increased competition and price pressure favouring consolidation.[33]

Second, new ways of financing M&As evidently played an important role in both cases. In particular, changes in the financial markets enabled firms to finance M&As using stock swaps instead of cash, nationally in the United States case, and internationally in the past decade. Third, each of the two waves was made possible by more permissive regulatory frameworks.

In the case of the United States, the M&A wave at the end of the nineteenth century helped to give birth to a national market and production system. It may well be that, what is occurring today as part of a secular trend towards more cross-border M&As, is the emergence of a global market for enterprises, as a complement to growing regional or global markets for products and services and an emerging international production system.

Notes

[1] See, e.g. "Marrying in haste", *Financial Times*, 12 April 2000.

[2] See Jensen and Ruback (1983), Mueller (1996), Sirower (1997) or Bild (1998) for surveys of several studies.

[3] Positive impacts on the share prices of the acquiring firm were observed by e.g. Asquith et al. (1983) and Franks and Harris (1989).

[4] See e.g. Morck et al. (1991), Singh and Montgomery (1987), Kitching (1967), Kusewitt (1985) and AT Kearney (1999).

[5] See e.g. Elgers and Clark (1980), Lubatkin (1987), Shelton (1988), Hunt et al. (1987) and Lahey and Conn (1990).

[6] For example, studying 276 United States international acquisitions made in the period 1975-1988, a positive impact on the market value of the bidding firms was found (Markides and Ittner, 1994). In the case of 103 German M&As during 1994-1998, deals concluded with an international partner typically resulted in rising share prices of the acquiring firm while 43 per cent of domestic M&As experienced reductions in share values (Jansen and Körner, 2000). United States firms were also found to provide poorer results through domestic M&As compared with foreign M&As by United States firms during the period 1978-

1986 (Morck and Yeung, 1991). A similar conclusion was drawn in a more recent study (Morck and Yeung, 1999).

[7] See e.g. Schenk (2000) and Cakici et al. (1996). Eun et al. (1996) concluded that, while Japanese acquirers benefited substantially from acquiring United States firms, British acquirers experienced wealth reductions.

[8] The use of accounting data is not without problems as firms can use various measures to manipulate published accounts.

[9] Another study of United Kingdom M&As, from 1955 to 1970, using a three-year horizon, showed that the profitability of assets of combined firms was not significantly different from that of firms that did not engage in M&A activity (Singh, 1975).

[10] While the bulk of the empirical studies are based on United States data, European studies tend to confirm these results (Mueller, 1980a).

[11] See e.g. Lichtenberg and Siegel (1987) and Lichtenberg (1992).

[12] See e.g. Ravenscraft and Scherer (1987), Scherer and Ross (1990) Hopkins (1999), Mueller (1980a), and Brealey and Myers (1988) for a discussion on different motives for M&As. The topic has also been

discussed by civil society, for example by NGOs such as the Consumer Unity and Trust Society of India (CUTS, 1999).

13   In some cases, a joint venture or strategic alliance may offer alternative ways for firms to access specific proprietary assets of other companies.

14   R. K. Krishna Kumar, Vice-Chairman, Tata Tea Ltd., at the UNCTAD Expert Meeting on Mergers and Acquisitions: Policies Aimed at Maximizing the Positive and Minimizing the Possible Negative Impact of International Investment, Geneva, 19-21 June 2000.

15   This does not mean that big is always better. For example, in innovation-driven industries characterized by rapid change, large organizations can be at a disadvantage vis-à-vis smaller entities in terms of creativity and flexibility.

16   The average interest rate paid by United States corporations was reduced by approximately 0.46 percentage points with each tenfold increase in company size (Scherer et al., 1975).

17   See, for example, Myers and Majluf, 1984.

18   For instance, while the main reason to allow the merger between two Brazilian companies, Companhia Cervejaria Brahma and Antarctica, in spite of their large market shares, was that significant cost reductions associated with economies of scale were sufficiently high to make it plausible to assume that the net effect on social welfare would not be negative, another argument that was influential in the debate was to let a national champion emerge that could be competitive in the regional market.

19   This conflict is particularly pronounced in so-called "outsider systems" of corporate governance with strong managers and widely-dispersed weak shareholders (Maher and Andersson, 1999).

20   This is reflected e.g. in the fact that firms pay retention bonuses to key staff in the case of some M&As.

21   For example, as a result of the merger between Astra (Sweden) and Zeneca (United Kingdom), the corporate headquarters was located in the United Kingdom, while responsibility for corporate R&D was placed in Sweden.

22   The survey of the literature was based on Andean Community General Secretariat, 1999; Asia-Pacific Economic Cooperation Secretariat, 1999; Association of South-East Asian Nations Secretariat, 1998; Economist Intelligence Unit, 1999; International Monetary Fund, 1999b; Lang, 1998; Tradeport, 2000; UNCTAD, 1999d, 1993, 1999f; United States Trade Representative, 2000; World Trade Organization, 1999. Information was also collected at the

websites of the East-Weat Association (http://www.ewba.org/regional.htm), the Investment Promotion Network (http://www.ipanet.net) and the Organization of American States (http://www.sice.oas.org/trl_e.asp).

23   Since the end of October 1997, foreign firms, in Zones 1 and 2 can get approval from the Board of Investment to change their equity ownership to majority or 100 per cent control, if local shareholders agree. Between November 1997 and March 1999, 253 companies applied for permission to increase their ownership share (Brimble, 2000).

24   It is estimated that about 70 countries today have adopted mandatory or voluntary antitrust merger notification systems. For more information, see UNCTAD (2000f).

25   See in this context the OECD Principles of Corporate Governance contained in UNCTAD (2000a), volume IV.

26   An illustrative example of the role of strategic countermoves was the concentration of deals in a short period of time in the aluminium industry in 1998. The announcements of Alcan Aluminium's acquisitions of Indian Aluminium and Ghana Bauxite in March 1998 were, within five months, followed by another 13 cross-border deal announcements in the same industry.

27   The outcome of the merger reviews in the case of WorldCom and Sprint by the competition authorities in both the United States and the European Union may for example have a chilling effect on future M&As.

28   See e.g. Moody (1904), Watkins (1927), Bain (1944), Nelson (1959), Bittlingmayer (1985), Lamoreaux (1985) and Chandler (1990).

29   These included financial institutions like the railroad financiers J. P. Morgan & Co. and Kidder Peabody, as well as National City Bank and First National Bank of New York. Sometimes manufacturers financed their own mergers, as with Standard Oil and Du Pont.

30   For example, in the United States hardware industry alone, there were more than 50 cartels for as many specialized product lines (Chandler, 1990).

31   In 1903, a circuit court decided in the Northern Securities case (upheld by the Supreme Court in 1904) that M&As were not exempt from the Sherman Act.

32   In more than a quarter of all consolidations between 1895 and 1904, ten firms or more were simultaneously involved in mergers (Nelson, 1959).

33   For a discussion of the role of increased price competition in the United States wave a century ago, see Lamoreaux (1985).

Chapter VI

FDI and Development: Does Mode of Entry Matter?

Introduction

Cross-border M&As, particularly those involving large firms, vast sums of money and major restructurings, are among the most visible faces of globalization. Not only do they dominate FDI flows in developed economies, they have also begun to take hold as a mode of FDI entry into developing and transition economies (chapter IV). As with globalization generally, the impact of M&As on development can be double-edged and uneven. Indeed, perhaps to a greater extent than many other aspects of globalization, cross-border M&As and the expanding global market for firm ownership and control in which they occur — raise questions about the balance of their benefits and costs for host countries. These questions arise despite the generally welcoming attitude towards inward FDI.

Concerns are expressed in political discussions and the media in a number of host countries that acquisitions as a mode of entry are less beneficial for economic development than greenfield investment, if not positively harmful. At the heart of these concerns is that foreign acquisitions (mergers, as noted in chapter IV, are rare in developing countries and economies in transition) do not add to productive capacity at the time of entry, but simply transfer ownership and control from domestic to foreign hands. This transfer is often accompanied by lay-offs and/or the closing

of some production or functional activities (e.g. R&D); it entails servicing the new owner in foreign exchange; and, if the acquirers are global oligopolists, it may well lead to market dominance. In fact, cross-border M&As can be used to reduce competition in domestic markets. They can lead to strategic firms or even entire industries (including key ones like banking) falling under foreign control, threatening local entrepreneurial and technological capacity-building. The concerns are not only economic, but also social, political and cultural. In industries like the media and entertainment, M&As may seem to threaten national culture or identity. A large shift of ownership of important enterprises from domestic to foreign hands may even be seen as eroding national sovereignty and amounting to recolonization.[1] When the acquisitions involve "fire sales" — sales of companies in distress, often at prices viewed as abnormally low — concerns become particularly acute. All these concerns can create the impression that greenfield FDI is "good", while FDI through cross-border M&As is "bad".

All of these concerns are further accentuated when they are placed in the broader context of globalization, rapid change, marginalization of some economies or groups within economies, and increasing inequality. (Witness the protests against various symbols of globalization.) TNCs are thought to benefit disproportionately from globalization, while local SMEs in developing countries are perceived as being affected adversely. M&As, particularly in their cross-border form, appear to be little more than a vehicle for the expansion of big business.

Concerns over cross-border M&As are by no means confined to developing countries. They are also expressed in many developed countries, sometimes more vehemently. When Japanese investors acquired Rockefeller Center in New York City and film studios in Hollywood, the United States media reacted with indignation.[2]   More recently, when Vodafone AirTouch (United Kingdom) sought to acquire Mannesmann (Germany), there was again indignation in some quarters. While nationalistic reactions to foreign takeovers are diminishing in force, they can be strong enough to lead host governments to intervene, particularly if takeovers are hostile.

A dispassionate analysis of the effects of M&As on development is therefore needed to throw light on the validity of these concerns, and especially on the validity of the view that greenfield FDI is better than FDI through M&As. Such an analysis must be based on an understanding of the driving forces of cross-border M&As and their global context, in particular, the emergence of a global market for firms. (This context and these forces have been discussed in the preceding two chapters.) The present chapter examines the impact of FDI through M&As on the development of host countries. The starting point is the impact of FDI in general on different areas of development, as identified in *WIR99* (UNCTAD, 1999a). The chapter then goes on to compare the impact of FDI through M&As with that of FDI through greenfield ventures and, where differences exist, suggests policies that could reduce the negative effects while strengthening the positive ones. Although direct investors sometimes have a real choice between entering a host country through greenfield FDI or entering it through M&As, the two modes are not always realistic alternatives — as when a telecommunication network is privatized or a large ailing firm needs to be rescued, and no domestic buyers can be found[3] (box VI.1). Hence the discussion below also considers situations in which M&As are the only realistic way for a country to receive FDI,[4] focusing on how M&As affect the performance of the acquired enterprise and the host economy.

Of course, in principle, both host countries and TNCs have other options. For countries, the priority is, in any event, to stimulate domestic investment and enterprise development, since FDI can only be a complement to domestic efforts. They can encourage domestic M&As (box VI.2) and establish public enterprises. They can also obtain international resources through strategic alliances, other non-equity arrangements for inter-firm cooperation and, of course, arm's

---

Box VI.1. To what extent are greenfield FDI and cross-border M&As alternatives?

A comparison of the impact of FDI through cross-border M&As with that of greenfield FDI assumes that the two modes of foreign entry constitute alternatives from the perspectives of both host countries and TNCs. In principle and even in practice this may be the case, but they are rarely perfect substitutes for each other. From a host country's perspective, substitutability depends on its characteristics, including its level of economic development, FDI policy, the institutional framework and specific circumstances.

Level of economic development. While both modes may be options in developed countries with a large pool of strong private enterprises and well-functioning markets for corporate control, this is not always the case in developing countries and economies in transition. For example, M&As are typically not a realistic alternative to greenfield investment in the least developed countries, in which investment opportunities may exist but there are few firms to acquire. In other developing countries with a more advanced industrial sector and more developed capital markets, the acquisition of a local firm can represent a realistic alternative to greenfield FDI. Mergers between local firms in many developing countries and developed country firms are typically not feasible because of large differences in size, technology or management experience. In general, the higher the level of development of a host country, the larger the supply of firms that may be targeted for cross-border M&As.

FDI policy. Another obvious prerequisite for cross-border M&As is that they have to be permitted by the national regulatory

/...

Box VI.1. To what extent are greenfield FDI and cross-border M&As alternatives? (concluded)

framework. The liberalization of FDI regimes has gone far, and most countries now actively promote the inflow of FDI. In many cases, liberalization applies to both greenfield FDI and cross-border M&As. However, in a number of developing countries, foreign takeovers are *de facto* (if not *de jure*) restricted. Even in some developed countries, authorization is needed for the acquisition of companies in certain industries. Policy liberalization as regards foreign acquisitions has been shown to have a strong impact on the pattern of inward FDI in countries with a strong industrial base. In Argentina, for example, cross-border M&As accounted for almost 60 per cent of total FDI inflows between 1992 and 1999. While privatization was initially responsible for the bulk of M&As, foreign acquisitions of private firms have gradually increased in importance, accounting for more than one-third of total inflows between 1996 and 1998 (Chudnovsky and López, 2000).

Institutional framework. The balance between cross-border M&As and greenfield FDI is also related to the institutional environment. For example, even among developed economies, the use of M&As is affected by differences in corporate governance and ownership structure. These help to explain the diverging patterns of M&As in the United States and the United Kingdom, on the one hand, and Germany and Japan on the other. In developing countries, underdeveloped asset markets and poor accounting standards may make it more difficult to assess accurately the value of corporate assets.

Exceptional circumstances. Examples include financial crises (as in Asia in 1997-1999) and large privatization programmes (as in Latin America or Central and Eastern Europe). Both produce, though for different reasons, a large one-off supply of firms in financial or competitive trouble. In both sets of circumstances, policy-makers have welcomed the cross-border acquisitions of local enterprises: greenfield FDI could not in these circumstances play the role of cross-border M&As in rescuing ailing companies and restructuring state-owned firms.

* * *

To sum up, even though there are a number of situations in which the two modes of FDI entry are not realistic alternatives, they remain alternatives often enough to justify the comparison of their impacts on development. From a host-country perspective, this also means that host countries can influence both forms of entry through various policy measures. Such measures, however, should be based not only on a realistic assessment of a host country's locational advantages, but also on an awareness of factors guiding firms' choices.

Firm-level factors were discussed in greater detail in chapter V. They can vary from industry to industry, depending on market structure and industry characteristics. High market concentration and high barriers to entry limit the probability of greenfield investment. This is the principal reason why, in such service industries as telecommunications, power generation and financial services, cross-border M&As are a predominant mode of entry. Similarly, in industries characterized by slow growth or excess capacity, firms are not likely to add new productive capacity, if they can acquire existing assets. It should be noted that the market power of existing firms can be affected by the introduction of new technology (like cellular phones in telecommunications) or through regulatory changes leading to a removal of barriers to entry and increasing the scope for greenfield investment.

The emergence of a knowledge-based economy and the liberalization of markets favour cross-border M&As. The former underlines the significance of skills and other knowledge-based assets for competitiveness and, consequently, leads to the increasing importance of asset-seeking FDI: of the two modes of FDI entry (leaving aside other modes and especially strategic alliances), only M&As can be used to access assets embodied in firms. The latter has increased competitive pressures, forcing firms to access assets or restructure *rapidly* and consolidate their operations in strategic response to competitors' moves, actual or expected (chapter V). As *speed* has become a critical parameter, the greenfield option is often ruled out as an entry mode at an early stage of corporate decision-making.

Source: UNCTAD.

length transactions. While countries need to consider these and other options, the analysis here focuses on greenfield investment vs. cross-border M&As, although other options are not neglected. In other words, the analysis takes as given a situation in which a country has decided that FDI is the preferred option, and the question is whether it matters that it is greenfield FDI or FDI via cross-border M&As.

Comparing cross-border M&As with greenfield investment often means considering counterfactuals — what might have happened if cross-border M&As had not taken place. Such

a counterfactual must take account of not only the industry and host-country context, but also of the broader setting of trade, technology and competition. The fact that this setting is changing rapidly, and that these changes are driving the current surge in cross-border M&As (see chapter V), is crucial to the analysis. FDI and trade liberalization, accelerating technological change, intensifying competition and integrated production systems mean that firms — in developing as well as developed economies, large and small — must upgrade and restructure to remain competitive. Macro-economic disturbances, such as financial crises

---

Box VI.2. A domestic merger: the sale of Kia Motors Corporation

In July 1997, Kia Motors Corporation, the second largest automobile company in the Republic of Korea, ran into a serious liquidity crisis. Attempts to save it in the ensuing few months failed, and the company was put under legal custody in April 1998. Kia was one of the country's ten largest business groups before its bankruptcy. It had a relatively specialized business portfolio, including passenger cars, commercial vehicles, specialized steel products and some other small companies, and was not a typical *chaebol* in that it had no family owner with a controlling share involved in company management. Because it was run by a professional management team and was more specialized in its business portfolio, it had a good image in the Republic of Korea and was regarded as a national champion. Because of its unique position in the economy, the creditors (i.e. the major banks) and the Government hesitated about what to do with the company.

After the Asian financial crisis reached the Korean economy in November 1997 and a new President took office, the Government announced in June 1998 that Kia would be sold through an international auction. Both domestic and foreign auto companies expressed their interest in acquiring it.

Major creditor banks decided to decapitalize the existing equity of Kia and infuse new capital amounting to around Won 1-1.5 trillion. This new equity would be sold to the company acquiring Kia. In other words, the acquiring firm would buy the new equity of Kia and also assume some part of its debt. It was also decided that Kia and Asia Motors, a firm specialized in commercial vehicles, would

be sold in a single deal. In the auction scheduled for 30 August 1998, five companies participated; three domestic firms (Hyundai, Daewoo and Samsung) and two United States companies (GM and Ford). The first auction failed to produce a deal because the terms of the bids offered by the companies failed to meet the condition laid out by the creditor banks. The second bidding on 25 September also failed to produce a successful bidder. By this time, GM had dropped out and only four firms submitted bids. The major problem was how much of the total debt of Kia and Asia Motors would be absorbed by the creditor banks. (The total debt amounted to Won 12.8 trillion.) After these two auctions had failed to produce a successful deal, the creditor banks further reduced the total debt to be assumed by the acquiring firm. On 11 October, Hyundai was finally selected from among four bidders because it asked for the smallest debt reduction. The deal was successfully completed in March 1999. Hyundai took over its largest competitor in the domestic market and decided to maintain Kia as a legally separate company for the time being.

This case shows that greenfield investment is not an alternative when it comes to a bankrupt company — but rescue by a domestic company may be. In restructuring failed companies in the aftermath of the Asian financial crisis, the creditors and the Government basically faced two choices, selling the company to a domestic firm or to a foreign firm. More precisely, it was a matter of selling the failed firm to an acquirer that offered the most favourable deal to the creditors.

Source: Jung, 2000.

(as in Asia in 1997-1999) and debt and fiscal problems (as in parts of Africa), intensify pressures on both firms and countries, making adjustment more difficult. So, too, does the need to change economic systems (as in Central and Eastern Europe). These circumstances clearly affect any comparison between the two modes of entry.

As emphasized in chapter IV, not all cross-border M&As are FDI in the normal sense. Some are portfolio investments (for measurement purposes, acquisitions of less than 10 per cent equity). Others are close kin to portfolio investments, being solely or primarily motivated by financial considerations, regardless of the equity share involved. Portfolio or portfolio-type cross-border M&As are not considered here, since the focus is on M&As as a mode of *FDI* entry. In any event, the share of portfolio and portfolio-type M&As in the total value of cross-border M&As appears to be relatively small (box IV.1 and figure IV.3). The present chapter thus focuses on the impact of cross-border M&As undertaken for *strategic* corporate reasons rather than for more or less immediate financial reasons.

Concerns as to the impact of cross-border M&As on host country development arise of course even when cross-border M&As go well from a corporate viewpoint. But there can be additional concerns arising from the possibility that M&As may not, in fact, go well. As discussed in the preceding chapter, half of all M&As do not live up to corporate-performance expectations of the parent firms, as measured by shareholder value. This may not matter for the development of host countries, especially when the performance of *acquired* firms benefits from M&As. Furthermore, greenfield investments face their own risks, and it is unclear that these are lower than those of M&As.[5] The risk of choosing the wrong target for acquisition may be greater in developing or transition economies, where corporate governance may be weak and corporate cultures different from those of acquirers from developed countries,[6] but the difficulties in maintaining or improving post-merger performance may still be smaller given the resource gap between the acquirer and the target. Resource flows are more likely to be in one direction (towards the newly acquired foreign affiliate) and the synergies between the parties may be less important.

As regards M&As that go well, efficient implementation from an investor's point of view need not, of course, imply a favourable impact on host-country development. This applies to FDI through M&As as well as to greenfield FDI. The main reason is that the objectives of TNCs and those of host economies do not necessarily coincide (UNCTAD, 1999a). In any event, both cross-border M&As and greenfield investments, regardless of whether they go well or not, can have undesirable effects on host countries. This again underlines the importance of policies to ensure that host countries benefit from FDI regardless of its mode of entry.

Apart from considerations related to whether M&As are well — or badly — done, the developmental impact of FDI through cross-border M&As — both in itself and in comparison with greenfield FDI — depends on a number of other factors. These include, in particular:

• The type of investment made through M&As and the motivation underlying it. Both direct effects and effects through linkages and spillovers vary according to whether an investment is natural-resource-seeking, market-seeking, efficiency-seeking or created-asset-seeking. Effects also depend on whether the choice of the M&A mode is based on a purely financial motivation, or on an economic one related to firm performance. In the case of purely financially motivated M&As, undertaken in the expectation of a rise in the value of the shares of the acquired firms or with a view to divesting ("stripping") some of the assets at higher prices, there may be a limited transfer of resources to the acquired enterprise, or none, or a negative impact.

• The situation of the host-country enterprises acquired through M&As. This factor influences the outcome in interaction with the investors' motivations. If M&As involve the purchase of competitive firms with a view to exploiting their assets for the benefit of an acquiring TNC, asset transfer to the host economy might be limited. But this need not exclude other benefits — those associated, for example, with more intense competition leading to more efficient local firms. The parent firm might also enhance the capabilities of its newly acquired affiliate, e.g. by giving it a world product mandate. On the other hand, if firms are purchased because they are not competitive, a transfer of additional assets to the acquired firm can take place. In many developing countries and, especially, economies in transition, the supply of competitive firms with capabilities similar to those of developed-country firms is limited, leaving ample room for substantial resource inflows through cross-border acquisitions.

- The environment in which an investment through M&As is made. Here the key factor is whether M&As take place in an industry or an economy with a robust, dynamic and expanding market, or in a static, stagnant or declining one.

- The time-frame within which the impact is considered. Effects at the time of entry may differ significantly from subsequent ones.

All of these factors will be examined below as appropriate. The discussion is organized into sections by the areas in which FDI most affects development (UNCTAD, 1999a): financial resources and investment; technology; employment and skills; export competitiveness; and market structure and competition. For each, the examination begins with a stylized summary of the general impact of FDI based on the discussion in *WIR99*. It goes on to consider the differences in impact of the two modes of entry and the impact of M&As on their own where greenfield FDI is not feasible. The analysis is often conceptual, but draws on empirical evidence and experience whenever possible. It concludes with an exploration of the policy implications in each area. The final section provides a summary and conclusions which also touch on the broader impact of cross-border M&As and policy implications.

A.   External financial resources and investment

In various ways FDI affects resource flows and investment in productive capacity in host countries (box VI.3). The flows of capital and income arising from the activities of foreign affiliates also affect the balance of payments and the allocation of benefits from foreign investment between host countries and foreign investors. In the discussion below the effects on financial resources and investment are considered separately.

1.   External financial resources

Investment through cross-border M&As adds to the financial resources of a host country at the time of entry,[7] as does greenfield FDI, to the extent that neither is financed by locally raised capital. Inflows of FDI via greenfield projects manifest themselves in new production facilities, while those via M&As transfer the ownership of local assets to foreign hands, placing investible resources in the hands of the former local owners in the form of cash or disposable shares. The effect on financial inflows is the same if the size of the TNC investment is identical. Both can result, in due course, in profit outflows and repatriated capital. (The question of whether or not the investible resources are actually invested is discussed below.)

There may, however, be two sorts of differences between the financial impacts according to the mode of entry. The first relates to the exchange-rate impact of the flows, particularly in the initial period. A foreign merger or acquisition typically places resources in the hands of the local owners of a firm *immediately*,[8] while the inflows involved in setting up new facilities in a greenfield project may take the form of "in kind" contributions, and a cash inflow may be spread over time and recipients. If a transaction is large, the former may, in the absence of appropriate policy measures, create greater pressures on the domestic currency than a greenfield investment of the same volume, leading to currency appreciation. Privatizations involving foreign buyers are a typical case in which the exchange rate may be affected by such sudden inflows. Intervention by monetary authorities via open market transactions and sterilization measures can neutralize most of the negative impact (currency appreciation with a negative impact on international balances and export performance, or inflation).[9] These actions have to strike the right balance between the costs (for example, the interest to be paid by the central bank on the financial instruments used to absorb excess foreign capital inflow) and the benefits (the avoidance of major disturbances in the domestic economy) of such intervention.

Box VI.3. FDI, external financial resources and investment

FDI affects the volume and characteristics of investible financial resources and actual investment in host countries. It also affects the balance of payments of host countries and the division of benefits from investment between them and other countries.

External financial resources for development. The net impact of FDI on the quantum of capital flows to developing countries is usually positive: it increases the inflow of foreign financial resources available for investment. Inflows of FDI have become the single most important source of private foreign savings for developing countries as a group (chapter I). The impact over time depends on the amount of capital brought from abroad by TNCs (equity inflows paid in "cash" and funds raised directly from international capital markets) less the volume of FDI-related financial transfers abroad (intra-company and other loan repayments and repatriated capital and profits) from the host country. During 1991-1997, each dollar repatriated from developing countries was matched by three dollars of new inflows.

As a source of finance FDI offers certain advantages over other sources of foreign finance to developing host countries. It has proved to be more stable than other types of financial flows, as reflected in the Asian financial crisis and the Mexican crisis of the mid-1990s. Direct investors show a longer-term commitment to host economies than lenders (particularly short-term lenders) and speculative portfolio investors. FDI is also easier to service than commercial loans, since profits tend to be linked to the performance and business cycles of the host economy. A part of FDI inflows, however, can be driven by short-term financial motives and thus behave just like speculative portfolio investments.

As a source of external finance, FDI complements domestic savings and contributes to growth through the indirect or direct financing of investment. An excess inflow of FDI (or any other type of capital inflow) in a short period may lead to the appreciation of the exchange rate of the national currency and reduce the competitiveness of exports, thus leading to the reduction of investment in export industries. It is also possible that FDI could effectively substitute for domestic savings, resulting in their reduction and enabling increased consumption or leading to capital

flight under certain condition. In the second-round effects, the increased consumption could induce an increase in investment through the accelerator effect. Unless there is unemployment and excess productive capacity to be utilized, this could bring the risk of overheating.

A profitable FDI project, with profits repatriated in foreign exchange, must necessarily result in greater *balance-of-payments* outflows than an identical national project financed locally. There are many projects, however, that can be undertaken only by foreign investors, or not at all, or could not be undertaken at comparable levels of efficiency by domestic firms. Moreover, comparisons of financial inflows and outflows cannot capture total balance-of-payments effects. This can only be done by evaluating the effects of all outputs and inputs. Whether FDI has a positive or negative impact on the host country's balance of payments depends on the following factors: the size of FDI inflows, net of disinvestment; outflows of direct investment income; the export and import propensities of foreign affiliates; the indirect impact of FDI on foreign-factor income outflows; the indirect impact of FDI on the export and import propensities of domestic firms; and the indirect impact of FDI on import demand by consumers in the host country.

The balance-of-payments effects of FDI and the country distribution of the value added by foreign affiliates can be affected by *transfer pricing* — the pricing of intra-firm transactions across national boundaries. TNCs have frequently considerable freedom in assigning prices in these transactions, particularly when there are no arm's length prices to serve as reference. This allows TNCs to shift profits between countries to lower their tax burdens or escape other restrictions on repatriating or declaring profits. The risk of unacceptable transfer pricing rises when there are large differences in tax regimes between countries and there are no double-taxation agreements in force. Concern about transfer pricing, greatest in the 1960s and 1970s, has declined as tax differences have narrowed, double-taxation agreements have proliferated and the desire to attract FDI has become widespread. Efforts to counter transfer pricing are now undertaken primarily by the tax authorities of major home countries like the United States and Japan.

/...

Secondly, there can be an important difference between the financial impacts of the two modes because cross-border M&As involve the *pricing* of firms. This is driven by many factors (box VI.4), and can raise problems. (Greenfield FDI does not normally raise issues concerning the value of the facility set up.) If an enterprise is sold at a price below its "correct" (social) price, there is a loss to the host economy.[10] The pricing of cross-border M&As may raise three sorts of problems:

• Under certain conditions, as when equity markets are underdeveloped or economic systems are in transition, it may be difficult to price assets correctly (box VI.4). Experience in economies of Central and Eastern Europe shows, for example, that, in the absence of capital markets or reference prices, there can be major problems in pricing the assets of state-owned enterprises. This increases the chances of a wrong valuation, and the prices received may be higher or lower than in the perceived valuation of a comparable greenfield project. The possibility of undervaluation increases if the negotiating position of the host country *vis-à-vis* foreign investors is weak, or if the host country does not make potential investors compete through bidding (Samonis, 2000). A careful consideration of the social benefits and costs to the host economy from FDI in a privatized enterprise is necessary to arrive at the right price. The way the bargaining process is carried out by privatization agents also influences the price. Much depends on their expertise, efficiency, honesty and independence. The right

management of the privatization process involving FDI requires many skills, especially in M&A techniques. After all, privatizations are just a variant of M&As.

• Pricing problems may arise even when there are active equity markets, if financial or other crises lead to firms being significantly under-valued. This allows foreign entrants to acquire them very cheaply. In the Asian crisis, the complaint was frequently voiced that foreign investors were able to snap up local firms at "fire sale" prices. While it is true that many firms were sold below what their sellers (and in some cases, buyers) considered their long-term value (Zhan and Ozawa, 2000), that may have been the only alternative to bankruptcy in some instances. In a number of cases, cross-border M&As served to save firms that could not raise finance elsewhere and added to foreign exchange resources in the host economy, an unlikely contribution from greenfield FDI in times of crisis. Under normal circumstances, the firms would not have needed a capital injection, or the financial system may have been able to provide additional liquidity. But the crisis-hit countries were caught in a severe credit crunch and many firms did not have the option of raising finances from local or international lenders. There could also have been additional gains from such cross-border M&As if the M&As had led to a restructuring of the acquired firms.

Cross-border M&As during a crisis may result in a net gain to a host economy even if the investors were to sell their

---

Box VI.3. FDI, external financial resources and investment (concluded)

Investment. Typically, FDI adds to productive capacity in a host country through the investment expenditures of affiliates. The value of investment expenditures by foreign affiliates is not necessarily the same as that of FDI inflows, since resources can be raised in local and international capital markets. Data on United States FDI abroad suggest that capital expenditures by foreign affiliates in host countries usually exceed the value of FDI inflows. FDI may also affect the volume of host-country investment indirectly by crowding in (stimulating entry of) or crowding out (inducing exit of) domestic investment.

Either is possible, depending on the activities undertaken by TNCs, the strength of local enterprises and the functioning of local factor markets. TNCs may crowd in domestic investment when they introduce new goods and services to the host economy, create local supply links and do not pre-empt local credit. They may crowd out domestic enterprises by entering activities already populated by local firms in which there is little room for further expansion, in which domestic firms are unable to compete with the foreign affiliates, or by using their size and "bankability" to gain privileged access to local capital markets.

Source: UNCTAD, 1999a.

acquisitions for a profit when markets recovered. This would be true if the profits made from the financial transactions were lower than the loss the economy would have suffered from the closure of the firms involved. There is little evidence to suggest, however, that most M&As in Asia

were undertaken for short-term financial reasons (Zhan and Ozawa, 2000). It may be argued that a better option would have been for governments or international institutions to provide liquidity to the stricken firms and so prevent fire sales, or to allow a debt standstill supervised by

---

Box VI.4. Is there a correct price in privatization-related M&As?

The correct market price of any productive asset is the present discounted value of future earnings adjusted for risk. This is "correct" in theory, assuming perfect foresight, full information on earning potential (including the impact of technological changes), no externalities (so that the private and social values of future earnings are equal) and no policy changes. Capital markets in developed countries provide a rough approximation in normal times, based on the existing prices of comparable assets and an assessment of technical change and other market imponderables. Even in these countries, M&As face pricing problems inherent in all asset pricing, and they are aggravated when they involve privatization. The difficulties are compounded when the firm being privatized is a utility with a local monopoly in a country without a functioning capital market. In privatization in a transition or developing economy, there may be no capital markets to throw up a comparable price or provide expert opinion on earning prospects.

There are two sets of factors affecting the price-setting process in privatizations:

- *The economic and political setting.* The risk element in pricing is affected by political and economic stability and general attitudes to FDI and privatization. The country "image" may affect not just prices, but also the numbers and origins of potential investors. A host country with a low rating as an investment destination may attract marginal players who in the long run perform badly. The nature and credibility of the policy reform process within which privatization takes place also affect risk. The strength and efficiency of the legal and judicial system of intellectual property protection and of the financial system will all affect prices. Broadly speaking, a clear political commitment to strong rules of the game may result in higher

general prices, but there may well be circumstances outside a government's direct control, e.g. pressure from neighbouring governments when strategic assets are involved.

- *The privatization process.* There are many ways to "create" a market for an enterprise being privatized. The best way is to get a large number of competitive bids from a variety of firms (domestic and foreign) and, if foreign firms are the only contenders, from established and trustworthy TNCs. Where the objective is to get a strategic partner with specific technological or other assets, however, there may need to be a trade-off between the up-front price and other conditions. For example, the privatization of telecommunications companies to foreign strategic investors has generally been by means of "controlled auctions" designed to achieve the highest possible price for the shares sold, from a limited number of pre-selected candidates that meet pre-established criteria. The price also depends on the market position of the enterprise being sold and the regulatory framework in place if it is a natural monopoly or oligopoly. It is further affected by prior restructuring and the performance conditions attached to the sale. (The less — or less efficient — the restructuring and the stronger the conditions, the lower the price.) The bargaining process itself is critical. The managers and workers of the firm being sold can become an important pressure group affecting a sale, influencing the choice of partner, the performance conditions, and the price. Sophisticated privatization operators use complex computerized optimizing techniques to evaluate bids. The buyers will use advanced techniques and high-powered teams in their turn — in addition, of course, to good old-fashioned pressure, lobbying, mystification and threats.

Source: UNCTAD.

adequate bankruptcy procedures. This option, however, was typically not open in the depths of the crisis: in a number of cases, M&As appeared to be the only solution, as not enough additional liquidity was available through official or banking sources.

• Another risk of M&As is that, during normal situations and with active stock markets, they allow for asset stripping. The acquired companies can be broken up by corporate raiders and their component parts sold off at a profit. This can have a further impact on financial resources, because the proceeds of asset sales can be repatriated to home countries. Asset stripping is often regarded with disfavour as it may involve speculation and financial manipulation for quick profit, with destructive effects on productive capacity. Indeed, it may be harmful if viable firms are bought, dismembered and sold off by entrants who do no restructuring or rationalization.[11] Certain types of asset stripping can, however, also serve a useful function. If asset stripping occurs when firms are managing their assets badly and places the viable assets under better management while disposing of the unviable ones, it improves the use of productive assets. In the case of privatization, asset stripping can be guarded against by governments retaining "golden shares" to enable them to influence or even veto corporate decisions they consider undesirable.

The impact of profit repatriation and transfer pricing on financial flows and the balance of payments of a host economy may differ according to the mode of entry. On the one hand, outflows of earnings are likely to begin sooner with M&As than with greenfield FDI when the acquired firm is profitable — though they may take longer where an affiliate has to be restructured. On the other hand, the scope for transfer pricing may be higher in greenfield projects than in cross-border M&As, at least initially. A parent firm may have greater leeway in setting intra-firm prices in greenfield ventures, since in M&As reference prices may be available from earlier transactions (that now become intra-firm). But this difference is unlikely to be very large, and it will most likely diminish over time. When a joint venture between local and foreign investors is taken over by the latter, the scope for transfer pricing may increase with the shift of control over the foreign affiliate and its transactions to foreign owners.

2.   Investment

As discussed, under normal conditions, there is little difference in the direct impacts of FDI through M&As and greenfield projects on absolute inflows of external financial resources. However, effects on host-country capital formation may differ under the two modes for given amounts of FDI. Greenfield FDI takes the form of a direct addition to host country production facilities once a project is completed, while M&As provide funds to local interests. Whether or not these funds are actually used for productive new investment depends on other factors. Where the investment opportunities exist, it is likely that productive investment will follow. In the case of privatization, one way to deal with this problem is that funds received are immediately deposited in an investment account of the acquired company, dedicated towards new investment (box VI.5).

Over the longer term, there is no reason to expect any difference in the impacts on capital formation of the two modes of entry. Both forms can be accompanied or followed by new (sequential) investment. Evidence from developing countries shows that sequential investment after cross-border M&As can be sizeable — so sizeable that a study of foreign acquisitions in Argentina (dominated by privatizations) and Chile (dominated by acquisitions of privately-owned companies) questions the distinction between the two modes of entry as regards their impact on investment. To quote:

"One of the more interesting survey results is that the frequent distinction between the purchase of existing assets versus greenfield investments is actually of relatively small significance in economic terms. In most instances when a foreign investor entered the host country's market through the purchase of domestic enterprises (whether wholly or through joint ventures), the initial purchase of assets ended up being only a small portion of the total investment." (Agosín, 1995, p. 3). "...During the 1990-

93 period, later investments of the privatized companies surveyed were responsible for 75 per cent of the FDI expended in further purchases of privatized assets in that country.[12] Furthermore, these same companies have additional investment plans for the 1994-96 period equal to 42 per cent of their original investments ... In the case of Chile, 10 of the 15 enterprises surveyed said that the initial investment or purchase of existing companies constituted only a small fraction of their subsequent investments" (Agosín, 1995, pp. 26).

Another study, comparing foreign acquisitions of private companies in Argentina during the 1990s with domestic acquisitions and domestic firms not participating in M&As, also yielded interesting results. It showed that increases in investments in firms acquired by foreign investors exceeded by a factor of two increases in investment in domestic M&A firms and by a factor of six those in domestic non-

M&A firms (Chudnovsky and López, 2000). In Peru, 35 per cent of the FDI inflows came through privatizations and resulted in an FDI stock of $8.5 billion by the end of 1999; the new owners committed themselves to additional investments of around $7 billion for the modernization and expansion of acquired facilities (UNCTAD, 2000d). In the Republic of Korea, cross-border M&As had larger sequential investments than greenfield FDI; during the period 1997-1999, the ratio of sequential to new investments was 125 per cent for cross-border M&As and 85 per cent for greenfield investments (Yun, 2000). In many M&A cases, this is not surprising as the new owner may have to undertake substantial investments in order to revitalize existing facilities. Sometimes, the new owner can be a minority foreign shareholder in a joint venture taking over the company in order to restructure it.

Privatizations in Central and Eastern Europe have also tended to lead to large sequential investments. In many cases, such

---

Box VI.5. Turning investible resources into investment: an example from Bolivia's privatization

Bolivia privatized its long distance telecommunication company ENTEL in 1995, through an international public bidding, open to national and foreign investors. ETI Euro Telecom International (an affiliate of Telecom Italia) made the winning bid. Through the capitalization of ENTEL, it agreed to inject fresh capital equal to $610 million in the exchange for a 50 per cent of equity participation (of the newly enlarged capitalized company) and 100 per cent management control. These resources were deposited in accounts of ENTEL to be used later for investments in the modernization and expansion of the company, in accordance to investment plans and the fulfillment of technical (quality) requirements. This arrangement stipulated that the privatized enterprise could not invest abroad until it had met its commitments to expand services in rural areas and in public telephone. Priority had to be given to:

• The installation of telephone services in every community of over 350 inhabitants;

• The installation of local services in every community of over 10,000 inhabitants;

• The replacement of manual and similar telephone exchanges with digital ones; and

• A five-fold increase in the number of public telephone booths.

The privatization contract also obliged the new owners of ENTEL's to submit an updated investment programme every three months, to be verified by the telecommunication regulator (SITTEL).

ENTEL enjoys exclusivity for long-distance services and its cooperatives for local services up to end-2001, on condition that it meets the goals of expansion and service improvement. These goals, too, are monitored and certified by the telecommunication regulator.

By March 2000, investment into ENTEL had reached $469 million, i.e. more than 75 per cent of the deposited amount.

Source: Government of Bolivia.

additional investments were fuelled by the rapid transfer of new technologies to the new affiliates (Hunya, 1997; Estrin, et al., 1995; Carlin, et al., 1994; Rojec, 1997). An UNCTAD survey of Central and Eastern European countries found that enterprises in the sample increased their capital investments by 28 per cent per year in the period preceding and 37 per cent per year in the period following privatization.[13] In Poland, there is evidence from the early phase of privatization (1992-1994) to suggest that investment outlays by firms privatized to foreign owners were higher and grew faster than in companies privatized to local entrepreneurs (Dabrowski, 1996).

Post-M&A sequential investments therefore reflect several factors, such as the need to revive a run-down plant or to meet growing demand. But where an acquired company needs restructuring and rationalization through the elimination of inefficient activities and the reduction of employment, there may be no new investment, at least in the short-term. In more advanced host countries, an acquired firm may be highly efficient and not in need of modernization. This may explain the weak sequential investment in cross-border M&As in Canada, as well as in other developed countries, where such asset-seeking investments are common (Chudy, Dery and Zahavich, 2000).[14]

In the case of privatizations, governments of host developing and transition economies have sometimes sought commitments from foreign investors to undertake further investments in the future. In telecommunication companies, performance targets relating to the expansion and modernization of public telecommunication facilities and improved service quality are generally a feature of privatization involving a strategic investor. For example, Bolivia, the Czech Republic, Latvia and South Africa, in addition to reinvestment of the purchase price in the privatized company, required future commitments from strategic investors to satisfy targets relating to network expansion, modernization and service quality set in advance by the governments (Eisenberg, 2000). Such commitments are often made in exchange for market or other privileges as well as a reduction in the initial prices. It is also customary for the investor to be made liable for precisely calibrated penalties should it fail to reach expansion and modernization goals. Monetary penalties are, however, not intended

to be so draconian as to frustrate the policy objective of expanding and modernizing the public telecommunication network as soon as practicable. Sometimes a non-monetary penalty, such as a reduction in the exclusivity period, is prescribed. A combination of monetary and non-monetary penalties were prescribed in the Czech Republic, Hungary and South Africa (Eisenberg, 2000). The evidence on the effectiveness of these commitments is mixed. In some cases they did not work (leading, nevertheless, to a reduction of the sale price) while in others they did, for example in Bolivia (box VI.5). It may well be that in some cases sequential investment would have taken place without these requirements, since, as noted earlier, such investment is quite common and sizeable in FDI related to privatization. Experience suggests, however, that most post-privatization commitments in regulated industries should be addressed through a well-designed regulatory regime based on service improvements expected from FDI rather than on privatization covenants.

What of the effects of M&As and greenfield FDI on the *crowding out* and *crowding in* of domestic firms? While an acquisition, by definition, involves the transfer of assets from local to foreign owners and so lowers the level of domestic ownership in the firm, its effects on other firms may or may not differ from those of greenfield entry. In final product markets, FDI entering through either mode may crowd out domestic firms if foreign affiliates are more efficient than locally owned firms. In fact, this may occur faster in the case of greenfield FDI, where TNCs are more likely to bring in newer technologies at the outset, than in M&As that involve taking over existing facilities. On the other hand, the acquisition of competitors in host economies can strengthen the competitive position of the firms involved, driving others out of the market (see section E below). This may more often be the case in market-seeking acquisitions than in asset- or efficiency-seeking ones. Crowding out of local firms can also occur if a foreign firm has privileged access to local factors (capital and skills) relative to local competitors, but this can occur with both modes of entry.

Case-study evidence on crowding out at the economy level (which does not distinguish between greenfield and M&A FDI) is inconclusive (UNCTAD, 1999a, pp. 172-173). In a recent study covering 32 developing countries (Agosín and Mayer, 2000), 17 showed neutral effects, 9 showed crowding out, and 6 showed crowding in. In general, therefore, there is little reason to expect a systematic difference with respect to crowding in and out between the two modes of entry.

Greenfield FDI and M&As may differ in their linkages with domestic suppliers, with different indirect effects on stimulating domestic entrepreneurship in intermediate product markets. An established local firm tends to have stronger linkages with other firms in the economy than a new foreign entrant as it takes time to establish local supply relations; these linkages are likely to persist after a merger or acquisition and may well be strengthened. A greenfield entrant, with long-standing supply links through its parent firm with enterprises overseas, may minimize transaction costs and risks by continuing to source overseas. As its information on the host country economy grows, local suppliers upgrade and/or its overseas suppliers undertake "follow on" FDI in the host country, its supply chains within the host country are likely to develop similarly to those of an M&A entrant. But linkages may not persist in acquired firms. If the local suppliers of an acquired firm turn out to be costly, unable to meet the quality and delivery needs of the acquirer or uneconomic to upgrade, they may well be replaced by foreign suppliers. In these circumstances, of course, greenfield FDI will also source its inputs abroad. Over the longer term, there will probably be no significant difference between the local linkages established by either mode of entry.

3. Summary

External financial resources

- FDI through M&As can bring in capital faster than greenfield investment does. This may or may not be an advantage to the host economy, depending, among others, on how well the capital inflow is managed from the macro-economic point of view. M&As carry a higher risk of reduced domestic (but not necessarily total) savings, permitting higher consumption with a possibility of potential inflationary pressures on the host economy.

- The financial implications of cross-border M&As may be affected by the mispricing

of assets in a host economy; greenfield FDI does not suffer from this. M&As can impose a cost on a host country when its firms or their assets are sold to foreigners "on the cheap" relative to their economic value. But, in some cases, there may be economic gains for a host economy if the alternative is bankruptcy and foreign acquisitions save or restructure troubled domestic firms. In the latter case, FDI through cross-border M&As performs a function that greenfield FDI, by definition, cannot perform.

- "Asset stripping" for short-term financial gain is another potential cost of entry through cross-border M&As. It can also lead to a faster outflow of funds.

Investment

- Differences between the two modes of entry may arise from the way the financial resources provided are used. In greenfield FDI, they are necessarily invested in the plant set up by a TNC. Proceeds obtained through cross-border M&As are fungible and can be used for productive as well as unproductive purposes.

- Over the longer term, both modes of entry are likely to provide similar investment inflows in similar situations. Thus, even in a case in which only cross-border M&As are feasible, as with some privatizations, there can be large sequential investments, particularly in capital-intensive enterprises like utilities that call for heavy investment.

- There is no clearly discernible difference between the two entry modes with respect to the crowding in and crowding out of domestic enterprises, though M&As are likely to have more beneficial linkage effects in the earlier phases of investment.

Policies

- Where maximizing long-term capital inflows is a policy objective, as when investment opportunities are plentiful and domestic savings fall short of investment requirements, there may be little reason for policies to differentiate between greenfield FDI and cross-border M&As. In order to make sure that sequential investment follows a foreign acquisition, some countries have inserted future investment commitments into privatization deals. As noted, the evidence on the effectiveness of these commitments is mixed. Countries could also consider structuring incentives in such a way that, following M&As, the creation of additional productive capacity by the new owners is encouraged.

- Countries could structure taxation rules in such a manner that they encourage the previous owners of firms sold in M&As to reinvest the proceeds obtained in productive capacities. In the case of privatizations, the funds obtained from foreign investors could be left with the newly acquired firm for investment purposes.

- Attracting the right kind of foreign partner in a cross-border merger or acquisition is important. Targeting may have a role to play here.

- To obtain the best prices in privatizations, a competitive and transparent tendering process is crucial. Careful attention must also be paid to the profile of the buyer and the quality of the offer.

- Pricing problems can be minimized by measures and institutions facilitating corporate valuation, such as appropriate accounting, reporting and auditing rules and well-functioning capital markets.

- The interests of domestic minority shareholders and other stakeholders need to be protected.[15] In particular, the host country's company law and stock-exchange rules may need to be strengthened to ensure that they include adequate guarantees for minority shareholders to be informed of and participate in decisions to sell or merge, including sufficient and timely information on potential foreign buyers. The minority shareholders' rights to dissent and to dispose of their shares need also to be protected.

- To prevent asset stripping or other corporate decisions that are likely to jeopardize development objectives, e.g. closures or relocation of productive activities abroad, governments of host countries can use such a device as "golden shares", which give them a veto over certain kinds of corporate decisions.

- The negotiating process is critical to the outcome of M&A deals — both private and privatization-related. In these negotiations, negotiators from developing countries and transition economies frequently face powerful companies with considerable legal and financial firepower. Governments can help in two ways: by providing technical advice and training domestic negotiators in the art and techniques of cross-border M&A negotiations; and by providing financial assistance to domestic firms to get the best national and international advice on their M&A deals.

- To help financially distressed but viable local companies (and where no other alternatives are available), governments can use proactive measures to attract specific types of M&A partners, such as matchmaking, securing outstanding debts or providing insurance for financial risks.

B.   Technology

Transforming and upgrading the technologies used in production and strengthening national technological capabilities, including the capacity to innovate, are major objectives of countries with respect to their development process. The transfer of technology and its efficient application and diffusion are therefore some of the most important benefits sought by developing countries from FDI (UNCTAD, 1999a). TNCs tend to be leading innovators. They are leading suppliers of technology to developing countries and economies in transition, through FDI and other (externalized) forms of transfer. They can also stimulate the development of innovatory capacities in host economies, thereby supplementing technology development that takes place through R&D in domestic firms and publicly funded institutions (box VI.6).

Box VI.6. FDI and the transfer, diffusion and generation of technology

Technology transfer. Generally TNCs are leading innovators in their industries. They transfer technologies by internalized modes — to the firms within their production systems, including the foreign affiliates they control — or externalized modes — to other firms, through licensing, minority joint ventures, subcontracting, strategic alliances or capital goods sales. Internalized technology transfer has the following characteristics:

- Generally TNCs transfer more modern and productive technologies to their affiliates than those available in host countries, especially developing and transition economies. However, the nature of the technology or process transferred reflects both the conditions in each host economy (wages, skills, supply capabilities, scale and so on) and the motivations of the TNCs concerned. Advanced host countries receive complex technologies or functions, while less developed ones receive simple technologies and processes.

- FDI may be a more expensive mode of transfer than externalized modes (e.g. licensing) where these are realistic alternatives. The latest and most valuable technologies, however, are not generally available on licence. Strategic inter-firm technology alliances, which may vary in form from equity joint ventures to contractual agreements, are another means by which technology transfers occur between foreign and local firms. These, however, mainly involve firms from developed countries and more advanced developing countries that have already built up some technological knowledge and capabilities. Moreover, firms in many host developing countries may find it difficult to implement efficiently even the mature technologies that are available by licensing or other contractual arrangements. Countries may therefore prefer FDI, as it provides the skills and knowledge needed for efficient implementation. FDI can also provide other benefits, such as export market access and brand names, not available in arm's-length technology purchases. And FDI can provide an effective means of updating technologies quickly, which is important for countries that lack the ability to improve and innovate on imported technologies. Taking these factors into account, FDI may often prove to be the cheapest long-term means of technology transfer.

- The techniques deployed in foreign affiliates are geared to local capabilities and exploit the existing comparative advantages of host countries. There is a risk that these advantages may remain static if the host economy does not strengthen its capabilities. TNCs may also restrict the access of particular affiliates to technology, in order to minimize inter-affiliate competition. They may hold back the upgrading of affiliate technology in line with growing local skills and capabilities or invest insufficiently in host country training and R&D, in accordance with their global corporate strategies.

- Foreign affiliates are generally in the forefront of new management and organizational techniques, quality management standards, training and marketing methods.

Technology diffusion. There may be positive spillover effects from foreign affiliates to a host economy through four channels:

- Competition with local firms, stimulating them to improve technological capabilities and raise productivity;

- Cooperation between affiliates and local suppliers and customers, stimulating technology spillovers to vertically linked firms and service providers;

- Labour mobility, particularly of highly trained personnel, from foreign affiliates to domestic firms including supply businesses set up by former TNC employees, often with the support of their former employers; and

- Proximity between foreign and local firms, leading to personal contact, reverse engineering, imitation and the formation of industrial clusters facilitating technological upgrading in host countries.

Technology generation. The impact of FDI on innovation capacity in host developing countries has so far been rather limited. TNCs tend to centralize R&D in their home countries

/...

1. Technology transfer and upgrading

To the extent that foreign investors enter a country to undertake value-adding activity in which they have a lasting interest, there is no reason to expect the mode of entry to make a major difference to the technology transfer involved. They would be interested in operating efficiently in either case and would presumably do whatever is needed in technological terms to ensure this. However, other things remaining the same, since a takeover involves working with an existing facility and a greenfield investment setting up a new one, the latter is more likely to involve newer equipment and work practices from inception.[16] This may mean that affiliates established through cross-border M&As have older technologies to start with, though this need not mean that these are less desirable. For instance, technologies in an acquired firm may be better adapted to the local environment or have a stronger learning base that allows them to be used more efficiently. Where the acquired firm has obsolete or inefficient equipment, the acquirer is very likely to inject new equipment, technologies and production methods to make it competitive.

In most developing countries and economies in transition, cross-border M&As, especially by developed-country TNCs, are likely to raise the level of hard and soft technologies and the related capabilities of acquired firms, because of the greater technological strengths that foreign investors usually have. Even in developed countries, where technological differences between M&A partners are relatively small, it has been observed that M&As tend to increase the productivity of acquired firms (Caves, 1998,[17] p. 1963; Modén, 1998). In developing countries, where the technological differences between domestic firms and foreign acquirers are often large, the impact on the acquired firm is likely to be correspondingly larger. However, the nature of the host economy, the activity concerned and the motivation of the investor will all make a difference to the technology transfer and upgrading that occur. The more open to international competition a host economy, or the more export-oriented the activity in question, the stronger is this effect likely to be. Similarly, the stronger the skill and technology base in a host economy and the greater the receptiveness of acquired firms, the faster and more effective will the transfers be. Needless to say, if M&As are not efficiently carried out because of the inadequate

---

Box VI.6. FDI and the transfer, diffusion and generation of technology (concluded)

and a few other advanced industrial countries, so as to reap economies of scale and linkages with technology and research centres. Developing countries attract only marginal shares of foreign affiliate research, and much of what they get relates to production (adaptation and technical support) rather than innovation. Still, in recent years, TNCs have located some strategic R&D in developing countries that have the required human resources.

In sum, the content of technology transfers by TNCs to their foreign affiliates in developing countries depends on the nature of the industry, the pace of technical change, and conditions in the host economy (the trade and competition regime and local skills and capabilities). The extent of spillovers to other domestic enterprises depends on technological and other

capabilities in the host economy, particularly among suppliers, and the strength of local technology institutions. Where local supply capabilities are low, spillovers will also be low. This may change over time as local capabilities increase and foreign affiliates gain familiarity with suppliers, taking on local flavour. The intensity of the spillover impact of FDI through competition will depend on the openness of the economy, domestic competition policy and the ability of local firms to take up competitive challenges and to restructure. The impact of FDI on the capacity of developing countries to innovate is low, because, with few exceptions, developing countries attract very small shares of TNCs' R&D. All these economic factors being given, TNCs will differ among themselves in their technological trajectories for reasons of corporate strategy.

Source: UNCTAD, 1999a.

assessment of technological complementarities, the benefits will be reduced or negated. Where the merging of two companies takes a long time, the benefits will take that much longer to realize.

There is one vital difference between the two modes of entry as regards the technology transfer and upgrading that may occur: M&As involve *existing local firms directly*, albeit under new ownership, while greenfield investments do not. The impact of the latter on other local firms' technology (through, e.g. competition and demonstration) is thus slower. Where the technological gap between foreign entrants and domestic firms is large, greenfield FDI may in fact drive some existing domestic firms out of the market. In that situation, to the extent that countries prefer to preserve capabilities already built up in local firms, they might prefer M&As. There may then be a case for incentives for M&As that save and strengthen technological capabilities in host country firms, similar to incentives to greenfield FDI that brings in new technologies.

As for *upgrading* technologies over time, much depends on the status of an acquired firm at the time ownership is transferred. If it needs considerable upgrading to bring it to competitive levels, there is likely to be relatively rapid change, as compared to a foreign greenfield facility near technical frontiers. On the other hand, if a facility is already technically efficient, there may be little upgrading for some time; in the long run, upgrading will occur in line with overall changes in the technical capabilities of a TNC and the position of the affiliate in its strategy and structure. Where an acquisition is made to access local technology, no upgrading may take place in the acquired firm, although it might occur in other facilities owned by the TNC. For example, in the Chilean mining industry, in which domestic and foreign firms already had modern technologies, there was little upgrading following cross-border M&As in the 1990s (Riveros, et al., 1995). On the other hand, in Swedish TNCs that acquired foreign firms to gain access to R&D in the latter, knowledge flows vis-à-vis the foreign acquisitions were found to be reciprocal, with flows to the acquired firm preceding those in the opposite direction (Bresman, et al., 1999). Upgrading in foreign affiliates established through acquisition may be slow where an acquired firm suffers from organizational "inertia" and its

integration into the TNC's system takes time; its inherited capabilities and habits can make it difficult for a new owner to introduce new technologies.

Apart from these considerations, however, the technological upgrading of affiliates over time should not differ much by mode of entry. The process depends more on the market orientation of the investment, local skills and capabilities in the host country, and corporate strategies (UNCTAD, 1999a). Evidence for Asia (Zhan and Ozawa, 2000), some Latin American countries (Argentina: Chudnovsky, et al., 1995; Mexican car industry: Mortimore, 1998) and Central and Eastern Europe (Zemplínerová and Jarolim, 2000) shows that FDI through cross-border M&As can lead to considerable technological upgrading. Such upgrading also occurred in foreign acquisitions in Sweden, according to a study of a sample of firms covering selected years during the period 1980-1994 (Modén, 1998). Foreign acquisitions increased both the labour and the total factor productivity of the acquired firms; moreover, the productivity improvements in them were greater than those observed in locally acquired firms.

The transfer of soft technologies, including management and organizational practices, is an important aspect of knowledge transfer within TNCs. Evidence from several studies suggests that foreign investors introduce new or improved management techniques to acquired firms (Allard and Lundborg, 1998, p. 45). This seems to be of particular importance in acquisitions of state-owned enterprises, including service providers. In Argentina, for instance, the principal contributions of foreign acquirers of gas and, to a lesser extent, electricity utilities lie in the organization of the new enterprises (Chudnovsky, et al., 1995, p. 10). Improved practices for effective corporate governance may also be transferred when acquisitions are made by TNCs from countries with well-developed private sectors and governance systems. At the same time, differences between the management styles of the acquired and the acquirer may create problems, since these need more time to be harmonized. It has been noted that successful acquisitions are often distinguished by the respect accorded to the local management culture (Allard and Lundborg, 1998). Finally, as regards management as well as other aspects, the scope and direction of technology transfer and upgrading will depend upon the roles assigned to firms after acquisition, with some becoming more restricted due to specialization within the global systems of the acquirers while other become centres of excellence for a particular product or function.

2. Technology diffusion

From the viewpoint of host-country development, what matters is not just the transfer of technology to foreign affiliates, but also, and more importantly, the wider dissemination of the technologies from those affiliates to other parts of the local economy. The local diffusion of technology by foreign affiliates depends on their linkages with the local economy and the spillovers captured by the local economy. If existing linkages by acquired firms are efficient, TNCs are likely to retain and strengthen them. Foreign affiliates established through M&As are likely to have stronger local links than greenfield FDI, which will take time and effort to develop such linkages. While this is true in the short- to medium-term, it may also be true in the long-term, because of the cumulative effects of building capabilities, contacts and trust. Thus, FDI through M&As may lead to a better diffusion of technology transferred by TNCs than FDI in greenfield sites. For example, in Swedish TNCs (Andersson, et al., 1996) and in foreign affiliates in some Central and Eastern European countries (Szanyi, 2000), greenfield foreign affiliates have been found to import more intermediate inputs from home countries than acquired firms. In the case of Swedish foreign affiliates, moreover, the difference between the two groups studied did not diminish over time. If, on the other hand, the local linkages of acquired firms are weak or inefficient, M&As will lead to a switching of supply chains abroad, with lower diffusion of new technologies locally. This case, however, will be no different from that of a greenfield investment sourcing overseas.

Policy efforts to strengthen linkages (and thereby technology diffusion) by imposing local content requirements are relevant to FDI through M&As, as well as greenfield projects. Their relevance is, however, constrained by their potential for distorting resource allocation and by the TRIMs agreement within WTO, which generally prohibits the imposition of certain performance requirements on foreign investors. Policies focusing on strengthening local supplier (and distributor) capabilities and, in particular, on inducing TNCs to retain existing linkages can, however, contribute to encouraging technology diffusion.

Technology diffusion from foreign affiliates to the host economy at large can also involve institutions such as research centres, universities, extension services and quality-assurance services. Foreign affiliates often use these institutions more actively than local firms in developing countries because of TNCs' greater technological awareness and skills. The impact of the mode of entry in this respect is likely to be similar to that noted with regard to diffusion to local firms with supply linkages. Where an acquired firm has strong and efficient institutional linkages, TNCs are likely to retain and enhance them, thereby contributing to the building up of national innovation systems. Where the linkages are weak or inefficient, they are likely to behave like greenfield entrants and build them gradually over time while relying initially on overseas linkages.

Technology diffusion can also take the form of spillovers to local competitors and other firms, by demonstration, competitive pressure, and the movement of technical and professional staff. These are unlikely to differ by mode of entry. (Competition issues as such are taken up in section E.)

3. Technology generation

Usually TNCs concentrate their technology generation efforts (R&D) in advanced countries. It is often feared by host countries with local R&D capabilities that cross-border M&As can cause innovative activity in acquired firms to be reduced, shifted elsewhere or shut down. How realistic is this fear? Where local R&D is uneconomic to start with (built up to adapt technologies for small-scale production in protected markets, often the main reason for R&D in developing countries) and becomes even more uneconomic in a liberalized environment, M&As may certainly reduce it. This may be a loss to the host economy if activities that are currently uneconomic could, with a certain measure of protection, become profitable in the future. The key factor here is the expected dynamic comparative advantage of these activities. Curtailing uneconomic R&D activities that cannot be made more efficient or better serve the market in the long run may allow for more rapid technology upgrading and release valuable human resources for other uses. Where local R&D *is* economic, however, and reduced by TNCs for strategic reasons (because it duplicates R&D elsewhere or does not suit their product or location strategy), it can be harmful for a host economy. This eliminates valuable capabilities built up with considerable effort and pulls the country down the technological ladder.

At the same time, where local R&D is economic, there is little reason to expect that acquiring TNCs in many industries will reduce it unless it duplicates what is being done elsewhere. TNCs tend to value a broad range of technological activity, aimed to suit different conditions and markets. The cost of R&D of certain kinds can be much lower in affiliates in developing countries or transition economies than in developed countries because of the lower costs of obtaining certain types of scientific and technical personnel.[18] Thus, TNCs can efficiently locate segments of R&D activity that suit the endowments of host economies and the competitive strengths of affiliates in them. In the case of efficiency-seeking or created-asset-seeking FDI, the acquisition of a firm with R&D capabilities can save the time and effort needed to build such capabilities from scratch. TNCs can then use the human and knowledge resources at their disposal to enhance the quality of existing R&D and integrate it into their larger research systems.

All this suggests that it would be rational for TNCs to increase R&D in acquired firms with prior R&D capabilities, especially if the motivation is efficiency-seeking or asset-seeking, although with the possibility of greater specialization in the context of their global systems and strategies. Where the host economy has other efficient sources of innovative activity, TNCs can use their local R&D facilities to monitor and tap into those sources. A greenfield affiliate in an economy with strong human resources may also invest in R&D, but this is likely to take much longer to develop. The greenfield affiliate may also attract trained researchers away from other facilities in a host country.

Systematic evidence is lacking, but there are examples of both decreasing and increasing R&D in acquired affiliates with R&D capabilities. For example, R&D in several acquired enterprises in Latin America has been

wound up or downscaled as production was reoriented towards less technology-intensive activities. In Hungary, on the other hand, when General Electric acquired Tungsram, it initially cut the latter's R&D activities, but later resumed and strengthened them.[19] In the Republic of Korea, the acquisition by Volvo of a unit from Samsung not only saved this unit from an uncertain future but also created the potential to turn it into a centre of excellence with a world product mandate from Volvo (box VI.7). Government policies can play a role in influencing the outcome, by either influencing the choice of the foreign partner (say, in a privatization or acquisition of a major private firm) or the acquirer's decision on locating technological activity (through incentives or persuasion).

Does the mode of entry make a difference to TNC investment in local technological activity? Given local skills, factor prices and institutions, would an investor who downgrades an acquired firm's technological activity undertake R&D in a greenfield affiliate? There is no strong *a priori* reason to expect this. It is unlikely that a TNC would close down efficient R&D in an acquired firm but would launch R&D in a new affiliate in the same setting. As noted, the opposite is likely because of the learning costs involved.

In the context of developed countries, it has been suggested that, when there are strong market, product, technological and organizational complementarities, M&As improve the technological performance of TNCs (Hagedoorn and Duysters, 2000). When both the acquiring and acquired firms are highly research-oriented and their resources complementary, M&As lead to increases in research output per researcher. This need not mean, of course, that R&D in the acquired firms necessarily increases. Furthermore, M&As can lead to a reduction of R&D in acquired firms if there is duplication of R&D or few complementarities between the acquired and acquiring firms. Where an acquired firm is well below the technological frontier, its R&D activity may be reoriented towards absorbing and improving existing technologies; this may lead to lower R&D spending, while raising its efficacy. Purely financial mergers, where the acquirer lacks the necessary technological capability or is not committed to technological excellence, may also lead to R&D reductions (Hagedoorn and Duysters, 2000).

The foreign acquisition of a *local technological leader* raises fear that the acquiring TNC will "strip" the local firm of its technological assets and innovatory activities to transfer them overseas, depriving the local economy of the revenues, spillovers and linkages that such assets and activities generate. This is one major reason why many developed countries seek to prevent the takeover of "national champions". The urge to protect champions is particularly strong in defence and other strategic technologies with strong linkage and spillover benefits. The risk of losing strategic assets in this way is certainly real, especially when the technology has strong spillover effects on other products and activities and these are captured by overseas firms. As noted, however, TNCs acquiring technologically strong firms tend to preserve their R&D capabilities and links with local technological sources even if they exploit their proprietary technologies for their own benefit. Indeed, it is in their interest to strengthen these capabilities by integrating them into their own research networks. This follows from the logic of asset-seeking FDI (Dunning, 1993), which is an increasingly important motive for outward FDI in developed countries (UNCTAD, 1998a).

Studies of acquisitions by TNCs in some developed countries support this reasoning. In Sweden, there was no "stripping" of R&D-related technological assets in a sample of acquired firms covering the period 1980-1994; on the contrary, R&D was strengthened in the acquired firms (Modén, 1998). Similarly, foreign acquisitions of R&D-oriented Danish firms led mainly to a strengthening of their R&D assets (Pedersen and Valentin, 1996, p. 171). Another study of Swedish TNCs, mentioned earlier, that examined acquisitions made mainly to gain access to the R&D of the acquired units, throws light on knowledge transfer in cross-border M&As. In the early stages of an acquisition, knowledge transfer was mostly one way, from the acquiring to the acquired unit. Over time, the transfer became more reciprocal and shifted from relatively articulated technologies (e.g. patents) to more tacit flows. The facilitators of knowledge transfers included telecommunication, visits and meetings (Bresman, et al., 1999).

While these findings apply primarily to M&As in the developed world, they are also relevant to some newly industrializing economies. Technology-seeking firms from

---

**Box VI.7. Turning an ailing unit into a centre of excellence:
Volvo's acquisition of Samsung's construction equipment division**

As a result of the Asian financial crisis, the Korean conglomerate (*chaebol*) Samsung Group decided in 1997 to divest from its loss-making and debt-ridden construction equipment division, Samsung Heavy Industries, and concentrate on shipbuilding and plant construction.[a] This would immediately enable the company to reduce its high debt-equity ratio and invest part of the proceeds into its core business.

Volvo Group of Sweden bought Samsung Heavy Industries in May 1998 for $500 million, saving it from an uncertain future. Moreover, Volvo decided to make the acquired company (re-named Volvo Construction Equipment Korea Co.) its global centre of

excellence for excavators. In the longer term, Volvo also intends to transform Volvo Korea into a global research and production centre for construction equipment in Asia and the world. In order to achieve these objectives, Volvo plans to set up a new R&D centre in the Republic of Korea whose task would be to develop new products, modify existing products and develop core parts for various other products. In April 1999, Volvo closed some plants in Sweden and Germany and transferred the production to its Changwon Plant in the Republic of Korea. In 1999 alone, Volvo invested an additional $200 million to strengthen its operations in the Republic of Korea.

Source: Jung, 2000.

[a]   In a separate deal, Samsung also sold its fork lift truck business to Clark Equipment Co. of the United States for $30 million.

Mexico, the Republic of Korea, Taiwan Province of China and other developing economies have been acquiring firms with strong technological assets in developed countries (particularly in Silicon Valley). Such M&As have boosted the technological base of the acquiring firms without apparent damage to the host economies. Recently, technology seeking M&As have also been undertaken by developed-country TNCs in the Republic of Korea (Zhan and Ozawa, 2000).

Notwithstanding the evidence cited above — and given the limited nature of available evidence in this regard and, in particular, the broader context of globalization and the greater opportunities open to TNCs to switch the location of various functions — the possible loss of (or decrease in) viable or promising R&D activities in host countries cannot be overlooked. Policy-makers may consider measures to preserve local R&D activities, particularly on grounds of infant technology development. In cases where firms with high R&D potential are offered for purchase by foreign investors, measures could be taken to encourage R&D in acquired firms after a change of ownership. This is particularly important in cases in which firms slated for acquisition are at the forefront of R&D activity. The objective should not necessarily always be to maintain local R&D regardless of cost; when local efforts cannot keep up with international frontiers or the longer-term chances of maintaining a successful local capability are slim, it may be more economical to let local R&D disappear. It is not easy to pick winners and losers, least of all in technology generation. Nevertheless, if a sound economic case can be made, governments may try to influence foreign acquirers to preserve established innovatory activities in important areas by means of carefully crafted financial incentives or public-private sector cooperation.

4. Summary

Technology transfer

- Both modes of entry can lead to similar technology transfers and upgrading in affiliates established through FDI. The content of the transfer depends on the needs of the acquired companies in a given context of local factor endowments, market conditions and affiliate orientation.

- One difference between the modes of entry lies in the speed of implementation. This depends in turn on the efficiency with which M&As are conducted and the absorptive capacity of the local enterprises. The greater the technological strengths and capabilities of acquired firms and the better managed the M&A process, the greater the likelihood that acquisitions would contribute to a rapid build-up of technological competence and activity.

- Greenfield FDI may transfer newer equipment and technology at inception, but entry through M&As may also be followed by technology transfers to foreign affiliates. Foreign affiliates established through M&As may, moreover, be able to absorb technologies faster because of capabilities already existing in the acquired firms. Much depends on the original technological status of the acquired enterprise.

- M&As can offer the benefit of involving local acquired enterprises directly in the technology transfer and upgrading, including soft technologies and especially improved organizational and managerial practices, while greenfield FDI does not: it transfers technology to a new affiliate and affects local firms through linkages and spillovers. The former may, therefore, be preferable in terms of saving and upgrading existing capabilities.

Diffusion

- The greater the capabilities and human-resource development in a host country, the more likely is diffusion to take place through linkages and spillovers from foreign affiliates, regardless of mode of entry.

- M&As may diffuse technology faster because their linkages are likely to be stronger.

Innovation

- Innovative activity may be downgraded by M&As in countries in which it is lagging behind world frontiers, but is likely to be enhanced where it is actually or potentially efficient. There may, however, be situations in which an acquiring TNC's location strategy leads it to scrap significant R&D activity in a host country even if it is efficient.

- Where good R&D capabilities exist, M&As may be able to tap them faster than greenfield investments. However, where an acquired firm suffers from significant technological inertia, the process may turn out to be slower.

- The stripping of technological assets by M&As is a risk, although probably a small one in most developing and transition economies.

Policies

- Within the context of an overall national technology policy, there may be a case for providing incentives to foreign acquirers that save and strengthen existing capabilities and firms, similar to the "pioneer" incentives provided by many countries to greenfield investors who bring valuable new technologies or export-oriented facilities. This should not involve actively discouraging greenfield entry, but only making takeovers more beneficial.

- On the R&D front, a government may consider encouraging the preservation of efficient local activity (particularly in strategic industries) through approximate negotiations with acquirers and by offering incentives.

- The stimulation of local diffusion needs policies to strengthen skills and technology support systems for supplier industries and competitors. It may be desirable to offer special incentives to investors that preserve and increase local supply and other linkages.

C. Employment and skills

Unemployment and a concentration of large numbers of workers in low-wage employment, with poor and insecure conditions of work, continue to plague most developing countries and economies in transition. Increasing gainful employment and shifting it towards higher-quality jobs are important to the development of these countries as is improving workers' skills. FDI affects the quantity and quality of employment and the development of skills in a number of ways (box VI.8).

1. Employment quantity

The direct impact of FDI through cross-border M&As on the quantity of employment is likely to differ markedly from that of greenfield FDI, especially at entry and in the short-term thereafter. A greenfield investment generates new employment, while an acquisition transfers responsibility for existing employees — who may then be laid off by the new owner. Lay-offs are likely for three main reasons: rationalizing and eliminating duplication, enhancing efficiency (particularly in privatized enterprises), and reducing excess capacity. Of course, the opposite might also happen, leading to increased employment. In the longer-term, employment in foreign affiliates acquired through M&As is likely to increase if the restructuring and integration that follows the acquisition is successful.

Employment effects are likely to vary according to the motivation of the foreign acquirer and the characteristics of the acquired firm.[20] A simple classification of motivations suggests the following:

- In *market-seeking* cross-border M&As, where TNCs acquire firms to access domestic or regional markets or international marketing networks, the direct effect on employment is likely to be neutral or positive in the short- to medium-term. A TNC is likely to retain the existing workforce to cater to its newly acquired market, and to raise employment if the market grows or if the affiliate increases its market share. Acquisitions by TNCs in the food industry in Costa Rica, for example, led to increased employment in some firms.[21]

- In *strategic-asset-seeking* M&As, TNCs also tend to maintain employment in acquired firms if, as is likely, the employees of these firms have valuable skills and capabilities. If M&As lead to productive synergies between the parties, operations are likely to expand and raise employment.[22]

Box VI.8. FDI, employment and skills

The **quantitative** effects of FDI on the volume of employment in a host country can be summarized as follows:

- FDI may increase employment directly by setting up new foreign affiliates or expanding existing affiliates, and indirectly by stimulating additional employment in suppliers and distributors (depending on the intensity of local linkages). In the medium-term, employment can also rise through multiplier effects from the new income generated by FDI or through the increased demand stimulated by improved efficiency and restructuring of competing firms.

- FDI can preserve employment by acquiring and restructuring firms that would otherwise go bankrupt.

- FDI decreases employment through the divestment and closure of foreign affiliates, the liberalization of protected (inefficient) activities, changes in parent company strategies, mergers between parent companies in home countries, or the restructuring of newly acquired firms in host countries with corresponding indirect effects.

The **qualitative** impacts of FDI on employment (on wages, job security and conditions of work, such as health and safety standards, hours of work and workers' rights), include the following:

- *Wages.* Foreign affiliates generally pay higher wages than domestic firms in similar activities. The difference is more marked in industries that demand higher levels of skills, technology and marketing and in export-oriented activities that need to ensure consistent quality and timely delivery. However, some export-oriented affiliates (especially those of TNCs from developing countries) may pay low wages because their *raison d'être* is tapping low-wage labour in simple assembly activities.

- *Job security.* Foreign affiliates tend to offer greater job security because of their size, competitive strength and need for a stable workforce. Investors, however, motivated by low wages offer insecure employment, since they can move to other countries as wages rise. New forms of work organization imported from home countries may also result in greater insecurity.

- *Other conditions of work.* Working conditions in foreign affiliates are generally better than in local firms. In particular, large and visible TNCs tend to comply with local and international standards and even with the labour standards in their home countries. This may not, however, be the case in low-end, labour-intensive industries.

In the area of *skills*, TNCs tend to upgrade employee skills in host countries by investing in training. Employees may leave foreign affiliates and carry their skills to other firms or set up their own firms. Generally TNCs induce or support local suppliers to train workers to meet their quality standards and influence local competitors or unrelated firms to emulate their training practices. They may also interact with local education and training institutions to improve practices, curricula and links with industry. Affiliates of firms on the frontiers of human-resource management are generally better at providing training than local firms. However, TNCs investing to take advantage of low-cost labour may do relatively little training, though they may still raise supervisory or technical skills to meet the standards of export markets. Skill upgrading feeds back into TNC activity: TNCs react to the availability of skills by raising the technological content of their investments, contributing to further learning and skill creation.

What determines the frequency, scope and intensity of these effects in a host country? The quantity of employment generated by FDI depends on the amount of net investment in new production activity, the nature of the activity (whether labour-intensive or capital-intensive) and the technology transferred. It also depends on market orientation. In market-seeking FDI, the size of a host-country market limits the amount of investment and hence employment, while in export-oriented FDI the market can be much larger and the potential for direct and indirect employment generation greater. Employment quality is also affected by the level of education and labour markets in a host economy and the activity and technology of the affiliate. In general, the more efficient the labour markets and the higher the skill levels in a host economy, the greater the chances of attracting FDI associated with high employment quality and good training practices.

Source: UNCTAD, 1999a.

- In *efficiency-seeking* M&As, where the acquired firms have low costs and the likelihood of improving technical efficiency or finding various synergies with the acquirers, the outcome will vary according to the technological status of the acquired firm, the extent of employment duplication between the acquired firm and the rest of the TNC, the trend of the market and the global strategy of the acquiring TNC. Acquired firms with poor technology or management or with substantial excess capacity are likely to lose employees as they are restructured. Those offering synergies may suffer some losses as duplicated functions are eliminated, but this may be offset by the strengthening of other functions, and employment may increase. Overall, the horizontal mega-mergers of the 1990s have led to considerable downsizing to realize synergies and focus on core competencies (Kang and Johansson, 2000, p.16). M&As in the world automotive industry during the 1990s have been followed by cuts in employment despite an increase in output.[23] In this industry, restructuring to improve efficiency in the context of global over-capacity has been taking place across the board, and greenfield FDI is less and less of an option for firms and countries that have established production capacity. M&As in the financial-service industries have also led to lay-offs. In Brazil, for example, the acquisition of local banks by foreign firms resulted in significant lay-offs (Vidotto, 1999). Staff reductions also followed the acquisitions of a number of Thai banks by foreign investors in the context of the recent financial crisis.[24]

- Cross-border M&As driven primarily by short-term *financial considerations* may have employment-reducing effects when restructuring is required and when financial markets or the managers in the home country treat post-acquisition employment reduction as an indication of restructuring. In other words, information on lay-offs can substitute for more detailed technical information (that markets may not have) on restructuring. This can create incentives for acquirers to undertake technically unnecessary redundancies where the need for signals is very strong.

Acquisitions driven by the quest for short-term financial gains may also lead to unemployment if gains are sought through asset stripping and the dismantling of production units. On the other hand, where the acquired firm is profitable and dynamic and M&As are a form of portfolio diversification, firms can show increasing employment because they now have more resources to invest.

Cross-border acquisitions in *privatizations* often lead to lay-offs after (and in some cases, before) the change of ownership. This was the case with the recent privatizations of electric power generation and distribution in Latin America involving the Spanish firm Endesa (ECLAC, 2000, p. 154), and the privatizations of telecommunication services in several developing countries and economies in transition.[25] Another example, this time from Asia, is that of the Manila Water Works, acquired by two TNCs in 1997; employment dropped from 7,370 to 4,580 employees (PSI, 2000).

In Central and Eastern Europe, where state-owned enterprises accounted for half or more of total employment prior to the onset of transition, privatization to cross-border investors (as well as to domestic ones) and the restructuring that followed led to large employment cuts in the acquired enterprises. A 1999 UNCTAD survey of the pre- and post-privatization performance of 23 major companies acquired by foreign investors in seven countries of Central and Eastern Europe found that employment in the enterprises decreased before as well as after privatization.[26] Nevertheless, the rate of decrease of employment in privatized enterprises was often smaller than the general rate of decline in employment in these countries and was more pronounced in the period preceding privatization. This suggests that other employers were less successful than foreign investors in preserving jobs, or that foreign investors acquired the more efficient of the privatized enterprises. There are inter-country differences in Central and Eastern Europe in the extent of employment reduction following privatization. Reductions of staff and sales of non-core businesses were more frequent in the early stage of privatization in the Czech Republic than in Poland and Hungary (Rojec, 1995).

The immediate loss of employment following an acquisition may not be a net loss to an economy if the local firm was in competitive difficulties and would have gone bankrupt in the absence of an acquisition. FDI entry through M&As in this case represents a *conservation of employment* even if the numbers employed are smaller than before. In crisis or transition economies, the employment conservation effect of cross-border M&As may be quite strong (Zhan and Ozawa, 2000; Hunya and Kalotay, 2000). For example, a study of early privatizations in Poland found that 90 per cent of foreign investors changed the organizational structure of the enterprises they bought, but only 20 per cent reduced employment (Jermakowicz, 1994). Employment also remained unchanged following privatization, according to a study on foreign-owned enterprises in Slovenia (Rojec, 1997).

Once the initial adjustment after privatization has been made, employment might well increase. This happened, for example, in the telecommunication industries of some developing countries. Growing markets, or increased demand, stimulated by lower post-acquisition prices for the products of privatized enterprises, can stimulate sequential investments leading to employment generation side-by-side with productivity increases. In the Czech Republic, Hungary and Poland, downsizing was often followed by large new investments and employment remained stable or increased (Hunya, 1997).

The *indirect employment effects* of M&As include effects on employment in other firms in the economy through linkages and through the "crowding out" or "crowding in" of domestic enterprises (UNCTAD, 1994a; UNCTAD, 1999a). As discussed in section B, if linkages in acquired firms are strong and internationally competitive, they are likely to be retained and strengthened by acquiring TNCs; this would lead to employment in supplier firms being maintained or increased. If linkages are weak or inefficient, there will be a switch to new sources, leading to a reduction of employment in former suppliers. This may be compensated for by an increase of employment in other suppliers if the switch is within the host economy. If the switch is to imports, however, there would be a larger loss of employment. In comparison with greenfield FDI, however, it is not clear that there is a net loss of employment. Greenfield investors would tend to rely on foreign suppliers to a greater extent, especially in the initial phase of their operations. Furthermore, even without foreign entry, inefficient local suppliers would lose ground if the economy opens up to competing imports. International competition would force all firms, local and foreign, to switch to the most economical sources.

As far as crowding in and out of local firms goes, the effects on employment can vary. In a saturated domestic market, a greenfield investment (once it is fully operational), if successful, will necessarily reduce employment in competing firms, while an acquisition of existing capacity will not. When domestic firms merge to strengthen their competitive position *vis-à-vis* incoming foreign competitors, there may be layoffs in these firms. On the other hand, if the market has excess or growing demand, domestic-market-oriented greenfield investment can flourish along with existing firms and add to employment in net terms. In such markets, firms entering through M&As will also expand their operations through sequential investments, adding to employment. In other words, M&As and greenfield FDI are unlikely to differ in their indirect employment effects, apart from short-term adjustment effects. In the case of export-oriented investments, the indirect effects of both modes on employment are again likely to be similar, since production is not constrained by domestic market size and demand.

The effects of M&As on employment quantity also raise broader economic issues. If a host economy has efficient labour markets and is expanding so that laid-off employees are quickly absorbed elsewhere, redundancies in any particular activity do not matter that much. Indeed, firm turnover and labour movement are a necessary, though often painful, feature of a dynamic economic change. It is when labour market conditions do not allow for rapid adjustments or when there are few other opportunities for employment that redundancies in particular firms raise social and economic problems. In developing countries characterized by high unemployment, insufficient training, infrastructure and lack of resources to upgrade workers' skills, these problems can be acute and the cost particularly high in terms of unemployment.

Problems caused by lay-offs following cross-border M&As call for government policies and measures by employers and trade unions to minimise the hardships and adjustment costs faced by wage-earners. One important step is to ensure that early consultations with worker representatives take place to discuss the reasons for any proposed M&As or privatizations and address the concerns and needs of workers. This is important not least because M&As increase anxiety over job security at all levels, highlighting the need for timely information and consultation. There is increasing recognition among countries, trade unions and company managers that consultations with employees in these situations are a corporate duty. A number of international labour instruments — notably the ILO Tripartite Declaration on Multinational Enterprises and Social Policy and the employment chapter of the OECD Guidelines for Multinational Enterprises — also call for such consultations (box VI.9). The European Union goes further in protecting employee's rights in the event of M&As (box VI.10).

In some cases of cross-border M&As in developing and transition economies, future commitments on employment, at least for a few years after a cross-border acquisition or privatization, are negotiated. This may be particularly important where social safety nets are weak or non-existent. For example, in Poland, the acquisition of two telecommunication equipment manufacturers by Siemens guaranteed continued employment of 100 per cent (in one acquisition) and 75 per cent (in the other), but only for 18 months (Floyd, 2000, p. 12). Such measures are transitional in nature. Some governments have incorporated workplace grants in M&As and privatization deals, in effect subsidizing wages (Kuruvilla, et al., 1998, for the Philippines; Phang, 1999, for the Republic of Korea) and, thereby, acquirers.

Obtaining employment commitments from M&A investors can be helpful in some cases. But for the society as a whole, a general policy of strengthened social safety nets may be more beneficial in the long run. Compensatory measures, including allowances for employees who resign voluntarily, can also be negotiated as part of a merger, acquisition or privatization deal. Indeed, as M&As grow in importance, the need to introduce, expand and strengthen social security systems, and in particular unemployment benefit systems, becomes more important than ever (Mody and Negishi, 2000, p. 11). A proactive safety net not only provides unemployment benefits, but also establishes training, retraining, counselling and guiding programmes for the unemployed. The financing of such programmes could come not only from fiscal, but also from privatization revenues. Governments can enter into partnerships with private companies with respect to proactive measures, including the provision of job search and mobility assistance, retraining and vocational training. Thus, the development of government-sponsored business advisory services and credit facilities linked to enterprise restructuring or privatization projects can enhance the mobility of laid-off employees (ILO, 1998). These mechanisms cannot, however, replace the Government as the main agent of social security and retraining.

2. Employment quality

Employment quality refers to wages and conditions of employment, such as contractual status, hours of work, industrial relations (including the right to organize and to collective bargaining) and equal opportunities. TNCs tend to offer high-quality employment unless they are in low-technology, export-oriented activities outside the purview of normal labour laws (UNCTAD, 1999a, pp. 267 and 270-271). Other things being equal, a greenfield venture is initially likely to offer higher quality employment, while the inertia inherent in M&As can lead the acquirer to preserve old, lower-quality norms. This effect is likely to erode as the acquired firms introduce new management practices and are integrated into the corporate culture of their parent firms. Over time, therefore, there should not be much difference between the two entry modes. Changes in employment conditions after a merger or acquisition may, however, have a stronger demonstration effect on other local firms in terms of employment practices than the practices in a greenfield affiliate, because of the stronger local linkages and contacts in the former case.

The impact on employment quality of foreign entry through M&As depends on the motives of the investor and the conditions in the acquired firm and the host economy.

Box VI.9. International guidelines on consultations, negotiations and other employee-related matters relevant for M&As

There are two international instruments that are explicitly addressed to TNCs and which, explicitly or implicitly, are relevant to cross-border M&A employment issues: the ILO Tripartite Declaration on Multinational Enterprises and Social Policy[a] (UNCTAD, 1996b) and the OECD Guidelines for Multinational Enterprises (OECD, 2000).

The Tripartite Declaration, in paragraph 26, provides that reasonable notice be given:

"26. In considering changes in operations (including those resulting from mergers, take-overs or transfers of production) which would have major employment effects, multinational enterprises should provide reasonable notice of such changes to the appropriate government authorities and representatives of the workers in their employment and their organisations so that the implications may be examined jointly in order to mitigate adverse effects to the greatest possible extent. This is particularly important in the case of the closure of an entity involving collective lay-offs or dismissals."

Paragraph 54 then stipulates that relevant information be made available:

"54. Multinational enterprises should provide workers' representatives with information required for meaningful negotiations with the entity involved and, where this accords with local law and practices, should also provide information to enable them to obtain a true and fair view of the performance of the entity or, where appropriate, of the enterprise as a whole."

And paragraph 56 provides for consultation:

"56. In multinational as well as in national enterprises, systems devised by mutual agreement between employers and workers and their representatives should provide, in accordance with national law and practice, for regular consultation on matters of mutual concern. Such consultation should not be a substitute for collective bargaining."

Similarly, the text of the revised OECD Guidelines, adopted by the Governments of the 29 member countries of the OECD and of Argentina, Brazil, Chile and Slovakia at the OECD ministerial meeting of 27 June 2000, states under the "Guideline on Employment and Industrial Relations":

"6. In considering changes in their operations which would have major effects upon the livelihood of their employees, in particular in the case of the closure of an entity involving collective lay-offs or dismissals, provide reasonable notice of such changes to representatives of their employees, and, where appropriate, to the relevant governmental authorities, and co-operate with the employee representatives and appropriate governmental authorities so as to mitigate to the maximum extent practicable adverse effects. In light of the specific circumstances of each case, it would be appropriate if management were able to give such notice prior to the final decision being taken. Other means may also be employed to provide meaningful co-operation to mitigate the effects of such decisions."[b]

"8. Enable authorized representatives of their employees to negotiate on collective bargaining or labour-management relations issues and allow the parties to consult on matters of mutual concern with representatives of management who are authorised to take decisions on these matters."

Both the ILO Tripartite Declaration and the OECD Guidelines are non-binding recommendations addressed to TNCs. However, they also indicate that these principles reflect good practice for both transnational and national enterprises, which, wherever relevant, should be subject to the same expectations in respect of their conduct in general and their social practices in particular.

Of relevance also are the OECD Principles of Corporate Governance (UNCTAD, 2000a). They recommend that the corporate governance systems of companies should recognize the rights of stakeholders, as established by law, and encourage active co-operation between corporations and stakeholders. Among others, the Principles recommend that:

/...

Market-seeking or strategic-asset-seeking M&As may upgrade employment quality to assure delivery and quality of products and retain skilled workers. However, M&As may also provide opportunities for an acquirer to negotiate changes in employment conditions with disadvantageous effects for workers, at least in the short run; an obvious example is the privatization of state-owned enterprises, in which employees' benefits may not be retained after acquisition. Another is the deunionization observed in some countries, when TNCs acquire plants that have delisted unions (Cooke, 2000a and 2000b). In acquisitions of firms in distress, takeovers may involve measures to lower wages and cut costs by reducing other benefits. At the same time, a reduction in the staff of privatized firms can lead to higher wages for the work force that remains. This is illustrated by domestic privatizations in Sri Lankan tea plantations (Salih, 1999), the Korean iron and steel industry, (Park, 1997) and Chinese foreign-invested state-owned enterprises (Fan Gang, et al., 1998).

Trade unions can play an important role in minimizing the negative impacts of the rapid growth in international production and maximizing the gains to labour (UNCTAD, 1994a; Bailey, et al., 1993). They can ensure workers' representation in the decision-making process affecting them and, in the context of lay-offs, enhance transparency, information flows and the discussion of alternatives. Some unions are also developing special initiatives to address the problems to which M&As can give rise, such as sudden lay-offs, changes in contractual status and conditions of work. Examples include the "employment pacts" that are being concluded between some trade unions and employers to guarantee employment and continued production over a period of time (ILO, 2000c, pp.17f).[27] Another example is the incorporation of "work-ownership" — a concept pioneered by the National Automobile, Aerospace, Transportation and General Workers' Union of Canada — into collective bargaining agreements. Under such agreements, firms acknowledge that the workers own the contribution to the product they make. Thus, a company cannot be sold off or work outsourced without the agreement also applying to an acquiring firm or newly established supplier (ILO, 2000c, p. 17).

Box VI.9. International guidelines on consultations, negotiations and other employee-related matters relevant for M&As (concluded)

"D. Where stakeholders participate in the corporate governance process, they should have access to relevant information" (UNCTAD, 2000a, vol. IV, p. 263). The annotation to this principle indicates that "Where laws and practice of corporate governance systems provide for participation by stakeholders, it is important that stakeholders have access to information necessary to fulfil their responsibilities" (UNCTAD, 2000a, vol. IV, p. 274).

Obviously, this provision is of immediate relevance to cross-border M&As.

Source: UNCTAD.

a   A number of ILO Conventions, as well as many other international arrangements, are of course also relevant to TNCs, even though they do not address them specifically. Among the ILO instruments perhaps particularly relevant in the context of M&As are the ILO Convention Concerning Termination of Employment (Convention 158, of 1982) (ILO, 2000a) and the ILO Recommendation Concerning Termination of Employment at the Initiative of the Employer (Recommendation 166, of 1982) (ILO, 2000b).

b   Paragraph 6 of the revised OECD Guideline on Employment and Industrial Relations reproduces verbatim the previous text of this guideline, except for the last two sentences which were added in the new version. The first new sentence suggests that the appropriate timing of the notice given to employees in the relevant situations should be prior to the final decision being taken, but this is qualified by the phrase "if management were able to" do so. Notice prior to the final decision is indeed a feature of the industrial relations laws and practices of a number of OECD countries. At the same time, the revised Guideline recognizes that giving notice to employees is not the only means to ensure an opportunity for meaningful co-operation to mitigate the effects of such decisions and the laws and practices of a number of OECD countries provide for other such means as defined periods during which consultations must be undertaken before decisions are implemented (see Commentary on Employment and Industrial Relations, OECD, 2000).

In the case of privatizations, employees who remain in a company may be offered stock options as part of a privatization package, strengthening their potential role in its management. However, this does not necessarily guarantee voting rights. In the Telmex (Mexico) privatization, for example, unionized workers bought 3 per cent of Telmex public shares as individuals and the union's retirement fund bought 1.4 per cent. This, however, did not give the union a seat on the company's board, although it was agreed that workers would be allowed to continue purchasing shares and would be entitled to a seat when their purchases reached 10 per cent of all shares. This goal was not reached as many workers cashed in their shares and others chose to exert direct control over their shares rather than hand them over to the union's share fund (ILO, 1998).

3. Skills

TNCs tend to invest more in training than local firms and to deploy more modern training practices and materials. They also bring in expatriates with specialized skills and establish strong linkages with training institutions and schools. The main difference between the two modes of TNC entry is likely to lie primarily in the short-term inertia associated with acquisitions. In the long-term, there is no reason to expect any important difference. Upgrading of skills has been observed, for example, in the auto-supplier industries in Mexico. Though cross-border M&As here reduced the number of local

supplier firms, they enhanced the quality of employment in the firms that survived. These firms were acquired from Mexican owners in the early 1990s, and incoming TNCs provided shop-floor training, as well as training in quality control, design, technical norms and specifications (Romijn, et al., 2000, pp. 36f). In Zimbabwe, an agro-processing firm, Olivine, a joint-venture with a TNC, provided training at all levels as earnings were reinvested to upgrade the firm's competitiveness (Romijn, et al., 2000, p. 25).

There is a risk that M&As may result in the best, most highly skilled employees of the acquired firms being transferred abroad for use elsewhere in a TNC network. This may be regarded as an undesirable brain drain for a host economy, though it may lead to higher welfare and skill creation for the employees concerned (and for the host economy if and when they return). However, where a host economy has such desirable skills at low cost, foreign employers can attract workers abroad by other means. A greenfield venture may also bid workers away from other firms and send them abroad, or foreign firms may hire workers without investing locally at all.

At the same time, the integration of an acquired affiliate into a TNC system can lead to such significant skill inflows as new work systems, management techniques and production technologies are introduced. The deliberate downgrading of skill levels in a newly acquired facility is fairly unlikely; it would make sense for a TNC to do this only if it went for an acquisition to access low-wage

---

Box VI.10. Employees' rights in the event of M&As in the European Union

The European Community's Council Directive 98/50 (1998) "on the approximation of the laws of the Member States relating to the safeguarding of employees' rights in the event of transfers of undertakings, businesses or parts of businesses" requires, in article 6, both the transferor and transferee to inform the representatives of their employees affected by a transfer of the date and reasons for the transfer, the economic and social implications for the employees, and any measures envisaged in relation to them. The information must be given in good time before the transfer

is carried out and, in any event, before employees are directly affected by the transfer as regards their employment and conditions of work. Representatives of employees should be consulted in good time on such measures, with a view to reaching an agreement. In addition, article 3 imposes an obligation on an acquiring company to respect established contracts of employment. Apart from the requirements on the provision of information and the consultations mentioned before, the Directive gives unions an influence on the acquisition process.

Source: European Community, 1998.

unskilled labour. This is unlikely to form the basis of a strategic acquisition, because setting up a new venture to access low-cost labour would be much simpler.

4. Summary

Employment quantity

• The employment effects of cross-border M&As and greenfield FDI differ in the first instance. Greenfield FDI directly and immediately creates new jobs, while M&As do not. On the contrary, there are several reasons why M&As may lead to lay-offs.

• However, not all cross-border M&As lead to direct employment losses. There are several conditions in which they add to employment even in the short-term, as when corporate decisions lead to the immediate expansion of capacity.

• If employment in acquired enterprises would have declined even further or disappeared entirely in the absence of cross-border M&As, as, for example, in cases in which firms go bankrupt, M&As conserve employment for a host economy.

• In the long-term, and taking indirect effects into account, there is no reason to expect a systematic difference between the two modes of entry on employment. Instead, differences will depend on the motivation underlying FDI.

• Lay-offs nevertheless cause economic loss and social problems. Wherever they occur, even for sound economic reasons, governments should therefore make provisions to deal with them, to retrain workers and to help create other employment opportunities by means, among others, of policies generally conducive to investment and enterprise development. Where social safety nets are lacking, large-scale lay-offs may create extreme distress.

Employment quality and skills

• Greenfield FDI may upgrade employment conditions more than M&As because the latter may tend to stick with the inherited

norms and practices for some time. Furthermore, cross-border M&As can be used to renegotiate work conditions and lead to their downgrading. Thereafter, M&As may upgrade employment quality faster to bring the new affiliates in line with corporate norms and competitive needs. Over time, there is no reason to expect any systematic difference between the two modes.

• There is, similarly, no reason to expect systematic differences in skill creation. If the integration of an acquired affiliate takes time and there are many inherited "bad work habits", however, retraining may take longer.

• There may be a risk of skill loss if an acquiring company transfers abroad the best jobs or the most qualified employees of an acquired firm. However, this is not likely in most cases: acquired firms are more likely to benefit from an inflow of new skills as technologies and management systems are integrated into the parent TNCs.

Policies

• As M&As typically create anxieties at all levels of a firm's staff structure, consultations are important. Early consultations and discussions with worker representatives can provide lead time for taking measures to minimize hardship through e.g. the retraining and relocation of workers. An appropriate mechanism for consultations can be helpful in this respect.

• As FDI through cross-border M&As increases the prospects for sudden and large-scale lay-offs from employment in the formal sector, it is more important than ever that countries adapt, expand and strengthen their social safety nets for workers and strengthen the domestic enterprise sector and its competitiveness so that it creates more jobs.

• Specific commitments and measures for employment retention have a role to play as short-term complementary measures, especially where safety nets are weak or non-existent.

- Trade unions play an important role in ensuring that qualitative gains in employment conditions achieved over time are not dissipated in the course of M&As, including cross-border M&As. Forms of information-sharing need to be found for M&As taking place in firms that lack formal worker representation.

D. Export competitiveness and trade

FDI can help developing countries exploit existing comparative advantages and build new ones. It is the principal means for them to enter the international production systems of TNCs that increasingly figure importantly in world trade, particularly in complex manufactures (box VI.11).

1. Building export competitiveness

There is an important difference between FDI through the two modes of entry when it comes to building export competitiveness in host economies. Greenfield entry may be the only feasible mode of foreign entry for many new export-oriented activities, particularly in export-processing zones, since there are generally few local firms with major export potential to acquire. In export-oriented activities that are closely integrated into international production chains — as in electronics — there is little scope for independent local firms. The skill and technological needs are very high and the transaction costs inherent in firms hitherto under different ownerships integrating their operations in fast-moving technologies are often prohibitive. Greenfield FDI is thus the dominant form of entry.

Greenfield and M&A FDI may, however, be real alternatives in the case of protected, locally-owned activities that need to raise competitiveness in the face of rapid trade and FDI liberalization. For the host economy or industry, greenfield investment would be preferable where restructuring local firms is costly and prolonged, and M&As where they could manage the restructuring quickly and effectively. In liberalizing economies,

M&As can be a valuable means of preserving and upgrading local capabilities. The automotive component industry has been restructured by cross-border M&As in Mexico, Brazil, Argentina (Mortimore, 1998) and more recently Thailand, when the alternative facing them was declining competitiveness and, in some cases, bankruptcy. Greenfield entry would also have provided competitive facilities, but may have led to a loss of local capabilities and a greater disruption of local supply chains and activities.

What of the export orientation of affiliates established by the two modes? The experience of Central and Eastern European economies provides a mixed picture. In Hungary, most new export-oriented enterprises located in export-processing zones were established through greenfield ventures but some privatized enterprises also became major exporters. In general, however, M&As were less export-oriented than greenfield investments (Éltető and Sass, 1997). In contrast, in the Czech Republic, the export intensity of affiliates established through M&As was not significantly different from that of greenfield investments. The major exporter in both cases was the automobile industry; the difference in export performance reflects its different evolution. In Hungary, foreign investment in automobiles was greenfield, since earlier it had no automobile industry. In the Czech Republic, the national incumbent Skoda was a well-established producer and exporter. After its sale to Volkswagen, the share of exports in Skoda's sales increased from 34 per cent in 1990 to 52 per cent in 1995 and 80 per cent in 1999; Skoda accounted for 76 per cent of the automobile exports of the country by 1998 (Zemplínerová and Jarolim, 2000). In Poland, the picture is unclear (Uminski, 2000). A survey of early privatizations (1990-1994) shows that the share of exports in sales increased in firms sold to foreign owners, while falling in locally owned firms (Dabrowski, 1996). A survey of 23 firms in seven Central and Eastern European countries shows that exports grew rapidly both before and after privatization, but faster before than after (39 and 34 per cent, respectively). In an example from a developing country, Costa Rica, acquisitions of local firms oriented towards the domestic market were partly redirected to the regional market, a process which, however, also involved an increase in imports (box VI.12).

Box VI.11. FDI, export competitiveness and trade

TNCs account for a large share of world exports and imports. Their role is greater in technology- and skill-intensive industries, the most dynamic and high value-added activities in trade. TNCs are increasingly setting up integrated production systems across countries, with considerable specialization by technology level and labour costs; thus, intra-firm trade is playing a greater role in some of the most advanced areas of trade. TNCs are also very active in sourcing natural resources and resource-based manufactures from developing countries and relocating simple labour-intensive activities and processes (within high technology industries) there to tap their low wages. Thus, TNC participation can help host countries raise exports in all kinds of industries by providing the missing elements, tangible as well as intangible, that they need to compete or by improving the local base of skills and capabilities. However, the impact of FDI on strengthening host countries' export competitiveness and their ability to compete with imports is not unambiguously positive: much depends on the nature of local skills and capabilities and on measures taken to improve these over time. To summarize the main effects of FDI:

- *Exploiting static comparative advantages.* FDI can be an effective means of providing the missing resources, such as the skills, training and technology, capital goods and intermediate inputs needed to exploit the host countries' existing comparative advantages. These advantages can be natural resources and low-wage unskilled labour in less developed countries, or the base of capabilities built up earlier (behind protective barriers) in more advanced countries with import-substituting experience. FDI may not, however, be sufficient to sustain export growth as wages rise and it becomes necessary to develop more skill-intensive and technology-intensive exports. TNCs can improve worker skills, but cannot upgrade the local base of education and capabilities. Unless the host country does this, there is a danger that TNC-based export growth will peak and then stagnate.

- *Creating dynamic comparative advantages*. In countries with adequate education and capabilities, TNCs can help create dynamic comparative advantages by

means of new skills and more advanced technologies. This has been the case with dynamic industries like electronics in some countries of South-East Asia. In countries with more advanced industrial and technology bases, TNCs can feed into innovation by setting up R&D centres and interacting with local research.

- *Providing access to international markets.* Successful exporting needs not only competitive products, but also marketing expertise and access to international markets. FDI can provide a major benefit in this respect, especially in markets in which established brand names and large distribution networks are important assets. Where trade is internal to TNCs, as in some high technology products, joining TNC networks is often a *conditio sine qua non* for increasing exports. On the other hand, foreign affiliates may have less freedom than domestic firms to choose export markets and diversify their product range. Those assigned to the low end of the value-added chain may stagnate relative to competent and technologically progressive local firms.

- *Raising local linkages.* To the extent that a foreign affiliate sources inputs locally, FDI in export-oriented industries links domestic suppliers indirectly to international markets. These enterprises may later be able to exploit these links further on their own. With trade liberalization, the decision of foreign affiliates to source their inputs locally or abroad is subject more to cost and delivery considerations than to host-government trade policies. When they first enter a new host country, TNCs may tend to use established overseas suppliers with whom they have strong linkages. However, there are advantages to having suppliers nearby, and TNCs invest in developing local suppliers when the cost of bringing them up to the necessary technical and quality levels is modest. Some of this takes place through FDI in supplier industries, including producer services. Where the costs of developing supplier industries are too high to induce such associated investment, promoting linkages needs government support to help local firms raise their skills and technology levels.

/...

Box VI.11. FDI, export competitiveness and trade (concluded)

Over time, the linkages of foreign affiliates and local firms tend to become similar as their information on local and foreign suppliers converges.

Statistical analyses show a positive link between FDI and manufactured export performance. The list of the most dynamic exporters in the developing world shows that the great majority depends heavily on TNC export operations (UNCTAD, 1999a). However, export-oriented TNC operations are concentrated in a few developing countries, with high technology export networks encompassing an even smaller number.

Inward FDI also affects the volume and composition of host-country imports. It has been found, in most cases, to lead to a net increase in imports (UNCTAD, 1996a, pp.73-85), adding to both arm's length and intra-firm purchases of goods and services. Some of these imports serve to complement domestic comparative advantages and strengthen export competitiveness. The composition of imports also tends to change, as production by foreign affiliates is often more technology-intensive than domestic production. The economic implications of increased imports by foreign investors depend upon the quantity, quality and prices of their products.

Source: UNCTAD, 1999a.

---

2. Reliance on imports versus local sources

Greenfield and M&A FDI may differ in the extent to which they rely on imported or local inputs. As noted earlier, greenfield projects tend, at least initially, to have weaker local linkages, relying more on foreign suppliers and intra-TNC trade. Acquired firms are likely to continue to rely on local suppliers with which they have established links, as long as the suppliers are competitive with alternative sources. Interestingly, the higher import propensity of greenfield FDI can persist over

a longer term, as Swedish data show (Andersson, et al., 1996, p. 66). In the Czech Republic as well, greenfield foreign enterprises were found to rely more on imported supplies than did acquired firms (Zemplínerová and Jarolim, 2000). In 1998, the imports-to-sales ratio of the former was 30 per cent higher than of firms acquired by TNCs.

In the services sector, however, where cross-border M&As are often an important means of foreign entry, the import propensities of acquisitions can be high. In Central and Eastern Europe, according to the 1999 UNCTAD survey that covered large infrastructure

---

Box VI.12. M&As and trade: the experience of firms in Costa Rica's food industry

A survey undertaken in early 2000 by the Ministry of External Trade of Costa Rica of ten companies in the country's food industry that had been acquired by foreign firms shows that export destinations are concentrated in neighboring countries, suggesting that some investors were seeking access to Central American markets through the acquisition. For example, two of the firms that were hitherto producing for the domestic market have emerged as regional exporters of dessert foods, while four others increased their export values, two of them significantly. Seven firms in the sample are centering their export activity on two to three subregional countries each.

On the other hand, eight of the ten surveyed firms display a negative trade balance with import values amounting from twice to five times as much as those of exports. It is not clear, however, from the available information whether this reflects a short- to medium-term effect due, for example, to the import of capital goods for strengthening or upgrading production capacities after acquisition, or an effect that might extend over a longer-term, due to import-sourcing of inputs that could persist and that is not offset by export earnings.

Source: Costa Rica, Ministry of Foreign Trade, 2000; and UNCTAD.

companies, the growth of imports accelerated significantly after privatization. Imports increased at 40 per cent per annum after privatization, as compared with 14 per cent per annum before it. This rapid growth in imports has to be evaluated in the context of a rapid growth in the provision of goods and services to customers at falling costs, as well as increased efficiency in downstream industries due to improved access to and the lower costs of producer services.

3. Summary

Building export competitiveness

- Many export-oriented activities, particularly those integrated into international production systems, are new to developing countries and involve greenfield FDI rather than M&As. However, M&As can play an important role in restructuring and reorienting firms coming to be exposed to international competition. This role is more important in large import-substituting economies with strong domestic capabilities and is likely to grow in significance.

- In European economies in transition, M&As have tended to be more domestic-market-seeking than greenfield investment, but there are striking exceptions. Much depends on the specific situation of the countries and industries involved.

Reliance on imports versus local sourcing

- FDI through cross-border M&As may rely more on local suppliers relative to greenfield foreign affiliates, which take time to establish local links. Although import reliance may be quite high, especially in acquisitions in capital- and technology-intensive industries, the preservation of links with local suppliers may be an advantage of FDI through cross-border M&As.

Policies

- Apart from general policies to strengthen competitiveness, governments could consider offering incentives for restructuring firms for export activity, just as they do for new export-oriented greenfield investments.

- Governments can target export-oriented TNCs for specific M&As. Governments can also directly influence the export performance of M&As through incentives linked to export performance (to the extent that they do not conflict with trading rules).

E.   Market structure and competition

FDI has complex effects on a host-country's market structure and competition. Large foreign affiliates can pose serious challenges for maintaining effective competition in host economies, by increasing market concentration or engaging in anti-competitive behaviour. They can also promote competition rather than restrict it (box VI.13).

1. Market structure

What difference does the mode of foreign entry make to market structure? Greenfield entry initially adds to the number of enterprises — potential competitors — in a host country, reducing market concentration. M&As leave the number of competitive firms intact. The net effect on market structure is, however, more complex than this. Greenfield FDI may not add to the number of competitors if the investing firm were present earlier in the market through trade or licensing agreements. It may increase concentration if the new foreign affiliate offsets the dominant market positions of incumbent firms, or takes a dominant market position itself. Cross-border M&As can, on the other hand, have a positive effect on competition if the entrants take over ailing domestic firms that would otherwise have been forced out of the market. They can also challenge established domestic oligopolies by merging with other domestic firms to create effective rivals.

One relevant difference between the two entry modes is that M&As can, in contrast to greenfield entry, be used to reduce competition via "monopolizing mergers and acquisitions" (UNCTAD, 1997a). This type of cross-border M&As can occur in the following situations:

- The acquiring firm was exporting substantially to a market before it buys a competing firm in it;

- A foreign firm with an affiliate already in the market acquires another, thereby acquiring a dominant or monopolistic market share;

- The investing TNC acquires a market leader with which it has previously competed;

- The acquisition is intended to suppress rather than develop the competitive potential of the acquired firm.

In addition, there can be important adverse effects on market structure and competition (as well as in the other areas of development considered in this chapter) of cross-border M&As that occur in other economies. For example:

- Parent firms of foreign affiliates located in a host country merge and consequently merge their affiliates, reducing local competition;

- A TNC with an affiliate in a host country acquires an enterprise in a third country that has been a source of import competition in the host country market;

Box VI.13. FDI, market structure and competition

Market structure

TNCs flourish in concentrated markets. Their main ownership advantages (in technology, product differentiation and organization) are found in oligopolistic industries with large firms. Consequently, their entry also tends to occur in concentrated industries. This may initially add to the number of firms, though it can force the exit of less efficient firms and thereby raise concentration levels. This is not necessarily anti-competitive conduct. If markets are contestable, the result can be a more efficient and competitive industrial structure. Much depends on the openness of a market to trade, the intensity of local competition, the actual conduct of leading firms and technology. The chances of abuse of market power are much greater in protected markets or in those in which the Government favours selected enterprises than in open ones. Patchy evidence suggests that FDI may be associated with reduced concentration in developed countries and with increased concentration in developing ones, where strong domestic firms are relatively scarce. As to effects on competition, the evidence from developing countries is mixed.

Competitive behaviour

TNC entry puts competitive pressure on domestic firms. There is evidence that this leads to an increase in product quality, variety and innovation in host economies. There is little evidence, however, that it leads to lower prices. Domestic firms may react to the competitive

pressure by enhancing capabilities or be forced out altogether. Both might be desirable outcomes from the economic point of view as long as they reflect genuine market forces rather than predatory behaviour by foreign affiliates. However, when domestic producers of low-quality, low-price goods and services go bankrupt and these products disappear, the low-income population is left in distress. Predatory conduct remains a significant risk, although recent investment and trade liberalization have raised contestability in national markets. Nevertheless, the urgency of an effective competition policy has not diminished for host economies.

Privatization of natural monopolies

Another important issue for many economies is the impact on competition of foreign purchases of state-owned companies that hold monopoly positions. The problem is particularly acute with respect to natural monopolies, where privatization has to be accompanied by (often complex and flexible) regulatory structures and rules. Developed countries are experimenting with different policies, like introducing competition in particular segments where several producers can operate (e.g. power generation), or regulating and assessing the operation of monopolies in different ways (yardstick competition, price setting or negotiated rates of return). The impact of foreign private ownership is in this context a part of the larger array of regulatory issues.

Source: UNCTAD, 1997a.

- Two foreign affiliates in a host economy merge, although their parent firms remain separate, eliminating competition between the two affiliates and leading to a dominant market position.

In general, it is horizontal M&As (i.e. M&As between firms making similar products) that cause the main problems for competition policy. However, vertical M&As can also raise competition issues. For instance, they may increase the potential for keeping rivals from sources of supply or raise barriers to new entry. To repeat, the final outcome for competition depends on the context. Higher concentration by itself does not indicate anti-competitive conduct; it may simply reflect scale and efficiency considerations. Cross-border M&As (or M&As with foreign affiliates) may be a way for domestic firms to stand up to large TNCs entering the market. The crucial issue is the size of the relevant market: national, regional or global. This differs from industry to industry. Much depends also on how contestable the market is. Where a market is open to import competition and new local and foreign investment, the domestic concentration level need not necessarily make a difference to effective competition.

Evidence available on the consequences of M&As for concentration is less than conclusive. Evidence in the form of government actions in developed countries, relating to cross-border as well as domestic M&As, suggests that the majority of M&As do not have negative effects on concentration. In the United States and the European Union, competition authorities scrutinize only a small minority of cross-border M&As to assess negative impacts on competition. An even smaller number of transactions is subject to such obligations as selling off parts of the business or is completely ruled out. In the United States, for example, in fiscal year 1999 (ending 30 September) only 1.6 per cent of 4,679 M&As transactions notified to anti-trust authorities resulted in enforcement actions, with only about 1 per cent being challenged in the end (United States, Department of Justice, 2000). The situation is similar in the European Union: in 1999, only 14 out of 292 transactions (less than 5 per cent) were challenged or subject to a second-phase investigation. An additional 19 cases were cleared during the first phase of investigation. In Japan, all 3,813 M&As notified in 1998 were cleared, although two transactions "were revised in response to concerns raised during pre-notification consultation" (*ibid.*, p. 7). However, the lack of official action does not necessarily mean that firms did not increase concentration: the authorities may have believed the M&As to be in the public interest even if concentration did increase.

Evidence is scarce in developing countries because many of them do not have competition laws or the resources to implement them. Even if they have such laws, they might not have merger control provisions. In one country that provides such evidence, the Republic of Korea, the situation seems to be similar to that in developed countries. The Korean Fair Trade Commission has ordered corrective measures for only 3 out of 132 cross-border M&As notified in 1998 (Yun, 2000, p.12). In Mexico, all 55 notified cases of cross-border acquisitions of Mexican firms in 1997 went through unhindered as "no competition risk was registered" (Mexico, Federal Commission on Competition, 1997, pp. 7-8).

At the same time, there are examples of M&As between TNCs and incumbent firms resulting in the TNCs assuming dominant or quasi-monopolistic positions. In India, for instance, Hindustan Lever Limited, the Indian subsidiary of Unilever, acquired its main local rival, Tata Oil Mills Company, to assume a dominant position in the toilet soap (75 per cent) and detergent (30 per cent) markets (Mehta, 1999, p. 24). Hindustan Lever Limited also acquired several local companies in other markets, such as the ice cream makers Dollops, Kwality and Milkfood. This raised its market share in the ice cream market from zero in 1992-1993 to 69 per cent in 1996-1997 and over 74 per cent in 1997-1998 (Kumar, 2000, pp.13 and 17). Smith Kline Beecham, with a 64 per cent share in the Indian market for health drinks, acquired two brands from the domestic producer Jagjit Industry Limited (Kumar, 2000, p. 17). In Mexico, a United States brewery Anheuser-Busch — already present in the Mexican market — acquired a controlling stake (50.2 per cent) in the Mexican brewery Grupo Modelo SA, the marker leader, in 1998. Although data on the combined market share of the two companies are not available, it is presumably higher than the 55 per cent held by Modelo in 1996.[28]

In the countries of Central and Eastern Europe, many industries had monopolistic structures before the transition to market-based systems. Privatization therefore raised the very real possibility of monopoly positions being maintained or strengthened (Zemplínerová and Jarolim, 2000). In the Czech Republic, concentration in manufacturing fell during 1989-1995 as a result of the splitting of large companies into smaller units but, in the second half of the 1990s, domestic mergers raised concentration in a number of industries. A number of the merged firms were later sold to foreign investors. However, an analysis of concentration ratios in 87 manufacturing industries in 1998 did not find any strong correlation between cross-border acquisitions and the share of the largest producer in an industry's sales, excluding imports (Zemplínerová and Jarolim, 2000, table 5). Of the 15 industries in which the share of the largest producer was above 50 per cent, only four showed a link between the share and cross-border M&As, probably because of the sale of domestic companies with high shares to foreign investors. In the remaining 11 cases there was no link between the high ratio and cross-border M&As. The introduction of imports reduced the shares of dominant firms in many industries (including the four foreign firms with high shares) sufficiently to alleviate competition concerns. In small economies imports are, of course, often the only way through which competition can be maintained.

Nevertheless, the threat of the abuse of market power is always present. TNCs in countries with weak regulatory frameworks are by no means immune to the temptation to use this power to achieve dominant positions or secure higher levels of protection. Indeed, in the first years of transition and privatization in Central and Eastern Europe, foreign investors sought and frequently secured monopoly positions or protected markets. In Hungary, for example, privatization programmes offered foreign firms attractive local companies with strong market positions for sale (Antalóczy and Sass, 2000).

2. Competitive behaviour

The competitive conduct of TNCs is perhaps even more important than their impact on market structure (box VI.13). While conduct is not expected to vary by mode of entry, in cross-border M&As, the assets of the acquiring company are supplemented by those of the acquired one, access to which may have been a major motive for the acquisition. This can give the new company significant competitive advantages over incumbent or overseas rivals, greater than those achieved through greenfield FDI. An example is the retail trade industry, where TNCs take over local retail chains and combine their advantages of global sourcing with the advantages of the established distribution network. Greenfield FDI does not enjoy this advantage, and takes more time to build up local assets.

Neither conceptual analysis nor empirical evidence suggests that foreign affiliates, once operational, differ in their competitive conduct because of the mode of entry. Both types have engaged in anti-competitive practices — and both have added to competition. Take anti-competitive behaviour. Firms investing abroad through greenfield ventures may try to restrict competition by using "market-allocation investment cartels". The Timken Roller Bearing Company is a good example. The United-States-based Timken arranged with its major international rival, a United Kingdom firm also called Timken, to enter new markets as partners (via joint ventures), fix prices, allocate territories and participate in cartels to restrict exports (UNCTAD, 1997a). Affiliates established by M&As can indulge in similar restrictive practices.

At the same time, both types of affiliates can add to market competition by their activities. As noted above, the injection of new technologies, management methods and marketing techniques can place incumbent firms under great competitive pressure. This pressure can be particularly beneficial in host economies with a history of protected markets and entrenched local oligopolies.

3. Summary

The effects of cross-border M&As on market structure and competition need close scrutiny by policy-makers in host countries. At the time of entry, M&As do not add to the number of competitors, as greenfield FDI does. In fact, M&As — unlike greenfield FDI — can be used deliberately to reduce the number of competitors serving a host-country market when the acquiring TNC already serves the market. At the same time, there are also scenarios in which M&As can actually prevent a reduction in the number of competitors with a potentially positive effect — by, for example, acquiring ailing domestic firms.

There is no evidence that, in the longer run, foreign affiliates created through M&As would behave differently from foreign affiliates established through greenfield FDI when it comes to anticompetitive practices. However, the potential for a direct reduction in competition at the time of entry, and the avenues this may open for anticompetitive practices, requires the attention of policy-makers, especially of competition authorities. As elaborated above, there are several typical constellations in which M&As take place that deserve the attention of policy-makers even if the primary objective of these deals is not to reduce competition.

As countries liberalize and reduce policy impediments to FDI and trade, competition policy becomes increasingly important in regulating market structure and competition. Competent regulatory bodies and frameworks become critical for ensuring that the risk of negative impacts (including the impacts of cross-border transactions) is minimized. The concluding section will return to this issue, emphasizing the challenges faced by policy-makers in developing countries in the demanding sphere of competition policy and regulation.

F.   Summary and conclusions

With the emergence of a market for firms spanning developed countries and increasingly also developing countries and economies in transition, TNCs have indicated a strong revealed preference for M&As as a mode of entry of FDI. In fact, cross-border M&As are becoming an important means by which firms reshape and restructure themselves under conditions of dynamic change and in the context of the globalization of markets for goods and services and the emergence of an international production system.

The essential difference between cross-border M&As and greenfield FDI is that the former by definition involve a transfer of assets

from domestic to foreign hands and, at least initially, do not add to the productive capacity of host countries. This, in turn, leads to a range of concerns over insufficient resource transfers, lay-offs, asset stripping (including the stripping of technological and innovatory capacities), and, above all, adverse effects on market structure and competition. These concerns are, furthermore, embedded in broader apprehensions regarding an erosion of national economic sovereignty, a weakening of national enterprises, and a loss of control over the direction of national development and the pursuit of social, cultural and political goals. These concerns, in turn, are linked to fears regarding globalization and the perceived power of large TNCs.

Such concerns need to be considered carefully. Their examination in the present chapter focussed on the impact of cross-border M&As in key areas of economic development and whether this impact differed from that of greenfield FDI. A good part of the discussion has been conceptual, and more empirical work is needed to understand the matter fully.

The discussion in the preceding sections suggests that, especially *at the time of entry and in the short term*, M&As (as compared to greenfield investment) may involve, in some respects, smaller benefits or larger negative impacts from the perspective of host-country development. To summarize:

*   Although FDI through both M&As and greenfield investment brings foreign financial resources to a host country, the financial resources provided through M&As do not always go into additions to the capital stock for production, as they do in the case of greenfield FDI. Hence a given amount of FDI through M&As may correspond to a smaller productive investment than the same amount of greenfield FDI, or to none at all. However, when the only realistic alternative for a local firm is closure, cross-border M&As can serve as "life preservers".

*   FDI through M&As is less likely to transfer new or better technologies or skills than greenfield FDI, at least at the time of entry. Moreover, it may lead directly to the downgrading or closure of local production or functional activities (e.g. R&D capabilities), or to their relocation in

line with the acquirer's corporate strategy. Greenfield FDI does not *directly* reduce the technological or other assets and capabilities in a host economy.

• FDI through M&As does not generate employment when it enters a country, for the obvious reason that no new production capacity is created in a merger or an acquisition. Furthermore, it may lead to lay-offs, although it can conserve employment if the acquired firm would have otherwise gone bankrupt. Greenfield FDI necessarily creates new employment at entry.

• FDI through M&As can increase concentration in host countries and lead to anti-competitive results; in fact, M&As can be used deliberately to reduce or eliminate competition. It can, however, prevent concentration from increasing when takeovers help preserve local firms that might otherwise have gone under. Greenfield FDI, by definition, adds to the number of firms in existence and cannot directly increase market concentration upon entry.

Most of the shortcomings of FDI through M&As in comparison with greenfield FDI relate to effects at entry or soon after entry. *Over the longer term*, when direct as well as indirect effects are taken into account, many differences between the impacts of the two modes diminish or disappear. To summarize:

• Cross-border M&As are often followed by sequential investments by the foreign acquirers — sometimes large, especially in special circumstances such as privatizations. Thus, over the longer term, FDI through M&As can lead to enhanced investment in production just as greenfield FDI does. The two modes are also likely to have similar effects regarding the crowding in and crowding out of domestic enterprises.

• Cross-border M&As can be followed by transfers of new or better technology (including organizational and managerial practices), especially when acquired firms are restructured to increase the efficiency of their operations. To the extent that TNCs invest in building local skills and technological capabilities, they do so regardless of how those affiliates were established.

• Cross-border M&As can generate employment over time, if sequential investments take place and if the linkages of acquired firms are retained or strengthened. Thus, in the longer run, differences between the two modes as regards employment generation tend to diminish and depend more on the motivation for entry than on the mode of entry. If employment reductions occur due to restructuring for greater efficiency, the consequences may be less disruptive than when greenfield FDI eliminates uncompetitive firms.

• The effects on market structure, whether negative or positive, can persist after entry. The capacity to engage in anticompetitive practices is greater with M&As that increase concentration, especially when they occur in weakly regulated oligopolistic industries.

In sum, host-country impacts of FDI are difficult to distinguish by mode of entry once the initial period has passed — with the possible exception of the impacts on market structure and competition.

In addition to the effects on the principal *individual* aspects of economic development summarized above, the overall impact of cross-border M&As as against greenfield investment also needs to be considered, taking into account the specific economic context and the development priorities of individual host countries. Particularly important here is the impact on economic restructuring. The restructuring of industries and activities is necessary for growth and development, especially under conditions of rapid technological change and increasing global competition. Such restructuring can of course also take place through domestic M&As and not only cross-border ones; Argentina offers interesting comparisons in this respect (box VI.14). Economic restructuring can also be important under exceptional circumstances, such as financial crises or transitions to market-based economic systems. Cross-border M&As may have a role to play here since they provide a package of assets that can be used for various types of restructuring and, furthermore, have the attributes of speed and the immediate involvement of local (acquired) firms; they can thus usefully supplement domestic resources and efforts. Greenfield investment, of course, can also help economic restructuring; but it has no role to play in conserving domestic enterprises and may, indeed, hasten the demise of weaker domestic firms if and when it out-competes them.

Finally, there are the broader apprehensions regarding a weakening of the national enterprise sector and a loss of control over the direction of national economic development and the pursuit of social, cultural and political goals. These issues acquire urgency when cross-border M&As result in industries thought to be strategic[29] coming under the control of foreign TNCs. They may acquire a yet further edge in developing countries since these countries are predominantly host rather than home countries for FDI in general and cross-border M&As in particular.

The basic question here is what role foreign firms should play in an economy, regardless of whether they enter through greenfield investment or cross-border M&As. It has to do with the extent of foreign ownership that a country can accept comfortably, and the economic, social, cultural and political consequences of such ownership. Many governments, local enterprises and civil-society groups feel that certain activities (e.g. the

media) should be exclusively or primarily in local hands.

There are no *a priori* solutions to these concerns. Each country needs to make its own judgement in the light of its conditions and needs and in the framework of its broader development objectives. It also needs to be aware of — and to assess — the trade-offs involved, whether related to efficiency, output growth, the distribution of income, access to markets or various non-economic objectives. And it needs to note as well that some of these concerns are raised by *all* FDI, although the specific nature of M&As may exacerbate them. The impact of cross-border M&As also depends on host-country circumstances:

• Under *normal circumstances* (i.e. in the absence of crises or systemic changes), and especially when cross-border M&As and greenfield investments are *real* alternatives, greenfield FDI is more useful to developing countries than cross-border M&As. Other things (motivations and capabilities) being equal, greenfield investment not only brings a package of resources and assets *but* simultaneously creates additional productive capacity and employment; cross-border M&As may bring the same package but do not create immediate additional capacity. Further-more, certain types of cross-border M&As

---

Box VI.14. The impact of cross-border M&As in Argentina in the 1990s

Between 1992 and 1999, cross-border M&As accounted for almost 60 per cent of FDI inflows in Argentina. In the early 1990s, most were related to privatizations; after 1993-1994, most were acquisitions of private firms, and accounted for one-third of FDI flows in 1996-1998. Domestic M&As also increased during the 1990s. Given these trends, an examination of the Argentinean experience is useful for understanding the effects of cross-border M&As on a developing economy.

To examine these effects, the performance of manufacturing firms participating in M&As in Argentina was compared with that of an appropriate control group of firms from the same industries and of similar size which did not participate in M&As.[a] Matching firms were arranged in pairs to compare, first, firms involved in M&As in general (i.e. both domestic

and cross-border M&As) with firms, both domestic and foreign not participating in M&As (sample A of firms in box table). Secondly, the performance of firms participating in cross-border M&As was compared *indirectly* with that of firms participating in domestic M&As by examining how each group performed relative to comparable non-M&A firms (samples B and C). And thirdly, the performance of the two groups (not necessarily including the same firms) was compared *directly* with each other (sample D). Since only three among the M&A firms in these samples were state-owned before the merger or take-over, the analysis yields findings primarily about M&As involving private companies. It is the first analysis of its kind in Argentina, and one of the few in developing countries. The key findings of these comparisons follow.

/...

Box VI.14. The impact of cross-border M&As in Argentina in the 1990s (continued)

Box table VI.14.1. The performance of foreign and domestic M&A and non-M&A firms in Argentina between 1992 and 1996

Item	Sample A[a] M&A firms (all)	Sample A[a] Non-M&A firms (all)	Sample B[b,c] M&A firms (foreign)	Sample B[b,c] Non-M&A firms (domestic)	Sample C[c,d] M&A firms (domestic)	Sample C[c,d] Non-M&A firms (domestic)	Sample D[e] M&A firms (foreign)	Sample D[e] M&A firms (domestic)
Number								
Firms	99	99	51	51	41	41	19	19
Increase in per cent in 1996 (1992=100)[f]								
Sales	51*	25	63**	25	24	28	64	44
Exports	143	122	138	110	111	58	145	48
Imports of inputs and final goods	56	34	25	31	58	70	161	214
Imports of capital goods	166	57	189	-15	23	-39	53	328
Investment in productive assets	92	52	85	13	36	18	65	97
Number of employees	-4	-5	1	-9	-18	2	3	-23
Productivity[g]	50	29	..	..	..	..	..	..
R&D expenditure	70	50	53	34	278	39	79	220
Thousands of dollars per enterprise								
Cumulative training expenditures between 1992 and 1996	569*	113	820	150	459	133	261	115
Per cent								
Improvements in product and process technology and organizational and managerial practices[h]	62.1*	55.8	61.6*	49.4	55.8	50.2	56.8	71
Ratios,[i] in per cent (1992 / 1996)								
Exports/sales	8.7 / 10.7	6.7 / 9.7	10.9 / 12.8	6 / 8	6.1 / 7.9	5 / 6.7	13.2 / 16	11.7 / 11.1
Imports of inputs and final goods/sales	9.6 / 11.1	7.3 / 8.2	9.1 / 11.2	7.8 / 7.7	9.2 / 9.1	3.8 / 6.4	3.9 / 7.1	6.2 / 8.6

Source: Chudnovsky and López (2000).

a   M&A firms include firms acquired by local or foreign investors between 1990 and 1996. Non-M&A firms include local firms as well as foreign affiliates that did not undergo a change of ownership.

b   M&A firms (foreign) are firms in which foreign investors have acquired at least 10 per cent of the total equity. Non-M&A firms include firms in which the entire equity is in the hands of domestic investors.

c   It should be noted that firms in samples B and C are not identical to those in sample A. In sample A, M&A firms were matched with non-M&A firms independently of whether the latter were domestic- or foreign-owned. Samples B and C, respectively, compared cross-border and domestic M&A firms with only domestic non-M&A firms and hence, had to replace some of the firms included in the control group in sample A.

d   M&A firms (domestic) are firms acquired by domestic investors. Non-M&A firms are those in which the entire equity is in the hands of domestic investors.

e   M&A firms (foreign) are firms in which foreign investors have acquired at least 10 per cent of the total equity. M&A firms (domestic) are those acquired by domestic investors.

f   Estimated as the increase in the average values for each group.

g   Since not all the firms surveyed provided data on productivity, only 37 pairs could be arranged in sample A to compare productivity between "M&As" and "non-M&As". In B, C and D the samples were too small to be representative.

h   The firms were asked to indicate whether they have or have not adopted 19 different types of possible improvements in the fields of product and process technology, labour organization, quality control, managerial routines, marketing, etc. For each firm, the percentage of improvements actually adopted was estimated relative to total possible improvements. Thus, the data in this row represent the averages of the ratios for these improvements.

i   Estimated as the average of firms' ratios.

*   indicates statistical significance at the 0.05 level.

**   indicates statistical significance at the 0.01 level.

Box VI.14. The impact of cross-border M&As in Argentina in the 1990s (concluded)

All M&A firms vs. all non-M&A firms. The average sales, productivity, exports, investment expenditures and imports of capital goods have grown much more rapidly in M&A firms than in non-M&A firms, with export propensity showing the smallest difference in growth (box table, sample A). M&A firms have also introduced more improvements in product and process technologies and in organizational and managerial practices. They have incurred larger expenditures on training and have increased their R&D expenditures more rapidly. Contrary to expectations, the average employment level has not fallen more in non-M&A firms, despite the fact that sales per employee have grown considerably faster in M&A firms than in their non-M&A counterparts. The average differences in performance between M&A firms and non-M&A firms were found to be statistically significant in the case of sales, training expenditures, and technological, organizational and managerial improvements.

Foreign vs. domestic M&As: indirect comparison. The performance of firms acquired through cross-border M&As *vis-à-vis* domestic non-M&A firms (box table, sample B) is superior for almost all of the variables examined, except imports. Surprisingly, employment in foreign M&A firms increased slightly while that in domestic non-M&A firms decreased considerably. The average differences in performance between foreign M&A firms and non-M&A firms were statistically significant in sales and in technological, organizational and managerial improvements. On the other hand, a comparison of domestic M&A firms with domestic non-M&A firms (sample C) does not provide any clear evidence of a better performance by the former. Sales by domestic M&A firms grew less than those of non-M&A firms. Moreover, whereas employment was significantly reduced in the former, it increased slightly in the latter. Domestic M&A showed stronger performance in training and technological, organizational and managerial changes, but the differences are not statistically significant. On the whole, these findings,

combined with those regarding the relative performance of foreign M&A firms as compared with non-M&A firms, suggest that firms acquired through cross-border M&As have tended to perform relatively better than those acquired through domestic M&As.

Foreign vs. domestic M&As: direct comparison. This comparison, based on a sample too small to be statistically significant, suggests that foreign M&A firms performed better in terms of sales and exports, while domestic M&A firms did better in investment, R&D expenditures, and technological, organizational and managerial improvements (sample D). As regards employment, domestic M&A firms have apparently rationalized more than foreign M&A firms, in which employment increased slightly.

Although these results must be interpreted cautiously, since their statistical significance is partial and the scope of the analysis limited, it seems plausible to conclude that M&A firms performed better than non-M&A firms, while firms acquired through cross-border acquisitions seemed to perform, relatively speaking, better than firms participating in domestic M&As. The direct comparison of these two groups, based on a limited sample of firms, did not produce clear evidence about the superiority of either of these groups. Nevertheless, the analysis tends to support the hypothesis that M&As, both foreign and domestic, were generally a useful tool for microeconomic restructuring in a context of far-reaching trade and investment liberalization and in the absence of any significant public policy to help local firms adapt to the new rules of the game after many years of inward-oriented economic regimes. In these circumstances, M&As turned out to be an important part of a market-driven restructuring strategy for Argentinean firms, a strategy which seemingly produced more efficient and competitive firms. This helped the economy of Argentina to restructure to meet the demands of a liberalizing and globalizing environment. The effects of this strategy on welfare and competition still remain to be explored.

Source: Chudnovsky and López, 2000.

a   The comparison used data from a survey conducted in 1997 by Argentina's National Institute of Statistics and Census, which included 1,639 manufacturing firms, representing 54 per cent of sales, 50 per cent of employment and 61 per cent of exports of the manufacturing sector, and providing data on sales, foreign trade, employment, innovation, manufacturing practices, investment and other variables for two years: 1992 and 1996.

involve a number of risks at the time of entry, from reduced employment through asset stripping to the slower upgrading of domestic technological capacity. And when M&As involve competing firms, there are, of course, the possible negative impacts on market concentration and competition, which can persist beyond the entry phase.

- Under *exceptional circumstances,* cross-border M&As can play a useful role, a role that greenfield FDI may not be able to play, at least within the desired time-frame. Particularly relevant here is a situation of crisis in which firms in a country experience several difficulties or face the risk of bankruptcy and no alternative to FDI (including public funding) is available. Large capital-intensive privatizations (or a large number of privatizations within the framework of a comprehensive privatization programme) may also fall in this category, because domestic firms may not possess (or be able to raise) the required funds or have other assets (such as modern managerial practices or technology) which are needed to make the privatized firms competitive. The need for rapid restructuring under conditions of intense competitive

pressures or overcapacity in global markets may also make host countries find the option of FDI through cross-border acquisitions of some of their firms useful. The advantage of M&As in such conditions is that they restructure existing capacities. In some of these circumstances, host countries have thus found it useful to relax cross-border M&A restrictions, extend incentives previously reserved for greenfield investment to FDI through M&As, and even make active efforts to attract suitable cross-border M&A partners.

Although there are countries in which exceptional circumstances may be overriding for some time (for example, for economies in transition implementing massive privatization programmes or countries experiencing financial crises), most countries are characterized by a mixture of normal and exceptional circumstances. Thus, even countries in sound economic condition might have a number of enterprises (or even entire industries) that are uncompetitive and require restructuring. And, of course, competitive enterprises can also be targets of cross-border M&As. The factors that influence the impact (box VI.15) of cross-border M&As on development — regardless of circumstances — were summarized in June

---

Box VI.15. Intergovernmental experts on cross-border M&As: views on impact

At an intergovernmental meeting organized by UNCTAD at Geneva, from 19 to 21 June 2000, experts from developed and developing countries and from economies in transition agreed on an "Outcome" of the meeting that included the following observations as regards the impact of cross-border M&As:

"The following possible positive effects were mentioned: immediate capital inflows; immediate or follow-up new investment and resulting job creation; job conservation as acquired ailing firms are rescued or acquired firms are able to grow; immediate transfer of technology, especially information technology, and of managerial and other skills, leading to improved competitiveness; transfer of marketing skills; improvement of corporate governance; access to, and

integration with, global markets and increased exports; restructuring of firms and industries; longer-term industry development perspective; greater efficiency and productivity and improved quality of services; and increased tax and privatization revenues."

"The following possible challenges were identified: immediate reduction of employment; increase of concentration; less competition; no addition to the capital stock at the time of entry; possible low pricing of sold assets due, for example, to a lack of expertise; shrinking of domestic stock markets; crowding out of local enterprises, especially SMEs; loss of indigenous brands; cost of arbitration; and increase in the foreign control of a host country's economy, of special concern in sectors considered of strategic importance for the country."

Source: UNCTAD, 2000e, paras. 5-6.

2000 in the "Outcome" of an intergovernmental Expert Meeting on Mergers and Acquisitions as follows (UNCTAD, 2000e, para. 7):

"The economic policy framework and the country's level of development are key. Other factors affecting the impact are: whether a short- or long-term perspective is taken to evaluate effects; the normal or exceptional circumstances (such as privatization programmes or financial crises) in which cross-border M&As take place; the motivation of the investor (e.g. market seeking or efficiency seeking); the situation of the acquired enterprise; and the availability of alternatives as regards modes of entry of investment."

Many of these factors — and the specific consequences of cross-border M&As — can be influenced by policy measures. This underlines the central message of *WIR99*, which dealt with FDI and development generally, namely that policy matters. Policy matters especially when it comes to the risks and negative effects associated with cross-border M&As. This is not to minimize the importance of various alternatives to cross-border M&As. For example, while cross-border M&As are an alternative to greenfield FDI, the viability of other options such as strategic alliances or public intervention must also be considered carefully. There may even be a role for international action (box VI.16).

Policy also matters (as in the case of domestic M&As) in that sectoral policies need to address a number of potential negative effects, e.g. as regards employment and resource utilization. In addition, FDI policies in general can be used to maximize the benefits and minimize the costs of cross-border M&As, through e.g. sectoral reservations, ownership regulations, size criteria, screening and/or incentives. Specific cross-border M&A policies can also be used for some of the same purposes, e.g. the screening of cross-border M&As to ensure that they meet certain criteria.

The most important policy instrument, however, is competition policy. The principal reason is that M&As can pose threats to competition, both at the time of entry and subsequently. The search for increased market share and market domination is one of the characteristics of business behaviour. In the new

knowledge-based economy, the search for market power — or even monopoly — is accentuated by the nature of the costs of knowledge-based production. As was recently observed: "the constant pursuit of that monopoly power becomes the central driving thrust of the new economy" (Summers, 2000, p. 2). Indeed, the threat of monopoly, or tight oligopoly, is potentially the single most important negative effect of cross-border M&As and therefore poses the single most important policy challenge. The challenge, more precisely, is to ensure that policies are in place to deal with those M&As that raise competitive concerns, and that they are implemented effectively.

Indeed, as FDI restrictions are liberalized worldwide, it becomes all the more important that regulatory barriers to FDI are not replaced by anticompetitive practices of firms.[30] This means that, as observed in *WIR97*, "the reduction of barriers to FDI and the establishment of positive standards of treatment for TNCs need to go hand in hand with the adoption of measures aimed at ensuring the proper functioning of markets, including, in particular, measures to control anticompetitive practices by firms" (UNCTAD, 1997a, p. XXXI).[31] This puts the spotlight squarely on coordinated competition policy as a means to assess and address the impact of cross-border M&As on host-country economies, although policies aimed at maintaining a well-defined contestability of markets also have a role to play (UNCTAD, 1997a). It also suggests that the culture of FDI liberalization that has become pervasive, combined with the growing importance of cross-border M&As as a mode of entry, has to be complemented by an equally pervasive culture recognizing the need to prevent anticompetitive practices of firms. In the context of cross-border M&As, this requires the adoption of competition laws and their effective implementation, paying full attention not only to domestic, but also to cross-border M&As, both at the entry stage and subsequently. M&A reviews are indeed the principal interface between FDI and competition policy. Thus, there is a direct, necessary and enlarging relationship between liberalization of FDI entry through M&As on the one hand and the importance of competition policy on the other.

Increasingly, however, competition policy can no longer be pursued effectively

Box VI.16. International support for firms in currency-related distress

Even domestic firms that are well-managed and profitable may find themselves in serious financial difficulties because of events beyond their control. For example, a sudden and steep depreciation of a country's currency can lead to a large increase in its domestic firms' import costs and liabilities denominated in foreign currencies. If the depreciation is furthermore part of a financial crisis for the country, the lack of access to finance, whether from national or international banks or from the government, can threaten the very survival of firms, especially in developing countries. In consequence, small and medium-sized enterprises, in particular, may go bankrupt or be taken over at fire-sale prices. This in turn can be a blow to the domestic enterprise sector — the cornerstone of economic development.

The principle of international financial assistance is that if *countries* are in trouble, special funds and facilities set up in the framework of international financial agencies come to their aid. Recent experience has highlighted some of the shortcomings of the existing arrangements, and ways and means of reshaping and strengthening the international financial architecture are being explored. This revised architecture might conceivably include, among other things, schemes to strengthen the ability of governments to help *firms* facing liquidity problems under crisis conditions.

During the recent Asian financial crisis, a number of countries have experimented with such schemes. Examples (see Stone, 1998) include the "Jakarta Initiative" under which over-exposed Indonesian firms approach their creditors for a standstill and the creditors provide new funding, if the firm is considered viable and creditors can reach consensus. In the Republic of Korea, the Financial Supervisory Committee has provisions for the exchange of short-term foreign debt owed to commercial banks for government-guaranteed debt of longer maturity. In Thailand, the Corporate Debt Restructuring Advisory Committee, chaired by the Bank of Thailand, has introduced a non-binding debt-restructuring scheme.

At the international and regional levels, recent schemes (which often are administered through national restructuring agencies in the countries concerned) include the following: [1]

- The International Finance Corporation (IFC), the private-sector arm of the World Bank, provides capital, generally in the form of long-term equity and loans, to enterprises in developing countries (IFC, 2000, p. 20). It also undertakes short-term interventions when necessary. In Indonesia, for instance, the IFC has set up a facility for trade finance and working capital to assist exporters with short-term finance (IFC, 2000, p. 32). In collaboration with Chase Capital Partners of Hong Kong (China) and other Asian investors, the IFC established a restructuring fund in 1999, the Asia Opportunity Fund, that is expected to disburse up to $1.1 billion over the next three to five years. In addition, it has established the Asian Debt Facility to provide loans and guarantees directly to companies about to be restructured (IFC, 2000, pp. 32-33). To date, the Asian Opportunity Fund has invested in six firms, while the Asian Debt Facility is yet to be utilized. Roughly 25 per cent of the finance available had been disbursed by mid-2000.

- The Asian Development Bank established the Asian Currency Crisis Support Facility in 1998. Japan pledged $30 billion, of which $100 million was made available during 1999 to five of the crisis-stricken economies. Governments can use the loans for a variety of purposes, including bank restructuring and corporate-debt restructuring. To date, Thailand has used $3 million from this facility for restructuring specialized financial institutions (ADB, 2000, pp. 164-165 and 266).

- EBRD activities reflect the concern over liquidity squeezes and currency risks in several ways. A significant proportion of EBRD operations involves the provision of working capital, notably in countries and situations where existing credit lines from the local banking system may not be renewed and access to foreign banking lines may be difficult during financial sector crises. On this basis, EBRD can relieve the liquidity squeeze on corporate borrowers with sound long term fundamentals and help relieve pressure on balance sheets from possible foreign exchange losses. Operation design and client selection are tailored to the Bank's mandate in economies in transition.

/...

through national action alone. The very nature of cross-border M&As — indeed the emergence of a global market for firms — puts the phenomenon into the international sphere. This means that competition authorities need to have in place, and to strengthen, cooperation mechanisms among themselves at the bilateral, regional and multilateral levels, in order to respond effectively to M&As and anti-competitive practices of firms that affect their countries.[32] The UNCTAD Set of Principles and Rules on Restrictive Business Practices is, to date, the only multilateral instrument in this area (box VI.17). International action is particularly important when dealing with cross-border M&As with global dimensions, especially for smaller countries that lack the

resources to mount and enforce such policies on their own (box VI.18).

* * *

In chapter V, an intriguing parallel was drawn between the emergence of a *national* market and production system in the United States during the last decade of the nineteenth century, in the wake of a massive domestic M&A wave, and the emergence at the present time of a *global* market for firms, as a complement of the evolving global market for products and services and the development of an international production system. The United States wave, and the quest for increased market power that was part and parcel of it,

---

Box VI. 16. International support for firms in currency-related distress (concluded)

Currency risks are managed and hedged to the extent possible, including through the use of local currency financing instruments in certain countries. In addition, the EBRD is also involved in programmes supported by the European Commission, the Group of 7 and individual donor countries designed to mitigate the high risk of operating in certain countries and sectors, including those vulnerable to financial crises.

The question arises whether the volume, coverage and terms of reference of such regional and international schemes ought to be extended so as to provide a *greater and more rapidly accessible* measure of financial support to firms — including small and medium-sized enterprises — in distress because of developments over which they have no influence.

The numerous problems associated with such schemes call for careful analysis. They

begin with the need to have in place appropriate national restructuring and bankruptcy procedures. They include the need to determine the form that a liquidity provision should take. And, in particular, they involve the need to define criteria and conditions for screening firms deserving assistance. The precise implementation modalities are likely to differ by country and industry, depending on the specific cause and extent of financial distress.   A monitoring of the firms' performance would also need to be in place and measures would need to be taken to avoid moral hazard. Nevertheless, if fostering domestic enterprise is important for development, it might be worthwhile considering whether international schemes along these lines could assume the role of a rescuer of well-functioning enterprises in developing countries hit by financial difficulties under exceptional circumstances, so that the stock of otherwise healthy domestic enterprises is preserved and continues to grow.

Source: UNCTAD.

a   Precursors of these included the Foreign Exchange Risk Coverage Trust Fund (Ficorca), established in 1983 in Mexico to restructure corporate foreign debt. Participating firms were able to swap foreign debt for peso-denominated debt under a Government-guaranteed exchange rate. Some 2,000 corporations participated and approximately $12.5 billion of debt was restructured. Similar arrangements are operational in Chile, Hungary, Poland. In the United Kingdom, the "London Approach" was introduced in 1989 and is another example of a Government-mediated approach to corporate debt restructuring. Between 1989 and 1997, the Government, in conjunction with the Bank of England, handled 160 cases (Stone, 1998).

caused the courts of that country (beginning in 1903) to interpret the (1890) Sherman Antitrust Act to cover M&As and, eventually, Congress to adopt (in 1914) the Clayton Act, which prohibited M&As likely to lessen competition, and the Federal Trade Commission Act, which created the Federal Trade Commission to police violations of the Act. This marked the beginning of M&A control in the United States and of a process which, over the nearly 100 years since then, has led to a further strengthening of that country's competition control system.[33] The Sherman Act also was the antecedent of similar legislation in other countries. Today, some 90 countries have adopted antitrust laws, most of which were introduced in the 1990s.

The world economy today may well be seeing the beginning of a similar challenge in terms of global market structure and competition. If the parallel with the United States experience is indicative, this could mean that what is already happening may be only the beginning of a massive consolidation process at the regional and global levels. If so, it is all the more important to put in place the necessary policy instruments to deal with this process. Among these policy instruments, competition policy has pride of place. In the end, a global market for firms may need a global approach to competition policy, an approach that takes the interests and conditions of developing countries fully into account.

Box VI.17. The UNCTAD Set of Principles and Rules on Restrictive Business Practices

The Set of Multilaterally Agreed Equitable Principles and Rules for the Control of Restrictive Business Practices was adopted by the United Nations General Assembly in 1980 as a voluntary instrument. It is addressed to Governments and stresses that States should adopt, improve and effectively enforce appropriate legislation and procedures for the control of restrictive business practices (RBPs), by domestic firms as well as TNCs. Since 1980, many States have adopted national competition legislations that include provisions on RBPs. The main objectives of the Set are:

- to ensure that RBPs do not impede or negate the realization of benefits from trade liberalization;

- to attain greater efficiency in international trade and development;

- to protect and promote social welfare in general and, in particular, the interests of consumers.

To this end, the Set calls for enterprises to refrain from practices including "mergers, takeovers, joint ventures or other acquisitions of control" (Section D,4(c)) when, "through an abuse or acquisition and abuse of a dominant position of market power, they limit access to markets or otherwise unduly restrain competition" (Section D,4). Hence, the Set calls for control of such M&As, especially when they adversely affect international trade and development.

Cross-border M&As should therefore be dealt with in a holistic way, taking into consideration their various developmental impacts, such as concentration of economic power, on the one hand, and the encouragement of innovation on the other. There is a need to regulate transactions that carry the highest possibility of anti-competitive behaviour (including cross-border M&As) to minimize their negative impacts on development. There is also a need for international co-operation in the area of cross-border M&A control, including through the exchange of information and co-operation in proceedings, subject, however, to confidentiality safeguards.

The Set established an institutional machinery within UNCTAD to monitor its application through regular exchanges of information on the implementation of the Set's recommendations, an annual review of developments by UNCTAD, consultations, continued work on a model law on RBPs, and wide-ranging technical assistance. These measures are meant to strengthen the capacity of the developing world to deal effectively with cross-border M&As. The next quinquennial review conference is scheduled for 25-29 September 2000, to review all aspects of the Set, including the role of competition policy in economic development.

Source: UNCTAD, 1996b.

Box VI.18. Technical assistance and international co-operation in the area of merger review

The growth of cross-border M&A activities draws increased attention of policy makers towards competition policy and merger review. The globalization of markets and production poses challenges for the design of appropriate competition policies and especially for an effective policy implementation. For developing countries, this applies both in the case when a local firm is directly involved in a merger or an acquisition, and when mergers take place between major foreign TNCs with indirect consequences for third countries. This growing international dimension of M&As may call for new initiatives to strengthen international co-operation between competition authorities in developed and developing countries.

Technical assistance in the area of competition policy already exists at both the bilateral and multilateral levels. At the multilateral level, UNCTAD, in co-operation with other organizations such as the World Bank, the WTO and the OECD, provides assistance to developing countries and economies in transition. The main types of requests for assistance include:

- States without competition legislation may request information about restrictive business practices (RBPs) or introductory seminars;

- States that are in the process of drafting legislation in the area may request information on legislation in other countries and seek drafting advice;

- States that have just adopted competition legislation may seek advice on setting up a competition authority, including the training of officials through workshops and on-the-job training with competition authorities that have more experience;

- States that have adopted legislation and which have experience in the control of RBPs may wish to consult one another on specific cases and exchange information;

- States that wish to revise their legislation might seek expert advice from competition authorities in other States.

In addition to the work that is currently conducted, it may be worth exploring how international co-operation (including regional co-operation) in this area may be strengthened. For example, non-confidential information on specific M&A cases could be made available to a greater extent to developing countries. Even countries without a merger review system may be interested in learning about the potential effects of major M&As, e.g. if there is risk for the creation and abuse of a dominant position in specific markets. In some cases, competition authorities in developing countries could benefit from technical assistance provided by developed country authorities to assess the likely impact of individual M&As on the market structure in their countries. Naturally, that would have to take important aspects into account, such as the confidentiality of some of the information submitted by the merging parties, the short time allowed for merger reviews and the problem of determining which developing countries may be concerned in an individual case.

Enhanced bilateral or regional co-operation and joint investigation of M&As may also be further explored. Bilateral or multilateral exchanges of information in the area of merger control are today limited to a few countries and sometimes based on personal relations. Nevertheless, the importance of close bilateral co-operation in reviews of individual merger cases has been recognized in many countries, as witnessed by the joint investigations and co-ordinated remedies of some large M&As conducted by the EU and the United States recently. Such contacts increasingly take place also among the competition authorities of developing countries. For example, in Brazil, an exchange of information and experience has taken place with competition authorities in Argentina, Mexico, the United States and Venezuela.

Source: UNCTAD.

Notes

[1]   In Latin America, for example, extensive purchases of local firms by Spanish investors have been dubbed *reconquista* ("New world conquest", *Time*, 1 May 2000, pp. 44-48), and the sale of well-known firms to foreign investors has generally aroused concern (see, for example, "The nationalist groundswell in Brazil", *The Economist*, 26 February 2000, pp. 67-68).

[2]   The purchases of the Center and the studios — Columbia Pictures and Tristar Pictures — proved to be bad investments. Both suffered losses soon after the purchase. The Center was repurchased by United States investors by the mid-1990s ("Rockefeller Center heads back to American hands", *International Herald Tribune*, 13 September 1995; "Sony's American dream turns sour", *International Herald Tribune*, 18 November 1994). On the press reaction, see, for example, "For sale: America", *Time*, 14 September 1987, pp. 52-62; or "The selling of America", *Fortune*, 23 May 1988, pp. 55-64.

[3]   In theory, of course, foreign direct investors could even then engage in greenfield investments. In some cases, they actually do because it may be more advantageous for them to start afresh than to rehabilitate an existing facility.

[4]   The two modes can also be linked with each other. For example, a foreign firm that enters a host country via an acquisition may immediately expand via new investment. If this investment is financed through an increase in the parent firm's equity stake in the affiliate, it constitutes greenfield FDI. Conversely, an affiliate established via a greenfield project may expand through acquisitions of local companies, which will be FDI if financed by the parent company.

[5]   M&As and greenfield investments also face different sets of information and strategic needs, and have different advantages and disadvantages. In M&As, the targeted firm embodies information on markets, inputs, factors and local policies, and comprises a set of ready-made skills, capabilities and routines. At the same time, it requires the acquirer to collect information on how good or useful these capabilities are and whether they can be efficiently digested. A greenfield investment does not have access to ready-made information or capabilities, but it also does not require the investor to digest alien skills and routines.

[6]   The risk would be reflected in the price, but this does not reduce the economic cost if a venture goes wrong. To the extent that this is a real possibility, and greenfield entry is able to make better-informed decisions, there may be a net cost associated with cross-border M&As. The appropriate policy response is to improve the availability of corporate information, the transparency of governance, and the efficiency of capital markets. This would be advisable in any case for attracting FDI in any form and, indeed, for promoting economic development.

[7]   Except in the case of an exchange of stock between the two companies involved in a merger or acquisition. However, this is much less frequent in developing countries than in developed countries.

[8]   It should, however, be noted that some large cross-border M&A transactions include long-term financing arrangements (some extending up to 20 years).

[9]   Alternatively, revenues in foreign currencies from the sale of state-owned firms can be kept in separate accounts and released only gradually. Also, under certain circumstances, appreciation can be desirable. This was the case in some countries during the Asian financial crisis as the sharp depreciation in exchange rates brought about a debilitating increase in the corporate debt-servicing liability denominated in foreign currency.

[10]   The loss of financial resources is due to the lower sale price of the assets sold; this does not necessarily affect the subsequent performance of the acquired firm or the subsequent development impact of a given acquisition. One example where the sale price of a privatized state-owned enterprise was perhaps far from optimal but the long-term performance of the acquired firm was positive is the purchase of Czech Skoda Auto by Volkswagen.

[11]   Asset stripping can, of course, be undertaken by domestic investors as well, as evidence from Hungary suggests. During privatizations in Hungary, foreign buyers usually paid the full price for enterprises, while local buyers often used "soft" payment techniques, arbitraging between the nominal price and the price they received after dismembering the purchased companies and selling the component assets at a premium (Mihályi, 2000).

[12]   Twenty-six privatized foreign affiliates and two greenfield affiliates were surveyed in Argentina.

[13]   The survey conducted from January to June 1999 reviewed the pre- and post-privatization performance of 23 major companies selected from 7 Central and Eastern European countries: Croatia, the

Czech Republic, Hungary, Latvia, Poland, Romania and Slovenia. In 22 of these companies, the performance of the two or three years following privatization could be followed up with detailed data. Data availability for the two years preceding privatization was more limited, but still satisfactory: 16 firms provided data in this respect. The combined asset value of these enterprises at the time of their privatization exceeded $5 billion, i.e. 8 per cent of the combined inward stock of the seven countries. The increase in investment before privatization was most likely due to the restructuring of these enterprises prior to their sale.

14 Another example of the acquisitions of competitive firms not leading to sequential investment includes acquisitions made with a view to achieving a financial gain, i.e. those related to portfolio investment. They can dominate cross-border M&As in some industries in developing countries, as appeared to have been the case in Chile in power generation and banking in the second half of the 1990s. This does not mean, however, that acquisitions of efficient firms cannot lead to sequential investment. Such acquisitions can be a preferred way to enter new markets, because they are faster than greenfield FDI, they save TNCs considerable effort and transaction costs, and do not intensify competition in the market. If this happens in a developing country like Argentina, it may lead to sequential expansionary investment, as seems to have been the case in the acquisitions covered by the study mentioned earlier (Chudnovsky and López, 2000).

15 This matter may be complicated by the fact that firms involved in cross-border M&As may be subject to different corporate-governance rules and practices. The OECD Principles of Corporate Governance may be of relevance here (UNCTAD, 2000a, vol. IV).

16 However, a greenfield investment may not use technology of the latest vintage if local factor endowments make the use of older vintages more economical. Similarly, TNCs may, where appropriate, deploy used equipment in a new plant.

17 The results cited do not distinguish between cross-border and other M&As but some studies suggest that, if anything, cross-border M&As generate better results at the firm level than domestic ones (see chapter V).

18 R&D in computer software clusters, such as those in Bangalore, India, is an example (see UNCTAD, 1995a, chapter III).

19 When General Electric acquired a majority share in Tungsram in 1990, its restructuring led to an initial reduction of R&D activities

in the latter (Weiszburg, 1997). This changed in 1994 when GE fully bought out Tungsram and made its research centre its only overseas R&D facility and re-focussed it on light source research (Marer and Mabert, 1997).

20 See chapter V; Hamill, 1993, pp. 95, 112-118; UNCTAD, 1999a, pp. 100-101. A study of 55 acquired firms in Denmark over the period 1975-1990 attempted to examine the relationship between the motivation of the acquirer and impact on employment: it showed that employment rose in all categories of firms for the first five years after the acquisition, showing a 30 per cent increase over the time of acquisition. Thereafter, paths diverged according to the motive for the acquisitions. Market-seeking acquisitions — generally with low technological assets — showed a decline in employment, reaching their original level of employment by the tenth year. Employment in affiliates established through strategic-asset-seeking and efficiency-seeking acquisitions continued to rise, with the latter showing more sustained rises. In the tenth year, employment in the asset-seeking firms was around 45 per cent higher than at the time of acquisition, while in efficiency-seeking M&As, it was 80 per cent higher (Pedersen and Valentin, 1996).

21 Data for four large firms in the food industry acquired by TNCs between 1995 and 1997 show that employment in 1999 increased in three cases and remained constant in one (Costa Rica, Ministry of Foreign Trade, 2000).

22 See, for example, the reference to asset-seeking firms in footnote 20 (Pedersen and Valentin, 1996).

23 Employment in the automotive industry in the Triad countries decreased by roughly one-quarter during the 1980s and continued to decline during the 1990s, despite an increase in output. In several developing countries (e.g. Argentina and Thailand), however, employment in the industry rose during the period 1990-1997, while in a few others (e.g. Brazil) it declined (Romijn, et al., forthcoming).

24 "More bank unions set up to protect staff", *The Nation*, 9 March 2000.

25 Based on data from the International Telecommunications Union (1993, 1996-1997 and 1999), and Hunya and Kalotay (2000). It should be noted that, in a number of countries, employment increased after privatization.

26 For example, Tatramat, the state-owned white goods company in Slovakia, employed 2,300 people in 1989, of whom 1,000 were laid off in 1990-1991. Of the remaining employees, 550, working in the

washing machine arm of the firm, were transferred to another part of Tatramat when Whirlpool (United States) acquired shares in a joint venture with Tatramat for the production of washing machines in 1992. In 1993, employment in the joint venture was reduced from 470 to 219, with the early retirement of some workers and the dismissal of others who did not accept the management systems and conditions introduced by Whirlpool (Ferencikova, 2000).

27 Examples include the *Standortssicherungsvereinbarungen* in Germany, the four-year agreements recently signed between the United Auto Workers Union and the auto producers in the United States, and the agreement between the International Association of Machinists and Boeing in the United States (ILO, 2000).

28 *The Wall Street Journal*, 11 September 1998, and http://wev.netlink.net/preparedfoods/1998/9807/latin.htm.

29 The definition of which industries are "strategic" differs from country to country.

It also changes over time.

30 Government actions, including incentives and market privileges to attract foreign investors, also contribute to an environment that provides scope for anti-competitive practices (UNCTAD, 1997a).

31 For a full discussion of the interrelationship between FDI, market structure and competition policy, see UNCTAD, 1997a.

32 For a detailed discussion of international cooperation in this area, see UNCTAD, 1997a. For a recent contribution to this discussion see United States, Department of Justice, 2000.

33 The most important additions came in 1950, when the Clayton Act was significantly amended, and in 1976, when the Hart-Scott-Rodino Antitrust Improvement Act was adopted to provide the Federal Government with the opportunity to review the impact on competition of M&As and other consolidations before they are completed (see www.usdoj.gov/atr; and www.ftc.gov for more information).

References

Agosín, Manuel (1995). "Foreign direct investment in Latin America", in Manuel R. Agosín, ed., *Foreign Direct Investment in Latin America* (Washington, D.C.: Inter-American Development Bank), pp. 1-37.

_____ and Ricardo Mayer (2000). "Foreign investment in developing countries: does it crowd in domestic investment?", UNCTAD Discussion Paper 146 (Geneva: United Nations), United Nations publication, UNCTAD/OSG/DP/146.

Allard, Philippa and Louise Lundborg (1998). "Foreign acquisitions of Swedish companies: a study of internal and external effects", ISA Studies on Foreign Direct Investment, No. 5 (Stockholm: Invest in Sweden Agency).

Andean Community General Secretariat (1999). *How to Do Business in the Andean Community: Trade and Investment Guide* (Lima: Andean Community General Secretariat).

Andersson, Thomas and Roger Svensson (1994). "Entry modes for direct investment determined by the composition of firm-specific skills", *Scandinavian Journal of Economics*, 96,4, pp. 551-560.

_____, Torbjörn Fredriksson and Roger Svensson (1996). *Multinational Restructuring, Internationalization and Small Economies: The Swedish Case*. Routledge Studies in International Business and the World Economy (London and New York: Routledge).

Antalóczy, Katalin and Magdolna Sass (2000). "Greenfield FDI in Hungary: is it better than privatization-related FDI?", paper presented at the UNCTAD and OeNB Seminar on FDI and Privatization in Central and Eastern Europe (Vienna, 2-3 March), mimeo.

Argentina, Centro de Estudios para la Producción (CEP) (2000). *Síntesis de la Economía Real*, No. 33 (Enero-Febrero).

Asia-Pacific Economic Cooperation Secretariat (APEC) (1999). *Guide to the Investment Regimes of the APEC Member Economies*, 4th ed. (Singapore: APEC).

Asian Development Bank (ADB) (2000). *Annual Report 1999* (Manila: ADB), also available on the internet at http://www.adb.org.

Asquith, Paul, Robert F. Bruner and David W. Mullins (1983). "The gains to bidding firms from merger", *Journal of Financial Economics*,11 (Special Issue), pp. 121-139.

Association of South-East Asian Nations Secretariat (ASEAN) (1998). *Compendium of Investment Measures in ASEAN Countries* (Jakarta: ASEAN Secretariat).

AT Kearney (1999). *Corporate Marriage: Blight or Bliss? A Monograph on Post-Merger Integration* (Chicago: AT Kearney.)

Automotive News (1997). *Market Data Book 1997* (Detroit: Automotive News).

_____ (2000). *Market Data Book 2000* (Detroit: Automotive News).

Bailey, Paul, Aurelio Parisotto and Geoffrey Renshaw, eds. (1993). *Multinationals and Employment: The Global Economy of the 1990s* (Geneva: ILO).

Bain, Joe S. (1944). "Industrial concentration and government anti-trust policy", in H.F. Williamson, ed., *The Growth of the American Economy* (New York: Prentice-Hall), pp. 708-729.

Baldwin, John R. (1995). *The Dynamics of Industrial Competition* (Cambridge: Cambridge University Press).

Bank for International Settlements (BIS) (various issues). *International Banking and Financial Market Developments* (Basel: BIS).

Baumol, W.J. (1967). *Business Behavior, Value and Growth* (New York: Macmillan).

Bild, Magnus (1998). *Valuation of Takeovers*, Ph.D. dissertation, Stockholm School of Economics (Stockholm: Elanders Gotab).

Bittlingmayer, George (1985). "Did antitrust policy cause the great merger wave?", *Journal of Law & Economics*, XXVII (April), pp. 77-118.

Brealey, Richard A. and Stewart C. Myers (1988). *Principles of Corporate Finance*, 3rd ed. (Singapore: McGraw Hill).

Bresman, Henrik, Julian Burkinshaw and Robert Nobel (1999). "Knowledge transfer in international acquisitions", *Journal of International Business Studies*, 30, 3 (third quarter), pp. 439-462.

Brimble, Peter (2000). "Mergers and acquisitions in Thailand", paper presented at the UNCTAD Seminar on Cross-border M&As and Sustained Competitiveness in Asia: Trends, Impacts and Policy Implications (Bangkok, 9-10 March 2000), mimeo.

Cakici, Nusrett, Chris Hessel and Kishore Tandon (1996). "Foreign acquisitions in the United States: effect on shareholder wealth of foreign acquiring firms, *Journal of Banking & Finance*, 20, pp. 307-329.

Carlin, Wendy, John Van Reenen and Toby Wolfe (1994). "Enterprise restructuring in the transition: an analytical survey of the case study evidence from Central and Eastern Europe", European Bank for Reconstruction and Development Working Paper 14 (London: EBRD).

Caves, Richard E. (1971). "International corporations: the industrial economics of foreign investment", *Economica*, 38 (February), pp. 1-27.

_____ (1998). "Industrial organization and new findings on the turnover and mobility of firms", *Journal of Economic Literature*, XXXVI(4), pp. 1947-1982.

Central Europe Online (2000). "MOL teams up with Slovnaft", *Central Europe Online*, http://www.centraleurope.com/investorinsight/business.php3?id=147907, 3 April 2000.

Chandler, Alfred (1990). *Scale and Scope: The Dynamics of Industrial Capitalism* (Cambridge: Harvard University Press).

Chudnovsky, Daniel Andrés López and Fernando Porta (1995). "New foreign direct investment in Argentina: privatization, the domestic market, and regional integration", in Manuel R. Agosín, ed., *Foreign Direct Investment in Latin America* (Washington, D.C.: Inter-American Development Bank), pp. 39-104.

_____, and Andrés López (2000). "The impact of M&As in Argentina in the 1990s" (Geneva: UNCTAD), mimeo.

Chudy, Tereasa, Christian Dery and Ted Zahavich (2000). "Cross-border mergers and acquisitions in Canada" (Geneva: UNCTAD), mimeo.

Ciucci, Pietro (1999). "Privatisation, capital market development and pension funds", paper presented at the OECD Advisory Group on Privatisation, 21-22 September 1999 (Paris: OECD), mimeo.

Coase, Ronald H. (1937). "The nature of the firm", *Economica*, 4 (November), pp. 386-405.

Consumer Unity and Trust Society (CUTS) (1999). *FDI, Mega-Mergers and Strategic Alliances: is Global Competition Accelerating Development or Heading towards World Monopolies?* (Jaipur: Jaipur Printer).

Cooke, William N. (2000a). "Human resource management strategies and foreign direct investment in the U.S.", forthcoming proceedings of the 12 th World Conference, International Industrial Relations Association, pp. 211-224, mimeo.

_____ (2000b). "Foreign direct investment and human resource management/labor relations strategies: implications for union representation", paper prepared for the conference on *Multinational Companies & Emerging Workplace Issues: Practice, Outcomes and Policy*, 1-3 April 2000, The Douglas A. Fraser Center for Workplace Issues College of Urban, Labor & Metropolitan Affairs (Wayne State University), mimeo.

Costa Rica, Ministry of Foreign Trade (2000). "Foreign investment in Costa Rica and the emerging role of M&As, strategic partnerships and management contracts"(San José: Ministry of Foreign Trade), survey prepared for UNCTAD, mimeo.

Curhan, Joan P., William H. Davidson and Rajan Suri (1977). *Tracing the Multinationals: A Sourcebook on U.S.-based Enterprises* (Cambridge, MA: Ballinger Publishing Company).

Dabrowski, J. (1996). "Efekty prywatyzacji przedsiebiorstw droga kapitalowa", *Transformacja Gospodarki* no. 67, IbnGR, Gdansk, Poland.

Dickerson, Andrew P., Heather D. Gibson and Euclid Tsakalotos (1997). "The impact of acquisitions on company performance: evidence from a large panel of UK firms", *Oxford Economic Papers*, 49, pp. 344-361.

Dunning, John H. (1993). *Multinational Enterprises and the Global Economy* (Harrow: Addison-Wesley).

_____ (1998). "Location and the multinational enterprise: a neglected factor?", *Journal of International Business Studies*, 29, 1, pp. 45-66.

_____ (2000). "The eclectic paradigm as an envelope for economic and business theories of MNE activity", *International Business Review*, 9, pp. 163-190.

_____ and John R. Dilyard (1999). "Towards a general paradigm of foreign direct and foreign portfolio investment", *Transnational Corporations*, 8, 1, pp. 1-52.

Economist Intelligence Unit (EIU) (1999). *Investing, Licensing & Trading* (London: EIU); available on the Internet (http://www.eiu.com).

Eisenberg, David. M. (2000). "Foreign direct investment in the context of the privatization of state-owned telecommunications companies in several countries with developing economies", memorandum to UNCTAD of 13 March 2000, mimeo.

Elgers, Pieter and J. Clark (1980). "Merger types and stockholder returns: additional evidence", *Financial Management*, 9, pp. 66-72.

Ellis, J. and J. Heinbockel (1999). *Global Retailing 2000: A Statistical and Conceptual View* (New York: Goldman Sachs Investment Research).

Éltetö, Andrea and Magdolna Sass (1997). "A külföldi befektetök döntését és vállalati müködését befolyásoló tényezök Magyarországon az exporttevékenység tükrében" [Factors influencing decisions and activity of foreign investors in Hungary in the light of their export patterns], *Közgazdasági Szemle*, No. 7.

Estrin, Saul, Josef C. Brada, Alan Gelb and Inderjit Singh, eds. (1995). *Restructuring and Privatization in Central and Eastern Europe: Case Studies of Firms in Transition* (London: M.E. Sharpe).

Eun, Cheol S., Richard Kolodny and Carl Sheraga (1996). "Cross-border acquisitions and shareholder wealth: tests of the synergy and internalization hypotheses, *Journal of Banking & Finance*, 20, pp. 1559-1582.

European Bank for Reconstruction and Development (EBRD) (2000). *Annual Report 1999* (London: EBRD), also available on the internet at http://www.ebrd.org.

European Community (1998). "Council Directive 98/50/EN of 29 June 1998 amending Directive 77/187/EEC on the approximation of the laws of the Member States relating to the safeguarding of employees' rights in the event of transfers of undertakings, business or parts of business" *Official Journal No. L 201* of 17 June 1998, pp. 0088-0092; available also on the Internet *EUR-Lex: Community Legislation in force*, Document 298L0050, http://europa.eu.int/eurlex/en/lif/dat/1998/en_398L0050.html.

Eurostat (2000). *European Union Direct Investment, Yearbook 1999* (Luxembourg: Office for Official Publications of the European Communities).

Expert (2000). "Baza dannykh Expert-200", http://www.raexpert.ru/expert200.htm, 2 March 2000.

Fan Gang, M. R. Lunati and D. O. Connor (1998). "Labour market aspects of state enterprise reform in China" (Paris: OECD, Development Centre), Technical Paper 141, mimeo.

Ferencikova, Sonia (2000). "Transition at Whirlpool-Tatramat (from joint venture to acquisition): case study", paper presented at the UNCTAD and OeNB Seminar on FDI and Privatization in Central and Eastern Europe (Vienna, 2-3 March), mimeo.

Floyd, David (2000). "FDI through cross-border acquisitions and greenfield sites, their impact on development and policy implications for the Polish economy", paper presented at the UNCTAD and OeNB Seminar on FDI and Privatization in Central and Eastern Europe (Vienna, 2-3 March), mimeo.

Franks, Julian R. and Robert S. Harris (1989). "Shareholder wealth effects of corporate takeovers: the U.K. experience 1955-1985", *Journal of Financial Economics*, 23, 2, pp. 225-249.

Freeman, Christopher and Carlota Perez (1988). "Structural crisis of adjustment, business cycles and investment behaviour", in Giovanni Dosi, Christopher Freeman, Richard Nelson, Gerald Silverberg and Luc Soete, eds., *Technical Change and Economic Theory* (London: Pinter Publishers), pp. 38-66.

Garrido, Celso (2000). "Crossborder mergers and acquisitions in Mexico during the nineties". Two case studies prepared for UNCTAD (Mexico City), mimeo.

Gonzales, Pedro, Geraldo M. Vasconcellos and Richard J. Kish (1998). "Cross-border mergers and acquisitions: the undervaluation hypothesis", *The Quarterly Review of Economics and Finance*, 38, 1, pp. 25-45.

Hagedoorn, John and Geert Duysters (2000). "The effect of mergers and acquisitions on the technological performance of companies in a high-tech environment" (Maastricht: MERIT, University of Maastricht), MERIT Research Memoranda 00-010, mimeo.

Hamill, J. (1993). "Cross-border mergers, acquisitions and strategic alliances", in P. Bailey, A. Parisotto and G. Renshaw, eds., *Multinationals and Employment: The Global Economy of the 1990s* (Geneva: ILO), pp. 95-123.

Harzing, Anne-Wil (1999). "Acquisitions versus greenfield investments: both sides of the picture" (Bradford: University of Bradford), mimeo.

Hausmann, Ricardo and Eduardo Fernandez-Arias (2000). "Foreign direct investment: good cholesterol?" Paper prepared for the seminar entitled *The New Wave of Capital Inflows: Sea Change or Just Another Tide?* (Washington, D.C.: Inter-American Development Bank), mimeo.

Hong Kong Industry Department (1999). *Survey of Regional Representation by Overseas Companies in Hong Kong 1999* (Hong Kong: Industry Department, Hong Kong Special Administrative Region).

Hong Kong Special Administrative Region of China (2000). "Hong Kong's detailed balance of payments accounts for 1998, 1999, and the four quarters of 1999", Press Release 19 June 2000.

Hopkins, H. Donald (1999). "Cross-border mergers and acquisitions: global and regional perspectives", *Journal of International Management*, 5, pp. 207-239.

Hunt, John, S.Lees, J. Grumbar, and P.D. Vivian (1987). *Acquisitions: The Human Factor* (London: London Business School).

Hunya, Gábor (1997). "Foreign investment enterprises in the investment process of the Czech Republic, Hungary and Poland", final report for the PHARE ACE project P95-2226-R, "Industrial investments: cornerstones in the next stage of the Central European transformation", mimeo.

_____ and Kálmán Kalotay (2000). "Privatization and foreign direct investment in Central and Eastern Europe" (Geneva: UNCTAD), forthcoming.

Hymer, Stephen H. (1960). *The International Operations of National Firms: A Study of Direct Foreign Investment* (Cambridge: The MIT Press).

International Finance Corporation (IFC) (1999). *Trends in Private Investment in Developing Countries* (Washington, D.C.: IFC).

_____ (2000). *Annual Report 1999* (Washington, D.C.: IFC), also available on the internet at http://www.ifc.org/publications/pubs/ar/ar.html.

International Institute for Management Development (IMD) (1999). *International Competitiveness Report* (Lausanne: IMD).

International Labour Organization (ILO) (1998). *Structural and Regulatory Changes and Globalization in Postal and Telecom-munications Services: The Human Resources Dimension* (Geneva: ILO), TMPTS/1998.

_____ (2000a). "Convention Concerning Termination of Employment at the Initiative of the Employer" (ILO Convention 158, adopted in 1982), *ILOLEX: The ILO Database on International Labour Standards*, http://www.ilolex.ilo.ch.

_____ (2000b). "Convention Concerning Termination of Employment at the Initiative of the Employer" (ILO Convention 166, adopted in 1982), *ILOLEX: The ILO Database on International Labour Standards*, http://www.ilolex.ilo.ch.

_____ (2000c). *The Social and Labour Impact of Globalization in the Manufacture of Transport Equipment* (Geneva: ILO), TMTE/2000.

International Monetary Fund (IMF) (1999a). *International Financial Statistics 1999* (Washington, D.C.: IMF).

_____ (1999b). *Annual Report on Exchange Arrangements and Exchange Restrictions* (Washington, D.C.: IMF).

International Telecommunications Union (ITU) (1993). *World Telecommunications Development Report 1993* (Geneva: ITU).

_____ (1996-1997). *World Telecommunications Development Report 1996-1997* (Geneva: ITU).

_____ (1999). *World Telecommunications Development Report 1999* (Geneva: ITU).

Invest in Sweden Agency (2000). *Klimatet för Utländska Investeringar i Sverige* (Stockholm: Invest in Sweden Agency).

Jansen, Stephan A. and Klaus Körner (2000). *Fusionsmanagement in Deutschland* (Witten: Institute for Mergers and Acquisitions (IMA), Universität Witten/Herdecke and Mercuri International).

Japan Bank for International Cooperation (2000). "JBIC FY 1999 survey: the outlook of Japanese foreign direct investment", *Journal of Research Institute for Development and Finance*, January, pp. 4-49.

Japan External Trade Organization (JETRO) (2000). *JETRO Toshi Hakusho 2000* (Tokyo: JETRO).

Japan, Ministry of International Trade and Industry (MITI) (1998). *Dai 26-kai Wagakuni Kigyo no Kagiai Jigyo Katsudo* (Tokyo: Ministry of Finance Printing Bureau).

_____ (1999). *Dai 27-kai Wagakuni Kigyo no Kagiai Jigyo Katsudo* (Tokyo: Ministry of Finance Printing Bureau).

_____ (2000). *Dai 28-kai Wagakuni Kigyo no Kaigai Jigyo Katsudo* (Tokyo: Ministry of Finance Printing Bureau).

Japan, Small and Medium-sized Enterprise Agency (1999). *Chushio Kigyo Hakusho: Heisei 11-nenban* (Tokyo: Ministry of Finance Printing Bureau).

_____ (2000). *Chushio Kigyo Hakusho: Heisei 12-nenban* (Tokyo: Ministry of Finance Printing Bureau).

Jensen, Michael C. and Richard S. Ruback (1983). "The market for corporate control: the scientific evidence", *Journal of Financial Economics*, 11, 1-4, pp. 5-50.

Jermakowicz, Wladyslaw, ed. (1994). "Foreign privatization in Poland" (Warsaw: Centre for Social & Economic Research), mimeo.

Jung, Ku-Hyun (2000). "Comments and background material for World Investment Report 2000", June 2000, (Geneva: UNCTAD), mimeo.

Kang, Nam-Hoon and Sara Johansson (2000). "Cross-border mergers and acquisitions: their role in industrial globalisation", STI Working Paper 2000/1 (Paris: OECD).

Kitching, John (1967). "Why do mergers miscarry?", *Harvard Business Review*, March-April, pp. 84-101.

KPMG (1999). *Unlocking Shareholder Value: The Keys to Success* (London: KPMG).

Kumar, Nagesh (2000). "Multinational enterprises and M&As in India: patterns and implications", paper presented at the UNCTAD Seminar on Cross-border M&A and Sustained Competitiveness in Asia: Trends, Impacts and Policy Implications (Bangkok, 9-10 March), mimeo.

Kuruvilla, S., C. Erickson, M. Anner, M. Amante and I. Ortiz (1998). "Globalization and employment relations in Philippines", draft prepared for the ILO Regional Office (Geneva: ILO), mimeo.

Kusewitt, John B. (1985). "An explanatory study of strategic acquisition factors relating to performance", *Strategic Management Journal*, 6, pp. 151-169.

Lahey, Karen E. and Robert L. Conn (1990). "Sensitivity of acquiring firms' return to alternative model specifications and disaggregation", *Journal of Business Finance & Accounting*, 17, 3, pp. 421-439.

Lamoreaux, Naomi R. (1985), *The Great Merger Movement in American Business, 1895-1904* (Cambridge and New York: Cambridge University Press).

Lang, Jeffrey (1998). "The international regulation of foreign direct investment: obstacles and evolution", *Cornell International Law Journal*, 31, 3, p. 455-466.

Lichtenberg, Frank R. (1992). *Corporate Takeovers and Productivity* (Cambridge, MA: MIT Press).

_____ and Donald Siegel (1987). "Productivity and changes in ownership of manufacturing plants", *Brookings Paper on Economic Activity*, 3, pp. 643-673.

Lubatkin, Michael H. (1987). "Merger strategies and stockholder value", *Strategic Management Journal*, 8, 1, pp. 39-53.

Magenheim, Ellen and Dennis C. Mueller (1988). "On measuring the effect of mergers on acquiring firm shareholders", in Coffee, John C., Louis Loisenstein and Susan Rose-Ackerman, eds., *Knights, Raiders and Targets: The Impact of the Hostile Takeover* (New York and Oxford: Oxford University Press), pp. 171-193.

Mahathir bin Mohamed (2000). "UNCTAD X: Statement by Malaysia. Speech delivered at the plenary session of UNCTAD X in Bangkok, Thailand, 12 February 2000" (Geneva: UNCTAD), mimeo.

Maher, Maria and Thomas Andersson (1999). "Corporate governance: effects on firm performance and economic growth" (Paris: OECD), mimeo.

Malaysia, Ministry of Finance (2000). *Investors' Guide, Economic Report 1999/2000* (Kuala Lumpur: Ministry of Finance).

Marer, Paul and Vincent Mabert (1997). "Foreign investment brings a clash of cultures: the story of GE Lighting Tungsram", *Transition Newsletter* No. 1 (January-February), (Washington D.C.: World Bank), http://www.worldbank. org/html/prddr/trans/janfeb97/art9.htm.

Markides, Constantinos C. and Christopher D. Ittner (1994). "Shareholder benefits from corporate international diversification: evidence from U.S. international acquisitions", *Journal of International Business*, 25, 2, pp. 343-366.

Mataloni, Raymond J. Jr. (2000). "An examination of the low rates of return of foreign-owned U.S. companies", *Survey of Current Business*, 80, 3 (March), pp. 55-73.

Mehta, Pradeep S. (1999). "Foreign direct investment, mega-mergers and strategic alliances: is global competition accelerating development or heading towards world monopolies?", *The Role of Competition Policy for Development in Globalizing World Markets*, UNCTAD Series on Issues in Competition Law and Policy (Geneva: United Nations), pp. 19-26.

Mexico, Federal Commission on Competition (1997). *Annual Economic Competition Report*, http://www.cfc.gob.mx/cfc.99i/reports.

Meyer, Klaus and Saul Estrin (1998). "Entry mode choice in emerging markets: greenfield acquisition and brownfield", *Center for East European Studies*, Copenhagen Business Schools, Working Paper No. 18, February 1998.

Mihályi, Peter (2000). "Privatization as a unique form of FDI: the case of Hungary", paper presented at the UNCTAD and OeNB Seminar on FDI and Privatization in Central and Eastern Europe (Vienna, 2-3 March), mimeo.

Modén, Karl-Markus (1998). "Foreign acquisitions of Swedish companies: effects on R&D and productivity" (Stockholm: Research Institute of Industrial Economics), mimeo.

Mody, Ashoka and Shoko Negishi (2000). "The role of cross-border mergers and acquisitions in Asian restructuring", paper presented at the UNCTAD Seminar on Cross-border M&As and Sustained Competitiveness in Asia: Trends, Impacts and Policy Implications (Bangkok, 9-10 March), mimeo.

MOL (1999). "Strategy presentation", http://www.mol.hu/english/01befekt/be10.htm, 26 October .

_____ (2000a). "MOL and Slovnaft join forces to create the Central European downstream champion", Press Release, http://www.mol.hu/english/01befekt/sajto/sajto0403.htm, 3 April.

_____ (2000b). "Creating the regional champion", PowerPoint Presentation, mimeo.

Moody, John (1904). *The Truth about Trusts* (New York and Chicago: Moody publishing company).

Morck, Randall and Bernard Yeung (1991). "Why investors value multinationality", *Journal of Business*, 64, 2, pp. 165-187.

_____ and Bernard Yeung (1999). "Why firms diversify: internalization vs. agency behavior", (New York: Stern School of Business, New York University), mimeo.

_____, Andrei Schleifer and Robert Vishny (1990). "Do managerial objectives drive bad acquisitions?", *Journal of Finance*, 45, 1, pp. 31-48.

Morosini, Piero, Scott Shane and Harbir Singh (1998). "National cultural distance and cross-border acquisition performance", *Journal of International Business Studies*, 29, 1, pp. 137-158.

Mortimore, Michael M. (1998). "Getting a lift: modernizing industry by way of Latin American integration schemes. The example of automobiles", *Transnational Corporations*, 7, 2 (August), pp. 97-136.

Mueller, Dennis C., ed. (1980a). *The Determinants and Effects of Mergers: An International Comparison* (Cambridge: Oelgeschlager, Gunn & Hain).

_____ (1980b). "The United States, 1962-1972" in Mueller, Dennis C., ed., *The Determinants and Effects of Mergers: An International Comparison* (Cambridge: Oelgeschlager, Gunn & Hain).

_____ (1996). "Antimerger policy in the United States: History and lessons", *Empirica*, 23, 3, pp. 229-253.

Myers, Stewart C. and Nicholas S. Majluf (1984). "Corporate financing and investment decisions when firms have information that investors do not have", *Journal of Financial Economics*, 13, 2 (June), pp. 187-221.

Nelson, Ralph L. (1959). *Merger Movements in American Industry 1895-1956* (Princeton: Princeton University Press).

Organisation for Economic Co-operation and Development (OECD) (1999). "Privatization trends", *Financial Market Trends*, 72 (February), pp. 129-145.

_____ (2000). "The OECD Guidelines for Multinational Enterprises", *OECD Online. Investment, Capital Movements, Services* http://www.oecd.org/daf/investment/guidelines/mnetext.htm.

_____ (various issues). *Quarterly National Accounts* (Paris: OECD).

Park, Young-Bum (1997). "Privatization and employment in the Republic of Korea", in R. van der Hoeven and G. Sziraczki, eds., *Lessons from Privatization: Labour Issues in Developing and Transitional Countries* (Geneva: ILO), pp. 21-46.

Pedersen, Torben and Finn Valentin (1996). "The impact of foreign acquisition on the evolution of Danish firms: a competence based perspective", in Nicolai J. Foss and Christian Knudsen, eds., *Towards a Competence Theory of the Firm* (London: Routledge), pp. 150-174.

Phang, H.S. (1999). "Employment policies in Korea after the crisis", Manila Social Forum, The New Social Agenda for Central, East and South-East Asia, 9-12 November (Manila: Asia Recovery Information Center/Asian Development Bank), http://www.aric.adb.org.

Pigato, Miria and Maura Liberatori (2000). "FDI through privatization in Sub-Saharan Africa" (Washington, D.C.: World Bank), mimeo.

Public Services International (PSI) (2000). "Privatisation-related M&As in transition and developing countries: water and energy". A report from Public Services International to UNCTAD, mimeo.

Ravenscraft, David J. and Frederick M. Scherer (1987). *Mergers, Sell-offs and Economic Efficiency* (Washington D.C.: The Brookings Institution).

Reid, Samuel Richardson (1968). *Mergers, Managers and the Economy* (New York: McGraw-Hill).

Riveros, Luis A., Jaime Vatter and Manuel R. Agosín (1995). "Foreign direct investment in Chile, 1987-93: utilization of comparative advantages and debt conversion", in Manuel R. Agosín, ed., *Foreign Direct Investment in Latin America* (Washington, D.C.: Inter-American Development Bank), pp. 105-136.

Rojec, Matija (1995). "Foreign direct investment and privatization in Central and Eastern Europe", ACE project, Final Report, Ljubljana, mimeo.

_____ (1997). "Lessons from foreign direct investment research in Slovenia", Ljubljana, mimeo.

Romijn, H., Rikkert van Assouw and Michael Mortimore (forthcoming). "TNCs, industrial restructuring and competitiveness in the automotive industry in NAFTA, MERCOSUR and ASEAN", in UNCTAD, *Coping with Globalization: Transnationals, Industrial Restructuring and Competitiveness in Developing Countries* (Geneva: United Nations), forthcoming.

Salih, Rozana (1999). "Country study on the social effects of privatisation", report prepared for the International Labour Organisation sub-regional meeting on "Privatisation-Social Effects and Restructuring", October, mimeo.

Samonis, Valdas (2000). "The Williams Lithuania deal in a comparative perspective", paper presented at the UNCTAD and OeNB Seminar on FDI and Privatization in Central and Eastern Europe (Vienna, 2-3 March), mimeo.

Sauvant, Karl P. (1990). "The tradability of services", in Patrick A. Messerlin and Karl P. Sauvant, eds., *The Uruguay Round: Services in the World Economy* (Washington, D.C. and New York: The World Bank and the United Nations Centre on Transnational Corporations), pp. 114-122.

Schenk, Hans (1996). "Bandwagon mergers, international competitiveness and government policy", *Empirica*, 23, 3, pp. 255-278.

_____ (1999). "Large mergers a matter of strategy rather than economics", paper prepared for UNCTAD, mimeo.

_____ (2000). "Are international acquisitions a matter of strategy rather than wealth creation?", *International Review of Applied Economics*, forthcoming.

Scherer, Frederick M., Alan Beckenstein, E. Kaufer and R.D. Murphey (1975). *The Economics of Multi-Plant Operation: An International Comparison Study* (Cambridge: Harvard University Press).

_____(1988). "The market for corporate control: the empirical evidence since 1980," *Journal of Economic Perspectives*, 2, 1, pp. 69-82.

_____ and David Ross (1990). *Industrial Market Structure and Economic Performance*, 3rd ed. (Boston: Houghton Nifflin Company).

Shelton, Lois M. (1988). "Strategic business fit and corporate acquisitions: empirical evidence", *Strategic Management Journal*, 9, 3, pp. 279-287.

Singh, Ajit (1975). "Take-overs, economic natural section, and the theory of the firm: evidence from the post-war United Kingdom experience", *Economic Journal*, 85 (Sept), pp. 497-515.

Singh, Harbir and Cynthia A. Montgomery, (1987). "Corporate acquisition strategies and economic performance", *Strategic Management Journal*, 8, 4, pp. 377-386.

Sirower, Mark L. (1997). *The Synergy Trap* (New York: Free Press).

Smith, George David and Richard Sylla (1993). "The deal of the century", *Andacity*, 4, pp. 26-31.

Stone, Mark R. (1998). "Corporate debt restructuring in East Asia: some lessons from international experience", IMF paper on policy analysis and assessment, PPAA/98/13 (Washington, D.C.: IMF).

Summers, Lawrence H. (2000). "The new wealth of nations", *Treasury News* (Washington, D.C.: The Department of the Treasury), http://www.treas.gov/press/releases/ps617.htm.

Szanyi, Miklós (2000). "Privatization vs. greenfield FDI in Hungary: a comparative analysis", paper presented at the UNCTAD and OeNB Seminar on FDI and Privatization in Central and Eastern Europe (Vienna, 2-3 March), mimeo.

Tradeport (2000). "Investment Climate Statement" (various countries); available on the internet, http://www.tradeport.org/ts/countries.

Uminski, Stanislaw (2000). "Foreign capital in privatisation process in Poland", mimeo.

United Nations (1973). *Multinational Corporations in World Development* (New York: United Nations), United Nations publication, Sales No. E.97. XVII.6.

United Nations Centre on Transnational Corporations (UNCTC)(1993). *From the Common Market to EC 92: Regional Economic Integration in the European Community and Transnational Corporation* (New York: United Nations), United Nations publication, Sales No. E.93.II.A.2.

United Nations Conference on Trade and Development (UNCTAD) (1993a). *World Investment Report 1993: Transnational Corporations and Integrated International Production* (New York: United Nations), United National publication, Sales No. E.93.II.A.14.

_____ (1994a). *World Investment Report 1994: Transnational Corporations, Employment and the Workplace* (New York and Geneva: United Nations), United Nations publication, Sales No. E.94.II.A.14.

_____ (1995a). *World Investment Report 1995:Transnational Corporations and Competitiveness* (New York and Geneva: United Nations), United Nations publication, Sales No. E.95.II.A.9.

_____ (1996a). *World Investment Report 1996: Investment, Trade and International Policy Arrangements* (New York and Geneva: United Nations), United Nations publication, Sales No. E.96.II.A.14.

_____ (1996b). *International Investment Instruments: A Compendium, vols. I, II and III* (New York and Geneva: United Nations), United Nations publication, Sales No. E.96.II.A.9, 10 and 11. The three-volume set: E.96.II.A.12.

_____ (1997a). *World Investment Report 1997: Transnational Corporations, Market Structure and Competition Policy* (New York and Geneva: United Nations), United Nations publication, Sales No. E.97.II.D.10 and Corr. 1.

_____ (1998a). *World Investment Report 1998: Trends and Determinants* (New York and Geneva: United Nations), United Nations publication, Sales No. E.98.II.D.5 and Corr.1.

_____ (1999a). *World Investment Report 1999: Foreign Direct Investment and the Challenge of Development* (New York and Geneva: United Nations), United Nations publication, Sales No. E.99.II.D.3 and Corr.1.

_____ (1999b). *Foreign Direct Investment in Africa: Performance and Potential* (New York and Geneva: United Nations), United Nations publication, UNCTAD/ITE/IIT/Misc.15.

_____ (1999c). *Transfer Pricing. UNCTAD Series on Issues in International Investment Agreements* (New York and Geneva: UNCTAD), United Nations publication, Sales No. E.99.II.D.8.

_____ (1999d). *Investment Policy Review: Egypt* (New York and Geneva: United Nations), United Nations publication, Sales No. E.99.II.D.20.

_____ (1999e). *Investment Policy Review: Uganda* (New York and Geneva: United Nations), United Nations publication, Sales No. E.99.II.D.24.

_____ (1999f). *Investment Policy Review: Uzbekistan* (New York and Geneva), United Nations publication, UNCTAD/ITE/IIP/Misc.13.

_____ (2000a). *International Investment Instruments: A Compendium, vols. IV and V* (New York and Geneva: United Nations), United Nations publications, Sales No. E.00.II.D.13 and 14.

_____ (2000b). *International Agreements: Flexibility for Development* (New York and Geneva: United Nations) United Nations publication, Sales No. E.00.D.II.6.

_____ (2000c). *UNCTAD Handbook of Statistics 2000: CD-ROM* (New York and Geneva: United Nations), United Nations publication, Sales No. E/F.00.II.D.1.

_____ (2000d). *Investment Policy Review: Peru* (Geneva: United Nations), United Nations publication, forthcoming.

_____ (2000e). Trade and Development Board, Commission on Investment, Technology and Related Financial Issues, Expert Meeting on Mergers and Acquisitions: Policies Aimed at Maximizing the Positive and Minimizing the Possible Negative Impact of International Investment, "Outcome of the Expert Meeting", document TD/B/COM.2/EM.7/L.1, 23 June 2000, mimeo.

_____ (2000f). "Model Law on Competition", Document No. TD/RBP/CONF.5/7, 12 July.

United Nations, Economic Commission for Latin America and the Caribbean (ECLAC) (2000). *Foreign Investment in Latin America and the Caribbean: 1999 Report* (Santiago de Chile: United Nations), United Nations publication, Sales No. E.00.II.G.4.

United States Trade Representative (2000). *1999 National Trade Estimate Report on Foreign Trade Barriers* (Washington D.C.: United States Trade Representative).

United States, Department of Commerce (various issues, a). "Foreign direct investment in the Unites States", *Survey of Current Business*.

_____ (various issues, b)."U.S. business enterprises acquired or established by foreign direct investors", *Survey of Current Business*.

United States, Department of Justice (2000). *International Competition Policy Advisory Committee to the Attorney General and the Assistant Attorney General for Antitrust: Final Report,* http://www.usdoj.gov/atr/icpac/finalreport.htm.

United States, Department of the Treasury, Office of International Investment (2000). "Exon-Florio provision", available on the Internet, http://www.ustreas.gov/oii.

United States, General Accounting Office (1995). *Foreign Investment: Implementation of Exon-Florio and Related Amendments* (Washington D.C.: General Accounting Office), p.4.

_____ (1999). *Foreign- and U.S.-Controlled Corporations that Did not Pay U.S. Income Taxes, 1989-1995* (Washington, D.C.: Government Printing Office).

United States, International Competition Policy Advisory Committee to the Attorney General and Assistant Attorney General for Antitrust (2000). *Final Report of the International Competition Policy Advisory Committee to the Attorney General and Assistant Attorney General for Antitrust;* available on the Internet, http://www.usdoj.gov/atr/icpac/finalreport.htm.

Vasconcellos, Geraldo M. and Richard J. Kish (1998). "Cross-border mergers and acquisitions: the European-US experience", *Journal of Multinational Financial Management*, 8, pp. 431-450.

Vidotto, Carlos (1999). "Opening up the banking sector in Brazil", in Euro-fiet, *Mergers and take-overs in the finance sector,* CNB-CUT Discussion Paper, Report, April 1999, (Brussels), pp. 13-30, updated for UNCTAD, 2000.

Watkins, Myron W. (1927). *Industrial Combinations and Public Policy* (Boston: Houghton Mifflin Co.).

Weiszburg, J. (1997). "General Electric Lighting - Tungsram" (Budapest: Budapest University of Economic Sciences), mimeo.

White and Case (2000). "Competition/Merger Control Regimes"; available on the Internet, http://whitecase.com.

Williamson, Oliver E. (1971). "The vertical integration of production: market failure considerations", *American Economic Review*, 61, pp. 112-23.

World Bank (1999). *World Development Indicators 1999* (Washington, D.C.: The World Bank).

_____ (2000a). *Global Development Finance 2000* (Washington, D.C.: The World Bank).

_____ (2000b). *World Development Indicators 2000* (Washington, D.C.: The World Bank).

_____ (2000c). *East Asia: Recovery and Beyond* (Washington, D.C.: The World Bank).

World Trade Organization (WTO) (1999). *Trade Policy Review* (Geneva: WTO). (Egypt, Guinea, Israel, Togo).

Yun, Mikyung (2000). "Cross-border M&As and their impact on the Korean economy", paper presented at the UNCTAD Seminar on Cross-border M&As and Sustained Competitiveness in Asia: Trends, Impacts and Policy Implications (Bangkok, 9-10 March), mimeo.

Zemplínerová, Alena and Martin Jarolim (2000). "FDI through M&A vs. greenfield FDI: the case of the Czech Republic", paper presented at the UNCTAD and OeNB Seminar on FDI and Privatization in Central and Eastern Europe (Vienna, 2-3 March), mimeo.

Zhan, Xiaoning James (forthcoming). "China's accession to WTO and FDI: an assessment", *Journal of Swiss China Chamber of Commerce*, forthcoming.

_____ and Terutomo Ozawa (2000). *Business Restructuring in Asia: Cross-border M&As in Crisis-affected Countries* (Copenhagen: Copenhagen Business School Press).

ANNEXES

Annex A. Additional text tables

Annex table A.I.1. **Receipts and payments of royalties and licence fees by affiliated firms and by country in Germany, Japan and the United States, 1985-1999**

(Millions of dollars)

Receipts

Year	Germany[a] Intra-firm German parent firms only[b]	Germany[a] Intra-firm Foreign affiliates in Germany[c]	Germany[a] Country as a whole	Japan Intra-firm Japanese parent firms only (intra-firm only)	Japan Country as a whole	United States Intra-firm United States parent firms only	United States Intra-firm Foreign affiliates in the United States	United States Country as a whole
1985	464	83	546	..	723	..	..	6 680
1986	597	122	780	708	906	5 994	180	8 113
1987	760	146	997	..	1 293	7 668	220	10 174
1988	884	124	1 081	..	1 637	9 238	256	12 139
1989	916	106	1 122	1 034	2 016	10 612	349	13 818
1990	1 210	236	1 547	..	2 479	12 867	383	16 634
1991	1 070	345	1 515	..	2 866	13 523	583	17 819
1992	1 089	472	1 680	2 370	3 061	14 925	733	20 841
1993	941	501	1 596	..	3 861	14 936	752	21 695
1994	1 077	496	1 720	..	5 185	19 250	1 025	26 712
1995	1 499	617	2 232	3 919	6 005	21 399	1 460	30 289
1996	1 669	655	2 457	..	6 683	22 719	1 837	32 470
1997	1 686	518	2 319	..	7 303	23 221	1 803	33 781
1998	1 707	748	2 640	..	7 388	24 712	2 049	36 808
1999	1 433	626	2 258	..	..	24 120	1 924	37 213

a Receipts for patents, inventions and processes. Data on the country as a whole for 1985 do not include non-affiliated firms.
b Firms with participation abroad of more than 10 per cent (until the end of 1989: more than 25 per cent; from 1990 until the end of 1999 more than 20 per cent).
c Firms with foreign participation of more than 20 per cent (until the end of 1989: more than 25 per cent; from 1990 until the end of 1999 more than 20 per cent).

Payments

Year	Germany[a] Intra-firm Foreign affiliates in Germany[b]	Germany[a] Intra-firm German parent firms only[c]	Germany[a] Country as a whole	United States Intra-firm Foreign affiliates in the United States	United States Intra-firm United States parent firms only	United States Country as a whole
1985	799	200	999	..	..	1 170
1986	1 225	248	1 556	799	118	1 401
1987	1 518	274	1 891	1 142	168	1 857
1988	1 761	312	2 186	1 285	141	2 601
1989	1 683	359	2 172	1 632	71	2 528
1990	2 271	491	2 935	1 967	239	3 135
1991	2 401	470	3 211	2 789	166	4 035
1992	2 532	451	3 211	3 207	189	5 161
1993	2 386	452	3 049	3 152	234	5 032
1994	2 281	471	3 087	3 513	420	5 852
1995	2 671	1 001	4 012	4 673	583	6 919
1996	2 339	910	3 609	4 645	761	7 837
1997	2 738	799	3 803	5 978	989	9 390
1998	2 020	833	3 208	7 205	1 169	11 292
1999	1 477	814	2 739	8 437	1 218	12 437

Source: UNCTAD, based on UNCTAD, FDI/TNC database; Germany, Deutsche Bundesbank, unpublished data; and United States, Department of Commerce.

a Payments for patents, inventions and processes. Data on the country as a whole for 1985 do not include non-affiliated firms.
b Firms with participation abroad of more than 10 per cent (until the end of 1989: more than 25 per cent; from 1990 until the end of 1999 more than 20 per cent).
c Firms with foreign participation of more than 20 per cent (until the end of 1989: more than 25 per cent; from 1990 until the end of 1999 more than 20 per cent).

Annex table A.II.1. **Geographical sources of inward FDI stock in Central and Eastern European countries, latest date available**

(Percentage)

Home region and country	Belarus, July 1998	Bosnia and Herzegovina, July 1998	Bulgaria, December 1998	Croatia, December 1998	Czech Republic, December 1998	Estonia, December 1999	Hungary, December 1998	Latvia, December 1999	Lithuania, December 1999	Macedonia, FYR, December 1998	Moldova, Republic, June 1999	Poland, December 1999	Romania, December 1999	Russian Federation, June 1999	Slovakia, December 1999	Slovenia, December 1998	Ukraine, December 1998
Central and Eastern Europe	**11.0**	**22.8**	**4.8**	**2.7**	**3.4**	**1.8**	**1.1**	**13.7**	**2.7**	**0.7**	**32.0**	**3.8**	**5.4**	..	**10.2**	**9.4**	**6.7**
Croatia	..	16.7	-	..	-	..	..	..	..	1.1	..	0.5	-	..	..	3.3	..
Czech Republic	..	..	0.7	0.2	-	..	..	..	..	-	..	0.1	0.7	..	8.6	5.4	..
Hungary	3.0	..	0.1	0.3	0.2	..	0.1	..	..	..	..	-	3.6	..	1.6	0.2	..
Russian Federation	..	..	2.8	0.3	0.1	1.4	..	7.3	..	..	29.4	3.2	0.1	..	..	0.1	6.7
Developed countries	**85.0**	**38.7**	**76.1**	**93.6**	**94.6**	**95.4**	**94.7**	**69.4**	**97.0**	**41.2**	**49.3**	**83.7**	**70.1**	**62.5**	**84.1**	**89.8**	**52.8**
European Union	**65.0**	**30.4**	**58.3**	**60.6**	**82.7**	**84.6**	**64.0**	**50.8**	**71.9**	**19.5**	**22.7**	**63.8**	**56.8**	**24.7**	**69.9**	**81.2**	**28.1**
Austria	3.0	4.2	7.2	19.3	11.5	1.1	11.7	0.9	..	7.4	1.2	2.3	5.1	..	16.9	37.5	2.8
Belgium	..	..	..	0.7	1.1	0.1	3.9	-	..	..	2.2	0.8	1.0	..	1.2	0.3	..
Denmark	..	2.6	0.1	0.7	0.9	4.1	0.4	13.7	10.5	..	..	1.5	0.2	..	..	1.4	..
Finland	..	..	-	..	0.1	30.1	0.6	5.1	23.6	..	..	0.6	0.2	2.2	..	..	..
France	..	2.5	1.3	1.6	4.7	0.2	6.1	-	-	0.2	..	11.0	7.2	1.4	4.2	12.8	..
Germany	25.0	16.9	8.0	27.9	29.6	2.5	28.0	8.4	2.0	1.3	6.4	17.3	10.2	8.1	22.0	12.3	8.3
Greece	..	..	7.8	..	-	..	..	..	..	3.2	3.9	-	2.7	..	..	..	..
Ireland	..	..	0.1	..	0.1	0.3	0.3	3.9	1.2	1.3	4.9	2.3	0.3	1.3	1.6	6.6	..
Italy	9.0	4.2	1.3	1.4	0.9	0.6	3.2	0.1	0.7	1.6	..	9.1	7.6	..	..	0.3	..
Luxembourg	..	..	..	..	0.4	0.2	..	-	3.5	..	4.0	-	3.5	..	..	3.8	..
Netherlands	25.0	..	5.8	3.9	27.1	1.6	15.5	2.9	1.0	4.0	..	9.2	11.6	3.8	15.0	3.8	9.5
Portugal	..	..	0.1	..	-	..	..	..	..	..	..	0.8	0.1	..	..	..	..
Spain	..	..	4.1	..	0.2	..	0.1	0.1	..	..	..	0.7	0.5	..	..	1.1	..
Sweden	..	..	0.2	2.6	1.4	41.1	0.7	8.2	28.1	..	..	2.2	1.4	1.9	..	0.3	..
United Kingdom	3.0	..	12.2	2.5	4.7	2.8	6.4	7.4	1.3	0.4	..	5.9	5.1	6.0	9.1	4.8	7.5
Other Western Europe	**3.0**	..	**4.8**	**2.8**	**2.8**	**6.7**	**16.2**	**8.6**	**4.4**	**18.5**	**6.5**	**3.2**	**3.4**	**2.8**	**1.2**	**4.0**	**6.3**
Liechtenstein	..	..	0.1	1.3	0.1	1.6	0.2	1.4	..	18.1	5.1	0.1	0.5	..	..	-	3.1
Norway	..	..	..	..	0.7	3.4	0.3	3.7	2.7	..	..	1.3	0.1	..	..	..	..
Switzerland	3.0	..	4.7	1.5	1.8	1.5	2.9	1.3	0.9	0.4	0.6	1.8	2.3	2.2	1.2	3.3	3.2
Other developed countries	**17.0**	**8.3**	**13.1**	**30.3**	**9.1**	**4.1**	**14.5**	**10.0**	**20.7**	**3.3**	**20.1**	**16.7**	**10.0**	**35.1**	**13.0**	**4.6**	**18.3**
Canada	..	..	-	0.7	0.3	0.1	0.2	0.1	..	..	0.7	0.7	1.3	..	..	0.1	..
Japan	..	..	0.7	..	0.5	0.1	1.9	..	..	..	..	1.1	0.1	..	..	0.1	..
United States	17.0	..	12.2	28.4	8.2	3.9	12.2	9.7	20.7	3.0	18.7	14.7	7.7	35.1	13.0	4.4	18.3
Developing countries	**4.0**	**33.5**	**4.8**	**1.6**	**2.0**	**2.0**	**2.1**	**8.4**	**0.3**	**55.8**	**0.5**	**5.1**	**24.8**	**22.6**	..	**0.8**	**15.0**
Africa	..	..	-	0.1	0.1	-	0.6	1.6	..	-	..	0.1	0.4	..	..	..	..
Latin America and the Caribbean	**4.0**	..	-	**1.5**	**0.3**	**0.5**	**0.3**	**3.1**	**0.3**	..	..	..	**1.7**	..	..	**0.1**	**3.0**
Developing Asia	..	**33.5**	**4.8**	-	**1.6**	**1.4**	**1.2**	**3.2**	..	**55.8**	**0.5**	**5.1**	**22.5**	**22.6**	..	**0.7**	**12.1**
Cyprus	..	..	..	..	1.2	0.1	..	..	..	55.4	0.5	-	7.9	22.6	..	0.3	5.4
Korea, Republic of	..	..	2.6	..	-	..	0.8	..	..	..	..	4.6	5.4	..	..	..	6.7
Turkey	..	12.1	1.4	..	-	..	-	-	..	0.4	..	0.3	4.4	..	..	0.1	..
The Pacific	..	..	..	..	..	..	..	**0.6**	..	..	**0.6**	..	-	..	..	..	..
Other and not specified	..	**4.9**	**14.2**	**6.0**	..	**0.2**	**2.2**	**9.0**	..	**2.3**	**18.2**	**7.4**	-	**14.9**	**5.7**	-	**25.5**
Memorandum item: Commonwealth of Independent States	..	..	3.2	0.3	0.1	1.4	0.5	7.9	..	..	29.7	3.2	0.3	0.8	..	0.1	6.7
Total	**100.0**	**100.0**	**100.0**	**100.0**	**100.0**	**100.0**	**100.0**	**100.0**	**100.0**	**100.0**	**100.0**	**100.0**	**100.0**	**100.0**	**100.0**	**100.0**	**100.0**

Note: The survey- and announcement-based figures presented in this table do not necessarily correspond to the balance-of-payments data.

Annex table A.II.2. Sectoral and industrial distribution of inward FDI stock in Central and Eastern European countries, latest date available

(Percentage)

Home region and country	Albania[a], December 1995	Belarus, July 1998	Bosnia and Herzegovina, July 1998	Bulgaria, December 1998	Croatia, December 1999	Czech Republic, December 1998	Estonia, December 1999	Hungary, December 1998	Latvia, December 1999	Lithuania, December 1999	Macedonia, FYR, December 1998	Moldova, Republic, June 1998	Poland, December 1999	Romania, December 1999	Russian Federation, June 1999	Slovakia, December 1999	Slovenia, December 1998	Ukraine, December 1998
PRIMARY SECTOR	**1.4**	**53.7**	**..**	**1.6**	**3.4**	**1.0**	**1.5**	**1.4**	**1.2**	**..**	**..**	**..**	**0.3**	**3.0**	**10.7**	**1.4**	**-**	**4.2**
Agriculture, hunting, forestry and fishing	1.4	..	..	0.2	..	0.2	1.2	0.9	0.7	..	..	..	0.1	3.0	..	0.2	-	3.3
Mining, quarrying, petroleum and gas	..	53.7	..	1.4	3.4	0.9	0.3	0.5	0.5	..	..	..	0.2	..	10.7	1.2	-	0.9
SECONDARY SECTOR	**17.1**	**46.3**	**32.7**	**49.4**	**41.1**	**45.8**	**22.8**	**37.3**	**17.1**	**30.0**	**91.2**	**33.0**	**49.2**	**43.8**	**35.3**	**49.1**	**51.5**	**43.5**
Food, beverages & tobacco	..	20.2	..	21.5	4.2	7.1	..	9.0	5.3	10.7	25.8	..	13.1	13.9	20.3	..	5.0	21.0
Textiles and apparel	..	8.2	..	1.0	..	1.6	..	1.6	2.1	0.7	2.2	..	0.7	3.5	..	..	1.1	1.2
Wood, furniture, paper, publishing and printing	..	4.2	..	2.1	..	4.8	..	1.8	2.5	..	0.3	..	5.7	..	4.9	..	10.9	..
Coke and petroleum products	..	0.4	..	-	1.5	1.6	..	..	-	12.9	20.9	..	..	..	2.3	..	-	..
Chemicals and chemical products	..	..	..	4.6	24.9	2.4	..	8.9	2.7	1.7	..	..	3.7	..	..	..	7.6	4.5
Rubber and plastic products	..	2.3	..	0.5	..	2.3	..	..	0.4	..	..	..	1.3	..	..	..	5.5	..
Non-metallic mineral products	..	0.3	..	..	7.8	9.5	..	2.3	0.9	1.5	21.2	..	5.9	..	..	..	3.4	..
Basic metals and products	..	10.6	..	8.4	..	3.4	..	3.0	1.9	..	20.6	..	1.1	..	3.1	..	2.2	4.1
Machinery and equipment	..	..	..	-	..	1.5	..	10.3	0.9	..	0.2	..	1.5	26.4	4.8	..	5.1	12.7
Electrical machinery and apparatus	..	..	..	1.3	2.7	4.5	..	..	0.4	1.8	..	..	3.6	..	..	..	4.1	..
Motor vehicles and other transport equipment	..	..	..	..	..	7.0	..	..	0.1	0.8	..	..	12.5	..	..	..	6.7	..
Other manufacturing and recycling	..	..	..	0.9	..	..	..	0.3	..	..	..	..	..	..	..	..	..	..
TERTIARY SECTOR	**81.5**	**..**	**62.7**	**49.0**	**44.2**	**53.2**	**75.2**	**61.4**	**72.7**	**35.0**	**8.8**	**56.0**	**50.5**	**53.1**	**35.5**	**49.6**	**48.5**	**39.7**
Electricity, gas, steam and water supply	..	..	..	-	..	4.7	1.8	17.3	2.6	..	..	36.0	1.3	..	..	0.5	0.4	..
Construction	5.1	..	10.3	1.3	1.2	1.0	1.0	1.6	0.3	..	..	..	5.5	2.3	..	2.0	0.2	6.2
Wholesale and retail trade & repair of motor vehicles	65.8	..	25.7	23.0	1.6	17.3	15.7	10.6	16.3	0.6	7.0	20.0	9.7	24.1	16.0	18.7	16.8	15.8
Hotels and restaurants	..	..	..	2.1	..	0.1	1.0	1.8	1.4	..	..	..	1.2	0.8	..	1.2	0.6	..
Transport, storage and communications	4.6	..	6.2	5.0	30.6	9.2	26.6	8.2	24.9	29.4	1.9	..	..	..	18.8	3.1	1.8	5.3
Financial intermediation	..	..	..	11.4	..	14.8	23.5	10.9	18.9	5.0	..	..	5.4	2.3	..	20.3	15.4	7.1
Real estate, renting and business activities	..	..	..	..	10.8	5.5	5.0	9.4	7.4	..	..	..	22.4	..	..	3.5	12.3	..
Public administration	..	..	..	5.4	..	0.5	0.1	0.1	0.6	..	..	..	0.5	..	..	..	..	..
Health and social services	..	..	..	..	..	..	0.6	1.4	0.3	..	..	..	..	..	..	0.3	0.9	4.0
Other community, social and personal service activities	..	..	..	..	..	-	..	..	..	..	..	..	4.5	..	..	..	..	..
Unspecified services	5.9	..	20.5	0.8	..	0.1	..	..	..	..	..	..	..	23.6	0.8	..	0.1	1.3
UNSPECIFIED	**..**	**..**	**4.6**	**..**	**11.3**	**..**	**0.5**	**..**	**9.0**	**35.0**	**..**	**11.0**	**-**	**..**	**18.4**	**..**	**..**	**12.6**
TOTAL	**100.0**	**100.0**	**100.0**	**100.0**	**100.0**	**100.0**	**100.0**	**100.0**	**100.0**	**100.0**	**100.0**	**100.0**	**100.0**	**100.0**	**100.0**	**100.0**	**100.0**	**100.0**

Source: UNCTAD, FDI/TNC database.

Note: The survey- and announcement-based figures presented in this table do not necessarily correspond to the balance-of-payments data.
a Number of firms.

Annex table A.II.3. **Central and Eastern Europe: FDI inflows by type, 1993-1999**

(Millions of dollars)

(a) Total FDI inflows

Country	1993	1994	1995	1996	1997	1998	1999[a]	1993-1999
Total Central and Eastern Europe	**6 981**	**6 200**	**14 568**	**13 399**	**19 889**	**21 149**	**23 372**	**105 559**
Albania	58	53	70	90	48	45	41	405
Belarus	18	11	15	73	200	149	225	689
Bosnia and Herzegovina	..	..	..	-2	1	10	10	19[c]
Bulgaria	40	105	90	109	505	537	770	2 157
Croatia	120	117	115	506	517	893	1 382	3 651
Czech Republic	654	869	2 562	1 428	1 300	2 720	5 108	14 641
Estonia	162	214	201	151	267	581	306	1 882
Hungary [b]	2 339	1 146	4 453	2 275	2 173	2 036	1 944	16 367
Latvia	45	214	180	382	521	357	366	2 064
Lithuania	30	31	73	152	355	926	486	2 053
Macedonia, TFYR	..	24	10	12	16	118	22	200[d]
Moldova, Republic	14	28	67	24	76	81	34	323
Poland	1 715	1 875	3 659	4 498	4 908	6 365	7 500	30 520
Romania	94	342	420	265	1 215	2 031	961	5 328
Russian Federation	1 211	640	2 016	2 479	6 638	2 761	3 309	19 056
Slovakia	168	245	195	251	206	631	322	2 018
Slovenia	113	128	176	186	321	165	90	1 179
Ukraine	200	159	267	521	624	743	496	3 009

(b) FDI equity inflows (cash basis)

Country	1993	1994	1995	1996	1997	1998	1999[a]	1993-1999
Total Central and Eastern Europe	**5 999**	**4 857**	**11 632**	**9 745**	**14 065**	**14 957**	**11 559**	**72 855**
Albania	58	53	70	90	48	45	43	407
Belarus	18	11	15	73	200	149	225	689
Bosnia and Herzegovina	..	..	0	-2	1	2	..	1[e]
Bulgaria	40	105	90	109	492	505	476	1 817
Croatia	88	105	83	437	320	591	1 146	2 769
Czech Republic	654	869	2 562	1 428	1 300	2 540	4 877	14 230
Estonia	93	143	101	18	97	412	162	1 026
Hungary	2 339	1 146	4 453	1 788	1 811	1 410	1 675	14 622
Latvia	45	214	180	219	357	209	188	1 411
Lithuania	30	31	73	152	218	772	372	1 648
Macedonia, TFYR	..	20	1	5	9	103	10	148[d]
Moldova, Republic	14	28	65	21	70	57	37	292
Poland	892	884	1 807	2 845	2 663	4 323	..	13 414[f]
Romania	37	188	207	151	655	1 346	656	3 240
Russian Federation	1 211	640	1 451	1 822	5 014	1 378	1 434	12 950
Slovakia	168	245	195	251	189	451	300	1 800
Slovenia	113	128	176	110	309	165	..	1 001[f]
Ukraine	200	49	103	228	313	499	..	1 392[f]

(c) FDI equity inflows paid in kind

Country	1993	1994	1995	1996	1997	1998	1999[a]	1993-1999
Total Central and Eastern Europe	**449**	**665**	**830**	**859**	**1 964**	**2 012**	**1 162**	**7 940**
Bosnia and Herzegovina	..	..	..	..	..	8	..	8[g]
Croatia	33	12	32	69	25	6	11	189
Hungary [b]	142	173	117	57	22	10	11	532
Lithuania	..	..	..	..	23	..	..	23[h]
Macedonia, TFYR	..	4	8	7	7	14	12	52[d]
Poland	217	212	298	314	453	281	..	1 775[f]
Romania	57	154	213	114	560	685	305	2 088
Russian Federation	..	..	..	..	562	767	823	2 152[i]
Slovenia	..	..	..	6	5	..	..	11[j]
Ukraine	..	110	161	291	307	241	..	1 110[k]

/...

Annex table A.II.3. **Central and Eastern Europe: FDI inflows by type, 1993-1999** *(continued)*

(d) Reinvested earnings

Country	1993	1994	1995	1996	1997	1998	1999[a]	1993-1999
Total Central and Eastern Europe	**227**	**425**	**906**	**319**	**321**	**227**	**615**	**3 050**
Bulgaria	..	..	..	..	-	50	-20	30[i]
Croatia	..	..	..	..	40	68	59	167[i]
Czech Republic	..	..	..	..	..	180	231	411[l]
Estonia	28	43	15	18	95	26	67	292
Latvia	..	..	..	35	53	60	89	237[c]
Lithuania	..	..	..	..	43	100	146	290[i]
Moldova, Republic	..	..	..	..	1	5	4	10[i]
Poland	199	382	888	244	25	-264	..	1474[f]
Russian Federation	..	..	..	..	..	..	38	38[m]
Slovakia	..	..	..	..	1	-	-	1[i]
Slovenia	..	..	..	21	58	..	..	79[j]
Ukraine	..	..	3	2	4	3	..	12[e]

(e) Intra-company loans

Country	1993	1994	1995	1996	1997	1998	1999[a]	1993-1999
Total Central and Eastern Europe	**449**	**425**	**1 318**	**2 534**	**3 473**	**3 810**	**1 801**	**13 810**
Albania	..	..	..	..	..	..	-2	- 2[m]
Bulgaria	..	..	..	..	13	-17	315	311[i]
Croatia	..	..	..	..	44	76	55	175[i]
Estonia	42	28	85	115	75	143	77	564
Hungary	..	..	..	487	362	627	269	1 745[c]
Latvia	..	..	..	128	112	88	90	417[c]
Lithuania	..	..	..	..	70	54	-32	92[i]
Moldova, Republic	..	..	2	3	4	20	-8	21[n]
Poland	407	397	666	1 095	1 767	2 025	..	6 357[f]
Russian Federation	..	..	565	657	1 062	616	1 014	3 914[n]
Slovakia	..	..	..	..	16	179	22	217[i]
Slovenia	..	..	..	50	-51	..	..	- 1[j]

Source: UNCTAD, FDI/TNC database.

Note: No official FDI data are available for Yugoslavia. This table reflects a data revision for the Russian Federation received after the closure of the *Report*.

[a] Preliminary.
[b] In Hungary, FDI equity in kind is not included in the FDI total.
[c] 1996-1999.
[d] 1994-1999.
[e] 1995-1998.
[f] 1993-1998.
[g] 1998.
[h] 1997.
[i] 1997-1999.
[j] 1996-1997.
[k] 1994-1998.
[l] 1998-1999.
[m] 1999.
[n] 1995-1999.

Annex table A.II.4. **Geographical distribution of outward FDI from Central and Eastern European countries**

(Percentage)

Home country and year — Host region and economy	Croatia 1999 outflows	Czech Republic 1998 stock	Estonia 1999 stock	Hungary 1999 outflows	Latvia 1999 stock	Russian Federation 1995-1999 outflows	Slovakia 1999 stock	Slovenia 1998 stock
Central and Eastern Europe	164.8	50.9	89.5	35.5	3.9	..	68.6	82.4
Bosnia and Herzegovina	39.2	-	..	..	..	..	..	3.6
Croatia	..	0.4	..	2.7	..	..	..	53.1
Czech Republic	-	..	..	..	-	..	35.9	0.7
Hungary	-1.1	0.7	..	..	..	..	9.7	4.0
Latvia	..	..	48.6	..	..	..	..	..
Lithuania	..	0.5	38.2	..	0.9	..	..	..
Macedonia, TFYR	14.9	..	..	..	..	..	..	4.0
Poland	93.1	3.8	..	4.5	-	..	2.6	6.8
Romania	..	0.6	..	23.5	..	..	..	0.8
Russian Federation	-	1.0	0.5	1.5	0.7	..	4.1	1.4
Slovakia	2.8	21.0	..	3.3	..	..	..	0.1
Slovenia	13.7	18.9	..	..	..	..	..	..
Ukraine	..	2.8	2.1	..	1.0	..	13.4	1.4
Developed countries	-85.9	31.9	1.1	58.8	4.9	..	24.3	19.1
European Union	24.4	22.4	-	29.5	3.7	..	22.5	13.0
Austria	9.2	2.1	..	7.4	..	..	..	3.6
Germany	4.8	9.3	..	2.9	3.2	..	2.3	6.8
Italy	4.2	0.2	..	..	..	..	..	1.5
Netherlands	..	3.2	-0.2	18.1	0.3	..	..	0.5
United Kingdom	6.2	1.4	..	..	-	..	20.2	1.2
Other Western Europe	-43.5	7.3	1.1	12.2	0.1	..	1.8	2.9
Other developed countries	-66.8	2.2	..	17.1	1.1	..	..	3.2
United States	-66.8	1.2	..	17.1	1.1	..	..	3.3
Developing countries	0.3	17.2	8.1	5.2	90.4	..	2.1	2.4
Africa	2.1	6.7	..	-	79.5	..	..	3.8
Liberia	..	..	..	..	79.5	..	..	3.2
Latin America and the Caribbean	-0.6	6.8	0.3	-	4.2	..	..	0.4
Virgin Islands	..	4.2	..	..	-	..	..	..
Developing Asia	-1.3	3.7	7.8	5.2	6.7	..	2.1	-1.8
Cyprus	-1.3	2.4	7.8	..	6.6	..	2.1	-2.6
Korea, Republic of	..	..	..	5.0	..	..	..	..
Other and not specified	20.9	-	1.4	1.6	0.8	..	5.0	-3.9
Total	100.0	100.0	100.0	100.0	100.0	..	100.0	100.0
Memorandum item: Commonwealth of Independent States	0.1	4.2	2.7	1.5	2.3	11.2	17.5	2.9

Source: UNCTAD, FDI/TNC database.

Note: The survey and announcement-based figures presented in this table do not necessarily correspond to the balance-of-payments data.

Annex table A.IV.1. **World cross-border M&As, by type
(horizontal, vertical, conglomerate) 1987-1999**
(Percentages)

Year	Number			Value		
	Horizontal M&As[a]	Vertical M&As[b]	Conglomerate M&As[c]	Horizontal M&As[a]	Vertical M&As[b]	Conglomerate M&As[c]
1987	51.3	4.6	44.1	54.6	17.3	28.1
1988	54.6	4.8	40.6	61.1	1.4	37.5
1989	55.8	5.3	38.9	58.6	6.6	34.8
1990	54.8	5.0	40.2	55.8	3.4	40.9
1991	54.1	5.6	40.3	54.5	4.0	41.5
1992	54.6	5.4	40.0	60.9	4.4	34.7
1993	54.5	5.7	39.9	53.3	5.2	41.5
1994	54.1	5.6	40.4	61.0	7.3	31.8
1995	53.0	5.6	41.4	65.5	2.7	31.8
1996	54.0	5.7	40.3	56.9	5.5	37.6
1997	54.1	5.2	40.7	58.1	4.9	37.0
1998	56.5	6.2	37.3	68.8	5.9	25.3
1999	56.2	6.2	37.6	71.2	1.8	27.0

Source: UNCTAD, cross-border M&A database, based on data from Thomson Financial Securities Data Company.

[a] Defined as deals that were concluded in the same industry (at the two-digit level of SIC codes) between the acquirer and the acquired firm.

[b] Defined as deals that fall under the following combinations of industries between the acquirer and the acquired firm: 0-57; 13,29,46-10,12,14; 13,29,46-49; 15,16,17-50; 15,16,17-57; 20-0; 20-51; 20-54; 20-58; 21-51; 22,23-51; 22,23-53,56; 24,25,26-0; 24,25,26-15,16,17; 24,25,26-57; 27-48; 27-51; 28-49,72,79,80,83,84; 28-51; 30,32-0; 30,32-15,16,17; 30,32-50; 33,34-10,12,14; 33,34-15,16,17; 33,34-50; 33,34-52,55,59; 31-51; 31-57; 35 except 357-50; 35 except 357-52,55,59; 357-57; 357-73,81,87; 36 except 366-50; 36 except 366-52,55,59; 366-48; 37 except 372, 376-40,41,42,44,47; 37 except 372, 376-75,76; 372,376-45; 38-48; 38-50; 38-52,55,59; 39-52,55,59; 48-78; 60,61,62,63,67-65; 60,61,62,63,67-73,81,87; 70-40,41,42,44,47 and 70-45 at the two-digit level of SIC codes.

[c] Defined as deals that are not categorized as horizontal or vertical M&As.

Annex table A.IV.2. **Cross-border M&As motivated by immediate financial gains and strategic reasons,**[a]

1987-1999

(Billions of dollars and number of deals)

Year	Total	World		Developed countries		Developing countries		CEE	
		Motivated by financial gains	Motivated by economic and strategic reasons	Motivated by financial gains	Motivated by economic and strategic reasons	Motivated by financial gains	Motivated by economic and strategic reasons	Motivated by financial gains	Motivated by economic and strategic reasons
Value in billion dollars									
1987	74.5	4.9	69.6	4.9	67.9	-	1.7	-	-
1988	115.6	4.8	110.9	4.5	108.2	0.3	2.6	-	-
1989	140.4	9.2	131.1	8.8	126.5	0.4	4.6	-	-
1990	150.6	26.1	124.5	17.3	116.9	8.8	7.3	-	0.3
1991	80.7	10.2	70.5	7.7	66.3	2.5	3.4	0.1	0.7
1992	79.3	17.4	61.9	14.9	53.7	2.3	5.8	0.2	2.4
1993	83.1	13.5	69.5	10.7	58.5	2.7	10.1	0.2	1.0
1994	127.1	12.9	114.1	7.9	102.9	4.7	10.3	0.4	1.0
1995	186.6	18.0	168.5	12.9	151.6	2.4	13.6	2.7	3.3
1996	227.0	27.0	200.0	19.6	169.1	7.1	27.6	0.3	3.3
1997	304.8	41.0	263.8	27.0	207.7	11.7	52.9	2.4	3.2
1998	531.6	59.8	471.2	33.1	412.1	25.9	54.9	0.8	4.3
1999	720.1	54.8	663.5	46.4	598.1	7.6	56.9	0.7	8.4
Number of deals									
1987	862	65	797	60	754	5	43	-	-
1988	1 480	84	1 396	73	1 333	11	62	-	1
1989	2 201	136	2 065	120	1 946	15	110	1	9
1990	2 503	194	2 309	164	2 135	29	160	1	14
1991	2 854	271	2 583	230	2 313	30	214	11	56
1992	2 721	263	2 457	215	2 102	36	239	12	116
1993	2 835	292	2 543	220	2 053	60	358	12	132
1994	3 494	377	3 115	270	2 486	87	488	20	141
1995	4 247	400	3 846	273	2 987	91	622	36	237
1996	4 569	406	4 162	260	3 168	116	760	30	234
1997	4 986	490	4 494	340	3 451	117	828	33	215
1998	5 597	504	5 089	378	3 888	103	986	23	215
1999	6 233	566	5 662	366	4 340	128	914	72	408

Source: UNCTAD, cross-border M&A database, based on data from Thomson Financial Securities Data Company.

Notes: Data are classified by region/economy of seller. The components may not add up to totals due to deals which cannot be classified by region.

[a] Defined as deals in which the acquirer is a finance company (buyout firm, venture capital company, merchant bank, commercial bank, etc.), acquiring a target firm whose main activity is non-financial. However, target firms of industrial combinations that are considered as aiming at operational rather than financial objectives are excluded. These involve financial companies with SIC codes as follows: 16, 44, 65, 83, 106, 107, 150, 151, 176, 183, 195, 201, 247, 310, 330, 334, 363, 439, 55 and 8. Furthermore, deals whose target firms engage in information retrieval services are also excluded.

Annex table A.IV.3. **Friendly vs. hostile cross-border M&A transactions, 1987-1999**

(Billions of dollars and number of deals)

Year	Total	World			Developed countries			Developing countries			Central and Eastern Europe		
		Friendly[a]	Hostile[b]	Neutral[c]	Friendly[a]	Hostile[b]	Neutral[c]	Friendly[a]	Hostile[b]	Neutral[c]	Friendly[a]	Hostile[b]	Neutral[c]
							Value in billion dollars						
1987	74.5	67.9	4.4	2.0	66.1	4.4	2.0	1.7	-	-	-	-	-
1988	115.6	83.1	26.0	5.5	80.4	26.0	5.3	2.7	-	0.1	-	-	-
1989	140.4	122.8	13.8	3.8	118.2	13.8	3.3	4.6	-	0.5	-	-	-
1990	150.6	139.2	1.3	4.3	128.8	1.3	4.0	10.1	-	0.4	0.3	-	-
1991	80.7	75.0	2.8	2.8	68.6	2.8	2.6	5.6	-	0.2	0.8	-	-
1992	79.3	73.2	2.9	2.9	63.2	2.9	2.3	7.4	-	0.6	2.6	-	-
1993	83.1	77.5	0.4	4.7	65.9	0.4	2.5	10.5	-	2.3	1.1	-	-
1994	127.1	122.4	0.7	3.6	107.4	0.7	2.4	13.8	-	1.1	1.1	-	0.2
1995	186.6	166.2	8.1	5.0	145.5	7.9	3.9	14.8	0.2	1.0	5.9	-	0.1
1996	227.0	206.4	6.8	11.0	172.4	6.6	7.2	30.6	0.2	3.6	3.4	-	0.2
1997	304.8	287.6	6.2	9.6	220.9	5.9	7.7	61.5	0.2	1.6	5.2	-	0.3
1998	531.6	511.9	2.7	11.2	431.2	2.7	7.1	75.2	-	3.8	4.8	-	0.3
1999	720.1	676.2	8.8	24.1	605.2	8.8	20.5	60.9	-	2.8	8.3	-	0.8
							Number of deals						
1987	862	814	10	36	767	10	35	47	-	1	-	-	-
1988	1 480	1 413	15	50	1 342	15	47	70	-	3	1	-	-
1989	2 201	2 074	12	113	1 957	12	95	110	-	15	7	-	3
1990	2 503	2 390	4	96	2 206	4	79	169	-	17	15	-	-
1991	2 854	2 752	4	86	2 460	4	69	226	-	16	66	-	1
1992	2 721	2 620	3	89	2 243	3	65	252	-	21	124	-	3
1993	2 835	2 728	3	97	2 205	3	61	385	-	32	138	-	4
1994	3 494	3 341	5	134	2 654	5	87	537	-	36	149	-	10
1995	4 247	4 091	14	136	3 174	12	70	662	2	47	254	-	19
1996	4 569	4 372	10	176	3 319	9	96	811	1	57	241	-	23
1997	4 987	4 833	9	130	3 685	8	87	907	1	34	239	-	9
1998	5 597	5 420	5	150	4 174	5	77	1 018	-	60	224	-	13
1999	6 233	5 942	10	264	4 528	10	156	994	-	44	415	-	64

Source: UNCTAD, cross-border M&A database, based on data from Thomson Financial Securities Data Company.

Note: The components may not add up to totals due to deals whose nature is unkown.

[a] The board recommended to accept an offer.
[b] The board officially rejected an offer, but the acquirer persisted with its take-over efforts.
[c] The management of the seller did neither accept nor reject an offer.

Annex table A.IV.4. Cross-border M&A deals with values of over $1 billion completed in 1999ᵃ

Rank	Value ($billion)	Acquiring company	Industry of the acquiring company	Home economy	Acquired company	Host economy	Industry of the acquired company
1	60.3	Vodafone Group PLC	Telecommunications	United Kingdom	AirTouch Communications	United States	Telecommunications
2	34.6	ZENECA Group PLC	Pharmaceuticals	United Kingdom	Astra AB	Sweden	Pharmaceuticals
3	32.6	Mannesmann AG	Metal and Metal Products	Germany	Orange PLC	United Kingdom	Telecommunications
4	21.9	Rhone-Poulenc SA	Chemicals and Allied Products	France	Hoechst AG	Germany	Chemicals and Allied Products
5	13.6	Deutsche Telekom AG	Telecommunications	Germany	One 2 One	United Kingdom	Telecommunications
6	13.2	Repsol SA	Oil and Gas; Petroleum Refining	Spain	YPF SA	Argentina	Oil and Gas; Petroleum Refining
7	12.6	Scottish Power PLC	Electric, Gas, and Water Distribution	United Kingdom	PacifiCorp	United States	Electric, Gas, and Water Distribution
8	10.8	Wal-Mart Stores (UK) Ltd	Investment & Commodity Firms, Dealers, Exc	United Kingdom	ASDA Group PLC	United Kingdom	Retail Trade-Food Stores
9	10.8	Aegon NV	Insurance	Netherlands	TransAmerica Corp	United States	Insurance
10	10.1	Global Crossing Ltd	Telecommunications	Bermuda	Frontier Corp	United States	Telecommunications
11	9.8	ABB AG	Electronic and Electrical Equipment	Switzerland	ABB AB	Sweden	Electronic and Electrical Equipment
12	9.1	Deutsche Bank AG	Commercial Banks, Bank Holding Companies	Germany	Bankers Trust New York Corp	United States	Commercial Banks, Bank Holding Companies
13	8.4	Mannesmann AG	Metal and Metal Products	Germany	Ing C Olivetti-Telecom Int	Italy	Telecommunications
14	8.2	Suez Lyonnaise des Eaux SA	Electric, Gas, and Water Distribution	France	TRACTEBEL SA	Belgium	Electric, Gas, and Water Distribution
15	7.8	Japan Tobacco Inc	Tobacco Products	Japan	RJ Reynolds International	Netherlands	Tobacco Products
16	7.7	HSBC Holdings PLC	Commercial Banks, Bank Holding Companies	United Kingdom	Republic New York Corp,NY	United States	Commercial Banks, Bank Holding Companies
17	7.5	British American Tobacco PLC	Tobacco Products	United Kingdom	Rothmans Intl BV(Richemont)	Netherlands	Tobacco Products
18	6.8	TRW Inc	Transportation Equipment	United States	LucasVarity PLC	United Kingdom	Business Services
19	6.6	General Electric Capital Corp	Credit Institutions	United States	Japan Leasing Corp	Japan	Credit Institutions
20	6.5	Ford Motor Co	Transportation Equipment	United States	Volvo-Worldwide Passenger Bus	Sweden	Transportation Equipment
21	6.3	Vivendi SA	Electric, Gas, and Water Distribution	France	United States Filter Corp	United States	Machinery
22	6.2	New Holland(New Holland Hldg)	Machinery	Netherlands	Case Corp	United States	Machinery
23	6.1	Dexia Belgium	Investment & Commodity Firms, Dealers, Exc	Belgium	Dexia France	France	Investment & Commodity Firms, Dealers, Exchanges
24	5.7	Sun Life and Provincial	Insurance	United Kingdom	Guardian Royal Exchange PLC	United Kingdom	Insurance
25	5.4	Renault SA	Transportation Equipment	France	Nissan Motor Co	Japan	Transportation Equipment
26	5.3	Total SA	Oil and Gas; Petroleum Refining	France	Petrofina SA	Belgium	Oil and Gas; Petroleum Refining
27	4.8	Roche Holding AG	Pharmaceuticals	Switzerland	Genentech Inc	United States	Pharmaceuticals
28	4.5	ALITALIA-Passenger and Cargo	Air Transportation and Shipping	Italy	KLM Royal Dutch-Passenger	Netherlands	Air Transportation and Shipping
29	4.4	Investors	Investment & Commodity Firms, Dealers, Exc	Iran, Islamic Republic of	Telecom Eireann(Ireland)	Ireland	Telecommunications
30	4.3	Punch Taverns(Texas Pacific)	Retail Trade-Eating and Drinking Places	United Kingdom	Allied Domecq-UK Retailing	United Kingdom	Retail Trade-Eating and Drinking Places
31	4.2	GEC PLC	Communications Equipment	United Kingdom	FORE Systems Inc	United States	Computer and Office Equipment Care Products

/...

Annex table A.IV.4. **Cross-border M&A deals with values of over $1 billion completed in 1999ᵃ (continued)**

Rank	Value ($billion)	Acquiring company	Home economy	Industry of the acquiring company	Acquired company	Host economy	Industry of the acquired company
32	4.1	Suez Lyonnaise des Eaux SA	France	Electric, Gas, and Water Distribution	Nalco Chemical Co	United States	Chemicals and Allied Products
33	3.5	ACE Ltd	Bermuda	Insurance	CIGNA Corp-US & International	United States	Insurance
34	3.4	Investor Group	France	Investment & Commodity Firms, Dealers, Exc	Energie Baden-Wuerttemberg AG	Germany	Electric, Gas, and Water Distribution
35	3.2	Investor Group	Australia	Investment & Commodity Firms, Dealers, Exc	National Provident Institution	United Kingdom	Insurance
36	3.2	British Steel PLC	United Kingdom	Metal and Metal Products	Koninklijke Hoogovens NV	Netherlands	Metal and Metal Products
37	3.1	Reckitt & Colman PLC	United Kingdom	Pharmaceuticals	Benckiser NV	Netherlands	Soaps, Cosmetics and Personal-Care Products
38	3.1	BC Telecom(Anglo-CA Telephone)	Canada	Communications Equipment	Telus Corp	Canada	Communications Equipment
39	3.1	Uniphase Corp	United States	Electronic and Electrical Equipment	JDS Fitel(Furukawa Elec Co)	Canada	Electronic and Electrical Equipment
40	3.0	Tabacalera SA	Spain	Food and Kindred Products	Seita	France	Tobacco Products
41	3.0	AES Corp	United States	Electric, Gas, and Water Distribution	National Power Drax Ltd	United Kingdom	Electric, Gas, and Water Distribution
42	2.9	Pinault-Printemps Redoute	France	Retail Trade-General Merchandise and Apparel	Gucci Group NV	Netherlands	Leather and Leather Products
43	2.9	Quebecor Printing Inc	Canada	Printing, Publishing, and Allied Services	World Color Press Inc	United States	Printing, Publishing, and Allied Services
44	2.8	Fortis AG	Belgium	Investment & Commodity Firms, Dealers, Exc	American Bankers Ins Group Inc	United States	Insurance
45	2.8	Verenigd Bezit VNU	Netherlands	Printing, Publishing, and Allied Services	Nielsen Media Research Inc	United States	Business Services
46	2.8	Huntsman ICI Holdings LLC	United States	Chemicals and Allied Products	ICI-Polyurethane,Titanium Dio	United Kingdom	Chemicals and Allied Products
47	2.7	CIT Group Inc	United States	Credit Institutions	Newcourt Credit Group Inc	Canada	Credit Institutions
48	2.6	HSBC Holdings PLC	United Kingdom	Commercial Banks, Bank Holding Companies	Safra Republic Holdings SA	Luxembourg	Commercial Banks, Bank Holding Companies
49	2.5	Burlington Resources Inc	United States	Oil and Gas; Petroleum Refining	Poco Petroleums Ltd	Canada	Oil and Gas; Petroleum Refining
50	2.5	Koninklijke Numico NV	Netherlands	Food and Kindred Products	General Nutrition Companies	United States	Retail Trade-Food Stores
51	2.4	AT&T Canada Inc	Canada	Telecommunications	MetroNet Communications Corporation	Canada	Telecommunications
52	2.3	Weyerhaeuser Co	United States	Wood Products, Furniture and Fixtures	MacMillan Bloedel Ltd	Canada	Wood Products, Furniture, and Fixtures
53	2.3	ING Groep NV	Netherlands	Insurance	BHF Bank	Germany	Commercial Banks, Bank Holding Companies
54	2.3	Buhrmann NV	Netherlands	Paper and Allied Products	Corporate Express Inc	United States	Miscellaneous Retail Trade
55	2.1	Anglo American Corp of SA Ltd	South Africa	Mining	Minorco SA	Luxembourg	Mining
56	2.1	GEC PLC	United Kingdom	Communications Equipment	Reltec Corp	United States	Communications Equipment
57	2.1	Edison Mission Energy(Edison)	United States	Electric, Gas, and Water Distribution	PowerGen PLC-Power Stations(2)	United Kingdom	Electric, Gas, and Water Distribution

/...

Annex table A.IV.4. Cross-border M&A deals with values of over $1 billion completed in 1999ᵃ (continued)

Rank	Value ($billion)	Acquiring company	Industry of the acquiring company	Home economy	Acquired company	Host economy	Industry of the acquired company
58	2.0	Repsol SA	Oil and Gas; Petroleum Refining	Spain	YPF SA	Argentina	Oil and Gas; Petroleum Refining
59	1.9	El du Pont de Nemours and Co	Chemicals and Allied Products	United States	Herberts Paints(Hoechst AG)	Germany	Chemicals and Allied Products
60	1.9	NTL Inc	Radio and Television Broadcasting Stations	United States	Diamond Cable Communications	United Kingdom	Radio and Television Broadcasting Stations
61	1.8	Stagecoach Holdings PLC	Transportation and Shipping (except air)	United Kingdom	Coach USA Inc	United States	Transportation and Shipping (except air)
62	1.8	Investor Group	Investment & Commodity Firms, Dealers, Exc	United States	Japan Telecom Co Ltd(Japan)	Japan	Telecommunications
63	1.8	Heidelberger Zement AG	Stone, Clay, Glass, and Concrete Products	Germany	Scancem AB	Sweden	Stone, Clay, Glass, and Concrete Products
64	1.8	Alcatel SA	Communications Equipment	France	XYLAN Corp	United States	Communications Equipment
65	1.8	Vedior Holding UK PLC(Vedior)	Business Services	United Kingdom	Select Appointments (Holdings)	United Kingdom	Business Services
66	1.8	News Corp Ltd	Printing, Publishing, and Allied Services	Australia	Fox/Liberty Networks	United States	Radio and Television Broadcasting Stations
67	1.7	Kensington Acquisition Sub Inc	Investment & Commodity Firms, Dealers, Exc	United States	Cellular Communications Intl	United States	Telecommunications
68	1.7	Sithe Energies(Cie Generale)	Electric, Gas, and Water Distribution	United States	GPU Inc-Power Plants(23)	United States	Electric, Gas, and Water Distribution
69	1.7	Global Crossing Ltd	Telecommunications	Bermuda	Racal Telecommunications Ltd	United Kingdom	Telecommunications
70	1.6	Electronic Data Systems Corp	Business Services	United States	MCI Systemhouse Inc(MCI)	Canada	Business Services
71	1.6	Giovanni Agnelli & Co	Investment & Commodity Firms, Dealers, Exc	Italy	Exor Group (IFI)	Luxembourg	Investment & Commodity Firms, Dealers, Exchanges
72	1.6	Atlas Copco North America Inc	Machinery	United States	Rental Service Corp	United States	Business Services
73	1.6	Koninklijke Philips Electronic	Electronic and Electrical Equipment	Netherlands	LG Electronics-Crystal Display	Republic of Korea	Electronic and Electrical Equipment
74	1.6	AXA	Insurance	France	Guardian Royal Exchange O/Sea	Multinationalᵇ	Insurance
75	1.6	Deutsche Verkehrs-Bank AG	Commercial Banks, Bank Holding Companies	Germany	Long Term Credit-Aviation Div	United Kingdom	Credit Institutions
76	1.5	Fortis International NV	Insurance	Netherlands	ASLK-CGER Banque	Belgium	Commercial Banks, Bank Holding Companies
77	1.5	ABB Transportation	Transportation and Shipping (except air)	Netherlands	Elsag Bailey Process	Netherlands	Measuring, Medical, Photo Equipment; Clocks
78	1.5	EMAP PLC	Printing, Publishing, and Allied Services	United Kingdom	Petersen Companies Inc	United States	Printing, Publishing, and Allied Services
79	1.5	Getronics NV	Business Services	Netherlands	Wang Laboratories Inc	United States	Prepackaged Software
80	1.4	Gannett UK Ltd(Gannett Co Inc)	Investment & Commodity Firms, Dealers, Exc	United Kingdom	Newsquest PLC	United Kingdom	Printing, Publishing, and Allied Services
81	1.4	Royal & Sun Alliance Insurance	Insurance	United Kingdom	Orion Capital Corp	United States	Insurance

/...

Annex table A.IV.4. Cross-border M&A deals with values of over $1 billion completed in 1999[a] (continued)

Rank	Value ($billion)	Acquiring company	Home economy	Industry of the acquiring company	Acquired company	Host economy	Industry of the acquired company
82	1.3	Principal Financial Group	United States	Investment & Commodity Firms, Dealers, Exc	BT Fund Management / BT Invest Services	Australia	Investment & Commodity Firms, Dealers, Exchanges
83	1.3	ABN-AMRO Holding NV	Netherlands	Commercial Banks, Bank Holding Companies	Bank America-Asian Retail	Taiwan Province	Commercial Banks, Bank Holding Companies
84	1.3	ING Groep NV	Netherlands	Insurance	Credit Commercial de France	France	Commercial Banks, Bank Holding Companies
85	1.3	Energy Partnership	United States	Electric, Gas, and Water Distribution	Ikon Energy/Multinet Gas	Australia	Electric, Gas, and Water Distribution
86	1.2	Imetal SA(Parfinance)	France	Mining	English China Clays PLC	United Kingdom	Mining
87	1.2	National Power PLC	United Kingdom	Electric, Gas, and Water Distribution	Union Fenosa Generacion SA	Spain	Electric, Gas, and Water Distribution
88	1.2	Enron Corp	United States	Electric, Gas, and Water Distribution	Enron Oil-Oil & Gas Prop,China	China	Oil and Gas; Petroleum Refining
89	1.2	Aegon UK(AEGON NV)	United Kingdom	Insurance	Guardian RE-UK Life, Pensions	United Kingdom	Insurance
90	1.2	XL Capital Ltd	Bermuda	Insurance	NAC Re Corp	United States	Insurance
91	1.2	Koninklijke Philips Electronic	Netherlands	Electronic and Electrical Equipment	VLSI Technology Inc	United States	Electronic and Electrical Equipment
92	1.1	Accor SA	France	Hotels and Casinos	Red Roof Inns Inc	United States	Hotels and Casinos
93	1.1	KBC Bancassurance Holding NV	Belgium	Commercial Banks, Bank Holding Companies	Ceskoslovenska Obchodni Banka	Czech Republic	Commercial Banks, Bank Holding Companies
94	1.1	Investor Group	United Kingdom	Investment & Commodity Firms, Dealers, Exc	CBS Corp-Westinghouse Nuclear	United States	Public Administration
95	1.1	Thyssen Aufzuege AG(Thyssen)	Germany	Machinery	Dover Corp-Elevator Business	United States	Construction Firms
96	1.1	RAG International Mining Gmbh	Germany	Mining	Cyprus Amax-US Coal Mining Ops	United States	Mining
97	1.1	Tyco International Ltd	United States	Miscellaneous Manufacturing	Siemens Electromechanical	Germany	Electronic and Electrical Equipment
98	1.1	Deutsche Post AG(Germany)	Germany	Business Services	Danzas Holding AG	Switzerland	Transportation and Shipping (except air)
99	1.1	Investor Group	Italy	Investment & Commodity Firms, Dealers, Exc	Bank Polska Kasa Opieki SA	Poland	Commercial Banks, Bank Holding Companies
100	1.1	Placer Dome Inc	Canada	Mining	Getchell Gold Corp	United States	Mining
101	1.1	Gecina	France	Real Estate; Mortgage Bankers and Brokers	Sefimeg(Artemis Immobilier)	France	Real Estate; Mortgage Bankers and Brokers
102	1.1	Dyckerhoff AG	Germany	Stone, Clay, Glass and Concrete Products	Lone Star Industries Inc	United States	Stone, Clay, Glass, and Concrete Products
103	1.1	Grupo Mexicano de Desarrollo	Mexico	Construction Firms	ASARCO Inc	United States	Mining
104	1.1	Schneider SA	France	Electronic and Electrical Equipment	Lexel(A Ahlstrom, NKT Holdings)	Denmark	Electronic and Electrical Equipment

/...

Annex table A.IV.4. **Cross-border M&A deals with values of over $1 billion completed in 1999ᵃ (concluded)**

Rank	Value ($billion)	Acquiring company	Industry of the acquiring company	Home economy	Acquired company	Host economy	Industry of the acquired company
105	1.0	Cap Gemini SA(Sogeti SA)	Prepackaged Software	France	Cap Gemini NV (Cap Gemini SA)	Netherlands	Prepackaged Software
106	1.0	Texas Utilities Australia Pty	Electric, Gas and Water Distribution	Australia	Kinetik Energy/Westar	Australia	Electric, Gas and Water Distribution
107	1.0	Huhtamaki Oy	Food and Kindred Products	Finland	Royal Packaging Inds Van Leer	Netherlands	Paper and Allied Products
108	1.0	JV-Norske,Abitibiti,Hansol	Paper and Allied Products	Republic of Korea	Hansol Paper-Korean Newsprint	Republic of Korea	Paper and Allied Products
109	1.0	Havas SA(Vivendi SA)	Advertising Services	France	Cendant Software Corp	United States	Prepackaged Software

Source: UNCTAD, cross-border M&A database, based on data provided by Thomson Financial Securities Data Company.

ᵃ For the M&A deals whose home economy is identical to the host economy, the ultimate parent economy is different. Therefore, they are considered as cross-border mergers and acquisitions. For details see box IV.4.

ᵇ Involving more than two countries.

Annex table A.IV.5. Modality of financing cross-border M&As, 1987-1999

(Billions of dollars and number of deals)

Year	Total	World Cash-based	Stock swap	Developed countries Cash-based	Stock swap	Developing countries Cash-based	Stock swap	Central and Eastern Europe Cash-based	Stock swap
				Value in billion dollars					
1987	74.5	71.6	1.5	71.0	0.4	0.6	1.1	-	-
1988	115.6	113.2	1.6	110.5	1.6	2.8	-	-	-
1989	140.4	128.3	11.2	123.8	10.7	4.5	0.5	-	-
1990	150.6	137.0	12.6	126.9	6.4	9.9	6.2	0.3	-
1991	80.7	78.0	2.3	71.4	2.3	5.8	-	0.8	-
1992	79.3	76.3	3.0	65.7	2.8	8.0	0.2	2.6	-
1993	83.1	68.7	14.3	55.7	13.4	11.8	0.9	1.2	-
1994	127.1	121.8	5.3	105.6	5.2	14.9	0.1	1.3	-
1995	186.6	172.8	13.8	151.9	12.7	14.9	1.0	5.9	-
1996	227.0	197.2	29.8	161.1	27.7	32.5	2.2	3.6	-
1997	304.8	272.4	32.4	212.5	22.2	54.5	10.1	5.4	0.1
1998	531.6	390.7	140.9	307.0	138.1	78.0	2.8	5.1	-
1999	720.1	458.7	261.4	383.8	260.8	64.0	0.5	9.1	-
				Number of deals					
1987	862	813	8	768	7	45	1	-	-
1988	1 480	1 407	14	1 341	12	65	2	1	-
1989	2 201	2 073	51	1 947	47	117	4	9	-
1990	2 503	2 349	45	2 160	39	174	6	15	-
1991	2 854	2 764	22	2 464	39	235	1	65	-
1992	2 721	2 671	48	2 272	39	270	5	128	-
1993	2 835	2 760	75	2 210	39	408	10	142	2
1994	3 494	3 423	71	2 693	39	569	6	159	2
1995	4 247	4 151	96	3 191	39	688	25	271	2
1996	4 569	4 456	113	3 338	39	855	21	262	2
1997	4 987	4 875	112	3 700	39	927	18	246	2
1998	5 597	5 463	134	4 145	39	1 076	13	238	-
1999	6 233	6 079	154	4 564	39	1 033	9	477	3

Source: UNCTAD, cross-border M&A database, based on data from Thomson Financial Securities Data Company.

Note: The components may not add up to totals due to deals with unknown modalities of financing and deals which cannot be classified by region.

Annex table A.IV.6. Cross-border M&A sales, by region/economy of seller, 1987-1999

(Millions of dollars)

Region/economy	1987	1988	1989	1990	1991	1992	1993	1994	1995	1996	1997	1998	1999
TOTAL WORLD	74 509	115 623	140 389	150 576	80 713	79 280	83 064	127 110	186 593	227 023	304 848	531 648	720 109
Developed countries	72 804	112 749	135 305	134 239	74 057	68 560	69 127	110 819	164 589	188 722	234 748	445 128	644 590
Western Europe	13 209	34 274	48 949	67 370	38 520	45 831	40 598	57 262	79 114	88 512	121 548	194 388	354 205
European Union	12 761	31 012	47 358	62 133	36 676	44 761	38 537	55 280	75 143	81 895	114 591	187 853	344 537
Austria	8	253	32	189	244	107	417	540	609	856	2 259	3 551	385
Belgium	919	793	805	4 469	814	493	2 201	1 026	1 710	8 469	5 945	6 865	17 353
Denmark	-	218	225	496	272	99	590	570	199	459	566	3 802	4 459
Finland	20	80	229	51	463	209	391	550	1 726	1 199	735	4 780	2 556
France	1 426	3 018	3 338	8 183	2 623	9 150	8 497	16 290	7 533	13 575	17 751	16 885	23 077
Germany	1 069	1 300	4 301	6 220	3 407	5 521	2 285	4 468	7 496	11 924	11 856	19 047	41 938
Greece	-	22	-	115	70	413	52	15	50	493	99	21	193
Ireland	36	205	735	595	282	81	1 453	242	587	724	2 282	729	7 485
Italy	621	3 095	3 003	2 165	3 865	3 672	3 754	6 909	4 102	2 764	3 362	4 480	11 039
Luxembourg	50	5	-	531	82	-	254	380	280	506	3 492	35	7 072
Netherlands	1 256	1 182	3 965	1 484	3 490	9 362	4 779	2 789	3 607	3 538	19 052	19 359	38 497
Portugal	9	11	768	213	194	668	356	63	144	793	86	427	211
Spain	938	723	1 593	3 832	5 373	4 668	1 967	3 615	1 257	1 463	4 074	5 700	5 252
Sweden	875	192	1 849	4 489	2 478	2 455	1 844	6 016	9 451	3 863	3 327	11 093	59 618
United Kingdom	5 534	19 917	26 515	29 102	13 020	7 863	9 699	11 807	36 392	31 271	39 706	91 081	125 403
Other Western Europe	448	3 262	1 591	5 237	1 844	1 070	2 061	1 982	3 971	6 617	6 958	6 535	9 668
Gibraltar	-	-	-	-	4	-	-	-	-	9	-	-	8
Guernsey	-	-	-	-	-	-	-	-	-	-	-	-	27
Iceland	-	-	-	-	1	-	-	-	-	4	-	-	-
Jersey	-	-	-	-	-	-	-	-	-	-	-	-	31
Liechtenstein	-	-	-	-	-	-	-	-	-	-	-	-	-
Monaco	-	669	21	-	-	-	-	-	-	-	752	9	277
Norway	10	239	601	668	843	487	1 887	397	271	2 198	2 660	1 182	5 211
Switzerland	438	2 353	969	4 569	997	582	174	1 585	3 692	4 407	3 545	5 344	4 114
North America	57 918	72 641	79 233	60 427	31 884	18 393	22 291	49 093	64 804	78 907	90 217	225 980	257 862
Canada	6 153	8 737	10 412	5 731	3 658	2 554	2 313	4 364	11 567	10 839	8 510	16 432	24 829
United States	51 765	63 904	68 821	54 697	28 226	15 839	19 978	44 730	53 237	68 069	81 707	209 548	233 032
Other developed countries	1 677	5 834	7 123	6 442	3 654	4 337	6 237	4 464	20 672	21 303	22 983	24 761	32 523
Australia	1 545	4 380	4 704	2 545	2 592	2 446	3 191	2 975	17 360	13 099	14 794	14 737	10 452
Israel	-	106	134	44	58	293	18	235	303	541	1 097	1 754	2 870
Japan	27	29	1 612	148	178	230	93	750	541	1 719	3 083	4 022	15 857
New Zealand	89	1 320	674	3 704	815	1 157	1 430	317	1 828	4 839	1 346	2 316	1 780
South Africa	17	-	-	-	10	211	1 506	187	640	1 106	2 664	1 932	1 565

/...

Annex table A.IV.6. **Cross-border M&A sales, by region/economy of seller, 1987-1999 (continued)**

(Millions of dollars)

Region/economy	1987	1988	1989	1990	1991	1992	1993	1994	1995	1996	1997	1998	1999
Developing countries	1 704	2 875	5 057	16 052	5 838	8 119	12 782	14 928	15 966	34 700	64 573	80 755	64 550
Africa	143	-	1 039	485	37	177	301	154	200	700	1 682	675	591
North Africa	143	-	24	-	1	139	242	100	10	211	680	456	363
Algeria	-	-	-	-	1	-	-	-	-	-	-	-	-
Egypt	143	-	24	-	-	131	177	17	10	171	102	48	249
Morocco	-	-	-	-	-	-	64	83	-	40	578	5	113
Sudan	-	-	-	-	-	8	-	-	-	-	-	-	-
Tunisia	-	-	-	-	-	-	-	-	-	-	-	402	-
Other Africa	-	-	1 015	485	36	38	59	54	191	489	1 002	220	229
Botswana	-	-	-	-	-	-	-	-	4	11	4	-	-
Cameroon	-	-	-	-	-	-	-	-	4	0	-	-	-
Cape Verde	-	-	-	-	-	-	-	-	-	-	-	-	83
Central African Republic	-	-	-	-	-	-	4	-	2	1	-	-	1
Congo	-	-	-	-	-	-	-	-	61	14	-	-	-
Congo, Democratic Republic of	-	-	-	-	-	-	-	-	-	89	-	-	-
Côte d'Ivoire	-	-	-	-	-	-	-	-	23	15	194	-	-
Ethiopia	-	-	-	-	-	-	-	-	-	-	-	-	36
Gabon	-	-	-	448	-	-	-	-	-	-	39	-	-
Ghana	-	-	-	-	-	-	-	1	4	48	52	-	39
Guinea	-	-	-	-	-	-	-	-	39	50	-	-	-
Kenya	-	-	15	-	-	-	-	-	-	25	-	-	-
Madagascar	-	-	-	-	-	-	-	-	-	58	0	-	-
Malawi	-	-	1 000	-	-	-	-	-	-	60	-	10	-
Mali	-	-	-	-	-	-	-	-	18	1	-	-	0
Mauritius	-	-	-	-	-	-	-	-	-	-	10	-	-
Mozambique	-	-	-	-	-	-	-	40	14	11	-	13	-
Namibia	-	-	-	-	36	-	-	-	-	-	3	-	-
Nigeria	-	-	-	-	-	-	-	-	-	-	-	12	-
Senegal	-	-	-	-	-	-	-	-	-	-	107	-	66
Sierra Leone	-	-	-	-	-	-	34	-	-	0	-	-	-
Swaziland	-	-	-	37	-	-	-	-	-	-	387	-	-
Uganda	-	-	-	-	-	-	-	-	-	55	29	11	-
United Republic of Tanzania	-	-	-	-	-	-	-	12	2	17	1	23	-
Zambia	-	-	-	-	-	-	21	-	18	27	173	150	2
Zimbabwe	-	-	-	-	-	38	-	1	1	7	2	-	2

/....

Annex table A.IV.6. **Cross-border M&A sales, by region/economy of seller, 1987-1999 (continued)**

(Millions of dollars)

Region/economy	1987	1988	1989	1990	1991	1992	1993	1994	1995	1996	1997	1998	1999
Latin America and the Caribbean	1 305	1 305	1 929	11 494	3 529	4 196	5 110	9 950	8 636	20 508	41 103	63 923	37 166
South America	196	1 148	322	7 319	2 901	2 109	2 840	7 324	6 509	16 910	25 439	46 834	34 271
Argentina	-	60	27	6 274	302	1 164	1 803	1 315	1 869	3 611	4 635	10 396	19 183
Bolivia	-	-	15	26	-	-	-	-	821	273	911	180	233
Brazil	196	287	2	217	158	174	624	367	1 761	6 536	12 064	29 376	9 396
Chile	-	38	260	434	338	517	276	891	717	2 044	2 427	1 595	4 032
Colombia	-	764	-	341	49	31	8	1 248	67	2 399	2 516	1 780	48
Ecuador	-	-	-	-	-	49	-	44	35	105	27	79	214
Guyana	-	-	-	17	7	-	-	-	-	-	1	-	23
Paraguay	-	-	-	-	-	-	-	-	-	27	2	11	-
Peru	-	-	-	-	15	174	62	3 082	945	844	911	162	865
Uruguay	-	-	18	-	-	-	5	40	19	19	-	36	-
Venezuela	-	-	-	11	2 032	-	62	337	278	1 072	1 946	3 220	278
Other Latin America and the Caribbean	1 110	157	1 607	4 176	628	2 088	2 270	2 627	2 127	3 598	15 663	17 089	2 894
Antigua and Barbuda	-	-	-	-	-	-	-	-	-	-	-	24	-
Aruba	-	-	-	-	-	3	-	-	-	-	23	-	-
Bahamas	30	83	27	120	210	915	79	214	2	104	32	28	-
Barbados	-	-	-	-	189	-	-	4	6	64	-	-	-
Belize	-	-	-	-	-	-	-	-	-	-	-	62	-
Bermuda	1 079	-	214	1 296	50	4	52	50	251	1 277	5 601	11 635	890
British Virgin Islands	-	-	-	143	6	-	-	89	412	254	19	4	13
Cayman Islands	-	5	374	170	138	41	-	-	-	245	-	-	122
Costa Rica	-	-	64	3	-	-	1	17	96	27	28	2	73
Cuba	-	-	-	-	-	-	-	-	299	-	300	38	-
Dominican Republic	-	-	-	-	-	-	-	-	0	46	-	28	674
El Salvador	-	-	-	-	-	-	-	-	40	-	41	978	1
Grenada	-	-	-	-	5	-	-	-	-	-	5	-	-
Guatemala	-	-	-	3	3	-	29	1	-	26	30	582	101
Haiti	-	-	-	-	-	-	-	-	-	-	-	2	-
Honduras	-	-	-	-	5	-	5	1	-	-	-	367	-
Jamaica	-	-	-	-	-	-	62	262	-	12	-	34	-
Mexico	1	54	395	2 326	10	961	1 864	1 913	719	1 428	7 927	3 001	784
Netherlands Antilles	-	-	533	8	0	-	-	2	291	-	-	86	-
Nicaragua	-	-	-	-	-	-	-	-	-	23	42	-	11
Panama	-	15	-	-	-	-	6	73	9	14	652	216	219
Puerto Rico	-	-	-	-	-	142	-	-	-	-	-	-	6
Saint Kitts and Nevis	-	-	-	-	-	-	-	-	-	78	-	-	-

/...

Annex table A.IV.6. **Cross-border M&A sales, by region/economy of seller, 1987-1999 (continued)**

(Millions of dollars)

Region/economy	1987	1988	1989	1990	1991	1992	1993	1994	1995	1996	1997	1998	1999
Trinidad and Tobago	-	-	-	-	17	22	177	2	-	-	205	-	-
West Indies	-	-	-	-	-	-	-	-	-	-	760	-	-
Developing Europe	-	-	-	-	62	132	23	86	112	78	238	19	1 437
Croatia	-	-	-	-	-	43	23	45	94	48	61	16	1 167
Malta	-	-	-	-	-	-	-	-	-	-	-	3	251
Slovenia	-	-	-	-	-	88	-	41	18	30	133	-	15
TFYR of Macedonia	-	-	-	-	-	-	-	-	-	-	-	-	4
Former Yugoslavia	-	-	-	-	62	-	-	-	-	-	-	-	-
Yugoslavia	-	-	-	-	-	-	-	-	-	-	45	-	-
Asia	256	1 569	2 089	4 073	2 182	3 614	7 347	4 701	6 950	13 368	21 293	16 097	25 262
West Asia	-	59	60	113	131	203	71	49	222	403	368	82	186
Abu Dhabi	-	-	-	-	-	-	-	-	-	-	-	-	-
Bahrain	-	-	-	-	-	58	4	-	-	-	-	-	30
Jordan	-	-	-	-	-	-	-	-	26	-	-	-	-
Kuwait	-	-	-	-	-	-	6	-	-	-	-	-	-
Lebanon	-	-	-	-	-	-	-	-	-	-	168	11	-
Oman	-	-	-	-	78	-	15	-	-	7	-	-	-
Qatar	-	-	-	-	43	-	12	-	-	-	-	-	-
Saudi Arabia	-	-	2	-	-	24	-	-	8	26	-	-	-
Syrian Arab Republic	-	-	-	-	-	-	-	-	-	-	-	-	3
Turkey	-	59	58	113	9	116	35	49	188	370	144	71	69
United Arab Emirates	-	-	-	-	-	-	-	-	-	-	56	-	84
Yemen	-	-	-	-	-	5	-	-	-	-	-	-	-
Central Asia	-	-	-	-	-	-	9	-	450	3 221	2 340	174	72
Armenia	-	-	-	-	-	-	-	-	-	-	-	173	30
Azerbaijan	-	-	-	-	-	-	-	-	-	1	-	-	-
Georgia	-	-	-	-	-	-	-	-	-	-	3	1	41
Kazakhstan	-	-	-	-	-	-	9	-	450	3 216	2 337	-	1
Uzbekistan	-	-	-	-	-	-	-	-	-	4	-	-	-
South, East and South-East Asia	256	1 510	2 029	3 960	2 051	3 411	7 267	4 652	6 278	9 745	18 586	15 842	25 003
Bangladesh	-	-	-	-	-	-	-	-	-	-	-	33	-
Brunei Darussalam	-	-	-	-	-	-	2	-	-	-	-	-	-
Cambodia	-	-	-	-	-	-	-	-	-	0	1	-	-
China	-	-	-	8	125	221	561	715	403	1 906	1 856	798	2 155
Hong Kong, China	181	1 046	826	2 620	568	1 674	5 308	1 602	1 703	3 267	7 330	938	3 152
India	-	-	-	5	-	35	96	385	276	206	1 520	361	776

/....

World Investment Report 2000:   Cross-border Mergers and Acquisitions and Development

Annex table A.IV.6. Cross-border M&A sales, by region/economy of seller, 1987-1999 (concluded)

(Millions of dollars)

Region/economy	1987	1988	1989	1990	1991	1992	1993	1994	1995	1996	1997	1998	1999
Indonesia	29	100	150	-	149	233	169	206	809	530	332	683	1 112
Lao People's Dem. Rep.	-	-	-	-	-	-	10	-	-	-	-	-	-
Macau	-	-	-	-	29	-	-	-	-	-	-	-	-
Malaysia	-	20	701	86	128	46	518	443	98	768	351	1 096	1 101
Mongolia	-	-	-	-	-	-	-	1	-	-	-	-	-
Myanmar	-	-	-	-	-	-	10	-	9	-	260	-	-
Nepal	-	-	-	-	-	-	2	-	13	-	-	-	-
Pakistan	-	-	-	1	-	22	5	-	-	-	-	-	-
Philippines	25	45	161	15	63	404	136	828	1 208	1 124	80	2 259	1 637
Republic of Korea	-	-	68	-	673	0	2	1	192	564	836	3 973	9 057
Singapore	21	262	114	1 143	237	276	362	355	1 238	593	294	468	2 060
Sri Lanka	-	-	-	1	-	-	30	10	126	35	275	96	18
Taiwan Province of China	-	38	9	11	-	3	16	16	42	50	601	24	2 070
Thailand	-	-	-	70	79	498	42	89	161	234	633	3 209	1 812
Viet Nam	-	-	-	-	-	-	-	2	1	6	63	-	52
The Pacific	-	-	-	-	28	-	2	37	67	46	257	41	95
Fiji	-	-	-	-	-	-	-	-	-	5	-	-	5
French Polynesia	-	-	-	-	-	-	-	-	-	2	-	-	-
Marshall Islands	-	-	-	-	-	-	-	-	16	-	-	-	-
Papua New Guinea	-	-	-	-	28	-	2	36	51	39	257	41	90
Solomon Islands	-	-	-	-	-	-	-	1	-	-	-	-	-
Central and Eastern Europe	-	-	27	285	818	2 602	1 155	1 333	5 938	3 601	5 526	5 101	9 124
Albania	-	-	-	-	-	-	-	-	1	-	-	-	5
Bulgaria	-	-	-	-	-	-	20	90	32	71	497	61	1 144
Czech Republic	-	-	-	-	-	-	164	408	2 364	507	671	362	2 494
Former Czechoslovakia	-	-	-	-	477	780	-	-	-	-	-	-	-
Estonia	-	-	-	-	-	-	-	-	28	23	64	149	139
Hungary	-	-	24	226	267	392	382	139	2 106	1 594	298	612	546
Latvia	-	-	-	-	-	-	-	3	23	57	63	11	23
Lithuania	-	-	-	-	-	-	-	9	-	-	12	632	424
Poland	-	-	4	-	74	1 396	197	357	983	993	808	1 789	3 561
Republic of Moldova	-	-	-	-	-	-	-	-	-	-	2	-	-
Romania	-	-	-	-	-	-	-	181	229	94	391	1 284	437
Russian Federation	-	-	-	59	-	33	309	63	100	95	2 681	147	184
Slovakia	-	-	-	-	-	-	21	83	4	138	38	54	41
Ukraine	-	-	-	-	-	-	-	-	66	30	1	0	127
Multinational[a]	-	-	-	-	-	-	-	30	100	-	-	665	1 846

Source: UNCTAD, cross-border M&A database, based on data provided by Thomson Financial Securities Data Company.

[a] Involving sellers in more than two countries.

Annex table A.IV.7. Cross-border M&A purchases, by region/economy of purchaser, 1987-1999

(Millions of dollars)

Region/economy	1987	1988	1989	1990	1991	1992	1993	1994	1995	1996	1997	1998	1999
TOTAL WORLD	74 509	115 623	140 389	150 576	80 713	79 280	83 064	127 110	186 593	227 023	304 848	531 648	720 109
Developed countries	71 874	113 413	135 786	143 216	77 635	74 431	72 498	116 597	173 732	198 257	272 042	511 430	677 296
Western Europe	33 068	49 690	74 265	92 567	42 473	49 753	43 010	75 943	92 539	110 628	154 035	324 658	519 490
European Union	32 617	40 141	71 365	86 525	39 676	44 391	40 531	63 857	81 417	96 674	142 108	284 373	497 709
Austria	-	-	21	236	208	62	169	23	157	4	242	302	1 675
Belgium	20	188	309	813	222	625	181	3 107	4 611	3 029	2 053	2 225	13 294
Denmark	16	63	261	767	573	258	372	172	152	638	1 492	1 250	4 378
Finland	58	172	979	1 136	568	8	98	417	471	1 464	1 847	7 333	2 922
France	3 244	5 486	17 594	21 828	10 380	12 389	6 596	6 717	8 939	14 755	21 153	30 926	82 951
Germany	1 634	1 857	3 468	6 795	6 894	4 409	4 412	7 608	18 509	17 984	13 190	66 728	84 421
Greece	-	-	100	3	16	19	127	21	-	2	2 018	1 439	249
Ireland	67	548	1 174	730	390	358	457	1 447	1 166	2 265	1 826	3 196	2 560
Italy	3 327	1 373	1 961	5 314	816	5 167	816	1 622	4 689	1 627	4 196	15 200	12 792
Luxembourg	59	80	-	734	1 023	415	1 555	244	51	1 037	973	891	2 515
Netherlands	2 716	2 350	3 292	5 619	4 251	5 304	2 848	8 714	6 811	12 148	18 472	24 280	48 429
Portugal	-	-	14	17	181	502	14	144	329	96	612	4 522	1 285
Spain	212	582	1 318	4 087	2 773	983	1 053	3 828	460	3 458	8 038	15 031	23 070
Sweden	1 645	3 104	2 645	12 572	2 882	1 813	1 923	3 118	5 432	2 058	7 625	15 952	7 627
United Kingdom	19 621	24 339	38 229	25 873	8 501	12 080	19 911	26 675	29 641	36 109	58 371	95 099	209 543
Other Western Europe	452	9 549	2 900	6 043	2 797	5 362	2 478	12 086	11 122	13 954	11 928	40 285	21 781
Gibraltar	-	-	-	-	3	-	-	-	-	-	-	-	-
Iceland	-	-	-	-	-	7	-	-	-	-	-	-	7
Jersey	-	-	-	-	-	-	-	-	-	-	-	-	8
Liechtenstein	-	-	-	160	-	-	-	62	10	-	142	-	-
Monaco	-	-	-	-	35	113	-	4	-	-	-	-	-
Norway	53	19	126	1 380	1 301	270	143	643	1 276	3 956	1 212	1 170	962
Switzerland	399	9 530	2 774	4 503	1 458	4 973	2 336	11 378	9 836	9 998	10 574	39 115	20 804
North America	32 138	38 577	47 862	30 766	20 702	17 190	25 534	33 610	69 833	69 501	99 709	173 039	131 131
Canada	3 727	14 397	9 002	3 139	4 106	2 155	4 129	5 079	12 491	8 757	18 840	35 618	18 705
United States	28 412	24 181	38 860	27 627	16 596	15 035	21 405	28 531	57 343	60 744	80 869	137 421	112 426
Other developed countries	6 668	25 146	13 659	19 883	14 461	7 488	3 955	7 044	11 360	18 128	18 297	13 733	26 675
Australia	2 513	9 355	5 561	3 806	1 472	676	1 852	1 602	6 145	9 283	11 745	8 147	9 258
Israel	-	-	-	28	28	61	393	143	106	484	254	791	427
Japan	3 156	13 514	7 525	14 048	11 877	4 392	1 106	1 058	3 943	5 660	2 747	1 284	9 792
New Zealand	685	2 253	569	1 854	883	923	252	44	573	1 180	785	997	1 381
South Africa	315	24	5	146	201	1 436	352	4 196	593	1 522	2 766	2 514	5 817

/...

Annex table A.IV.7. **Cross-border M&A purchases, by region/economy of purchaser, 1987-1999 (continued)**

(Millions of dollars)

Region/economy	1987	1988	1989	1990	1991	1992	1993	1994	1995	1996	1997	1998	1999
Developing countries	2 614	2 180	3 990	7 035	3 057	4 827	10 439	10 164	12 779	28 127	32 544	19 204	41 245
Africa	100	-	-	-	229	309	54	25	52	625	34	163	414
North Africa	-	-	-	-	-	309	54	9	11	8	-	3	8
Egypt	-	-	-	-	-	-	18	-	-	-	-	-	8
Libyan Arab Jamahiriya	-	-	-	-	-	309	-	5	-	-	-	3	-
Morocco	-	-	-	-	-	-	36	4	-	8	-	-	-
Tunisia	-	-	-	-	-	-	-	-	11	-	-	-	-
Other Africa	100	-	-	-	229	-	-	16	41	618	34	160	406
Botswana	-	-	-	-	-	-	-	-	4	-	-	-	-
Central African Republic	-	-	-	-	-	-	-	-	-	63	-	-	-
Gabon	-	-	-	-	229	-	-	-	-	-	-	-	-
Ghana	-	-	-	-	-	-	-	-	35	506	-	137	-
Kenya	100	-	-	-	-	-	-	-	-	-	-	-	-
Liberia	-	-	-	-	-	-	-	-	-	15	-	-	-
Mauritius	-	-	-	-	-	-	-	-	-	4	34	7	-
Namibia	-	-	-	-	-	-	-	-	-	11	-	-	-
Nigeria	-	-	-	-	-	-	-	-	2	-	-	-	-
Uganda	-	-	-	-	-	-	-	-	-	-	-	-	406
Zambia	-	-	-	-	-	-	-	-	-	15	-	-	-
Zimbabwe	-	-	-	-	-	-	-	16	-	4	-	16	-
Latin America and the Caribbean	142	100	992	1 597	387	1 895	2 507	3 653	3 951	8 354	10 720	12 640	24 939
South America	-	10	91	130	269	594	1 795	682	3 405	5 939	6 038	9 510	3 202
Argentina	-	-	-	10	181	-	71	62	1 984	321	1 170	3 545	860
Bolivia	-	-	-	-	-	-	-	-	-	0	-	-	-
Brazil	-	2	2	-	45	63	439	158	379	1 167	2 357	3 517	1 901
Chile	-	-	-	-	-	443	828	293	794	3 827	1 497	591	206
Colombia	-	-	-	-	-	-	11	10	91	272	157	436	4
Ecuador	-	-	-	-	-	-	-	22	50	45	-	-	-
Peru	-	-	-	-	-	-	-	7	62	237	44	47	222
Suriname	-	-	-	-	2	-	-	-	-	-	-	-	-
Uruguay	-	-	-	-	-	8	-	120	3	-	-	25	-
Venezuela	-	7	89	120	41	80	446	10	42	71	813	1 348	10
Other Latin America and the Caribbean	142	91	901	1 467	118	1 300	712	2 971	546	2 415	4 682	3 130	21 737
Bahamas	-	83	-	1	-	17	-	9	142	344	23	51	460
Barbados	-	-	-	-	-	-	-	-	-	-	15	2	-
Belize	-	-	-	-	-	-	55	1	25	-	-	63	319
Bermuda	9	-	24	483	115	130	112	189	17	703	1 189	2 139	18 815

/...

Annex table A.IV.7. **Cross-border M&A purchases, by region/economy of purchaser, 1987-1999 (continued)**

(Millions of dollars)

Region/economy	1987	1988	1989	1990	1991	1992	1993	1994	1995	1996	1997	1998	1999
British Virgin Islands	2	-	-	-	-	-	4	44	62	260	56	-	22
Cayman Islands	-	-	-	-	-	-	24	530	-	207	99	99	81
Costa Rica	-	-	-	-	-	-	-	-	2	7	3	-	-
Cuba	-	-	-	-	-	-	-	8	-	-	-	-	-
Dominican Republic	-	-	-	-	-	-	-	-	-	-	48	-	109
Guatemala	-	-	-	-	-	-	-	-	-	-	-	-	-
Jamaica	-	-	-	16	-	10	-	-	4	-	-	-	-
Mexico	-	-	837	680	3	888	309	2 190	196	867	3 154	673	1 839
Netherlands Antilles	132	8	16	288	-	11	33	-	99	7	7	-	-
Panama	-	-	24	-	-	245	175	-	-	17	89	100	92
Trinidad and Tobago	-	-	-	-	-	-	7	-	-	3	100	5	-
Developing Europe													
Croatia	-	-	-	-	-	-	7	-	-	1	100	1	12
Malta	-	-	-	-	-	-	7	-	-	-	0	1	3
Slovenia	-	-	-	-	-	-	-	-	-	-	-	-	5
TFYR of Macedonia	-	-	-	-	-	-	-	-	-	2	-	-	4
Asia	2 372	2 080	2 998	5 438	2 441	2 624	7 843	6 486	8 755	19 136	21 690	6 399	15 875
West Asia	170	124	253	2 112	113	105	1 013	1 199	1 697	1 589	3 797	399	5 254
Abu Dhabi	-	-	-	528	-	-	-	-	-	-	-	-	-
Bahrain	-	-	168	1 537	-	-	811	300	-	-	1 472	45	33
Cyprus	-	-	-	-	-	-	-	-	-	41	1 881	-	60
Iran, Islamic Republic of	-	-	-	-	-	-	-	-	-	-	-	-	4 382
Kuwait	170	-	83	-	112	-	-	-	4	648	-	-	109
Lebanon	-	-	-	-	-	-	21	-	3	0	58	-	-
Oman	-	-	-	-	-	-	-	-	-	42	8	55	-
Qatar	-	-	-	-	-	-	-	-	-	-	-	-	-
Saudi Arabia	-	-	-	-	-	100	182	630	1 671	350	334	217	3
Turkey	-	-	2	-	-	-	-	11	19	356	43	4	90
United Arab Emirates	-	124	-	48	1	-	-	257	-	153	2	77	540
Yemen	-	-	-	-	-	5	-	-	-	-	-	-	37
Central Asia	-	-	-	-	-	-	-	-	450	-	-	-	-
Kazakhstan	-	-	-	-	-	-	-	-	450	-	-	-	-
South, East and South-East Asia	2 202	1 956	2 745	3 325	2 329	2 518	6 830	5 287	6 608	17 547	17 893	6 001	10 621
Afghanistan	-	-	-	-	-	-	-	-	-	-	-	-	-
Bangladesh	-	-	-	-	-	13	-	-	12	-	-	-	-
Brunei Darussalam	-	-	-	-	-	-	202	-	31	189	-	-	-
China	-	17	202	60	3	573	485	307	249	451	799	1 276	497

/...

Annex table A.IV.7. **Cross-border M&A purchases, by region/economy of purchaser, 1987-1999 (concluded)**

(Millions of dollars)

Region/economy	1987	1988	1989	1990	1991	1992	1993	1994	1995	1996	1997	1998	1999
Hong Kong, China	2 166	1 649	773	1 198	1 342	1 263	4 113	2 267	2 299	2 912	8 402	2 201	1 822
India	-	22	11	-	1	3	219	109	29	80	1 287	11	21
Indonesia	-	260	-	49	3	16	50	32	163	218	676	39	277
Malaysia	-	-	27	144	149	148	774	812	1 122	9 635	894	1 059	1 292
Philippines	-	-	-	-	14	-	25	42	153	190	54	1	584
Republic of Korea	7	-	235	33	187	72	74	500	1 392	1 659	2 379	187	1 718
Singapore	7	8	764	438	570	294	849	1 174	892	2 018	2 888	530	4 048
Sri Lanka	-	-	-	-	-	-	-	2	-	-	-	26	8
Taiwan Province of China	29	-	464	1 385	-	131	-	30	122	4	433	628	230
Thailand	-	-	269	18	59	1	38	12	144	180	55	43	115
Viet Nam	-	-	-	-	-	6	-	1	-	11	27	-	10
The Pacific	-	-	-	-	-	-	28	-	22	8	-	-	5
Fiji	-	-	-	-	-	-	-	-	-	-	-	-	5
Nauru	-	-	-	-	-	-	28	-	-	-	-	-	-
Papua New Guinea	-	-	-	-	-	-	-	-	13	8	-	-	-
Vanuatu	-	-	-	-	-	-	-	-	9	-	-	-	-
Central and Eastern Europe	8	-	6	-	14	22	113	329	59	501	175	1 007	1 550
Bulgaria	8	-	-	-	-	-	-	-	-	3	60	-	800
Czech Republic	-	-	6	-	-	-	19	51	48	176	60	142	6
Former Czechoslovakia	-	-	-	-	-	4	-	-	-	-	-	-	-
Estonia	-	-	-	-	-	-	-	22	-	15	1	12	7
Hungary	-	-	-	-	-	-	62	-	2	-	6	64	121
Latvia	-	-	-	-	-	-	18	-	-	-	-	-	-
Lithuania	-	-	-	-	-	-	-	-	-	-	-	-	2
Poland	-	-	-	-	14	-	8	11	8	23	45	465	135
Romania	-	-	-	-	-	-	-	-	-	-	0	-	-
Russian Federation	-	-	-	-	-	18	6	245	-	242	2	301	54
Slovakia	-	-	-	-	-	-	-	1	2	42	1	-	425
Ukraine	-	-	-	-	-	-	-	-	-	-	-	23	1
Unspecified	13	30	606	325	4	-	-	10	-	-	4	-	-
Multinational[a]	-	-	-	-	3	-	14	10	23	139	83	8	19

Source: UNCTAD, cross-border M&A database, based on data provided by Thomson Financial Securities Data Company.

[a] Involving purchasers from more than two economies.

Annex table A.IV.8. **M&As and greenfield investment in foreign affiliates operating in the United States,**

1980-1998

Year	Expenditures (billion dollars)				Number			
	Total	M&As	Greenfield	Share of M&As	Total	M&As	Greenfield	Share of M&As
1980	12.2	9.0	3.2	73.7	1659	721	938	43.5
1981	23.2	18.2	5.1	78.2	1332	462	870	34.7
1982	10.8	6.6	4.3	60.7	1108	395	713	35.6
1983	8.1	4.8	3.2	59.9	775	299	476	38.6
1984	15.2	11.8	3.4	77.9	764	315	449	41.2
1985	23.1	20.1	3.0	86.9	753	390	363	51.8
1986	39.2	31.4	7.7	80.3	1040	555	485	53.4
1987	40.3	33.9	6.4	84.2	978	543	435	55.5
1988	72.7	64.9	7.8	89.2	1424	869	555	61.0
1989	71.2	59.7	11.5	83.9	1580	837	743	53.0
1990	65.9	55.3	10.6	83.9	1617	839	778	51.9
1991	25.5	17.8	7.7	69.7	1091	561	530	51.4
1992	15.3	10.6	4.7	69.2	941	463	478	49.2
1993	26.2	21.8	4.5	83.0	980	554	426	56.5
1994	45.6	38.8	6.9	84.9	1036	605	431	58.4
1995	57.2	47.2	10.0	82.5	1124	644	480	57.3
1996	79.9	68.7	11.2	86.0	1155	686	469	59.4
1997	69.7	60.7	9.0	87.1	1112	640	673	57.6
1998[a]	201.0	180.7	20.3	89.9	1087	673	414	61.9

Source: UNCTAD, based on data provided in United States, Department of Commerce, various issues a, b.

[a] Preliminary.

Note: Investment expenditures include funds raised in local as well as international markets. For details, see box IV.3.

Annex table A.IV.9. Cross-border M&As, by sector and industry of seller, 1987-1999

(Millions of dollars)

Sector/industry	1987	1988	1989	1990	1991	1992	1993	1994	1995	1996	1997	1998	1999
Total	**74 509**	**115 623**	**140 389**	**150 576**	**80 713**	**79 280**	**83 064**	**127 110**	**186 593**	**227 023**	**304 848**	**531 648**	**720 109**
Primary	**10 795**	**3 911**	**1 941**	**5 170**	**1 164**	**3 637**	**4 201**	**5 517**	**8 499**	**7 935**	**8 725**	**10 599**	**9 417**
Agriculture, hunting, forestry, and fishing	343	1 809	225	221	548	301	406	950	1 019	498	2 098	6 673	593
Mining, quarrying and petroleum	10 452	2 102	1 717	4 949	617	3 336	3 795	4 568	7 480	7 437	6 628	3 926	8 824
Manufacturing	**42 393**	**73 727**	**89 596**	**75 495**	**36 176**	**43 222**	**43 204**	**69 321**	**84 462**	**88 522**	**121 379**	**263 206**	**275 148**
Food, beverages and tobacco	3 803	14 462	8 719	12 676	5 127	9 398	7 751	13 528	18 108	6 558	22 053	17 001	26 404
Textiles, clothing and leather	617	812	1 720	1 281	731	760	1 173	1 431	2 039	849	1 732	1 632	4 297
Wood and wood products	2 013	1 793	9 176	7 765	2 714	1 588	2 031	4 262	4 855	5 725	6 854	7 237	10 650
Publishing, printing, and reproduction of recorded media	1 196	11 741	6 544	2 305	353	5 192	1 183	2 747	1 341	10 853	2 607	12 798	9 564
Coke, petroleum and nuclear fuel	3 980	17 868	9 151	6 480	5 676	1 596	1 479	4 216	5 644	13 965	11 315	67 280	29 662
Chemicals and chemical products	16 836	5 008	18 368	12 275	5 773	5 581	11 393	20 061	26 984	15 430	35 395	31 806	86 489
Rubber and plastic products	1 696	3 620	1 387	2 745	574	228	265	997	4 313	3 943	2 306	2 264	3 106
Non-metallic mineral products	1 249	2 452	3 887	5 630	1 113	5 410	2 204	5 201	2 726	2 840	6 153	8 100	10 974
Metal and metal products	1 459	1 606	6 399	4 426	2 246	2 534	2 252	2 743	2 515	8 728	9 853	8 376	9 502
Machinery and equipment	832	2 878	2 078	1 750	1 140	1 087	1 661	3 312	5 103	4 301	7 546	8 918	21 003
Electrical and electronic equipment	7 135	6 998	12 771	6 114	8 361	6 198	3 895	3 432	5 581	7 573	7 897	35 819	38 003
Precision instruments	1 056	3 596	2 626	3 992	1 112	1 080	4 495	1 882	2 023	3 300	3 322	9 251	6 830
Motor vehicles and other transport equipment	315	889	5 215	7 390	995	2 211	2 743	4 988	2 657	4 150	4 189	50 767	17 937
Other manufacturing	208	4	1 556	666	261	360	680	522	575	308	158	1 958	729
Tertiary	**21 321**	**37 986**	**48 851**	**69 911**	**43 297**	**32 384**	**35 649**	**52 270**	**93 632**	**130 232**	**174 744**	**257 843**	**435 443**
Electric, gas, and water	61	116	1 028	609	1 072	1 847	1 783	2 510	12 240	21 274	29 620	32 249	48 694
Construction	416	295	813	533	279	651	331	838	1 738	4 410	602	1 434	3 083
Trade	4 319	10 013	12 377	9 095	7 904	5 703	7 537	8 753	10 159	27 928	21 664	27 332	36 388
Hotels and restaurants	2 304	6 829	3 316	7 263	1 293	1 408	1 412	2 335	3 247	2 416	4 445	10 332	4 535
Transport, storage and communications	309	2 182	3 578	14 460	3 757	3 035	6 559	13 540	8 225	17 523	17 736	51 445	167 776
Finance	7 360	14 471	14 616	21 722	14 188	13 178	12 168	10 568	31 059	36 693	50 836	83 432	111 761
Business services	6 237	3 009	5 264	11 831	5 100	3 808	3 664	8 406	9 715	13 154	26 480	42 497	47 743
Public administration and defence	-	-	-	-	-	-	-	-	605	-	111	395	1 770
Education	-	-	7	5	33	-	421	18	-	4	179	42	69
Health and social services	-	86	460	469	84	237	261	2 463	946	336	3 396	641	377
Community, social and personal service activities	315	984	7 363	3 858	9 554	2 474	1 404	2 319	12 110	6 494	19 656	7 976	13 247
Other services	-	3	30	66	33	44	110	520	3 588	-	19	69	-
Unknown[a]	-	-	-	-	76	37	10	1	-	334	-	-	102

Source : UNCTAD, cross-border M&A database, based on data provided by Thomson Financial Securities Data Company.

a Includes non-classified establishments.

Annex table A.IV.10. Cross-border M&As, by sector and industry of purchaser, 1987-1999

(Millions of dollars)

Sector/industry	1987	1988	1989	1990	1991	1992	1993	1994	1995	1996	1997	1998	1999
Total	**74 509**	**115 623**	**140 389**	**150 576**	**80 713**	**79 280**	**83 064**	**127 110**	**186 593**	**227 023**	**304 848**	**531 648**	**720 109**
Primary	**1 425**	**4 398**	**2 976**	**2 131**	**1 556**	**2 978**	**4 155**	**5 032**	**7 951**	**5 684**	**7 150**	**5 455**	**9 544**
Agriculture, hunting, forestry, and fishing	846	2 078	1 466	47	471	204	65	154	182	962	1 541	1 497	235
Mining, quarrying and petroleum	579	2 320	1 511	2 084	1 085	2 775	4 090	4 878	7 769	4 723	5 609	3 958	9 309
Manufacturing	**50 308**	**71 747**	**95 149**	**79 908**	**44 985**	**35 287**	**36 837**	**72 549**	**93 784**	**88 821**	**133 202**	**257 220**	**309 032**
Food, beverages and tobacco	4 454	19 774	15 484	13 523	5 212	6 383	7 668	7 872	22 546	9 684	21 439	16 922	30 486
Textiles, clothing and leather	259	608	1 636	3 363	1 401	406	3 767	332	1 569	778	1 254	3 062	1 986
Wood and wood products	1 374	3 115	5 637	6 717	2 244	1 743	2 933	2 483	6 466	3 143	6 157	13 131	9 040
Publishing, printing, and reproduction of recorded media	1 426	8 951	6 518	2 363	689	5 022	1 998	4 866	2 332	7 829	6 774	12 050	12 663
Coke, petroleum and nuclear fuel	12 624	15 360	9 384	7 051	6 199	1 442	2 243	3 499	6 679	12 994	11 860	67 665	28 260
Chemicals and chemical products	15 405	4 332	19 335	15 260	4 043	5 142	4 605	31 473	28 186	18 555	38 664	34 822	78 532
Rubber and plastic products	1 169	3 528	2 609	1 904	411	710	387	176	4 852	659	2 363	2 790	1 171
Non-metallic mineral products	2 126	1 865	2 983	6 183	911	3 939	2 404	5 232	2 740	4 585	6 965	8 823	11 229
Metal and metal products	1 654	2 729	5 992	3 076	1 874	2 308	2 046	2 475	1 472	13 395	8 512	7 947	51 157
Machinery and equipment	2 451	2 288	2 567	1 906	1 171	671	1 239	2 416	3 760	2 463	4 767	4 553	14 799
Electrical and electronic equipment	5 737	6 474	17 062	7 190	19 346	5 057	4 608	4 822	7 576	6 660	9 093	29 062	39 662
Precision instruments	920	1 251	1 511	2 861	445	619	1 415	1 135	2 809	3 033	4 757	7 209	3 912
Motor vehicles and other transport equipment	496	1 470	4 357	8 369	928	1 633	1 437	5 271	2 267	4 411	5 072	48 904	24 220
Other manufacturing	214	3	74	143	113	214	88	497	528	633	5 527	280	1 916
Tertiary	**22 776**	**39 221**	**42 264**	**68 423**	**33 985**	**40 965**	**42 028**	**49 519**	**84 824**	**132 414**	**164 457**	**268 486**	**401 520**
Electric, gas, and water	66	1 034	771	332	1 072	1 012	1 250	830	10 466	16 616	18 787	27 527	55 110
Construction	882	2 740	1 181	257	695	316	177	1 350	1 160	6 955	2 546	1 336	3 006
Trade	3 123	4 109	4 356	6 205	3 739	2 870	6 186	5 636	8 854	15 176	16 515	19 624	17 473
Hotels and restaurants	331	3 561	1 534	3 066	340	323	569	997	3 402	1 713	2 482	2 799	3 343
Transport, storage and communications	560	1 062	5 004	4 785	1 367	1 596	4 048	10 480	6 085	11 424	14 735	30 165	118 759
Finance	11 183	13 218	23 402	43 671	22 395	30 406	24 589	24 268	45 368	61 304	82 616	142 066	167 220
Business services	5 600	9 888	4 949	6 377	3 100	3 298	3 532	3 972	4 843	17 084	14 721	22 889	28 235
Public administration and defence	103	1 952	13	667	-	-	81	0	31	1	102	-	668
Education	-	-	216	-	4	-	420	-	-	-	98	30	56
Health and social services	-	14	155	530	41	221	203	154	263	265	321	738	21
Community, social and personal service activities	928	1 640	678	2 469	1 206	835	906	1 332	3 366	1 857	11 000	19 887	7 629
Other services	-	3	5	66	27	88	69	500	986	20	534	1 426	2
Unknown[a]	-	258	-	114	187	50	45	10	34	104	38	488	14

Source : UNCTAD, cross-border M&A database, based on data provided by Thomson Financial Securities Data Company.

a Includes non-classified establishments.

Annex table A.IV.11. Sales of cross-border M&As in the United States, by sector and industry, 1987-1999

(Millions of dollars)

Sector/industry	1987	1988	1989	1990	1991	1992	1993	1994	1995	1996	1997	1998	1999
Primary	**10 383**	**1 661**	**665**	**3 741**	**234**	**1 617**	**1 485**	**1 178**	**1 492**	**3 121**	**2 163**	**1 140**	**3 792**
Agriculture, hunting, forestry, and fishing	-	1 450	47	-	127	38	78	384	34	357	240	215	464
Mining, quarrying and petroleum	10 383	211	618	3 741	107	1 579	1 407	794	1 458	2 764	1 923	925	3 328
Secondary	**30 151**	**38 184**	**40 625**	**28 791**	**9 694**	**6 745**	**12 618**	**24 652**	**29 857**	**27 632**	**27 898**	**148 982**	**62 571**
Food, beverages and tobacco	1 921	3 422	1 215	2 212	839	502	1 334	5 162	6 635	609	1 452	1 181	1 366
Textiles, clothing and leather	511	450	881	580	187	26	230	224	1 459	82	24	451	94
Wood and wood products	239	667	2 009	536	50	3	549	1 606	1 294	799	2 004	946	1 218
Publishing, printing, and reproduction of recorded media	481	10 504	3 736	1 384	109	303	753	1 163	195	8 459	1 403	10 445	7 064
Coke, petroleum and nuclear fuel	1 177	5 485	2 627	2 091	599	326	641	476	2 917	489	2 009	53 859	595
Chemicals and chemical products	14 162	3 446	14 502	8 977	2 026	2 250	5 959	11 388	9 789	5 626	11 361	5 974	12 312
Rubber and plastic products	1 549	2 906	1 022	1 963	356	66	121	138	344	2 725	992	191	682
Non-metallic mineral products	728	1 622	1 000	3 775	444	1 400	243	191	1 137	323	1 083	1 578	3 117
Metal and metal products	813	534	5 029	997	469	440	124	778	462	1 204	817	2 255	2 374
Machinery and equipment	792	1 868	1 450	486	263	175	549	1 053	1 223	2 222	1 795	5 245	14 681
Electrical and electronic equipment	6 437	3 626	3 582	3 551	3 429	327	1 758	762	2 502	2 550	3 005	18 020	13 839
Precision instruments	1 047	3 396	2 198	1 601	748	771	295	1 327	1 040	818	517	4 940	2 769
Motor vehicles and other transport equipment	161	258	973	357	170	85	-	382	797	1 674	1 399	43 738	2 412
Other manufacturing	135	-	402	282	7	71	62	3	64	53	39	158	49
Tertiary	**11 231**	**24 059**	**27 531**	**22 165**	**18 298**	**7 477**	**5 876**	**18 900**	**21 888**	**36 987**	**51 646**	**59 426**	**166 625**
Electric, gas, and water	-	-	300	191	-	7	14	47	7	589	120	2 924	14 367
Construction	23	119	596	76	15	175	158	536	27	253	132	183	1 619
Trade	2 376	8 812	9 592	4 189	1 161	1 150	1 295	5 616	1 488	13 200	9 035	11 623	8 995
Hotels and restaurants	2 142	2 518	1 663	5 321	281	102	236	246	681	793	1 570	2 031	1 850
Transport, storage and communications	193	1 166	1 604	425	92	89	528	3 862	401	4 447	2 142	10 946	77 905
Finance	2 698	9 581	4 170	4 650	7 411	3 654	1 410	2 184	4 957	14 177	17 528	14 123	42 542
Business services	3 582	1 065	3 148	3 759	936	253	1 555	3 430	3 480	2 843	8 394	16 741	14 413
Public administration and defence	-	-	-	-	-	-	-	-	-	-	26	-	1 100
Education	-	-	-	-	3	-	421	18	-	1	114	-	9
Health and social services	-	86	338	51	53	92	48	2 321	819	270	2 373	66	53
Community, social and personal service activities	217	713	6 096	3 437	8 325	1 932	212	610	7 349	416	10 214	790	3 774
Other services	-	-	25	66	21	24	-	30	2 680	-	-	-	-
Total	**51 765**	**63 904**	**68 821**	**54 697**	**28 226**	**15 839**	**19 978**	**44 730**	**53 237**	**68 069**	**81 707**	**209 548**	**233 032**

Source: UNCTAD, cross-border M&A database, based on data provided by Thomson Financial Securities Data Company.

Note: Data are based on information on the United States as a seller country. Totals include amounts which cannot be allocated by sector/industry.

Annex table A.IV.12. Sales of cross-border M&As in the European Union, by sector and industry, 1987-1999

(Millions of dollars)

Sector/industry	1987	1988	1989	1990	1991	1992	1993	1994	1995	1996	1997	1998	1999
Primary	**155**	**750**	**153**	**544**	**162**	**157**	**181**	**357**	**882**	**1 219**	**374**	**5 642**	**3 564**
Agriculture, hunting, forestry, and fishing	155	-	11	-	75	67	53	120	67	22	86	5 486	69
Mining, quarrying and petroleum	-	750	143	544	88	90	129	237	815	1 197	288	156	3 494
Secondary	**7 110**	**22 181**	**30 441**	**34 364**	**18 975**	**28 382**	**21 370**	**34 712**	**32 207**	**27 717**	**56 940**	**57 306**	**151 043**
Food, beverages and tobacco	1 165	9 891	4 972	6 409	3 073	6 945	2 060	6 210	4 708	3 109	9 275	10 210	21 894
Textiles, clothing and leather	106	322	816	580	303	677	825	1 142	511	608	1 488	614	4 012
Wood and wood products	1 192	994	3 501	6 449	2 188	1 040	397	2 180	1 160	1 591	3 274	2 024	4 267
Publishing, printing, and reproduction of recorded media	612	888	2 674	644	209	4 851	385	1 354	871	1 682	906	2 049	2 151
Coke, petroleum and nuclear fuel	112	5 234	245	2 353	2 808	578	382	2 265	1 261	3 360	2 623	1 993	6 063
Chemicals and chemical products	2 383	1 128	2 988	1 646	2 580	2 917	3 719	8 181	15 094	2 886	20 081	9 799	70 321
Rubber and plastic products	147	272	150	655	146	161	56	355	176	926	538	369	2 292
Non-metallic mineral products	165	770	729	1 685	452	3 453	1 782	4 045	1 398	492	3 496	971	5 290
Metal and metal products	395	494	832	2 907	786	1 211	1 848	1 115	522	6 354	4 978	2 484	5 566
Machinery and equipment	40	508	338	820	730	525	1 006	1 867	3 103	978	4 165	2 627	3 389
Electrical and electronic equipment	679	1 069	7 492	1 225	4 703	4 872	1 594	1 034	1 818	2 610	1 858	14 563	14 188
Precision instruments	-	200	341	1 665	339	271	4 064	416	872	1 369	2 194	1 335	2 041
Motor vehicles and other transport equipment	43	407	4 211	7 013	411	746	2 662	4 098	669	1 724	1 969	6 479	8 933
Other manufacturing	73	4	1 152	313	248	135	590	450	45	27	96	1 789	637
Tertiary	**5 495**	**8 082**	**16 765**	**27 225**	**17 510**	**16 222**	**16 976**	**20 211**	**42 054**	**52 954**	**57 277**	**124 906**	**189 873**
Electric, gas, and water	-	116	320	418	134	874	301	676	5 605	9 601	8 906	20 716	22 322
Construction	385	92	213	409	129	356	108	206	1 192	2 711	141	1 136	1 115
Trade	1 585	477	1 817	3 780	5 896	3 610	3 831	1 420	5 954	11 178	8 186	11 114	22 378
Hotels and restaurants	19	2 705	796	1 780	748	624	318	882	1 183	780	1 911	7 179	1 200
Transport, storage and communications	117	335	1 525	1 610	1 099	1 232	2 290	5 937	3 263	5 610	5 456	10 923	72 303
Finance	2 834	2 615	9 193	13 136	5 560	6 689	8 063	6 277	17 878	10 745	15 836	49 146	37 866
Business services	458	1 474	1 704	5 539	2 855	2 241	1 431	3 113	3 202	7 296	8 923	19 846	25 458
Public administration and defence	-	-	-	-	-	-	-	-	385	-	85	-	196
Education	-	-	7	-	-	-	-	-	-	-	11	14	58
Health and social services	-	-	121	418	31	52	22	36	67	24	824	126	118
Community, social and personal service activities	98	266	1 068	136	1 047	525	572	1 197	2 468	5 010	6 979	4 637	6 861
Other services	-	3	-	-	12	20	41	465	856	-	19	69	-
Total	**12 761**	**31 012**	**47 358**	**62 133**	**36 676**	**44 761**	**38 537**	**55 280**	**75 143**	**81 895**	**114 591**	**187 853**	**344 537**

Source : UNCTAD, cross-border M&A database, based on data provided by Thomson Financial Securities Data Company.

Note : Data are based on information on the countries in the European Union as sellers. Totals include amounts which cannot be allocated by sector/industry.

Annex table A.IV.13. **Purchases of cross-border M&As in the United States, by sector and industry, 1987-1999**

(Millions of dollars)

Sector/Industry	1987	1988	1989	1990	1991	1992	1993	1994	1995	1996	1997	1998	1999
Primary	**46**	**67**	**142**	**400**	**231**	**1 175**	**1 782**	**1 684**	**862**	**2 819**	**940**	**2 513**	**353**
Agriculture, hunting, forestry, and fishing	-	-	-	-	24	-	-	114	18	467	154	523	100
Mining, quarrying and petroleum	46	67	142	400	207	1 175	1 782	1 571	845	2 352	786	1 990	254
Secondary	**22 848**	**18 367**	**26 040**	**13 341**	**7 198**	**7 236**	**11 710**	**12 997**	**28 762**	**23 888**	**33 763**	**48 962**	**50 676**
Food, beverages and tobacco	1 304	7 245	1 464	4 394	806	2 659	3 055	804	4 750	2 970	5 804	4 111	1 516
Textiles, clothing and leather	-	242	-	191	715	120	206	14	454	89	52	1 727	244
Wood and wood products	316	217	4 080	804	445	605	138	930	1 706	905	652	4 198	3 961
Publishing, printing, and reproduction of recorded media	393	287	1 276	720	152	72	197	953	452	350	971	574	564
Coke, petroleum and nuclear fuel	9 208	6 388	1 528	2 050	1 185	471	1 903	1 091	1 538	4 847	4 073	13 115	4 352
Chemicals and chemical products	7 806	1 221	4 270	655	1 266	2 069	2 330	4 776	13 106	4 016	4 050	4 939	7 083
Rubber and plastic products	42	64	269	25	25	94	327	52	433	107	554	650	300
Non-metallic mineral products	848	221	863	480	161	27	172	354	52	85	40	4 700	1 359
Metal and metal products	266	8	307	425	147	116	1 006	193	528	5 537	1 687	1 069	2 083
Machinery and equipment	1 891	957	929	1 075	189	109	435	886	1 035	703	3 237	2 531	3 567
Electrical and electronic equipment	288	488	6 830	980	2 077	331	583	1 600	3 271	1 305	3 770	4 350	7 321
Precision instruments	206	824	641	1 174	27	319	971	678	801	1 064	2 005	3 604	1 901
Motor vehicles and other transport equipment	279	204	3 559	275	-	108	307	529	461	1 520	1 528	3 289	14 937
Other manufacturing	2	-	24	94	3	137	80	139	176	391	5 339	105	1 489
Tertiary	**5 517**	**5 516**	**12 678**	**13 886**	**8 982**	**6 621**	**7 883**	**13 849**	**27 719**	**34 036**	**46 165**	**85 495**	**61 397**
Electric, gas and water	5	-	-	81	9	-	665	441	5 800	8 222	7 676	18 211	14 983
Construction	2	1 530	70	53	140	148	37	837	299	47	102	448	28
Trade	152	669	1 998	2 355	224	646	492	1 206	2 518	2 491	4 359	2 202	2 161
Hotels and restaurants	296	390	745	-	192	59	-	666	86	411	2 104	1 358	401
Transport, storage and communications	138	117	2 827	268	209	270	1 114	3 549	1 883	2 574	3 282	4 185	3 380
Finance	4 415	2 306	4 738	6 733	6 171	3 716	4 300	4 980	12 844	14 754	19 969	31 736	28 925
Business services	244	329	1 737	2 349	873	1 320	632	929	1 750	4 355	2 920	9 855	7 810
Education	-	-	9	-	4	-	-	-	-	1	95	-	51
Health and social services	-	14	155	-	41	221	186	117	45	242	58	224	2
Community, social and personal service activities	266	163	395	2 047	1 121	172	389	940	1 586	919	5 152	15 850	3 655
Other services	-	5	5	-	-	70	69	185	909	20	448	1 426	2
Total	**28 412**	**24 181**	**38 860**	**27 627**	**16 596**	**15 035**	**21 405**	**28 531**	**57 343**	**60 744**	**80 869**	**137 421**	**112 426**

Source : UNCTAD, cross-border M&A database, based on data provided by Thomson Financial Securities Data Company.

Note : Data are based on information on the United States as an acquiring country. Totals include amounts which cannot be allocated by sector/industry.

Annex table A.IV.14. Purchases of cross-border M&As in the European Union, by sector and industry, 1987-1999

(Millions of dollars)

Sector/industry	1987	1988	1989	1990	1991	1992	1993	1994	1995	1996	1997	1998	1999
Primary	**846**	**1 823**	**1 618**	**1 423**	**845**	**1 154**	**1 742**	**239**	**4 946**	**738**	**944**	**1 931**	**4 052**
Agriculture, hunting, forestry, and fishing	846	1 505	1 466	47	441	91	9	25	119	89	677	872	135
Mining, quarrying and petroleum	-	318	153	1 376	403	1 062	1 733	214	4 827	650	267	1 059	3 917
Secondary	**20 845**	**22 456**	**51 603**	**48 106**	**20 984**	**21 847**	**15 662**	**40 704**	**40 150**	**39 903**	**65 886**	**164 312**	**215 633**
Food, beverages and tobacco	2 295	2 728	12 300	6 110	3 397	2 714	2 022	5 535	7 338	4 578	5 978	6 927	19 489
Textiles, clothing and leather	54	152	1 310	2 806	589	225	3 404	274	386	500	1 113	1 317	1 595
Wood and wood products	261	1 225	1 137	4 698	1 161	628	1 731	1 336	3 017	485	2 491	7 536	3 835
Publishing, printing, and reproduction of recorded media	976	5 611	3 496	840	527	4 879	802	2 895	1 357	3 841	1 852	10 785	7 167
Coke, petroleum and nuclear fuel	1 817	2 372	3 070	2 297	3 971	719	105	1 572	1 584	1 786	5 043	50 074	22 749
Chemicals and chemical products	6 534	2 201	12 580	12 313	963	2 179	781	16 385	12 406	12 993	26 180	15 183	65 390
Rubber and plastic products	1 015	142	1 941	1 801	236	516	15	77	3 746	419	1 687	1 951	734
Non-metallic mineral products	1 278	1 390	1 255	4 572	476	2 287	1 997	3 625	2 503	3 139	6 281	3 343	8 708
Metal and metal products	1 238	1 154	4 460	2 006	1 343	1 285	477	1 341	387	3 190	5 654	4 489	48 373
Machinery and equipment	372	1 142	213	368	670	208	620	1 265	2 096	939	1 380	1 443	10 660
Electrical and electronic equipment	4 048	3 244	8 846	2 162	6 539	4 582	2 347	1 813	1 791	3 917	2 388	13 422	16 178
Precision instruments	712	417	269	822	393	272	360	436	1 742	1 863	2 523	2 924	1 570
Motor vehicles and other transport equipment	84	675	719	7 284	714	1 352	995	3 805	1 452	2 081	3 150	44 841	8 971
Other manufacturing	162	3	8	29	7	3	8	348	345	174	168	79	214
Tertiary	**10 925**	**15 836**	**18 144**	**36 995**	**17 848**	**21 384**	**23 125**	**22 913**	**36 321**	**56 033**	**75 279**	**118 130**	**278 024**
Electric, gas and water	-	950	745	251	1 064	916	552	353	4 108	5 623	10 645	7 967	37 770
Construction	346	137	909	113	555	108	135	99	220	495	357	54	770
Trade	2 795	2 229	1 468	2 698	2 150	1 638	4 568	3 044	4 404	8 566	7 064	15 204	14 024
Hotels and restaurants	6	323	376	2 761	69	69	168	33	2 002	851	143	398	2 466
Transport, storage and communications	61	648	1 704	3 769	367	1 007	1 876	5 491	3 534	3 760	6 218	11 693	92 670
Finance	2 397	6 439	9 996	24 079	12 458	16 625	14 497	11 669	19 905	28 641	43 311	71 001	109 936
Business services	4 804	1 691	2 604	1 962	1 096	886	1 123	1 773	1 174	7 474	4 226	8 540	17 079
Public administration and defence	103	1 952	-	667	-	-	53	-	6	-	-	-	-
Education	-		207	-	-	-	-	-	-	-	3	-	3
Health and social services	-	-	-	444	-	-	17	36	59	24	249	112	9
Community, social and personal service activities	412	1 463	136	252	77	118	136	110	903	601	3 058	3 161	3 297
Other services	-	3	-	-	12	18	-	305	8	-	5	-	-
Total	**32 617**	**40 141**	**71 365**	**86 525**	**39 676**	**44 391**	**40 531**	**63 857**	**81 417**	**96 674**	**142 108**	**284 373**	**497 709**

Source : UNCTAD, cross-border M&A database, based on data provided by Thomson Financial Securities Data Company.

Note : Data are based on information on the countries in the European Union as acquirors. Totals include amounts which cannot be allocated by sector/industry.

Annex table A.IV.15. **Sales of cross-border M&As in Japan, by sector and industry, 1987-1999**

(Millions of dollars)

Sector/industry	1987	1988	1989	1990	1991	1992	1993	1994	1995	1996	1997	1998	1999
Primary	-	-	-	-	-	-	-	-	-	-	-	-	-
Secondary	27	29	1 601	132	168	124	55	297	177	1 037	219	13	5 608
Wood and wood products	27	-	-	-	-	-	-	-	-	-	-	1	-
Publishing, printing, and reproduction of recorded media	-	-	-	-	-	-	-	0	-	-	-	-	-
Coke, petroleum and nuclear fuel	-	-	-	-	-	64	-	-	-	-	-	-	-
Chemicals and chemical products	-	-	-	20	147	-	-	-	-	688	-	-	-
Rubber and plastic products	-	-	-	-	-	-	-	-	-	-	-	-	108
Non-metallic mineral products	-	-	-	-	-	-	-	-	52	-	-	-	-
Metal and metal products	-	-	-	-	-	-	-	17	-	1	-	-	12
Machinery and equipment	-	29	32	-	21	-	-	-	-	-	-	-	83
Electrical and electronic equipment	-	-	1 569	112	-	36	25	22	125	245	219	12	14
Precision instruments	-	-	-	-	-	6	30	58	-	83	-	-	-
Motor vehicles and other transport equipment	-	-	-	-	-	-	-	200	-	-	-	-	5 391
Other manufacturing	-	-	-	-	-	19	-	-	-	20	-	-	-
Tertiary	-	-	11	16	10	106	38	452	364	682	2 864	4 010	10 249
Trade	-	-	4	-	10	38	-	2	222	283	30	-	28
Hotels and restaurants	-	-	-	-	-	-	-	229	9	-	-	-	-
Transport, storage and communications	-	-	7	-	-	20	11	5	-	-	133	32	2 533
Finance	-	-	-	-	-	8	-	195	22	-	2 661	2 029	7 592
Business services	-	-	-	-	-	30	27	8	111	14	41	1 948	96
Education	-	-	-	5	-	-	-	-	-	-	-	-	-
Health and social services	-	-	-	-	-	10	-	-	-	-	-	-	-
Community, social and personal service activities	-	-	-	11	-	-	-	14	-	386	-	-	-
Total	27	29	1 612	148	178	230	93	750	541	1 719	3 083	4 022	15 857

Source: UNCTAD, cross-border M&A database, based on data provided by Thomson Financial Securities Data Company.

Note: Data are based on information on Japan as a seller country. Totals include amounts which cannot be allocated by sector/industry.

Annex table A.IV.16. **Purchases of cross-border M&As in Japan, by sector and industry, 1987-1999**

(Millions of dollars)

Sector/Industry	1987	1988	1989	1990	1991	1992	1993	1994	1995	1996	1997	1998	1999
Primary	-	1 200	-	20	-	-	-	-	-	-	5	-	-
Mining, quarrying and petroleum	-	1 200	-	20	-	-	-	-	-	-	5	-	-
Secondary	1 704	8 434	3 983	7 816	9 247	1 820	371	217	1 096	1 956	1 450	186	9 379
Food, beverages and tobacco	-	62	157	728	59	92	-	20	-	31	0	-	7 975
Textiles, clothing and leather	-	79	51	155	35	10	1	-	122	165	2	-	2
Wood and wood products	-	1 067	-	30	2	-	-	-	-	36	-	8	-
Publishing, printing, and reproduction of recorded media	-	52	14	42	10	-	-	-	-	-	7	-	3
Coke, petroleum and nuclear fuel	-	24	50	78	70	-	-	-	-	-	-	-	-
Chemicals and chemical products	1 023	789	1 745	500	270	202	126	-	3	19	94	46	40
Rubber and plastic products	-	2 593	365	35	23	40	1	-	7	-	62	0	15
Non-metallic mineral products	-	253	28	845	55	1 100	120	13	-	-	-	31	279
Metal and metal products	63	1 197	388	544	313	265	-	21	3	1 190	1	4	3
Machinery and equipment	36	179	89	301	206	6	97	9	11	155	8	-	3
Electrical and electronic equipment	533	2 129	483	2 950	7 977	60	23	90	770	111	1 156	62	626
Precision instruments	-	8	569	848	13	-	-	-	-	-	18	-	163
Motor vehicles and other transport equipment	-	2	33	743	159	35	4	64	180	249	102	12	269
Other manufacturing	50	-	12	18	56	12	-	-	-	-	-	23	-
Tertiary	1 452	3 880	3 541	6 098	2 630	2 563	735	841	2 847	3 704	1 292	1 098	414
Electric, gas and water	-	-	-	-	-	-	-	-	-	-	-	-	21
Construction	-	35	-	59	-	-	-	-	-	-	4	-	-
Trade	4	448	450	624	965	289	17	497	1 560	3 447	316	557	26
Hotels and restaurants	-	2 427	189	305	-	-	22	-	-	-	-	-	-
Transport, storage and communications	320	100	45	279	328	-	-	2	123	215	249	127	307
Finance	843	447	2 597	3 371	790	1 597	165	342	985	-	573	411	29
Business services	35	424	150	1 358	547	152	113	-	179	43	151	2	31
Education	-	-	-	-	-	-	420	-	-	-	-	-	-
Community, social and personal service activities	250	-	110	103	1	525	-	-	-	-	-	-	-
Total	3 156	13 514	7 525	14 048	11 877	4 392	1 106	1 058	3 943	5 660	2 747	1 284	9 792

Source : UNCTAD, cross-border M&A database, based on data provided by Thomson Financial Securities Data Company.

Note : Data are based on information on Japan as an acquiring country. Totals include amounts which cannot be allocated by sector/industry.

Annex table A.IV.17. **Sales of cross-border M&As in South, East and South-East Asia, by sector and industry, 1987-1999**

(Millions of dollars)

Sector/Industry	1987	1988	1989	1990	1991	1992	1993	1994	1995	1996	1997	1998	1999
Primary	-	**120**	-	**15**	**46**	-	**93**	**211**	**82**	**3**	**1 705**	**247**	**167**
Agriculture, hunting, forestry, and fishing	-	20	-	-	27	-	-	198	6	3	1 284	218	47
Mining, quarrying and petroleum	-	100	-	15	19	-	93	14	77	1	421	29	120
Secondary	**56**	**33**	**1 483**	**1 621**	**719**	**863**	**971**	**1 402**	**1 668**	**3 344**	**7 035**	**8 689**	**11 274**
Food, beverages and tobacco	-	-	664	847	31	270	324	354	258	46	3 648	1 440	541
Textiles, clothing and leather	-	13	8	0	15	-	78	22	27	90	74	10	33
Wood and wood products	-	7	477	40	-	31	29	121	117	94	240	780	1 026
Publishing, printing, and reproduction of recorded media	27	-	-	39	-	17	-	135	166	24	32	56	51
Coke, petroleum and nuclear fuel	29	-	150	37	540	32	50	58	86	473	478	538	2 686
Chemicals and chemical products	-	-	151	-	2	27	37	167	286	451	349	3 660	939
Rubber and plastic products	-	-	3	5	5	-	-	24	9	107	49	139	10
Non-metallic mineral products	-	-	-	-	59	-	9	1	43	1	87	643	984
Metal and metal products	-	-	-	29	3	223	159	30	234	110	1 493	102	593
Machinery and equipment	-	-	-	13	14	1	60	226	126	91	86	756	1 619
Electrical and electronic equipment	-	13	19	574	46	109	187	237	217	1 258	295	484	2 509
Precision instruments	-	-	-	-	-	-	7	7	0	51	0	56	62
Motor vehicles and other transport equipment	-	-	11	6	3	23	11	14	91	539	189	21	219
Other manufacturing	-	-	-	31	-	130	26	6	9	11	14	5	3
Tertiary	**200**	**1 358**	**546**	**2 324**	**1 287**	**2 549**	**6 204**	**3 039**	**4 528**	**6 398**	**9 846**	**6 906**	**13 563**
Electric, gas, and water	-	-	-	-	-	-	40	147	4	1 012	4 904	819	1 496
Construction	-	-	-	35	83	-	40	35	330	394	222	13	129
Trade	7	-	10	275	167	171	1 304	767	384	619	132	495	662
Hotels and restaurants	91	185	199	71	110	419	132	58	1 168	99	487	275	604
Transport, storage and communications	-	11	182	1 388	102	807	1 853	370	780	3 135	1 188	2 062	2 914
Finance	25	1 081	69	122	587	249	1 867	836	876	928	1 704	2 522	6 136
Business services	77	80	82	433	236	892	435	711	404	212	1 175	691	1 335
Public administration and defence	-	-	-	-	-	-	-	-	-	-	-	8	243
Education	-	-	-	-	-	-	-	-	-	-	1	-	1
Health and social services	-	-	-	-	-	-	5	1	10	-	1	8	2
Community, social and personal service activities	-	1	5	-	2	11	529	115	571	51	34	13	42
Total	**256**	**1 510**	**2 029**	**3 960**	**2 051**	**3 411**	**7 267**	**4 652**	**6 278**	**9 745**	**18 586**	**15 842**	**25 003**

Source: UNCTAD, cross-border M&A database, based on data provided by Thomson Financial Securities Data Company.

Note: Data are based on information on the countries in South, East and South-East Asia as sellers.   Totals include amounts which cannot be allocated by sector/industry.

Annex table A.IV.18. **Sales of cross-border M&As in the five Asian countries most affected by the financial crisis,[a] by sector and industry, 1987-1999**

(Millions of dollars)

Sector/industry	1987	1988	1989	1990	1991	1992	1993	1994	1995	1996	1997	1998	1999
Primary	-	120	-	15	45	-	93	59	76	3	367	146	47
Agriculture, hunting, forestry, and fishing	-	20	-	-	26	-	-	45	-	3	-	117	47
Mining, quarrying and petroleum	-	100	-	15	19	-	93	14	76	1	367	29	-
Secondary	29	7	943	54	648	285	196	248	457	935	5 134	5 087	8 125
Food, beverages and tobacco	-	-	632	14	-	11	126	78	16	30	3 424	1 359	67
Textiles, clothing and leather	-	-	-	0	8	-	1	-	-	79	67	1	33
Wood and wood products	-	7	-	40	-	-	-	89	50	40	238	557	1 007
Publishing, printing, and reproduction of recorded medi	-	-	-	-	-	-	-	-	-	24	-	-	-
Coke, petroleum and nuclear fuel	29	-	150	-	540	28	-	5	83	291	112	230	1 417
Chemicals and chemical products	-	-	150	-	2	0	17	35	101	38	87	1 263	930
Rubber and plastic products	-	-	-	-	5	-	-	15	3	77	14	139	2
Non-metallic mineral products	-	-	-	-	59	-	9	-	7	1	87	637	781
Metal and metal products	-	-	-	-	-	212	31	11	139	7	812	6	125
Machinery and equipment	-	-	-	-	14	0	-	1	25	8	-	756	1 488
Electrical and electronic equipment	-	-	-	-	19	35	-	-	29	131	107	108	2 055
Precision instruments	-	-	-	-	-	-	-	-	-	-	-	27	-
Motor vehicles and other transport equipment	-	-	11	-	-	-	11	11	-	209	186	0	219
Other manufacturing	-	-	-	-	-	-	-	3	4	2	1	5	3
Tertiary	25	38	137	102	400	895	577	1 260	1 935	1 619	807	5 633	6 547
Electric, gas, and water	-	-	-	-	-	-	-	5	4	41	56	808	994
Construction	-	-	-	-	23	-	-	-	-	8	-	-	3
Trade	-	-	-	83	43	-	20	532	144	113	37	409	349
Hotels and restaurants	-	-	-	-	55	-	89	1	538	43	318	86	492
Transport, storage and communications	-	-	-	-	1	374	54	178	745	907	167	1 925	1 323
Finance	25	-	69	18	230	23	372	470	443	443	158	2 073	2 619
Business services	-	38	68	1	49	498	36	4	41	66	71	330	523
Public administration and defence	-	-	-	-	-	-	-	-	-	-	-	-	243
Health and social services	-	-	-	-	-	-	5	1	10	-	-	-	2
Community, social and personal service activities	-	-	-	-	-	-	-	70	11	-	-	1	-
Total	54	165	1 080	171	1 093	1 180	866	1 567	2 468	2 558	6 308	10 866	14 719

Source : UNCTAD, cross-border M&A database, based on data provided by Thomson Financial Securities Data Company.

Note : Data are based on information on the five crisis-hit countries as sellers. Totals include amounts which cannot be allocated by sector/industry.
[a] Indonesia, Malaysia, Philippines, Republic of Korea and Thailand.

Annex table A.IV.19.　Sales of cross-border M&As in Latin America and the Caribbean, by sector and industry, 1987-1999

(Millions of dollars)

Sector/industry	1987	1988	1989	1990	1991	1992	1993	1994	1995	1996	1997	1998	1999
Primary	196	38	578	65	159	599	304	2 337	211	560	1 445	829	287
Agriculture, hunting, forestry, and fishing	188	38	100	19	5	-	257	213	77	97	137	331	10
Mining, quarrying and petroleum	8	-	479	46	154	599	47	2 123	134	463	1 308	498	277
Secondary	-	1 110	908	1 731	982	1 060	1 971	2 807	2 918	8 497	11 184	19 825	20 422
Food, beverages and tobacco	-	13	-	791	4	345	1 019	1 434	800	1 564	4 801	2 655	1 056
Textiles, clothing and leather	-	-	-	-	-	-	21	-	29	23	1	115	94
Wood and wood products	-	-	370	410	-	95	342	62	80	644	700	231	532
Publishing, printing, and reproduction of recorded media	-	81	64	-	-	-	45	59	-	-	-	97	113
Coke, petroleum and nuclear fuel	-	764	-	300	534	161	22	55	103	1 553	2 074	1 057	15 804
Chemicals and chemical products	-	42	471	17	412	140	241	154	1 325	2 738	265	11 127	472
Rubber and plastic products	-	-	-	-	-	-	5	54	25	-	337	184	-
Non-metallic mineral products	-	60	-	8	-	-	98	597	18	1 054	623	564	938
Metal and metal products	-	-	-	-	2	245	63	312	309	390	486	2 454	245
Machinery and equipment	-	-	-	-	-	-	19	-	2	346	231	71	753
Electrical and electronic equipment	-	-	2	151	-	-	86	9	160	111	1 349	799	292
Precision instruments	-	-	-	-	-	-	1	-	3	70	8	27	-
Motor vehicles and other transport equipment	-	150	-	15	24	73	10	72	64	5	305	445	102
Other manufacturing	-	-	-	40	7	-	-	-	-	-	3	-	22
Tertiary	1 110	158	443	9 698	2 388	2 538	2 835	4 806	5 508	11 451	28 474	43 268	16 456
Electric, gas, and water	-	-	-	-	-	967	1 403	1 252	1 397	4 274	8 277	4 754	5 703
Construction	-	-	-	-	-	-	5	35	14	3	30	3	63
Trade	-	-	15	-	33	18	208	8	115	467	2 743	2 755	2 329
Hotels and restaurants	31	83	62	23	-	3	200	198	-	296	93	193	69
Transport, storage and communications	-	-	208	8 556	2 046	146	581	2 807	1 871	1 398	3 496	23 723	1 730
Finance	1 079	75	157	8	309	1 352	430	291	1 411	4 141	6 994	8 902	3 902
Business services	-	-	-	1 111	-	7	10	16	35	521	6 170	456	918
Public administration and defence	-	-	-	-	-	-	-	-	-	-	-	218	-
Health and social services	-	-	-	-	-	41	-	0	30	-	-	407	11
Community, social and personal service activities	-	-	-	-	-	4	-	200	634	352	670	1 859	1 731
Total	1 305	1 305	1 929	11 494	3 529	4 196	5 110	9 950	8 636	20 508	41 103	63 923	37 166

Source : UNCTAD, cross-border M&A database, based on data provided by Thomson Financial Securities Data Company.

Note : Data are based on information on the countries in Latin America and the Caribbean as sellers. Totals include amounts which cannot be allocated by sector/industry.

Annex table A.IV.20. Sales of cross-border M&As in Central and Eastern Europe,[a] by sector and industry, 1989-1999

(Millions of dollars)

Industry/sector	1989	1990	1991	1992	1993	1994	1995	1996	1997	1998	1999
Primary	-	-	-	-	-	**10**	**11**	**24**	**186**	**23**	**26**
Agriculture, hunting, forestry, and fishing	-	-	-	-	-	-	2	-	4	13	-
Mining, quarrying and petroleum	-	-	-	-	-	10	8	24	183	10	26
Secondary	**25**	**226**	**772**	**2 362**	**721**	**712**	**1 956**	**1 612**	**2 701**	**1 815**	**2 417**
Food, beverages and tobacco	-	-	72	305	438	243	731	505	256	821	679
Textile, clothing and leather	-	-	40	-	-	12	8	-	5	11	8
Wood and wood products	-	-	-	278	10	2	53	141	194	96	109
Publishing, printing, and reproduction of recorded media	5	1	11	21	-	-	17	63	30	5	60
Coke, petroleum and nuclear fuel	2	-	-	-	38	49	9	203	588	303	931
Chemicals and chemical products	-	75	134	138	53	25	174	179	398	317	173
Rubber and plastic products	-	-	-	-	-	-	168	82	123	2	1
Non-metallic mineral products	-	-	42	235	-	8	58	276	462	66	29
Metal and metal products	-	-	1	73	38	100	49	34	329	29	55
Machinery and equipment	-	-	7	-	6	3	29	27	1	41	17
Electrical and electronic equipment	-	150	89	40	120	99	94	48	37	92	60
Precision equipment	-	-	-	18	-	-	-	-	45	-	-
Motor vehicles and other transport equipment	19	-	377	1 255	19	171	566	55	233	32	293
Other manufacturing	-	-	-	-	-	-	1	-	1	-	-
Tertiary	**2**	**59**	**60**	**339**	**457**	**696**	**4 083**	**2 044**	**2 876**	**3 278**	**7 868**
Electric, gas and water	-	-	-	-	26	185	1 881	251	331	119	90
Construction	-	-	-	22	-	21	31	3	8	38	26
Trade	2	-	60	47	21	32	93	193	34	64	335
Hotels and restaurants	-	-	-	-	110	24	4	73	24	11	102
Transport, storage and communications	-	-	-	108	280	155	1 613	992	114	1 400	1 859
Finance	-	-	-	162	17	278	437	477	2 218	1 564	4 898
Business activities	-	-	-	0	2	-	6	8	55	79	196
Community, social and personal service activities	-	59	0	-	-	2	17	48	92	4	362
Unspecified	-	-	**48**	**32**	-	-	-	-	-	-	-
Total	**27**	**285**	**880**	**2 733**	**1 178**	**1 419**	**6 050**	**3 679**	**5 764**	**5 116**	**10 310**

Source: UNCTAD, cross-border M&A database, based on data provided by Thomson Financial Securities Data Company.

a   Includes the countries of the former Yugoslavia.

Annex table A.IV.21. **Transaction values of cross-border M&As of privatized firms, by country of seller, 1987-1999**

(Billions of dollars)

Country/economy[a]	1987	1988	1989	1990	1991	1992	1993	1994	1995	1996	1997	1998	1999	1987-1999 total
Brazil	-	0.1	-	-	-	0.1	-	-	-	2.9	6.0	19.9	2.8	31.9
Argentina	-	-	-	0.6	0.1	1.1	1.3	0.5	0.8	0.4	0.4	5.5	15.6	26.4
Australia	-	0.4	-	-	-	0.8	0.5	0.1	4.2	5.2	6.9	2.6	3.7	24.3
Germany	-	-	-	0.6	0.7	0.6	0.1	0.6	0.2	-	1.0	0.1	5.1	9.0
Belgium	-	-	-	0.1	-	-	1.4	0.4	0.6	5.6	-	-	0.6	8.7
Sweden	-	-	-	-	-	0.6	0.1	4.4	0.2	0.7	-	2.4	-	8.3
Poland	-	-	-	-	0.1	1.4	0.2	0.2	0.6	0.8	0.6	0.9	2.7	7.5
France	0.2	0.2	-	-	0.2	0.1	0.1	1.4	1.5	0.3	0.6	1.3	0.1	5.9
Venezuela	-	-	-	-	2.0	-	-	0.0	0.1	0.2	0.8	2.3	-	5.4
Philippines	-	-	-	-	0.1	0.4	-	0.6	0.1	-	3.1	0.8	0.1	5.3
Peru	-	-	-	-	-	0.2	0.1	3.1	0.8	0.6	0.4	-	-	5.1
Spain	-	-	-	0.2	0.5	-	0.2	0.1	0.2	0.1	2.0	1.2	0.1	4.7
Kazakhstan	-	-	-	-	-	-	-	-	0.5	1.9	2.3	-	-	4.6
Mexico	-	-	-	1.8	-	0.3	-	-	-	0.1	2.1	-	0.3	4.6
Italy	-	-	0.3	0.1	-	0.5	0.6	0.9	0.3	0.6	0.0	1.1	0.2	4.6
United Kingdom	-	0.1	-	0.1	0.1	0.4	0.2	0.3	0.5	1.8	0.5	0.5	-	4.5
Hungary	-	-	-	0.2	0.3	0.3	0.3	0.1	1.6	1.4	0.2	-	-	4.3
Netherlands	-	-	-	-	0.1	-	0.5	-	1.2	0.2	-	0.1	2.3	4.3
Colombia	-	-	-	0.3	-	-	-	-	-	1.3	2.0	-	-	3.8
Czech Republic	-	-	-	-	-	-	-	0.3	1.9	0.2	-	0.1	1.2	3.7
Austria	-	-	-	0.2	-	-	0.1	0.3	-	-	-	2.8	-	3.5
New Zealand	-	-	0.4	0.6	-	0.3	0.2	0.1	0.1	0.2	0.1	-	0.6	2.7
Romania	-	-	-	-	-	-	-	0.2	0.2	0.1	0.3	1.2	0.4	2.4
Russian Federation	-	-	-	-	-	-	0.3	-	0.1	-	1.9	-	-	2.3
Chile	-	-	0.1	-	-	0.1	-	0.6	0.1	0.3	-	-	1.1	2.2
Ireland	-	-	-	-	-	-	-	-	-	0.3	0.8	-	1.0	2.2
Thailand	-	-	-	-	-	-	-	-	-	-	-	1.7	0.4	2.0
Bulgaria	-	-	-	-	-	-	-	0.1	-	0.1	0.5	0.1	1.1	1.8
Finland	-	0.1	-	-	-	-	0.1	-	0.8	0.1	-	-	0.7	1.8
Bolivia	-	-	-	-	-	-	-	-	0.7	-	0.9	-	0.1	1.7
South Africa	-	-	-	-	-	-	-	-	-	-	1.3	0.2	0.2	1.7
Czechoslovakia	-	-	-	-	0.5	0.8	0.2	-	-	-	-	-	-	1.5
Croatia	-	-	-	-	-	-	-	-	0.1	-	0.1	-	1.2	1.3
Canada	0.2	-	0.3	-	0.1	0.2	-	0.3	-	-	-	-	-	1.2
Pakistan	-	-	-	-	-	-	-	-	-	1.1	-	-	-	1.1
Nigeria	-	-	1.0	-	-	-	-	-	-	-	-	-	-	1.0
El Salvador	-	-	-	-	-	-	-	-	-	-	-	0.9	-	0.9
Portugal	-	-	-	-	-	0.4	-	-	-	0.2	-	0.2	-	0.9
Panama	-	-	-	-	-	-	-	0.1	-	-	0.7	-	0.1	0.8
Morocco	-	-	-	-	-	-	0.1	0.1	-	-	0.5	-	0.1	0.8
Lithuania	-	-	-	-	-	-	-	-	-	-	-	0.5	0.3	0.8
Greece	-	-	-	-	-	0.4	0.1	-	-	0.1	0.1	-	0.1	0.8
Guatemala	-	-	-	-	-	-	-	-	-	-	-	0.5	0.1	7.0
Dominican Republic	-	-	-	-	-	-	-	-	-	-	-	-	0.6	0.6
Hong Kong, China	-	-	-	-	-	-	-	-	-	0.6	-	-	-	0.6
Indonesia	-	-	-	-	-	-	-	-	-	0.3	-	0.1	0.2	0.6
Sri Lanka	-	-	-	-	-	-	-	-	0.1	-	0.2	0.1	-	0.5
India	-	-	-	-	-	-	-	-	-	-	-	-	0.4	0.4
Republic of Korea	-	-	-	-	-	-	-	-	-	-	-	-	0.4	0.4
China	-	-	-	-	-	-	0.1	0.1	-	-	0.1	-	0.1	0.4
TOTAL WORLD	0.7	1.0	2.1	4.9	5.1	9.2	7.0	15.4	18.1	28.8	37.3	47.6	44.5	221.7

Source: UNCTAD, cross-border M&A database, based on data provided by Thomson Financial Securities Data Company.

[a] Ranked in descending order of the transaction value during the period 1987-1999.

Annex table A.IV.22. Cross-border M&As of privatized firms, 1987-1999

(Billions of dollars)

Year	World	Developed countries				Developing countries				Central and Eastern Europe
		Total	European Union	Japan	United States	Total	Africa	Latin America and the Caribbean	South East and South-East Asia	
(a) By country of acquiror										
1987	0.7	0.7	0.3	-	0.3	-	-	-	-	-
1988	1.0	1.0	0.5	-	0.4	-	-	-	-	-
1989	2.1	2.1	1.3	-	0.4	-	-	-	-	-
1990	4.9	4.6	2.2	0.1	2.2	0.1	-	-	0.1	-
1991	5.1	5.0	2.3	0.1	2.4	0.1	-	-	0.1	-
1992	9.2	8.4	4.8	0.2	2.0	0.7	-	0.5	0.2	-
1993	7.0	5.5	3.6	-	1.4	1.4	-	1.0	0.4	0.1
1994	15.4	13.4	9.2	-	3.5	2.0	-	0.6	0.6	-
1995	18.1	16.2	10.3	0.3	4.6	1.9	-	0.7	0.8	-
1996	28.8	24.7	12.9	0.2	9.3	3.8	0.1	2.5	1.1	0.2
1997	37.3	29.4	11.8	0.2	13.9	7.9	-	3.2	2.5	0.1
1998	47.6	43.0	27.1	-	12.1	4.3	-	2.5	1.7	0.3
1999	44.5	42.2	33.1	-	7.3	1.5	-	0.9	0.6	0.8
(b) By country of seller										
1987	0.7	0.6	0.2	-	-	-	-	-	-	-
1988	1.0	0.9	0.4	-	-	0.1	-	0.1	-	-
1989	2.1	1.1	0.3	-	-	1.1	1.0	0.1	-	-
1990	4.9	2.0	1.3	-	-	2.8	-	2.8	-	0.2
1991	5.1	1.9	1.7	-	0.1	2.4	-	2.2	0.1	0.8
1992	9.2	4.4	3.1	-	-	2.4	-	1.8	0.4	2.5
1993	7.0	4.1	3.4	-	-	1.9	0.1	1.6	0.2	1.0
1994	15.4	8.9	8.4	-	-	5.5	0.1	4.6	0.7	0.9
1995	18.1	9.9	5.6	-	-	3.7	0.1	2.9	0.2	4.5
1996	28.8	15.4	10.0	-	-	10.7	0.3	6.1	2.3	2.7
1997	37.3	13.3	5.1	-	-	20.5	1.0	13.4	3.5	3.5
1998	47.6	12.4	9.7	-	-	32.3	0.3	29.2	2.7	2.9
1999	44.5	14.9	10.3	-	-	23.9	0.2	20.8	1.5	5.7

Source: UNCTAD, cross-border M&A database, based on data from Thomson Financial Securities Data Company.

Annex B. Statistical annex

Tables

Annex tables

DEFINITIONS AND SOURCES

A. General definitions

1. Transnational corporations

Transnational corporations (TNCs) are incorporated or unincorporated enterprises comprising parent enterprises and their foreign affiliates. A *parent enterprise* is defined as an enterprise that controls assets of other entities in countries other than its home country, usually by owning a certain equity capital stake. An equity capital stake of 10 per cent or more of the ordinary shares or voting power for an incorporated enterprise, or its equivalent for an unincorporated enterprise, is normally considered as a threshold for the control of assets.[1] A *foreign affiliate* is an incorporated or unincorporated enterprise in which an investor, who is resident in another economy, owns a stake that permits a lasting interest in the management of that enterprise (an equity stake of 10 per cent for an incorporated enterprise or its equivalent for an unincorporated enterprise). In the *World Investment Report*, subsidiary enterprises, associate enterprises and branches are all referred to as *foreign affiliates* or *affiliates*.

- *Subsidiary:* an incorporated enterprise in the host country in which another entity directly owns more than a half of the shareholders's voting power and has the right to appoint or remove a majority of the members of the administrative, management or supervisory body.

- *Associate:* an incorporated enterprise in the host country in which an investor owns a total of at least 10 per cent, but not more than a half, of the shareholders' voting power.

- *Branch:* a wholly or jointly owned unincorporated enterprise in the host country which is one of the following: (i) a permanent establishment or office of the foreign investor; (ii) an unincorporated partnership or joint venture between the foreign direct investor and one or more third parties; (iii) land, structures (except structures owned by government entities), and /or immovable equipment and objects directly owned by a foreign resident; (iv) mobile equipment (such as ships, aircraft, gas- or oil-drilling rigs) operating within a country other than that of the foreign investor for at least one year.

2. Foreign direct investment

Foreign direct investment (FDI) is defined as an investment involving a long-term relationship and reflecting a lasting interest and control of a resident entity in one economy (foreign direct investor or parent enterprise) in an enterprise resident in an economy other than that of the foreign direct investor (FDI enterprise or affiliate enterprise or foreign affiliate).[2] FDI implies that the investor exerts a significant degree of influence on the management of the enterprise resident in the other economy. Such investment involves both the initial transaction between the two entities and all subsequent transactions between them and among foreign affiliates, both incorporated and unincorporated. FDI may be undertaken by individuals as well as business entities.

Flows of FDI comprise capital provided (either directly or through other related enterprises) by a foreign direct investor to an FDI enterprise, or capital received from an FDI enterprise by a foreign direct investor. There are three components in FDI: equity capital, reinvested earnings and intra-company loans.

- *Equity capital* is the foreign direct investor's purchase of shares of an enterprise in a country other than its own.

- *Reinvested earnings* comprise the direct investor's share (in proportion to direct equity participation) of earnings not distributed as dividends by affiliates or earnings not remitted to the direct investor. Such retained profits by affiliates are reinvested.

- *Intra-company loans* or *intra-company debt transactions* refer to short- or long-term borrowing and lending of funds between direct investors (parent enterprises) and affiliate enterprises.

FDI stock is the value of the share of their capital and reserves (including retained profits) attributable to the parent enterprise, plus the net indebtedness of affiliates to the parent enterprise.[3] FDI flow and stock data used in the *World Investment Report* are not always defined as above, because these definitions are often not applicable to disaggregated FDI data. For example, in analysing geographical and industrial trends and patterns of FDI, data based on approvals of FDI may also be used because they allow a disaggregation at the country or industry level. Such cases are denoted accordingly.

3. Non-equity forms of investment

Foreign direct investors may also obtain an effective voice in the management of another business entity through means other than acquiring an equity stake. These are non-equity forms of FDI, and they include, *inter alia*, subcontracting, management contracts, turnkey arrangements, franchising, licensing and product sharing. Data on transnational corporate activity through these forms are usually not separately identified in balance-of-payments statistics. These statistics, however, usually present data on royalties and licensing fees, defined as "receipts and payments of residents and non-residents for: (i) the authorised use of intangible non-produced, non-financial assets and proprietary rights such as trademarks, copyrights, patents, processes, techniques, designs, manufacturing rights, franchises, etc., and (ii) the use, through licensing agreements, of produced originals or prototypes, such as manuscripts, films, etc."[4]

B. Availability, limitations and estimates of FDI data presented in the *World Investment Report*

1. FDI flows

Data on FDI flows in annex tables B.1 and B.2, as well as most of the tables in the text, are on a net basis (capital transactions' credits less debits between direct investors and their foreign affiliates). Net decreases in assets or net increases in liabilities are recorded as credits (recorded with a positive sign in the balance of payments), while net increases in assets or net decreases in liabilities are recorded as debits (recorded with a negative sign in the balance of payments). In the annex tables, as well as in the tables in the text, the negative signs are deleted for practical use. Hence, FDI flows with a negative sign in the *World Investment Report* indicate that at least one of the three components of FDI (equity capital, reinvested earnings or intra-company loans) is negative and not offset by positive amounts of the remaining components. These are instances of reverse investment or disinvestment.

UNCTAD regularly collects published and unpublished national official FDI data directly from central banks, statistical offices or national authorities on an aggregated and disaggregated basis for its FDI/TNC database. These data constitute the main source for the reported data on FDI. These data are further complemented by the data obtained from other international organizations such as the International Monetary Fund (IMF), the World Bank, the Organisation for Economic Co-operation and Development (OECD) and the Economic Commission for Latin America and the Caribbean (ECLAC), as well as UNCTAD's own estimates.

For the purpose of assembling balance-of-payments statistics for its member countries, IMF publishes data on FDI inflows and outflows in the *Balance of Payments Statistics Yearbook*. The same data are also available in the *International Financial Statistics* of IMF for certain countries. Data from IMF used in the *World Investment Report* were obtained directly from the CD-ROMs of IMF containing balance-of-payments statistics and international financial statistics. For this year's *Report, International Financial Statistics* and *Balance-of-Payments* CD-ROMs, June 2000, were used.

For those economies for which data were not available from national official sources or the IMF or for those for which available data do not cover the entire period of 1980-1999 that is used in the *World Investment Report 2000*, data from the World Bank's *World Development Indicators 2000* CD-ROM were used. However, this reports net FDI flows (FDI inflows less FDI outflows) and FDI inward flows. Consequently, data on FDI outflows were estimated by subtracting FDI inward flows from net FDI flows. In those economies in Latin America and the Caribbean for which the data are not available from one of these sources, data from ECLAC were supplemented. Furthermore, data on the FDI outflows of the OECD, as presented in its publication, *Geographical Distribution of Financial Flows to Developing Countries,* are used as proxy for FDI inflows. As these OECD data are based on FDI outflows to developing economies from the member countries of the Development Assistance Committee (DAC) of OECD,[5] inflows of FDI to developing economies may be underestimated. In some economies, FDI data from large recipients and investors are also used as proxies.

Table 1. List of economies for which at least one component of FDI inflows is not available [a] from IMF, 1980-1998

Equity investment	Reinvested earnings	Intra-company loans
Developed countries:		
Austria,[b] Canada, Denmark,[c] Iceland,[d] Ireland, Israel,[e] Japan,[f] Sweden[g] and the United Kingdom[h]	Austria, Belgium and Luxembourg, Denmark, Finland,[i] France,[l] Germany,[k] Greece,[l] Iceland,[m] Ireland,[m] Italy, Japan,[n] Norway,[o] Portugal,[p] South Africa, Spain and Sweden[q]	Austria,[r] Denmark,[s] Greece,[t] Iceland,[u] Italy, Japan,[f] Spain,[m] and Switzerland,[v]
Developing economies:		
Africa:		
Angola,[w] Benin,[x] Botswana,[y] Burkina Faso,[z] Burundi,[t,u] Central African Republic,[aa] Comoros,[ab] Congo,[ac] Côte d'Ivoire,[ab] Djibouti, Egypt, Gabon,[ae] Gambia,[ag] Ghana,[ag] Guinea,[ah] Kenya,[ae] Lesotho,[x] Libyan Arab Jamahiriya,[l] Mali, Mauritius, Morocco,[l] Niger,[aj] Nigeria, Rwanda,[aj] Seychelles,[e] Sierra Leone,[ak] Somalia, Togo,[al] United Republic of Tanzania and Zambia,[e]	Algeria, Angola,[am] Botswana,[y] Burkina Faso,[an] Burundi, Cameroon,[ao] Cape Verde,[ap] Central African Republic,[aq] Chad,[ar] Comoros,[as] Congo,[at] Côte d'Ivoire,[b] Egypt, Equatorial Guinea, Gambia,[au] Ghana,[av] Guinea,[b,v] Kenya,[b] Lesotho, Liberia,[aw] Libyan Arab Jamahiriya,[ax] Madagascar, Malawi, Mali,[ay] Mauritania, Mauritius,[az] Mozambique, Niger,[ba] Nigeria, Rwanda,[bb] Sierra Leone,[bc] Somalia, Sudan, Togo,[bd] Tunisia, Uganda,[be] United Republic of Tanzania and Zimbabwe[bf]	Algeria, Benin,[bg] Botswana,[bh] Burundi, Cameroon,[i] Cape Verde, [bj] Chad,[bk] Comoros,[bl] Côte d'Ivoire,[b] Djibouti, Equatorial Guinea, Gambia,[bm] Ghana,[bn] Guinea,[bo] Kenya,[bp] Lesotho,[bq] Liberia,[br] Libyan Arab Jamahiriya,[bs] Madagascar,[bt] Malawi, Mauritania, Morocco, [bs] Mozambique, Seychelles,[bv] Sierra Leone,[bc] Sudan, Togo,[q] Tunisia,[bw] Uganda, United Republic of Tanzania, Zambia,[e] and Zimbabwe,[bx]
Latin America and the Caribbean:		
Antigua and Barbuda,[d] Aruba, Colombia,[by] El Salvador,[bz] Guyana, Honduras,[ca] Paraguay,[y] Peru,[x] Saint Kitts and Nevis,[d, al] Saint Lucia,[d] Saint Vincent and the Grenadies,[d] and Suriname,[cb]	Antigua and Barbuda,[d] Aruba, Bahamas, Barbados,[cc] Belize,[u] Bolivia,[cd] Chile,[cc] Dominica,[ce] Dominican Republic,[cf] El Salvador,[cg] Grenada,[ch] Guyana,[ci] Haiti, Jamaica,[cj] Netherlands Antilles,[ck] Paraguay,[m] Saint Kitts and Nevis,[d] Saint Lucia,[cl] Saint Vincent and the Grenadies,[d, ck] Suriname, Uruguay[q] and Venezuela[by]	Argentina,[o] Belize,[cm] Bolivia,[cn] Brazil,[o] Chile, Colombia,[bu] Costa Rica,[co] Dominica,[bg] Dominican Republic,[o] Ecuador, El Salvador,[cp] Grenada,[cq] Guatemala,[cl, bd] Guyana,[cr] Haiti, Honduras,[cc] Netherlands Antilles,[ck] Nicaragua, Paraguay,[cl, bh] Peru,[s] Saint Lucia,[cs] Saint Vincent and the Grenadies,[cs, bh] Trinidad and Tobago,[ct] Uruguay[cu] and Venezuela[by]
Developing Europe:		
..	Croatia,[cv] TFYR Macedonia and Slovenia	Croatia,[cv] TFYR Macedonia[co] and Slovenia
West Asia:		
Bahrain,[z] Cyprus,[n] Jordan,[cw] and Saudi Arabia	Bahrain,[z] Cyprus,[av] Iran (Islamic Republic of), Jordan, Kuwait, Saudi Arabia, Syrian Arab Republic, Turkey[n] and Yemen	Bahrain,[bt] Cyprus,[cy] Iran (Islamic Republic of), Kuwait, Oman, Syrian Arab Republic, Turkey and Yemen
Central Asia:		
..	Armenia,[aw] Azerbaijan, Georgia, Kazakhstan,[p] Kyrgystan,[av] and Turkmenistan	Armenia,[cy] Georgia, Kyrgystan[av] and Turkmenistan[bz]
South, East and South-East Asia:		
Indonesia,[c] Lao People's Democratic Republic,[bl] Malaysia and Maldives	Bangladesh, Cambodia,[cz] China,[da] India, Indonesia, Republic of Korea,[e] Lao People's Democratic Republic and Malaysia, Mongolia, Myanmar, Nepal, Pakistan,[cf] Philippines, Singapore, Sri Lanka,[d] and Thailand	Bangladesh,[db] Cambodia,[dc] China,[dd] India, Republic of Korea,[g] Lao People's Democratic Republic,[cx] Maldives, Mongolia, Myanmar, Nepal, Pakistan,[cf] Philippines,[g] Singapore and Sri Lanka,[de]
The Pacific:		
Kiribati,[f] Papua New Guinea,[de] Tonga[df] and Vanuatu[dg]	Kiribati,[v] Solomon Islands, Tonga	Kiribati, Papua New Guinea, [p] Solomon Islands,[dh] Tonga[di] and Vanuatu [y, u]

Finally, in those economies for which data were not available from either of the above-mentioned sources or only partial data (quarterly or monthly) were available, estimates were made by annualizing the data if they are only partially available (monthly or quarterly) from either the IMF or national official sources; using data on cross-border mergers and acquisitions (M&As) and their growth rates; and using UNCTAD's own estimates.

Not all economies record every component of FDI flows. Tables 1 and 2 summarize the availability of each component of FDI during 1980-1998 from the IMF for, respectively, FDI inflows and FDI outflows. Comparison of data among economies should therefore be made bearing these limitations in mind.

Table 1. List of economies for which at least one component of FDI inflows is not available [a] from IMF, 1980-1998 (concluded)

Equity investment	Reinvested earnings	Intra-company loans
Central and Eastern Europe:		
Republic of Moldova,[dj] Russian Federation,[dj] and Ukraine	Albania, Belarus,[dk] Bulgaria,[dl] Czech Republic,[dm] Hungary, Latvia,[dh] Lithuania,[dj] Republic of Moldova,[do] Poland,[m] Romania, Russian Federation,[dm] Slovakia[dj] and Ukraine	Albania, Belarus,[dp] Bulgaria,[dq] Czech Republic, Hungary,[dr] Latvia,[dn] Lithuania,[dj, bz] Republic of Moldova,[dj] Poland,[m] Romania, Russian Federation,[do] Slovakia[dj] and Ukraine

Source: UNCTAD, based on International Monetary Fund, *International Financial Statistics* CD-ROM, June 2000.

[a]   Economies not available at least one year are all reported in the table.
[b]   1997-1998
[c]   1981-1982
[d]   1980-1985
[e]   1980-1988
[f]   1985-1990
[g]   1980-1996
[h]   1980-1983
[i]   1980
[j]   1982-1993
[k]   1998
[l]   1980-1990
[m]   1980-1989
[n]   1980-1995
[o]   1980-1991
[p]   1995
[q]   1980-1981
[r]   1982-1989 and 1991-1998
[s]   1983-1998
[t]   1991-1997
[u]   1993
[v]   1983
[w]   1980-1990 and 1992-1996
[x]   1980-1984
[y]   1988
[z]   1982-1989
[aa] 1988 and 1992-1994
[ab] 1990 and 1992-1995
[ac] 1986 and 1988
[ad] 1990-1992 and 1997-1998
[ae] 1993-1994
[af] 1981
[ag] 1984
[ah] 1992 and 1994
[ai] 1981 and 1986-1995
[aj] 1992-1993 and 1995-1996
[ak] 1984-1985 and 1988-1995
[al] 1994
[am] 1985-1990, 1992 and 1994-1996
[an] 1987-1989
[ao] 1989-1990 and 1992-1993
[ap] 1986, 1988, 1992 and 1997

[aq] 1980-1981, 1983, 1985-1988 and 1991-1994
[ar] 1984-1989, 1991 and 1993-1994
[as] 1989 and 1992-1995
[at] 1987-1988
[au] 1981, 1989 and 1991-1997
[av] 1985-1998
[aw] 1982 and 1986-1987
[ax] 1984-1998
[ay] 1980-1987 and 1991
[az] 1980-1987, 1991 and 1994-1998
[ba] 1990
[bb] 1992-1993 and 1995-1998
[bc] 1981
[bd] 1991
[be] 1991-1992
[bf] 1980-1981 and 1985-1994
[bg] 1982-1984
[bh] 1989
[bi] 1983-1984
[bj] 1986-1997
[bk] 1984-1985, 1988, 1991 and 1993-1994
[bl] 1988-1995
[bm] 1987-1989 and 1991-1997
[bn] 1982-1998
[bo] 1986-1988, 1991 and 1993-1998
[bp] 1981-1986 and 1990-1998
[bq] 1986-1994
[br] 1982 and 1986-1987
[bs] 1991-1998
[bt] 1989-1998
[bu] 1995-1998
[bv] 1989-1993
[bw] 1981, 1984, 1986-1987 and 1993
[bx] 1983-1984 and 1987-1994
[by] 1980-1993
[bz] 1996
[ca] 1980 and 1990-1992
[cb] 1985-1986
[cc] 1980-1986

[cd] 1986
[ce] 1987-1985
[cf] 1980-1992
[cg] 1992-1993, 1995-1996 and 1988
[ch] 1982-1985
[ci] 1980-1981 and 1992-1995
[cj] 1980-1986 and 1988
[ck] 1987
[cl] 1980-1987
[cm] 1980-1993 and 1996-1998
[cn] 1980-1986 and 1993-1998
[co] 1997
[cp] 1984, 1992-1993 and 1998
[cq] 1982-1985, 1987 and 1989
[cr] 1982-1983 and 1985
[cs] 1986-1987
[ct] 1986 and 1996
[cu] 1980-1981 and 1993-1995
[cv] 1993-1996
[cw] 1988-1996
[cx] 1995-1998
[cy] 1993-1994 and 1996-1997
[cz] 1992
[da] 1982-1996
[db] 1983-1984, 1990-1992 and 1997
[dc] 1992-1995
[dd] 1982-1996
[de] 1980-1994
[df] 1984-1986 and 1989
[dg] 1988-1989 and 1991-1998
[dh] 1980-1986 and 1988-1991
[di] 1991-1993
[dj] 1994
[dk] 1993-1996
[dl] 1990-1997
[dm] 1994-1997
[dn] 1992-1996
[do] 1994-1996
[dp] 1993-1995
[dq] 1990-1996
[dr] 1991-1995

Table 2. List of economies for which at least one component of FDI outflows is not available [a] from the IMF, 1980-1998

Equity investment	Reinvested earnings	Intra-company loans
Developed countries:		
Austria,[b] Canada, Denmark,[c] Ireland, Israel,[d] Japan,[e] Sweden,[f] and Switzerland[u]	Austria, Belgium and Luxembourg, Denmark, Finland,[h] France,[i] Iceland,[h] Israel,[k,l] Italy, Japan,[f] New Zealand,[am] Norway,[bz] Portugal[k,l,ca] South Africa and Spain	Austria,[m] Denmark,[n] Iceland,[o,p,q] Ireland, Israel,[r] Italy, Japan[e] Portugal,[s] Spain[t] and Switzerland[u]
Developing economies:		
Africa:		
Benin,[h,v] Botswana,[k,u,w,x] Cape Verde,[y,z] Côte d'Ivoire, Egypt,[t,aa,ab] Kenya,[d,ac] Lesotho, Mauritius, Namibia,[ad] Niger,[c,ae] Seychelles and Swaziland[k,p,af]	Algeria, Angola, Benin,[ag] Botswana[ah,ai] Burkina Faso, Burundi, Cameroon,[d,q,aj] Cape Verde,[ak] Chad, Central African Republic, Egypt, Gabon, Guinea, Kenya,[al,am] Lesotho, Libyan Arab Jamahiriya, Mauritania, Mauritius,[an,ao] Morocco,[b,ap] Niger,[aj,aq,ar] Senegal,[ah,as] Swaziland,[b] Tunisia and Zimbabwe	Algeria, Angola, Botswana,[s,at] Burkina Faso, Burundi, Cameroon,[d,au] Cape Verde, Central African Republic, Chad, Comoros, Côte d'Ivoire, Gabon, Guinea, Kenya,[aq] Libyan Arab Jamahiriya, Mauritania, Mauritius,[s] Morocco, Seychelles,[av] Tunisia and Zimbabwe
Latin America and the Caribbean:		
Bahamas,[aw] Barbados,[ax] Bolivia,[b,ay] Brazil,[az] Colombia,[ba] Costa Rica,[b,aj,bb] Dominica, Haiti, Uruguay,[ak] and Venezuela[an]	Argentina,[y] Aruba, Bahamas, Barbados,[bc] Belize, Bolivia,[k,bd] Brazil, Chile,[dec] Colombia,[ab] Dominica, El Salvador, Haiti, Jamaica, Netherlands Antilles,[t] Peru, Trinidad and Tobago, Uruguay and Venezuela,[az,bf]	Argentina,[g] Aruba, Bahamas,[aj,bg] Barbados,[bh] Belize, Bolivia, Brazil,[bi] Chile, Colombia,[ab] Costa Rica,[bc,bj] El Salvador, Netherlands Antilles,[at,bj] Peru, Trinidad and Tobago and Venezuela,[bf,bl]
Developing Europe:		
..	Croatia,[bm] Malta,[bn] and Slovenia	Croatia,[bm] Malta,[bo] and Slovenia
West Asia:		
Cyprus,[ac,bp] and Jordan	Cyprus,[ac,bp] Jordan, Kuwait and Turkey	Bahrain, Cyprus,[x] Kuwait, Turkey and Yemen
Central Asia		
Armenia	Armenia, Azerbaijan, Kazakhstan and Kyrgyzstan	Azerbaijan, Kazakhstan and Kyrgyzstan
South, East and South-East Asia:		
Indonesia	Bangladesh, China, India, Indonesia, Republic of Korea,[b,bq] Pakistan, Philippines, Singapore, Sri Lanka and Thailand	Bangladesh, China,[br] India, Indonesia, Pakistan, Philippines, Singapore, Sri Lanka and Thailand
The Pacific:		
Fiji,[g,bg] Kiribati, Papua New Guinea and Tonga	Fiji,[bk] and Papua New Guinea	Fiji,[az] Kiribati and Tonga
Central and Eastern Europe:		
Bulgaria,[bo] Republic of Moldova,[bs] Russian Federation,[ax] Slovakia,[bg] and Ukraine	Belarus, Bulgaria, Czech Republic,[bt] Estonia,[au] Hungary, Latvia,[au] Lithuania,[bs] Republic of Moldova, Poland,[t] Romania, Russian Federation,[bu] Slovakia,[bo,bv,bw] and Ukraine	Belarus, Bulgaria,[bw] Czech Republic, Estonia,[aa] Hungary, Lithuania,[bx] Republic of Moldova, Poland,[t,by] Romania, Russian Federation,[bu] Slovakia,[bv] and Ukraine

Source: UNCTAD, based on International Monetary Fund, *International Financial Statistics* CD-ROM, June 2000.

[a]   Economies not available at least one year are all reported in the table.

b	1997-1998	aa	1992	ba	1980-1993		
c	1981-1982	ab	1994-1998	bb	1982-1988		
d	1980-1988	ac	1996-1997	bc	1980-1986		
e	1985-1990	ad	1996-1998	bd	1987-1996		
f	1980-1996	ae	1986-1995	be	1984-1991		
g	1980-1983	af	1986	bf	1982		
h	1981	ag	1981-1984	bg	1993		
i	1983-1993	ah	1980-1981	bh	1987		
j	1986-1989	ai	1985	bi	1983-1998		
k	1980	aj	1995	bj	1980-1990		
l	1982-1984	ak	1997	bk	1980-1987		
m	1982-1998	al	1988-1989	bl	1984-1993		
n	1983-1998	am	1996-1997	bm	1993-1996		
o	1986-1987	an	1988	bn	1993-1995		
p	1990	ao	1990-1998	bo	1998		
q	1992-1993	ap	1991-1994	bp	1987-1994		
r	1989-1994	aq	1980-1985	bq	1980-1994		
s	1984-1985	ar	1987-1993	br	1982-1996		
t	1980-1989	as	1983-1995	bs	1995-1996		
u	1983	at	1990-1994	bt	1993-1997		
v	1983-1984	au	1992-1995	bu	1994-1996		
w	1990-1992	av	1989-1993	bv	1993-1994		
x	1995-1998	aw	1991	bw	1996		
y	1989	ax	1994	bx	1992-1996		
z	1994-1995	ay	1981-1983	by	1991-1995		
		az	1984	bz	1980-1991		
				ca	1980-1991		

The following sections give details of how FDI flow data for each economy used in the *Report* were obtained.

a.   *FDI inflows*

Those economies for which national official sources data were used for the period, 1980-1999, or part of it, are listed below.

Period	Economy
1980-1999	Bolivia, Chile, Finland, Republic of Korea, Taiwan Province of China and Turkey.
1986-1999	Ecuador and the United States
1988-1999	Iceland and Slovenia
1989-1999	Armenia and Hungary
1990-1999	Angola, Antigua and Barbuda, Aruba, Australia, Bahamas, Benin, Botswana, Brazil, Bulgaria, Burundi, Canada, Côte d'Ivoire, Czech Republic, Dominica, Dominican Republic, France, Germany, Ghana, Grenada, Guatemala, Indonesia, Jamaica, Kenya, Lesotho, Madagascar, Malaysia, Mozambique, Namibia, Netherlands, Pakistan, Paraguay, Philippines, Saint Kitts and Nevis, Saint Lucia, Saint Vincent and the Grenadines, Seychelles, Singapore, Slovakia, Sri Lanka, Switzerland, Thailand, Tunisia, United Republic of Tanzania, United Kingdom, Venezuela, Viet Nam and Zimbabwe
1991-1999	Cyprus, Haiti, Lao People's Democratic Republic, Nicaragua, Romania, South Africa and Swaziland
1992-1999	Albania, Argentina, Austria, Belarus, Estonia, Guyana, Kazakhstan, Latvia, Lithuania, Republic of Moldova, Mongolia, Russian Federation and Ukraine
1993-1999	Croatia and Kuwait
1994-1999	Cambodia, Honduras, Kyrgyzstan, TFYR Macedonia, Spain and Zambia
1994 and 1999	Azerbaijan
1995-1999	Denmark, Norway and Sweden
1996-1999	Portugal
1997-1999	Peru and Trinidad and Tobago
1998-1999	Ireland, Italy, Hong Kong China, Japan and Morocco
1999	Belgium and Luxembourg, China, El Salvador, India, Mauritius and New Zealand
1989-1998	Colombia
1990-1998	Ethiopia, Malawi, Senegal and Togo
1991-1998	Poland
1992-1998	Burkina Faso and Niger
1993-1998	Mali and Uganda
1995-1998	Egypt
1996-1998	Gambia
1997-1998	Tajikistan
1994-1997	Georgia
1995-1996	Uzbekistan
1994-1995	Turkmenistan

As mentioned above, one of the main sources for annex table B.1 is the IMF. Those economies for which IMF data were used for the period, 1980-1999, or part of it, are listed below.

Period	Economy
1980-1999	Israel, Malta and Panama
1984-1985, 1989 and 1996-1999	Sudan
1980-1998	Barbados, Belgium and Luxembourg, China, Costa Rica, Fiji, Jordan, Libyan Arab Jamahiriya, Mauritius, Mexico, New Zealand, Nigeria, Oman, Papua New Guinea, Saudi Arabia, Solomon Islands, Vanuatu, and Yemen
1980-1993 and 1995-1998	Rwanda
1980-1995 and 1998	Mauritania
1980 and 1982-1998	Bahrain
1980-1981, 1986-1988 and 1993-1998	Uruguay
1980-1993, 1995 and 1998	El Salvador
1981-1998	Bangladesh
1981 and 1984-1998	Belize
1986-1998	Cape Verde, Guinea and Maldives.
1989-1998	Myanmar
1991-1998	India
1993-1998	Syrian Arab Republic
1994-1998	Iran (Islamic Republic of)
1995-1998	Azerbaijan
1996-1998	Nepal
1998	Georgia
1980-1997	Greece, Ireland, Italy, Japan and Morocco
1996-1997	Turkmenistan
1980-1996	Peru and Trinidad and Tobago
1989-1996	Equatorial Guinea
1994-1996	Tajikistan
1980-1995	Cameroon, Gabon, Netherlands Antilles, Portugal, Sierra Leone and Suriname
1981, 1987-1989 and 1991-1995	Gambia
1987-1995	Comoros
1992-1995	Djibouti
1980-1994	Central African Republic, Egypt, Norway and Sweden.
1981-1994	Denmark
1981, 1984-1985 and 1990-1994	Brunei Darussalam
1983 and 1985-1994	Kiribati
1984-1989 and 1991-1994	Chad
1992-1994	Uzbekistan
1994	New Caledonia
1980-1993	Honduras and Spain
1984-1993	Tonga
1992-1993	Cambodia
1980-1992	Mali
1991-1992	Uganda
1980-1991	Algeria, Argentina, Austria, Niger and Zambia
1980-1990	Cyprus, Poland, South Africa and Swaziland
1988-1990	Lao People's Democratic Republic
1980-1989	Antigua and Barbuda, Australia, Bahamas, Botswana, Brazil, Burkina Faso, Canada, Côte d'Ivoire, Dominican Republic, France, Germany, Ghana, Guatemala, Haiti, Indonesia, Jamaica, Kenya, Malaysia, Netherlands, Pakistan, Paraguay, Philippines, Saint Kitts and Nevis, Saint Lucia, Saint Vincent and the Grenadines, Senegal, Seychelles, Singapore, Sri Lanka, Thailand, Tunisia, Togo, United Kingdom, Venezuela and Zimbabwe
1980-1984 and 1986-1989	Lesotho
1980-1984 and 1989	Benin
1980 and 1986-1989	Mozambique
1982-1989	Dominica and Grenada.
1983-1989	Switzerland
1985-1989	Angola and Burundi
1989	Madagascar and Nicaragua
1980-1988	Colombia and Congo
1980-1981 and 1987-1988	Hungary
1980-1981, 1983, 1985 and 1987	Malawi
1980-1987	Iceland
1982-1987	Liberia
1980-1985	Ecuador, Guyana and the United States
1982-1985	Somalia
1980	Qatar

Those economies for which World Bank data were used for the period, 1980-1999, or part of it, are listed below.

Period	Economy
1980-1998	Democratic Republic of the Congo
1990-1998	Lebanon
1991-1998	Congo and Liberia
1992-1998	Algeria
1994-1998	Samoa and Tonga
1995-1998	Central African Republic and Chad
1996-1998	Cameroon, Comoros, Djibouti and Sierra Leone
1997-1998	Equatorial Guinea and Uzbekistan
1998	Turkmenistan
1996-1997	Mauritania
1997	El Salvador and Kiribati
1995-1996	Guinea-Bissau
1983-1995	Nepal
1994	Rwanda
1992-1993	Zambia
1992	Uruguay
1980-1990	India
1990	Haiti
1989	Czech Republic
1987	Myanmar

Those economies for which ECLAC data were used for the period, 1980-1999, or part of it, are listed below.

Period	Economy
1990-1996	Cayman Islands
1996	Suriname and Netherlands Antilles
1990-1997	Bermuda, Cuba and Virgin Islands

Those economies for which FDI inflows data were unavailable from the above-mentioned sources, the estimates of UNCTAD are used by employing the following methodologies:

• *Annualized data*

Estimates were applied by annualizing quarterly data obtained from either national official sources or the IMF for the economies and the years listed below.

(a)   National official sources

Year	Latest quarter	Economy
1999	Third quarter	Colombia and Mexico.

(b)   IMF

Year	Latest quarter	Economy
1999	First quarter	Nepal and Vanuatu.

• *Proxy*

One of the main methodologies for estimating FDI inflows for economies for which the data are not available is that OECD data on outward flows from DAC member countries are used as proxy for FDI inflows. Those economies for which this methodology is applied for the period, 1980-1998, or part of it, are listed below (these data were available until 1998 only at the time of the compilation of inflow data).

Period	Economy
1980-1981, 1986-1992 and 1996-1998	Somalia
1984-1992, 1994 and 1997-1998	Guinea-Bissau
1996-1998	Gabon
1980-1990 and 1993-1997	Iraq
1980-1981 and 1991-1997	Afghanistan

Period	Economy
1982-1983 and 1986-1997	Macau China
1987-1997	Democratic People's Republic of Korea
1985-1986, 1988-1993 and 1995-1996	New Caledonia
1996	Bosnia and Herzegovina
1980-1995	United Arab Emirates
1980-1983 and 1990-1995	Sudan
1984-1995	Qatar
1995	Brunei Darussalam
1982-1994	Gibraltar
1981, 1983-1988 and 1990-1993	Samoa
1980-1987 and 1989-1991	Djibouti
1990-1991	Burkina Faso
1980-1981 and 1988-1990	Liberia
1980, 1982, 1985 and 1988-1990	Uganda
1982-1986 and 1990	Gambia
1989-1990	Congo
1980-1989	Bermuda, Cayman Islands, Cuba, Iran (Islamic Republic of), Kuwait, Lebanon and the United Republic of Tanzania.
1980 and 1982-1989	Virgin Islands
1982, 1984, 1986 and 1988-1989	Malawi
1983-1989	Syrian Arab Republic
1985 and 1987-1989	Namibia
1980-1988	Ethiopia and Madagascar
1981-1988	Equatorial Guinea
1985-1988	Benin
1980-1987	Yugoslavia (Former)
1987	Nicaragua
1980, 1983-1984 and 1986	Myanmar
1981-1982 and 1986	Viet Nam
1980 and 1982-1985	Maldives
1980-1981 and 1983-1985	Guinea
1981-1985	Mozambique
1980-1984	Angola and Burundi.
1980-1983	Chad
1980-1982	Nepal

Outflows of FDI from large investors were also used as a proxy. Those economies for which this methodology was used for the period, 1980-1998, or part of it, are listed below.

Proxy countries	Period	Economy
United States only	1997-1998	Netherlands Antilles

- *Cross-border M&As*

Data on cross-border M&As and their growth rates were used to estimate FDI inflows. Those economies for which this methodology was used are listed below.

Period	Economy
1999	Bermuda, Central African Republic, Gibraltar and Uruguay

- *Estimates of UNCTAD*

Estimates of UNCTAD using national and secondary sources and information have been applied to the economies or the periods if FDI inflow data from the above-mentioned sources are not available. Those economies for which estimates of UNCTAD were used for the period, 1980-1998, or part of it, are listed below.

Period	Economy
1995-1996 and 1998-1999	Kiribati
1996-1999	Brunei Darussalam, Qatar and United Arab Emirates.
1997-1999	Bosnia and Herzegovina, Cayman Islands, New Caledonia and Suriname.
1998-1999	Afghanistan, Cuba, Greece, Democratic Republic of Korea, Macau China and Virgin Islands
1988 and 1999	Djibouti
1989 and 1999	Ethiopia
1999	Algeria, Bahrain, Bangladesh, Barbados, Belize, Burkina Faso, Cameroon, Cape Verde, Chad, Comoros, Congo, Democratic Republic of the Congo, Costa Rica, Egypt, Equatorial Guinea, Fiji, Gabon, Gambia, Georgia, Guinea, Guinea-Bissau, Jordan, Lebanon, Liberia, Libyan Arab Jamahiriya, Malawi, Maldives, Mali, Mauritania, Myanmar, Netherlands Antilles, Niger, Nigeria, Oman, Papua New Guinea, Poland, Rwanda, Samoa, Saudi Arabia, Senegal, Sierra Leone, Solomon Islands, Somalia, Tajikistan, Tonga, Togo, Turkmenistan, Uganda, Uzbekistan and Yemen.
1990-1993 and 1998	Iran (Islamic Republic of)
1990-1992 and 1998	Syrian Arab Republic
1995-1998	Gibraltar
1980-1997	Hong Kong (China)
1997	Bermuda
1991-1992	Iraq
1988-1989	Viet Nam
1986	Namibia

b.   FDI outflows

Those economies for which national official sources data were used for the period, 1980-1999, or part of it, are listed below.

Period	Economy
1980-1999	Bolivia, Chile, Finland, Republic of Korea, Malaysia, Taiwan Province of China, United Kingdom and the United States.
1983-1999	Zimbabwe
1987 and 1990-1999	Turkey
1988-1999	Iceland and Slovenia
1990 and 1998-1999	Morocco
1990-1999	Australia, Bahamas, Botswana, Brazil, Burundi, Canada, Côte d'Ivoire, France, Germany, Jamaica, Kuwait, Namibia, Netherlands, Nigeria, Pakistan, Philippines, Seychelles, Singapore, Switzerland, Thailand, Tunisia, and Venezuela
1991-1999	Cyprus, Hungary, Romania, South Africa and Swaziland
1992-1999	Argentina, Aruba, Austria, Estonia, Latvia, and Slovakia
1993-1999	Croatia, Czech Republic, Indonesia and the Russian Federation
1994-1999	Kazakhstan, Spain, Republic of Moldova and Ukraine
1995-1999	Denmark, Kenya, Lithuania, Malta, Norway and Sweden
1996-1999	Portugal
1998-1999	Azerbaijan, Hong Kong (China), Ireland, Italy and Japan
1999	Armenia, Belgium, El Salvador, India, Luxembourg, Mauritius and Trinidad and Tobago.
1990-1998	Senegal and Togo.
1991-1998	Poland
1992-1998	Mexico and Niger.
1993-1998	Burkina Faso
1996-1998	Benin, The Former Yugoslav Republic of Macedonia and Mali
1998	Tajikistan
1995-1997	Peru
1992-1993 and 1996	Guyana
1995-1996	Uganda
1990-1994	Bangladesh
1992-1995	Albania

As mentioned above, one of the main sources for annex table B.2 is the IMF. Those economies for which IMF data were used for the period, 1980-1999, or part of it, are listed below.

Period	Economy
1980-1999	Israel
1995-1999	Bulgaria
1980-1998	Barbados, Belgium, Colombia, Costa Rica, Fiji, Luxembourg and New Zealand
1980-1992 and 1994-1998	Egypt
1980-1982 and 1987-1998	Libyan Arab Jamahiriya
1982-1998	China
1988-1998	Mauritius
1993-1998	India
1991-1998	Belize
1990-1998	Bahrain
1997-1998	Bangladesh and Dominica.
1998	Armenia
1980-1997	Japan
1982-1988 and 1997	Uruguay
1988-1997	Cape Verde
1990-1997	Ireland and Italy.
1991-1997	Morocco
1997	Kyrgyzstan
1980-1996	Jordan
1993-1996	Dominican Republic
1996	El Salvador and Guinea
1980-1995	Cameroon, Netherlands Antilles and Portugal
1985-1995	Sri Lanka
1980-1994	Gabon
1980-1983, 1985-1989 and 1991-1994	Chad
1981-1994	Denmark, Norway and Sweden
1981, 1990 and 1993-1994	Angola
1982-1994	Central African Republic
1993-1994	Malta
1994	Kiribati
1980-1993	Spain
1990-1993	Tonga
1980-1991	Algeria, Austria and Niger
1980-1983 and 1989-1991	Argentina
1989-1991	Equatorial Guinea and Czechoslovakia (Former)
1990-1991	Haiti
1980-1990	Papua New Guinea, South Africa and Swaziland
1985 and 1987-1990	Cyprus
1990	Comoros and Romania
1980-1989	Australia, Brazil, Canada, France, Germany, Kenya, Kuwait, Netherlands, Poland, Senegal, Seychelles, Singapore and Thailand
1981-1989	Tunisia
1981 and 1983-1989	Venezuela
1981 and 1989	Burundi
1983-1989	Switzerland
1984-1989	Pakistan
1986-1989	Iceland
1989	Bahamas
1986-1988	Mauritania
1988	Lesotho
1983-1987	Trinidad and Tobago
1980-1986	Burkina Faso
1982-1986	Yemen
1983-1985	Botswana
1981-1984	Benin
1981	Guinea-Bissau

Those economies for which FDI outflows data were unavailable from the above-mentioned sources, the estimates of UNCTAD are used by employing the following methodologies:

• *Proxy*

Inflows of FDI to large recipient economies were used as a proxy. Those economies for which this methodology was used for the period, 1980-1998, or part of it, are listed below.

Proxy countries	Period	Economy
United States only	1981-1999	Bermuda, Panama and United Arab Republic
	1996-1999	Netherlands Antilles
	1998	Cape Verde and Guinea
	1997-1998	Angola and Uganda
	1995-1998	Saint Kitts and Nevis and Trinidad and Tobago
	1993-1998	Virgin Islands
	1995-1996	Gabon
	1995	Central African Republic and Chad
	1994-1998	Guatemala
	1994-1995 and 1997-1998	Guyana
	1993-1998	Antigua and Barbuda, Ecuador, Haiti and Honduras
	1981-1988	Bahamas
	1989-1991 and 1995-1996	Uruguay
	1982-1997 and 1999	Lebanon
	1980-1997	Liberia
	1996	Nicaragua and Syrian Arab Republic.
	1992-1994	Bosnia and Herzegovina
	1988-1989 and 1994-1996	Oman
	1981-1996 and 1999	Saudi Arabia
	1992 and 1997-1998	Dominican Republic
	1992-1993	Ireland
	1984-1989	Ireland
	1984-1988	Argentina
	1982-1989	Nigeria
	1981-1991	Mexico
	1981-1986 and 1988-1989	Bahrain
China, United States, Germany and Sweden	1997	Hong Kong (China)
European Union, China, United States and Japan	1996	Hong Kong (China)
European Union, China and United States	1980-1995	Hong Kong (China)
European Union	1992-1996	Iran (Islamic Republic of)
European Union and United States	1991-1996	Greece
	1980-1992	India and Indonesia
	1980-1989	Philippines
United States, Germany and Sweden	1997-1998	Greece
United States and Sweden	1997-1998	Saudi Arabia
Germany only	1997-1998	Iran (Islamic Republic of)

• *Annualized data*

In the case of unavailability of data from the above-mentioned sources, estimates were applied by annualizing quarterly data obtained from either national official sources or the IMF for the economies and the years listed below.

(a) National official sources

Year	Latest quarter	Economy
1999	Third quarter	Egypt

(b) IMF

Year	Latest quarter	Economy
1999	Third quarter	Colombia and Iceland

• *World Bank*

The World Bank reports only data on net FDI flows and FDI inward flows. Therefore, for selected economies FDI outward flows were estimated by subtracting FDI inflows from net FDI flows. This methodology was used for the economies and years listed below.

Period	Economy
1980-1998	Paraguay
1982-1984, 1990-1992 and 1996-1998	Mozambique
1982-1984, 1986-1988 and 1990-1998	Ethiopia

Period	Economy
1990-1998	Maldives, Samoa and Solomon Islands
1991, 1995 and 1998	Lao People's Democratic Republic
1993, 1995 and 1998	Nicaragua
1996-1998	Cameroon, Mauritania, Nepal and Sri Lanka
1996 and 1998	Mongolia
1998	Lebanon
1991-1997	Congo
1995-1997	Azerbaijan
1996-1997	Kyrgyzstan
1997	Guinea and Jordan
1983-1989 and 1995-1996	Bangladesh
1986-1988 and 1990-1996	Saint Vincent and the Grenadines
1990-1991 and 1995-1996	Saint Lucia
1991 and 1995-1996	Angola
1993-1996	Belarus
1996	Dominica
1990-1995	Benin and Sierra Leone
1991-1995	Comoros
1990-1994	Saint Kitts and Nevis and Trinidad and Tobago
1992-1994	Uruguay
1994	Malawi
1985-1990 and 1993	Syrian Arab Republic
1990-1993	Oman
1992-1993	Bulgaria
1993	Egypt
1983-1984, 1986-1988 and 1990-1992	Madagascar
1985 and 1990-1992	Lesotho
1982-1990	Iran (Islamic Republic of)
1984-1990	Guinea-Bissau
1987-1990	Belize
1985-1989	Tonga
1987-1989	Burkina Faso
1980-1981	Botswana
1980	Mexico

- *Cross-border M&As*

Data on cross-border M&As and their growth rates were used to estimate FDI outflows. Those economies are listed below.

Period	Economy
1998-1999	Cayman Island and Peru
1995-1998	Qatar
1996 and 1998	Ghana
1997-1998	Oman
1991-1996	Brunei Darussalam
1995	Nepal
1993	Cambodia

- *Estimates of UNCTAD*

Those economies for which information from national and secondary sources and information were used for the period, 1980-1999, or part of it, are listed below.

Period	Economy
1992 and 1999	Haiti
1995-1999	Bosnia and Herzegovina
1995, 1997 and 1999	Mongolia
1996-1999	Central African Republic, Chad and Malawi.
1997-1999	Belarus, Brunei Darussalam, Gabon and Syrian Arab Republic
1997 and 1999	Ghana
1998-1999	Jordan and Uruguay.
1999	Angola, Antigua and Barbuda, Bahrain, Bangladesh, Barbados, Belize, Benin, Burkina Faso, Cape Verde, China, Costa Rica, Dominica, Dominican Republic, Ecuador, Ethiopia, Fiji, Greece, Guatemala, Guyana, Honduras, Iran (Islamic Republic of), Kyrgyzstan, Libyan Arab Jamahiriya, TFYR Macedonia, Mali, Mexico, Nepal, New Zealand, Nicaragua, Niger, Oman, Paraguay, Poland, Qatar, Saint Kitts and Nevis, Samoa, Senegal, Sri Lanka, Togo, Uganda and the Virgin Islands.
1996-1998	Albania
1980-1997	Cayman Islands
1994	Peru
1992	Czech Republic

Up to 1994, the United States data on FDI outflows and outward stocks were adjusted for the financial sector of the Netherlands Antilles. This is because considerable intra-company loans between United States parent enterprises and their financial affiliates in the Netherlands Antilles are in many respects more akin to portfolio investment than to FDI. Since that year, however, the United States Department of Commerce has changed its methodology in reporting FDI outward flows to the Netherlands Antilles by excluding investment in the finance sector reported under intra-company loans.

2. FDI stocks

Annex tables B.3 and B.4, as well as some tables in the text, present data on FDI stocks at book value or historical cost, reflecting prices at the time when the investment was made.

For a large number of economies (as indicated in the footnotes of annex tables B.3 and B.4), FDI stocks are estimated by either cumulating FDI flows over a period of time or adding flows to an FDI stock that has been obtained for a particular year from national official sources or the IMF data series on assets and liabilities of direct investment.

In this year's *Report* the IMF data on assets and liabilities of direct investment were also used for some countries. Those economies for which IMF data were used for the period, 1980-1999, or part of it, are listed below.

Country/economy	Inward stock	Outward stock
Austria	1980-1989	1980-1989
Bahrain	1989-1998	1989-1998
Belgium and Luxembourg	1981-1998	1981-1997
Bulgaria	None	1998
Colombia	1980-1998	1980-1998
Denmark	1991-1998	1991-1998
Estonia	1996	None
France	None	1987-1989
Italy	None	1980-1998
Japan	1980-1998	1980-1998
Kyrgyzstan	1993-1998	None
Latvia	1995-1999	None
Malaysia	1980-1994	None
Namibia	1989	None
Netherlands	1980-1989	1980-1989
New Zealand	1989-1999	1989-1999
Norway	None	1980-1987
Peru	None	1993-1998
Romania	None	1990-1999
Spain	None	1980-1989
Swaziland	1981-1990	1980-1990
Sweden	None	1982-1985
Uruguay	None	1983-1987
Venezuela	None	1980-1989

C. Data revisions and updates

All FDI data and estimates in the *World Investment Report* are continuously revised. Because of the on-going revision, FDI data reported in the *World Investment Report* may differ from those reported in earlier *Reports* or other publications of UNCTAD. In particular, recent FDI data are being revised in many economies according to the fifth edition of the balance-of-payments manual of IMF. Because of this, the data reported in last year's report may be completely or partly changed in *WIR2000*. Major changes were observed in the following countries:

Austria

With the reporting period of 1998, FDI statistics were adjusted to the recommendations of the fifth edition of the balance-of-payments manual, so that FDI also includes loans between affiliated enterprises (except between banks), the private purchase and sale of real estate and property, as well as reinvested earnings. The OENB only started collecting data with a breakdown by economic sectors with the reporting period of 1997. Since 1995, the surveys on FDI stock also cover enterprises with a nominal capital of less than ATS 1 million provided their total assets exceed ATS 100 million.

Finland

From 1999 onwards, inter-company trade credits are included in FDI. As from 1998, direct investment enterprises' reinvested earnings are calculated according to the current operating performance concept, i.e. excluding capital gains and losses; the accrual principle is applied.

Germany

From the reporting period of 1999 onwards, enterprises' cross border participating interests amounting to 10 per cent or more of the capital or voting rights are deemed to be direct investment (before 1999: 20 per cent, before 1990: 25 per cent). Data for reinvested earnings follow the accrual principle. Short-term intra-company loans and trade credits, as well as reverse investments are included in FDI flows since 1996. From June 1990 (stock) and July 1990 (flow) onwards, FDI data relate to unified Germany.

Hong Kong (China)

The Census and Statistics Department compiled, for the first time, a set of FDI statistics for Hong Kong (China) in 2000, following international standards as stipulated in the *Balance of Payments Manual*, fifth edition, published by IMF. The compiled data are for 1998 and 1999 only. Data on investment position, flows and income are reported. The broad geographical and industrial distribution of such data are also available. These official data for 1998 are available in *the External Direct Investment Statistics of Hong Kong 1998*, published by the Census Statistics Department.

Ireland

Data on FDI are compiled by the Balance-of-Payments Section of the Central Statistics Office (CSO). In Spring 2000, a new quarterly series of balance-of-payments statistics was introduced, beginning with the reporting period of 1998 and following a complete overhaul of CSO collection and compilation system. The results are now being presented, for the first time, with a geographic breakdown and in line with international standards. These changes result in a discontinuity in long-term time series data and, therefore, new data from 1998 onwards are not comparable with the earlier series. However, it is envisaged to revise earlier data accordingly at a later stage.

Portugal

Trade credits between affiliated companies and reinvested earnings are included in FDI since 1996. Data are collected through annual surveys, carried out in 1997 (for 1995 and 1996 inward data) and in 1998 (for 1996 and 1997 outward data). No stock data are available prior to 1996.

United Kingdom

From the reporting period of 1997 onwards, the threshold was lowered to 10 per cent (prior to 1997: 20 per cent). Among further changes, which accompanied the implementation of the latest version of international guidelines, with the reporting period of 1997 onwards, is the exclusion of the Channel Islands and the Isle of Man from the definition of the economic territory of the United Kingdom – their data is now reported separately under "UK offshore islands". Data for the period prior to 1997 were not revised to take into account these changes.

D. Data verification

In compiling data for this year's *Report*, requests for verifications and confirmation were made to national official sources for virtually all economies to reflect the latest data revisions and accuracy. In addition, web sites of certain national official sources were also consulted. This verification process continued until end of June 2000. Any revisions made after this process are not reflected in the *Report*.

Below is a list of economies for which data were checked through either means. For the economies which are not mentioned below, the UNCTAD Secretariat could not have the data verified or confirmed by respective governments.

Communiqué

Albania, Antigua and Barbuda, Armenia, Aruba, Australia, Austria, Azerbaijan, Bahamas, Belarus, Belgium and Luxembourg, Bolivia, Botswana, Brazil, Bulgaria, Burundi, Cambodia, Canada, Croatia, Cyprus, Denmark, Dominica, Dominican Republic, Ecuador, Estonia, Finland, France, Germany, Ghana, Grenada, Guatemala, Guyana, Honduras, Hungary, Iceland, Indonesia, Ireland, Italy, Jamaica, Kazakhstan, Kenya, Kuwait, Lao People's Democratic Republic, Latvia, Lesotho, Lithuania, TFYR Macedonia, Madagascar, Malaysia, Mauritius, Moldova, Mongolia, Morocco, Mozambique, Myanmar, Namibia, Netherlands, New Zealand, Nicaragua, Nigeria, Norway, Pakistan, Philippines, Poland, Portugal, Republic of Korea, Russian Federation, Rwanda, Saint Kitts and Nevis, Saint Lucia, Saint Vincent and the Grenadines, Seychelles, Singapore, Slovakia, Slovenia, South Africa, Spain, Sri Lanka, Swaziland, Sweden, Switzerland, Thailand, Trinidad and Tobago, Tunisia, Turkey, Ukraine, United Republic of Tanzania, United Kingdom, Venezuela, Viet Nam, Zambia and Zimbabwe.

Web site

Angola, Argentina, Chile, Colombia, Costa Rica, El Salvador, Haiti, Hong Kong (China), India, Israel, Japan, Kyrgyzstan, Malta, Paraguay, Peru, Taiwan Province of China and United States.

E. Definitions and sources of the data in annex tables B.5 and B.6

These two annex tables show the ratio of inward and outward FDI flows to gross fixed capital formation or gross domestic capital formation (annex table B.5) and inward and outward FDI stock to GDP (annex table B.6), respectively. All of these data are in current prices.

The data on GDP were obtained from UNCTAD Secretariat. For some economies such as Taiwan Province of China, the data are supplemented from national sources. The data on gross fixed capital formation were obtained from IMF's international-financial-statistics CD-ROM, June 2000.

For economies for which data on gross fixed capital formation were unavailable, the following data were used:

Gross capital formation:

Barbados, Nigeria, Oman, Romania, Suriname and Syrian Arab Republic.

Gross investment:

Ethiopia and Indonesia.

In the case of economies for which gross fixed capital formation data were unavailable for the IMF, such as Taiwan Province of China, the data are supplemented from national sources or World Bank data on gross domestic fixed investment, obtained from the *World Development Indicators 2000* CD-ROM.

For annex table B.5, figures exceeding 100 per cent may result from the fact that, for some economies, the reported data on gross fixed capital formation do not necessarily accurately reflect the value of capital formation and that FDI flows do not necessarily translate into capital formation.

Data on FDI are from annex tables B.1-B.4.

Notes

---

[1]   In some countries, an equity stake of other than 10 per cent is still used. In the United Kingdom, for example, a stake of 20 per cent or more was a threshold until 1997.

[2]   This general definition of FDI is based on OECD, *Detailed Benchmark Definition of Foreign Direct Investment*, third edition (Paris, OECD, 1996) and International Monetary Fund, *Balance of Payments Manual*, fifth edition (Washington, D.C., IMF, 1993).

[3]   There are, however, some exceptions. For example, in the case of Germany, loans granted by affiliate enterprises to their parent enterprises are not deducted from the stock.

[4]   International Monetary Fund, op. cit., p. 40.

[5]   Includes Austria, Belgium, Canada, Denmark, Finland, France, Germany, Italy, Japan, the Netherlands, Norway, Spain, Sweden, the United Kingdom and the United States.

Annex table B.1.   **FDI inflows, by host region and economy, 1988-1999**

(Millions of dollars)

Host region/economy	1988-1993 (Annual average)	1994	1995	1996	1997	1998	1999
World	**190 629**	**255 988**	**331 844**	**377 516**	**473 052**	**680 082**	**865 487**
Developed countries	**140 088**	**145 135**	**205 693**	**219 789**	**275 229**	**480 638**	**636 449**
Western Europe	**80 974**	**82 967**	**119 012**	**114 940**	**138 986**	**259 924**	**315 123**
European Union	**78 511**	**76 866**	**114 387**	**108 604**	**128 574**	**248 675**	**305 058**
Austria	768	2 102	1 904	4 426	2 654	4 567	2 813
Belgium and Luxembourg	8 613	8 514	10 689	14 064	11 998	22 691	15 862
Denmark	1 168	5 006	4 195	742	2 801	6 716	7 454
Finland	472	1 577	1 063	1 109	2 114	12 144	3 023
France	13 976	15 580	23 681	21 960	23 178	29 495	39 101
Germany	3 052	7 135	12 025	6 572	11 097	21 163	26 822
Greece	987	981	1 053	1 058	984	700[a]	900[a]
Ireland	787	838	1 447	2 618	2 743	8 579	18 322
Italy	4 105	2 199	4 842	3 546	3 700	3 065	4 901
Netherlands	8 058	7 266	12 220	15 052	14 463	41 682	33 785
Portugal	1 854	1 270	685	1 368	2 278	2 802	570
Spain	10 814	8 876	6 161	6 585	6 375	11 863	9 355
Sweden	2 586	6 269	14 453	5 070	10 963	19 560	59 968
United Kingdom	21 271	9 253	19 969	24 435	33 227	63 649	82 182
Other Western Europe	**2 463**	**6 100**	**4 625**	**6 335**	**10 413**	**11 249**	**10 065**
Gibraltar	50[a]	- 1[a]	1[a]	1[a]	1[a]	1[a]	8[a]
Iceland	11	- 2	- 9	84	149	148	66
Norway	455	2 736	2 409	3 172	3 627	3 599	6 577
Switzerland	1 948	3 366	2 223	3 078	6 636	7 500	3 413
North America	**50 117**	**53 302**	**68 029**	**94 091**	**117 249**	**208 021**	**300 594**
Canada	5 336	8 207	9 257	9 636	11 761	21 705	25 061
United States	44 781	45 095	58 772	84 455	105 488	186 316	275 533
Other developed countries	**8 997**	**8 866**	**18 652**	**10 758**	**18 994**	**12 693**	**20 732**
Australia	6 105	4 600	12 376	6 127	7 732	6 345	5 422
Israel	331	432	1 337	1 382	1 622	1 850	2 256
Japan	737	912	39	200	3 200	3 192	12 741
New Zealand	1 802	2 543	3 659	2 231	2 623	745	-1 063
South Africa	22	380	1 241	818	3 817	561	1 376
Developing countries	**46 919**	**104 920**	**111 884**	**145 030**	**178 789**	**179 481**	**207 619**
Africa	**3 472**	**5 632**	**4 699**	**5 522**	**6 896**	**7 519**	**8 949**
North Africa	**1 388**	**2 312**	**1 207**	**1 215**	**2 356**	**2 300**	**2 992**
Algeria	11	18	5	4	7	5	6[a]
Egypt	730	1 256	596	637	888	1 077	1 500[a]
Libyan Arab Jamahiriya	105	- 79	- 107	- 135	- 82	- 152	- 100[a]
Morocco	275	551	335	357	1 079	329	847
Sudan	- 6[b]	-[a]	-[a]	-	98	371	371
Tunisia	273	566	378	351	366	670	368
Other Africa	**2 084**	**3 320**	**3 493**	**4 307**	**4 540**	**5 220**	**5 958**
Angola	208	170	472	181	412	1 114	1 814

/...

Annex table B.1.   **FDI inflows, by host region and economy, 1988-1999 (continued)**

(Millions of dollars)

Host region/economy	1988-1993 (Annual average)	1994	1995	1996	1997	1998	1999
Benin	54	14	8	25	26	35	31
Botswana	- 20	- 14	70	71	100	90	112
Burkina Faso	3	18	10	17	13	10	10[a]
Burundi	-	-	2	-	-	2	-
Cameroon	- 14	- 9	7	35	45	50	40[a]
Cape Verde	1	2	26	29	12	9	15[a]
Central African Republic	- 5	4	3	5	6	5	13[a]
Chad	7	27	13	18	15	16	15[a]
Comoros	1	-	-	2	2	2	2[a]
Congo	5	5	3	8	9	4	5[a]
Congo, Democratic Republic of	- 3	1	1	2	1	-	1[a]
Côte d'Ivoire	64	118	268	302	450	314	279
Djibouti	-	1	3	5	5	6	5[a]
Equatorial Guinea	14	17	127	376	20	24	120[a]
Ethiopia	2	21	32	13	68	178	90[a]
Gabon	22	- 100	- 113	312[a]	143[a]	211[a]	200[a]
Gambia	7	10	8	12	13	14	15[a]
Ghana	34	233	107	120	83	56	115
Guinea	18	-	-	24	17	18	20[a]
Guinea-Bissau	2[c]	-[a]	1	1	10[a]	-[a]	3[a]
Kenya	24	4	32	13	40	42	42
Lesotho	127	273	275	286	269	262	136
Liberia	200	14	21	17	15	16	10[a]
Madagascar	15	6	10	10	14	16	58
Malawi	13	9	25	44	22	70	60[a]
Mali	-	17	123	47	74	36	40[a]
Mauritania	6	2	7	5	3	-	2[a]
Mauritius	25	20	19	37	55	12	49
Mozambique	16	35	45	73	64	213	384
Namibia	54	98	153	129	84	77	114
Niger	17	8	16	20	25	9	15[a]
Nigeria	968	1 959	1 079	1 593	1 539	1 051	1 400[a]
Rwanda	9	1	2	2	3	7	5[a]
Senegal	19	67	35	7	176	71	60[a]
Seychelles	19	30	40	30	54	55	60
Sierra Leone	4	- 3	- 2	5	4	5	1[a]
Somalia	- 13	1	1	-[a]	-[a]	-[a]	-[a]
Swaziland	55	25	33	- 62	- 48	51	- 4
Togo	5	16	38	27	23	42	35[a]
Uganda	9	88	125	120	175	210	180[a]
United Republic of Tanzania	7	50	150	149	158	172	183
Zambia	99	40	97	117	207	198	163
Zimbabwe	3	41	118	81	135	444	59
Latin America and the Caribbean	**13 136**	**30 091**	**32 816**	**45 890**	**69 172**	**73 767**	**90 485**
South America	**6 534**	**15 183**	**18 909**	**31 572**	**47 629**	**51 348**	**72 053**
Argentina	2 266	3 490	5 315	6 522	8 755	6 526	23 153
Bolivia	79	130	374	426	879	957	1 016
Brazil	1 534	2 590	5 475	10 496	18 743	28 480	31 397
Chile	993	2 733	2 956	4 633	5 219	4 638	9 221
Colombia	571	1 445	968	3 112	5 639	2 907	1 396[a]
Ecuador	208	531	470	491	695	831	636
Guyana	108[d]	107	74	93	53	47	48
Paraguay	63	138	155	246	270	423	306
Peru	154	3 084	2 000	3 226	1 702	1 930	2 068
Suriname	- 105	- 30	- 21	7[a]	12[a]	10[a]	5[a]

/...

Annex table B.1. **FDI inflows, by host region and economy, 1988-1999 (continued)**

(Millions of dollars)

Host region/economy	1988-1993 (Annual average)	1994	1995	1996	1997	1998	1999
Uruguay	51[d]	155	157	137	126	164	200[a]
Venezuela	612	813	985	2 183	5 536	4 435	2 607
Other Latin America and the Caribbean	**6 601**	**14 908**	**13 907**	**14 318**	**21 544**	**22 419**	**18 432**
Antigua and Barbuda	38	25	31	19	24	26	12
Aruba	65[e]	- 59	1	84	196	84	394
Bahamas	12	23	107	88	210	147	145
Barbados	10	13	12	13	15	16	15[a]
Belize	15	15	21	17	12	18	3[a]
Bermuda	1 544[a]	1 079[a]	1 350[a]	2 100[a]	1 700[a]	2 400[a]	184[a]
Cayman Islands	117[a]	532[a]	490[a]	410[a]	2 000[a]	3 500[a]	1 800[a]
Costa Rica	173	298	337	427	483	559	450[a]
Cuba	4[a]	14[a]	9[a]	12[a]	13[a]	30[a]	15[a]
Dominica	15	23	54	18	21	9	13
Dominican Republic	144	207	414	97	421	700	1 353
El Salvador	15	..	38	- 5	11	872	231
Grenada	16	19	20	19	35	51	43
Guatemala	134	65	70	77	85	673	147
Haiti	6	- 3	7	4	4	11	30
Honduras	45	42	69	90	128	99	230
Jamaica	120	130	147	184	203	369	520
Mexico	3 705	10 973	9 526	9 186	12 831	10 238	11 233[a]
Netherlands Antilles	19	22	10	11[a]	103[a]	151[a]	70[a]
Nicaragua	41[e]	40	75	97	173	184	300
Panama	2	393	267	410	1 256	1 206	22
Saint Kitts and Nevis	25	15	20	35	20	34	77
Saint Lucia	37	32	30	17	47	84	87
Saint Vincent and the Grenadines	14	47	31	43	55	28	25
Trinidad and Tobago	175	516	299	355	1 000	732	633
Virgin Islands	112[a]	447[a]	470[a]	510[a]	500[a]	200[a]	400[a]
Developing Europe	**221**	**420**	**483**	**1 026**	**1 020**	**1 459**	**2 315**
Bosnia and Herzegovina	..	..	..	- 2[a]	1[a]	10[a]	10[a]
Croatia	120[f]	117	115	506	517	893	1 382
Malta	52	152	182	325	165	273	811
Slovenia	49	128	176	185	321	165	90
TFYR Macedonia	..	24	10	12	16	118	22
Asia	**29 854**	**68 606**	**73 324**	**92 434**	**101 575**	**96 504**	**105 621**
West Asia	**1 996**	**1 756**	**14**	**2 429**	**4 979**	**6 206**	**6 711**
Bahrain	239	208	431	2 048	329	181	300[a]
Cyprus	78	46	80	50	68	56	65
Iran, Islamic Republic	- 86	2	17	26	53	24	85[a]
Iraq	-	-[a]	2[a]	-[a]	-[a]	..	..
Jordan	9	3	13	16	361	310	151[a]
Kuwait	13[f]	..	7	347	20	59	72
Lebanon	3	7	35	80	150	200	250[a]
Oman	121	76	46	75	53	106	70[a]
Qatar	23	132[a]	94[a]	35[a]	55[a]	70[a]	50[a]
Saudi Arabia	389	350	-1 877	-1 129	3 044	4 289	4 800[a]
Syrian Arab Republic	84	251	100	89	80	80	75[a]
Turkey	665	608	885	722	805	940	783
United Arab Emirates	111	62[a]	399[a]	130[a]	100[a]	100[a]	160[a]

Annex table B.1.   **FDI inflows, by host region and economy, 1988-1999 (continued)**

(Millions of dollars)

Host region/economy	1988-1993 (Annual average)	1994	1995	1996	1997	1998	1999
Yemen	347	11	- 218	- 60	- 139	- 210	- 150[a]
Central Asia	**745**	**896**	**1 655**	**2 053**	**3 079**	**3 141**	**2 762**
Armenia	7[b]	8	25	18	52	232	130
Azerbaijan	..	22	330	627	1 115	1 023	691
Georgia	..	8	5	45	111	265	96[a]
Kazakhstan	686[d]	660	964	1 137	1 321	1 152	1 587
Kyrgyzstan	10[f]	38	96	47	83	109	35
Tajikistan	..	10	15	16	4	30	29[a]
Turkmenistan	..	100	100	108	108	130	80[a]
Uzbekistan	43[d]	50	120	55	285	200	113[a]
South, East and South- East Asia	**27 113**	**65 954**	**71 654**	**87 952**	**93 518**	**87 158**	**96 148**
Afghanistan	-[g]	-[a]	-[a]	-[a]	-[a]	-[a]	-[a]
Bangladesh	4	11	2	14	141	308	150[a]
Brunei Darussalam	4	6	13[a]	11[a]	5[a]	4[a]	5[a]
Cambodia	44[d]	69	151	294	168	121	135
China	8 852	33 787	35 849	40 180	44 236	43 751	40 400[a]
Hong Kong, China	3 689[a]	7 828[a]	6 213[a]	10 460[a]	11 368[a]	14 776	23 068
India	234	973	2 144	2 426	3 577	2 635	2 168
Indonesia	1 269	2 109	4 346	6 194	4 677	- 356	-3 270
Korea, Democratic People's Republic	103[a]	7[a]	14[a]	-[a]	-[a]	-[a]	-[a]
Korea, Republic of	956	991	1 357	2 308	3 088	5 215	10 340
Lao People's Democratic Republic	10	59	88	128	86	45	79
Macau, China	-	4[a]	2[a]	6[a]	3[a]	-[a]	1[a]
Malaysia	3 320	4 581	5 816	7 296	6 513	2 700	3 532
Maldives	5	9	7	9	11	12	10[a]
Mongolia	5[d]	7	10	16	25	19	30
Myanmar	137[b]	126	277	310	387	315	300[a]
Nepal	3	7	8	19	23	12	132[a]
Pakistan	266	419	719	918	713	507	531
Philippines	770	1 591	1 459	1 520	1 249	1 752	737
Singapore	3 982	8 550	7 206	8 984	8 085	5 493	6 984
Sri Lanka	82	166	65	133	435	206	202
Taiwan Province of China	1 160	1 375	1 559	1 864	2 248	222	2 926
Thailand	1 899	1 343	2 000	2 405	3 732	7 449	6 078
Viet Nam	319	1 936	2 349	2 455	2 745	1 972	1 609
The Pacific	**236**	**172**	**563**	**158**	**126**	**231**	**248**
Fiji	55	68	70	2	16	76	30[a]
Kiribati	-	-	-[a]	-[a]	1	-[a]	-[a]
New Caledonia	13	10	-[a]	-[a]	10[a]	5[a]	3[a]
Papua New Guinea	133	57	455	111	29	110	170[a]
Vanuatu	18	30	31	33	30	27	26[a]
Samoa	3	3	3	4	4	3	2[a]
Solomon Islands	13	2	2	6	34	9	15[a]
Tonga	-	2	2	2	3	2	2[a]
Central and Eastern Europe	**3 623**	**5 932**	**14 267**	**12 697**	**19 034**	**19 963**	**21 420**
Albania	39[d]	53	70	90	48	45	41
Belarus	12[d]	11	15	73	200	149	225
Bulgaria	35[e]	105	90	109	505	537	770
Czech Republic	502[b]	869	2 562	1 428	1 300	2 720	5 108

Annex table B.1. **FDI inflows, by host region and economy, 1988-1999 (concluded)**

(Millions of dollars)

Host region/economy	1988-1993 (Annual average)	1994	1995	1996	1997	1998	1999
Estonia	114[d]	214	201	151	267	581	306
Hungary	1 033	1 146	4 453	2 275	2 173	2 036	1 944
Latvia	36[d]	214	180	382	521	357	366
Lithuania	20[d]	31	73	152	355	926	486
Moldova, Republic of	16[d]	28	67	24	76	81	34
Poland	478	1 875	3 659	4 498	4 908	6 365	7 500[a]
Romania	72[g]	342	420	265	1 215	2 031	961
Russian Federation	956[d]	640	2 016	2 479	6 638	2 761	2 861
Slovakia	111[e]	245	195	251	206	631	322
Ukraine	200[d]	159	267	521	624	743	496

Memorandum:

Least developed countries: [h]

Total	**1 361**	**1 168**	**2 001**	**2 394**	**2 524**	**3 715**	**4 527**
Africa	822	844	1 641	1 632	1 772	3 062	3 798
Latin America and the Caribbean	6	- 3	7	4	4	11	30
Asia and the Pacific	533	327	352	758	748	642	700
Asia	499	292	316	715	679	603	657
West Asia	347	11	- 218	- 60	- 139	- 210	- 150
South, East and South-East Asia	151	281	533	775	817	813	807
The Pacific	34	35	36	43	69	39	43

Oil-exporting countries: [i]

Total	**12 482**	**24 277**	**23 268**	**30 662**	**39 116**	**28 401**	**27 162**
Africa	2 308	3 787	2 321	2 986	3 327	4 030	5 233
North Africa	*1 119*	*1 761*	*872*	*857*	*1 179*	*1 600*	*1 774*
Other Africa	*1 189*	*2 026*	*1 449*	*2 129*	*2 148*	*2 430*	*3 459*
Latin America and the Caribbean	4 779	12 963	11 655	12 642	20 941	17 193	16 126
South America	*899*	*1 474*	*1 829*	*3 101*	*7 110*	*6 224*	*4 259*
Other Latin America and the Caribbean	*3 880*	*11 489*	*9 825*	*9 541*	*13 831*	*10 970*	*11 866*
Asia	5 395	7 527	9 293	15 034	14 848	7 177	5 804
West Asia	*802*	*831*	*- 881*	*1 533*	*3 653*	*4 829*	*5 537*
South, East and South-East Asia	*4 593*	*6 696*	*10 175*	*13 501*	*11 195*	*2 348*	*267*
All developing countries minus China	37 269	71 133	76 035	104 850	134 553	135 730	167 219
Asia and the Pacific	29 532	68 777	73 887	92 592	101 701	96 736	105 869
Africa including South Africa	3 494	6 012	5 940	6 340	10 713	8 080	10 325

Source: UNCTAD, FDI/TNC database.

[a] Estimates. For details, see "definitions and sources" in annex B.
[b] Annual average from 1989 to 1993.
[c] Annual average from 1988 to 1992.
[d] Annual average from 1992 to 1993.
[e] Annual average from 1990 to 1993.
[f] 1993.
[g] Annual average from 1991 to 1993.
[h] Least developed countries include: Afghanistan, Angola, Bangladesh, Benin, Burkina Faso, Burundi, Cambodia, Cape Verde, Central African Republic, Chad, Comoros, Democratic Repunlic of Congo, Djibouti, Equatorial Guinea, Ethiopia, Gambia, Guinea, Guinea-Bissau, Haiti, Kiribati, Lao People's Democratic Republic, Lesotho, Liberia, Madagascar, Malawi, Maldives, Mali, Mauritania, Mozambique, Myanmar, Nepal, Niger, Rwanda, Samoa, Sierra Leone, Solomon Islands, Somalia, Sudan, Togo, Uganda, United Republic of Tanzania, Vanuatu, Yemen and Zambia. Not included are Bhutan, Eritrea, Sao Tome and Principe and Tuvalu due to unavailability of data.

ⁱ Oil-exporting countries include: Algeria, Angola, Bahrain, Brunei Darussalam, Cameroon, Congo, Ecuador, Egypt, Gabon, Indonesia, Islamic Republic of Iran, Iraq, Kuwait, Libyan Arab Jamahiriya, Malaysia, Mexico, Nigeria, Oman, Qatar, Saudi Arabia, Trinidad and Tobago, Tunisia, United Arab Emirates and Venezuela.

Note: For Nigeria, FDI inflows excluding reinvested earnings in oil prospecting companies are as follows:
FDI inflows, in millions of dollars.

Year	1990	1991	1992	1993	1994	1995	1996	1997	1998	1999
FDI inflows	1 300	566	678	1 933	357	796	81	139	418	358

Annex table B.2. **FDI outflows, by home region and economy, 1988-1999**

(Millions of dollars)

Home region/economy	1988-1993 (Annual average)	1994	1995	1996	1997	1998	1999
World	**221 357**	**282 902**	**357 537**	**390 776**	**471 906**	**687 111**	**799 928**
Developed countries	**197 581**	**240 487**	**306 822**	**331 963**	**404 153**	**651 873**	**731 765**
Western Europe	**115 639**	**133 665**	**174 080**	**204 381**	**246 464**	**444 747**	**533 244**
European Union	**107 220**	**120 684**	**158 990**	**182 266**	**223 662**	**425 495**	**509 824**
Austria	1 177	1 257	1 131	1 934	1 987	2 765	2 797
Belgium and Luxembourg	6 528	1 371	11 603	8 026	7 252	28 845	24 928
Denmark	1 622	4 162	2 334	1 970	3 715	3 955	8 214
Finland	1 469	4 297 *	1 497	3 595	5 287	18 646	4 192
France	24 246	24 381	15 760	30 419	35 591	45 471	107 952
Germany	18 383	18 859	39 049	50 804	40 733	91 159	50 596
Greece	12[b]	- 90[a]	66[a]	- 18[a]	4[a]	- 47[a]	- 21[a]
Ireland	400	438	820	727	1 008	3 906	5 418
Italy	5 545	5 239	7 024	8 697	10 414	14 096	2 958
Netherlands	12 886	17 664	20 165	31 224	29 243	51 373	45 858
Portugal	271	287	688	776	1 667	2 901	2 679
Spain	2 675	3 934	4 076	5 397	12 522	19 042	35 414
Sweden	6 925	6 685	11 215	4 667	12 652	24 365	19 549
United Kingdom	25 083	32 199	43 562	34 047	61 586	119 018	199 289
Other Western Europe	**8 419**	**12 981**	**15 090**	**22 115**	**22 802**	**19 252**	**23 421**
Gibraltar	..	..	..	..	..	..	..
Iceland	9	23	24	63	55	74	85
Norway	1 031	2 166	2 856	5 900	5 016	2 545	5 420
Switzerland	7 379	10 793	12 210	16 152	17 732	16 633	17 916
North America	**44 633**	**82 548**	**103 538**	**97 524**	**122 032**	**177 338**	**168 717**
Canada	5 309	9 296	11 464	13 098	22 515	31 286	17 816
United States	39 323	73 252	92 074	84 426	99 517	146 052	150 901
Other developed countries	**37 309**	**24 274**	**29 204**	**30 058**	**35 657**	**29 788**	**29 803**
Australia	3 235	2 483	3 801	6 064	6 460	2 323	3 604
Israel	316	742	733	1 042	834	830	702
Japan	32 472	18 089	22 508	23 442	26 059	24 152	22 743
New Zealand	837	1 725	- 336	-1 534	- 46	752	1 641[a]
South Africa	450	1 236	2 498	1 044	2 351	1 731	1 114
Developing countries	**23 509**	**42 124**	**50 259**	**57 763**	**64 335**	**33 045**	**65 638**
Africa	**1 001**	**528**	**175**	**- 43**	**1 617**	**648**	**935**
North Africa	**25**	**103**	**194**	**101**	**429**	**371**	**317**
Algeria	17[c]	..	..	..	..	..	..
Egypt	25	43	93	5	129	45	47[a]
Libyan Arab Jamahiriya	- 43	28	83	63	282	304	250[a]
Morocco	23[d]	24	15	30	9	20	18
Sudan	..	..	..	..	..	..	..
Tunisia	3	8	3	2	9	2	3
Other Africa	**975**	**425**	**- 19**	**- 144**	**1 188**	**277**	**618**
Angola	-[d]	- 2	- 222[a]	-[a]	- 1[a]	- 1[a]	-[a]

/...

Annex table B.2.   FDI outflows, by home region and economy, 1988-1999 (continued)

(Millions of dollars)

Home region/economy	1988-1993 (Annual average)	1994	1995	1996	1997	1998	1999
Benin	- 58[d]	- 9[a]	- 12[a]	12	12	2	7[a]
Botswana	9[d]	9	41	- 1	4	3	3
Burkina Faso	2[e]	7	-	-	1	5	1[a]
Burundi	_[f]	-	-	-	-	-	-
Cameroon	24	-	-	- 57[a]	- 66[a]	- 55[a]	..
Cape Verde	-	-	-	-	-	_[a]	_[a]
Central African Republic	5	7	6[a]	6[a]	5[a]	5[a]	5[a]
Chad	12[b]	-	12[a]	8[a]	10[a]	5[a]	7[a]
Comoros	_[d]	3[a]	_[a]	..	..	..	..
Congo	4[b]	5[a]	3[a]	8[a]	9[a]	..	..
Congo, Democratic Republic of	..	..	..	..	..	..	..
Côte d'Ivoire	105[d]	40	56	33	34	36	27
Djibouti	..	..	..	..	..	..	..
Equatorial Guinea	_[g]	..	..	..	..	..	..
Ethiopia	8[d]	3[a]	8[a]	5[a]	5[a]	4[a]	5[a]
Gabon	15	-	- 1[a]	- 1[a]	15[a]	5[a]	6[a]
Gambia	..	..	..	..	..	..	..
Ghana	..	..	..	150[a]	47[a]	30[a]	70[a]
Guinea	..	..	..	-	- 16[a]	_[a]	..
Guinea-Bissau	1[h]	..	..	..	..	..	..
Kenya	_[c]	..	13	25	5	14	30
Lesotho	_[i]	..	..	..	..	..	..
Liberia	119	85[a]	- 96[a]	- 430[a]	1 028[a]	..	..
Madagascar	_[i]	..	..	..	..	..	..
Malawi	..	1[a]	..	2[a]	_[a]	6[a]	3[a]
Mali	..	..	..	4	5	27	15[a]
Mauritania	_[j]	..	..	5[a]	3[a]	5[a]	..
Mauritius	15	1	4	3	3	14	6
Mozambique	_[i]	..	..	_[a]	_[a]	_[a]	..
Namibia	4[d]	- 6	- 4	- 22	1	- 1	2
Niger	9	4	2	18	8	10	15[a]
Nigeria	661	179	104	42	58	107	92
Rwanda	..	..	..	..	..	..	..
Senegal	8	17	- 3	2	-	10	5[a]
Seychelles	2	13	16	13	10	3	9
Sierra Leone	_[d]	- 1[a]	3[a]	..	..	..	..
Somalia	..	..	..	..	..	..	..
Swaziland	9	54	28	- 32	- 20	10	- 14
Togo	7[d]	-	6	13	4	22	15[a]
Uganda	..	..	3	- 1	- 4[a]	_[a]	300[a]
United Republic of Tanzania	..	..	..	..	..	..	..
Zambia	..	..	..	..	..	..	..
Zimbabwe	12	13	13	51	28	9	9
Latin America and the Caribbean	**6 930**	**6 094**	**7 305**	**5 823**	**15 050**	**9 405**	**27 325**
South America	**1 398**	**3 139**	**3 773**	**4 140**	**8 642**	**8 428**	**8 329**
Argentina	310	1 013	1 497	1 600	3 656	2 166	1 195
Bolivia	2	2	2	2	2	3	3
Brazil	521	618	1 163	520	1 660	2 609	1 401
Chile	165	911	752	1 188	1 866	2 797	4 855
Colombia	67	149	256	328	810	529	16[a]
Ecuador	- 1[e]	- 2[a]	2[a]	1[a]	_[a]	_[a]	_[a]
Guyana	_[k]	_[a]	_[a]	- 1	_[a]	_[a]	_[a]
Paraguay	13	83[a]	28[a]	_[a]	49[a]	13[a]	20[a]
Peru	10[k]	7[a]	8	- 16	85	40[a]	220[a]
Suriname	..	..	..	..	..	..	..
Uruguay	3	_[a]	- 26[a]	11[a]	13	5[a]	10[a]
Venezuela	309	358	91	507	500	267	609

Annex table B.2.   **FDI outflows, by home region and economy, 1988-1999 (continued)**

(Millions of dollars)

Home region/economy	1988-1993 (Annual average)	1994	1995	1996	1997	1998	1999
Other Latin America and the Caribbean	**5 532**	**2 954**	**3 532**	**1 683**	**6 408**	**977**	**18 996**
Antigua and Barbuda	- 1[e]	- 1[a]	- 2[a]	- 1[a]	- 2[a]	.[a]	1[a]
Aruba	3[k]	2	2	-	- 2	1	- 7
Bahamas	-	-	-	-	-	1	-
Barbados	2	1	3	4	1	-	2[a]
Belize	1[f]	2	2	6	4	5	5[a]
Bermuda	48[a]	378[a]	501[a]	- 144[a]	2 104[a]	- 363[a]	15 099[a]
Cayman Islands	65[a]	300[a]	450[a]	400[a]	1 800[a]	100[a]	100[a]
Costa Rica	4	5	6	6	7	8	7[a]
Cuba	..	..	..	..	..	..	..
Dominica	..	..	..	1[a]	-	2	2[a]
Dominican Republic	5[k]	12	15	14	1[a]	1[a]	6[a]
El Salvador	..	..	..	2	..	..	3
Grenada	..	..	..	..	..	..	..
Guatemala	..	- 20[a]	- 24[a]	2[a]	1[a]	2[a]	2[a]
Haiti	- 7[d]	.[a]	1[a]	1[a]	.[a]	.[a]	.[a]
Honduras	.[d]	- 3[a]	- 2[a]	- 2[a]	- 1[a]	- 1[a]	1[a]
Jamaica	61[e]	53	66	93	57	82	95
Mexico	179	1 058	- 263	38	1 108	1 363	800[a]
Netherlands Antilles	2	1	-	-1 242[a]	-2 427[a]	- 613[a]	137[a]
Nicaragua	.[e]	..	.[a]	- 9[a]	..	.[a]	- 2[a]
Panama	288	- 210[a]	329[a]	860[a]	313[a]	1 218[a]	979[a]
Saint Kitts and Nevis	.[d]	.[a]	- 2[a]	- 2[a]	- 2[a]	- 1[a]	- 1[a]
Saint Lucia	.[l]	..	5[a]	16[a]	..	..	..
Saint Vincent and the Grenadines	1[d]	.[a]	.[a]	.[a]	..	..	..
Trinidad and Tobago	.[d]	.[a]	1[a]	1[a]	1[a]	1[a]	266
Virgin Islands	4 882[e]	1 378[a]	2 444[a]	1 639[a]	3 444[a]	- 830[a]	1 500[a]
Developing Europe	**28**	**7**	**24**	**68**	**228**	**125**	**109**
Bosnia and Herzegovina	.[k]	4[a]	8[a]	29[a]	- 2[a]	.[a]	.[a]
Croatia	19[e]	7	6	24	186	98	34
Malta	.[e]	- 1	5	6	17	15	30
Slovenia	9	- 3	6	8	26	11	44
TFYR Macedonia	..	..	..	-	1	1	1[a]
Asia	**15 528**	**35 484**	**42 738**	**51 885**	**47 418**	**22 818**	**37 239**
West Asia	**857**	**-1 225**	**- 879**	**2 369**	**- 352**	**-4 339**	**1 169**
Bahrain	32	199	- 16	305	48	181	200[a]
Cyprus	12	22	28	48	44	85	158
Iran, Islamic Republic	- 42[a]	6[a]	3[a]	.[a]	61[a]	17[a]	30[a]
Iraq	..	..	..	..	..	..	..
Jordan	- 10	- 23	- 27	- 43	.[a]	10[a]	15
Kuwait	564	-1 519	-1 022	1 740	- 969	-1 867	223
Lebanon	2[a]	- 2[a]	- 2[a]	- 2[a]	- 3[a]	-2 671[a]	- 1[a]
Oman	.[a]	5[a]	1[a]	1[a]	10[a]	10[a]	10[a]
Qatar	..	..	30[a]	40[a]	20[a]	20[a]	30[a]
Saudi Arabia	210[a]	81[a]	13[a]	180[a]	195[a]	- 472[a]	- 125[a]
Syrian Arab Republic	56	..	..	1[a]	3[a]	2[a]	2[a]
Turkey	23[d]	49	113	110	251	367	645
United Arab Emirates	11[a]	- 42[a]	1[a]	- 11[a]	- 11[a]	- 20[a]	- 18[a]
Yemen	..	..	..	..	..	..	..
Central Asia	**-**	**-**	**176**	**37**	**67**	**157**	**354**
Armenia	..	..	..	..	..	12	13

Annex table B.2. **FDI outflows, by home region and economy, 1988-1999 (continued)**

(Millions of dollars)

Home region/economy	1988-1993 (Annual average)	1994	1995	1996	1997	1998	1999
Azerbaijan	..	..	175[a]	36[a]	64[a]	137	336
Georgia	..	..	..	..	..	..	..
Kazakhstan	..	-	-	-	1	8	4
Kyrgyzstan	..	..	..	-[a]	1[a]	-	1[a]
Tajikistan	..	..	..	..	..	-	..
Turkmenistan	..	..	..	..	..	..	..
Uzbekistan	..	..	..	..	..	..	..
South, East and South-East Asia	**14 671**	**36 708**	**43 442**	**49 479**	**47 703**	**27 000**	**35 716**
Afghanistan	..	..	..	..	..	..	..
Bangladesh	-	-	- 65[a]	28[a]	3	3	5[a]
Brunei Darussalam	17[b]	-[a]	20[a]	40[a]	10[a]	10[a]	20[a]
Cambodia	2[e]	..	..	..	..	..	..
China	1 962	2 000	2 000	2 114	2 563	2 634	2 500[a]
Hong Kong, China	6 086[a]	21 437[a]	25 000[a]	26 531[a]	24 407[a]	16 973	19 895
India	7	83	117	239	113	48	167
Indonesia	78	609	603	600	178	44	72
Korea, Democratic People's Republic	..	..	..	..	..	..	..
Korea, Republic of	966	2 300	3 072	4 249	3 230	3 893	2 548
Lao People's Democratic Republic	..	..	-[a]	..	..	-[a]	..
Macau, China	..	..	..	..	..	..	..
Malaysia	326	2 329	2 488	3 768	2 626	785	1 640
Maldives	-[d]	-[a]	-[a]	- 1[a]	- 3[a]	-[a]	..
Mongolia	..	..	1[a]	-[a]	2[a]	-[a]	1[a]
Myanmar	..	..	..	..	..	..	..
Nepal	..	..	-[a]	12[a]	- 5[a]	-[a]	3[a]
Pakistan	7	-	-	7	- 25	5	1
Philippines	91	302	98	182	136	160	128
Singapore	1 171	4 577	6 281	6 935	8 859	-1 525	3 943
Sri Lanka	3	8	7	-[a]	-[a]	-[a]	5[a]
Taiwan Province of China	3 825	2 640	2 983	3 843	5 243	3 836	4 420
Thailand	132	422	835	932	367	134	368
Viet Nam	..	..	..	..	..	..	..
The Pacific	**23**	**12**	**16**	**29**	**22**	**49**	**30**
Fiji	15	-	- 3	10	30	31	25[a]
Kiribati	..	-	..	..	..	..	..
New Caledonia	..	..	..	..	..	..	..
Papua New Guinea	5[h]	..	..	..	..	..	..
Vanuatu	..	..	..	..	..	..	..
Samoa	5[d]	3[a]	3[a]	4[a]	4[a]	3[a]	5[a]
Solomon Islands	- 3[d]	9[a]	16[a]	15[a]	- 12[a]	14[a]	..
Tonga	-	..	..	..	..	..	..
Central and Eastern Europe	**267**	**291**	**456**	**1 051**	**3 417**	**2 193**	**2 526**
Albania	14[k]	9	12	10[a]	10[a]	1[a]	..
Belarus	- 8[e]	5[a]	13[a]	4[a]	2	2	-
Bulgaria	8[k]	..	- 8	- 29	- 2	-	5
Czech Republic	56[k]	120	37	153	25	175	197
Czechoslovakia (former)	12[m]	..	..	..	..	..	..
Estonia	4[k]	2	2	40	137	6	74
Hungary	13[b]	49	43	- 3	431	481	249
Latvia	- 1[k]	- 65	- 65	3	6	54	-
Lithuania	..	..	1	-	27	4	9
Moldova, Republic of	..	18	-	-	-	-	-[a]
Poland	8[b]	29	42	53	45	316	200[a]

/...

Annex table B.2. **FDI outflows, by home region and economy, 1988-1999 (concluded)**

(Millions of dollars)

Home region/economy	1988-1993 (Annual average)	1994	1995	1996	1997	1998	1999
Romania	9d	1	3	2	-	-	12
Russian Federation	142e	101	358	771	2 597	1 011	2 144
Slovakia	12k	14	8	52	95	146	- 372
Ukraine	..	8	10	- 5	42	- 4	7

Memorandum:

Least developed countries: n
Total	**113**	**111**	**- 335**	**- 298**	**1 047**	**111**	**386**
Africa	116	99	- 290	- 357	1 060	91	373
Latin America and the Caribbean	- 7d	-	1	1	-	-	-
Asia and the Pacific	2	12	- 46	58	- 13	21	13
Asia	-	-	- 65	39	- 6	4	8
West Asia	..	..	..	..	..	..	..
South, East and South-East Asia	-	-	- 65	39	- 6	4	8
The Pacific	2d	12	19	19	- 8	17	5

Oil-exporting countries: o
Total	**2 354**	**3 326**	**1 939**	**7 300**	**4 093**	**724**	**4 129**
Africa	678	243	- 15	88	315	383	367
North Africa	*- 25*	*60*	*101*	*96*	*300*	*326*	*271*
Other Africa	*703*	*183*	*- 116*	*- 8*	*15*	*56*	*97*
Latin America and the Caribbean	489	1 416	- 167	549	1 611	1 634	1 678
South America	*310*	*358*	*95*	*510*	*502*	*270*	*612*
Other Latin America and the Caribbean	*179*	*1 058*	*- 262*	*39*	*1 109*	*1 364*	*1 066*
Asia	1 187	1 667	2 121	6 663	2 167	-1 292	2 084
West Asia	*775*	*-1 271*	*- 990*	*2 255*	*- 647*	*-2 132*	*350*
South, East and South-East Asia	*412*	*2 938*	*3 111*	*4 408*	*2 814*	*839*	*1 732*
All developing countries minus China	17 356	40 124	48 259	55 649	61 772	30 411	63 138
Asia and the Pacific	15 529	35 495	42 754	51 914	47 440	22 867	37 269
Africa including South Africa	1 404	1 764	2 673	1 001	3 968	2 379	2 049

Source: UNCTAD, FDI/TNC database.

a   Estimates. For details, see "definitions and sources" in annex B.
b   Annual average from 1991 to 1993.
c   Annual average from 1988 to 1991.
d   Annual average from 1990 to 1993.
e   1993.
f   Annual average from 1989 to 1993.
g   Annual average from 1989 to 1992.
h   Annual average from 1988 to 1990.
i   Annual average from 1990 to 1992.
j   1988.
k   Annual average from 1992 to 1993.
l   Annual average from 1990 to 1991.
m   Annual average from 1989 to 1991.
n   Least developed countries include: Afghanistan, Angola, Bangladesh, Benin, Burkina Faso, Burundi, Cambodia, Cape Verde, Central African Republic, Chad, Comoros, Democratic Repunlic of Congo, Djibouti, Equatorial Guinea, Ethiopia, Gambia, Guinea, Guinea-Bissau, Haiti, Kiribati, Lao People's Democratic Republic, Lesotho, Liberia, Madagascar, Malawi, Maldives, Mali, Mauritania, Mozambique, Myanmar, Nepal, Niger, Rwanda, Samoa, Sierra Leone, Solomon Islands, Somalia, Sudan, Togo, Uganda, United Republic of Tanzania, Vanuatu, Yemen and Zambia. Not included are Bhutan, Eritrea, Sao Tome and Principe and Tuvalu due to unavailability of data.
o   Oil-exporting countries include: Algeria, Angola, Bahrain, Brunei Darussalam, Cameroon, Congo, Ecuador, Egypt, Gabon, Indonesia, Islamic Republic of Iran, Iraq, Kuwait, Libyan Arab Jamahiriya, Malaysia, Mexico, Nigeria, Oman, Qatar, Saudi Arabia, Trinidad and Tobago, Tunisia, United Arab Emirates and Venezuela.

Annex table B.3. **FDI inward stock, by host region and economy, 1980, 1985, 1990, 1995, 1998 and 1999** [a]

(Millions of dollars)

Host region/economy	1980	1985	1990	1995	1998	1999
World	**495 200**	**763 357**	**1 761 198**	**2 743 391**	**4 015 258**	**4 771 981**
Developed countries	**373 960**	**545 243**	**1 380 827**	**1 967 538**	**2 690 129**	**3 230 800**
Western Europe	**200 713**	**254 007**	**770 434**	**1 127 337**	**1 545 983**	**1 757 208**
European Union	**185 669**	**236 441**	**723 455**	**1 050 270**	**1 451 159**	**1 652 322**
Austria	3 163	3 762	9 884	17 532	24 006	23 363
Belgium and Luxembourg	7 306	18 447	58 388	116 570	165 322	181 184 [b]
Denmark	4 193	3 613	9 192	23 801	30 377	37 830 [b]
Finland	540	1 339	5 132	8 465	16 455	16 540
France	22 862 [c]	33 636 [c]	86 508	143 673	168 496	181 974
Germany	36 630	36 926	111 232	165 914	198 773	225 595 [b]
Greece	4 524	8 309	14 016 [d]	19 306 [d]	22 048 [d]	22 948 [d]
Ireland	3 749	4 649	5 502 [e]	11 706 [e]	25 647 [e]	43 969 [e]
Italy	8 892	18 976	57 985	63 456	103 094	107 995 [b]
Netherlands	19 167	24 952	73 564	124 506	181 449	215 234 [b]
Portugal	2 863 [f]	3 796 [f]	9 769 [f]	17 579	22 446	20 513
Spain	5 141	8 939	65 916	106 900	118 921	112 582
Sweden	3 626	5 071	12 461	31 089	50 986	68 035
United Kingdom	63 014	64 028	203 905	199 772	323 138	394 560
Other Western Europe	**15 043**	**17 566**	**46 979**	**77 067**	**94 825**	**104 886**
Gibraltar	..	32 [g]	197 [g]	363 [g]	366 [g]	374 [g]
Iceland	.. [h, i]	64 [i]	147	129	466	529
Norway	6 577 [j]	7 412 [j]	12 391	19 513	24 308 [k]	30 885 [k]
Switzerland	8 506	10 058	34 245	57 063	69 685	73 099 [b]
North America	**137 195**	**249 249**	**507 783**	**658 734**	**954 990**	**1 253 555**
Canada	54 149	64 634	112 872	123 181	143 234	166 266
United States	83 046	184 615	394 911	535 553	811 756	1087 289 [b]
Other developed countries	**36 053**	**41 987**	**102 609**	**181 467**	**189 156**	**220 037**
Australia	13 173	25 049	73 611	102 114	102 420	118 600
Israel [l]	727	1 131	2 012	5 256	10 110	12 366
Japan	3 270	4 740	9 850	33 508	26 065	38 806 [b]
New Zealand	2 363	2 043	7 938	25 574	34 889	33 217
South Africa	16 519	9 024	9 198	15 016	15 672	17 048 [b]
Developing countries	**121 240**	**218 114**	**377 380**	**739 499**	**1 240 976**	**1 438 484**
Africa	**19 235**	**29 240**	**44 104**	**66 430**	**84 372**	**93 066**
North Africa	**9 608**	**14 353**	**20 941**	**30 818**	**35 341**	**38 162**
Algeria [l]	1 320	1 281	1 316	1 377	1 393	1 399
Egypt [m]	2 257	5 699	11 039	14 096	16 698	18 198
Libyan Arab Jamahiriya	..	..	382 [n]	444 [n]	75 [n]	.. [h,n]
Morocco [l]	189	440	917	3 034	4 800	5 647
Sudan [l]	8	57	29	28	497	868
Tunisia	5 835 [o]	6 876 [o]	7 259	11 839	11 878	12 075
Other Africa	**9 627**	**14 887**	**23 163**	**35 612**	**49 031**	**54 904**
Angola [l]	61	675	1 024	2 922	4 628	6 442

Annex table B.3. **FDI inward stock, by host region and economy, 1980, 1985, 1990, 1995, 1998 and 1999** [a]

(Millions of dollars)

Host region/economy	1980	1985	1990	1995	1998	1999
Benin [l]	32	34	159	381	467	498
Botswana	698 [p]	947 [p]	1 309 [p]	1 126	1 298	1 359
Burkina Faso [l]	18	24	39	74	113	123
Burundi [l]	7	23	29	33	35	35
Cameroon [l]	330	1 125	1 044	1 062	1 192	1 232
Cape Verde	..	..	4 [q]	38 [q]	87 [q]	102 [q]
Central African Republic [l]	50	77	95	76	92	105
Chad [l]	123	187	243	305	354	369
Comoros	..	..	15 [r]	17 [r]	23 [r]	25 [r]
Congo [s]	309	479	564	585	606	611
Congo, Democratic Republic of [m]	330	242	171	176	180	181
Côte d'Ivoire [l]	525	707	973	1 621	2 687	2 966
Djibouti [t]	3	3	6	14	30	35
Equatorial Guinea	..	6 [g]	25 [g]	239 [g]	659 [g]	779 [g]
Ethiopia [l]	110	114	120	178	438	528
Gabon [l]	512	833	1 208	954	1 620	1 820
Gambia [l]	22	21	35	79	118	133
Ghana [l]	229	272	315	822	1 081	1 196
Guinea [t]	2	2	70	132	191	211
Guinea-Bissau [m]	-	4	8	17	29	32
Kenya [l]	344	434	626	689	784	826
Lesotho [u]	4	19	149	1 337	2 154	2 290
Liberia [u]	72	464	1 657	1 719	1 767	1 777
Madagascar [l]	37	48	104	169	209	268
Malawi [l]	100	137	185	250	386	446
Mali [s]	13	34	39	163	321	361
Mauritania [l]	.. [h]	33	51	86	94	96
Mauritius [l]	20	37	163	251	355	404
Mozambique [l]	15	17	42	201	551	935
Namibia	1 935 [c]	1 951 [c]	2 047	1 708	1 440	1 520
Niger [l]	188	203	284	361	415	430
Nigeria [l]	2 405	4 417	8 072	14 065	18 249	19 649
Rwanda [l]	54	133	213	228	240	245
Senegal [l]	150	191	277	393	647	707
Seychelles [v]	37	87	187	304	443	503
Sierra Leone [l]	77	66	.. [h]	.. [h]	-	2
Somalia [l]	29	4	.. [h]	.. [h]	.. [h]	.. [h]
Swaziland	243 [w]	104	336	539	480	476
Togo [l]	176	210	268	307	399	434
Uganda [l]	9	7	4	275	780	960
United Republic of Tanzania [l]	47	91	93	325	804	987
Zambia [s]	322	416	979	1 247	1 769	1 932
Zimbabwe [x]	4	5	.. [h]	160	820	879
Latin America and the Caribbean	**44 095**	**62 918**	**118 300**	**204 932**	**404 621**	**485 604**
South America	**29 672**	**42 474**	**68 650**	**114 602**	**268 593**	**331 143**
Argentina	5 344	6 563	9 085 [y]	27 828	47 114	62 289
Bolivia	420	592	1 026	1 564	3 827	4 843
Brazil	17 480	25 664	37 143	42 530	132 734	164 105
Chile	886	2 321	10 067	15 547	30 038 [z]	39 258 [z]
Colombia	1 464	2 654	4 904	8 563	18 125	19 521 [b]
Ecuador	719	982	1 626	3 434 [aa]	5 452 [aa]	6 088 [aa]
Guyana [l]	.. [h]	.. [h]	.. [h]	350	542	591
Paraguay [l]	218	298	402	973	1 911	2 217
Peru	898	1 152	1 302	5 541	7 998	8 573
Suriname	..	..	..	..	..	..

Annex table B.3.　**FDI inward stock, by host region and economy, 1980, 1985, 1990, 1995, 1998 and 1999** [a]

(Millions of dollars)

Host region/economy	1980	1985	1990	1995	1998	1999
Uruguay [ab]	700	748	882	1 296	1 723	1 923
Venezuela	1 604	1 548	2 260	6 975	19 129	21 736
Other Latin America and the Caribbean	**14 423**	**20 444**	**49 650**	**90 330**	**136 028**	**154 460**
Antigua and Barbuda [ab]	23	94	292	437	506	518
Aruba	..	..	131 [ac]	202 [ac]	566 [ac]	961 [ac]
Bahamas [t]	298	294	336	493	938	1 082
Barbados [l]	102	124	169	225	269	284
Belize [l]	12	10	72	147	193	196
Bermuda [l]	5 132	8 052	13 849	24 705	30 905	31 088
Cayman Islands [ad]	223	1 479	1 749	3 320	9 230	11 030
Costa Rica	672	957	1 447	2 733 [aa]	4 201 [aa]	4 651 [aa]
Cuba [v]	-	-	3	45	100	115
Dominica	..	6 [g]	66 [g]	192 [g]	240 [g]	252 [g]
Dominican Republic	239	265	572	1 707 [aa]	2 924 [aa]	4 276 [aa]
El Salvador	154	181	212	293	1 172 [z]	1 403 [z]
Grenada [ab]	1	13	70	167	273	316
Guatemala [l]	701	1 050	1 734	2 209	3 043	3 190
Haiti [l]	79	112	149	163	182	212
Honduras [l]	92	172	383	620	937	1 167
Jamaica [l]	501	458	727	1 505	2 261	2 781
Mexico	2 090 [ae]	1 984 [ae]	22 424	41 130	60 783	72 016 [b]
Netherlands Antilles [af]	569	56	206	322	587	657
Nicaragua [l]	109	109	114	353	807	1 107
Panama	2 353 [f]	3 034 [f]	2 090 [f]	3 171 [f]	6 064	6 086 [b]
Saint Kitts and Nevis [u]	1	32	160	244	332	409
Saint Lucia [v]	93	197	315	510	658	745
Saint Vincent and the Grenadines [x]	1	9	48	181	307	331
Trinidad and Tobago	976	1 719	2 093	3 634 [aa]	5 721 [aa]	6 354 [aa]
Virgin Islands [v]	2	40	240	1 622	2 832	3 232
Developing Europe	**156**	**286**	**1 131**	**3 246**	**7 555**	**9 773**
Bosnia and Herzegovina	..	..	..	..	..	..
Croatia	..	..	..	482 [f]	2 733	4 028
Malta [l]	156	286	465	972	1 736	2 547
Slovenia	..	..	666 [ag]	1 759	2 907	2 997 [b]
TFYR Macedonia	..	..	..	33 [ah]	179 [ah]	200 [ah]
Asia	**56 587**	**124 500**	**211 632**	**461 988**	**741 311**	**846 677**
West Asia	**.. [h]**	**27 654**	**30 199**	**40 471**	**54 085**	**60 796**
Bahrain	65 [c]	399 [c]	552	2 403	4 962	5 262 [b]
Cyprus [l]	460	789	1 146	1 478	1 652	1 717
Iran, Islamic Republic [m]	1 893	1 711	970	792	895	980
Iraq	..	..	..	..	..	..
Jordan [af]	155	493	615	627	1 313	1 464
Kuwait [l]	30	33	32	52	479	551
Lebanon [s]	20	34	53	105	535	785
Oman [m]	538	1 257	1 778	2 282	2 517	2 587
Qatar [l]	83	77	55	435	595	645
Saudi Arabia [l]	.. [h]	21 828	22 501	22 423	28 627	33 427
Syrian Arab Republic	..	37 [ai]	374 [ai]	963 [ai]	1 212 [ai]	1 287 [ai]
Turkey	107	360	1 320	5 103 [aa]	7 570 [aa]	8 353 [aa]
United Arab Emirates [l]	409	482	751	1 769	2 099	2 259

Annex table B.3. **FDI inward stock, by host region and economy, 1980, 1985, 1990, 1995, 1998 and 1999** [a]

(Millions of dollars)

Host region/economy	1980	1985	1990	1995	1998	1999
Yemen [s]	68	155	53	2 039	1 631	1 481
Central Asia	..	..	..	3 957	13 379	16 340
Armenia	..	..	..	34	324	441
Azerbaijan	..	..	..	352 [ah]	3 117 [ah]	3 808 [ah]
Georgia	..	..	..	32	210	306 [b]
Kazakhstan	..	..	..	2 915	7 929	9 728
Kyrgyzstan	..	..	..	144	383	419 [b]
Tajikistan	..	..	..	25 [ah]	75 [ah]	104 [ah]
Turkmenistan	..	..	..	200 [ah]	546 [ah]	626 [ah]
Uzbekistan	..	..	..	255 [aj]	795 [aj]	908 [aj]
South, East and South-East Asia	**58 843**	**96 846**	**181 434**	**417 559**	**673 847**	**769 541**
Afghanistan [l]	11	12	12	12	13	13
Bangladesh	63	112	147 [ak]	180 [ak]	642 [ak]	792 [ak]
Brunei Darussalam [l]	19	33	30	68	88	93
Cambodia	..	..	191 [al]	498	681	605
China	6 252 [am]	10 500 [am]	24 763 [am]	137 436 [am]	265 603 [k]	306 003 [k]
Hong Kong, China	22 929 [p]	28 393 [p]	46 826 [p]	70 951	109 334 [k]	132 402 [k]
India	1 177	1 075	1 593 [ak]	5 610 [ak]	14 248 [ak]	16 416 [ak]
Indonesia	10 274	24 971	38 883	50 601	68 458	65 188
Korea, Democratic People's Republic	..	..	572 [r]	641 [r]	642 [r]	642 [r]
Korea, Republic of	1 140	2 160	5 186	9 443	19 043	27 984
Lao People's Democratic Republic [l]	2	2	14	212	472	551
Macau, China [af]	2	10	11	18	27	28
Malaysia	5 169	7 388	10 318	28 732 [an]	45 241 [an]	48 773 [an]
Maldives [t]	5	3	25	61	93	103
Mongolia	..	..	..	26 [aj]	86 [aj]	116 [aj]
Myanmar [af]	5	5	173	1 090	2 103	2 403
Nepal [ad]	1	2	12	39	93	225
Pakistan	688	1 079	1 928	5 552	9 247	9 778
Philippines	1 281	2 601	3 268	6 086	9 305	11 199
Singapore	6 203	13 016	28 564	59 582	72 416 [k]	79 401 [k]
Sri Lanka	231	517	681 [ak]	1 297 [ak]	2 071 [ak]	2 273 [ak]
Taiwan Province of China	2 405	2 930	9 735 [ak]	15 736 [ak]	20 070 [ak]	22 996 [ak]
Thailand	981	1 999	8 209	17 452	20 461 [k]	26 539 [k]
Viet Nam [l]	7	38	294	6 238	13 410	15 019
The Pacific	**1 167**	**1 170**	**2 213**	**2 903**	**3 117**	**3 365**
Fiji	358	393	402 [d]	739 [d]	832 [d]	862 [d]
Kiribati	..	-	- [ap]	1 [ap]	3 [ap]	4 [ap]
New Caledonia	..	-	40 [ai]	91 [ai]	105 [ai]	108 [ai]
Papua New Guinea	748	683	1 582	1 667	1 614 [k]	1 784 [k]
Samoa [ad]	-	-	8	23	34	36
Solomon Islands [m]	28	32	69	125	174	189
Tonga	..	- [aq]	- [aq]	9 [aq]	16 [aq]	18 [aq]
Vanuatu [t]	33	62	110	249	339	364
Central and Eastern Europe	**-**	**-**	**2 991**	**36 355**	**84 153**	**102 697**
Albania	..	..	..	201 [aj]	384 [aj]	425 [aj]
Belarus	..	..	..	50 [aj]	472 [aj]	697 [aj]
Bulgaria	..	..	4 [ac]	337 [ac]	1 488 [ac]	2 258 [ac]

/...

Annex table B.3. **FDI inward stock, by host region and economy, 1980, 1985, 1990, 1995, 1998 and 1999** [a]

(Millions of dollars)

Host region/economy	1980	1985	1990	1995	1998	1999
Czech Republic	..	..	1 360 [ar]	7 352	14 375	16 246
Estonia	..	..	..	731 [f]	1 822	2 441
Hungary	..	..	569	10 007	15 862	19 095
Latvia	..	..	..	616	1 558	1 885
Lithuania	..	..	97 [ag]	352	1 625	2 063
Moldova, Republic of	..	..	..	94	275	335
Poland	..	..	109	7 843	22 479	29 979
Romania	..	..	766	1 150	4 335	5 441
Russian Federation	..	..	..	5 465	14 166	16 541
Slovakia	..	..	87 [ar]	1 248	2 502	2 044
Ukraine	..	..	..	910	2 811	3 248

Memorandum:

Least developed countries: [as]						
Total	2 189	3 851	7 092	16 054	24 286	28 602
Africa	1 894	3 354	6 129	11 362	17 827	21 625
Latin America and the Caribbean	79	112	149	163	182	212
Asia and the Pacific	216	386	814	4 528	6 277	6 765
Asia	155	292	627	4 131	5 728	6 172
West Asia	68	155	53	2 039	1 631	1 481
South, East and South-East Asia	88	137	574	2 092	4 097	4 692
The Pacific	61	94	187	398	549	593
Oil-exporting countries: [at]						
Total	31 556	86 969	156 810	246 429	343 306	377 905
Africa	13 028	21 386	31 908	47 343	56 339	61 401
North Africa	*9 411*	*13 856*	*19 996*	*27 756*	*30 044*	*31 647*
Other Africa	*3 617*	*7 529*	*11 912*	*19 587*	*26 295*	*29 753*
Latin America and the Caribbean	6 133	7 405	49 033	89 528	133 008	156 741
South America	*2 743*	*3 121*	*4 912*	*11 973*	*28 408*	*32 667*
Other Latin America and the Caribbean	*3 066*	*3 703*	*24 517*	*44 764*	*66 504*	*78 370*
Asia	12 395	58 178	75 869	109 557	153 959	159 763
West Asia	*.. [h]*	*25 786*	*26 638*	*30 157*	*40 172*	*45 709*
South, East and South-East Asia	*15 461*	*32 392*	*49 231*	*79 400*	*113 786*	*114 053*
All developing countries minus China	114 988	207 614	352 617	602 063	975 373	1 132 481
Asia and the Pacific	57 754	125 670	213 845	464 890	744 428	850 042
Africa including South Africa	35 754	38 263	53 302	81 446	100 044	110 114

Source: UNCTAD, FDI/TNC database.

[a] For the countries for which the stock data are estimated by either cumulating FDI flows or adding flows to FDI stock in a particular year, notes are given belows.
[b] Estimated by adding flows to the stock of 1998.
[c] Stock data prior to 1989 are estimated by subtracting flows.
[d] Estimated by adding flows to the stock of 1989.
[e] Estimated by adding flows to the stock of 1986.
[f] Stock data prior to 1996 are estimated by subtracting flows.
[g] Estimated by accumulating flows since 1982.
[h] Negative accumulation of flows. However, this value is included in the regional and global total.
[i] Stock data prior to 1988 are estimated by subtracting flows.
[j] Stock data prior to 1987 are estimated by subtracting flows.
[k] Estimated by adding flows to the stock of 1997.
[l] Estimated by accumulating flows since 1970.

m   Estimated by accumulating flows since 1975.
n   Estimated by accumulating flows since 1988.
o   Stock data prior to 1990 are estimated by subtracting flows.
p   Stock data prior to 1994 are estimated by subtracting flows.
q   Estimated by accumulating flows since 1986.
r   Estimated by accumulating flows since 1987.
s   Estimated by accumulating flows since 1971.
t   Estimated by accumulating flows since 1973.
u   Estimated by accumulating flows since 1980.
v   Estimated by accumulating flows since 1976.
w   Stock data prior to 1981 are estimated by subtracting flows.
x   Estimated by accumulating flows since 1978.
y   1990 stock is estimated by subtracting the flow of 1991.
z   Estimated by adding flows to the stock of 1995.
aa Estimated by adding flows to the stock of 1990.
ab Estimated by accumulating flows since 1977.
ac Estimated by accumulating flows since 1990.
ad Estimated by accumulating flows since 1974.
ae Stocks up to 1989 are estimated by accumulating flows since 1970.
af Estimated by accumulating flows since 1972.
ag Stock data prior to 1993 are estimated by subtracting flows.
ah Estimated by accumulating flows since 1994.
ai Estimated by accumulating flows since 1985.
aj Estimated by accumulating flows since 1992.
ak Estimated by adding flows to the stock of 1988.
al Stock data prior to 1995 are estimated by subtracting flows.
am Stock data prior to 1997 are estimated by subtracting flows.
an Estimated by adding flows to the stock of 1994.
ap Estimated by accumulating flows since 1983.
aq Estimated by accumulating flows since 1984.
ar Stock data prior to 1992 are estimated by subtracting flows.
as Least developed countries include: Afghanistan, Angola, Bangladesh, Benin, Burkina Faso, Burundi, Cambodia, Cape Verde, Central African Republic, Chad, Comoros, Democratic Republic of Gongo, Djibouti, Equatorial Guinea, Ethiopia, Gambia, Guinea, Guinea-Bissau, Haiti, Kiribati, Lao People's Democratic Republic, Lesotho, Liberia, Madagascar, Malawi, Maldives, Mali, Mauritania, Mozambique, Myanmar, Nepal, Niger, Rwanda, Western Samoa, Sierra Leone, Solomon Islands, Somalia, Sudan, Togo, Uganda, United Republic of Tanzania, Vanuatu, Yemen and Zambia. Not included are Bhutan, Eritrea, Sao Tome and Principe and Tuvalu due to unavailability of data.
at Oil-exporting countries include: Algeria, Angola, Bahrain, Brunei Darussalam, Cameroon, Congo, Ecuador, Egypt, Gabon, Indonesia, Islamic Republic of Iran,Iraq, Kuwait, Libyan Arab Jamahiriya, Malaysia, Mexico, Nigeria, Oman, Qatar, Saudi Arabia, Trinidad and Tobago, Tunisia, United Arab Emirates and Venezuela.

Note: For data on FDI stock which are calculated as an accumulation of flows, price changes are not taken into account.

Annex table B.4. **FDI outward stock, by home region and economy, 1980, 1985, 1990, 1995, 1998 and 1999** [a]

(Millions of dollars)

Home region/economy	1980	1985	1990	1995	1998	1999
World	523 156	707 133	1 716 364	2 870 624	4 065 798	4 759 333
Developed countries	506 834	674 682	1 634 099	2 607 095	3 649 951	4 276 961
Western Europe	234 717	318 903	866 450	1 468 414	2 135 313	2 574 926
European Union	212 602	292 654	789 401	1 303 241	1 920 431	2 336 631
Austria	530	1 343	4 273	11 702	17 451	17 522
Belgium and Luxembourg	6 037	9 551	40 636	88 526	134 533 [b]	159 461 [b]
Denmark	2 065	1 801	7 342	24 703	33 821	42 035 [c]
Finland	737	1 829	11 227	14 993	29 407	31 803
France	23 599 [d]	37 072 [d]	110 119	184 388	227 815	298 012
Germany	43 127	59 909	151 581	268 419	370 311	420 908 [c]
Greece	853 [e]	853 [e]	853 [e]	865 [e]	803 [b]	783 [b]
Ireland	..	202 [f]	2 150 [f]	4 037 [f]	9 678 [f]	15 096 [f]
Italy	7 319	16 600	57 261	109 176	165 412	168 370 [c]
Netherlands	42 135	47 772	109 005	179 557	260 538	306 396 [c]
Portugal	116 [g]	187 [g]	504 [g]	3 712 [g]	9 221	9 605
Spain	1 931	4 455	15 652	35 155	69 178	97 553
Sweden	3 721 [h]	10 768	49 491	73 143	93 537	104 985
United Kingdom	80 434	100 313	229 307	304 865	498 724	664 103
Other Western Europe	22 115	26 249	77 049	165 173	214 882	238 295
Gibraltar	..	..	..	..	..	..
Iceland	63 [i]	63 [i]	75	180	342	420
Norway	561	1 093	10 888	22 514	33 004 [j]	38 423 [j]
Switzerland	21 491	25 093	66 086	142 479	181 536	199 452 [c]
North America	243 955	294 161	515 350	817 120	1 141 501	1 309 813
Canada	23 777	43 127	84 829	118 105	160 936	178 347
United States	220 178	251 034	430 521	699 015	980 565	1 131 466 [c]
Other developed countries	28 162	61 618	252 299	321 561	373 137	392 222
Australia	2 260	6 653	31 411	48 237	62 152	55 266
Israel	179 [k]	661 [k]	1 169	3 937	6 171	6 873 [c]
Japan	19 610	43 970	201 440	238 452	270 038	292 781 [c]
New Zealand	392	1 371	3 269	7 630	5 775	7 187
South Africa	5 722	8 963	15 010	23 305	29 001	30 115 [c]
Developing countries	16 323	32 426	81 907	258 265	403 920	468 744
Africa	991	6 814	12 249	14 499	16 340	16 974
North Africa	310	460	891	974	1 864	2 181
Algeria [l]	98	156	183	233	233	233
Egypt [m]	39	91	163	405	584	630
Libyan Arab Jamahiriya [n]	162	207	517	175	824	1 074
Morocco	..	..	14 [o]	131 [o]	190 [o]	208 [o]
Sudan	..	..	..	..	..	..
Tunisia	11 [k]	6 [k]	15	30	33	35
Other Africa	680	6 355	11 357	13 525	14 476	14 793
Angola	..	..	..	..	..	..

/...

Annex table B.4. **FDI outward stock, by home region and economy, 1980, 1985, 1990, 1995, 1998 and 1999**[a]

(Millions of dollars)

Home region/economy	1980	1985	1990	1995	1998	1999
Benin [p]	-	2	.. [q]	.. [q]	.. [q]	.. [q]
Botswana	440 [r]	440 [r]	447	650	258	261
Burkina Faso [s]	3	3	.. [q]	-	8	9
Burundi	..	..	- [t]	- [t]	- [t]	- [t]
Cameroon [u]	23	53	150	227	49	49
Cape Verde	..	..	1 [t]	4 [t]	5 [t]	5 [t]
Central African Republic [v]	-	2	18	46	62	67
Chad [w]	-	1	36	84	107	114
Comoros	..	..	1 [o]	7 [o]	7 [o]	7 [o]
Congo	..	..	..	..	..	..
Congo, Democratic Republic of	..	..	..	..	..	..
Côte d'Ivoire	..	..	..	..	103 [x]	130 [x]
Djibouti	..	..	..	..	..	..
Equatorial Guinea	..	..	- [t]	- [t]	- [t]	- [t]
Ethiopia	..	..	..	18 [y]	32 [y]	37 [y]
Gabon [s]	78	103	164	206	225	231
Gambia	..	..	..	..	..	..
Ghana	..	..	..	..	227 [x]	297 [x]
Guinea	..	..	..	..	.. [q, x]	.. [q, x]
Guinea-Bissau	..	..	..	..	..	..
Kenya [v]	18	60	99	112	156	186
Lesotho	..	..	- [z]	- [z]	- [z]	- [z]
Liberia [aa]	48	361	453	717	1 315	1 315
Madagascar	..	..	..	..	..	..
Malawi	..	..	..	..	8	11 [c]
Mali [v]	22	22	22	22	57	72
Mauritania	..	..	3 [ab]	3 [ab]	15 [ab]	15 [ab]
Mauritius	..	..	1 [z]	93 [z]	113 [z]	119 [z]
Mozambique	..	..	..	..	..	..
Namibia	..	..	80	20	38	39
Niger [s]	2	8	54	109	145	160
Nigeria [p]	5	5 193	9 653	10 957	11 164	11 256
Rwanda	..	..	..	..	..	..
Senegal [n]	7	43	49	96	107	112
Seychelles [ac]	14	44	61	94	120	129
Sierra Leone	..	..	..	..	..	..
Somalia	..	..	..	..	..	..
Swaziland	19	9	38	136	94	80
Togo [ad]	2	2	7	35	75	90
Uganda	..	..	..	..	..	..
United Republic of Tanzania	..	..	..	..	..	..
Zambia	..	..	..	..	..	..
Zimbabwe	..	10 [ae]	88 [ae]	137 [ae]	225 [ae]	234 [ae]
Latin America and the Caribbean	**9 025**	**13 827**	**20 378**	**48 165**	**77 372**	**104 580**
South America	**7 032**	**8 124**	**11 512**	**24 804**	**45 761**	**53 974**
Argentina	6 128 [af]	6 079 [af]	6 105 [af]	10 696	18 184	19 277
Bolivia	- [ag]	1 [ag]	9	18	25	27
Brazil	652	1 361	2 397	5 941 [ah]	10 730 [ah]	12 131 [ah]
Chile	42	102	178	2 810 [ai]	8 660 [ai]	13 515 [ai]
Colombia	136	301	402	1 028	2 381	2 397 [c]
Ecuador	..	..	..	..	..	..
Guyana	..	..	..	2 [y]	1 [y]	1 [y]
Paraguay [ac]	32	45	78	238	300	320
Peru	3	38	63	133	239	459 [c]
Suriname	..	..	..	..	..	..

Annex table B.4. FDI outward stock, by home region and economy, 1980, 1985, 1990, 1995, 1998 and 1999 [a]

(Millions of dollars)

Home region/economy	1980	1985	1990	1995	1998	1999
Uruguay	16 [aj]	32	42 [ak]	21 [ak]	50 [ak]	60 [ak]
Venezuela	23	165	2 239	3 918	5 191	5 787
Other Latin America and the Caribbean	**1 993**	**5 703**	**8 866**	**23 362**	**31 611**	**50 606**
Antigua and Barbuda	..	..	..	..	..	..
Aruba	..	..	..	10 [y]	10 [y]	4 [y]
Bahamas [al]	285	154	1 535	1 184	1 185	1 185
Barbados [l]	5	12	23	32	38	40
Belize	..	..	..	10 [am]	24 [am]	29 [am]
Bermuda [al]	724	2 002	1 550	2 321	3 918	19 017
Cayman Islands [an]	10	740	868	1 940	4 240	4 340
Costa Rica [w]	7	27	44	67	87	94
Cuba	..	..	..	..	..	..
Dominica	..	..	..	..	3 [ao]	5 [ao]
Dominican Republic	..	..	..	38 [y]	53 [y]	59 [y]
El Salvador	..	..	..	..	2 [x]	5 [x]
Grenada	..	..	..	..	..	..
Guatemala	..	..	..	..	..	..
Haiti	..	..	..	..	..	..
Honduras	..	..	..	..	..	..
Jamaica [l]	5	5	42	308	540	635
Mexico	136 [ap]	533 [ap]	575 [ap]	4 132	5 825	6 625 [c]
Netherlands Antilles [ac]	9	10	21	23	.. [q]	.. [q]
Nicaragua	..	..	..	..	..	..
Panama [al]	811	2 204	4 188	4 573	6 964	7 943
Saint Kitts and Nevis	..	..	..	..	..	..
Saint Lucia	..	..	..	..	..	..
Saint Vincent and the Grenadines	..	..	..	..	..	..
Trinidad and Tobago	..	15 [ae]	20 [ae]	21 [ae]	24 [ae]	290 [ae]
Virgin Islands	..	..	..	8 704 [y]	12 957 [y]	14 457 [y]
Developing Europe	**-**	**-**	**258**	**1 225**	**1 642**	**1 749**
Bosnia and Herzegovina	..	..	..	13 [y]	41 [y]	41 [y]
Croatia	..	..	..	703	992	1 024
Malta	..	..	..	5 [aq]	43 [aq]	73 [aq]
Slovenia	..	..	258 [ar]	504	563	607
TFYR Maeedonia	..	..	..	..	3 [x]	4 [x]
Asia	**6 294**	**11 747**	**48 929**	**194 237**	**308 357**	**345 206**
West Asia	**1 548**	**2 231**	**6 406**	**6 078**	**3 755**	**4 925**
Bahrain	628 [as]	657 [as]	719	1 044	1 577	1 777 [c]
Cyprus	..	- [at]	8 [at]	122 [at]	299 [at]	457 [at]
Iran, Islamic Republic	..	..	..	77 [au]	154 [au]	184 [au]
Iraq	..	..	..	..	..	..
Jordan [n]	117	120	110	17	.. [q]	.. [q]
Kuwait [v]	568	930	3 662	2 798	1 702	1 925
Lebanon [al]	1	40	.. [q]	.. [q]	.. [q]	.. [q]
Oman [al]	1	40	7	5	26	36
Qatar	..	..	..	30 [aq]	110 [aq]	140 [aq]
Saudi Arabia [al]	228	420	1 811	1 685	1 588	1 463
Syrian Arab Republic	..	..	..	..	6 [x]	8 [x]
Turkey	..	..	..	268 [am]	996 [am]	1 641 [am]

Annex table B.4. **FDI outward stock, by home region and economy, 1980, 1985, 1990, 1995, 1998 and 1999** [a]

(Millions of dollars)

Home region/economy	1980	1985	1990	1995	1998	1999
United Arab Emirates [al]	5	19	99	66	24	6
Yemen	..	4 [av]	5 [av]	5 [av]	5 [av]	5 [av]
Central Asia	-	-	-	-	159	513
Armenia	..	..	..	..	12 [aw]	25 [aw]
Azerbaijan	..	..	..	..	137 [aw]	473 [aw]
Georgia	..	..	..	..	..	..
Kazakhstan	..	..	..	-	10	14
Kyrgyzstan	..	..	..	..	- [aw]	2 [aw]
Tajikistan	..	..	..	..	..	..
Turkmenistan	..	..	..	..	..	..
Uzbekistan	..	..	..	..	..	..
South, East and South-East Asia	**4 746**	**9 517**	**42 522**	**188 159**	**304 442**	**339 769**
Afghanistan	..	..	..	..	..	..
Bangladesh	..	..	- [o]	.. [o, q]	.. [o, q]	.. [o, q]
Brunei Darussalam	..	..	..	71 [am]	131 [am]	151 [am]
Cambodia	..	..	..	2 [y]	2 [y]	2 [y]
China	-	131	2 489 [ax]	15 802 [ax]	23 113 [ax]	25 613 [ax]
Hong Kong, China [ay]	148	2 345	13 242	85 156	153 067	172 962
India	235 [az]	250 [az]	281 [az]	494 [ai]	894 [ai]	1 061 [ai]
Indonesia	..	49 [ap]	25 [ap]	1 295	2 117	2 189
Korea, Democratic People's Republic	..	..	..	..	..	..
Korea, Republic of	127	461	2 301	10 233	20 288	22 418
Lao People's Democratic Republic	..	..	..	..	..	..
Macau, China	..	..	..	..	..	..
Malaysia	197	1 374	2 671	11 143	15 240	16 880 [c]
Maldives	..	..	..	..	..	..
Mongolia	..	..	..	1 [aq]	3 [aq]	4 [aq]
Myanmar	..	..	..	..	..	..
Nepal	..	..	..	..	..	..
Pakistan	40	129	250	403	467	468
Philippines	171	171	155	1 220	1 698	1 858
Singapore	3 718	4 387	7 808	35 050	47 371	51 314 [c]
Sri Lanka	..	1 [at]	8 [at]	37 [at]	36 [at]	41 [at]
Taiwan Province of China	97	204	12 888 [ba]	25 144 [ba]	38 066 [ba]	42 486 [ba]
Thailand	13	14	404	2 173	1 978 [b]	2 346 [b]
Viet Nam	..	..	..	- [au]	- [au]	- [au]
The Pacific	**13**	**37**	**94**	**138**	**209**	**234**
Fiji [an]	2	15	87	132	203	228
Kiribati	..	..	..	- [bb]	- [bb]	- [bb]
New Caledonia	..	..	..	..	..	.. -
Papua New Guinea	10	22	7 [ax]	7 [ax]	7 [ax]	7 [ax]
Samoa	..	..	..	..	..	..
Solomon Islands	..	..	..	..	..	..
Tonga	..	..	..	- [am]	- [am]	- [am]
Vanuatu	..	..	..	..	..	..
Central and Eastern Europe	**-**	**25**	**358**	**5 264**	**11 927**	**13 628**
Albania	..	..	..	48 [au]	69 [au]	69 [au]
Belarus	..	..	..	..	4 [ao]	5 [ao]

Annex table B.4. **FDI outward stock, by home region and economy, 1980, 1985, 1990, 1995, 1998 and 1999** [a]

(Millions of dollars)

Home region/economy	1980	1985	1990	1995	1998	1999
Bulgaria	..	..	..	34 [bc]	4	8 [c]
Czech Republic	..	..	..	345	804	908
Estonia	..	..	..	68 [bd]	198	272
Hungary	..	..	197	383	1 101	1 553
Latvia	..	..	..	231	281	281
Lithuania	..	..	..	1	16	26
Moldova, Republic of	..	..	..	18	19	20
Poland	..	25 [k]	95	539	1 165	1 365
Romania	..	..	66	121	122	133
Russian Federation	..	..	..	3 015	7 377	8 586
Slovakia	..	..	..	374	668	296 [c]
Ukraine	..	..	..	87	98	105

Memorandum:

Least developed countries: [be]

	1980	1985	1990	1995	1998	1999
Total	77	406	533	739	1 574	1 653
Africa	77	401	528	796	1 597	1 670
Latin America and the Caribbean	..	..	..	..	..	..
Asia and the Pacific	-	4	5	.. [q]	.. [q]	.. [q]
Asia	-	4	5	.. [q]	.. [q]	.. [q]
West Asia	..	4	5	5	5	5
South, East and South-East Asia	-	-	-	.. [q]	.. [q]	.. [q]
The Pacific	-	-	-	-	-	-

Oil-exporting countries: [bf]

	1980	1985	1990	1995	1998	1999
Total	2 203	10 011	22 682	38 537	46 846	50 989
Africa	416	5 808	10 844	12 234	13 113	13 509
North Africa	*310*	*460*	*877*	*843*	*1 674*	*1 973*
Other Africa	*106*	*5 348*	*9 966*	*11 391*	*11 439*	*11 536*
Latin America and the Caribbean	160	714	2 843	8 088	11 064	12 729
South America	*24*	*166*	*2 248*	*3 936*	*5 216*	*5 814*
Other Latin America and the Caribbean	*136*	*548*	*595*	*4 153*	*5 849*	*6 915*
Asia	1 628	3 489	8 995	18 214	22 669	24 751
West Asia	*1 431*	*2 066*	*6 299*	*5 705*	*5 181*	*5 531*
South, East and South-East Asia	*197*	*1 423*	*2 696*	*12 509*	*17 488*	*19 220*
All developing countries minus China	16 323	32 295	79 418	242 463	380 808	443 131
Asia and the Pacific	6 307	11 785	49 022	194 376	308 566	345 441
Africa including South Africa	6 713	15 778	27 259	37 804	45 341	47 089

Source: UNCTAD, FDI/TNC database.

[a] For the countries for which the stock data are estimated by either cumulating FDI flows or adding flows to FDI stock in a particular year, notes are given below.

[b] Estimated by adding flows to the stock of 1997.

[c] Estimated by adding flows to the stock of 1998.

[d] Stock data prior to 1987 are estimated by subtracting flows.

[e] Stock data prior to 1997 are estimated by subtracting flows.

[f] Estimated by accumulating flows since 1984.

[g] Stock data prior to 1991 are estimated by accumulating flows since 1972. From 1991 to 1995 stocks were estimated by subtracting flows to the stock of 1996.

[h] Stock data prior to 1982 are estimated by subtracting flows.

[i] Stock data prior to 1988 are estimated by subtracting flows.

[j] Estimated by adding flows to the stock of 1996.

[k] Stock data prior to 1990 are estimated by subtracting flows.

[l] Estimated by accumulating flows since 1970.

[m] Estimated by accumulating flows since 1977.

[n] Estimated by accumulating flows since 1972.

[o] Estimated by accumulating flows since 1990.

[p] Estimated by accumulating flows since 1979.

[q] Negative accumulation of flows. However, this value is included in the regional and global total.

[r] Stock data prior to 1994 are estimated by subtracting flows.

[s] Estimated by accumulating flows since 1974.

[t] Estimated by accumulating flows since 1989.

[u] Estimated by accumulating flows since 1973.

[v] Estimated by accumulating flows since 1975.

[w] Estimated by accumulating flows since 1978.

[x] Estimated by accumulating flows since 1996.

[y] Estimated by accumulating flows since 1993.

[z] Estimated by accumulating flows since 1988.

[aa] Estimated by using the inward stock of the United States as a proxy and accumulating flows since 1994.

[ab] Estimated by accumulating flows since 1986.

[ac] Estimated by accumulating flows since 1976.

[ad] Estimated by accumulating flows since 1971.

[ae] Estimated by accumulating flows since 1983.

[af] Stock data prior to 1991 are estimated by subtracting flows.

[ag] Stock data up to 1985 are estimated by accumulating flows since 1980.

[ah] Estimated by adding flows to the stock of 1990.

[ai] Estimated by adding flows to the stock of 1992.

[aj] Stock data prior to 1983 are estimated by subtracting flows.

[ak] Estimated by adding flows to the stock of 1987.

[al] Estimated by using the inward stock of the United States as a proxy and accumulating flows since 1993.

[am] Estimated by accumulating flows since 1991.

[an] Estimated by accumulating flows since 1980.

[ao] Estimated by accumulating flows since 1997.

[ap] Estimated by using the inward stock of the United States as a proxy.

[aq] Estimated by accumulating flows since 1995.

[ar] Stock data prior to 1993 are estimated by subtracting flows.

[as] Stock data prior to 1989 are estimated by subtracting flows.

[at] Estimated by accumulating flows since 1985.

[au] Estimated by accumulating flows since 1992.

[av] Estimated by accumulating flows since 1982.

[aw] Estimated by accumulating flows since 1998.

[ax] Estimated by adding flows to the stock of 1989.

[ay] Estimated by using the inward stock of the United States and China as a proxy and accumulating flows since 1994.

[az] Stock data prior to 1992 are estimated by subtracting flows.

[ba] Estimated by adding flows to the stock of 1988.

[bb] Estimated by accumulating flows since 1994.

[bc] Stock data prior to 1998 are estimated by subtracting flows.

[bd] Stock data prior to 1996 are estimated by subtracting flows.

[be] Least developed countries include: Afghanistan, Angola, Bangladesh, Benin, Burkina Faso, Burundi, Cambodia, Cape Verde, Central African Republic, Chad, Comoros, Democratic Republic of Gongo, Djibouti, Equatorial Guinea, Ethiopia, Gambia, Guinea, Guinea-Bissau, Haiti, Kiribati, Lao People's Democratic Republic, Lesotho, Liberia, Madagascar, Malawi, Maldives, Mali, Mauritania, Mozambique, Myanmar, Nepal, Niger, Rwanda, Western Samoa, Sierra Leone, Solomon Islands, Somalia, Sudan, Togo, Uganda, United Republic of Tanzania, Vanuatu, Yemen and Zambia. Not included are Bhutan, Eritrea, Sao Tome and Principe and Tuvalu due to unavailability of data.

[bf] Oil-exporting countries include: Algeria, Angola, Bahrain, Brunei Darussalam, Cameroon, Congo, Ecuador, Egypt, Gabon, Indonesia, Islamic Republic of Iran,Iraq, Kuwait, Libyan Arab Jamahiriya, Malaysia, Mexico, Nigeria, Oman, Qatar, Saudi Arabia, Trinidad and Tobago, Tunisia, United Arab Emirates and Venezuela.

Note: For data on FDI stock which are calculated as an accumulation of flows, price changes are not taken into account.

Annex table B.5. **Inward and outward FDI flows as a percentage of gross fixed capital formation, by region and economy, 1988-1998**

(Percentage)

Region/economy	1988-1993 (Annual average)	1994	1995	1996	1997	1998
World						
inward	4.1	4.6	5.4	5.9	7.5	11.1
outward	*4.9*	*5.2*	*5.8*	*6.2*	*7.6*	*11.5*
Developed countries						
inward	4.0	3.5	4.5	4.8	6.2	10.9
outward	*5.6*	*5.9*	*6.7*	*7.2*	*9.2*	*14.8*
Western Europe						
inward	5.7	5.6	6.8	6.5	8.5	15.2
outward	*8.1*	*8.9*	*9.9*	*11.6*	*15.1*	*26.0*
European Union						
inward	5.8	5.5	6.9	6.5	8.3	15.3
outward	*8.0*	*8.6*	*9.6*	*11.0*	*14.5*	*26.2*
Austria						
inward	2.2	4.8	3.7	8.7	5.8	9.6
outward	*3.4*	*2.9*	*2.2*	*3.8*	*4.3*	*5.8*
Belgium and Luxembourg						
inward	19.7	17.1	17.8	24.2	22.1	40.6
outward	*14.9*	*2.8*	*19.3*	*13.8*	*13.3*	*51.6*
Denmark						
inward	4.7	18.9	12.4	2.1	8.2	18.5
outward	*6.5*	*15.7*	*6.9*	*5.7*	*10.9*	*10.9*
Finland						
inward	1.7	10.4	5.1	5.2	9.8	51.3
outward	*5.4*	*28.2*	*7.2*	*16.8*	*24.4*	*78.8*
France						
inward	*5.9*	*6.5*	*8.1*	*7.6*	*9.1*	*11.0*
outward	10.3	10.2	5.4	10.5	13.9	17.0
Germany						
inward	0.9	1.6	2.3	1.3	2.6	5.1
outward	*5.4*	*4.2*	*7.5*	*10.3*	*9.6*	*22.1*
Greece						
inward	5.5	5.3	4.8	4.4	3.9	2.6
outward	*-a*	*-0.5*	*0.3*	*-*	*-*	*-0.2*
Ireland						
inward	10.5	9.3	12.7	19.1	16.9	45.0
outward	*5.3*	*4.8*	*7.2*	*5.3*	*6.2*	*20.5*
Italy						
inward	1.9	1.2	2.4	1.6	1.8	1.4
outward	*2.6*	*2.8*	*3.5*	*3.9*	*5.0*	*6.6*
Netherlands						
inward	14.2	11.3	15.7	19.3	19.8	55.2
outward	*22.6*	*27.4*	*25.9*	*40.0*	*40.1*	*68.0*
Portugal						
inward	10.0	6.1	2.8	5.3	8.8	10.1
outward	*1.5*	*1.4*	*2.8*	*3.0*	*6.5*	*10.5*
Spain						
inward	10.2	9.2	5.3	5.6	5.8	9.0
outward	*2.5*	*4.1*	*3.5*	*4.6*	*11.4*	*14.4*
Sweden						
inward	6.4	23.1	42.9	13.6	35.2	59.8
outward	*17.1*	*24.7*	*33.3*	*12.5*	*40.6*	*74.4*
United Kingdom						
inward	12.0	5.6	10.9	12.5	15.1	25.7
outward	*14.1*	*19.6*	*23.7*	*17.4*	*28.0*	*48.0*

/...

Annex table B.5. **Inward and outward FDI flows as a percentage of gross fixed capital formation, by region and economy, 1988-1998**

(Percentage)

Region/economy	1988-1993 (Annual average)	1994	1995	1996	1997	1998
Other Western Europe						
inward	3.0	7.3	4.8	6.7	12.0	12.4
outward	*10.4*	*15.5*	*15.5*	*23.4*	*26.2*	*21.3*
Gibraltar						
inward	..	..	..	..	..	..
outward	..	..	..	..	..	..
Iceland						
inward	0.9	-0.2	-0.9	6.4	10.7	8.4
outward	*0.8*	*2.4*	*2.3*	*4.8*	*3.9*	*4.2*
Norway						
inward	1.8	10.8	7.9	9.4	10.3	9.8
outward	*4.1*	*8.5*	*9.4*	*17.6*	*14.2*	*6.9*
Switzerland						
inward	3.6	5.8	3.4	5.1	13.2	14.4
outward	*13.5*	*18.8*	*18.6*	*27.0*	*35.3*	*32.0*
North America						
inward	5.2	4.7	5.6	7.1	8.2	13.2
outward	*4.7*	*7.3*	*8.6*	*7.4*	*8.5*	*11.3*
Canada						
inward	4.7	8.1	9.4	9.2	9.9	18.8
outward	*4.7*	*9.2*	*11.7*	*12.5*	*18.9*	*27.1*
United States						
inward	5.3	4.4	5.3	7.0	8.0	12.8
outward	*4.6*	*7.1*	*8.3*	*7.0*	*7.6*	*10.0*
Other developed countries						
inward	0.8	0.6	1.2	0.7	1.4	1.1
outward	*3.3*	*1.7*	*1.8*	*2.0*	*2.7*	*2.6*
Australia						
inward	8.9	5.9	15.0	6.7	8.2	7.3
outward	*4.7*	*3.2*	*4.6*	*6.6*	*6.8*	*2.7*
Israel						
inward	2.8	2.5	6.4	6.2	7.6	9.3
outward	*2.7*	*4.3*	*3.5*	*4.7*	*3.9*	*4.2*
Japan						
inward	-	-	-	-	0.3	0.3
outward	*3.2*	*1.3*	*1.5*	*1.7*	*2.2*	*2.4*
New Zealand						
inward	23.3	24.4	29.0	16.0	20.0	7.3
outward	*10.8*	*16.5*	*-2.7*	*-11.0*	*-0.4*	*7.4*
South Africa						
inward	0.1	1.8	5.2	3.5	15.8	2.5
outward	*2.3*	*6.0*	*10.4*	*4.5*	*9.7*	*7.8*
Developing countries						
inward	4.6	8.3	7.6	9.1	10.8	11.5
outward	*2.1*	*3.4*	*3.4*	*3.8*	*3.8*	*2.4*
Africa						
inward	4.9	8.7	6.7	7.6	8.9	8.8
outward	*1.8*	*1.3*	*0.4*	*-*	*2.7*	*1.0*
North Africa						
inward	3.1	5.9	3.0	2.8	5.3	4.6
outward	*-*	*0.4*	*0.7*	*0.4*	*1.4*	*1.1*

/...

Annex table B.5. **Inward and outward FDI flows as a percentage of gross fixed capital formation, by region and economy, 1988-1998**

(Percentage)

Region/economy	1988-1993 (Annual average)	1994	1995	1996	1997	1998
Algeria						
inward	-	0.1	-	-	-	-
outward	0.1[b]	..	..	..	..	..
Egypt						
inward	4.4	11.9	5.2	5.1	6.1	6.1
outward	0.2	0.4	0.8	-	0.9	0.3
Libyan Arab Jamahiriya						
inward	2.8	-2.2	-3.3	-3.1	-2.0	-3.9
outward	-1.1	0.8	2.6	1.4	6.9	7.8
Morocco						
inward	4.8	8.8	4.7	5.0	15.6	4.1
outward	0.4[c]	0.4	0.2	0.4	0.1	0.3
Sudan						
inward	-0.2[d]	-	-	-	3.8	14.7
outward	..	..	..	..	..	..
Tunisia						
inward	8.8	13.4	8.7	7.7	7.8	13.6
outward	-	0.2	-	-	0.2	-
Other Africa						
inward	**8.1**	**13.0**	**11.9**	**14.5**	**13.8**	**14.7**
outward	**5.6**	**2.6**	**-**	**-0.6**	**4.1**	**0.9**
Angola						
inward	19.9	13.7	51.2	31.2	23.1	73.8
outward	-[c]	-0.2	-24.1	-	-	-
Benin						
inward	20.9	5.3	2.1	6.6	6.8	8.5
outward	-20.6[c]	-3.3	-3.2	3.1	3.2	0.5
Botswana						
inward	-2.0	-1.4	6.4	6.7	8.8	7.5
outward	0.8[c]	0.9	3.7	-	0.4	0.3
Burkina Faso						
inward	0.5	4.7	1.8	2.6	1.9	1.5
outward	-0.5	1.8	-	-	0.2	0.8
Burundi						
inward	0.5	-	1.9	-	-	3.7
outward	-[d]	0.1	0.5	-	-	-
Cameroon						
inward	-0.7	-0.9	0.6	2.5	3.1	3.1
outward	1.2	-	-	-4.0	-4.5	-3.4
Cape Verde						
inward	1.2	1.2	12.6	15.0	6.1	4.5
outward	0.6	0.2	0.3	0.1	-	-
Central African Republic						
inward	-3.1	3.6	2.0	13.5	6.3	3.6
outward	3.0	7.2	4.0	16.6	5.7	3.6
Chad						
inward	9.4	19.5	7.8	9.3	6.8	6.6
outward	13.9	0.4	7.2	4.0	4.6	2.0
Comoros						
inward	3.6	0.5	2.3	5.0	5.2	5.1
outward	2.2[c]	7.7	0.3	..	..	..
Congo						
inward	1.1	0.6	0.4	1.2	1.8	0.7
outward	0.8[a]	0.6	0.4	1.2	1.8	..
Congo, Democratic Republic of						
inward	-0.4	0.2	0.2	0.5	0.2	-
outward	..	..	..	..	..	..

Annex table B.5. **Inward and outward FDI flows as a percentage of gross fixed capital formation, by region and economy, 1988-1998**

(Percentage)

Region/economy	1988-1993 (Annual average)	1994	1995	1996	1997	1998
Côte d'Ivoire						
inward	7.5	14.3	20.9	22.4	29.6	15.7
outward	*13.2ᶜ*	*4.8*	*4.4*	*2.4*	*2.3*	*1.8*
Djibouti						
inward	1.5ᵃ	2.5	7.6	11.2	10.5	13.4
outward	*..*	*..*	*..*	*..*	*..*	*..*
Equatorial Guinea						
inward	37.2	20.0	108.4	135.2	6.5	6.2
outward	*0.3*	*..*	*..*	*..*	*..*	*..*
Ethiopia						
inward	0.2	2.7	3.5	1.2	6.5	16.0
outward	*0.7*	*0.4*	*0.9*	*0.4*	*0.5*	*0.4*
Gabon						
inward	1.8	-11.3	-10.5	23.7	10.5	11.8
outward	*1.2*	*-*	*-*	*-*	*1.1*	*0.3*
Gambia						
inward	10.3	14.8	10.0	14.4	18.0	18.7
outward	*..*	*..*	*..*	*..*	*..*	*..*
Ghana						
inward	3.9	19.0	7.8	8.4	5.1	3.4
outward	*..*	*..*	*..*	*10.5*	*2.9*	*1.8*
Guinea						
inward	3.7	-	0.1	3.3	2.3	2.6
outward	*..*	*..*	*..*	*-*	*-2.2*	*-*
Guinea-Bissau						
inward	2.6ᵉ	0.8	1.8	1.6	17.1	3.6
outward	*1.7ᶠ*	*..*	*..*	*..*	*..*	*..*
Kenya						
inward	1.6	0.3	1.7	0.7	2.1	2.2
outward	*_ᵇ*	*..*	*0.7*	*1.4*	*0.2*	*0.8*
Lesotho						
inward	33.6	57.0	48.2	52.3	48.1	60.5
outward	*_ᵉ*	*..*	*..*	*..*	*..*	*..*
Liberia						
inward	201.4	14.1	21.1	17.1	15.1	16.1
outward	*119.8*	*85.6*	*-96.6*	*-432.8*	*1035.1*	*..*
Madagascar						
inward	4.2	1.8	2.8	2.2	3.2	3.4
outward	*0.2ᵉ*	*..*	*..*	*..*	*..*	*..*
Malawi						
inward	5.0	2.8	12.3	19.6	8.9	36.5
outward	*..*	*0.3*	*..*	*0.9*	*0.4*	*2.9*
Mali						
inward	-	3.9	20.5	7.6	12.6	5.7
outward	*..*	*..*	*..*	*0.6*	*0.8*	*4.3*
Mauritania						
inward	3.2	1.3	3.8	4.0	1.8	-
outward	*0.3*	*..*	*..*	*4.0*	*1.8*	*2.3*
Mauritius						
inward	3.3	1.9	1.9	3.3	5.0	1.3
outward	*1.9*	*-*	*0.4*	*0.2*	*0.3*	*1.4*
Mozambique						
inward	2.0	3.5	4.9	13.4	9.8	26.7
outward	*_ᵉ*	*..*	*..*	*-*	*-*	*-*
Namibia						
inward	12.0	15.1	21.2	17.2	12.4	12.9
outward	*0.7*	*-0.9*	*-0.5*	*-2.9*	*0.1*	*-0.2*

Annex table B.5. **Inward and outward FDI flows as a percentage of gross fixed capital formation, by region and economy, 1988-1998**

(Percentage)

Region/economy	1988-1993 (Annual average)	1994	1995	1996	1997	1998
Niger						
inward	6.9	5.0	9.5	11.1	13.8	4.3
outward	3.8	2.2	1.2	9.7	4.5	4.9
Nigeria						
inward	30.3	50.5	23.9	35.4	25.2	12.7
outward	20.7	4.6	2.3	0.9	1.0	1.3
Rwanda						
inward	2.8	1.1	1.1	1.0	0.9	2.2
outward	..	..	..	..	..	..
Senegal						
inward	2.6	12.6	5.2	0.9	20.7	7.7
outward	1.1	3.3	-0.5	0.2	-0.1	1.1
Seychelles						
inward	21.7	23.0	26.2	18.0	31.7	26.3
outward	1.9	10.1	10.4	7.9	5.8	1.4
Sierra Leone						
inward	7.6	-4.0	-3.1	10.5	29.9	19.2
outward	-	-1.6	5.0	..	..	..
Somalia						
inward	-5.9	0.5	0.5	-	-	-
outward	..	..	..	..	..	..
Swaziland						
inward	28.7	7.5	7.8	-17.4	-11.1	35.8
outward	4.8	16.3	6.6	-9.0	-4.6	7.0
Togo						
inward	1.7	13.7	19.3	14.1	12.6	20.2
outward	2.4	0.1	2.9	6.7	2.4	10.8
Uganda						
inward	1.7	11.7	12.2	12.4	17.1	20.4
outward	..	..	0.3	-0.1	-0.4	-
United Republic of Tanzania						
inward	0.7	4.5	14.6	13.9	14.0	13.8
outward	..	..	..	..	..	..
Zambia						
inward	27.3	9.0	20.5	24.6	40.3	44.3
outward	..	..	..	..	..	..
Zimbabwe						
inward	0.2	2.8	6.8	4.2	8.0	39.8
outward	0.8	0.9	0.8	2.7	1.7	0.8
Latin America and the Caribbean						
inward	**5.2**	**8.8**	**9.3**	**12.3**	**16.2**	**16.6**
outward	*0.9*	*1.3*	*1.2*	*1.5*	*2.6*	*2.8*
South America						
inward	**4.3**	**6.7**	**7.2**	**11.6**	**15.8**	**17.5**
outward	*1.0*	*1.4*	*1.4*	*1.5*	*2.9*	*2.9*
Argentina						
inward	8.2	6.8	11.5	13.2	15.4	11.0
outward	1.1	2.0	3.2	3.3	6.4	3.7
Bolivia						
inward	10.8	14.7	35.9	35.6	57.0	48.2
outward	0.2	0.2	0.2	0.2	0.1	0.1
Brazil						
inward	1.8	2.3	3.8	7.0	11.7	18.4
outward	0.6	0.5	0.8	0.3	1.0	1.7

Annex table B.5. **Inward and outward FDI flows as a percentage of gross fixed capital formation, by region and economy, 1988-1998**

(Percentage)

Region/economy	1988-1993 (Annual average)	1994	1995	1996	1997	1998
Chile						
inward	13.0	23.1	19.0	27.1	27.2	25.0
outward	*2.2*	*7.7*	*4.8*	*7.0*	*9.7*	*15.1*
Colombia						
inward	7.8	7.8	4.7	14.8	26.2	17.5
outward	*0.9*	*0.8*	*1.2*	*1.6*	*3.8*	*3.2*
Ecuador						
inward	9.1	17.0	14.1	14.5	18.5	20.1
outward	*-g*	*-*	*-*	*-*	*-*	*-*
Guyana						
inward	..[h]	43.0	26.4	30.0	15.9	22.5
outward	*-h*	*-*	*-*	*-0.3*	*-*	*-*
Paraguay						
inward	4.7	7.8	7.5	11.3	12.4	22.3
outward	*1.0*	*4.7*	*1.3*	*-*	*2.2*	*0.7*
Peru						
inward	2.4	29.2	14.2	23.5	10.6	12.5
outward	*0.2[h]*	*-*	*-*	*-0.1*	*0.5*	*0.3*
Suriname						
inward	-18.0	-3.5	-2.1	0.6	1.2	1.0
outward	*..*	*..*	*..*	*..*	*..*	*..*
Uruguay						
inward	3.5	6.3	6.2	5.0	4.4	5.1
outward	*0.3*	*-*	*-1.0*	*0.4*	*0.5*	*0.2*
Venezuela						
inward	5.9	7.9	7.7	19.6	34.8	25.6
outward	*3.0*	*3.5*	*0.7*	*4.6*	*3.1*	*1.5*
Other Latin America and the Caribbean						
inward	**7.3**	**13.6**	**18.6**	**14.8**	**17.3**	**14.5**
outward	***0.8***	***1.0***	***0.2***	***1.4***	***1.6***	***2.5***
Antigua and Barbuda						
inward	26.2	15.3	17.3	8.7	9.8	13.3
outward	*-0.7g*	*-0.6*	*-1.1*	*-0.5*	*-0.8*	*-*
Aruba						
inward	..	..	..	..	..	..
outward	*..*	*..*	*..*	*..*	*..*	*..*
Bahamas						
inward	1.9	3.8	15.3	..	..	..
outward	*-*	*-*	*-*	*..*	*..*	*..*
Barbados						
inward	4.0	5.6	4.5	5.3	4.4	5.5
outward	*0.6*	*0.5*	*1.3*	*1.4*	*0.4*	*0.3*
Belize						
inward	12.4	12.1	16.3	12.1	8.3	11.5
outward	*0.9d*	*1.6*	*1.6*	*4.1*	*2.7*	*2.9*
Bermuda						
inward	..	..	..	..	..	..
outward	*..*	*..*	*..*	*..*	*..*	*..*
Cayman Islands						
inward	..	..	..	..	..	..
outward	*..*	*..*	*..*	*..*	*..*	*..*
Costa Rica						
inward	13.9	18.1	19.5	26.4	25.8	24.4
outward	*0.3*	*0.3*	*0.3*	*0.4*	*0.4*	*0.3*

Annex table B.5. Inward and outward FDI flows as a percentage of gross fixed capital formation, by region and economy, 1988-1998

(Percentage)

Region/economy	1988-1993 (Annual average)	1994	1995	1996	1997	1998
Cuba						
inward	..	..	..	..	..	..
outward	..	..	..	..	..	..
Dominica						
inward	27.4	41.2	78.3	26.8	27.4	14.6
outward	..	..	..	*1.8*	*1.1*	*4.1*
Dominican Republic						
inward	7.8	8.3	16.0	3.4	12.6	16.9
outward	*0.2h*	*0.5*	*0.6*	*0.5*	-	-
El Salvador						
inward	1.7	..	2.1	-0.3	0.6	44.0
outward	..	..	..	*0.1*	..	..
Grenada						
inward	22.4	21.8	23.7	19.5	32.1	39.3
outward	..	..	..	..	..	..
Guatemala						
inward	10.3	3.5	3.3	3.7	3.1	20.7
outward	..	*-1.1*	*-1.1*	-	-	-
Haiti						
inward	2.5	-2.3	2.3	1.0	1.0	2.4
outward	*-3.5c*	-	*0.3*	*0.3*	-	-
Honduras						
inward	5.8	4.3	7.3	9.5	10.8	6.4
outward	*-c*	*-0.3*	*-0.2*	*-0.2*	-	-
Jamaica						
inward	11.0	9.9	8.9	9.7	9.4	18.6
outward	*4.1c*	*4.0*	*4.0*	*4.9*	*2.6*	*4.1*
Mexico						
inward	6.9	13.5	20.6	15.5	16.4	11.6
outward	*0.3*	*1.3*	*-0.6*	-	*1.4*	*1.5*
Netherlands Antilles						
inward	..	..	..	..	..	..
outward	..	..	..	..	..	..
Nicaragua						
inward	9.5d	10.0	16.7	18.1	27.0	25.8
outward	*-g*	..	-	*-1.7*	..	-
Panama						
inward	0.3	21.5	13.0	19.9	54.7	45.9
outward	*34.7*	*-11.5*	*16.0*	*41.8*	*13.6*	*46.4*
Saint Kitts and Nevis						
inward	31.7	18.2	24.2	54.0	16.1	25.5
outward	*0.2c*	*-0.4*	*-2.4*	*-3.1*	*-1.6*	*-0.8*
Saint Lucia						
inward	34.5	26.2	28.9	13.9	33.2	71.1
outward	*0.2i*	..	*4.5*	*13.1*	..	..
Saint Vincent and the Grenadines						
inward	24.2	77.4	38.5	54.1	63.3	27.6
outward	*1.6*	*-0.5*	*1.0*	*1.0*	..	..
Trinidad and Tobago						
inward	25.4	51.3	37.0	37.3	65.2	46.9
outward	*-c*	-	*0.1*	*0.1*	-	-
Virgin Islands						
inward	..	..	..	..	..	..
outward	..	..	..	..	..	..
Developing Europe						
inward	**5.5**	**6.8**	**5.7**	**10.6**	**9.7**	**13.0**
outward	***0.4***	**-**	***0.2***	***0.4***	***2.2***	***1.1***

Annex table B.5. **Inward and outward FDI flows as a percentage of gross fixed capital formation, by region and economy, 1988-1998**

(Percentage)

Region/economy	1988-1993 (Annual average)	1994	1995	1996	1997	1998
Bosnia and Herzegovina						
inward	..	..	..	..	..	..
outward	..	..	..	..	..	..
Croatia						
inward	7.1[g]	5.7	3.9	12.4	10.5	17.3
outward	*1.1[g]*	*0.3*	*0.2*	*0.6*	*3.8*	*1.9*
Malta						
inward	7.8	18.8	17.6	33.9	19.5	32.5
outward	*0.1[g]*	*-0.1*	*0.5*	*0.7*	*2.0*	*1.8*
Slovenia						
inward	4.0[a]	4.4	4.4	4.4	7.5	3.5
outward	*0.3[a]*	*-0.1*	*0.1*	*0.2*	*0.6*	*0.2*
TFYR Macedonia						
inward	..	5.2	2.3	2.6	3.4	26.4
outward	*..*	*..*	*..*	*0.2*	*0.2*	*0.3*
Asia						
inward	**4.3**	**8.1**	**7.1**	**8.2**	**9.0**	**9.6**
outward	***2.5***	***4.4***	***4.4***	***4.8***	***4.4***	***2.4***
West Asia						
inward	**1.1**	**1.6**	**-**	**1.6**	**3.1**	**3.9**
outward	***0.6***	***-1.3***	***-0.8***	***1.6***	***-0.2***	***-2.7***
Bahrain						
inward	26.0	18.2	42.5	271.1	43.3	20.8
outward	*3.5*	*17.4*	*-1.6*	*40.4*	*6.3*	*20.8*
Cyprus						
inward	5.6	3.0	4.7	2.8	4.4	3.5
outward	*0.8*	*1.4*	*1.6*	*2.7*	*2.8*	*5.3*
Iran, Islamic Republic						
inward	-	-	-	-	0.1	-
outward	*-*	*-*	*-*	*-*	*0.2*	*-*
Iraq						
inward	..	..	..	..	..	..
outward	*..*	*..*	*..*	*..*	*..*	*..*
Jordan						
inward	0.7	0.1	0.7	0.8	19.3	16.8
outward	*-0.7*	*-1.2*	*-1.4*	*-2.1*	*-*	*0.5*
Kuwait						
inward	0.4	..	0.2	7.9	0.5	1.6
outward	*17.5*	*-45.9*	*-27.7*	*39.5*	*-23.7*	*-51.9*
Lebanon						
inward	0.4[c]	0.2	1.0	2.0	3.8	4.2
outward	*0.2[c]*	*-*	*-*	*-*	*-*	*-56.2*
Oman						
inward	7.3	3.8	2.2	3.6	1.9	3.1
outward	*-*	*0.2*	*-*	*-*	*0.4*	*0.3*
Qatar						
inward	1.9	7.3	5.0	2.1	3.1	3.9
outward	*..*	*..*	*1.6*	*2.4*	*1.1*	*1.1*
Saudi Arabia						
inward	1.9	1.6	-7.5	-4.7	11.1	16.6
outward	*1.0*	*0.4*	*-*	*0.7*	*0.7*	*-1.8*
Syrian Arab Republic						
inward	1.6	1.9	0.7	0.6	0.6	0.6
outward	*1.8*	*..*	*..*	*-*	*-*	*-*

Annex table B.5. **Inward and outward FDI flows as a percentage of gross fixed capital formation, by region and economy, 1988-1998**

(Percentage)

Region/economy	1988-1993 (Annual average)	1994	1995	1996	1997	1998
Turkey						
inward	2.0	1.9	2.2	1.6	1.6	1.9
outward	*-c*	*0.2*	*0.3*	*0.2*	*0.5*	*0.7*
United Arab Emirates						
inward	1.5	0.6	3.7	1.2	0.9	0.9
outward	*0.2*	*-0.4*	*-*	*-*	*-0.1*	*-0.2*
Yemen						
inward	25.3c	0.2	-9.5	-4.1	-10.5	-22.6
outward	*..*	*..*	*..*	*..*	*..*	*..*
Central Asia						
inward	**4.1**	**7.5**	**12.9**	**15.1**	**25.5**	**28.3**
outward	*..*	*-*	*3.5*	*0.7*	*1.3*	*2.5*
Armenia						
inward	0.2c	6.1	12.2	6.2	19.5	71.2
outward	*..*	*..*	*..*	*..*	*..*	*3.5*
Azerbaijan						
inward	..	2.5	73.1	67.9	78.0	64.2
outward	*..*	*..*	*38.8*	*3.9*	*4.5*	*8.6*
Georgia						
inward	..	19.4	3.9	16.4	29.5	66.1
outward	*..*	*..*	*..*	*..*	*..*	*..*
Kazakhstan						
inward	8.8h	12.8	21.0	31.4	36.7	30.4
outward	*..*	*-*	*-*	*-*	*-*	*0.2*
Kyrgyzstan						
inward	1.7g	27.7	31.2	11.3	37.2	50.3
outward	*..*	*..*	*..*	*-*	*0.4*	*0.3*
Tajikistan						
inward	..	2.1	5.1	3.3	0.9	7.5
outward	*..*	*..*	*..*	*..*	*..*	*-*
Turkmenistan						
inward	..	..	..	..	..	..
outward	*..*	*..*	*..*	*..*	*..*	*..*
Uzbekistan						
inward	1.4h	1.3	2.0	0.8	5.3	5.1
outward	*..*	*..*	*..*	*..*	*..*	*..*
South, East and South-East Asia						
inward	**5.5**	**9.1**	**8.1**	**9.1**	**9.8**	**10.5**
outward	*3.0*	*5.2*	*5.1*	*5.3*	*5.2*	*3.4*
Afghanistan						
inward	..	..	..	..	..	..
outward	*..*	*..*	*..*	*..*	*..*	*..*
Bangladesh						
inward	0.1	0.3	-	0.3	2.9	6.2
outward	*-*	*-*	*-1.4*	*0.5*	*-*	*-*
Brunei Darussalam						
inward	..	..	..	..	..	..
outward	*..*	*..*	*..*	*..*	*..*	*..*
Cambodia						
inward	18.1h	15.5	23.5	36.1	28.6	28.0
outward	*0.7g*	*..*	*..*	*..*	*..*	*..*
China						
inward	6.4	17.3	14.7	14.3	14.6	12.9
outward	*1.4*	*1.0*	*0.8*	*0.8*	*0.8*	*0.8*

Annex table B.5. **Inward and outward FDI flows as a percentage of gross fixed capital formation, by region and economy, 1988-1998**

(Percentage)

Region/economy	1988-1993 (Annual average)	1994	1995	1996	1997	1998
Hong Kong, China						
inward	16.5	20.1	14.6	21.7	19.8	29.6
outward	*27.2*	*55.0*	*58.7*	*55.1*	*42.5*	*33.9*
India						
inward	0.4	1.4	2.4	2.6	3.8	2.9
outward	-	*0.1*	*0.1*	*0.3*	*0.1*	-
Indonesia						
inward	3.1	3.8	6.7	8.9	6.8	-0.8
outward	*0.2*	*1.1*	*0.9*	*0.9*	*0.3*	-
Korea, Democratic People's Republic						
inward	..	..	..	..	..	..
outward	..	..	..	..	..	..
Korea, Republic of						
inward	1.0	0.7	0.8	1.2	1.8	5.5
outward	*1.0*	*1.6*	*1.7*	*2.2*	*1.9*	*4.1*
Lao People's Democratic Republic						
inward	10.8	60.8	19.3	23.6	18.2	14.4
outward	*0.1^j*	..	-	..	..	-
Macau, China						
inward	-	0.2	0.1	0.4	0.2	-
outward	..	..	..	..	..	..
Malaysia						
inward	20.7	15.7	15.5	17.0	15.1	13.9
outward	*2.0*	*8.0*	*6.6*	*8.8*	*6.1*	*4.0*
Maldives						
inward	7.1	11.7	9.6	12.4	15.2	15.3
outward	*0.5^c*	*0.4*	*-0.3*	*-1.7*	*-4.5*	*-0.7*
Maldives						
inward	7.1	11.7	9.6	12.4	15.2	15.3
outward	*0.5c*	*0.4*	*-0.3*	*-1.7*	*-4.5*	*-0.7*
Mongolia						
inward	4.9^g	4.1	3.9	5.9	10.0	7.0
outward	..	..	*0.4*	-	*0.8*	-
Myanmar						
inward	3.3^d	1.4	1.9	1.6	1.7	1.4
outward	..	..	..	..	..	..
Nepal						
inward	0.5	0.8	0.9	1.9	2.2	1.3
outward	..	..	-	*1.2*	*-0.5*	-
Pakistan						
inward	3.5	4.5	7.1	8.9	7.5	5.6
outward	-	-	-	-	*-0.3*	-
Philippines						
inward	7.8	10.5	8.9	7.8	6.2	12.8
outward	*0.9*	*2.0*	*0.6*	*0.9*	*0.7*	*1.2*
Singapore						
inward	29.2	36.1	25.6	25.6	22.1	17.6
outward	*8.6*	*19.3*	*22.3*	*19.7*	*24.2*	*-4.9*
Sri Lanka						
inward	4.2	5.3	1.9	4.0	11.8	5.2
outward	*0.2*	*0.3*	*0.2*	-	-	-
Taiwan Province of China						
inward	2.9	2.3	2.4	3.0	3.4	0.4
outward	*9.5*	*4.4*	*4.5*	*6.1*	*7.9*	*6.1*
Thailand						
inward	5.4	2.3	2.8	3.2	7.8	25.1
outward	*0.4*	*0.7*	*1.2*	*1.2*	*0.8*	*0.5*

Annex table B.5. **Inward and outward FDI flows as a percentage of gross fixed capital formation,
by region and economy, 1988-1998**

(Percentage)

Region/economy	1988-1993 (Annual average)	1994	1995	1996	1997	1998
Viet Nam						
inward	45.4[d]	49.0	42.8	37.9	36.8	25.3
outward	..	..	..	..	..	..
The Pacific						
inward	**17.4**	**14.0**	**42.0**	**8.3**	**4.8**	**15.0**
outward	***2.8***	***-0.1***	***-1.1***	***4.3***	***12.4***	***16.5***
Fiji						
inward	30.4	30.7	27.3	1.1	6.4	39.8
outward	*8.3*	*-0.1*	*-1.1*	*4.3*	*12.4*	*16.5*
Kiribati						
inward	0.6	2.1	1.4	3.3	4.8	2.4
outward	..	*0.1*	..	..	..	..
New Caledonia						
inward	..	..	..	..	..	..
outward	..	..	..	..	..	..
Papua New Guinea						
inward	14.5	7.1	47.5	7.6	2.2	9.7
outward	*0.6[f]*	..	..	..	..	..
Vanuatu						
inward	39.2	52.4	42.8	54.8	48.0	41.4
outward	..	..	..	..	..	..
Samoa						
inward	..	..	..	..	..	..
outward	..	..	..	..	..	..
Solomon Islands						
inward	..	..	..	..	..	..
outward	..	..	..	..	..	..
Tonga						
inward	3.3	9.3	9.3	9.4	14.0	9.3
outward	-	..	..	..	..	..
Central and Eastern Europe						
inward	**3.7**	**4.4**	**9.2**	**6.8**	**10.5**	**12.9**
outward	***0.2***	***0.2***	***0.3***	***0.6***	***1.9***	***1.4***
Albania						
inward	..	..	..	..	..	..
outward	..	..	..	..	..	..
Belarus						
inward	0.1[h]	0.2	0.3	1.8	3.9	2.5
outward	*-g*	-	*0.3*	-	-	-
Bulgaria						
inward	1.7[c]	7.9	4.5	8.1	44.0	37.9
outward	*0.6[h]*	..	*-0.4*	*-2.1*	*-0.1*	-
Czech Republic						
inward	6.0[d]	7.4	15.4	7.7	8.1	17.5
outward	*0.6[h]*	*1.0*	*0.2*	*0.8*	*0.2*	*1.1*
Estonia						
inward	17.6[h]	34.8	21.8	12.9	20.6	38.3
outward	*0.6[h]*	*0.4*	*0.3*	*3.4*	*10.6*	*0.4*
Hungary						
inward	15.3	13.7	52.8	23.6	21.4	18.3
outward	*0.2[a]*	*0.6*	*0.5*	-	*4.2*	*4.3*
Latvia						
inward	5.0[h]	26.4	26.7	41.0	49.3	27.8
outward	*-0.2[h]*	*-8.0*	*-9.7*	*0.3*	*0.6*	*4.2*

Annex table B.5. **Inward and outward FDI flows as a percentage of gross fixed capital formation, by region and economy, 1988-1998**

(Percentage)

Region/economy	1988-1993 (Annual average)	1994	1995	1996	1997	1998
Lithuania						
inward	1.0[h]	2.3	4.6	8.4	15.2	35.4
outward	..	..	-	-	*1.2*	*0.2*
Moldova, Republic of						
inward	2.7[h]	5.2	29.1	7.2	20.4	23.0
outward	..	*3.4*	*-0.2*	*-0.2*	*0.1*	-
Poland						
inward	3.4	10.5	15.5	15.1	14.5	15.8
outward	-	*0.2*	*0.2*	*0.2*	*0.1*	*0.8*
Romania						
inward	1.7[a]	5.6	5.5	3.3	15.8	25.3
outward	*0.2[c]*	-	-	-	-	-
Russian Federation						
inward	1.4[h]	1.1	2.8	2.8	7.9	5.6
outward	*0.4[g]*	*0.2*	*0.5*	*0.9*	*3.1*	*2.1*
Slovakia						
inward	2.8[c]	6.1	4.1	3.6	2.7	7.6
outward	*0.3[h]*	*0.3*	*0.2*	*0.7*	*1.3*	*1.8*
Ukraine						
inward	0.9[h]	1.3	2.3	4.0	5.9	8.8
outward	..	-	-	-	*0.4*	-
Memorandum:						
Least developed countries: [k]						
Total						
inward	**6.3**	**3.6**	**5.3**	**5.5**	**5.3**	**8.1**
outward	*1.6*	*1.3*	*-3.1*	*-2.3*	*7.2*	*0.6*
Africa						
inward	**6.5**	**6.5**	**12.0**	**12.1**	**11.8**	**20.1**
outward	*2.9*	*2.5*	*-5.8*	*-5.1*	*12.7*	*1.1*
Latin America and the Caribbean						
inward	**2.5**	**-2.3**	**2.3**	**1.0**	**1.0**	**2.4**
outward	*-3.5[c]*	-	*0.3*	*0.3*	-	-
Asia and the Pacific						
inward	**6.0**	**1.7**	**1.5**	**2.5**	**2.3**	**2.1**
outward	-	-	*-1.0*	*0.6*	-	-
Asia						
inward	5.8	1.5	1.3	2.4	2.2	2.0
outward	-	-	*-1.0*	*0.6*	-	-
West Asia						
inward	25.3[c]	0.2	-9.5	-4.1	-10.5	-22.6
outward	..	..	..	..	..	..
South, East and South-East Asia						
inward	2.1	2.0	2.5	2.8	2.7	2.8
outward	-	-	*-1.0*	*0.6*	-	-
The Pacific						
inward	27.4	38.8	33.6	41.2	37.2	31.9
outward	..	..	..	..	..	..
Oil-exporting countries: [l]						
Total						
inward	**4.1**	**8.9**	**8.5**	**9.9**	**11.3**	**8.9**
outward	*0.9*	*1.3*	*0.8*	*2.4*	*1.3*	*0.2*
Africa						
inward	**5.1**	**9.9**	**5.8**	**7.2**	**7.2**	**7.6**
outward	*1.7*	*1.0*	*0.2*	*0.2*	*1.2*	*1.0*
North Africa						
inward	3.0	5.8	2.8	2.6	3.4	4.1
outward	-	*0.4*	*0.9*	*0.3*	*1.8*	*1.3*

Annex table B.5. **Inward and outward FDI flows as a percentage of gross fixed capital formation, by region and economy, 1988-1998**

(Percentage)

Region/economy	1988-1993 (Annual average)	1994	1995	1996	1997	1998
Other Africa	-	-	-	-	-	-
inward	14.7	26.1	16.9	25.1	19.2	17.7
outward	*9.2*	*2.4*	*-1.3*	-	-	*0.4*
Latin America and the Caribbean						
inward	**7.0**	**13.4**	**18.2**	**16.7**	**20.7**	**15.2**
outward	*0.7*	*1.5*	*-0.3*	*0.7*	*1.6*	*1.4*
South America	-	-	-	-	-	-
inward	6.7	10.3	10.7	19.7	33.5	26.5
outward	*2.7*	*2.5*	*0.6*	*3.2*	*2.4*	*1.1*
Other Latin America and the Caribbean						
inward	7.1	13.9	20.9	15.9	17.3	12.2
outward	*0.3*	*1.3*	*-0.6*	-	*1.4*	*1.5*
Asia						
inward	**2.9**	**5.4**	**5.4**	**7.8**	**7.5**	**4.7**
outward	*0.7*	*1.2*	*1.2*	*3.5*	*1.1*	*-0.9*
West Asia						
inward	0.6	1.5	-1.3	1.9	4.2	5.5
outward	*0.7*	*-2.3*	*-1.5*	*2.9*	*-0.7*	*-2.4*
South, East and South-East Asia						
inward	8.0	8.0	10.0	12.0	10.0	3.7
outward	*0.7*	*3.5*	*3.0*	*3.9*	*2.5*	*1.3*
All developing countries minus China						
inward	**4.3**	**6.6**	**6.2**	**7.9**	**9.9**	**11.1**
outward	*2.2*	*3.9*	*4.0*	*4.5*	*4.5*	*2.9*
Asia and the Pacific						
inward	**4.4**	**8.1**	**7.2**	**8.2**	**9.0**	**9.6**
outward	*2.5*	*4.4*	*4.4*	*4.8*	*4.4*	*2.4*
Africa including South Africa						
inward	**3.9**	**7.0**	**6.3**	**6.6**	**10.5**	**7.5**
outward	*1.9*	*2.9*	*3.7*	*1.3*	*4.8*	*2.7*

Source: UNCTAD, FDI/TNC database.

a   Annual average from 1991 to 1993.
b   Annual average from 1988 to 1991.
c   Annual average from 1990 to 1993.
d   Annual average from 1989 to 1993.
e   Annual average from 1988 to 1992.
f   Annual average from 1988 to 1990.
g   1993.
h   Annual average from 1992 to 1993.
i   Annual average from 1990 to 1991.
j   1991.
k   Least developed countries include: Afghanistan, Angola, Bangladesh, Benin, Burkina Faso, Burundi, Cambodia, Cape Verde, Central African Republic, Chad, Comoros, Democratic Repunlic of Congo, Djibouti, Equatorial Guinea, Ethiopia, Gambia, Guinea, Guinea-Bissau, Haiti, Kiribati, Lao People's Democratic Republic, Lesotho, Liberia, Madagascar, Malawi, Maldives, Mali, Mauritania, Mozambique, Myanmar, Nepal, Niger, Rwanda, Western Samoa, Sierra Leone, Solomon Islands, Somalia, Sudan, Togo, Uganda, United Republic of Tanzania, Vanuatu, Yemen and Zambia. Not included are Bhutan, Eritrea, Sao Tome and Principe and Tuvalu due to unavailability of data.
l   Oil-exporting countries include: Algeria, Angola, Bahrain, Brunei Darussalam, Cameroon, Congo, Ecuador, Egypt, Gabon, Indonesia, Islamic Republic of Iran, Iraq, Kuwait, Libyan Arab Jamahiriya, Malaysia, Mexico, Nigeria, Oman, Qatar, Saudi Arabia, Trinidad and Tobago, Tunisia, United Arab Emirates and Venezuela.

Annex table B.6. Inward and outward FDI stocks as a percentage of gross domestic product,
by region and economy, 1980, 1985, 1990, 1995 and 1998

(Percentage)

Region/economy	1980	1985	1990	1995	1998
World					
inward	4.9	6.7	8.6	9.6	13.7
outward	*5.4*	*6.4*	*8.6*	*10.2*	*14.1*
Developed countries					
inward	4.7	6.1	8.3	8.8	12.1
outward	*6.4*	*7.5*	*9.8*	*11.7*	*16.4*
Western Europe					
inward	5.5	8.5	10.9	12.7	17.6
outward	*6.5*	*10.7*	*12.2*	*16.5*	*24.3*
European Union					
inward	5.3	8.3	10.7	12.4	17.3
outward	*6.1*	*10.3*	*11.7*	*15.4*	*22.9*
Austria					
inward	4.0	5.7	6.2	7.6	11.3
outward	*0.7*	*2.0*	*2.7*	*5.1*	*8.2*
Belgium and Luxembourg					
inward	5.9	22.0	28.3	40.1	61.7
outward	*4.9*	*11.4*	*19.7*	*30.4*	*50.2*
Denmark					
inward	6.3	6.2	6.9	13.2	17.4
outward	*3.1*	*3.1*	*5.5*	*13.7*	*19.4*
Finland					
inward	1.1	2.5	3.8	6.7	13.1
outward	*1.4*	*3.4*	*8.3*	*11.9*	*23.4*
France					
inward	3.4	6.4	7.2	9.4	11.7
outward	*3.6*	*7.1*	*9.2*	*12.0*	*15.9*
Germany					
inward	4.0	5.3	6.8	6.9	9.3
outward	*4.7*	*8.6*	*9.2*	*11.1*	*17.3*
Greece					
inward	11.3	24.9	16.9	16.6	18.3
outward	*2.1*	*2.6*	*1.0*	*0.7*	*0.7*
Ireland					
inward	19.5	24.5	12.2	18.6	32.7
outward	*..*	*1.1*	*4.8*	*6.4*	*12.4*
Italy					
inward	2.0	4.5	5.3	5.8	8.8
outward	*1.6*	*3.9*	*5.2*	*10.0*	*14.1*
Netherlands					
inward	11.1	19.5	25.9	31.5	48.0
outward	*24.5*	*37.3*	*38.4*	*45.4*	*68.9*
Portugal					
inward	10.0	16.0	14.1	16.8	20.8
outward	*0.4*	*0.8*	*0.7*	*3.5*	*8.6*
Spain					
inward	2.4	5.4	13.4	19.1	21.5
outward	*0.9*	*2.7*	*3.2*	*6.3*	*12.5*
Sweden					
inward	2.9	5.0	5.4	13.4	22.5
outward	*3.0*	*10.7*	*21.5*	*31.6*	*41.3*
United Kingdom					
inward	11.7	14.0	20.8	18.0	23.3
outward	*15.0*	*21.9*	*23.4*	*27.4*	*35.9*

/...

Annex table B.6. **Inward and outward FDI stocks as a percentage of gross domestic product, by region and economy, 1980, 1985, 1990, 1995 and 1998**

(Percentage)

Region/economy	1980	1985	1990	1995	1998
Other Western Europe					
inward	9.0	11.0	13.4	16.6	22.7
outward	*13.1*	*16.5*	*22.0*	*35.8*	*51.6*
Gibraltar					
inward	..	..	..	..	..
outward	..	..	..	..	..
Iceland					
inward	-	2.2	2.3	1.8	5.6
outward	*1.9*	*2.2*	*1.2*	*2.6*	*4.1*
Norway					
inward	10.4	11.7	10.7	13.3	16.7
outward	*0.9*	*1.7*	*9.4*	*15.4*	*22.6*
Switzerland					
inward	8.4	10.8	15.0	18.6	26.5
outward	*21.1*	*27.0*	*28.9*	*46.3*	*69.1*
North America					
inward	4.6	5.7	8.3	8.7	10.5
outward	*8.2*	*6.7*	*8.4*	*10.7*	*12.5*
Canada					
inward	20.6	18.6	19.7	21.5	23.9
outward	*9.0*	*12.4*	*14.8*	*20.6*	*26.9*
United States					
inward	3.1	4.6	7.1	7.6	9.5
outward	*8.1*	*6.2*	*7.8*	*9.9*	*11.5*
Other developed countries					
inward	2.7	2.6	3.0	3.1	4.3
outward	*2.1*	*3.8*	*7.3*	*5.6*	*8.5*
Australia					
inward	8.8	15.6	24.9	28.9	28.1
outward	*1.5*	*4.2*	*10.6*	*13.6*	*17.1*
Israel					
inward	3.3	4.7	3.8	6.0	11.1
outward	*0.8*	*2.7*	*2.2*	*4.5*	*6.8*
Japan					
inward	0.3	0.4	0.3	0.7	0.7
outward	*1.9*	*3.3*	*6.8*	*4.6*	*7.1*
New Zealand					
inward	10.6	9.1	18.4	42.6	66.2
outward	*1.7*	*6.1*	*7.6*	*12.7*	*11.0*
South Africa					
inward	21.3	16.3	8.6	11.2	13.4
outward	*7.4*	*16.2*	*14.1*	*17.4*	*24.8*
Developing countries					
inward	5.4	9.1	10.5	13.4	20.0
outward	*0.9*	*1.6*	*2.6*	*4.9*	*6.7*
Africa					
inward	6.0	9.5	12.4	19.9	21.1
outward	*0.4*	*2.8*	*4.5*	*5.4*	*4.8*
North Africa					
inward	9.6	11.4	11.2	17.3	15.9
outward	*0.3*	*0.4*	*0.5*	*0.6*	*0.9*

/...

Annex table B.6. **Inward and outward FDI stocks as a percentage of gross domestic product, by region and economy, 1980, 1985, 1990, 1995 and 1998**

(Percentage)

Region/economy	1980	1985	1990	1995	1998
Algeria					
inward	3.1	2.2	2.1	3.3	3.0
outward	*0.2*	*0.3*	*0.3*	*0.6*	*0.5*
Egypt					
inward	9.8	16.4	25.6	23.9	20.2
outward	*0.2*	*0.3*	*0.4*	*0.7*	*0.7*
Libyan Arab Jamahiriya					
inward	..	..	1.3	2.2	0.3
outward	*0.4*	*0.7*	*1.7*	*0.9*	*3.2*
Morocco					
inward	1.0	3.4	3.5	9.2	13.3
outward	*..*	*..*	*-*	*0.4*	*0.5*
Sudan					
inward	0.1	0.5	0.2	0.4	4.9
outward	*..*	*..*	*..*	*..*	*..*
Tunisia					
inward	66.7	83.0	59.0	65.7	59.3
outward	*0.1*	*-*	*0.1*	*0.2*	*0.2*
Other Africa					
inward	**4.4**	**8.2**	**13.7**	**22.9**	**27.7**
outward	***0.5***	***5.4***	***11.7***	***13.9***	***10.9***
Angola					
inward	1.8	9.9	13.2	57.8	69.6
outward	*..*	*..*	*..*	*..*	*..*
Benin					
inward	2.2	3.2	8.6	18.9	20.1
outward	*-*	*0.2*	*-*	*-*	*-*
Botswana					
inward	67.4	78.1	38.6	24.6	26.1
outward	*42.5*	*36.3*	*13.2*	*14.2*	*5.2*
Burkina Faso					
inward	1.4	1.7	1.4	3.1	4.6
outward	*0.2*	*0.2*	*-*	*-*	*0.3*
Burundi					
inward	0.7	2.0	2.6	3.3	3.6
outward	*..*	*..*	*-*	*-*	*-*
Cameroon					
inward	4.9	13.8	9.4	13.3	13.7
outward	*0.3*	*0.6*	*1.3*	*2.9*	*0.6*
Cape Verde					
inward	..	..	1.3	9.0	21.1
outward	*..*	*..*	*0.4*	*1.1*	*1.2*
Central African Republic					
inward	6.2	8.9	6.4	6.7	8.8
outward	*-*	*0.2*	*1.2*	*4.0*	*5.9*
Chad					
inward	11.9	18.9	15.1	21.1	21.1
outward	*-*	*0.1*	*2.2*	*5.8*	*6.4*
Comoros					
inward	..	..	6.0	8.1	12.1
outward	*..*	*..*	*0.4*	*3.2*	*3.5*
Congo					
inward	18.1	22.2	20.1	27.9	30.4
outward	*..*	*..*	*..*	*..*	*..*
Congo, Democratic Republic of					
inward	2.2	3.4	1.8	2.8	2.9
outward	*..*	*..*	*..*	*..*	*..*

/...

**Annex table B.6. Inward and outward FDI stocks as a percentage of gross domestic product,
by region and economy, 1980, 1985, 1990, 1995 and 1998**

(Percentage)

Region/economy	1980	1985	1990	1995	1998
Côte d'Ivoire					
inward	5.2	10.1	9.0	16.2	24.2
outward	..	..	..	..	*0.9*
Djibouti					
inward	1.0	1.0	1.3	2.8	5.6
outward	..	..	..	..	..
Equatorial Guinea					
inward	..	7.0	19.2	145.7	121.5
outward	..	..	-	*0.1*	-
Ethiopia					
inward	2.7	2.0	1.5	3.2	6.9
outward	..	..	..	*0.3*	*0.5*
Gabon					
inward	12.0	22.7	20.3	19.2	34.1
outward	*1.8*	*2.8*	*2.7*	*4.2*	*4.7*
Gambia					
inward	8.9	9.4	11.2	20.7	28.6
outward	..	..	..	..	..
Ghana					
inward	5.2	6.0	5.4	12.7	15.1
outward	..	..	..	..	*3.2*
Guinea					
inward	-	0.2	2.5	3.6	5.0
outward	..	..	..	..	-
Guinea-Bissau					
inward	-	2.7	3.3	6.8	13.2
outward	..	..	..	..	..
Kenya					
inward	4.8	7.1	7.3	7.6	7.6
outward	*0.2*	*1.0*	*1.2*	*1.2*	*1.5*
Lesotho					
inward	1.2	7.9	23.9	156.9	279.0
outward	..	..	-	-	-
Liberia					
inward	6.4	42.4	137.9	859.6	568.0
outward	*4.3*	*33.0*	*37.7*	*358.5*	*422.7*
Madagascar					
inward	0.9	1.7	3.4	5.4	5.6
outward	..	..	..	..	..
Malawi					
inward	8.1	12.2	10.2	17.1	22.9
outward	..	..	..	..	*0.5*
Mali					
inward	0.8	2.8	1.6	6.6	12.1
outward	*1.3*	*1.8*	*0.9*	*0.9*	*2.2*
Mauritania					
inward	-	4.8	5.0	8.1	10.5
outward	..	..	*0.2*	*0.2*	*1.7*
Mauritius					
inward	1.8	3.5	6.2	6.3	8.5
outward	..	..	-	*2.4*	*2.7*
Mozambique					
inward	0.5	0.5	2.0	10.4	14.4
outward	..	..	..	..	..
Namibia					
inward	85.5	137.2	83.8	51.2	48.0
outward	..	..	*3.3*	*0.6*	*1.3*
Niger					
inward	7.4	14.1	11.8	21.9	20.6
outward	-	*0.6*	*2.3*	*6.6*	*7.2*

/...

Annex table B.6. **Inward and outward FDI stocks as a percentage of gross domestic product, by region and economy, 1980, 1985, 1990, 1995 and 1998**

(Percentage)

Region/economy	1980	1985	1990	1995	1998
Nigeria					
inward	2.6	5.5	28.3	50.0	50.5
outward	*-*	*6.4*	*33.9*	*39.0*	*30.9*
Rwanda					
inward	4.6	7.8	8.2	17.2	11.8
outward	*..*	*..*	*..*	*..*	*..*
Senegal					
inward	5.0	7.4	4.9	8.7	13.3
outward	*0.2*	*1.7*	*0.9*	*2.1*	*2.2*
Seychelles					
inward	24.9	51.7	50.7	59.8	78.8
outward	*9.4*	*25.9*	*16.6*	*18.5*	*21.3*
Sierra Leone					
inward	6.4	5.5	-	-	-
outward	*..*	*..*	*..*	*..*	*..*
Somalia					
inward	4.8	0.5	-	-	-
outward	*..*	*..*	*..*	*..*	*..*
Swaziland					
inward	41.8	28.9	39.1	42.5	40.5
outward	*3.3*	*2.4*	*4.5*	*10.7*	*7.9*
Togo					
inward	15.5	27.5	16.5	23.4	26.4
outward	*0.2*	*0.3*	*0.4*	*2.7*	*4.9*
Uganda					
inward	-	0.2	-	4.8	12.9
outward	*..*	*..*	*..*	*..*	*..*
United Republic of Tanzania					
inward	0.9	1.3	2.2	7.0	9.9
outward	*..*	*..*	*..*	*..*	*..*
Zambia					
inward	8.3	18.5	29.8	35.7	52.8
outward	*..*	*..*	*..*	*..*	*..*
Zimbabwe					
inward	-	-	-	2.2	14.5
outward	*..*	*0.2*	*1.0*	*1.9*	*4.0*
Latin America and the Caribbean					
inward	**5.7**	**8.6**	**10.5**	**11.9**	**19.5**
outward	***1.3***	***2.0***	***1.9***	***2.4***	***3.3***
South America					
inward	**6.1**	**9.1**	**8.7**	**8.7**	**17.9**
outward	***1.5***	***1.8***	***1.5***	***1.9***	***3.1***
Argentina					
inward	6.9	7.4	6.4	9.9	13.9
outward	*8.0*	*6.9*	*4.3*	*3.8*	*5.4*
Bolivia					
inward	8.4	11.6	21.1	23.3	44.6
outward	*-*	*-*	*0.2*	*0.3*	*0.3*
Brazil					
inward	7.4	11.5	8.0	6.0	17.1
outward	*0.3*	*0.6*	*0.5*	*0.8*	*1.4*
Chile					
inward	3.2	14.1	33.2	26.2	40.4
outward	*0.2*	*0.6*	*0.6*	*4.7*	*11.7*
Colombia					
inward	4.4	7.6	12.2	10.6	20.0
outward	*0.4*	*0.9*	*1.0*	*1.3*	*2.6*

Annex table B.6. **Inward and outward FDI stocks as a percentage of gross domestic product, by region and economy, 1980, 1985, 1990, 1995 and 1998**

(Percentage)

Region/economy	1980	1985	1990	1995	1998
Ecuador					
inward	6.1	8.1	15.2	19.1	28.2
outward	..	..	..	..	..
Guyana					
inward	-	-	-	56.3	73.8
outward	..	..	..	0.3	0.1
Paraguay					
inward	4.9	6.5	7.6	10.8	17.5
outward	0.7	1.0	1.5	2.6	2.7
Peru					
inward	4.3	6.1	4.0	9.4	12.5
outward	-	0.2	0.2	0.2	0.4
Suriname					
inward	..	..	..	..	..
outward	..	..	..	..	..
Uruguay					
inward	6.9	15.8	10.5	7.2	8.2
outward	0.2	0.7	0.5	0.1	0.2
Venezuela					
inward	2.7	2.6	4.7	9.0	20.1
outward	-	0.3	4.6	5.1	5.5
Other Latin America and the Caribbean					
inward	**5.0**	**7.6**	**14.5**	**22.5**	**24.0**
outward	***0.8***	***2.4***	***3.0***	***4.3***	***3.7***
Antigua and Barbuda					
inward	20.9	46.5	74.5	88.6	82.9
outward	..	..	..	..	..
Aruba					
inward	..	..	15.1	16.4	46.6
outward	..	..	..	0.8	0.8
Bahamas					
inward	22.3	12.7	10.8	14.2	22.8
outward	21.3	6.6	49.4	34.2	28.8
Barbados					
inward	11.8	10.3	9.9	12.1	11.6
outward	0.6	1.0	1.3	1.7	1.6
Belize					
inward	6.4	5.0	17.7	25.0	28.6
outward	..	..	..	1.7	3.6
Bermuda					
inward	837.1	774.2	871.0	1211.0	1427.2
outward	118.1	192.5	97.5	113.8	180.9
Cayman Islands					
inward	..	..	355.5	479.8	1124.3
outward	..	..	176.4	280.3	516.4
Costa Rica					
inward	13.9	24.4	25.3	30.3	40.3
outward	0.1	0.7	0.8	0.7	0.8
Cuba					
inward	-	-	-	0.2	0.4
outward	..	..	..	..	..
Dominica					
inward	..	5.7	39.9	86.3	96.1
outward	..	..	..	..	1.3
Dominican Republic					
inward	3.6	5.9	8.1	14.3	18.2
outward	..	..	..	0.3	0.3

/...

Annex table B.6. **Inward and outward FDI stocks as a percentage of gross domestic product, by region and economy, 1980, 1985, 1990, 1995 and 1998**

(Percentage)

Region/economy	1980	1985	1990	1995	1998
El Salvador					
inward	4.3	4.7	4.4	3.1	9.9
outward	..	..	..	..	-
Grenada					
inward	1.7	9.8	31.7	60.6	92.9
outward	..	..	..	..	..
Guatemala					
inward	8.9	10.8	22.7	15.1	16.0
outward	..	..	..	..	..
Haiti					
inward	5.4	5.6	5.0	6.2	4.7
outward	..	..	..	..	..
Honduras					
inward	3.6	4.7	12.5	15.6	17.6
outward	..	..	..	..	..
Jamaica					
inward	18.7	22.7	17.1	28.7	32.0
outward	*0.2*	*0.2*	*1.0*	*5.9*	*7.6*
Mexico					
inward	0.9	1.1	8.5	14.4	14.3
outward	-	*0.3*	*0.2*	*1.4*	*1.4*
Netherlands Antilles					
inward	65.6	5.1	13.2	13.1	23.4
outward	*1.1*	*0.9*	*1.3*	*0.9*	-
Nicaragua					
inward	5.1	4.1	11.3	18.7	39.0
outward	..	..	..	..	..
Panama					
inward	66.4	56.2	39.3	40.1	65.8
outward	*22.9*	*40.8*	*78.8*	*57.8*	*75.6*
Saint Kitts and Nevis					
inward	2.1	40.5	102.0	104.8	114.1
outward	..	..	..	..	..
Saint Lucia					
inward	70.1	90.7	75.7	93.0	97.4
outward	..	..	..	..	..
Saint Vincent and the Grenadines					
inward	2.0	7.5	24.4	68.9	102.6
outward	..	..	..	..	..
Trinidad and Tobago					
inward	15.7	23.7	41.3	68.4	93.3
outward	..	*0.2*	*0.4*	*0.4*	*0.4*
Virgin Islands					
inward	..	..	..	..	..
outward	..	..	..	..	..
Developing Europe					
inward	**13.8**	**28.2**	**5.8**	**7.6**	**15.7**
outward	..	..	*1.5*	*2.9*	*3.3*
Bosnia and Herzegovina					
inward	..	..	..	..	..
outward	..	..	..	*0.9*	*2.3*
Croatia					
inward	..	..	..	2.6	13.1
outward	..	..	..	*3.7*	*4.7*
Malta					
inward	13.8	28.2	20.1	30.0	43.5
outward	..	..	..	*0.1*	*1.1*

/...

Annex table B.6. **Inward and outward FDI stocks as a percentage of gross domestic product,
by region and economy, 1980, 1985, 1990, 1995 and 1998**

(Percentage)

Region/economy	1980	1985	1990	1995	1998
Slovenia					
inward	..	..	3.8	9.4	14.5
outward	*..*	*..*	*1.5*	*2.7*	*2.8*
TFYR Macedonia					
inward	..	..	..	1.6	5.5
outward	*..*	*..*	*..*	*..*	*-*
Asia					
inward	**4.9**	**9.3**	**10.2**	**13.6**	**20.2**
outward	***0.7***	***1.0***	***2.8***	***6.1***	***9.0***
West Asia					
inward	**-**	**8.2**	**6.5**	**7.1**	**7.6**
outward	***0.7***	***1.3***	***3.4***	***1.2***	***0.5***
Bahrain					
inward	2.1	10.8	13.8	43.8	92.7
outward	*20.5*	*17.7*	*18.0*	*19.0*	*29.5*
Cyprus					
inward	21.4	32.6	20.6	16.8	18.6
outward	*..*	*-*	*0.2*	*1.4*	*3.4*
Iran, Islamic Republic					
inward	2.0	2.2	1.0	0.8	0.5
outward	*..*	*..*	*..*	*-*	*-*
Iraq					
inward	..	..	..	..	..
outward	*..*	*..*	*..*	*..*	*..*
Jordan					
inward	4.0	9.6	15.3	9.5	17.6
outward	*3.0*	*2.3*	*2.7*	*0.3*	*-*
Kuwait					
inward	0.1	0.2	0.2	0.2	1.8
outward	*2.0*	*4.3*	*19.8*	*10.5*	*6.4*
Lebanon					
inward	0.5	0.9	1.9	0.9	3.1
outward	*-*	*1.1*	*-*	*-*	*-*
Oman					
inward	9.1	12.6	16.9	16.6	16.8
outward	*-*	*0.4*	*-*	*-*	*0.2*
Qatar					
inward	1.1	1.2	0.7	5.7	5.1
outward	*..*	*..*	*..*	*0.4*	*0.9*
Saudi Arabia					
inward	-	25.2	21.5	17.8	22.7
outward	*0.1*	*0.5*	*1.7*	*1.3*	*1.3*
Syrian Arab Republic					
inward	..	0.2	1.6	1.9	2.1
outward	*..*	*..*	*..*	*..*	*-*
Turkey					
inward	0.2	0.5	0.9	3.0	3.8
outward	*..*	*..*	*..*	*0.2*	*0.5*
United Arab Emirates					
inward	1.4	1.8	2.2	4.4	4.4
outward	*-*	*-*	*0.3*	*0.2*	*-*
Yemen					
inward	1.3	2.5	1.1	55.2	30.6
outward	*..*	*-*	*0.1*	*0.1*	*-*

Annex table B.6. **Inward and outward FDI stocks as a percentage of gross domestic product,
by region and economy, 1980, 1985, 1990, 1995 and 1998**
(Percentage)

Region/economy	1980	1985	1990	1995	1998
Central Asia	-	-	-	-	-
inward	..	..	..	8.8	25.6
outward	..	..	..	-	*0.5*
Armenia					
inward	..	..	..	1.2	17.4
outward	..	..	..	..	*0.6*
Azerbaijan					
inward	..	..	..	14.6	76.1
outward	..	..	..	..	*3.3*
Georgia					
inward	..	..	..	1.1	3.8
outward	..	..	..	..	..
Kazakhstan					
inward	..	..	..	14.6	35.7
outward	..	..	..	-	-
Kyrgyzstan					
inward	..	..	..	9.7	20.5
outward	..	..	..	..	-
Tajikistan					
inward	..	..	..	3.9	7.6
outward	..	..	..	..	..
Turkmenistan					
inward	..	..	..	4.6	33.3
outward	..	..	..	..	..
Uzbekistan					
inward	..	..	..	2.5	5.6
outward	..	..	..	..	..
South, East and South-East Asia					
inward	7.9	9.7	11.2	15.0	23.3
outward	*0.8*	*1.0*	*2.8*	*7.1*	*11.3*
Afghanistan					
inward	0.5	0.3	0.1	0.3	0.6
outward	..	..	..	..	..
Bangladesh					
inward	0.4	0.5	0.5	0.5	1.5
outward	..	..	-	-	-
Brunei Darussalam					
inward	0.4	0.9	0.8	1.4	1.7
outward	..	..	..	1.4	*2.5*
Cambodia					
inward	..	..	13.4	17.0	22.3
outward	..	..	..	-	-
China					
inward	3.1	3.4	7.0	19.6	27.6
outward	-	-	0.7	*2.3*	*2.4*
Hong Kong, China					
inward	80.5	81.4	62.6	51.0	65.7
outward	*0.5*	*6.7*	*17.7*	*61.2*	*92.0*
India					
inward	0.7	0.5	0.5	1.7	3.4
outward	*0.1*	*0.1*	-	*0.1*	*0.2*
Indonesia					
inward	14.2	28.6	34.0	25.0	77.3
outward	..	-	-	*0.6*	*2.4*

/...

Annex table B.6. **Inward and outward FDI stocks as a percentage of gross domestic product,
by region and economy, 1980, 1985, 1990, 1995 and 1998**
(Percentage)

Region/economy	1980	1985	1990	1995	1998
Korea, Democratic People's Republic					
inward	..	..	3.0	10.8	11.3
outward	..	..	..	..	..
Korea, Republic of					
inward	1.8	2.3	2.0	2.1	6.1
outward	*0.2*	*0.5*	*0.9*	*2.2*	*6.5*
Lao People's Democratic Republic					
inward	0.4	0.1	1.6	11.9	42.6
outward	..	..	..	..	..
Macau, China					
inward	..	0.6	0.3	0.2	0.4
outward	..	..	..	..	..
Malaysia					
inward	21.1	23.7	24.1	32.9	67.0
outward	*0.8*	*4.4*	*6.2*	*12.8*	*22.6*
Maldives					
inward	11.3	3.8	17.1	22.5	23.2
outward	..	..	..	..	..
Mongolia					
inward	..	..	..	2.8	8.1
outward	..	..	..	*0.1*	*0.3*
Myanmar					
inward	-	-	0.7	1.0	1.2
outward	..	..	..	..	..
Nepal					
inward	-	-	0.3	0.9	2.1
outward	..	..	..	..	..
Pakistan					
inward	2.9	3.5	4.8	9.1	14.4
outward	*0.2*	*0.4*	*0.6*	*0.7*	*0.7*
Philippines					
inward	3.9	8.5	7.4	8.2	14.3
outward	*0.5*	*0.6*	*0.3*	*1.6*	*2.6*
Singapore					
inward	52.9	73.6	76.3	70.0	85.8
outward	*31.7*	*24.8*	*20.9*	*41.2*	*56.1*
Sri Lanka					
inward	5.7	8.7	8.5	10.0	13.2
outward	..	-	*0.1*	*0.3*	*0.2*
Taiwan Province of China					
inward	5.8	4.7	6.1	6.0	7.8
outward	*0.2*	*0.3*	*8.0*	*9.7*	*14.7*
Thailand					
inward	3.0	5.1	9.6	10.4	17.5
outward	-	-	*0.5*	*1.3*	*1.7*
Viet Nam					
inward	0.2	0.6	4.5	30.8	54.5
outward	..	..	..	-	-
The Pacific					
inward	**28.5**	**24.0**	**28.6**	**25.1**	**29.4**
outward	***0.3***	***1.0***	***2.1***	***1.9***	***3.3***
Fiji					
inward	29.7	34.4	30.5	37.0	35.7
outward	*0.2*	*1.3*	*6.6*	*6.6*	*8.7*
Kiribati					
inward	..	-	1.2	2.5	5.6
outward	..	..	..	-	-

Annex table B.6. **Inward and outward FDI stocks as a percentage of gross domestic product,**
by region and economy, 1980, 1985, 1990, 1995 and 1998

(Percentage)

Region/economy	1980	1985	1990	1995	1998
New Caledonia					
inward	..	-	1.6	2.5	2.9
outward	..	..	..	..	..
Papua New Guinea					
inward	29.4	28.2	49.1	33.1	43.6
outward	*0.4*	*0.9*	*0.2*	*0.1*	*0.2*
Vanuatu					
inward	29.0	52.3	71.9	105.0	137.8
outward	..	..	..	..	..
Samoa					
inward	0.4	0.8	5.4	14.5	15.7
outward	..	..	..	..	..
Solomon Islands					
inward	23.8	20.0	32.8	38.3	54.7
outward	..	..	..	..	..
Tonga					
inward	..	0.2	0.7	5.2	9.0
outward	..	..	..	-	-
Central and Eastern Europe	**-**	**-**	**-**	**-**	**-**
inward	..	..	**1.5**	**5.2**	**12.1**
outward	..	-	*0.3*	*0.8*	*1.7*
Albania					
inward	..	..	..	8.3	12.6
outward	..	..	..	*2.0*	*2.3*
Belarus					
inward	..	..	..	0.3	3.3
outward	..	..	..	..	-
Bulgaria					
inward	..	..	-	2.6	12.3
outward	..	..	..	*0.3*	-
Czech Republic					
inward	..	..	4.3	14.5	26.1
outward	..	..	..	*0.7*	*1.5*
Estonia					
inward	..	..	..	20.2	35.6
outward	..	..	..	*1.9*	*3.9*
Hungary					
inward	..	..	1.7	22.4	33.2
outward	..	..	*0.6*	*0.9*	*2.3*
Latvia					
inward	..	..	..	13.8	25.2
outward	..	..	..	*5.2*	*4.5*
Lithuania					
inward	..	..	4.4	5.8	15.2
outward	..	..	..	-	*0.1*
Moldova, Republic of					
inward	..	..	..	6.6	17.2
outward	..	..	..	*1.3*	*1.2*
Poland					
inward	..	..	0.2	6.6	15.1
outward	..	-	*0.2*	*0.5*	*0.8*
Romania					
inward	..	..	2.0	3.2	10.4
outward	..	..	*0.2*	*0.3*	*0.3*
Russian Federation					
inward	..	..	..	1.6	5.0
outward	..	..	..	*0.9*	*2.6*

Annex table B.6. **Inward and outward FDI stocks as a percentage of gross domestic product, by region and economy, 1980, 1985, 1990, 1995 and 1998**

(Percentage)

Region/economy	1980	1985	1990	1995	1998
Slovakia					
inward	..	..	0.6	7.2	12.1
outward	..	..	..	*2.2*	*3.2*
Ukraine					
inward	..	..	..	2.5	6.6
outward	..	..	..	*0.2*	*0.2*
Memorandum:					
Least developed countries: [a]					
Total					
inward	**1.8**	**3.4**	**4.4**	**6.9**	**7.4**
outward	*0.7*	*2.7*	*1.0*	*1.1*	*1.9*
Africa					
inward	**2.3**	**4.8**	**7.3**	**16.4**	**21.5**
outward	*0.7*	*4.5*	*2.8*	*3.7*	*5.4*
Latin America and the Caribbean					
inward	**5.4**	**5.6**	**5.0**	**6.2**	**4.7**
outward	*..*	*..*	*..*	*..*	*..*
Asia and the Pacific					
inward	**0.6**	**0.9**	**1.1**	**2.8**	**2.6**
outward	*..*	*-*	*-*	*-*	*-*
Asia					
inward	0.5	0.7	0.9	2.6	2.4
outward	*..*	*-*	*-*	*-*	*-*
West Asia					
inward	1.3	2.5	1.1	55.2	30.6
outward	*..*	*-*	*0.1*	*0.1*	*-*
South, East and South-East Asia					
inward	0.3	0.4	0.8	1.3	1.7
outward	*..*	*..*	*-*	*-*	*-*
The Pacific					
inward	17.9	24.2	34.6	51.9	65.6
outward	*..*	*..*	*..*	*-*	*-*
Oil-exporting countries: [b]					
Total					
inward	**3.4**	**10.4**	**14.0**	**17.8**	**22.2**
outward	*0.3*	*1.3*	*2.7*	*3.3*	*3.5*
Africa					
inward	**6.8**	**10.1**	**15.1**	**24.9**	**23.4**
outward	*0.2*	*2.6*	*5.5*	*6.7*	*5.7*
North Africa					
inward	12.7	13.7	13.6	20.1	17.1
outward	*0.3*	*0.4*	*0.6*	*0.6*	*1.0*
Other Africa	*-*	*-*	*-*	*-*	*-*
inward	2.8	6.6	19.1	38.7	42.4
outward	*-*	*5.7*	*21.5*	*27.3*	*22.6*
Latin America and the Caribbean					
inward	**1.9**	**2.6**	**8.9**	**14.4**	**17.1**
outward	*-*	*0.3*	*0.9*	*2.2*	*2.1*
South America	*-*	*-*	*-*	*-*	*-*
inward	3.6	4.0	7.7	11.7	23.1
outward	*-*	*0.3*	*4.2*	*4.7*	*5.0*
Other Latin America and the Caribbean					
inward	1.3	2.0	9.1	15.4	15.4
outward	*-*	*0.3*	*0.2*	*1.4*	*1.4*

/...

Annex table B.6. **Inward and outward FDI stocks as a percentage of gross domestic product, by region and economy, 1980, 1985, 1990, 1995 and 1998**

(Percentage)

Region/economy	1980	1985	1990	1995	1998
Asia					
inward	**2.9**	**16.5**	**17.5**	**17.7**	**26.5**
outward	*0.7*	*1.3*	*2.7*	*3.0*	*3.9*
West Asia					
inward	-	11.2	9.8	9.3	9.6
outward	*0.6*	*1.4*	*3.7*	*1.8*	*1.2*
South, East and South-East Asia					
inward	15.2	26.5	30.6	27.0	70.5
outward	*0.8*	*1.2*	*1.7*	*4.2*	*10.8*
All developing countries minus China					
inward	**5.6**	**10.0**	**10.9**	**12.5**	**18.6**
outward	*1.0*	*1.8*	*2.9*	*5.3*	*7.6*
Asia and the Pacific					
inward	**5.0**	**9.4**	**10.3**	**13.6**	**20.3**
outward	*0.7*	*1.0*	*2.8*	*6.1*	*9.0*
Africa including South Africa					
inward	**9.0**	**10.5**	**11.5**	**17.4**	**19.4**
outward	*2.1*	*5.2*	*7.2*	*9.4*	*9.8*

Source: UNCTAD, FDI/TNC database.

[a]   Least developed countries include: Afghanistan, Angola, Bangladesh, Benin, Burkina Faso, Burundi, Cambodia, Cape Verde, Central African Republic, Chad, Comoros, Democratic Repunlic of Congo, Djibouti, Equatorial Guinea, Ethiopia, Gambia, Guinea, Guinea-Bissau, Haiti, Kiribati, Lao People's Democratic Republic, Lesotho, Liberia, Madagascar, Malawi, Maldives, Mali, Mauritania, Mozambique, Myanmar, Nepal, Niger, Rwanda, Western Samoa, Sierra Leone, Solomon Islands, Somalia, Sudan, Togo, Uganda, United Republic of Tanzania, Vanuatu, Yemen and Zambia. Not included are Bhutan, Eritrea, Sao Tome and Principe and Tuvalu due to unavailability of data.

[b]   Oil-exporting countries include: Algeria, Angola, Bahrain, Brunei Darussalam, Cameroon, Congo, Ecuador, Egypt, Gabon, Indonesia, Islamic Republic of Iran, Iraq, Kuwait, Libyan Arab Jamahiriya, Malaysia, Mexico, Nigeria, Oman, Qatar, Saudi Arabia, Trinidad and Tobago, Tunisia, United Arab Emirates and Venezuela.

Selected UNCTAD publications on transnational corporations and foreign direct investment

A. Individual studies

International Investment Instruments: A Compendium, vol. IV, 319 p. Sales No. E.00.II.D.13. $55, vol. V, 505 p. Sales No. E.00.II.D.14. $55.

FDI Determinants and TNCs Strategies: The Case of Brazil. 195 p. Sales No. E.00.II.D.2, $35.

World Investment Report 1999: Foreign Direct Investment and the Challenge of Development. 536 p. Sales No. E.99.II.D.3. $45.

World Investment Report 1999: Foreign Direct Investment and Challenge of Development. An Overview. 75 p. Free-of-charge.

Investment Policy Review of Uganda. 75 p. Sales No. E.99.II.D.24. $15.

Investment Policy Review of Egypt. 113 p. Sales No. E.99.II.D.20. $19.

Science, Technology and Innovation Policy Review of Colombia. 175 p. Sales No. E.99.II.D.13. $23.

Foreign Direct Invesment in Africa: Performance and Potential. 89 p. UNCTAD/ITE/IIT/Misc. 15.

Investment Policy Review of Uzbekistan. 64 p. UNCTAD/ITE/IIP/Misc. 13. Free-of-charge.

The Financial Crisis in Asia and Foreign Direct Investment: An Assessment. 101 p. Sales No. GV.E.98.0.29. $20.

Science, Technology and Innovation Policy Review of Jamaica. 172 p. Sales No. E.98.II.D.7. $42.

World Investment Report 1998: Trends and Determinants. 430 p. Sales No. E.98.II.D.5. $45.

World Investment Report 1998: Trends and Determinants. An Overview. 67 p. Free-of-charge.

Bilateral Investment Treaties in the mid-1990s. 314 p. Sales No. E.98.II.D.8. $46.

Handbook on Foreign Direct Investment by Small and Medium-sized Enterprises: Lessons from Asia. 200 p. Sales No. E.98.II.D.4. $48.

Handbook on Foreign Direct Investment by Small and Medium-sized Enterprises: Lessons from Asia. Executive Summary and Report on the Kunming Conference. 74 p. Free-of-charge.

International Investment Towards the Year 2002. 166 p. Sales No. GV.E.98.0.15. $29. (Joint publication with Invest in France Mission and Arthur Andersen, in collaboration with DATAR.)

World Investment Report 1997: Transnational Corporations, Market Structure and Competition Policy. 420 p. Sales No. E.97.II.D.10. $45.

World Investment Report 1997: Transnational Corporations, Market Structure and Competition Policy. An Overview. 70 p. Free-of-charge.

International Investment Towards the Year 2001. 81 p. Sales No. GV.E.97.0.5. $35. (Joint publication with Invest in France Mission and Arthur Andersen, in collaboration with DATAR.)

World Investment Directory. Vol. VI: West Asia 1996. 192 p. Sales No. E.97.II.A.2. $35.

World Investment Directory. Vol. V: Africa 1996. 508 p. Sales No. E.97.II.A.1. $75.

Sharing Asia's Dynamism: Asian Direct Investment in the European Union. 192 p. Sales No. E.97.II.D.1. $26.

Transnational Corporations and World Development. 656 p. ISBN 0-415-08560-8 (hardback), 0-415-08561-6 (paperback). £65 (hardback), £20.00 (paperback). (Published by International Thomson Business Press on behalf of UNCTAD.)

Companies without Borders: Transnational Corporations in the 1990s. 224 p. ISBN 0-415-12526-X. £47.50. (Published by International Thomson Business Press on behalf of UNCTAD.)

The New Globalism and Developing Countries. 336 p. ISBN 92-808-0944-X. $25. (Published by United Nations University Press.)

Investing in Asia's Dynamism: European Union Direct Investment in Asia. 124 p. ISBN 92-827-7675-1. ECU 14. (Joint publication with the European Commission.)

World Investment Report 1996: Investment, Trade and International Policy Arrangements. 332 p. Sales No. E.96.II.A.14. $45.

World Investment Report 1996: Investment, Trade and International Policy Arrangements. An Overview. 51 p. Free-of-charge.

International Investment Instruments: A Compendium. Vol. I. 371 p. Sales No. E.96.II.A.9; Vol. II. 577 p. Sales No. E.96.II.A.10; Vol. III. 389 p. Sales No. E.96.II.A.11; the 3-volume set, Sales No. E.96.II.A.12. $125.

World Investment Report 1995: Transnational Corporations and Competitiveness. 491 p. Sales No. E.95.II.A.9. $45.

World Investment Report 1995: Transnational Corporations and Competitiveness. An Overview. 51 p. Free-of-charge.

Accounting for Sustainable Forestry Management. A Case Study. 46 p. Sales No. E.94.II.A.17. $22.

Small and Medium-sized Transnational Corporations. Executive Summary and Report of the Osaka Conference. 60 p. Free-of-charge.

World Investment Report 1994: Transnational Corporations, Employment and the Workplace. 482 p. Sales No. E.94.II.A.14. $45.

World Investment Report 1994: Transnational Corporations, Employment and the Workplace. An Executive Summary. 34 p. Free-of-charge.

Liberalizing International Transactions in Services: A Handbook. 182 p. Sales No. E.94.II.A.11. $45. (Joint publication with the World Bank.)

World Investment Directory. Vol. IV: Latin America and the Caribbean. 478 p. Sales No. E.94.II.A.10. $65.

Conclusions on Accounting and Reporting by Transnational Corporations. 47 p. Sales No. E.94.II.A.9. $25.

Accounting, Valuation and Privatization. 190 p. Sales No. E.94.II.A.3. $25.

Environmental Management in Transnational Corporations: Report on the Benchmark Corporate Environment Survey. 278 p. Sales No. E.94.II.A.2. $29.95.

Management Consulting: A Survey of the Industry and Its Largest Firms. 100 p. Sales No. E.93.II.A.17. $25.

Transnational Corporations: A Selective Bibliography, 1991-1992. 736 p. Sales No. E.93.II.A.16. $75. (English/French.)

Small and Medium-sized Transnational Corporations: Role, Impact and Policy Implications. 242 p. Sales No. E.93.II.A.15. $35.

World Investment Report 1993: Transnational Corporations and Integrated International Production. 290 p. Sales No. E.93.II.A.14. $45.

World Investment Report 1993: Transnational Corporations and Integrated International Production. An Executive Summary. 31 p. ST/CTC/159. Free-of-charge.

Foreign Investment and Trade Linkages in Developing Countries. 108 p. Sales No. E.93.II.A.12. $18.

World Investment Directory 1992. Vol. III: Developed Countries. 532 p. Sales No. E.93.II.A.9. $75.

Transnational Corporations from Developing Countries: Impact on Their Home Countries. 116 p. Sales No. E.93.II.A.8. $15.

Debt-Equity Swaps and Development. 150 p. Sales No. E.93.II.A.7. $35.

From the Common Market to EC 92: Regional Economic Integration in the European Community and Transnational Corporations. 134 p. Sales No. E.93.II.A.2. $25.

World Investment Directory 1992. Vol. II: Central and Eastern Europe. 432 p. Sales No. E.93.II.A.1. $65. (Joint publication with the United Nations Economic Commission for Europe.)

The East-West Business Directory 1991/1992. 570 p. Sales No. E.92.II.A.20. $65.

World Investment Report 1992: Transnational Corporations as Engines of Growth. 356 p. Sales No. E.92.II.A.19. $45.

World Investment Report 1992: Transnational Corporations as Engines of Growth: An Executive Summary. 30 p. Sales No. E.92.II.A.24. Free-of-charge.

World Investment Directory 1992. Vol. I: Asia and the Pacific. 356 p. Sales No. E.92.II.A.11. $65.

Climate Change and Transnational Corporations: Analysis and Trends. 110 p. Sales No. E.92.II.A.7. $16.50.

Foreign Direct Investment and Transfer of Technology in India. 150 p. Sales No. E.92.II.A.3. $20.

The Determinants of Foreign Direct Investment: A Survey of the Evidence. 84 p. Sales No. E.92.II.A.2. $12.50.

The Impact of Trade-Related Investment Measures on Trade and Development: Theory, Evidence and Policy Implications. 108 p. Sales No. E.91.II.A.19. $17.50. (Joint publication with the United Nations Centre on Transnational Corporations.)

Transnational Corporations and Industrial Hazards Disclosure. 98 p. Sales No. E.91.II.A.18. $17.50.

Transnational Business Information: A Manual of Needs and Sources. 216 p. Sales No. E.91.II.A.13. $45.

World Investment Report 1991: The Triad in Foreign Direct Investment. 108 p. Sales No.E.91.II.A.12. $25.

B. IIA Issues Paper Series

Employment. UNCTAD Series on issues in international investment agreements. 69 p. Sales No. E.00.II.D.15. $12.

Taxation. UNCTAD Series on issues in international investment agreements. 111 p. Sales No. E.00.II.D.5. $12.

International Investment Agreements: Flexibility for Development. UNCTA3D Series on issues in international investment agreements. 185 p. Sales No. E.00.II.D.6. $12.

Taking of Property. UNCTAD Series on issues in international investment agreements. 83 p. Sales No. E.00.II.D.4. $12.

Trends in International Investment Agreements: An Overview. UNCTAD Series on issues in international investment agreements. 112 p. Sales No. E.99.II.D.23. $ 12.

Lessons from the MAI. UNCTAD Series on issues in international investment agreements. 31 p. Sales No. E.99.II.D.26. $ 12.

National Treatment. UNCTAD Series on issues in international investment agreements. 104 p. Sales No. E.99.II.D.16. $12.

Fair and Equitable Treatment. UNCTAD Series on issues in international investment agreements. 64 p. Sales No. E.99.II.D.15. $12.

Investment-Related Trade Measures. UNCTAD Series on issues in international investment agreements. 64 p. Sales No. E.99.II.D.12. $12.

Most-Favoured-Nation Treatment. UNCTAD Series on issues in international investment agreements. 72p. Sales No. E.99.II.D.11. $12.

Admission and Establishment. UNCTAD Series on issues in international investment agreements. 72p. Sales No. E.99.II.D.10. $12.

Scope and Definition. UNCTAD Series on issues in international investment agreements. 96p. Sales No. E.99.II.D.9. $12.

Transfer Pricing. UNCTAD Series on issues in international investment agreements. 72p. Sales No. E.99.II.D.8. $12.

Foreign Direct Investment and Development. UNCTAD Series on issues in international investment agreements. 88p. Sales No. E.98.II.D.15. $12.

Admission et établissement. CNUCED Collection consacrée aux problèmes relatifs aux accord internationaux d'investissements. 55 p. Sales No. F.99.II.D.10. $12.

C. Serial publications

Current Studies, Series A

No. 30. *Incentives and Foreign Direct Investment.* 98 p. Sales No. E.96.II.A.6. $30. (English/French.)

No. 29. *Foreign Direct Investment, Trade, Aid and Migration.* 100 p. Sales No. E.96.II.A.8. $25. (Joint publication with the International Organization for Migration.)

No. 28. *Foreign Direct Investment in Africa.* 119 p. Sales No. E.95.II.A.6. $20.

No. 27. *Tradability of Banking Services: Impact and Implications.* 195 p. Sales No. E.94.II.A.12. $50.

No. 26. *Explaining and Forecasting Regional Flows of Foreign Direct Investment.* 58 p. Sales No. E.94.II.A.5. $25.

No. 25. *International Tradability in Insurance Services.* 54 p. Sales No. E.93.II.A.11. $20.

No. 24. *Intellectual Property Rights and Foreign Direct Investment.* 108 p. Sales No. E.93.II.A.10. $20.

No. 23. *The Transnationalization of Service Industries: An Empirical Analysis of the Determinants of Foreign Direct Investment by Transnational Service Corporations.* 62 p. Sales No. E.93.II.A.3. $15.

No. 22. *Transnational Banks and the External Indebtedness of Developing Countries: Impact of Regulatory Changes.* 48 p. Sales No. E.92.II.A.10. $12.

No. 20. *Foreign Direct Investment, Debt and Home Country Policies.* 50 p. Sales No. E.90.II.A.16. $12.

No. 19. *New Issues in the Uruguay Round of Multilateral Trade Negotiations.* 52 p. Sales No. E.90.II.A.15. $12.50.

No. 18. *Foreign Direct Investment and Industrial Restructuring in Mexico.* 114 p. Sales No. E.92.II.A.9. $12.

No. 17. *Government Policies and Foreign Direct Investment.* 68 p. Sales No. E.91.II.A.20. $12.50.

The United Nations Library on Transnational Corporations
(Published by Routledge on behalf of the United Nations.)

Set A (Boxed set of 4 volumes. ISBN 0-415-08554-3. £350):
Volume One: *The Theory of Transnational Corporations.* 464 p.
Volume Two: *Transnational Corporations: A Historical Perspective.* 464 p.
Volume Three: *Transnational Corporations and Economic Development.* 448 p.
Volume Four: *Transnational Corporations and Business Strategy.* 416 p.

Set B (Boxed set of 4 volumes. ISBN 0-415-08555-1. £350):
Volume Five: *International Financial Management.* 400 p.
Volume Six: *Organization of Transnational Corporations.* 400 p.
Volume Seven: *Governments and Transnational Corporations.* 352 p.
Volume Eight: *Transnational Corporations and International Trade and Payments.* 320 p.

Set C (Boxed set of 4 volumes. ISBN 0-415-08556-X. £350):
Volume Nine: *Transnational Corporations and Regional Economic Integration.* 331 p.
Volume Ten: *Transnational Corporations and the Exploitation of Natural Resources.* 397 p.
Volume Eleven: *Transnational Corporations and Industrialization.* 425 p.
Volume Twelve: *Transnational Corporations in Services.* 437 p.

Set D (Boxed set of 4 volumes. ISBN 0-415-08557-8. £350):
Volume Thirteen: *Cooperative Forms of Transnational Corporation Activity.* 419 p.
Volume Fourteen: *Transnational Corporations: Transfer Pricing and Taxation.* 330 p.
Volume Fifteen: *Transnational Corporations: Market Structure and Industrial Performance.* 383 p.
Volume Sixteen: *Transnational Corporations and Human Resources.* 429 p.

Set E (Boxed set of 4 volumes. ISBN 0-415-08558-6. £350):
Volume Seventeen: *Transnational Corporations and Innovatory Activities.* 447 p.
Volume Eighteen: *Transnational Corporations and Technology Transfer to Developing Countries.* 486 p.

Volume Nineteen: *Transnational Corporations and National Law*. 322 p.
Volume Twenty: *Transnational Corporations: The International Legal Framework*. 545 p.

D. Journals

Transnational Corporations (formerly *The CTC Reporter*).

Published three times a year. Annual subscription price: $45; individual issues $20.

ProInvest, a quarterly newsletter, available free of charge.
United Nations publications may be obtained from bookstores and distributors throughout the world. Please consult your bookstore or write to:

United Nations Publications

Sales Section
United Nations Office at Geneva
Palais des Nations
CH-1211 Geneva 10
Switzerland
Tel: (41-22) 917-1234
Fax: (41-22) 917-0123
E-mail: unpubli@unorg.ch

OR

Sales Section
Room DC2-0853
United Nations Secretariat
New York, NY 10017
U.S.A.
Tel: (1-212) 963-8302 or (800) 253-9646
Fax: (1-212) 963-3489
E-mail: publications@un.org

All prices are quoted in United States dollars.

For further information on the work of the Division on Investment, Technology and Enterprise Development, UNCTAD, please address inquiries to:

United Nations Conference on Trade and Development
Division on Investment, Technology and Enterprise Development
Palais des Nations, Room E-9123
CH-1211 Geneva 10
Switzerland
Telephone: (41-22) 907-5707
Telefax: (41-22) 907-0194
E-mail: medarde.almario@unctad.org

QUESTIONNAIRE

World Investment Report 2000:
Cross-border Mergers and Acquisitions and Development

Sales No. E.00.II.D.20

In order to improve the quality and relevance of the work of the UNCTAD Division on Investment, Technology and Enterprise Development, it would be useful to receive the views of readers on this and other similar publications. It would therefore be greatly appreciated if you could complete the following questionnaire and return to:

Readership Survey
UNCTAD Division on Investment, Technology and Enterprise Development
United Nations Office in Geneva
Palais des Nations
Room E-9123
CH-1211 Geneva 10
Switzerland

1. Name and address of respondent (optional):

   _____

   _____

   _____

   _____

2. Which of the following best describes your area of work?

Government	☐	Public enterprise	☐
Private enterprise institution	☐	Academic or research	☐
International organization	☐	Media	☐
Not-for-profit organization	☐	Other (specify) _____	

3. In which country do you work? _____

4. What is your assessment of the contents of this publication?

Excellent	☐	Adequate	☐
Good	☐	Poor	☐

5. How useful is this publication to your work?

    Very useful ☐   Of some use ☐   Irrelevant ☐

6. Please indicate the three things you liked best about this publication:

    _____

    _____

    _____

7. Please indicate the three things you liked least about this publication:

    _____

    _____

    _____

8. If you have read more than the present publication of the UNCTAD Division on Investment, Enterprise Development and Technology, what is your overall assessment of them?

    Consistently good ☐   Usually good, but with some exceptions ☐

    Generally mediocre ☐   Poor ☐

9. On the average, how useful are these publications to you in your work?

    Very useful ☐   Of some use ☐   Irrelevant ☐

10. Are you a regular recipient of *Transnational Corporations* (formerly *The CTC Reporter*), the Division's tri-annual refereed journal?

    Yes ☐   No ☐

    If not, please check here if you would like to receive a sample
    copy sent to the name and address you have given above ☐

Foreword

The Environment Policy Committee and the Committee on Fiscal Affairs have carried out joint work on taxation and environment, in particular on implementation strategies of environmental taxes (see "Implementation Strategies for Environmental Taxes", OECD, 1995, forthcoming). This compendium on environmental taxes in OECD countries is an expanded and updated version of an earlier survey (1993). The Secretariat wishes to express its gratitude to the Delegates to the "Joint Sessions on Taxation and Environment" for their cooperation in the preparation of this document, and to Ms Béatrice Fournier, consultant, for preparing the report.

TABLE OF CONTENTS

Tables

I. CONTEXT AND SCOPE OF THE SURVEY

This paper is a revised version of the "OECD Environment Monographs No. 71: Environmental Taxes in OECD Countries: A Survey" Paris 1993[1]. Like the original paper it draws on material provided by Member countries in response to a questionnaire circulated by the OECD Secretariat in January 1994. The questionnaire asked for an update of the information provided in the 1993 survey[2].

The role of environmental taxes in OECD countries has been growing both politically and economically. In the late 1980's it was foreseen by many observers that reduced government intervention could lead to a more prominent role for economic instruments, particularly taxes, providing incentives to change polluter behaviour. The report " Managing The Environment: The Role of Economic Instruments"[3] concludes that "the role of charges has been extended, although their revenue raising capabilities have remained the dominant function". The report goes on "Although an increasing number of charge schemes show incentive purposes, not much evidence exists that such instruments will replace direct regulation, as part of a process towards reducing government intervention." As can be seen from the overview of recent policy trends below, there is a great deal of interest in developing the use of existing excises on goods such as energy to take more account of environmental considerations. These considerations now play a significant role in the design of tax systems in many Member countries.

This survey is on the use of taxation as an instrument of environmental policy, rather than on the use of market-based instruments in general. Recent OECD work[4] already provides an overview of the use of all forms of market-based instruments, including environmental charges, deposit-refund systems, product charges (indirect taxes) and tradeable permit systems. Thus, this survey focuses on the subset of market-based environmental instruments which form part of the tax system of Member countries, or which have a character closely related to other fiscal instruments.

The survey covers a rather broad range of taxes. It covers not only taxes which are explicitly recognised as having an environmental purpose (reduce environmental damage), but also covers a number of areas of the tax system where the structure of existing taxes may be seen as having significant effects on the environment, although their purpose originated in revenue considerations.

Defining the scope of the work is inevitably imprecise. Similar measures in different countries may be variously defined as taxes, charges, levies, fees or duties, and it is not the intention to enter into semantic discussions of the borderline between these various concepts. The definitions applied in one language cannot necessarily be given exact counterparts in other languages.

The identification of tax measures which have not been introduced with a specific environmental objective but which nonetheless have an impact on the environment is also by nature imprecise. If not all then a significant number of existing tax measures could be argued to have some effect on the environment. The present survey limits itself, as did the first survey, to specific areas where the environmental dimension is relatively clear and uncontroversial, particularly on the taxation of energy and motor vehicles.

The paper concentrates on general issues of pollution, and does not consider the environmental issues associated with resource utilisation, including the utilisation of land resources.

II. RELATIVE IMPORTANCE OF ECOTAX REVENUES

In a survey of this character it would be of interest to have information on the economic importance of environmental taxes measured for example as percentage of GDP. Such information would facilitate comparisons between countries and add to what is already known on differences in tax structures between countries. However, compatible and reliable data of this kind are not readily available.

The "Revenue Statistics of OECD Member Countries"[5] does not have a special classification for environmental taxes. The taxes covered in this survey are found under different headings in the "Revenue Statistics". Recurrent taxes on vehicles are placed under subheading 5211 (paid by households) and 5212 (paid by others), while taxes on for example petrol are placed under subheading 5121. The heading 5121 also includes most of the taxes readily recognised as environmental taxes including for example carbon taxes. Unfortunately, the details under this heading vary from country to country which makes it impossible to present a compatible picture for all the Member countries. Even where a rather detailed specification is provided, it still leaves a certain arbitrariness to the selection of relevant excises.

Nevertheless, a number of taxes from the countries that have so far introduced a carbon tax have been selected either because they relate to energy and transport, or to some other environmental problem such as waste. The countries include: Denmark, Finland, the Netherlands, Norway and Sweden. The boxes are not necessarily exhaustive as regards environmental taxes because as mentioned above, the selection process is somewhat arbitrary. Using Revenue Statistics as a source for this information has the advantage of using a well known statistical source providing reliable and comparable data. However, in order to get comparable data, it means that the data has about a two-year lag. Furthermore, due to the limitations in the selection of taxes included in the box, comparisons between the countries on the basis of the information in the boxes should only be done with these limitations in mind. The readers are invited to refer to Table 6 for further data on tax revenues from Vehicle Taxes and Motor Fuels Taxes.

Box 1.

Taxes/excises with environmental implications in **Denmark** in per cent of total tax revenue						
	1980	1985	1990	1991	1992	1993
From 5121 Excises:						
Duty on Petrol	2.18	1.49	1.45	1.36	1.36	1.29
Motor vehicle registration duty	1.76	3.71	2.03	2.07	2.02	1.91
Sale of vehicle number plates	0.03	0.09	0.07	0.07	0.07	0.06
Duty on electricity	0.72	0.67	1.11	1.10	0.95	0.81
Duty on certain oil products	1.01	0.44	0.81	0.93	0.97	1.09
Duty on certain retail containers	0.06	0.06	0.10	0.11	0.11	0.08
Duty on gas	0.03	0.00	0.01	0.01	0.01	0.01
Duty on extraction and import of raw materials	0.01	0.01	0.03	0.03	0.03	0.03
Duty on disposable tableware	-	0.01	0.02	0.02	0.01	0.01
Duty on insecticides, herbicides in small containers, etc.	-	0.00	0.00	0.00	0.00	0.00
Duty on coal etc.	-	0.07	0.22	0.22	0.18	0.17
Duty on waste	-	-	0.10	0.12	0.11	0.12
Duty on CFC	-	-	0.01	0.00	0.00	0.00
Duty on CO_2	-	-	-	-	0.36	0.76
5211 Weight duty on automobiles paid by households	1.08	0.69	0.71	0.82	0.73	0.70
5212 Weight duty on automobiles paid by others	0.62	0.38	0.41	0.30	0.27	0.26
Total in per cent of total tax revenue	7.50	7.61	7.08	7.16	7.19	7.30
Total in per cent of GDP	3.41	3.73	3.45	3.50	3.55	3.65

Source: OECD, Revenue Statistics of OECD Member Countries.

The time period depicted in Box 1 shows the introduction of a number of new excises in *Denmark*. These new excises are of limited revenue importance except for the CO_2 tax. It is also clear that traditional excises on fuels, electricity and vehicles are by far the most important when looking at revenue. Over the period 1994 - 1998 the government has announced that environmental taxes - in particular on energy - will increase substantially.

In *Finland*, taxes on liquid fuels in percent of total tax revenues have been increasing since 1990. This is likely to continue in view of repeated rise in the carbon tax rate. At present the tax is split into a "fiscal" component with tax differentiation for diesel and gasoline, and a "carbon/energy" component (which replaced the pure carbon component).

Box 2.

Taxes/excises with environmental implications in **Finland** in per cent of total tax revenue.						
	1980	1985	1990	1991	1992	1993
From 5121 Excises:						
Taxes on Liquid Fuels	4.24	3.30	2.45	2.82	3.14	3.83
Excise on Motor Cars	2.01	2.12	1.77	1.03	0.89	0.73
Stock-Building Levies on Liquid	0.13	0.18	0.12	0.11	0.12	0.11
Tax on Electricity	0.55	0.74	-	-	-	0.30
Oil Damage Levy	0.00	0.01	0.02	0.01	0.02	0.02
Oil Waste Levy	-	-	0.01	0.02	0.01	0.01
From 5211: Motor Vehicles Tax Paid by Households	-	-	-	-	-	-
From 5211: Motor Vehicles Tax Paid by Others	0.29	0.36	0.36	0.38	0.37	0.40
Total in per cent of total tax revenue	7.21	6.71	4.72	4.37	4.53	5.40
Total in per cent of GDP	2.66	2.74	2.14	2.05	2.12	2.47

Source: OECD, Revenue Statistics of OECD Member Countries.

The *Netherlands* has a number of specific environmental levies. Most of these do not bring in much revenue but it is worth noting that the levies on water and air pollution contribute around 1.23 per cent of total tax revenue in 1993. The levy on air pollution shows a growing importance over the period.

Box 3.

Taxes/excises with environmental implications in the **Netherlands** in per cent of total tax revenue.						
	1980	1985	1990	1991	1992	1993
From 5121 Excises:						
Excise on petrol	1.83	1.70	1.61	1.57	1.74	1.89
Excise on mineral oil	0.42	0.35	0.77	0.77	0.82	1.06
Levies for Nuclear reactor	-	-	-	-	-	-
Levies on noise pollution	-	0.06	-	-	-	-
Levies on air pollution	0.04	0.05	0.29	0.37	0.56	0.58
Levies on petroleum products	-	-	0.07	0.05	0.04	0.05
5211 Motor vehicle tax and license paid by households	0.66	0.69	0.76	0.70	0.72	0.82
5212 Motor vehicle tax and license paid by others	0.86	0.91	1.00	0.92	0.95	1.08
From 5213 levies on water pollution	0.53	0.59	0.62	0.59	0.63	0.65
Total in per cent of total tax revenue	4.34	4.35	5.12	4.97	5.46	6.12
Total in per cent of GDP	1.94	1.92	2.28	2.35	2.57	2.94

Source: OECD, Revenue Statistics of OECD Member Countries.

In *Norway* excise taxes on fuels and transport are responsible for a sizeable part of total tax revenue (nearly 11 per cent). The importance of the CO_2-tax has been growing since 1991. The introduction of the CO_2-tax has been accompanied by a phasing out of the basic excise charge on energy.

Box 4.

Taxes/excises with environmental implications in **Norway** as per cent of total tax revenue.						
	1980	1985	1990	1991	1992	1993
From 5121 Excises:						
Excise on petrol	1.72	1.70	2.31	2.47	2.86	2.78
Vehicles transfer tax	2.06	3.15	1.49	1.28	1.54	1.54
Electric energy	1.13	1.04	1.12	1.05	1.06	1.12
Oil and gas products	2.78	4.99	2.87	2.96	2.64	2.52
Mineral oil	0.08	0.04	0.36	0.64	0.61	0.52
CO_2 tax	-	-	-	0.25	0.59	0.68
5211 Motor vehicles tax paid by households	0.34	0.46	0.58	0.67	0.79	0.83
5212 Motor vehicles tax paid by others	0.52	0.55	0.68	0.69	0.77	0.76
Total in per cent of total tax revenue	8.64	11.94	9.40	9.99	10.86	10.75
Total in per cent of GDP	4.07	5.68	4.35	4.70	5.05	4.92

Source: OECD, Revenue Statistics of OECD Member Countries.

Box 5.

Taxes/excises with environmental implications in **Sweden** as per cent of total tax revenue.						
	1980	1985	1990	1991	1992	1993
From 5121 Excises:						
Taxes on Petrol and Fuel	1.63	2.73	2.27	2.29	2.47	3.00
Sales Tax on Motor Vehicles	0.21	0.28	0.26	0.21	0.20	0.18
Tax on Energy Consumption	1.99	3.01	2.16	2.07	2.17	2.07
Taxes on Electricity From Certain Sources	-	0.25	0.13	0.12	0.14	0.14
From 5211: Motor Vehicles Tax Paid by Households	0.48	0.34	0.26	0.27	0.26	0.28
From 5212: Motor Vehicles Tax Paid by Others	0.96	0.72	0.67	0.74	0.69	0.67
Total in per cent of total tax revenue	5.27	7.33	5.77	5.69	5.92	6.34
Total in per cent of GDP	2.57	3.67	3.20	3.00	2.96	3.17

Source: OECD, Revenue Statistics of OECD Member Countries.

In *Sweden*, revenues from taxes on petrol and fuel are the only ones showing a growing trend in terms of total tax revenue, leading revenues from all ecotaxes to be growing in importance. In terms of GDP, revenues from ecotaxes are nearly as high as their 1990 level..

In *Denmark*, *Finland* and *the Netherlands* environmental taxes show a growing importance in terms of revenue source to the governments and in terms of GDP. Norway is leading both in terms of GDP and total tax revenues, with nearly 11 per cent of total tax revenues and 5 per cent of GDP. *Denmark* is next with 7.3 per cent of total tax revenues and 3.7 per cent of GDP.

III. NEW POLICY TRENDS

This section provides a brief overview of some major trends in environmental taxation. The trends cover two broad categories of countries. The first group consists of those countries that have introduced a major restructuring of the tax system as part of a tax reform with the aim of replacing or reducing distortionary taxes. A shift in tax structure away from income taxation towards VAT and other indirect taxes including environmental taxes is often seen as beneficial, because it can help reduce structural problems in the economy. The tax systems are often given considerable responsibility for structural problems connected with for example the functioning of labour and capital markets. As mentioned already, explicit environmental considerations tend to play a growing role in the design of tax reforms. Arguments to this effect were for example part of the reasons presented for the *Danish* tax reform in 1993. The proposals to Parliament stressed the need to shift taxation away from wage income and onto consumption/production which have a negative effect on the environment. A similar set of policy objectives form the basis for considerations on the evolution of the tax system in *the Netherlands*, *Sweden* and *Norway*. The restructuring concerns mainly energy taxes. The other broad group consists of countries that in general use environmental taxes on a smaller scale e.g *Austria*, *Germany*, *Belgium* and *France*. For this group of countries, there is also an increase in the use of environmental taxes both new- and existing ones but of a more narrow nature i.e. not in the context of a major tax reform.

There also seems to be a trend towards stressing the incentive effects of environmental taxes. Existing taxes, on for instance energy, are being restructured in order to give consumers an environmentally correct incentive in their use of energy.

Many of the recent developments in environmental taxation in OECD countries can be summarised under three headings. First, there has been a continuing growth in the use of *Product Charges*. Second, *Energy Taxation* has been reformed in a number of countries and has included taxation of the transport sector, particularly vehicles. Third, the use of *Committees and Task Forces* into environmental taxes has been used in a number of countries. These three headings are considered in turn.

3.1   Product charges or taxes

Product charges are taken here to include charges on specific goods which can be seen as being introduced to correct externalities. In this way these charges differ from excises on specific goods which have traditionally been levied for fiscal reasons.

In *Belgium*, several new charges have been added or are under consideration. A tax on disposable razors (BF 10) has been introduced; disposable cameras are taxed (BF 300) if they are not recycled; some drink containers are taxed (BF 15/litre) if they are not submitted to a deposit-refund system and cannot be reused or recycled.

The major *Danish* tax reform implemented from January 1994 has introduced several new charges and increased existing ones. A tax on the consumption of ground surface water by households has been introduced. There are plans to introduce a tax on waste water from both households and industry from 1997. There is now a new tax on shopping bags made of plastic or paper (DKr 0.5 per bag). The charges on waste have been increased and remain differentiated according to whether the waste is incinerated or goes into landfill sites. The province of Prince-Edward-Island in *Canada* is in the process of developing a tax on promotional material and newspapers in consultation with stakeholders. *Italy* has abolished the tax on plastic carrier bags as of March 1994 replacing it with a recycling contribution levied on virgin polyethylene (basic substance used for their production). Since January 1993 the *Italian provinces* have been able to levy a special tax for the purpose of organising waste disposal and control of discharges and emissions. A somewhat similar scheme has been introduced in *Turkey* from the beginning of 1994 when the Environmental Clean-Up Tax was introduced. The tax is levied on waste and waste water and applies to both households and non-households. The aim of the tax is to change behaviour and reduce pollution but also to raise revenue.

In the *United Kingdom* the intention to introduce a tax on waste disposal in landfill sites has been announced. The intention is to encourage businesses and consumers to produce less waste, to dispose of less waste in landfill sites and to recover more value from more of the waste which is produced, for example through recycling. The new tax will be introduced in 1996 and a consultation paper setting out details of the proposal and inviting views will be published in early 1995.

3.2   Transport taxes and energy taxes

Several countries have recently announced substantial changes to existing energy taxes, especially those relating to transport. For example, in *Sweden* all excises on energy (including petrol etc.) will be indexed to retail price inflation for the period 1994 to 1998. The sulphur tax and taxes on power production are not covered by the indexation. In *Australia*, there has been an increase in petrol taxes and in the leaded/unleaded differential. In the Netherlands, the government agreed to increase the excise duty on petrol in real terms as well as the annual car tax for LPG-driven cars. These measures are not intended to lead to an increase in the collective tax burden : they will be offset by equal reductions elsewhere. The *United Kingdom* has pre-announced increases in petrol taxes, on average at least 5 pence, over and above the rate of inflation for the next several years in order to help meet the commitments to reduce greenhouse gas emissions. As a result of the *United States* budget process for 1993, there is a 4.3 cent per gallon increase in a wide range of fuels, some of which had previously been untaxed.

Aside from these general increases in fuel taxation, changes in the structure of taxation has also taken place in other countries. Increases in fuel taxes is an integral part of the *Danish* tax reform. The projected increase in fuel taxes in the period up to 1998 is a reversal of the reduction in these excises in 1990 carried on in order to discourage cross-border shopping especially into Germany. This has been made possible by an increase in German excises. It is still the official Danish policy to target excise rates so as to avoid cross-border shopping problems. Denmark has also used part of the revenue increase from petrol to finance a car-scrapping scheme, which pays a premium to car owners scrapping cars that are older than ten years. In *Finland*, the excise duty on fuels was restructured as of January 1994. The carbon component in the excise was replaced by an "EU-type" carbon/energy component. A new mode of tax differentiation was introduced for both diesel and car petrol. The "kilometre" tax has been discontinued in *Sweden*, being replaced instead by a special tax on diesel fuels with a marked differentiation between standard-, light- and urban area diesel. Hence, diesel is now subject to this special tax, the general energy tax and the carbon dioxide tax. Within the limits of a certain quota, biodiesel (diesel produced from plants) are exempted from excises in *Italy*. Environment friendly diesel powered vehicles registered before December 1994 are exempt from road surtax for a period of three years. Finally, in *Portugal* the tax differential in favour of unleaded petrol is being phased out on the grounds that unleaded petrol sales as a proportion of total petrol sales are now around the EU-average.

Aside from excises on fuels, other taxes on motoring have been changed. In the *United Kingdom* a large increase in the taxation of company cars has taken place. This is also the case in *Denmark* and *Belgium*. In *Portugal,* the vehicle registration taxes has been reviewed in order to make them administratively more simple and increase their rates. *Austria* introduced a new car registration tax in January 1992. The tax base is the sales price and the tax rate depends on the standard fuel consumption of the car.

Other energy taxes have been altered. As part of the tax reform in *Denmark*, the excises on electricity and coal will be increased gradually in the period up until 1999. As a result of this increase the excises on coal and electricity will correspond to the excise on oil in respect of energy content. The *United Kingdom* has introduced a reduced rate of VAT on domestic fuels, along with an extensive set of changes to the benefit system to protect those on low incomes. In 1992, *Sweden* introduced a charge on NO_x emissions (which is refunded to the group of plants that pay the charge in proportion to energy produced). As from 1996, the charge system will gradually apply to smaller plants. In the Netherlands, all energy users (with some adjustments for the industries) are subject to a tax on fossil fuels. Plans are underway to introduce a regulatory energy tax on 1 January 96.

Following the recent vote to introduce VAT in *Switzerland*, the Federal council has now proposed a CO_2 tax, which would be introduced (at the earliest) in 1996. The proposed tax will rise to ECU 22.5 per ton of CO_2. Industries which are exposed to international competition and which have a fossil-fuel energy intensity of over 3 per cent in relation to their gross production value will get reliefs. Up to one third of the revenues will be earmarked for environmental purposes, the rest will be redistributed to households and businesses. The environmental effects are supposed to be positive, with no significant economic effects.

Taxes on volatile organic compounds (VOC), which can result in smog, ozone problems, damages to the nerve system etc. have also been discussed in *Switzerland*. The Swiss tax, which is expected in 1995-1996, will be introduced over a period of time increasing to over ECU 3 per kilo. Border taxes on imports are allowed under the law, but will not be applied unless necessary on competitive or environmental grounds.

3.3   Commissions, Committees and Task Forces

Committees, Commissions of Enquiry, Task Forces etc. continue to be established regularly to examine the interface between taxation and the environment. The traditional use of such groups has been to forge consensus on the need to use economic instruments, rather than command and control methods, in environmental policies. This function is still important in *Canada*, where a Commission in Ontario suggested the use of environmental taxes at the provincial level, including a carbon tax, taxes on road use and taxes on water use. Following the election of a liberal government at the Federal level, a Task Force was set up, involving government industry and environmental organisations. The mandate of the Task Force is to identify barriers and disincentive to sound environmental practices, and to find effective ways in which to use economic instruments to protect the environment. The Task Force has submitted its report late 1994[6].

A Ministerial Working Party was set up in *Denmark* in 1993 to analyze the need for a more extensive use of environmental taxes on industry. The importance of recycling the revenues raised in order to conserve industry's international competitiveness was stressed. The Working Party has published a half-way report which concludes that a more widespread use of environmental taxes on industry is needed if Denmark is to meet a number of environmental commitments. A number of organisations (industry, as well as trade unions) have had the opportunity to comment on the report and the government is now analysing these comments with a view to future policy in the area.

A Parliamentary Commission has been set up in *Sweden* to look at how to structure a tax system to take more into account environmental considerations. This will involve an evaluation of the successes or otherwise of existing environmental taxes, and the prospect of a further shift in the tax base in order to provide funds to lower social charges. Finally, the revision of the *Finnish* energy tax system was in response to a report of the Environmental Economics Committee.

The *Netherlands* are planning to undertake an interministerial study to look into the possibilities of a further broadening of taxation on an environmental basis. Furthermore, the Government has announced a study on how the tax-system can support environmental objectives. This study is to be undertaken by non-governmental experts.

Under the auspices of the Nordic Council of Ministers, the Nordic Contact Group for Environmental Economics has published a report on the use of economic instruments in Nordic environmental policy[7]. Among other, the report gives an overview of the main environmental problems in the Nordic area and a comparative overview of the economic instruments applied in the area.

Following the Belgium Ecotax Law, the Belgium Ecotax Commission, consisting of 13 experts in a number of fields was set up to follow up the implementation of new ecotaxes. The Commission was given broad powers to amend the existing law, to propose the introduction of new ecotaxes and even the abolishment of existing ones. The amendment of the Ecotax Law by the government is possible without consultation with the Ecotax Commission.

3.4   Other trends

It is also worth noting that the income tax system is also influenced by environmental considerations in some countries. In the 1992-93 budget *Australia* amended the income tax system to allow immediate deduction for expenditures for certain environmental purposes. The deductible expenditure must be incurred in connection with preventing, combating, cleaning etc. pollution or waste produced by the taxpayers business. Both *Canada* and the Netherlands have a scheme of Accelerated Cost Allowance which can be used in connection with equipment for energy conservation and equipment to reduce air and water pollution.

IV. TAXATION OF MOTOR FUELS AND VEHICLE RELATED TAXES

Road transport is the subject of a number of different taxes in most OECD countries. Existing taxes apply primarily to motor vehicles and to the fuels they consume. There is considerable scope for environmental objectives to be reflected through the restructuring of existing taxes rather than the introduction of wholly new ones.

4.1   Motor fuel taxes

Motor fuel is generally subject to a number of different taxes: general consumption or VAT taxes, excise taxes, storage and security levies, and environmental taxes. The overall tax burden on motor fuels thus tends to be high - usually higher than for other goods, reflecting in part both the elasticity and the breadth of this tax base. Existing taxes on motor fuels include:

a) **VAT or general consumption taxes**. Among OECD countries, only Australia and the United States do not have a VAT, general consumption tax or turnover tax (at the federal level). Among those countries that do, the general VAT rates range from 3 per cent for Japan to 25 per cent for Sweden and Denmark. VAT treatment of energy[8], including motor fuels, varies among countries.

   In some countries different rates of tax are applied to different motor fuels: Ireland taxes petrol at 21 per cent, automotive diesel at 12,5 per cent; amongst other countries, aviation fuel is exempt in European Union Countries. In Switzerland, only motor fuels among all energy sources are subject to VAT/turnover tax; in Sweden only aviation fuel is exempt. (See Table 1 in annex for a summary and comparison of general, motor fuels and energy-related VAT rates in OECD countries in 1994).

   It is important to note that Value Added Taxation in virtually all countries applies effectively only to households. The tax is rebated or refunded to industrial, commercial and agricultural users who are registered for VAT, and to electricity generators. This refund is equal to 100 per cent of the tax in most countries. However, Portugal refunds only 50 per cent, except for heavy passenger vehicles, for public transport and for agricultural tractors since March 1992. In Denmark, VAT on the purchase and running costs including fuel of vehicles designed to seat no more than 9 persons are not deductible. In Finland, all fuels used in transport are subject to the VAT, including purchases by industry.

b) **Excise Taxes**. All OECD countries levy excise taxes on motor fuel. These excise taxes tend to be product-specific (usually highest on petrol) and are most often specific (i.e. quantity-related) taxes rather than ad-valorem (price-related). Diesel fuel is often taxed at a different rate than petrol. In OECD Europe the tax rate for diesel is usually lower, reflecting the greater use of diesel fuel by commercial vehicles. In the United States, the rate for diesel is higher, reflecting the extra costs of highway construction and repair imposed by heavy diesel vehicles, but lower than in most countries. In Australia, rebates on diesel fuel excise taxes are available for certain mining operations (at approximately 90 per cent) and primary production (at 100 per cent). A number of countries have also introduced a tax differential in favour of lead free petrol.

Among countries which have a federal form of government, States in the United States and provinces in Canada levy their own excise taxes on motor fuel. In the United States, the state excise taxes are often higher than the federal taxes. Municipalities, counties and other local governments may also levy taxes on motor fuels.

c) **Special taxes**. Besides VAT and excise taxes, motor fuels are also subject to a number of special taxes in different countries. These include environmental taxes (Denmark, Finland, the Netherlands, Norway, Sweden and the United States[9]) discussed in Section VII, fuel storage taxes (in some EC countries, to fund emergency stocks), taxes to fund public works on related infrastructure (France, Japan, New Zealand, the United States), taxes to fund national industry R&D (France), taxes to help finance the social security system (Belgium), franchise fees (Australia) and petroleum tax (Japan) and various other business taxes and sales taxes. Excise taxes, however, still comprise some 95 per cent of the special (non-VAT) taxes levied on motor fuels. Refer to Tables 2 and 3 in Annex for more detailed information on motor fuel taxes.

The next three charts present end-user prices and taxes paid for leaded, unleaded and diesel, for the countries where the fuel is available and for those countries that the data on prices and taxes existed for the two years 1990 and 1993[10]. Prices and taxes are converted to U.S. dollars using Purchasing Power Parities to account for the difference in the cost of living in each country. Prices and taxes paid on diesel are those paid by industry, and are exclusive of Value Added Taxes.

One direct observation is that end-user prices and the tax burden greatly vary across OECD countries, with the United States having the lowest prices. Differences in prices are in part explained by differences in tax burden, but also by other factors such as adequate infrastructure for the transport of fossil fuels. Prices have generally increased since 1990, and rising tax burdens appear to be the major reason for those rising prices. Countries that have introduced CO_2 taxes, like Finland and Norway have had large increases in prices, as well as in tax burden, but other countries like Germany, Greece and the United Kingdom have had a more than proportional increase in tax burden.

Leaded gasoline is usually more expensive than unleaded gasoline, and the tax differential between leaded and unleaded gasoline would appear as the major factor. With the exception of Denmark and Portugal, the price of leaded gasoline has increased in all countries from 1990 to 1993. The price of diesel has also increased in most countries, except Austria, New Zealand, Portugal, Sweden and the United States. If it were not for tax increases in Austria, Portugal, Sweden and the United States, the price of diesel would have fallen even more. In New Zealand, the tax burden has fallen proportionately more than the price.

Prices and Taxes on Gasoline:
UNLEADED (95 RON)
in U.S. Purchasing Power Parities per litre

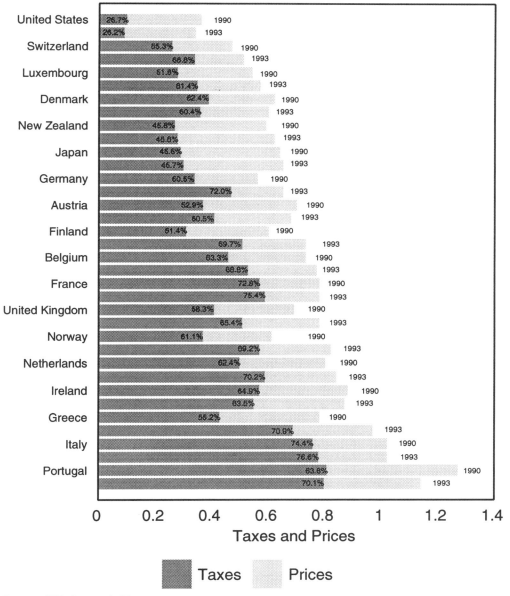

Source: IEA Quarterly Report
"Energy Prices and Taxes", 1st Quarter, 1994.

19

Prices and Taxes on Gasoline:
LEADED
in U.S. Purchasing Power Parities per litre

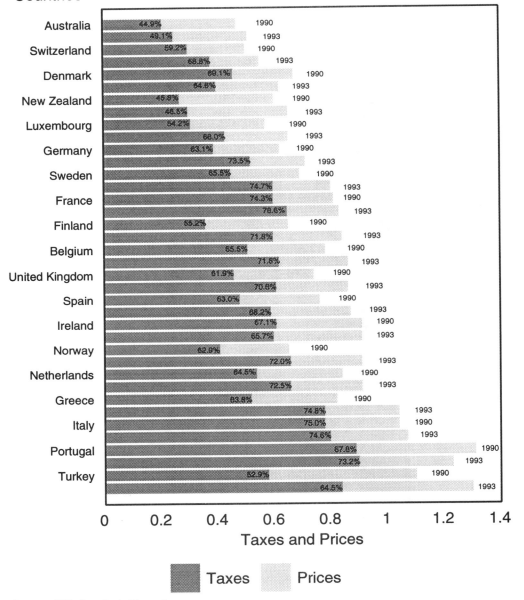

Source: IEA Quarterly Report
"Energy Prices and Taxes", 1st Quarter, 1994.

20

Effective Prices and Taxes
on DIESEL used by Industry
in U.S. Purchasing Power Parities per litre

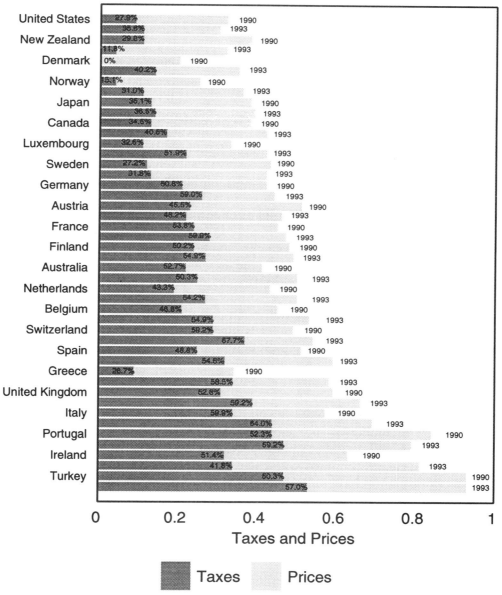

Countries

Taxes and Prices

Taxes   Prices

Source: IEA Quarterly Report
"Energy Prices and Taxes", 1st Quarter, 1994.

4.2　Vehicle-related taxes

Motor vehicles are often taxed according to their physical or fuel-use characteristics, and/or the use to which they are put. These taxes are primarily revenue-raising measures, and vary widely among OECD countries. However, vehicle-related taxes, particularly negative taxes (tax expenditures) relating to commuting expenses, do have the potential to alter behaviour for environmental purposes, particularly when tied to infrastructure reform. Existing vehicle-related taxes include:

a) **Sales taxes on new motor vehicles**. These taxes are in many cases higher than on other goods, or are imposed in addition to the general sales tax. In Belgium, motor vehicles (new or second-hand) attract both the normal VAT and a "taxe de mise en circulation". In Belgium, a maximum of 50 per cent is rebated through the VAT system, while the remaining part of the professional use is accepted as a deductible charge in income taxes. In the Netherlands, motor vehicles are subject to VAT and to one extra tax on private cars and motorbikes. There is also a special car tax in the United States, levied on the sale of new cars with above-average fuel consumption. This so-called gas-guzzler tax ranges from US$1 000 to US$7 700 per car. While such taxes may discourage purchase of new cars (except in Belgium), and hence reduce the number of vehicles on the road, they may also result in consumers keeping older, less technologically clean, vehicles for a longer time, thus increasing the potential for emissions. In a bill put forward to the Parliament, the Swedish government proposed that the sales tax on electric cars and cars that can run on both electricity and other fuel should be abolished for a period of three years with a start from 1 January 1995.

b) **Recurrent annual charges**. Such charges commonly take the form of fees for the registration or use of motor vehicles. These may be an annual lump-sum tax (*e.g.* the British Vehicle Excise Duty of £135 per annum), or may be related to certain characteristics of the motor vehicle, such as engine capacity. In most countries, annual charges for the use of commercial vehicles differ from those for private motor cars. In the United Kingdom, the Vehicle Excise Duty on commercial freight vehicles is higher than that for cars, and is related to vehicle weight. In some countries the annual registration charge is a local tax, either in the sense that the revenues accrue to local governments, or that the tax level is determined at a local level (*e.g.* France).

Possibilities exist for the differentiation of the tax on new cars and the annual charges for registration according to the "environmental" attributes of different vehicles. In some countries, a tax incentive has been introduced for "clean" cars (*e.g.* cars meeting certain emissions standards, or fitted with catalytic converters), and, for environmental reasons, a number of countries have recently begun to differentiate these taxes by engine size or other factors affecting fuel use. The pattern of one-off and recurrent charges on the ownership and use of private motor cars and commercial vehicles in OECD countries is summarised in Table 4. The taxes levied on commercial vehicle sales, ownership and use are generally more complex than the taxes on private cars, and the pattern of differentiation more long-standing.

c) **Tax treatment of company cars and commuting expenses**. Countries pursue a wide range of practices with regard to the fiscal treatment of cars provided by employers to their employees ("company cars"), and to expenditures incurred by private individuals in the course of commuting to work. In the former case, the main issue is the extent to which remuneration of employees through the provision of income in kind is fiscally-privileged, relative to monetary remuneration. In the latter case, there are two main issues. One issue is the extent to which allowing tax deductibility for commuting costs encourages individuals to commute longer distances than they would have done in the absence of tax deductibility. The other is whether the structure of tax deductibility encourages commuting using certain modes of transport - especially, using private cars - rather than other, less environmentally-damaging, modes. Both of the "encouragement" effects usually apply to company cars as well. These various provisions are summarised in Table 5.

4.3   New trends in motor fuels and vehicle taxation

Until very recently, taxation of motor vehicles and motor fuels had focused primarily if not exclusively on raising revenue. A few countries are now beginning to implement coordinated fiscal and environmental policies, aimed at reducing motor vehicle related pollution. Examples from some OECD countries of recent policy changes to take greater account of environmental considerations in the taxation of road transport include the following:

a) In **Austria**, an environmental tax on car registration was introduced on 1 January 1992. This tax is based on the sales price of new cars and on the average petrol consumption. At the same time, the VAT rate on new vehicles was reduced from 32 per cent to 20 per cent and the VAT rate on electric cars has been cut by half to 10 per cent.

Since 1 May 1993, the vehicle tax on passenger cars will be assessed on the basis of engine power and no longer on cylinder volume. From 1 January 1995, cars without catalytic converter are imposed a surtax of 20 per cent.

b) In **Finland**, the State Budget for 1990 introduced a package of environmental measures. These included an increase in the tax rate on motor fuels, and a restatement of the reasons for the tax in terms of environmental objectives. Finland operates a system of taxes on cars which is differentiated according to whether they are equipped with a catalytic converter. Tax differentiation in favour of lead-free petrol was introduced in 1986. Moreover, the excise on both diesel and car petrol is differentiated, since 1993, in favour of sulphur-free (diesel) and reformulated (petrol) qualities.

c) **Germany** has a vehicle tax system, which includes higher tax rates for high-pollutant petrol and diesel cars, to accelerate the introduction of low-pollutant vehicles, especially cars fitted with catalytic converters.

d) In **Greece**, a law introduced in March 1990 provided an exemption for new cars fitted with a catalytic converter from the road surtax and the initial lump sum tax for a period of five years. The exemption was given provided the buyer had already scrapped his old car. The Greek authorities find the results very satisfactory. Around 300 000 old cars were scrapped and pollution considerably reduced.

e) In recent years, in the **Netherlands** a "variabilisation" of car costs has been implemented, by increasing the excise duties on motor fuel. In the period 1990-1994, the excise on petrol has been increased by an average of 40%, the excise on diesel by 70%. For the taxes on new cars and the annual road taxes, the possibilities for differentiation of the tariff or introduction of tax reliefs, both related to environmental considerations are under study.

f) **Norway** has a system of differentiated taxes on car prices, with a tax advantage given to cars fitted with catalytic converters. Also during 1994 tax advantages are maintained for cars powered by electricity or gas.

g) In **Sweden**, in a bill put forward to the Parliament, the government proposed that the sales tax on electric cars and cars that can run on both electricity and other fuels should be abolished for a period of three years, starting 1 January 1995.

h) In **Belgium**, a "Tax on bringing in circulation" (taxe de mise en circulation) was introduced for new motorcars on 1 June 1992 and it has been extended to second-hand cars since 1 June 1993. This tax is based on the engine power of the car. The possibility to deduct expenditures incurred by private individuals using their own car to commute has been substantially reduced over the last five years. Also the fiscal privilege of the use of company cars has been reduced and the fiscal treatment of commuting expenses refunded by the employer has been altered, introducing a clear advantage for those who make use of public transportation means.

The revenues which Member countries derive from taxes on road transport are set out in Table 6.

Five countries have recently instituted carbon taxes on motor fuels as part of overall carbon tax schemes: Denmark, Finland, Norway, Sweden, and the Netherlands. (For a more detailed description see section VII below). In Finland and Norway these taxes are a small addition to existing motor fuel taxes. The Netherlands introduced a general tax on fuels in 1992, this tax has two components: a CO_2 emission and an energy content. The total revenue (GLd 1.5 billion in 1993) is strictly for the purpose of raising revenue for the general budget. In Norway, the tax as levied on motor fuels in 1994 is NKr 0.82 per litre for petrol and NKr O.41 for diesel. The Government estimates that revenues will reach NKr 2 650 million per year.

In Sweden, a carbon tax was imposed on motor and other fossil fuels as of 1 January 1991. The part of the tax levied on motor fuels amounted to SKr 0.58 per litre for petrol and SKr 0.92 for diesel oil. Other energy taxes were reduced by 50 per cent at the same time. In 1994, the CO_2 tax on petrol amounted to 0.77 SKr per litre[11] and to SKr 0.957 for diesel. The CO_2 tax on all fossil fuel is equivalent to SKr 0.333 per kg of CO_2.

The Finnish carbon tax on fossil fuels was replaced, as from January 1994, by a combined carbon/energy tax. Tax rates were raised again for 1995. The 1995 tax rate on petrol consists of: 1) a basic excise of Mk 2.61 for standard quality (Mk 2.56 for reformulated); 2) plus a carbon/energy surtax of Mk 0.123; 3) and, an additional tax of Mk 0.45 per litre if leaded. For standard diesel the basic excise is Mk 1.65 and the carbon/energy rate Mk 0.135. For sulphur-free quality the basic rate is Mk 0.15 per litre lower.

V. TAXATION OF OTHER ENERGY PRODUCTS

Taxation of other energy products varies widely between OECD Member countries. There are also substantial differences in the tax burden on individual energy products within Member countries. Only rarely has any attempt been made to tax all sources of energy on a consistent basis, and very large differences in tax rates for different types of energy can be encountered, reflecting domestic political pressures (low or negative taxation of coal in some countries), or the desire to reduce the tax burden on fuels predominantly used as industrial inputs. This section also describes some measures reported by some OECD countries, taken to introduce systems of energy taxation exhibiting an explicit environmental rationale.

Taxes by Fuel

Among petroleum products, and apart from motor fuels, light and heavy fuel oil are frequently taxed. These taxes vary by product, by country, and according to use. As with motor fuels, other energy sources are generally and variously subject to VAT, excise taxes and special taxes of different kinds. For a summary of applicable VAT rates, see Table 1. For a summary of taxes on other energy products, see Table 7.

Light fuel oil

In general, **household** use of light fuel oil is subject to the VAT (in all countries which have a VAT[12] (except Switzerland[13]). These consumers are also liable for emergency stock fees (for Austria, Finland, France, Germany, the Netherlands and Switzerland); environmental taxes (Finland, the Netherlands, Norway, Sweden and the United States); R&D fees (France); inspection fees (Belgium); a number of general excise taxes on mineral oils or petroleum products (Australia, Austria, Belgium, Denmark, Finland, Germany, Greece, Ireland, Italy, Japan, Luxembourg, the Netherlands, New Zealand, Portugal, Spain, Sweden, Switzerland and the United Kingdom); and, in the United States various state and local sales taxes.

Industrial use of light fuel oil is subject to all of these same taxes but usually not to the VAT paid by industrial users which is refunded through the VAT credit mechanism, and is not borne as a cost. Only in Portugal, among countries with general consumption taxes, are certain industrial, agricultural and commercial users fully reimbursed for VAT on their light oil consumption while for all other purposes, it is 50 per cent reimbursed.

Heavy fuel oil

Industrial users of heavy fuel oil are subject to excise taxes in Australia, Austria[14], Finland, Germany, Greece, Italy, the Netherlands, New Zealand, Norway, Spain, Sweden, Switzerland and the United Kingdom. In Belgium, an excise tax on heavy fuel oil was introduced on 1 January 1993. From the start, the tax was differentiated according to the sulphur content of the fuel. If the sulphur content does not exceed one per cent, the tax rate is BF 250/ton, otherwise it is BF 750/ton. In Finland, Germany, the Netherlands and the UK, electricity generators are also subject to these taxes. Special storage fees are charged to these customers for emergency storage funds in Austria, Finland, France, Germany, the Netherlands and Switzerland; and they are subject to environmental taxes in Finland, the Netherlands, Norway (a sulphur tax), Sweden (SO_2 tax) and the United States. In the United States heavy fuel oil is subject to state and local sales taxes.

Natural gas

Natural gas is subject to resource taxes in Australia and to sales taxes and resource taxes in the United States (2-6 per cent). In countries with a VAT, household consumption of natural gas is generally subject to the tax (exceptions are Greece, Luxembourg, Norway, and Spain). In Belgium, households pay an additional levy on energy of BF 0.1367/megajoule. A few countries impose various excise taxes (France, Germany, Italy, Japan, Sweden and Switzerland). Spain has a municipal tax of 1.5 per cent; Finland and the Netherlands, impose environmental taxes (for industry and households); and New Zealand collects an R&D fee as well.

Coal

Coal is the least taxed of all primary energy sources. Most coal taxes consist of a VAT levied on household use (Austria, Belgium, France, Germany, Ireland, Italy, Japan, the Netherlands, New Zealand, Spain, Sweden and the United Kingdom). In addition, other kinds of special taxes are levied variously as follows: an excise tax on household use (Denmark); an environmental tax (Finland, the Netherlands and the United States); a resource tax (New Zealand); a fee to fund emergency stock (Switzerland); and customs duties (Switzerland). In Sweden, households and non-industrial consumption is subject to general energy tax, carbon dioxide tax and sulphur tax; industrial consumption is subject to a reduced carbon dioxide tax (25% of general level).

Electricity

Electricity, like gas, is subject primarily to the VAT (effectively for households only, in Austria, Belgium, Canada, Denmark, Finland, France, Germany, Greece, Ireland, Italy, Japan, Luxembourg, the Netherlands, New Zealand, Norway, Portugal, Spain, Sweden and the United Kingdom), and to sales taxes in the United States. Household consumption is subject to an excise tax in Denmark, Greece and Norway; industrial and household consumption is subject to excise taxes in Finland, Italy, and Japan; household and non-industrial consumption is subject to an excise tax in Sweden and to a levy on energy in Belgium. Local taxes are levied on coal use in France, Italy, and Spain. In Germany, a special tax of 8 per cent levied on all electricity to subsidise domestic coal, was reduced to 7.75 per cent in 1992.

In the Netherlands, the introduction of the tax on uranium-235 is postponed until 1997. The rate of the tax to be paid by nuclear power plants is Gld 31.95 per gramme.

VI. EMISSIONS TAX

France introduced in 1985, for a duration of five years, a parafiscal tax on polluting emissions into the atmosphere, which was extended on 11 May 1990 and broadened in terms of both rates and taxpayers. The rate is FF 150/tonne. The taxpayers are as follows:

- operators of fuel installations with a total capacity of over 20 thermal MW;

- operators of waste incineration facilities with a capacity of over 3 tonnes per hour;

- operators of plant emitting over 150 tonnes per year of sulphur, nitrogen oxide and hydrochloric acid compounds or non-methane hydrocarbons, solvents and other volatile organic compounds.

The Environment and Energy Agency (ADEME) administers this tax, which is paid by about 1 400 taxable persons. The revenue is used for the installation of suitable equipment, the development of atmospheric pollution prevention, reduction or measurement techniques, and the financing of air quality monitoring. The gross revenue for 1993 and 1994 is respectively FF 197 million and FF 169 million.

VII. ENVIRONMENTAL TAXATION OF ENERGY

The taxes described above have been levied primarily for revenue-raising purposes, and not as attempts to achieve behaviour modification, that is to reduce pollution. Systematic taxation of fuels according to their environmental characteristics is a comparatively recent idea, and whilst carbon taxes or other environmental taxes on energy sources have been discussed in many countries, only a few have so far implemented any systematic energy tax structure along environmental lines.

As noted in previous sections, five countries have implemented carbon taxes: Denmark, Finland, the Netherlands, Norway and Sweden. What follows is more detailed information on the structure and administration of these carbon taxes. The tables describe the various excise taxes that were imposed on energy products over the last two years.

7.1   Denmark

In Denmark, a carbon dioxide tax was first introduced in 1992 as part of a tax package, which comprised eight laws which included a CO_2 tax on energy consumption and various subsidy schemes for promoting means to produce electricity and heat from less carbon-rich fuels such as natural gas and biofuels, and to increase energy efficiency. The CO_2 tax was imposed on all types of CO_2 emissions sources in Denmark except gasoline, natural gas and biofuels, and was based on the CO_2 content of each fuel at combustion. The overall rate was 100 DKr per tonne CO_2. In 1993, the total net revenue of the CO_2 tax was DKr 3.174 million.

Generally, 50 per cent of the CO_2 tax was reimbursed to businesses registered under the VAT law, except the CO_2 tax on diesel used for motor fuels which could not be reimbursed. Further reimbursement for the other 50 per cent was possible: 50 per cent of the tax that exceeded 1 per cent of the refund base, 75 per cent of the tax beyond 2 percent of the refund base and 90 per cent of the tax beyond 3 per cent of the refund base could be reimbursed. The refund base is the difference between the total sales liable to VAT including exports and the total purchase liable to VAT including imports. If the CO_2 tax was beyond 3 per cent of the refund base and if the company had been subject to an energy audit, a subsidy was granted corresponding to the part of the CO_2 tax that had not been reimbursed according to the above mentioned rules. However, companies always had to pay DKr 10 000 per year. This arrangement was made to compensate businesses that rely heavily on energy in their production processes. The carbon tax was not reimbursed to households.

Aviation, shipping and gas consumption on refineries were exempted from CO_2 charges. It was considered most appropriate to impose CO_2 tax on electricity at the final consumption and to calculate the tax according to the CO_2 content in coal based electricity. With a view to support or compensate the CO_2-free or CO_2-low production of electricity, a special law was passed according to which a subsidy of DKr .10 per KWh could be given to producers of electricity for the quantity of electricity produced by renewable energy and renewable fuels or by decentralised heat and power generation based on natural gas. Furthermore, a subsidy of DKr 0.17 per KWh was granted on electricity produced by wind power, water power, biogas and biofuels.

Before the introduction of the CO_2 tax, there were already excise duties imposed on energy products. Leaded and unleaded gasoline have been imposed at different rates since the mid-1980s. The market share of unleaded gasoline is nearly 100 per cent in 1994. Besides excise duties, consumers of fuels and energy products have to pay Value Added Tax at a rate of 25 per cent. The following table compares the rates of the excise duty and the CO_2 tax for 1993 and 1994.

Tax Rates on Fuels and Electricity: Denmark

Energy source	Unit	Excise Tax:		Carbon Tax:	
		1993	1994	1993	1994
Unleaded Petrol[a]	DKr/litre	2.25	2.45	-	-
Leaded Petrol[a]	DKr/litre	2.90	3.10	-	-
Diesel Oil, light	DKr/litre	1.67	1.67	0.27[b]	0.27[b]
Diesel Oil, ordinary	DKr/litre	1.77	1.77	0.27[b]	0.27[b]
Light Fuel Oil	DKr/litre	1.49[c]	1.49[c]	0.27[d]	0.27[d]
Heavy Fuel Oil	DKr/kg	1.66[c]	1.66[c]	0.32[d]	0.32[d]
Fuel tar	DKr/kg	1.50	1.50	0.28	0.28
Kerosine, heating	DKr/litre	1.49	1.49	0.27	0.27
Kerosine	DKr/litre	1.77	1.77	0.27	0.27
Coal	DKr/tonne	690[c]	690[c]	242[d]	242[d]
Petroleum Coke	DKr/tonne	690	690	323	323
Lignite	DKr/tonne	505	505	178	178
Gas used as motor fuel	DKr/litre	1.18	1.18	0.16	0.16
Other Gas (LPG)	DKr/kg	2.00	2.00	0.30	0.30
Refinery gas	DKr/kg	2.00	2.00	0.29	0.29
Electricity	DKr/kWh	0.27	0.30	0.10	0.10
Electricity, heating	DKr/kWh	0.24	0.27	0.10	0.10

Notes:
a) An Environmental Pool tax on gasoline has been levied since 1.4.1993 at 0.025 DKr/litre and was increased to 0.04 DKr/litre
b) The CO_2 tax is not refundable to industrial consumers
c) The excise tax on LFO/HFO and coal is refundable to industry
d) The carbon tax on LFO/HFO and coal is only 50% refundable to industry

The 1994 tax reform increased the excise tax rates on electricity, motor fuels and coal, but did not affect the CO_2 tax rates. The next table shows the total charges imposed before and after the tax reform, that is in 1993 and in 1994. The tax reform will be fully implemented in 1998. The tax rates shown are VAT-inclusive (25 per cent).

The charge on gasoline increased by DKr 0.20/litre in 1994, and will increase gradually until 1998. The increase in the tax on diesel will take place in the years 1995 to 1997, and will be DKr 0.35/litre in 1997. The charge on electricity is to increase by DKr 0.19 to DKr 0.46 from 1994 to 1998. On top of that the consumer will pay the CO_2 tax of DKr 0.10 each year.

Fuels	Unit	1993	1994	1995	1996	1997	1998
Gasoline, leaded	DKr/litre	3.63	3.88	4.44	4.66	4.73	4.79
Gasoline unleaded	DKr/litre	2.81	3.06	3.63	3.85	3.91	3.98
Diesel, ordinary:	DKr/litre	2.55	2.55	2.84	2.86	2.99	2.99
of which CO_2 Tax	DKr/litre	0.34	0.34	0.34	0.34	0.34	0.34
Diesel, light:	DKr/litre	2.43	2.43	2.71	2.74	2.86	2.86
of which CO_2 Tax	DKr/litre	0.34	0.34	0.34	0.34	0.34	0.34
Autogas	DKr/litre	1.68	1.68	1.88	2.04	2.13	2.13
Electricity:	DKr/KWh	0.46	0.50	0.54	0.58	0.63	0.70
of which CO_2 Tax	DKr/KWh	0.13	0.13	0.13	0.13	0.13	0.13
Electr., heating:	DKr/KWh	0.42	0.46	0.49	0.53	0.58	0.62
of which CO_2 tax	DKr/KWh	0.13	0.13	0.13	0.13	0.13	0.13
Coal:	DKr/tonne	1165	1165	1265	1378	1490	1603
of which CO_2 Tax	DKr/tonne	303	303	303	303	303	303

7.2   Finland

In January 1990, Finland introduced Europe's first explicit carbon tax, imposed on fossil fuels according to their carbon content. This carbon tax was initially set at the comparatively low level of Mk 24.5 per ton of carbon. The carbon tax was incorporated - as a surtax - into the excise duty on fossil fuels. In 1993, the tax rate was doubled to Mk 50, and a new mode of tax differentiation was introduced for diesel oil and petrol.

The excise duty on fuels was restructured as of January 1994, and the tax rates were raised. At present, the tax is split into a "fiscal" component with tax differentiations for diesel and petrol, and a "carbon/energy" component (which replaced the pure carbon component). The relative weights of the carbon content and the energy content are 60/40 in terms of total revenues. The tax rates are raised again for 1995: the carbon rate was set at Mk 141 per ton of carbon (Mk 38.3 per ton of CO_2) and the energy rate at Mk 3.5 per MWh. The excise tax rates as from 1 January 1995, and for 1993 and 1994 are as follows:

Tax Rates on Fuels and Electricity: Finland

Fuels	Unit	Basic tax:			Energy/CO$_2$ tax:		
		1993	1994	1995	1993[f]	1994	1995
Unleaded Petrol[a,c]	Mk/litre	2.35	2.36	2.61	0.05	0.071	0.123
Leaded Petrol[a,c]	Mk/litre	2.35	2.81	3.06	0.50	0.071	0.123
Diesel Oil[b,c]	Mk/litre	0.87	1.65	1.65	0.27	0.078	0.135
Light Fuel Oil[c]	Mk/litre	0.042	0.042	0.0428	0.0417	0.08	0.137
Heavy Fuel Oil[c]	Mk/kg	0.025	0.025	0.0255	0.0417	0.093	0.160
Coal	Mk/tonne	-	-	-	33.38	67.2	116.1
Peat[d]	Mk/MWh	-	-	-	4.17	4.3	3.5
Natural Gas[e]	Mk/nm^3	-	-	-	0.0209	0.065	0.112
Electricity:							
Nuclear	Mk/kWh	0.015	0.015	0.015	0.0062	0.0062	0.009
Hydro	Mk/kWh	0.015	-	-	-	0.002	0.004
Imported	Mk/kWh	0.015	0.007	0.013	0.0062	0.0062	0.009

Note:
a) Basic Tax 0.05 Mk/litre lower for reformulated petrol
b) Basic Tax 0.15 Mk/litre lower for sulphur-free diesel
c) Additional Precautionary stock feeds are imposed on liquid fuels
d) Peat is exempt from carbon component
e) Only 50% of the rate is applied to natural gas in 1995
f) Before the introduction of the Energy/CO$_2$ tax in 1994, there was an Environmental Damage Tax.

Exemptions or reduced rates are not applied for industries. Products used as raw materials in industrial production, or used as fuels for planes and certain vessels are exempted from the tax. Estimated total revenues for 1995 from the basic tax on energy products amount to Mk 10 200 million and to 2 400 million from the additional energy/CO$_2$ tax, and for 1994, to Mk 8 800 million and Mk 1 450 million respectively.

7.3 The Netherlands

When it was introduced in 1988, the environmental charge on fuels replaced a system of programme specific levies, raising revenue for specific types of environmental expenditure. The environmental charge on fuels was developed in response to a perceived need for an integral system for financing environmental policy expenditures. Fuel was chosen as the tax base, because it was felt that this would provide a "general" link with the polluter-pays-principle. Many pollution problems are directly related to fuel usage. Furthermore, fuel use was considered to be a rough indicator for economic activities resulting in pollution.

Since 1988, the tax base has been changed considerably over the years. In 1990, a CO_2-component was added to the tax base, providing Gld 150 million of extra revenue. Refinery gas was added to the tax base in 1991. The earmarking received various criticisms, and since July 1992 revenues are for the general budget, with the Minister of Finance being primarily responsible. In 1992, the entire tax base was changed to one based 50/50 on energy/carbon content. The next table gives the tax rates on different types of fuels, derived from their energy and carbon content applicable on 1 January 1993, 1994 and 1995. In addition to excise duties and the environmental tax, there is also a compulsory storage charge imposed at Gld 0.0135 per litre on leaded and unleaded gasoline, diesel and light fuel oil. The revenues from the environmental tax for 1995 are expected to amount to Gld 1 400 million or about 1.3 per cent of total tax revenue.

Tax Rates on Fuels: Netherlands

Fuels	Unit	Excise Duties:			Environmental Tax		
		1993	1994	1995	1993	1994	1995
Unleaded Petrol	Gld/litre	0.9715	1.0815	1.082	0.0241	0.0266	0.0251
Leaded Petrol	Gld/litre	1.093	1.2193	1.2193	0.0241	0.0241	0.0251
Diesel Oil	Gld/litre	0.5552	0.6352	0.6352	0.0266	0.0266	0.0277
Light Fuel Oil	Gld/litre	0.1026	0.1026	0.1023	0.0265	0.0265	0.0275
Heavy Fuel Oil	Gld/tonne	34.24	34.24	34.24	31.04	31.04	32.33
LPG	Gld/tonne	-	78.72	78.72	31.83	31.83	33.08
Coal	Gld/tonne	-	-	-	22.64	22.64	23.38
Blast Furnace, cokes oven, refinery and coal gas	Gld/GJ	-	-	-	220.57	220.57	236.82
Natural Gas 0-10 mn m³	Gld/m³	-	-	-	20.79	20.79	21.55
>10 mn m³	Gld/m³	-			13.67	13.67	14.10
Residuals (traded) Petrocokes	Gld/tonne	-	-	-	31.03	31.03	32.47
Liquid	Gld/tonne	-	-	-	31.04	31.04	32.33
Gaseous	Gld/1000 GJ	-	-	-	220.57	220.57	236.82

7.4   Norway

In Norway, the current tax system for fossil fuels already include taxes on atmospheric emissions of CO_2, SO_2 and lead, in addition to the general Value Added Tax of 22 percent. Both the petrol and mineral oil tax contain a CO_2 element. A carbon tax has also been introduced for gas and oil combustion on the continental shelf and as from 1 July 1992, a carbon tax was introduced for certain coal and coke applications. Moreover, the petrol tax has been differentiated based on lead content and the mineral oil tax based on sulphur content.

CO_2 taxes were introduced on 1 January 1991, starting at a rate of NKr 0.60/litre which was increased to NKr 0.80/litre on 1 January 1992, to NKr 0.82 on 1 January 1994 and then to NKr 0.83 on 1 January 1995. Besides its environmental importance, the CO_2 tax represents an important element of the national budget. In 1994, the tax on CO_2 gave state revenues of about 6 billion NKr.

Petrol also faces a basic tax which was on 1 January 1994 NKr 3.78/litre of leaded gasoline and NKr 3.12/litre of unleaded gasoline.The basic tax on petrol differentiates leaded petrol and unleaded petrol since 1986. The lead surcharge since 1990 was increased many times from 0.43 NKr/l on 1 January 1990, to 0.53 on 1 January 1991, to 0.65 NKr/litre on 1 January 1992 and to 0.66 NKr/litre on 1 January 1994. Since 1995, the rate is also differentiated for leaded petrol : below 0.05 g of lead per litre of petrol the rate is NKr 3.79, and above 0.05 g of lead per litre the rate is NKr 4.24.

The SO_2 tax is levied on light and heavy fuel oils and is calculated on each 0.25 per cent of sulphur content and per litre. Oil with lower sulphur content than 0.05 per cent is exempted. The tax rate is 0.07 NKr per litre light fuel oil and 0.63 NKr per litre of heavy fuel oil and has remained unchanged since 1 January 1991.

The next table gives the tax rates on different types of fuels, derived from their energy and carbon content applicable in Norway in 1 January 1993 and 1994.

Tax Rates on Fuels and Electricity: Norway

Fuels	Unit	Excise Duties:			CO$_2$ Tax			SO$_2$ Tax		
		1993	1994	1995	1993	1994	1995	1993	1994	1995
Unleaded Petrol	NKr/litre	3.07	3.12	3.57	0.80	0.82	0.83	-	-	-
Leaded Petrol	NKr/litre	3.72	3.78	4.24[a]	0.80	0.82	0.83	-	-	-
Diesel Oil	NKr/litre	2.45[b]	2.45	2.87	0.40	0.41	0.415	0.07	0.07	0.07
Light Fuel Oil	NKr/litre	0	-	-	0.40	0.41	0.415	0.07	0.07	0.07
Heavy Fuel Oil[c]	NKr/litre	6	-	-	0.40	0.41	0.415	0.63	0.63	0.63
Coal	NKr/kilo	-	-	-	0.40	0.41	0.415	-	-	-
Natural Gas[d]		-	-	-	-	-	-	-	-	-
Electricity consumption	NKr/kWh	0.046	0.051	0.052	-	-	-	-	-	-
Production	Nkr/kwk	0.012	0.0122	0.0152	-	-	-	-	-	-

Note:
a) The rate for leaded gasoline with less than 0.05 g of lead per litre is NKr 3.79, and above 0.05g/l the rate is NKr 4.24/litre
b) As of 1 October 1993.
c) The sulphur tax is for each 0.25% content of sulphur. However, the tax is rebated if the sulphur content is removed before its end-use. Since 1 January 1992, oil with a sulphur content lower than 0.05 percent is exempted.
d) No consumption of natural gas

7.5   Sweden

In Sweden, a bill passed in May 1990 introduced a carbon tax as part of a systematic reform of energy taxation to take account of various forms of polluting emissions. A carbon tax amounting to SKr 0.25 per kg of carbon dioxide was introduced on 1 January 1991, levied on oil, coal, natural gas and liquid petroleum gas and petrol, at the following rates: SKr 720/m^3 on oil products, SKr 620/tonne of coal, SKr 535/1000 m^3 of natural gas and SKR 750/tonne of liquified petroleum gas. This tax was also imposed on domestic air traffic, at a rate of SKr 0.79 per kg of fuel consumed plus a tax calculated at the rate of SKr 12 per kg of hydrocarbons and nitrogen oxides assumed to be emitted. Since 1991, sulphur in diesel and heating oils, coal and peat is also subject to a tax amounting for coal and peat to 30 SKr/kg of sulphur, and for oil products to SKr 27 for each tenth of a per cent by weight of the sulphur content. If sulphur emission control measures are applied, all or part of the tax can be refunded. Anticipated revenues in fiscal year 1993-94 were some SKr 230 million. The same rates will also apply in 1995.

Tax Rates on Fuels and Electricity: Sweden[a,b]

Fuels	Unit	Energy Tax			Carbon dioxide Tax		
		1993	1994	1995	1993	1994	1995
Unleaded Petrol[c]	SKr/litre	3.14	3.14	3.22	0.74	0.77	0.79
Leaded Petrol	SKr/litre	3.65	3.65	3.81	0.74	0.77	0.79
Diesel Oil[d,e] used as propellant							
class 1	SKr/litre	1.31	1.31(1.41)	1.42	0.92	0.96	0.98
class 2	SKr/litre	1.59	1.60	1.64	0.92	0.96	0.98
class 3	SKr/litre	1.84	1.86	1.91	0.92	0.96	0.98
Light and Heavy Fuel Oil[e]	SKr/m³	540	562	577	920	957	982
Coal	SKr/tonne	230	239	245	800	832	854
Natural Gas[g]	SKr/1000m	175	182	187	680	707	725
LPG[g]	SKr/tonne	105	109	112	960	998	1024
Consumption tax on Electricity[h]	SKr/kWh	8.5	8.8	9.0	0	0	0
Biomass	SKr/tonne	0	0	0	0	0	0
Biofuels[i]							
- pure ethanol and vegetable oils	SKr/litre	0	0	0	0	0	0
- ethanol and methanol used in mixtures with other fuel components	SKr/litre	0.80	0.80	0.82	0	0	0

Notes:
a) The excise rates do not include the sulphur tax.
b) Sweden applies reduced excise rates on fuels and electricity consumed by manufacturing industry. No energy tax is paid on such consumption, but only 25% of the carbon dioxide tax. The reduced tax rates do not apply to fuels used for propulsion of cars, lorries and buses.
c) As from 1 December 1994, Sweden applies a differentiated energy tax on unleaded petrol based on the environmental quality of the products (based on the sulphur-, lead-, benzene-, and phosphorous contents and vapour pressure).
The tax rate for class 2 is SKr 3.14 per litre (in 1995 3.22/litre) and for class 3 SKr 3.20 per litre (1995 3.28/litre) Class 1 is reserved for future more environmental friendly petrol.
d) As of 1 October 1993, the mileage tax is replaced by a special tax on diesel oil used as a propellant. The mileage tax was based on the type of vehicle and the weight of the vehicle. The special tax on diesel is included in the energy tax presented.
e) From 1 January 1991 until 1 July 1994 three different rates of energy tax applied on oil products based on the environmental quality of the products. As from 1 July 1994 the differentiation has been shifted from the energy tax to an equal differentiation of the special tax on diesel. On 1 July 1994 the diesel tax on class 1 fuel was increased by SKr 0.1 per litre.
f) As from 1 January 1995, natural gas used as a propellant is taxed with an energy tax of SKr 1 498/1000 m³.
g) On LPG used as a propellant the following taxes are levied (energy tax = E, CO$_2$-tax = C)
In 1993 E=SKr 0.85/litre, C=0.48/litre. In 1994 E=0.88/litre and C=0.50/litre. In 1995 E=0.90/litre and C=0.51/litre.
h) Reduced rates applies when consumed for electricity-, gas-, water-, or heating supplies and when consumed in certain areas, mainly in the northern parts of Sweden. Electricity consumed by manufacturing industry are exempt. There are also two additional taxes on electricity which apply to the production of electricity in nuclear plants (SKr 0.002 per KWh) and power stations built before 1977 (SKr 0.02 if built before 1973 and SKr 0.01 if built between 1973 and 1977). These taxes are paid by the producer and are not refunded to the manufacturing industry.
i) As from 1 January 1995, biofuels are taxed with the same rates as diesel or petrol. But the government allows the above listed reduced excise rates for ethanol, methanol and vegetable oils used in pilot projects.

Sweden introduced a new energy and carbon tax system at the beginning of 1993. The carbon dioxide tax for manufacturing industry and commercial agriculture was reduced to 25% of the general level. At the same time, the energy tax on fuels and electricity was abolished for manufacturing and commercial horticulture. The new system replaced the previous system of energy and carbon dioxide tax reduction for energy intensive industry and commercial horticulture. Transitional regulation applied for the industry during 1993-1994, thus regulations limit the amount of carbon dioxide tax for the industry to 1.2% of the sale value of their manufactured products. Transitional regulations apply for commercial horticulture during 1993-95. The revenue effect of the abolished energy tax and the reduced carbon dioxide tax for industry was balanced by an increase of the carbon dioxide tax, from SKr 0.25 to SKr 0.32 per kg of CO_2, for non industrial consumers, as well as an increase of energy tax on electricity for non-industrial consumers.

On 1 January 1994, the carbon dioxide tax (among other indirect taxes) was increased by 4 percent. Total revenue from excises on fossil fuels (including petrol) and electricity for fiscal years 1993/94 was SKr 38.7 billion. The carbon dioxide tax raised 11.3 billion for the period.

Fossil fuels are also submitted to the Value Added Tax at a rate of 25 percent. From the start of 1992 a direct charge of SKr 40 per kg of nitrogen oxide emissions was also levied from large furnaces with an annual production of at least 50 GWh. The revenues are to be redistributed to the furnaces on the basis of the amount of energy produced. As from 1996, the charge system will gradually apply to smaller plants with an energy production of 25-50 GWh/year. The extension is to be made in two steps. The first step is to be taken on 1 January 1996 when the charge threshold will be lowered from 50 GWh to 40 GWh. Finally, on 1 January 1997, the threshold will be reduced to 25 GWh.

As from 1 December 1994, Sweden applies two different rates on excise duty on unleaded petrol. The aim of this measure is to encourage a changeover to more environment-friendly petrol. The reduced rate for environmental class 2 is linked to established technical characteristics including e.g. sulphur, lead, benzene and phosphorus contents. The rate differs by some 0.6 SKr and amount of SKr 3.22 for class 2 and SKr 3.28 for class 3.

VIII. ENVIRONMENTAL TAXATION OF AGRICULTURAL INPUTS

Taxes on agricultural fertilisers and pesticides have been introduced (or are under consideration) in a number of OECD countries:

-- **Australia**: Most goods used in the course of a primary production business are exempt from wholesale sales tax. For example, a registered farmer could purchase goods such as pesticides and fertilizers free from sales tax. When these goods are acquired by non-exempt purchasers they are subject to sales tax at the general rate of 21 per cent. The aim of the exemptions for primary producers is to prevent the taxation of business inputs; similar exemptions apply to manufacturing and mining.

-- **Austria**: A fertilizer levy was introduced in 1986 at a low level, raising about Sch 1 billion in 1990 and 1991. Despite the low level, the levy has had a significant effect on fertiliser use.

-- **Belgium**: A tax on surplus manure (to finance the organisation "Mestbank" responsible for manure disposal) has been levied since 1991 by the Flemish Region. The charge consists of two components; a base charge levied on the nitrogen and phosphate content of surplus manure and a disposal charge based on the quantities disposed by "Mestbank" in each year. From 1995, some pesticides will be submitted to a tax levied by the federal government.

-- **Denmark**: The retail sale of pesticides sold in containers less than 1 kg or 1 litre is subject to a tax. The rate is 1/6 of the wholesale value including the tax but excluding the VAT. When the tax is paid in connection with imports, the rate is 20 per cent of the producer price. Pesticides sold in larger quantities than mentioned above are subject to a tax of 3 % of the wholesale price excluding discount and VAT. When the tax is paid in connection with imports the rate is 20 per cent of the producer price.

-- **Finland**: The fertilisers tax, based on the phosphorous and nitrogen content, was repealed as of June 1994. Finland still operates a pesticide registration and control fee.

-- In the **Netherlands** a surplus manure tax is levied on the production of animal manure. The amount of the tax is specified in terms of the weight of phosphate produced on the farm per hectare per year. Farms producing less than 125 kg per hectare per year pay no tax. For farms producing between 125 and 200 kg per hectare per year, the rate of tax is Gld 0.25 per kg, and for farms producing in excess of 200 kg per hectare per year the tax rate is Gld 0.50 per kg. Total revenues amount to about Gld 35 million.

-- **Norway**: has levied both a fertilizer tax and a pesticides tax since 1988. The fertilizer tax is paid by the wholesalers. The tax rates are calculated on a quantitative basis: the rates in 1994 are NKr 1.21 per kg content of nitrogen and NKr 2.30 per kg content of phosphorus. These rates were increased substantially the first years, but have been less than price-adjusted since 1991. The tax amounts to approximately 20 per cent of the product price, but this depends on the nitrogen content in each type of fertilizer. The expected revenue from the environmental tax on fertilizers in 1994 is NKr 165 million. The pesticides tax is paid by the pesticide importers. The tax rate is 13 per cent of the wholesale price, and the expected revenue in 1994 is NKr 22 million. It comes in addition to a 6 per cent control charge on pesticides, which finances control and approval of pesticides.

-- **Sweden**: A fertilizer charge has been levied since 1984. As from November 1994, the rate is SKr 1.60 per kg of nitrogen and SKr 30 per gram of cadmium if the cadmium content is more than 5 gram per tonne of phosphorous. A pesticide charge is levied at SKr 20 per kg of active substance.

IX. TAXATION OF OTHER GOODS AND SERVICES

Considerable scope exists within multiple-rate systems of VAT or other sales taxes for the re-classification of goods for environmental purposes, subjecting environmentally-damaging goods and services to higher tax rates, and including goods and services which benefit the environment amongst those taxed at lower rates. It is, of course, difficult to distinguish environmental from non-environmental reasons for the classification of services in particular tax brackets. However, in the public debate about taxation, environmental motives have been occasionally advanced for particular indirect tax structures. In the Netherlands, for example, environmental groups have recently promoted the differentiation of VAT, currently at 6 and 17.5 per cent, according to the environmental characteristics of products. A low VAT tariff on repairs and a high tariff on consumer durables would aim to extend the economic life of durables and stimulate repairs.

Product taxes specifically introduced with environmental objectives are described in Table 8. They include taxes on the following goods:

-- *Batteries*: in Sweden environmentally-harmful batteries are taxed more heavily. A charge on new lead-acid batteries is also levied in certain parts of Canada. In Belgium, a new tax on batteries will come into force on 1 July 1995.

-- *Plastic carrier bags*: in Italy and Denmark (also on paper bags).

-- *Drinks sold in disposable containers*: bear environmental taxes in Belgium (Since 1 April 1994, the rate is BF 15/l, for beer and soft drinks only if the disposable containers are not reusable, or if an annually increasing per cent of them is not being recycled, or if they are not submitted to a deposit-refund system), Denmark (DKr 0.5 to 2.25 per container), Finland (soft drinks, beer and other alcohol beverages in 1995; disposable containers Mk 4/litre, return/refilling exempt; return from material Mk 1/litre), and certain parts of Canada (US$0.05 to US$0.10 for alcohol beverage containers). In some countries, taxes on disposable drinks containers are refundable if the container is recycled.

-- *Pesticides in small quantities*: (i.e. for retail sale) are taxed in Denmark at 20 per cent of the producer price.

-- *Tires*: new tires bear environmental charges in certain parts of Canada.

-- *CFCs and/or halons*: are subject to environmental taxes in Denmark and the United States.

-- *Disposable razors*: are being taxed in Belgium since 31 January 1994 at a rate of BF 10.

-- *Disposable cameras*: are taxed in Belgium since 1 July 1994 at a rate of BF 300, unless they are recycled.

X. ENVIRONMENTAL PROVISION IN DIRECT TAXATION

Evidence on the extent to which the direct tax systems of OECD countries have been employed for environmental purposes is summarised in Table 9. In principle, the system of corporate taxation would provide scope for incentives to encourage investments in cleaner technologies, and the replacement of older, more-polluting, capital equipment. Such incentives would move in the opposite direction to the trend to limit the scope for special deductions and allowances that has been a common feature of tax reforms during the 1980s.

XI. LANDING CHARGES AND OTHER TAXATION OF AIR TRANSPORT

Table 10 summarises information provided in the questionnaire replies about the extent of landing charges and other taxes on aviation with an environmental impact. Where airports are in public ownership a particular difficulty is encountered in identifying the borderline between fiscal measures such as taxes, and non-fiscal measures, such as the charges levied by airports for services provided. In some cases, where the charges are applied only to certain airports where noise disturbance is a particular problem, the matter is clear. Where charges apply more generally, it may be difficult to separate charges for services from the fiscal element.

XII. WATER CHARGES AND TAXES

Similar difficulties are encountered in determining whether charges made for the provision of water to domestic and industrial consumers and for water-borne waste disposal services have a fiscal character, or are to be regarded as charges related to the cost of providing the relevant service. In the replies to the questionnaire, comprehensive details were provided of water and water services charges by two countries, France and the Netherlands, and a number of other countries mentioned similar issues.

France

A "water resource charge" in the form of a flat rate per cubic metre has been levied since 1966 by local water basins on water extraction and consumption, and on modifications to the basin structure. The applicability of the charge varies amongst basins but is equal within each basin. The amount of the charge depends on the type of water extracted (surface or ground), and on the particular risks of each geographic zone.

In addition, a "water pollution charge" has been levied since 1968 on domestic and non-domestic water discharges. The charge is based on location within regional water basins, and is calculated on different bases for water pollution from domestic and non-domestic sources.

-- **Non domestic**: the substances covered by the charge are specified in a list. The charge applies to private and public sources discharging at least the equivalent of a population of 200. If users are connected to the public sewerage system the charge applies only to sources which exceed 6 000 cubic metres per annum. Each emissions source is assessed individually and allocated an emissions class. The charge is then calculated on the basis of the emissions class and level of activity of the individual source ie the maximum normal daily discharge per month. End-of-pipe measurement can also be used either by demand from the basin authority or the user.

-- **Domestic**: the charge applies to all municipalities with more than 400 inhabitants, and, unlike the non-domestic charge, applies even if discharge is below 6 000 cubic metres per annum. The charge is levied as a surcharge on the price per cubic metre of water distributed. The exact level is calculated by the municipality, based on:

i) daily discharge per inhabitant fixed for five years;

ii) the number of inhabitants (seasonal inhabitants are weighted with a factor of 0.4);

iii) an agglomeration factor increasing as a function of the discharge per municipality. The rate varies according to a coefficient reflecting the constraints of collecting the effluent.

Total revenue from the water resource charge and the water pollution charge together amounted to FF 6.5 billion in 1993 and 8.0 billion in 1994.

Netherlands

In the Netherlands a "ground water charge" has been levied since 1983 by the provinces on ground water extraction. The rate is approximately Gld 0.01 per cubic metre of extracted water. Total revenue is about Gld 10 million which is spent on ground water research and damages. Since 1995, there is also a tax on ground water levied by the central government. The rates are Gld 0.34 per cubic metre for the water companies and Gld 0.17 per cubic metres for the other industries. The revenue is estimated at Gld 310 million in 1995. The 1991 tariffs for drinking water used by households were:

- made with ground water : Gld 1.60 per m^3
- made with infiltration water : Gld 2.35 per m^3
- made with surface water : Gld 2.69 per m^3

Also, a "surface water pollution tax" has been levied since 1969. It applies to firstly, the pollution of state waters (state tax), secondly, the pollution of non-state waters (local tax), and, thirdly, the contribution in respect of direct or indirect connection to a purification plant operated by a public body not pursuing an active form of water quality management (local tax).

The rate is determined by the quantity and/or nature of the waste matter, pollutants or noxious matter and the manner in which they are discharged. If the discharged matter combines with oxygen, the criterion is daily surface water discharge expressed in inhabitant equivalents (the average quantity of oxygen-using material which is discharged into surface water per inhabitant per 24-hour period). If the matter does not combine with oxygen (i.e. heavy metals or phosphate), the criterion is the number of units of weight released per unit of time (24-hour period, year) into surface water or a purification plant, expressed in pollution units. The charge is levied on enterprises according to size in inhabitant equivalents (i.e.). Different rates apply to small enterprises with discharges below 3 i.e., and medium enterprises with discharges between 3 and 1,000 i.e. For large enterprises the tax is paid on the basis of end-of-pipe measurement. In addition to enterprises the charge is also levied on households.

The rate is determined by the cost of the measures to counter and prevent pollution of surface waters. In the case of the state tax the rates applicable for 1994 is Gld 55 per i.e. For discharges on state waters out of purification plant managed by a water board this rate is reduced to 8%. In case of local taxes, rates in 1994 vary from Gld 54.60 to Gld 129 per i.e. Aggregate revenues are Gld 28 million for the state tax, and Gld 1,629 million for the local tax.

Other similar taxes and charges mentioned in the questionnaire replies included:

-- In **Australia**, the state of New South Wales has levied an environment levy since 1989-90 on Water Board customers. The rates applied are A$ 80 for water and sewage facilities, and A$ 25 per annum for water facilities only. The levy is expected to raise a total revenue of some A$ 440 million, earmarked for a programme of environmental policy measures. This environmental levy was limited to five years and so has ceased on 1 January 1994.

-- In **Belgium**, the Flemish and Wallonne Regions have introduced in 1990 taxes on withdrawal and water pollution.

-- In **Denmark**, within the framework of the tax reform, a tax on water distributed in pipelines was introduced. The water tax is payable on groundwater and surface water and is introduced gradually from 1994-1998. The rate in 1994 is DKr 1 per cubic metre (exclusive VAT) but will in 1998 reach a level of DKr 5 per cubic metre (exclusive VAT). Only the Household sector is paying this new tax, such that agriculture and industry sectors are exempted. A tax on waste water is considered for introduction in 1997. Furthermore municipal charges on sewage exist.

-- In **Finland** there is a municipal water charge and a waste water charge. In addition, the State levies a water protection charge and a fish management charge. The water protection charge is imposed on heavy polluters and is earmarked for water protection activities of the State. The revenue from this charge was Mk 2,3 million in 1993 and is Mk 2,2 million in 1994 (estimation). The fish management charge is imposed on polluters and builders in the watercourse and is earmarked for financing the costs incurred by the State in order to preserve the stock of fish. The revenue from this charge was Mk 3,6 million in 1993 and is Mk 3,5 million in 1994.

-- In **Ireland** a water supply charge and a sewage disposal charge are levied by local authorities. Charges are also made on licences for water emissions.

-- In **Germany**, a waste water charge has been levied nation-wide since 1981. The charge is levied on the direct discharge of waste water into water bodies (direct discharges) rather than the discharge into waste water facilities (indirect discharges). The operators of the waste water treatment plants, who are liable to pay the charge, apportion the related costs to the users served by the system.

The waste water charge depends on the noxiousness of the waste water, which, as a rule, is determined on the basis of a number of parameters (oxydisable substances, organohalogens, metals, toxicity to fish, and, since 1991, phosphorus and nitrogen). Based on an assessment system specified by law, the noxiousness determined for each parameter is expressed in units of noxiousness. The number of units of noxiousness is, as a rule, determined by the official notice in which the discharge is authorised and in which the values to be complied with according to the provisions of water legislation are specified, as well as by the annual volume of waste water. If the values are not complied with, the charge will be increased accordingly. The rate of charge per unit of noxiousness has been regularly and gradually increased since

1981: it was DM 12 in 1981 and was gradually raised to DM 60 in 1993 and will rise to DM 70 from 1 January 1997.

To induce dischargers to comply with the standards of generally acknowledged rules of technology, or with the state-of-the-art standards in the case of hazardous substances, well before the date specified in the law, the rate of charge is decreased by 75 per cent. The rate will be decreased by 50 per cent in 1999 if the administrative provisions on waste water have been fully complied with. The charge may be offset against investment made in water protection measures. Therefore, the charge should be regarded as a means to ensure the use of modern technologies as early as possible. It has made a substantial contribution to a considerable reduction in emissions. The total income from the charge was DM 344 million in the assessment year 1991; DM 234 million of this sum was spent on water protection measures, while DM 62 million was spent on administrating the levy of the charge.

-- In **Turkey**, a water waste charge is applied to both households and non-households on their water consumption.

XIII. WASTE DISPOSAL AND MANAGEMENT CHARGES

Table 11 summarises information on fiscal or quasi-fiscal waste disposal and management charges levied by OECD countries. As with water charges, some of these measures can be seen as explicit or implicit payment for various services - the provision of rubbish dumps, insurance against future environmental hazards, and so on.

Notes

1. OCDE/GD(93)161

2. The survey also draws from the IEA quarterly publication "Energy Prices and Taxes" whenever data is missing from countries replies.

3. OECD (1994): Managing the environment: The Role Of Economic Instruments, OECD Paris, 1994.

4. Op. cit., OECD (1994).

5. OECD(1994): Revenue Statistics of OECD Member Countries - 1965-1993, OECD Paris, 1994.

6. *Economic Instruments and Disincentives to Sound Environmental Practices*, Final Report of the Task Force, November 1994, Canada.

7. *The Use of Economic Instruments in Nordic Environmental Policy*, TemaNord, 1994:561, Copenhagen, 1994. The Nordic Council of Ministers consists of Denmark, Finland, Iceland, Norway and Sweden. The Nordic Council promotes cooperation between the governments of its Member countries in a wide range of fields.

8. For VAT treatment of other energy sources including other petroleum products, electricity, and coal see the following Section V.

9. In the United States, the environmental damage taxes are the Superfund and Oil Spill taxes, which apply to crude oil and imported petroleum products in general.

10. The data is based on information contained in the IEA Quarterly Report, *Energy Prices and Taxes*, 1st quarter, 1994. Data on unleaded gasoline differs from the one presented in Table 2 in annex since prices and taxes in the figures are for premium unleaded gasoline (95 RON) instead of regular unleaded gasoline (92 RON).

11. The CO_2 tax on all fossil fuels is equivalent to SKr 0.333 per kg of CO_2.

12. New Zealand and Canada have a Goods and Services Tax, which is close to a VAT tax system; Switzerland has a turnover tax; and Japan has a general consumption tax.

13. Energy consumption in Switzerland is generally exempt from the turnover tax, with the exception of motor fuels (petrol and automotive diesels).

14. Since 1 January 1992.

TABLES

Table 1. **Rates of VAT or general consumption taxes levied on energy products in OECD countries in 1994**

Countries[a]	General Rate	Motor Fuels Households	Diesel Industrial[b]	Light fuel oil residential	Light fuel oil industrial[b]	Heavy Fuel Oil[b]	Applied to residential use only Gas	Electricity	Coal
Austria	20	20	0	20	0	0	20	0	20
Belgium[f]	20.5	20.5	0	20.5	0	0	20.5	20.5	12
Canada[c]	7	7	0	7	0	0	7	7	7
Denmark	25	25	0	25	0	0	25	25	0
Finland	22	22	22	22	0	0	22	22	22
France	18.6	18.6	0	18.6	0	0	18.6	18.6	18.6
Germany	15	15	0	15	0	0	15	15	15
Greece	18	18	0	18	0	0	0	18	0
Iceland	24.5	24.5	0	24.5	0	0	0	24.5	0
Ireland	12.5	21	0	12.5	0	0	12.5	12.5	12.5
Italy	19	19	0	19	0	0	9	9	9
Japan	3	3	3	3	3	3	3	3	3
Luxembourg[d]	15	15[d]	0	12	0	0	15	15	0
Mexico	10	10	0	10	0	0	10	10	10
Netherlands	17.5	17.5	0	17.5	0	0	17.5	17.5	17.5
New Zealand	12.5	12.5	0	12.5	0	0	12.5[e]	12.5[e]	12.5[e]
Norway[f]	22	22	0	22	0	0	22	20[g]	22
Portugal[f]	5	16	5[h]	5[h]	5[h]	5	5	5	16
Spain[f]	15	15	0	15	0	0	15	15	15
Sweden	25	25	0	25	0	0	25	25	25
Switzerland[f]	5.84	6.2	6.2	0	0	0	0	0	0
Turkey[f,i]	15	15	0	15	0	0	8[i]	15[i]	15[i]
United Kingdom	17.5	17.5	0	8[i]	0	0	8	8	8

Notes:
a) Australia and the United States are the only countries that do not have a VAT, general consumption tax or turnover tax.

b) 70-80 per cent of total automotive diesel oil is sold to industry and commerce, and the VAT paid by industry is usually 100 per cent refunded in most countries.

c) Canadian provinces impose either a GST or a retail tax in addition to the federal GST.

46

d) Luxembourg applies a different VAT rate on leaded and unleaded gasoline, with unleaded facing a rate of 12 percent since 1 January 1993.

e) Applies to New Zealand industry as well.

f) The VAT rates were increased on 1 January 1995 in Norway, Portugal, Spain and Switzerland to 23%, 17%, 16% and 6.5% respectively. Belgium and Turkey had both increased the VAT in 1994 from 19.5 to 20.5 percent in Belgium, and from 13 to 15 percent in Turkey.

g) This is a national average rate: general taxes for household rates vary between regions and over time in Norway.

h) Since 24 March 1992, in Portugal, VAT (5%) is 100% reimbursed only for heavy passenger vehicles, for public transport (except rent-a-car), diesel oil for machines (non matriculated vehicles) and for agriculture tractors; for the other purposes, it is 50% reimbursed.

i) VAT rates vary in Turkey according to the product:

The general rate:
29 February 1992 - 31 October 1993: 13%
1 November 1993 to present: 15%

Gas:
1 January 1991 - 30 October 1993: 6%
1 November 1993 to present: 8%

Electricity:
1 December 1990 - 30 October 1993: 12%
1 November 1993 to present: 15%

Steam coal:
1 January 1992 - 30 October 1993: 12%
1 November 1993 to present: 15%

j) Prior to 1 April 1994, light fuel oil for households was exempt from VAT in the United Kingdom.

Source: Energy Prices and Taxes, First Quarter, 1994, IEA/OECD, 1994.

47

Table 2. Total taxes as per cent of end-user price for automotive fuels

	1990		1991		1992		1993		1994	
	Gasoline[a] households	Diesel industrial	Gasoline[a] households	Diesel industrial	Gasoline[a] households	Diesel industrial	Gasoline[a] households	Diesel industrial	Gasoline[a] households	Diesel industrial
Australia	44.9	52.7	46.8	48.8	46.2	47.7	49.1	50.3	n.a.	n.a.
Austria[a]	54.1	45.5	55.7	46.5	60.7	48.8	60.8	48.2	63.9	49.1
Belgium	65.5	46.8	66.6	46.3	70.0	54.0	71.8	54.9	74.2	57.3
Canada[a,b]	42.4	34.5	42.2	34.7	46.2	39.0	48.7	40.5	50.0	41.6
Denmark	69.1	0.0	67.8	20.9	67.2	39.7	64.6	40.2	68.0	41.5
Finland	55.2	50.2	61.2	51.7	68.0	53.7	71.8	54.9	n.a.	62.3
France	74.3	53.8	75.2	54.2	77.2	57.8	78.6	59.9	80.8	65.1
Germany	63.1	50.8	67.6	51.8	72.4	58.0	73.5	59.0	76.9	62.5
Greece	63.8	26.7	67.6	42.2	69.1	57.9	74.8	58.5	75.1	62.6
Iceland	67.7	19.7	67.1	19.7	69.6	19.7	65.4	19.7	n.a.	n.a.
Ireland	67.1	51.4	66.2	49.8	66.6	51.5	65.6	41.8	67.3	44.2
Italy	74.9	59.9	75.9	64.6	75.8	66.3	74.6	64.0	76.1	65.1
Japan[a]	45.6	35.1	46.3	36.0	47.6	35.5	48.2	37.1	n.a.	n.a.
Luxembourg	54.2	32.6	54.9	32.0	62.0	45.7	66.0	51.9	68.7	56.3
Mexico	n.a.	n.a.	12.5	0	9.1	0	9.1	0	9.1	0
Netherlands	64.5	43.3	68.1	45.9	72.4	49.6	72.5	54.2	75.9	59.7
New Zealand	45.7	29.7	45.4	11.8	46.6	11.8	46.5	11.8	48.0	11.9
Norway	62.9	15.1	68.1	24.3	71.4	22.6	72.1	31.0	67.3	46.0
Portugal	67.8	52.3	72.2	56.3	75.4	62.6	73.2	59.2	73.5	59.4
Spain	63.0	48.8	65.4	51.1	69.8	57.4	68.2	54.6	68.6	56.9
Sweden[c]	65.5	27.2	67.7	30.3	69.2	32.3	74.7	31.7	76.5	48.3
Switzerland	59.2	59.1	59.5	58.6	62.5	61.7	68.8	67.8	71.3	68.9
Turkey	52.9	50.3	59.6	53.5	63.7	56.0	64.5	57	66.2	58.6
United Kingdom	61.9	52.8	66.0	56.5	69.5	59.2	70.6	59.2	73.5	63.6
United States[a]	26.7	27.9	32.9	34.1	33.9	35.6	30.7	35.6	34.4	39.6

48

Notes:
a) Taxes as per cent of end-user prices are for premium leaded gasoline for all countries except Austria, Canada, Japan and the United States where it is no longer sold. Percentage for these countries are for regular unleaded gasoline (92 RON).

b) Commencing 1st January 1991, the Federal Government introduced a Goods and Services tax of 7 per cent. This replaced the Manufacturers' sales tax. Percentages are expressed in terms of prices excluding GST for diesel only - (as this is refunded to industrial/commercial uses).

c) There was also an additional mileage tax levied on vehicles that use diesel fuel. As from 1 October 1993 the mileage tax was replaced with a diesel tax levied on the fuel.

Source: Energy prices and taxes, Fourth Quarter, 1994, IEA/OECD 1994.

Table 3. Taxes on motor fuels

Country	Taxes	Leaded petrol (households)	Unleaded petrol (households)	Diesel fuel (industrial)	LPG, methane and other motor fuel
Australia (Cwealth)	Excise duty[b]	$A 0.29573/litre (0.2749)[a]	$0.29573/litre (0.2749)[a]	$A 0.29573/litre (0.2749)[a]	n.a.
(NSW)	Petroleum license fee	$A 0.0686/litre	$A0.0686/litre	$A0.069/litre (0.063)[a]	n.a.
(SA)		0.0911/litre	$A 0.0896/litre	$A 0.1023/litre	n.a.
Austria	Excise duty	Prohibited since 1 Nov 93, prev: Sch 6.43/litre	Sch 4.52/litre (4.01)	Sch 3.03/litre (3.03)	Sch 3.61/kg
	Special tax on fossil oil, payable on import and domestic production of crude oil, and import of oil products	Approx. Sch 0.1/litre (0.1)	Approx. Sch 0.1/litre (0.1)	Approx. Sch. 0.11/litre (0.11)	Approx. Sch 0.1/l (0.1)
	Emergency Stock fee	Sch 0.1/litre	Sch 0.1 litre	Sch 0.1/litre	
	VAT	20%	20%		20%
Belgium	Excise duty	BF 19.50/litre (18.44)[a]	BF 16.75/litre (15.51)[a]	BF 11.7/litre (11.331)[a]	Nil
	VAT	20.5%	20.5%		20.5%
Canada[c]	Excise tax	n.a.	(C$ 0.125/litre)	(C$ 0.04/litre)	--
	Goods and services tax	7%	7%		7%
Denmark	Excise duty	Dkr 2.66/litre (2.54)[a]	Dkr 2.45/litre (2.25)	Dkr 1.67/litre (1.67)	Dkr 1.24[d]
	Environment pool tax[e]	Dkr 0.4/litre	Dkr 0.4/litre	Dkr 0.27/litre	Dkr 0.16/litre
	VAT	25%	25%		25%

50

Country	Tax type				
Finland	Excise duty (basic rate)	Mk 2.81/litre (2.35)	Mk 2.31/litre (2.35)	Mk 1.10/litre (0.87)	0
	Carbon/Energy tax in 94 (Environmental damage tax in 93)	Mk 0.071/litre (0.5)	Mk 0.071/litre	Mk 0.078/litre (0.27)	0
	Precautionary stock fee	Mk 0.043/litre (0.043)	Mk 0.043/litre (0.043)	Mk 0.023/litre (0.023)	0
	Oil pollution fee	Mk 0.0017/litre (0.0017)	Mk 0.0017/litre (0.0017)	Mk 0.0018/litre (0.0018)	0
	VAT	22%	22%	22%	22%
France	Excise duty[f]	FF 3.647/litre	FF 3.307/litre	FF 2.11/litre	no information
	VAT	18.6%	18.6%		18.6%
Germany	Excise duty	DM 1.08/litre (0.92)	DM 0.98/litre (0.82)	DM 0.620[a]/litre (0.550)[a]	DM 0.31/litre
	Emergency Storage Fund	DM 0.0072/litre	DM 0.0072/litre	DM 0.0066/litre	
	VAT	15%	15%		15%
Greece	Excise duty	Drs 120/litre (120)	Drs 120/litre (120)	Drs 68/litre (68)	no information
	VAT	18%	18%		18%
Iceland	Excise duty	97% of c.i.f. value	97% of c.i.f. value		
	Special excise tax	IKr 24.99/litre	IKr 24.99/litre		
	VAT	24.5%	24.5%		
Ireland	Excise duty	Ir£ 0.299/litre (0.287)	Ir£ 0.273/litre (0.2614)	Ir£ 0.235/litre (0.223)	no information
	VAT	21%	21%		21%

(Table 3. Cont'd)

Country	Taxes	Leaded petrol (households)	Unleaded petrol (households)	Diesel fuel (industrial)	LPG, methane and other motor fuel
Italy	Excise duty	L 1019.05/litre (946.30)[a]	L 911.04/litre (856.69)[a]	L 676.04/litre (662)[a]	L 652.62/kg
	VAT	19%	19%		19% (LPG and nat. gas)
Japan	Petroleum tax	Y 2.04 per l of crude oil	Y 2.04 per l of crude oil	Y 2.04 per l of crude oil	Y 670 per tonne of LPG[d]
	Gasoline (petrol) tax	Y 48.6 per litre	Y 48.6 per litre		
	Local road tax	Y 5.2 per litre	Y 5.2 per litre		
	Light oil (diesel) delivery tax			Y 32.1 per litre	
	LPG tax				Y 17.5 per kg[d]
	Consumption tax	3%	3%	3%	3%
Luxembourg	Excise tax	Luxfr 14.36/litre (13.87)[a]	Luxfr 12.26/litre (11.50)[a]	Luxfr 9.50/litre (8.727)[a]	no information
	VAT	15%	12%		
Mexico[g]	Excise tax	191.76%-142.15%	163.74%-96.79%	92.93%-80.04%	
	VAT	10%	10%		10%
Netherlands	Excise duty	Gld 1.21930 per l (1.14719)[a]	Gld 1.08150 per l (1.007)[a]	Gld 0.6352/l (0.593)[a]	Gld 78.72 per tonne (LPG only)
	Environment fuel tax	Gld 0.0251 per kl	Gld 0.0751 per l	Gld 0.0277 per l	Gld 33.08 per tonne
	VAT	17.5%	17.5%		17.5%

Country	Tax				
New-Zealand	Land transport fund	NZ$ 0.094/l (0.0825)[a]	NZ$ 0.094/l (0.0825)[a]		
	Consolidated Fund	0.208 (0.22)[a]	0.208 (0.22)[a]		
	Lead taxes	NZ$ 0.021/l (0.0245)[a]			
	Petroleum Market Monitoring levy	NZ$ 0.00025/l (0.00025)	NZ$ 0.00025/l (0.00025)	NZ$ 0.00025/l (0.00025)	
	Local taxes	NZ$ 0.0066/l (0.0066)	NZ£ 0.0066/l (0.0066)	0.0033/l (0.0033)	
	GST	12.5%	12.5%	12.5%	12.5%
Norway[h]	Excise duty	Nkr 3.78/litre (3.72)	Nkr 3.12/litre (3.07)	Nkr 2.45/litre (2.25)[a]	0
	CO_2 tax	Nkr 0.82/litre (0.80)	Nkr 0.82/litre (0.80)	Nkr 0.41/litre (0.40)	0
	Sulphur tax			Nkr 0.07/litre	
	VAT	22%	22%		22%
Portugal[i]	Excise duty	Esc 92/litre	Esc 85/litre	Esc 58/litre	Esc 7.5/kg (fuel oil)
	VAT	16%	16%	5%	5%
Spain	Excise duty	Pta 60.5/litre (57.5)[a]	Pta 55.5/litre (52.6)[a]	Pta 40.3/litre (38.5)[a]	Pta 118.8 per ton of LPG used as motor fuel Pta 1 100 per ton of LPG used for heating purposes
	VAT	15%	15%	15%	15%

(Table 3. Cont'd.)

Country	Taxes	Leaded petrol (households)	Unleaded petrol (households)	Diesel fuel (industrial)	LPG, methane and other motor fuel
Sweden[j]	CO_2 tax	SK 0.77/litre (0.74)	SK 0.77/litre (0.74)	SK 0.957/litre (0.920)	SK 0.50/litre (LPG) (0.49)
	Petrol tax[j]	SK 3.650/litre (3.650)	SK 3.140/litre (3.140)		SK 0.80/litre (methanol) (0.80) SK 0.80/litre (Ethanol)[k] (0.80)
	Energy tax[j]			Standard: SK 0.562/l (0.540) Light: SK 0.302/l (0.290) Urban area: SK 0.005/l (0.090) (levied on sulphur and HC content)	SK 0.88/l (LPG) (0.85)
	Sulphur tax [only levied on oil that contains more than 0.1% sulphur by weight]			SK 27/m³ for each 0.1% content by weight	
	Diesel tax[l]			SK 1.3 per litre	
	VAT	25%	25%		25%
Switzer- land	Excise tax	FS 0.8/l (0.745)[a]	FS 0.719/l (0.669)[a]	FS 0.759/l (0.7327)[a]	no information
	Emergency fund	FS 0.0177/l (0.0185)	FS 0.0177/l (0.0185)	FS 0.0115/l (0.0129/l)	no information
	Turnover tax	6.2% (retail)	6.2% (retail)	6.2% (retail) 9.3%(whlsale)	6.2% (retail)

Turkey	Liquid fuels consumption tax (introduced in 1984)	(TL 3893/l)[p]	(TL 3790/l)[p]	(TL 2000/l)[p]	n.a.
	VAT and other ad valorum taxes/duties are also levied	15%	15%	15%	15%
United Kingdom	Excise duty	33.14 pence/litre (29.9)[a]	28.32 pence/litre (25.4)[a]	27.7 pence/litre (24.8)[a]	12.93 pence/litre[d]
	VAT	17.5%	17.5%	17.5%	17.5%
United States[m]	Federal motor fuels[n,o]:				
	Highway motor fuels	$0.184/gallon	$0.184/gallon	$0.244/gallon	$0.184/gallon[p]
	Non-commercial aviation	$0.194/gallon	$0.194/gallon	n.a.	$0.194/gallon
	Recreational motor boats	$0.184/gallon	$0.184/gallon	$0.244/gallon	$0.184/gallon[p]
	Outdoor power equipment	$0.184/gallon	$0.184/gallon	n.a.	$0.184/gallon
	Inland waterway transportation	$0.234/gallon	$0.234/gallon	$0.234/gallon	$0.234/gallon
	Rail transportation	n.a.	n.a.	$0.069/gallon	n.a.
	State motor fuels tax (median as of 12/93)	$0.190/gallon	$0.190/gallon	$0.185/gallon	n.a.

Notes:

a) If there is a footnote [a], it is an average value. Otherwise, it is the value at 1 January 1994. Values in parentheses are for 1993. The VAT rate does not appear if the VAT payments are eventually reimbursed to the firms.

b) As of 1 February 1994, leaded and unleaded gasoline do not have the same excise rates in Australia: they are respectively 0.31750 and 0.30750 up until 31 July 1994, and $A0.34099/litre and $A0.320088/litre; and the diesel fuel, on the same date, was increased to 0.30750 per litre.

c) In Canada, leaded gasoline has been phased out. Federal excise taxes on motive fuels do not apply to propane or compressed natural gas used as motive fuel. Also, these taxes do not apply to ethanol or methanol when these fuels are the main component of a motive fuel. In the case of fuels that have gasoline as their main component, the excise tax is not applied to the ethanol or methanol portions of blended fuels, provided the ethanol or methanol is produced from biomass or renewable feedstocks. Provinces also levy taxes on motor fuels that range from C$0.09 to C$0.157 per litre. Several provinces have exemptions or lower tax rates for certain alternative fuels, such as methanol and ethanol.

d) Values are for 1991 - Denmark, Japan.

e) In May 1992, a CO_2 tax of 100 DKK (overall rate) per tonne of CO_2 was introduced on private energy consumption in Denmark. It includes all types of CO_2 emissions sources in Denmark except gasoline. In January 1993, a CO_2 tax of 50 DKK per tonne was levied on VAT registered companies.

f) Estimated calculations based on prices and taxes in France as expressed in IEA publication.

(*Notes* to table 3. *cont'd.*)

g) Motor fuels in Mexico have an established public price. The excise tax is a variable rate calculated as the difference between the cost which is the result of adding to the reference oil price on the Houston spot market, the freight, and applying commissions, a quality adjustment and the established public price. The figures showed are the values for January and June 1994 respectively.

h) The sulphur tax rate in Norway is 0.07 Nkr per 0.25% of SO_2 content.

i) Values for Portugal are for 1994.

j) As of 1.1.1993, the energy tax on diesel in Sweden is differentiated by classes with regard to environmental effects, while the CO_2 tax is levied at a constant rate. Since 1 December 1994, the gasoline tax in Sweden is also differentiated by classes with regard to environmental effects.

k) If fuel content is 100% ethanol, then there is no tax in Sweden.

l) The diesel special tax replaced the mileage tax as of 1 October 1993 in Sweden.

m) Although the federal government in the U.S. does not impose different rates of tax on leaded and unleaded gasoline, it imposes certain restrictions on the use of leaded gasoline. It required all new cars to have catalytic converters after 1974 and is scheduled to ban the use of leaded gasoline after 1995.

n) The federal motor fuels excise tax rates include the $0.001 per gallon leaking Underground Storage Tank Trust Fund Tax.

o) A non-refundable credit is allowed for ethanol used as a fuel if the equivalent partial exemption from the motor fuels tax is not used. The credit is generally $0.54 per gallon, but is $0.64 per gallon for a limited amount of production by some small producers.

p) A tax is imposed on compressed natural gas that is sold for use as a fuel in a motor vehicle or motor boats. The rate of tax is $0.4854 per thousand cubic meter.

Table 4. **Taxes on sale, registration and use of motor vehicles**

	One-off taxes on sale or initial registration of motor vehicles	**Annual or recurrent taxes on registration or use of motor vehicles**
Australia	The Commonwealth levies **wholesales sales tax** at 16 per cent on passenger motor vehicles whose wholesale value is less than A$ 32 486; 21 per cent on trucks and four wheel drive vehicles; and a split rate of 16/45 per cent on motor vehicles whose wholesale value exceeds A$ 32 486 (the 45 per cent rate applies to the wholesale value exceeding this threshold). Imported passenger motor vehicles currently attract **import duty** at the rate of 30 per cent.	The States and Territories levy fees for annual registration, third party compulsory insurance and driver's licenses. Fees for commercial vehicles are generally higher than the fees for private vehicles. For example, in Victoria the annual registration fee for a private vehicle in the metropolitan area is A$ 420.50, as well as a Transport Accident Charge of A$ 280.50. In most States, fees for trucks vary depending on power-mass ratios.
Austria	**Investment allowance of 20 per cent,** applicable to investments in noise-reduced trucks. The higher VAT rate (32 per cent) was replaced by a standard rate of 20 per cent; VAT for electric vehicles: 10 per cent. A new Car Registration Tax was introduced on 1st January 1992. While the tax base is the selling price, the tax rate depends on the standard fuel consumption of the car.	**Motor Vehicle Tax** based on the engine power of passenger cars, on cylinder volume for passenger cars (tax differentiation between catalyst and non-catalyst cars), on loading capacity for trucks, and on net weight for buses. **Road Transport duty** levied on lorries and trailers. Fla-rate monthly charge, in two payload bands. For lorries below 8 tonnes, the charge is Sch 150 per month; above 8 tonnes Sch 300. For trailers below 8 tonnes, Sch 130 per month; above 8 tonnes, Sch 260. Foreign vehicles are taxed at Sch 0.35 per tonne.

(Table 4. Cont'd)

One-off taxes on sale or initial registration of motor vehicles	Annual or recurrent taxes on registration or use of motor vehicles

Belgium

VAT at 20.5 per cent
Motor vehicle registration charge of 2 500 BF since 1.7.1990.

Road tax levied on power (passenger transport vehicles) or weight (goods transport vehicles), adjusted annually on 1 July with CPI. Rates applicable in 1993 for cars:

4CV:BF 1 884	13CV:BF 14 352
5CV:BF 2 364	14CV:BF 16 608
6CV:BF 3 408	15CV:BF 18 864
7CV:BF 4 452	16CV:BF 24 708
8CV:BF 5 496	17CV:BF 30 552
9CV:BF 6 540	18CV:BF 36 396
10CV:BF 7 584	19CV:BF 42 240
11CV:BF 9 840	20CV:BF 48 072
12CV:BF 12 096	

For each additional CV + BF 2 628

Motor vehicle registration charge:

Capacity in litres	Horse power	KW	New & 6 month to <1 year	< 6 months	1 to < 2 years	2 to < 3 years	3 to < 4 years	4 to < 5 years	5 to < 6 years	6 to < 7 years	7 to < 8 years	8 to < 9 years	9 to < 10 years	10 & over
0.1 - 1.5	0 to 8	0 to 70	2 500	12 500	2 500	2 500	2 500	2 500	2 500	2 500	2 500	2 500	2 500	2 500
1.6 - 1.9	9 & 10	71 to 85	5 000	25 000	4 500	4 000	3 500	3 000	2 500	2 500	2 500	2 500	2 500	2 500
2.0 - 2.1	11	86 to 100	20 000	40 000	18 000	16 000	14 000	12 000	10 000	8 000	6 000	4 000	2 500	2 500
2.2 - 2.7	12 to 14	101 to 110	35 000	55 000	31 500	28 000	24 500	21 000	17 500	14 000	10 500	7 000	3 500	2 500
2.8 - 3.0	15	111 to 120	50 000	70 000	45 000	40 000	35 000	30 000	25 000	20 000	15 000	10 000	5 000	2 500
3.1 - 3.4	16 & 17	121 to 155	100 000	130 000	90 000	80 000	70 000	60 000	50 000	40 000	30 000	20 000	10 000	2 500
3.5 & +	18 & +	156 & +	200 000	230 000	180 000	160 000	140 000	120 000	100 000	80 000	60 000	40 000	20 000	2 500

Canada

Automotive air conditioner tax levied on vehicle air conditioners at C $ 100 per unit.

Vehicle excise tax levied on heavy automobiles (over 2 007 kg). Increasing scale, starting at C $ 30 per vehicle.

One province has a tax levied on the purchase of fuel inefficient passenger cars and sport utility vehicle. A subsidy of $ 100 is provided for cars with a highway fuel efficiency rating of less than 6 litres per 100 km.

Denmark

The Vehicle registration tax:

The registration tax is payable when the vehicle is registered with police for the first time. Different rates are used for motor vehicles destined for different purposes. Generally, the rate is higher for private vehicles than for cars used for commercial purposes.

For example:

    Private cars of value:
    - less than or equal to 34.400 Dkr: 105%
    - more than 34.400 Dkr:
        on the first 34.400: 36.120 Dkr
        on the remainder: 180%
    Taxis of value:
    - less than or equal to 6.100 DKr: 0%
    - more than 6.100 DKr:
        on the first 6.100 DKr: 0%
        on the remainder: 20%

All provinces impose annual fees for the registration or use of motor vehicles. In general, the fees depend on the type of vehicles and in most cases on the weight of the vehicle.

The weight tax:

For this tax, the base of taxation of private cars is the dead weight of the car. For a private car with a dead weight between 801 and 1.100 kg the tax amounts to 2.260 Dkr per year.

For lorries and trailers the basis of assessment is the permitted total weight of the vehicle. For an articulated vehicle with 5 axels and a permitted total weight of 40 (16 + 24) tonnes the tax amounts to 8.800 Dkr.

(Table 4. Cont'd)

	One-off taxes on sale or initial registration of motor vehicles	Annual or recurrent taxes on registration or use of motor vehicles
Finland	**Value added tax** **Vehicle excise tax**: the amount of the tax for passengers-cars, delivery vans (see also below) and other motor-cars weighing less than 1 800 kg is the taxation value of the vehicle plus 2% less 4 600 FIM. For delivery vans designed exclusively for the transports of goods, the rate is 35% and for motor-cycles 20-70% of the taxable value, varying with the cylinder capacity. Cars with low emissions are allowed a special deduction of 4 500 FIM, which is deducted from the taxable value of the car.	**Annual tax on diesel-driven vehicles** levied on all vehicles using fuel other than petrol. Rates (examples): - passengers cars 150 FIM/100 kg of total weight - delivery vans 27 FIM/100 kg - lorries 27-63 FIM/100 kg **Annual tax on motor vehicles** levied on passenger cars and delivery vans: - 300 FIM/a for old vehicles (registr. before 1994) - 500 FIM/a for new vehicles New tax; levied as of 1-6-1994 **Road taxes** applicable to motor vehicles registered abroad **Fuel charge** to balance the difference between the taxes on diesel oil and the fuel used in the diesel motor vehicle New charge; levied as of 15-4-1993
Germany	Value Added Tax on acquisition:15% Tax on motoring: mineral oil tax + VAT on mineral oil tax Tax on insurance: 7% Registration charge: 35-50 DM	**Motor vehicle Tax** on vehicles licensed for use on public roads. Tax on cars is based on cylinder capacity; rates depend on date of registration, pollutant emission and type of engine: Annual tax rate per 100 cc cylinder capacity: DM 13.20 for low-pollutant cars; DM 18.80 for other petrol-engined cars, registered 1985 or earlier; DM 21.60 for other petrol-engined cars registered 1986 or later. Tax rates for diesel engined cars DM 23.90 (since 1-1-94) higher in each case. Tax on motorcycles DM 3.60 per 25 cc cylinder capacity. Tax on commercial vehicles based on maximum permissible weight. (Tax accounts for approx. 3 per cent of road haulage costs).

60

Greece[*]

Taxes on registration and use of motor vehicles:

Initial tax registration (Lump Sum Tax) levied on cars as below:

I.

Private passengers cars estimated on cubic capacity	Rate of Lump Sum Tax as per cent on taxable values
0 - 1 200	8%
1 201 - 1 800	12%
1 801 - and over	15%

II.   All the other cars are subjected to this lump sum tax equal to the corresponding road surtax as the case may be (since 1-1-1994).

[*] In Greece, a law introduced in March 1990 provided an exemption from the road surtax and the initial registration tax for a period of five calendar years, on the condition that his owner had already withdrawn from circulation and scrapped his old car.

Iceland

Value added tax (24.5%).

Vehicle registration fee of IKr 5 475 on initial registration, and IKr 2 300 for subsequent changes.

Motor vehicle excise duty, based on cylinder capacity (rate 30-75 %)

Weight-distance tax levied on non-petrol vehicles (non gasoline fuels, including diesel, are exempt from other taxes). For vehicles under 4 000 kg owners have the option of a flat annual rate ranging from IKr 96 000 to IKr 250 000 depending on the weight of the vehicle. Others are charged per kilometre driver with charges ranging from IKr 6.57 to IKr 25.16 per km, depending on the weight of the vehicle.

Annual Automobile Tax levied on weight, at IKr 4.22 per kg, with 50 per cent surcharge for vehicles above 1 000 kg. Minimum rate IKr 5 764; maximum rate IKr 36 432.

Inspection fee charged for annual inspection of vehicles over two years old. For vehicles under 5 000 kg, the charge is IKr 2480, and IKr 4950 for vehicles over 5 000 kg. An additional IKr 330 is charged for a mandatory emission test.

(Table 4. Cont'd)

	One-off taxes on sale or initial registration of motor vehicles	Annual or recurrent taxes on registration or use of motor vehicles
Ireland	**Value added tax (21%)** **Sales tax** based on retail price 20.7% for private vehicles below 2,012 cc; 24.7% above; 12.5% for commercial car drive and vans and 0.0% for other commercial vehicles.	**Road Tax** on private cars based on cylinder capacity: -1 000 cc a flat rate of IR£ 92 applies, 1 001 - 1 500 cc: IR£ 12.50 per 100 cc 1 501 - 1 700 cc: IR£ 14.50 per 100 cc 1 701 - 2 000 cc: IR£ 16.00 per 100 cc 2 001 - 2 500 cc: IR£ 19.50 per 100 cc Electrically propelled vehicles: IR£ 92 flat rate. 2 501 - 3 000 cc: IR£ 22.00 per 100 cc + 3 000 cc: IR£ 80.00 (flat rate) per 100 cc.
Italy	**Registration tax** on purchase of new and used vehicles, at a variety of rates depending on type and size of vehicle (eg: motorcycles, L 120 000 Cars from L 150 000; lorries with a load of 8 tonnes from L 170 000)(1993-94). **VAT at 19 per cent** **Car extra charge** for fuel motor vehicles over 21 CV powered measured in "fiscal CV" from L 5 000 000 to 12 000 000 (luxury good).	**Annual tax** on all motor vehicles and caravans. Levied in relation to cylinder volume (light motorcycles), power (motorcycles, cars, coaches), load (lorries and trailers) or lump sum (caravans). Power is measured in "fiscal CV" - an ad hoc unit based on cylinder volume. Further, different rates of tax apply to petrol and gas-oil motor vehicles. Tax rates are the sum of components for central and regional government; the latter can be varied within limits by the regional authority, and there is thus some regional variation in overall tax rates. Four wheels traction car extra charge from L 150 000 to 840 000.
Japan	**Consumption tax** at 3 per cent.	**Motor Vehicle Tonnage Tax** (national): Passenger vehicles Y 6 300 per 0.5 tonnes; Lorries and buses below 2.5 tonnes: Y 4 400 per tonne; Lorries and buses above 2.5 tonnes Y 6 300 per tonne; Light motor vehicles Y 4 400 per vehicle; The rate for commercial vehicles is Y 2 800 per tonne.

62

Automobile Acquisition Tax at 5 per cent of purchase price (3% for commercial vehicles).

Automobile Tax levied according to cylinder capacity. Rates applicable to non-commercial vehicles (commercial vehicles in brackets):

660 - 1 000 cc:	Y 29 500 (Y 7 500)
1 000 - 1 500 cc:	Y 34 500 (Y 8 500)
1 500 - 2 000 cc:	Y 39 500 (Y 9 500)
2 000 - 2 500 cc:	Y 45 000 (Y 13 800)
2 500 - 3 000 cc:	Y 51 000 (Y 15 700)
3 000 - 3 500 cc:	Y 58 000 (Y 17 900)
3 500 - 4 000 cc:	Y 66 500 (Y 20 500)
4 000 - 4 500 cc:	Y 76 500 (Y 23 600)
4 500 - 6 000 cc:	Y 88 000 (Y 27 200)
+ 6 000 cc:	Y 111 000(Y 40 700)

Lorries: (4-5 tonnes capacity): Y 25 500 (Y 18 500)
Buses: Y 49 000 (14 500)

Tax rate was halved in 1990 and 1991 to taxpayers replacing old trucks and buses with new ones conforming to 1988-1989 emissions standards.

Light vehicle tax (local) levied on motorcycles and light vehicles according to cylinder capacity.

Tax on property or use of motor vehicles levied on the value of motor vehicles up to 10 years old[*].

Type	Car Value (thousands of Nuevos pesos)	Rate
A	jusqu'à 147	2%
B	de 147 à 251	6.25%
C	au-dessus de 251	10%

The value of previous model-year vehicles is updated according to annuel changes on the National Consumer Price Index and a discount of 10% for each passed year is granted, so that vehicles older than 10 years do not pay the tax.
For vehicles imported in 1990 or fefore, tax rate is 1.75%.

[*] These rates are updated every quarter according to relative changes on the CPI. This table is valid for the last quarter of 1994.

Mexico

Tax on new motor vehicles levied on the value of the first sale, according to the following table:

Lower Limit (Nuevos Pesos)	Upper Limit (Nuevos Pesos)	Fix Payable Amount (Nuevos Pesos)	% rate Paid on the Difference between Sales Value and Lower Limit
0.01	39 440.05	0	2
39 440.06	47 328.05	788.80	5
47 328.06	55 216.08	1 183.20	10
55 216.09	70 992.05	1 972.00	15
70 992.06	ou plus	4 338.40	17

(Table 4. Cont'd)

	One-off taxes on sale or initial registration of motor vehicles	Annual or recurrent taxes on registration or use of motor vehicles
Netherlands	Value added tax at 17.5 per cent. **Sales Tax** levied on net value : Cars: 45.2 %, the resulting amount diminished with Gld 3.394 (petrol engine) or Gld 2 116 (diesel engine) Motorcycles: (A) for motorcycles with a net value not higher than Gld 4 700: 10.2% of the net value (B) for motorcycles with a net value higher than Gld 4 700: 20.7% of the net value, the resulting amount diminished with Gld 494.	**Vehicle excise duty** levied according to type, weight and fuel used.
Norway	**Import tax** levied on road motor vehicles (weight based component 50%). Electric vehicles exempt. Average import-tax is approx. NKr 70 000 per car. **License tax** levied on road motor vehicles assembled in Norway (weight based component 50%). Electric vehicles exempt. **Registration tax on vehicles** previously licensed in Norway.	**Vehicle excise duty** levied on weight, number of axles, vehicle type and fuel.
Portugal	**Value added tax at 16%** (since March 1992). **Vehicle excise duty** levied on cylinder capacity. Rates/cc (1994): -1000 cc: ESC 251/cc 1001-1250 cc: ESC 573/cc 1251-1500 cc: ESC 1 340/cc 1501-1750 cc: ESC 1 933/cc 1751-2000 cc: ESC 3 264/cc 2001-2500 cc: ESC 3 147/cc above 2500 cc: ESC 1 981/cc	**Municipal vehicle tax** levied on cars and motorcycles. Modified in 1994, the **Commercial driving tax** is levied according to the weight and manner in which vehicle is used.

Spain	**Motor vehicle tax.** (levied by municipalities) based on engine power for passenger cars, passenger capacity for buses, loading capacity for trucks and cylinder volume for motorcycles. **Vehicle registration tax** levied at 13% of the VAT tax base.
Sweden	**Vehicle excise duty** levied on weight, number of axles, vehicle type and fuel. **Sales tax levied on weight.** **Sales tax** levied on environmental qualxties from 1 July 1992 for vehicles of model year 1993 or later.
Switzerland	**Kilometre tax** levied on diesel passenger vehicles, lorries, buses and trailers (abolished 1 October 1993 and replaced by a special diesel tax on diesel fuel used in lorries, buses and cars). **Import tax** **Motor vehicle tax.**

Motorway tax if SF30 per year levied on all vehicles below 3.5 tonnes:

Lorries and semi-trailers:

3.5 - 11 tonnes:	SF 500
11 - 16 tonnes:	SF 1 500
16 - 19 tonnes:	SF 2 000
over 19 tonnes:	SF 3 000

Trailers:

3.5 - 8 tonnes:	SF 500
8 - 10 tonnes:	SF 1 000
over 10 tonnes:	SF 1 500
Motor coach:	SF 500.

Turkey	**Motor Vehicle Tax** levied on all motor vehicles - based on weight, type and cylinder capacity. Paid twice annually by registered owner. **VAT** on cars at a rate of 23% and on other vehicles at a rate of 15. **Motor Vehicles Acquisition Tax** levied according to the weight and the type **Supplementary tax on acquisition** of motor vehicles at 12% of list price on sale of new cars. **Environment Fund** at 25% of the Supplementary Motor Vehicles Acquisition Tax.
United Kingdom	**VED** on lorries is set according to the number of axles, weight, and type of vehicle. **VAT** on new cars, at standard rate of 17.5 per cent. **Vehicle Excise Duty** payable as an annual lump sum on all vehicles (with a few exceptions). Set at £135 for private cars since 30 november 1994.

(Table 4. Cont'd)

	One-off taxes on sale or initial registration of motor vehicles	Annual or recurrent taxes on registration or use of motor vehicles
United States	**The gas guzzler excise tax** is imposed on the sale of autos whose fuel efficiency is less than 22.5 miles per gallon. The tax varies from $1 000 to $7 700 depending on the fuel efficiency.	A tax is imposed on the use of trucks weighing at least 55 000 pounds. For those trucks weighing no more than 75 000 pounds, the tax is $100 per year plus $22 for each 1 000 pounds in excess of 55 000 pounds. For those trucks weighing more than 75 000 pounds, the tax is $550.
	The luxury car tax is imposed on the first retail sale of any passenger vehicle in an amount equal to 10 per cent of the extent to which the sales prices exceeds $30 000. The $30 000 threshold is indexed for inflation.	State and local governments may impose a periodic registration, operator's license, parking, and inspection fees, as well as property taxes.
	A tax is imposed on the first sale of heavy trucks in an amount equal to 12 per cent of the sales price.	
	A tax is imposed on the sale of tyres for highway vehicles. For tyres whose weight exceeds 40 pounds but whose weight does not exceed 70 pounds, the tax is $0.15 per pound in excess of 40 pounds. For tyres whose weight exceeds 70 pounds but whose weight does not exceed 90 pounds, the tax is $4.50 plus $0.30 per pound in excess of 70 pounds. For tyres whose weight exceeds 90 pounds, the tax is $10.50 plus $0.50 cents per pound in excess of 90 pounds.	
	State and local governments impose a one-time sales tax and/or title fee.	

Table 5. Fiscal charges and incentives for commuting expenses and company cars

Australia

A fringe benefits tax applies to all employer provided cars where the car is used by an employee for private purposes or is taken to be available for private use. The benefit is valued in one of two ways, firstly with reference to the value of the car and the amount of private use, or secondly, with reference to the operating cost of the car when the benefit arises. The aim of the tax is to ensure that all benefits in kind are subject to the same level of taxation as remuneration in the form of wages and salaries. In 1992-93 this tax raised some A$600 million.

Belgium

For taxpayers who use private transport for commuting purposes : deduction of commuting expenditures is limited to 6BF/km.
Taxpayers who do not use the possibility to deduct 6BF/km and who live more than 75 km from their place of work, may deduct (in addition to the deduction for professional expenses) per year:

    75-100km: 3 000 BF; 101-125km: 5 000 BF; + 126 km: 7 000 BF

Income tax exemption for commuting expenditures refunded by employers:

    a) if taxpayer deducts 6BF/km and does not prove the use of public transport regularly : nil
    b) if taxpayer provides proof of use of public transport: the amount the employer is obliged to refund
    c) other cases: 5 000 BF

Private use of company cars is taxed as follow:

Horsepower	BF added to salary for each km
4	5.3
5	6.2
6	6.9
7	7.6
8	8.3
9	9.0
10	10.0
11	10.9
12	11.6
13	12.3
14	12.8
15	13.3
16	13.7
17	14.0
18	14.3
19 and more	14.6

The employee who has the use of a company car for private means is (for tax purposes) assumed to use this car for private reasons at least 5 000 km/year.

(Table 5. Cont'd)

Fiscal charges and incentives for commuting expenses and company cars

Canada

Income tax is applied to the personal benefit of employer-paid automobile expenses.

Denmark

Commuting expenses are limited deductible:
("km" denotes the commuting distance between home and workplace)

    0-24km : no deduction

    25-100km: the deduction rate is determined by the Danish Taxation Council. In 1993, the deduction rate for a commuting distance between home and workplace of 21-54km was DKR 1.17 per km. For the part of distance exceeding 54km the deduction rate was DKR 0.2925 per km.

    + 101km: 25 per cent of the rate mentioned above is deductible.

Company cars which are available for private use are taxed 20-30 per cent of the value of the car. The first three years the value of the car is the price of the car as new. After the first three years the value of the car is 75 per cent of this price.

Finland

Private benefit of cars (and fuel) provided by employers is subject to income tax. The car scales used to value this benefit relate to the price, age and engine capacity of the vehicle as well as to the private mileage. In most cases the taxable benefit is between 1 500 and 3 000 FIM per month. The total amount of taxable benefit (income) in kind of a company car was FIM 1 800 million, to 76 000 persons, in 1992. Income tax raised from this taxation in 1992 was roughly FIM 1 000 million.

Exempt income is the benefit of collective transport, provided by the employer, between home and the place of work. Exempt as well is the reimbursement for business travel up to 1.73 FIM/km.

Actual commuting expenditures (except the "first" 2 000 FIM/a), using the cheapest means of transport, are deductible from income tax base. The maximum deduction is 16 000 FIM/a. In 1992, deductions were accepted to the total amount of FIM 3 100 million (to 883 000 persons). This is equivalent to ca. FIM 1 500 million in lost revenue.

Germany

Commuting expenses are deductible from the income tax base
- to the actual amount in case of public transport,
- and with a flat rate of DM 0.70 per km for private cars.

Additional benefits paid by the employer for commuting expenses
- are tax-free in case of public transport,
- are tax-deductible to a minimum flat rate of 15% calculated on the basis of a flat rate of DM 0.70 per km.
Car pooling in company cars is tax-free.

The VAT paid on the purchase of commercial vehicles and private cars for professional use is deductible.
Depreciations are written-down in 4 years (commercial vehicles), or in 5 years (professional used private cars).

Ireland

Commercial motoring expenses allowable against profits only where cost of the vehicle exceeds IR 10 000 i.e. tax deductible amount: (10 000 vehicles value) x running costs.
Capital allowances for cars restricted to a maximum of IR 10 000.

Netherlands

Deductibility of commuting expenses.

Distance	Other transport deductible	Public transport deductible
0 - 10 km	--	--
11 - 15 km	Gld 870	Gld 870
16 - 20 km	Gld 1180	Gld 1180
21 - 30 km	Gld 1950	Gld 1950
31 - 40 km	Gld 1950	Gld 2440
41 - 50 km	Gld 1950	Gld 3270
51 - 60 km	Gld 1950	Gld 3670
61 - 70 km	Gld 1950	Gld 4140
71 - 80 km	Gld 1950	Gld 4310
over 81 km	Gld 1950	Gld 4390

Deductibility of commuting expenses.

Distance	Public transport reimbursed tax free	Other transport reimbursed tax free
0 - 10 km	Gld 820	-
11 - 15 km	Gld 2 020	Gld 1 820
16 - 20 km	Gld 2 400	Gld 2 200
21 - 30 km	Gld 3 210	Gld 3 010
31 - 40 km	Gld 3 800	Gld 3 010
41 - 50 km	Gld 4 800	Gld 3 010
51 - 60 km	Gld 5 290	Gld 3 010
61 - 70 km	Gld 5 860	Gld 3 010
71 - 80 km	Gld 6 100	Gld 3 010
over 81 km	Gld 6 200	Gld 3 010

The maximum tax-free reimbursement for business travel is Gld 0.57 per km

(Table 5. Cont'd)

Fiscal charges and incentives for commuting expenses and company cars

Spain
The private benefit of cars provided by employers is subject to personal income tax. The benefit, in the case of supply, is the acquisition cost for the employer and in the case of use, an annual 15% of this cost if the vehicle belongs to the employer, or the amount paid by the employer to allow this use, in other cases. Commuting expenses are not deductible from the income tax base.

Sweden
The private benefit of cars and fuel provided by employers is subject to income tax and employers' social contributions. The aim is to achieve fiscal neutrality between those paid wholly in cash and those who realise the benefit of a company car in kind.

Switzerland
Tax deductibility for commuting expenses (public transport and private cars)(equivalent to SF 150-200 million in lost revenue at federal level in 1990-1991)

Turkey
Transportation expenditures made by employers for the mass transport of employees to and from work are excluded from income tax. Private benefit of cars and fuel provided by employers is subject to income tax.

United Kingdom
The private benefit of cars and fuel provided by employers is subject to income tax, and employers' national insurance contributions.From 1 April 1991, a new system was introduced to tax the annual benefit of a car, based on 35% of the list price of the car with discounts for the age of the vehicle and business mileage. The benefit of fuel will continue to be taxed on the basis of engine capacity. The aim is to achieve broad fiscal neutrality between those paid wholly in cash and those who receive the benefit in kind of a company car. The income tax charges applies to about 1.8 million company cars, of which about 1 million are also subject to the fuel charge. Income tax raised from this taxation in 1993/94 was 1500 million pounds (cars) and 200 million pounds (fuel), with a further 70 million pounds (fuel) from employers' national insurance contributions.

United States
Employer-provided transit passes, tokens, fare cards, and reimbursements for such items are included in the gross income of the employee if they are used for commuting but only to the extent that their value exceeds $60 per month. Employer provided parking is also included in the gross income of the employee but only to the extent that its value exceeds $155 per month.

70

Table 6. **Revenues from vehicle taxes and taxes on motor fuels**

I. **Revenues from one-off taxes on sale or initial registration and annual or recurrent taxes of private motor vehicles**

Country	Description	Revenue
Australia(C[th])	Wholesale sales tax	$A 780 million in 1992-93
	Import duty	..
(Victoria)	Motor vehicle registration	$A 311 million in 1992-93
	Stamp duty on vehicle registration	$A 223 million in 1992-93
	Drivers' licenses	$A 90 million in 1992-93
	Road taxes	$A 6 million in 1992-93
Austria	Road transport duty	Sch 2.9 billion in 1991 Sch 2.9 billion in 1992 Sch 3 billion in 1993
	Motor vehicle tax (partly earmarked)	Sch 6.5 billion in 1991 Sch 6.7 billion in 1992 Sch 6.4 billion in 1993
	VAT	..
Belgium	Value added tax (one-off tax on sale) Taxe de mise en circulation (one-off tax on sale) Taxe de Circulation (annual)	BF 30 billion in 1993 (estimate) BF 4.8 billion in 1993 BF 31 billion in 1993

71

(Table 6. Cont'd)

Country	Description	Revenue
Canada	Excise tax on automotive air conditioners	C$ 70 million in 1990-91 C$ 80 million in 1991-92
	Excise tax on heavy automobiles	less than C$ 2.5 million in 1990-91 C$ 1.5 million in 1991-92
	Goods and Service Tax	..
Denmark	Vehicle registration tax	DKr 8256 million in 1991 DKr 8532 million in 1992 Dkr 7997 million in 1993
	Weight tax	DKr 4548 million in 1991 DKr 4213 million in 1992 DKr 4225 million in 1993
	Third party liability insurance	Dkr 894 million in 1991 DKr 855 million in 1992 DKr 856 million in 1993
	VAT	..
Finland	Vehicle excise tax	FIM 1609 million in 1993 FIM 1720 million in 1994 (estimation)
	Annual tax on diesel-driven vehicles	FIM 885 million in 1993 FIM 930 million in 1994 (estimation)
	Road taxes on motor vehicles registered abroad	included in tax cited above
	Fuel charge	included in tax cited above
	Annual tax on motor vehicles	FIM 650 million in 1994 (estimation)

72

Country	Tax	Revenue
Germany	Motor vehicle tax	DM 11 billion in 1991
		DM 13.3 billion in 1992
		DM 14.1 billion in 1993
	VAT	..
Iceland	Motor vehicle excise duty	IKr 2.2 billion in 1994
	Weight distance tax	IKr 2.115 billion in 1994
	Annual automobile tax	IKr 1.83 billion in 1994
	Vehicle registration fee (earmarked for motor vehicle bureau)	..
	VAT	..
Ireland	Sales tax	IR£ 261 million in 1990 (209 m in 1991)
	Road tax	IR£ 161 million in 1990 (184 m in 1991)
Italy	VAT	..
	Registration tax	L 732 billion (1990)
		L 696 billion (1992)
		L 753 billion (1993)
	Annual vehicle tax	L 2 052 billion (1990)
		L 2 865 billion (1992)
		L 1 190 billion (1993)
	Annual diesel, LPG, Methane car surcharge	L 1 320 billion (1990)
		L 1 826 billion (1992)
		L 270 billion (1993)
	VAT	..

73

Country	Description	Revenue
Japan	Automobile Acquisitions Tax (local)	Y 549.0 billion in 1994
	Automobile tax (local)	Y 1 478.3 billion in 1994
	Light vehicle tax (local)	Y 98.2 billion in 1994
	Motor Vehicle Weight Tax (national)	Y 916.0 billion in 1994
	Consumption tax	..
Mexico	New motor vehicles tax	NS 1 248 million new pesos in 1994
	Property or use of motor vehicles tax	NS 2 693 million new pesos in 1994
	Gasoline and diesel tax	NS 19 639 million new pesos in 1994
Netherlands	Motor vehicle tax	Gld 4.751 billion (1993) Gld 5.335 billion (estimates for 1995)
	Value added tax	..
	Sales tax	Gld 3.300 billion (1993) Gld 4.040 billion (estimates for 1995)
Norway	Import tax	NKr 4.2 billion (1993)
	Registration tax	NKr 0.98 billion (1993)
	Vehicle excise duty	NKr 3.0 billion (1993)
	VAT	..
Portugal	Value added tax	Esc 62 billion (1991) Esc 97 billion (1993)
	Vehicle excise duty	Esc 68.5 billion (1991) Esc 103 billion (1993)
	Special motorcycle tax	Esc 81 million (1990) (abolished)
	Municipal vehicle tax	Esc 4.6 million (1991) Esc 7.6 million (1992)

Country	Tax	Revenue
	Commercial driving tax	Esc 2.7 million (1990) Esc 9.4 million (1992)
Spain	Vehicle registration tax	Pta 116.1 billion (1993)
Sweden	Sales tax (weight)	SKr 1.85 billion in 1991/92 SKr 1.27 billion in 1993 SKr 1.45 billion in 1994 (expected)
	Vehicle excise duty	SKr 4.1 billion in 1991/92 SKr 4.09 billion in 1993 SKr 4.11 billion in 1994 (expected)
	Kilometre tax (a)	SKr 3.3 billion in 1991/92 SKr 2.74 billion in 1993
	VAT	..
Switzerland	Import tax	SF 284 million (1990)
	Turnover tax	..
Turkey	Motor vehicles acquisition tax	TL 5 363 577 million (1993)
	Supplementary acquisition tax on motor vehicles	TL 6 051 311 million (1993)
	Motor vehicle tax	TL 2 086 039 million (1993)
	VAT	..
United kingdom	Vehicle Excise Duty	£ 3600 million (1993/94)
	VAT on new cars	approx. £2.6 billion

Country	Description	Revenue
United States	Gas Guzzler Excise Tax	US$ 175 million (FY 1991) US$ 144 million (FY 1992) US$ 134 million (FY 1993)
	Luxury Car Tax	US$ 293 million (FY 1992) US$ 344 million (FY 1993)
	Sale of Heavy Trucks	US$ 946 million (FY 1992) US$ 1 199 million (FY 1993)
	Sale of Tyres	US$ 287 million (FY 1992) US$ 305 million (FY 1993)
	Use of Trucks	US$ 605 million (FY 1992) US$ 630 million (FY 1993)
	State and local fees for vehicle title, registration, inspection and operators' licenses	US$ 10 837 million (FY 1989) US$ 11 771 million (FY 1992)

II.   Revenues from taxes on motor fuels

Country	Description	Revenue
Australia	Production excise duty	A$ 1.232 billion in 1989-90 A$ 1.24 billion in 1990-91
(C[th])	Petroleum excise duty	A$ 116 million in 1992-93 A$ 7.2 billion in 1992-93
(NSW) (Victoria) (Queensland)	Petroleum franchise fees	A$ 493 billion in 1992-93 A$ 350 million in 1992-93 Nil- no franchise fee
Austria	Mineral oil excise duty (unearmarked since 1987)	Sch 19,618 billion in 1990 Sch 20.7 billion in 1991 Sch 25.2 billion in 1992 Sch 25.3 billion in 1993

	Special tax on fossil oil	Sch 505 million in 1990 Sch 600 million in 1991 Sch 543 million in 1992 Sch 516 million in 1993
	VAT on motor fuels	approx. Sch 6 billion p.a.
Belgium	Excise duty	BFr 81.6 billion in 1990 BFr 108.2 billion in 1993
	Levy on energy	BFr 0.7 billion in 1993
	VAT	BFr 16.8 billion in 1989 BFr 19.7 billion in 1991
Canada	Excise tax on Gasoline and Diesel Fuel	C$ 3.38 billion in 1991-92
	unleaded/leaded differential	C$ 20 million in 1990 C$ 35 million in 1989
	Goods and Services Tax	..
Denmark	Energy taxes (coal, electricity, gas, oil and petrol)	DKr 5446 million in 1991 DKr 5651 million in 1992 DKr 5611 million in 1993
	VAT	..
	CO_2-tax	Dkr 1401 million in 1992 Dkr 3177 million in 1993
Finland	Excise duty (basic rate): unleaded leaded diesel	 FIM 5 102 million in 1993 FIM 676 million in 1993 FIM 1 476 million in 1993
	Excise Duty (carbon/energy): unleaded leaded diesel	 FIM 7 million in 1993 FIM 132 million in 1993 FIM 396 million in 1993
	Precautionary stock fee: petrol diesel	 FIM 106 million in 1993 FIM 39 million in 1993
	Oil pollution fee: petrol diesel	 FIM 4 million in 1993 FIM 3 million in 1993
	VAT (22%)	..

(Table 6. Cont'd.)

Country	Description	Revenue
France	Excise duty: leaded/unleaded differential	FF 1.08 billion in 1990 FF 2.50 billion in 1991
	VAT	..
Germany	Excise duty:	
	unleaded petrol	DM 21.662 billion in 1991 DM 28.3 billion in 1992
	leaded petrol	DM 6.795 billion in 1991 DM 5.8 billion in 1992
	diesel	DM 12.410 billion in 1991 DM 14.7 billion in 1992
	VAT	..
Iceland	Excise duty	IKr 4.325 billion in 1994
	Special excise duty	IKr 1.6 billion in 1994
	VAT	..
Ireland	Leaded petrol excise duty	IR£ 287 million in 1990 IR£ 263 million in 1991
	Unleaded petrol excise duty	IR£ 62 million in 1990 IR£ 84 million in 1991
	Diesel excise duty	IR£ 167 million in 1990 IR£ 176 million in 1991
	LPG excise duty	IR£ 1 million in 1990 and 1991
	Estimated tax expenditures: unleaded petrol LPG	IR£ 6 million (1990) IR£ 1 million (1990)
	VAT	..

78

Country	Tax	Value
Italy	Petrol	L 15 177 billion (1990) L 16 569 billion (1993)
	Unleaded petrol	L 382 billion (1990) L 2 165 billion (1993)
	Diesel fuel	L 9 652 billion (1990) L 14 709 billion (1993)
	LPG	L 466 billion (1993)
	Value Added Tax	..
Japan	Petroleum tax	Y 525 billion in 1994
	Gasoline Tax	Y 2 091.8 billion in 1994
	Light oil (diesel fuel) delivery tax	Y 1 236.3 billion in 1994
	Local road tax	Y 256.0 billion in 1994
	LPG tax	Y 30.0 billion in 1994
	Consumption tax	..
Mexico	Gasoline and diesel tax	N$ 19 639 million new pesos in 1994
Netherlands	General funding tax (including CO_2 tax of Gld 150 m and a temporary surcharge on leaded light oils of Gld 32.5 million)	GLD 926.5 million in 1991
	Gld 123 million are earmarked for public transport improvements)	
	Fuel excise duty gasoline	Gld 3.910 billion in 1993
	Fuel excise duty petrol	Gld 5.224 billion in 1993
	VAT	..
Norway	Excise duty (including CO_2 tax): gasoline	NKr 8.1 billion in 1991 NKr 9.6 billion in 1993
	mineral oil	NKr 2.2 billion in 1991 Nkr 2.4 billion in 1993
	VAT	..

(Table 6.Cont'd.)

Country	Description	Revenue
Portugal	Excise duty	Esc 293.2 billion in 1991 Esc 349 billion in 1993
Spain	VAT	..
Sweden	Mineral oil excise duty (including petrol, diesel and heating oil)	Pta 1104.3 billion in 1993 Pta 1096.8 billion in 1992
	Petrol tax	SEK 22 107 million in 1993-94 SEK 22 544 million in 1994-95
	whereas:	
	Carbon dioxide	SEK 4 231 million in 1993-94 SEK 4 442 million in 1994-95
	Tax on other energy	SEK 16 150 million in 1993-94 SEK 19 549 million in 1994-95
	whereas: Carbon dioxide	SEK 6 963 million in 1993-94 SEK 7 717 million in 1994-95
	Energy tax on electricity	SEK 5 793 million in 1993-94 SEK 6 110 million in 1994-95
	Energy tax on fuel	SEK 1 965 million in 1993-94 SEK 3 300 million in 1994-95
	Diesel tax	SEK 1 400 million in 1993-94 SEK 2 422 million in 1994-95
	Total tax on petrol and other energy	SEK 38 257 million in 1993-94 SEK 42 093 million in 1994-95
	VAT	..
Switzerland	Excise duty, Turnover tax on gasoline Excise duty, Turnover tax on mineral oils Excise duty, Turnover tax on gas Excise duty, Turnover tax on coal	SF 2 348 million (1990) SF 20 million (1990) SF 3 million (1990) SF 0.44 million (1990)

Turkey	Liquid fuels consumption tax	TL 12 215 696	million in 1993
	Customs duty on motor fuels	TL 4 358 943	million in 1993
	VAT and other ad valorem taxes and duties are also levied	..	
United Kingdom	Excise duty on leaded petrol	£ 4423	million (1993/94)
	Excise duty on unleaded petrol	£ 4408	million (1993/94)
	Excise duty on diesel fuel	£ 3658	million (1993/94)
	VAT	..	
United States	Federal Motor Fuels:		
	Highway Motor Fuels tax	US$ 18 707	million (FY 1992)
		US$ 19 310[c]	million (FY 1993)
	Non-commercial Aviation	US$ 256	million (FY 1992)
		US$ 166	million (FY 1993)
	Recreational Motor boat	US$ 151	million (FY 1992)
		US$ 163	million (FY 1993)
	Outdoor Power Equipment	US$ 43	million (FY 1992)
		US$ 45	million (FY 1993)
	Inland Waterway Transportation	US$ 70	million (FY 1992)
		US$ 80	million (FY 1993)
	Rail Transportation	US$ 80	million (FY 1992)
		US$ 85	million (FY 1993)
	Leaking Underground storage Tank Tax[b]	US$ 148	million (FY 1992)
	State motor fuels (includes taxes on gasoline, diesel oil and other fuels used in motor vehicles, including aircraft fuel).	US$ 22 198	million (FY 1992)

Notes:

a) The kilometre tax was abolished in Sweden on 1 October 1993 and replaced by a special diesel tax.

b) Includes separate tax used to support the Leaking Underground Storage Tank Trust Fund.

Table 7. Non-VAT taxes for Energy other than Motor Fuels

Country	Petroleum products: Light Oil Industrial (households)	Petroleum Products: Heavy Oil Industrial	Gas Industrial (households)	Electricity Industrial (households)	Coal Industrial (households)
Australia[a]	Excise tax $A 0.086/l	Excise tax $A 0.086/l	State sales taxes[c]	State sales taxes[c]	n.a.
Austria	Stock fee: Sch 9.92/100kg (Sch 12.08/100kg) Mineral oil tax: Sch 57/100 kg (Sch 77/100kg)	Stock fee: Sch 9.92/100kg Mineral oil tax: Sch 20.0/100kg	0	0	0
Belgium	Levy on energy: BF 0.34/litre Inspection fee: BF 0.21/litre	Levy on energy: if sulphur (<1%): BF 250/1 000kg otherwise BF 750/1 000kg	Levy on energy[d] BF 0.01367/Megajoule	Levy on energy[e] BF 55/Mwh	0
Canada[f]	0	0	0	0	0
Denmark	Excise tax[b] DKr 1 490/KI Environment tax[b,g] DKr 270/KI	Excise tax DKr 1 660/KI Environment tax[g] DKr 320/KI	Excise tax as for LFO on heat equivalent basis	Excise tax (DKr 0.300/kWh) Environment tax[g,b] DKr 0.100/kWh	Excise tax[b] DKr 690/t Environment tax[b,g] DKr 242/t
Finland	Excise tax[b,h] Mk 0.042/l Additional tax[b] (carbon/energy): Mk 0.08/l Precautionary stock fee:[b] Mk 0.023/l Oil pollution fee:[b] Mk 0.0019/l	Excise tax[h] Mk 0.025/kg Additional tax (carbon/energy): Mk 0.093/kg Precautionary stock fee: Mk 0.019/kg Oil pollution fee: Mk 0.0022/kg	Additional tax (carbon/energy):[b] Mk 0.065/m^3	Excise and additional tax[b]: Nuclear: Mk 0.021/kWh Hydro: Mk 0.002/kWh Imported electricity: Mk 0.013/kWh	Additional tax (carbon/energy):[b] Mk 67.2/t
France	Special taxes to hydro carbon fund and IFP N/A	Special taxes to hydro carbon fund and IFP N/A	Special tax FF 82.08/10^7 kcal for industrial consumption over 18 000 GJ/year	Local taxes Composite National Rate 0.5%, (8.5%)	0[b]

Germany	Excise tax[b]: DM 80.0/1000litres Storage fund[b] DM 7.81/t	Excise tax DM 30/t for industry; DM 55/t for electricity generation; Storage fund 7.3 DM/t	Excise tax[b] 0.476/100kwh	Special tax for support of coal industry[b] 8.5%	0[b]
Greece	Excise tax[b]: Drs 48 569/1000l	Excise tax Drs 1200/t	-	-	-
Iceland	0	0	0	0	0
Ireland	Excise tax[b,i]: IR£ 37.30/1000 litres (industrial, agricultural uses and heating) IR£ 4.40/1000 litres (horticultural purposes)	Excise duty (Industry and electricity generation): IR£ 10.68/1000litres	0[b]	0[b]	0[b]
Italy	L 676/l	L 45/l	Excise tax: L 282.82/kg (L 245/kg)	Excise taxes: Local and State taxes at various rates	0[b]
Japan	Petroleum tax: Y 2 040 per kl of crude oil	Petroleum tax: Y 2 040 per kl of crude oil	Petroleum tax: Y 720/t of LNG Y 670 of LPG	Electric Power Promotion Tax Y 0.445/kwh	0
Luxembourg	Excise tax[b,h]: Lux Francs 210/1000 litre	Excise tax: Lux Francs 550/t	0[b]	0[b]	0[b]
Mexico	Petroleum and gas extraction fee Additional petroleum and gas extraction fee for participation to the states	Petroleum and gas extraction fee Additional petroleum and gas extraction fee for participation to the states	Petroleum and gas extraction fee Additional petroleum and gas extraction fee for participation to the states	-	-
Netherlands	Excise tax[b]: Gld 115.2/1000 litres Env. tax[b]: Gld 26.5/1000 litres	Excise tax[b]: Gld 34.24/tonne Env. tax[b]: Gld 31.04/tonne	0-10 mm m^3: Env. tax: Gld 20.79/m^3 >10 mm m^3 Env. Tax : Gld 13.67/m^3	0[b]	Env. tax : Gld 22.64/tonne
New-Zealand	:	:	:	:	:

(Table 7. Cont'd.)

Country	Petroleum products: Light Oil Industrial (households)	Petroleum Products: Heavy Oil Industrial	Gas Industrial (households)	Electricity Industrial (households)	Coal Industrial (households)
Norway	CO_2 tax NKr 0.410/l[b] Sulphur Tax NKr 0.07/l[b]	CO_2 tax NKr 0.41/l Sulphur tax NKr 0.07/l and per 0.25% sulphur content	no consumption	Excise tax: NKr 0.051/kwh Tax on industry NKr 0.0122/kwh	CO_2 tax[b]: NKr 0.41/kg
Portugal	..	..	No consumption	0[b]	0 (unimportant consumption for households)
Spain	Excise tax[b]: Ptas 11 800/kl	Excise tax: Ptas 2 003/t	0[b]	0[b]	0[b]
Sweden[l]	Carbon dioxide tax: SKr 0.239/l (SKr .957/l) General energy tax:[k-p] (SKr 0.562/litre)	Carbon dioxide tax: SKr 0.239/l	Carbon dioxide tax: SKr 0.177/m³ (SKr 0.707/m³) General energy tax:[k] (SKr 0.182/m³)	General energy tax:[k] (SKr 3.6-8.8/kwh)	Carbon dioxide tax: SKr 0.208/kg (SKr 0.832/kg) General energy tax[k]: (SKr 0.239/kg) Sulphur tax: SKr 30/kg
Switzerland	Excise tax[b]: SF 3.18/kl Emergency fund[b]: SF 16.69/kl	Excise tax: SF 3.18kl Emergency fund: SF 16.69 kl	Excise tax[b] SF 2.06/t	0[b]	Special tax for emergency fund[b]N/A
Turkey	0[b]	0	0[b]	0[b]	0[b]
United Kingdom	Excise tax: .. (£ 16.40/1000 litre)	Excise tax: £ 11.67/t	0[b]	0[b]	0[b]

United States	Hazardous Substances Superfund Tax of $0.097 per barrel on domestic and imported products[m]. The Oil Spill Liability Trust Fund Tax of $0.05 per barrel on domestic and imported crude oil and imported petroleum products was temporarily suspended as of July 1, 1993. It may be reapplied if the Oil Spill Liability Trust Fund balance drops below $1 billion[n]. Some state and local governments impose severance taxes on oil.	Hazardous Substances Superfund Tax of $0.097 per barrel on domestic and imported crude oil and imported petroleum products[m]. The Oil Spill Liability Trust Fund Tax of $0.05 per barrel on domestic and imported petroleum products was temporarily suspended as of July 1, 1993. It may be reapplied if the Oil Spill Liability Trust Fund balance drops below $1 billion[n]. Some state and local governments impose severance taxes on oil.	Some state and local governments impose severance taxes on natural gas.	Some state and local governments impose taxes on public utilities	Black lung disability tax of US $1.10 per ton of coal (except lignite) from underground mines and US $0.55 per ton of coal from surface mines. Rate is capped at 4.4 per cent of 1xe price of coal when sold by the producer. Some state and local governments impose severance taxes on coal.

Notes: Values in parentheses are for households, otherwise it is for industrial use, for 1.1.1994. VAT rates apply for households only (see table 1 for VAT rates).

a) Values for 1993.
b) Identical values for industry and households - many countries where this applies.
c) Concerning the gas tax, South Australia imposes a 5% levy on gross sales revenue (paid by the gas authority) and Victoria imposes an energy consumption levy on major users of natural gas to encourage conservation. Concerning the electricity tax, South Australia imposes a 5% tax on gross sales revenue (paid by electricity authority)
d) For Belgium domestic use and assimilated non-domestic use.
e) For low voltage (for domestic use) in Belgium.
f) Sales tax and resource royalties may apply in some Canadian provinces.
g) The environment tax was established on 15 May 1992 in Denmark and was refundable to industry until 1st January 1993. After 1st January 1993, only 50% of the tax is refundable to industry.
h) Since 1st January 1993 (Finland, Luxembourg).
i) The excise tax is zero when light fuel oil is used by Irish fisherman.
k) Energy tax for industrial use is abolished from 1st January 1993 in Sweden. As of 1st January 1993, the "excise tax in Sweden was differentiated by classes with regard to environmental effects:
from 1.1.1994 to 1.7.1994 the rate for Class 1 = 5 SEK/m^3, Class 2 = 302 SEK/m^3, Class 3 = 562 SEK/m^3. Since 1.7.1994, there is no longer any differentiation. The rate is now 562 SEK/m^3.
l) A sulphur tax is levied on the sulphur content in oil, coal and peat in Sweden. On oil the tax rate is Skr 27 for each 0,1% sulphur content by weight. On peat and coal the tax rate is Skr 30 000 for each ton of sulphur.
m) The Hazardous Substances Superfund in the U.S. is used to clean-up hazardous emergencies and abandoned uncontrolled hazardous waste sites.
n) The Oil Spill Liability Trust Fund is used for oil pollution and clean-up as well as for compensating individuals for damages caused by oil spills.

Table 8. Environmental tax provisions relating to other goods and services

Country	Item	Description	Revenue
Australia (Commonwealth)	CFC	$A 0.23 per kg levy introduced in 1989 on production and import to cover costs of administering CFC phase-out.(The States also have licensing and quantity based charges for CFCs)	$A 0.15 million in 1989
	Recycled paper	Certain paper products made from 100% recycled paper are exempt from Wholesale sales tax .	Estimated revenue loss less than $A0.5 million
	Some solar power equipment used for heating purposes and goods used to convert internal combustion engines to LPG or natural gas.	Exempt from Wholesale Tax.	
Austria	Tires	(under discussion)	
Belgium	Disposable razors	BF 10 per razor (from 31 January 1994)	
	Beverage containers	Since 1 April 1994, a tax of BF 15/litre (minimum BF 7) is levied on containers of beer and some soft drinks if they are not submitted to a deposit-refund system and if they are not reusable or an annually increasing per cent of them is not being recycled, BF 380 if not recycled (1 july 1994)	
	Paper, pesticides, batteries, packaging of ink, glue, oil and solvents.	Dates of coming into force are under discussion.	
	Disposable cameras	BF 300 if not recycled (1 July 1994)	
Canada	Ontario, Manibota	Alcohol beverage containers : C$ 0.05 to C$ 0.10 on non-refillable containers	
	Certain provinces	Tyres : C$ 2 to C$ 4 per tire	
	Manibota	Quarry minerals : C$ 0.10 per tonne	
	Prince Edward Island	Newsprint and promotional material (under discussion)	
	British Columbia	Lead-acid batteries : C$ 5 per battery	

Denmark

	Description	Revenue
Raw materials	The excise duty is levied on extraction and export of sand, gravel etc. at the rate of DKR 5 per cubic metre.	Dkr 120 million in 1993
Certain retail packaging	The excise duty is levied on containers for beverage, soft drinks, fruit juice, spirits, vinegar and oils etc. The tax rate is between DKR 0.38 - 2.28 per container depending on the size and the type of the container.	DKr 305 million in 1993
Carrier bags of plastic and paper	An excise duty on carrier bags of plastic and paper with a possible content of minimum 5 litre was introduced 1 January 1994. For bags of paper the tax rate is DKR 9 per kilo and for bags of plastic the tax rate is DKR 20 per kilo.	n.a.
Disposable tableware	The excise duty is levied on plastic and paper cups, plates, cutlery etc. The tax rate is one-third of the wholesale value including the tax rate but excluding VAT. In connection with imports the tax rate is 50 per cent.	DKr 58 million in 1993
Pesticides	The retail sale of pesticides sold in containers less than 1 kg or 1 litre is subject to a tax. The rate is 1/6 of the whole sale value including the tax but excluding the VAT. When the tax is paid in connection with imports the rate is 20 per cent of the producer price. Pesticides sold in larger quantities than mentioned above are subject to a tax of 3 per cent of the wholesale price excluding discounts and VAT. When the tax is paid in connection with imports the rate is 20 per cent of the producer price.	Dkr 11 million in 1993
CFC and halons	The excise duty is levied on the use of CFC's and halons or products containing these. The tax rate is DKR 30 per kilo of the products.	DKr 5.1 million in 1993
Rechargeable batteries	A charge is levied on rechargeable nickel/cadmium batteries. The revenue of this excise duty is earmarked for covering the costs of a collection arrangement for used rechargeable batteries. The rate is DKR 2 per single battery and DKR 8 per battery attached to technical devices or apparatus.	DKr 7.8 million in 1993
Light bulbs	An excise duty on ordinary light bulbs exists while energy saving light bulbs are exempt from this duty. This difference in taxation between ordinary and energy saving light bulbs is a measure taken in order to encourage the use of energy saving light bulbs.	n.a.

(Table 8. Cont'd)

Country	Item	Description	Revenue
Finland	Beverage containers	"Surtax" levied since 1976 on beer and soft drinks in non-reusable glass, metal and other containers. Rates are 3 Mk/litre on soft drinks in non-returnable metal or glass containers, 2 Mk/litre on soft drinks in other non-returnable containers. Approved return systems allow exemption from the surtax. Surtax of 1 Mk/litre applied to beer in non-returnable containers. Amendment in June 1994: Beer and other alcohol beverage containers 4 FIM/l For approved return system: - refillables: exempt - use as raw material: 1 FIM/l	Surtax revenues: - soft drinks: Mk 35 million (in 1990) Mk 19 million (in 1993); - beer: Mk 30 million (in 1990) Mk 16 million (in 1993).
	Lubrification oil	Waste oil charge at the rate of 0.25 FIM per kg	FIM 21 million (in 1993)
	Fertilizers	Excise tax on fertilizers: 2.60 FIM/kg N + 1.70 FIM/kg P (repealed as of 16-6-1994)	FIM 516 million (in 1993)
France	Paper, pulp and board	Revenues partly used for promoting waste paper recovery	
	Tax in billboards, advertisements and signs or advertising sites	Fixed by municipal councils	
Iceland	Plastic bags	8 IKr per bag	n.a.
Italy	Polyethylene	Levied on polyethylene as primary product of carrier bags (since March 18, 1994)	n.a
Mexico	-	-	-
Norway	Beverage containers	Also levied since 1988 on disposable beverage containers per litre: **Liquor and wine:** NKr 2.50 (1991) NKr 3.00 (1993) **Beer:** NKr 3.50 (1991) NKr 3.00 (1993)	NKr 41 million in 1991 NKr 48 million in 1993 NKr 13 million in 1993 NKr 11 million in 1993

88

Country	Product	Description	Revenue
		Carbonated drinks: 9.50 (1991) 9.30 (1994) **Non-carbonated drinks:** NKr 9.50 (1991) NKr 9.30 (1994) **Non-reusable beverage containers:** (since 1994) NKr 0.70	NKr 60 million in 1991 NKr 24 million in 1993 NKr 59 million in 1991 NKr 65 million in 1993 NKr 95 million in 1994
Portugal	Batteries, packaging, glass, plastic, coal ashes, mining and tyres	These products are subject to different protocol for collection and recycling between the authorities and the related industry	
	Mineral oils obtained from recycling of used oils	Not subject to Excise Duty on motor fuels	
Sweden	Beverage containers[a]	Levied since 1973 on beverage containers, per container depending on volume (paper and cardboard exempt): Returnable SKr 0.08 Disposable SKr 0.10-0.25	SKr 110 million for 1991-92
	Batteries	Levied on batteries per kg: HgOx SKr 23 NiCd SKr 25 Pb SKr 32	SKr 17 million for 1991-92
United States	Ozone-depleting chemicals	Ozone-depleting chemical excise tax imposed on CFCs, halons, carbon tetrachloride, and methyl chloroform. The rates are proportional to the ozone-depleting potential of each chemical and range from US $0.137 to US $13.70 per pound (in 1991) and US $0.435 to US $ 43.5 per pound (in 1994). The tax is also imposed on imported products containing (or manufactured with) these ozone-depleting chemicals.	US $ 886 million in FY 1991 US $ 580 million in FY 1992

Notes: a) Abolished in May 1993.

Table 9. **Tax incentives for environmental investments**

Country	Eligibility	Details
Australia (Commonwealth)	Environmental-related capital expenditures	Deduction for expenditures incurred after 18 August 1992 for the purpose of preventing, combating or recycling pollution, or treating, cleaning up, removing or storing waste.
	Mine site re-habilitation expenditure	Since 1.6 1991 rehabilitation expenditures are fully tax-deductible in year they are incurred, except for plant and machinery and housing and welfare.
	Measures to prevent land degradation	Full tax deductibility for certain capital costs
	Water conservation or conveyance expenditure on environmental studies	Deductible over 10 years, or project life if less.
Austria	Energy saving measures in private households	Expenditures are within certain limitations deductible from the tax base.
	Low-noise lorries	Investment allowance of 20% instead of 10% capital tax exemption.
	Investments of enterprises in the environmental field	Capital tax exemption.
Belgium	Investments which do not have a negative effect on the environment or are designed to minimise negative effects on the environment	Investment deduction at 10 percentage points above inflation.
Canada	Water and air pollution control investments at sites operating before 1974.	Accelerated depreciation or Capital Cost Allowance.
	Energy saving equipment	Accelerated depreciation.
Denmark[a]	Operating equipment and agricultural machinery approved for environmental improvements on small farms (elapsed 31.12.1992) Since 1993, no tax incentives for environmental investments exist. Instead incentives are given as grants.	Deductible

Country	Item	Treatment
Finland	Investments in air and water pollution control	Accelerated depreciation at maximum of 25% of purchase price annually for four years.
France	Pollution reducing equipment - industrial water treatment plant - air cleaning facilities and electrical vehicles	Accelerated depreciation
	Energy saving equipment	Accelerated depreciation
Ireland	Land drainage and reclamation; cages in offshore and inshore fishing	Capital allowances
	Income from woodlands managed on a commercial basis	Exempt from tax. Relief from Capital Acquisitions Tax and Stamp Duty in some circumstances.
	Expenditures incurred by trader on plant and machinery provided for environmental purposes (1992)	Accelerated allowance of 25% no longer available.
	Business contributions to local authority expenditure on effluent control.	Capital allowance available as if expenditure directly incurred by business
	Expenditure for control of farmyard pollution.	Accelerated capital allowances (50% instead of 25%) for two year period from April 91
	Expenditure incurred by trader on plant and machinery provided for environmental purposes.	Accelerated capital allowances (25%)
Japan	Energy efficiency improving	Choice of special initial depreciation of 30% of acquisition cost, in addition to ordinary depreciation or tax credit of acquisition cost.
	Pollution preventing equipment	Special initial depreciation of 18% of acquisition cost, in addition to ordinary depreciation.
	Recycling equipment	Special initial depreciation of 14% of acquisition cost, in addition to ordinary depreciation.
	Air, water and noise abatement facilities	Reduction of income, corporate, municipal fixed property tax.
	Asbestos emission reduction facilities	Exemption from municipal and fixed property taxes.
	Nine types of industry that are collecting and/or developing markets for recyclable resources.	A reserve fund for promoting recyclable resources.

(Table 9. Cont'd)

Country	Eligibility	Details
Mexico	Immediate deduction of investments in new fixed assets permanently located in the national territory and out of the three more congested and polluted cities (Mexico, Guadalajara and Monterrey)	An immediate deduction of 91% on equipment used to prevent and control environment pollution
	Accelerated depreciation of equipment used to control environment pollution	A depreciation rate of 50% a year
Netherlands	Energy-efficiency improving expenditure and pollution prevention equipment.	Accelerated depreciation (available since September 1991).
Norway	In Norway, investments are liable to duty with a percentage of 7%. However, are exempted from the investment tax: -- industrial investments aimed to decrease emissions to water and air -- agricultural investments aimed to ameliorate the environment -- environmentally-related investments concerning municipal handling of ordinary and hazardous waste.	
Portugal	Tools machines and other equipments destined exclusively or principally for: solar or geothermal energy generation, other alternative energy forms, energy generated from waste, incineration, oil or natural gas, exploration costs, pollution measurement or control costs.	Reduced VAT (5%)
	Personal expenditure on renewable energy forms.	Income tax deductible up to a ceiling.
	Investment related to environmental protection of air and water	Reduction of charge and granting of subsidies on a case by case basis
Switzerland	Energy efficiency improving expenditure.	Reduction of taxable income (for individuals)
	Energy saving, new heating systems, solar energy and other resource saving (water, air) equipment.	Accelerated depreciation (for companies)

Turkey	
Energy-saving investments	Since 1980, investments which are aimed at achieving savings of energy can be deducted from relevant earnings.
R&D expenditures aimed at developing and utilising high technologies	Since 1985, can be deferred for three years without paying deferment fee or interest, up to 20% of Corporation Tax, provided that this does not exceed the amount actually spent.
United States	
Solar and geo-thermal energy property	A non-refundable credit equal to 10 per cent of basis is allowed for investment in solar and geothermal energy property.
Electricity Produced from Renewable Sources	A non-refundable credit of 1.5 cents per kilowatt hour is allowed for the domestic production of electricity from wind and biomass.
Electric Vehicles	A non-refundable credit is allowed for 10 per cent of the cost of certain electric vehicle. The maximum credit is $ 4 000.
Reforestation expenditures	A non-refundable credit of 10 per cent is allowed for expenditures (up to $10 000 per year per taxpayer) associated with forestation or reforestation of commercial woodlands. These expenditures may also be amortized over a seven-year period.
Soil and water Conservation Expenditures	Farmers may expense certain soil or water conservation expenditures which would otherwise be chargeable to a capital account.
Pollution Control, Sewage, Solid waste and Hazardous Waste facilities	Interest on debt issued by state or local governments for the purposes of financing pollution control, sewage, solid waste, and hazardous waste facilities may be exempt from Federal income taxation.

Notes:

a) In Denmark, incentives for environmental investments are given as government grants. Examples of projects or processes that are covered by grant schemes are given below:
-- Electricity produced by renewable energy sources.
-- Energy saving measures implemented by firms with a considerable use of energy in the production process.
-- New installations that make use of renewable energy sources.
-- Collection of waste oil.

Table 10. **Taxes and charges on aircraft (noise pollution)**

Country	Description
Australia	Aircraft noise charge (under discussion)
Belgium	Aircraft noise charge on landings at Brussels (Zaventem) airport since 1st October 1991, differentiated according to type of aircraft and time of day.
Canada	Although Canada does not have a tax based on noise levels, there is an excise tax of C$ 0.04 per litre on aviation fuel and C$ 0.085 per litre on aviation gasoline.
France	"Aircraft noise charge" levied since 1973 for landings at Roissy and Orly airports has been extended to four other airports: Lyon, Marseilles, Nice and Toulouse. The tax applies to any aircraft weighting over 2 tonnes.
Germany	Aircraft noise charge on landings at German airports: the charge is based on noise level of aircraft type.
Netherlands	"Aircraft noise pollution charge" levied since 1982 on civilian aircraft landings from user of aircraft as surcharge on landing fees. Amount of the tax is determined annually based on noise prevention expenditure and noise level of aircraft type. Total revenue, Gld 39 million.
Norway	"Aircraft noise tax", based on noise level of aircraft, levied since 1st November 1990 at Fornebu and Bodø airports.
Portugal	Special tax on aircraft levied on all aircraft weighing more than 1.4 tonnes and less than 15 years old. Rates of tax applicable: Since 1994: 1.4 - 1.8 tonnes Esc 106 000 1.8 - 2.5 tonnes Esc 159 000 2.5 - 4.2 tonnes Esc 212 000 4.2 - 5.7 tonnes Esc 318 000 + 5.7 tonnes Esc 530 000
Sweden	A tax per kg emitted HC and NOx is levied on domestic air since 1st March 1989. Since 1st January 1991, a tax on carbon dioxide in air fuel is levied on domestic air traffic. Tax level per litre of fuel SKr 1.00; there is also a tax per kg emitted HC and NOx Skr 12. Total revenues for 1994 expected to be approx Skr 170 millions.
Switzerland	"Aircraft landing tax" levied since 1980 by noise classes per take-off: Class 1/SF 400, class 2/SF 265, class 3/SF 200, class 4/SF 135, class 5/SF 0. (new and modified aircraft are exempt until they are attributed to a noise class). "Light aircraft landing tax" levied since 1988 by degree to which noise limit is undercut per take-off. Tax per tonne: Category A (below noise limit) SF 7 Category B (0 - 1.9 dB) SF 4 Category C (2 - 4.9 Db) SF 2 Category D (5 Db) SF 0

Table 11. **Waste disposal and management charges**

Country	Description	Rate	Revenue
Australia	There are many waste disposal and management charges schemes operating, however responsibility for these lies with the State and local governments.	For example: the Victorian Landfill Levy Rates are based on weight and volume, plus a 10 per cent charge to recover administrative costs.	A\$ 6 million (this revenue is distributed between the Recycling and Recovery Council and the Waste Management Council)
Austria	Contaminated sites clean-up charge		Sch 167 million (1992) Sch 216 million (1993)
Belgium	Federal level: - Charge on export, import and transit of waste - Charge on toxic waste Regions: - Charges on waste disposal and waste management (including charges on waste water) are under the jurisdiction of the regions.	BF 500 per declaration plus BF 200 per export form.	
Canada[a]	Waste policy under jurisdiction of provinces and territories		
Denmark	Excise duty on waste: (Recycling businesses are generally exempt or have a possibility of reimbursement) - waste delivered to landfill sites - waste delivered incineration plants	 DKr 195/t DKr 160/t	DKr 527.6 million (in 1993)

(Table 11.Cont'd)

Country	Description	Rate	Revenue
Finland	Municipal waste charge: a municipal user charge		FIM 400 million (1992)
	Waste oil charge (levied since 1987 on lubricant oils produced for domestic use or imported. Earmarked for hazardous waste (especially waste oil) management.	FIM 0.25/kg	FIM 20.5 million (1993) FIM 22.0 million (1994, estimation)
	Hazardous waste processing charge; a commercial charge imposed on municipalities and firms using the services of Ekokem Ltd, a hazardous waste processing plant jointly owned by the State, the municipalities and the industry.		FIM 130 million (1992) FIM 140 million (1993)
	Nuclear waste management charge; fund contributions to the State Nuclear Waste Management Fund.	FIM 12-16Mwh	Contrib. accumulated to 3 000 million FIM.
France	Waste oil charge levied since 1979 on production of lubricating oils per tonne	FF 150/tonne	FF 103 million in 1993 FF 116 million in 1994
	A tax on the dumping of waste and similar products was introduced in 1992 concerning any facility for the storage of domestic refuse and similar products. The general aim of the tax is the phasing out of all traditional refuse dumps by the year 2002.	FF 20 per tonne in 1994 FF 25 per tonne in 1995 FF 30 per tonne in 1996 FF 35 per tonne in 1997 FF 40 per tonne in 1998	FF 170 million in 1993 (incomplete year) FF 395 million in 1994
	Tax for domestic refuse collection		FF 10 billion in 1992
Germany	Domestic refuse disposal charge	DM 70-200 per tonne	
	Hazardous waste disposal charge	DM 50-150 tonne (average)	
	Waste disposal taxes already implemented by 4 Länder; a Federal charge is currently under consideration		

96

Country	Charge	Rate	Revenue
Iceland	Waste management fee	Charged by local authority at various rates	n.a.
	Hazardous waste disposal charge	From IKr 34.24/kg to IKr 304.10/kg	n.a.
Ireland	Waste disposal charge (administered by local authority)	no details	
Italy	Domestic refuse disposal charge depending on the use of the surface:		
	- residence	L 2975/m2 (average for 1994)	
	- others	L 6500 to 20 000 m2 (average for 1994)	L 420.9 billion (1994)
Mexico	1. Charge on residual water discharged (per cubic meter):		
	Disponibility zone 1	N$ 0.5528	n.a.
	Disponibility zone 2	N$ 0.1381	n.a.
	Disponibility zone 3	N$ 0.0551	n.a.
	Disponibility zone 4	N$ 0.0276	n.a.
	2[b]. Charge on pollutants on water discharged (per kilogram of chemical demand of oxygen on discharge):		
	Disponibility zone 1	N$ 0.3593	n.a.
	Disponibility zone 2	N$ 0.0896	n.a.
	Disponibility zone 3	N$ 0.0358	n.a.
	Disponibility zone 4	N$ 0.0178	n.a.
	3[b]. Charge on pollutants on water discharged (per kilogram of solid substances on discharged):		
	Disponibility zone 1	N$ 0.6358	n.a.
	Disponibility zone 2	N$ 0.1588	n.a.
	Disponibility zone 3	N$ 0.0635	n.a.
	Disponibility zone 4	N$ 0.0316	n.a.
Netherlands	Domestic refuse disposal charge 50-250 Gld per tonne		Gld 2 191 million (estimate for 1995)
	Waste tax for dumping waste:		
	- at landfill sites	Gld 29.2 per tonne	Gld 275 million (estimate for 1995)
	- for incineration	nil	
	Municipal waste charge (households)		Gld 1 899 million (estimate for 1995)

(Table 11.Cont'd)

Country	Description	Rate	Revenue
Norway	Waste oil charge levied since 1988 per litre	NKr 0.50 From 1.1.94:NKr 1.00	NKr 28 million (1993) Nkr 30 million (1994)
Portugal	Waste water disposal in the natural environment	Variable (depending on pollutant)	n.a.
	Air quality control	Variable (under study)	
	Waste disposal in sewerage systems	Municipal charges	n.a.
Spain	Waste Disposal Charge	No details	
Sweden	Municipalities may differentiate waste charges as an incentive to separation of waste.	no details	
Turkey	A solid waste charge and water waste charge referred as Environmental Clean Up Tax is levied on households and non-households as from the beginning of 1994.	The monthly amount of the solid waste charge differs from 25 000 TL up to 100 000 TL for households and 25 000 TL up to 5 000 000 TL for non households. A reduction of 50% is applied to the mentioned amounts in municipalities with a population of less than 5 000.	The levy is administrated by municipalities and estimated revenue from the tax is 3 500 billion TL in 1994.
United Kingdom	Waste disposal in landfill sites	Proposed	
United States	Hazardous Substances Superfund excise taxes imposed on hazardous chemicals.	$ 0.22 to $ 4.87 per ton	$ 254 million in FY 1992
	Some States and local governments impose fees for trash collection and dumping		

98

Notes :

a) Examples of initiatives in some provinces of Canada include waste discharge permit fees, surcharges on extra-strength waste water discharges, waste dumping charges.

b) The charges for 2. and 3. are applied on the amount of pollutants obtained by subtracting the admitted maximum values of pollutants established in the Official Mexican Rules and the Ecological Equilibrium Law from those discharged.

MAIN SALES OUTLETS OF OECD PUBLICATIONS
PRINCIPAUX POINTS DE VENTE DES PUBLICATIONS DE L'OCDE

ARGENTINA – ARGENTINE
Carlos Hirsch S.R.L.
Galería Güemes, Florida 165, 4° Piso
1333 Buenos Aires   Tel. (1) 331.1787 y 331.2391
Telefax: (1) 331.1787

AUSTRALIA – AUSTRALIE
D.A. Information Services
648 Whitehorse Road, P.O.B 163
Mitcham, Victoria 3132   Tel. (03) 873.4411
Telefax: (03) 873.5679

AUSTRIA – AUTRICHE
Gerold & Co.
Graben 31
Wien I   Tel. (0222) 533.50.14
Telefax: (0222) 512.47.31.29

BELGIUM – BELGIQUE
Jean De Lannoy
Avenue du Roi 202
B-1060 Bruxelles   Tel. (02) 538.51.69/538.08.41
Telefax: (02) 538.08.41

CANADA
Renouf Publishing Company Ltd.
1294 Algoma Road
Ottawa, ON K1B 3W8   Tel. (613) 741.4333
Telefax: (613) 741.5439
Stores:
61 Sparks Street
Ottawa, ON K1P 5R1   Tel. (613) 238.8985
211 Yonge Street
Toronto, ON M5B 1M4   Tel. (416) 363.3171
Telefax: (416)363.59.63
Les Éditions La Liberté Inc.
3020 Chemin Sainte-Foy
Sainte-Foy, PQ G1X 3V6   Tel. (418) 658.3763
Telefax: (418) 658.3763

Federal Publications Inc.
165 University Avenue, Suite 701
Toronto, ON M5H 3B8   Tel. (416) 860.1611
Telefax: (416) 860.1608
Les Publications Fédérales
1185 Université
Montréal, QC H3B 3A7   Tel. (514) 954.1633
Telefax: (514) 954.1635

CHINA – CHINE
China National Publications Import
Export Corporation (CNPIEC)
16 Gongti E. Road, Chaoyang District
P.O. Box 88 or 50
Beijing 100704 PR   Tel. (01) 506.6688
Telefax: (01) 506.3101

CHINESE TAIPEI – TAIPEI CHINOIS
Good Faith Worldwide Int'l. Co. Ltd.
9th Floor, No. 118, Sec. 2
Chung Hsiao E. Road
Taipei   Tel. (02) 391.7396/391.7397
Telefax: (02) 394.9176

CZECH REPUBLIC – RÉPUBLIQUE TCHÈQUE
Artia Pegas Press Ltd.
Narodni Trida 25
POB 825
111 21 Praha 1   Tel. 26.65.68
Telefax: 26.20.81

DENMARK – DANEMARK
Munksgaard Book and Subscription Service
35, Nørre Søgade, P.O. Box 2148
DK-1016 København K   Tel. (33) 12.85.70
Telefax: (33) 12.93.87

EGYPT – ÉGYPTE
Middle East Observer
41 Sherif Street
Cairo   Tel. 392.6919
Telefax: 360-6804

FINLAND – FINLANDE
Akateeminen Kirjakauppa
Keskuskatu 1, P.O. Box 128
00100 Helsinki
Subscription Services/Agence d'abonnements :
P.O. Box 23
00371 Helsinki   Tel. (358 0) 12141
Telefax: (358 0) 121.4450

FRANCE
OECD/OCDE
Mail Orders/Commandes par correspondance:
2, rue André-Pascal
75775 Paris Cedex 16   Tel. (33-1) 45.24.82.00
Telefax: (33-1) 49.10.42.76
Telex: 640048 OCDE
Orders via Minitel, France only/
Commandes par Minitel, France exclusivement :
36 15 OCDE
OECD Bookshop/Librairie de l'OCDE :
33, rue Octave-Feuillet
75016 Paris   Tel. (33-1) 45.24.81.81
(33-1) 45.24.81.67
Documentation Française
29, quai Voltaire
75007 Paris   Tel. 40.15.70.00
Gibert Jeune (Droit-Économie)
6, place Saint-Michel
75006 Paris   Tel. 43.25.91.19
Librairie du Commerce International
10, avenue d'Iéna
75016 Paris   Tel. 40.73.34.60
Librairie Dunod
Université Paris-Dauphine
Place du Maréchal de Lattre de Tassigny
75016 Paris   Tel. (1) 44.05.40.13
Librairie Lavoisier
11, rue Lavoisier
75008 Paris   Tel. 42.65.39.95
Librairie L.G.D.J. - Montchrestien
20, rue Soufflot
75005 Paris   Tel. 46.33.89.85
Librairie des Sciences Politiques
30, rue Saint-Guillaume
75007 Paris   Tel. 45.48.36.02
P.U.F.
49, boulevard Saint-Michel
75005 Paris   Tel. 43.25.83.40
Librairie de l'Université
12a, rue Nazareth
13100 Aix-en-Provence   Tel. (16) 42.26.18.08
Documentation Française
165, rue Garibaldi
69003 Lyon   Tel. (16) 78.63.32.23
Librairie Decitre
29, place Bellecour
69002 Lyon   Tel. (16) 72.40.54.54
Librairie Sauramps
Le Triangle
34967 Montpellier Cedex 2   Tel. (16) 67.58.85.15
Tekefax: (16) 67.58.27.36

GERMANY – ALLEMAGNE
OECD Publications and Information Centre
August-Bebel-Allee 6
D-53175 Bonn   Tel. (0228) 959.120
Telefax: (0228) 959.12.17

GREECE – GRÈCE
Librairie Kauffmann
Mavrokordatou 9
106 78 Athens   Tel. (01) 32.55.321
Telefax: (01) 32.30.320

HONG-KONG
Swindon Book Co. Ltd.
Astoria Bldg. 3F
34 Ashley Road, Tsimshatsui
Kowloon, Hong Kong   Tel. 2376.2062
Telefax: 2376.0685

HUNGARY – HONGRIE
Euro Info Service
Margitsziget, Európa Ház
1138 Budapest   Tel. (1) 111.62.16
Telefax: (1) 111.60.61

ICELAND – ISLANDE
Mál Mog Menning
Laugavegi 18, Pósthólf 392
121 Reykjavik   Tel. (1) 552.4240
Telefax: (1) 562.3523

INDIA – INDE
Oxford Book and Stationery Co.
Scindia House
New Delhi 110001   Tel. (11) 331.5896/5308
Telefax: (11) 332.5993
17 Park Street
Calcutta 700016   Tel. 240832

INDONESIA – INDONÉSIE
Pdii-Lipi
P.O. Box 4298
Jakarta 12042   Tel. (21) 573.34.67
Telefax: (21) 573.34.67

IRELAND – IRLANDE
Government Supplies Agency
Publications Section
4/5 Harcourt Road
Dublin 2   Tel. 661.31.11
Telefax: 475.27.60

ISRAEL
Praedicta
5 Shatner Street
P.O. Box 34030
Jerusalem 91430   Tel. (2) 52.84.90/1/2
Telefax: (2) 52.84.93
R.O.Y. International
P.O. Box 13056
Tel Aviv 61130   Tel. (3) 49.61.08
Telefax: (3) 544.60.39
Palestinian Authority/Middle East:
INDEX Information Services
P.O.B. 19502
Jerusalem   Tel. (2) 27.12.19
Telefax: (2) 27.16.34

ITALY – ITALIE
Libreria Commissionaria Sansoni
Via Duca di Calabria 1/1
50125 Firenze   Tel. (055) 64.54.15
Telefax: (055) 64.12.57
Via Bartolini 29
20155 Milano   Tel. (02) 36.50.83
Editrice e Libreria Herder
Piazza Montecitorio 120
00186 Roma   Tel. 679.46.28
Telefax: 678.47.51
Libreria Hoepli
Via Hoepli 5
20121 Milano   Tel. (02) 86.54.46
Telefax: (02) 805.28.86
Libreria Scientifica
Dott. Lucio de Biasio 'Aeiou'
Via Coronelli, 6
20146 Milano   Tel. (02) 48.95.45.52
Telefax: (02) 48.95.45.48

JAPAN – JAPON
OECD Publications and Information Centre
Landic Akasaka Building
2-3-4 Akasaka, Minato-ku
Tokyo 107   Tel. (81.3) 3586.2016
Telefax: (81.3) 3584.7929

KOREA – CORÉE
Kyobo Book Centre Co. Ltd.
P.O. Box 1658, Kwang Hwa Moon
Seoul   Tel. 730.78.91
Telefax: 735.00.30

MALAYSIA – MALAISIE
University of Malaya Bookshop
University of Malaya
P.O. Box 1127, Jalan Pantai Baru
59700 Kuala Lumpur
Malaysia   Tel. 756.5000/756.5425
                        Telefax: 756.3246

MEXICO – MEXIQUE
Revistas y Periodicos Internacionales S.A. de C.V.
Florencia 57 - 1004
Mexico, D.F. 06600   Tel. 207.81.00
                        Telefax: 208.39.79

NETHERLANDS – PAYS-BAS
SDU Uitgeverij Plantijnstraat
Externe Fondsen
Postbus 20014
2500 EA's-Gravenhage   Tel. (070) 37.89.880
Voor bestellingen: Telefax: (070) 34.75.778

NEW ZEALAND
NOUVELLE-ZÉLANDE
Legislation Services
P.O. Box 12418
Thorndon, Wellington   Tel. (04) 496.5652
                        Telefax: (04) 496.5698

NORWAY – NORVÈGE
Narvesen Info Center – NIC
Bertrand Narvesens vei 2
P.O. Box 6125 Etterstad
0602 Oslo 6   Tel. (022) 57.33.00
                        Telefax: (022) 68.19.01

PAKISTAN
Mirza Book Agency
65 Shahrah Quaid-E-Azam
Lahore 54000   Tel. (42) 353.601
                        Telefax: (42) 231.730

PHILIPPINE – PHILIPPINES
International Book Center
5th Floor, Filipinas Life Bldg.
Ayala Avenue
Metro Manila   Tel. 81.96.76
                        Telex 23312 RHP PH

PORTUGAL
Livraria Portugal
Rua do Carmo 70-74
Apart. 2681
1200 Lisboa   Tel. (01) 347.49.82/5
                        Telefax: (01) 347.02.64

SINGAPORE – SINGAPOUR
Gower Asia Pacific Pte Ltd.
Golden Wheel Building
41, Kallang Pudding Road, No. 04-03
Singapore 1334   Tel. 741.5166
                        Telefax: 742.9356

SPAIN – ESPAGNE
Mundi-Prensa Libros S.A.
Castelló 37, Apartado 1223
Madrid 28001   Tel. (91) 431.33.99
                        Telefax: (91) 575.39.98

Libreria Internacional AEDOS
Consejo de Ciento 391
08009 – Barcelona   Tel. (93) 488.30.09
                        Telefax: (93) 487.76.59

Llibreria de la Generalitat
Palau Moja
Rambla dels Estudis, 118
08002 – Barcelona
                (Subscripcions) Tel. (93) 318.80.12
                (Publicacions) Tel. (93) 302.67.23
                        Telefax: (93) 412.18.54

SRI LANKA
Centre for Policy Research
c/o Colombo Agencies Ltd.
No. 300-304, Galle Road
Colombo 3   Tel. (1) 574240, 573551-2
                        Telefax: (1) 575394, 510711

SWEDEN – SUÈDE
Fritzes Customer Service
S–106 47 Stockholm   Tel. (08) 690.90.90
                        Telefax: (08) 20.50.21

Subscription Agency/Agence d'abonnements :
Wennergren-Williams Info AB
P.O. Box 1305
171 25 Solna   Tel. (08) 705.97.50
                        Telefax: (08) 27.00.71

SWITZERLAND – SUISSE
Maditec S.A. (Books and Periodicals - Livres
et périodiques)
Chemin des Palettes 4
Case postale 266
1020 Renens VD 1   Tel. (021) 635.08.65
                        Telefax: (021) 635.07.80

Librairie Payot S.A.
4, place Pépinet
CP 3212
1002 Lausanne   Tel. (021) 341.33.47
                        Telefax: (021) 341.33.45

Librairie Unilivres
6, rue de Candolle
1205 Genève   Tel. (022) 320.26.23
                        Telefax: (022) 329.73.18

Subscription Agency/Agence d'abonnements :
Dynapresse Marketing S.A.
38 avenue Vibert
1227 Carouge   Tel. (022) 308.07.89
                        Telefax: (022) 308.07.99

See also – Voir aussi :
OECD Publications and Information Centre
August-Bebel-Allee 6
D-53175 Bonn (Germany) Tel. (0228) 959.120
                        Telefax: (0228) 959.12.17

THAILAND – THAÏLANDE
Suksit Siam Co. Ltd.
113, 115 Fuang Nakhon Rd.
Opp. Wat Rajbopith
Bangkok 10200   Tel. (662) 225.9531/2
                        Telefax: (662) 222.5188

TURKEY – TURQUIE
Kültür Yayinlari Is-Türk Ltd. Sti.
Atatürk Bulvari No. 191/Kat 13
Kavaklidere/Ankara   Tel. 428.11.40 Ext. 2458
Dolmabahce Cad. No. 29
Besiktas/Istanbul   Tel. 260.71.88
                        Telex: 43482B

UNITED KINGDOM – ROYAUME-UNI
HMSO
Gen. enquiries   Tel. (071) 873 0011
Postal orders only:
P.O. Box 276, London SW8 5DT
Personal Callers HMSO Bookshop
49 High Holborn, London WC1V 6HB
                        Telefax: (071) 873 8200
Branches at: Belfast, Birmingham, Bristol,
Edinburgh, Manchester

UNITED STATES – ÉTATS-UNIS
OECD Publications and Information Center
2001 L Street N.W., Suite 650
Washington, D.C. 20036-4910 Tel. (202) 785.6323
                        Telefax: (202) 785.0350

VENEZUELA
Libreria del Este
Avda F. Miranda 52, Aptdo. 60337
Edificio Galipán
Caracas 106   Tel. 951.1705/951.2307/951.1297
                        Telegram: Libreste Caracas

Subscription to OECD periodicals may also be
placed through main subscription agencies.

Les abonnements aux publications périodiques de
l'OCDE peuvent être souscrits auprès des
principales agences d'abonnement.

Orders and inquiries from countries where Distributors have not yet been appointed should be sent to:
OECD Publications Service, 2 rue André-Pascal,
75775 Paris Cedex 16, France.

Les commandes provenant de pays où l'OCDE n'a
pas encore désigné de distributeur peuvent être
adressées à : OCDE, Service des Publications,
2, rue André-Pascal, 75775 Paris Cedex 16, France.

5-1995

OECD PUBLICATIONS, 2 rue André-Pascal, 75775 PARIS CEDEX 16
PRINTED IN FRANCE
(97 95 08 1) ISBN 92-64-14489-7 - No. 47987 1995